Complete with an extraordinary array of visual illustrations, this book covers important topics needed for an introductory text in New Testament in a way that is both understandable and well-informed. It emphasizes many details that help students discover the biblical text in new ways they would rarely get on their own.

CRAIG S. KEENER, F. M. and Ada Thompson professor of biblical studies, Asbury Theological Seminary

What a welcome update to an already cutting-edge introduction to the New Testament! The strength of the first edition was its ability to make connections: connecting today's reader to the ancient Mediterranean world of the New Testament and connecting the best of academic research with the life and ministry of the church. This second revised edition maintains the connections of the first and improves upon them. It does not disappoint.

Burge and Green have done a phenomenal job of connecting seminary students, undergraduates, pastors, and church leaders to the historically contingent and relevant message of the first-century authors so that modern interpreters can preach, teach, and apply that same message in our current contexts. It's an ideal textbook in many ways. I'm pleased to give *The New Testament in Antiquity* my highest recommendation. Well done!

MAX LEE, associate professor of New Testament, North Park University

For years I have searched in vain for a book that would introduce students to the New Testament—with clear outlines, graphic images, historical contexts, timelines, maps, and bibliographies. My search is over; this is that book.

SCOT MCKNIGHT, professor of New Testament, Northern Seminary

Since this is a text that has shaped my teaching for many years, I'm pleased to see the revised version retains its rigorous historical context, which has continually set an excellent foundation for informed theological conversation. The vivacity of a thorough revision guarantees that I and my students will remain exposed to the fresh wisdom and beauty of New Testament study.

AMY L. PEELER, associate professor of New Testament, Wheaton College and Graduate School

I've assigned *The New Testament in Antiquity* for years, with appreciation for the wealth of information the first edition offered students: photographs to help them visualize life in the New Testament world; sidebars with information on social, historical, and cultural backgrounds; quotations from primary sources; maps and charts galore. The new edition keeps these distinctives, but the revisions to the layout, organization, and the text itself make the volume even more accessible to students—including those with little preparation for the study of the New Testament. This comprehensive, comprehensible introduction is a valuable asset for the classroom.

C. A. REEDER, professor of New Testament, Religious Studies Department, Westmont College

Few, if any, New Testament surveys can rival this one in terms of its multiple strengths: academic rigor, accessible and engaging style, and visual appeal. This balance means the text appeals equally to both students and professors—a rare accomplishment. The first edition was excellent; the revision is even better.

MARK L. STRAUSS, university professor of New Testament, Bethel Seminary

THE NEW TESTAMENT IN
ANTIQUITY

2ND EDITION

THE NEW TESTAMENT IN ANTIQUITY

2ND EDITION

A SURVEY OF THE NEW TESTAMENT WITHIN
ITS CULTURAL CONTEXTS

GARY M. BURGE
GENE L. GREEN

ZONDERVAN ACADEMIC

The New Testament in Antiquity, 2nd Edition

Requests for information should be addressed to:
Zondervan, *3900 Sparks Dr. SE, Grand Rapids, Michigan 49546*

ISBN 978-0-310-53132-6 (hardcover)

ISBN 978-0-310-53133-3 (ebook)

Cover design: Chris Tobias—Tobias' Outerwear for Books
Cover photo: Courtesy of Heritage Auctions, HA.com
Interior design: Kait Lamphere

Printed in China

19 20 21 22 23 24 25 26 27 28 29 30 31 32 /GPC/ 20 19 18 17 16 15 14 13 12 11 10 9 8 7 6 5 4 3 2 1

To our many students,
who continue to inspire us

CONTENTS

PREFACE

It has been eleven years since the first edition of *The New Testament in Antiquity* came into service. It has been gratifying to see its use in so many colleges, seminaries, and churches as a reliable and helpful textbook. This second edition is not a quick cosmetic retouching of the first, but a vigorous overhaul. We received numerous suggestions and corrections from New Testament scholars and these have been carefully reviewed and most adopted. Fully 25 percent of the text has been substantially rewritten, many of the photographs updated, and bibliographies brought up to date. We see the text as an ongoing project that should see many revisions as its use continues to grow. Another major change is the loss of one of our authors. The present edition is the work of Gary Burge and Gene Green; Lynn Cohick's other commitments led to her decision to step away from the revision.

A variety of textbooks promise to survey the New Testament for the beginning student. Each volume comes with its own pedagogical, historical, even theological priorities. This volume is no different. We sought to write a textbook that is firmly rooted in our tradition yet is conversant with the academic field we represent.

Four goals focused our efforts. First, we wanted to offer a volume that was academically rigorous. Too often evangelical introductions sacrifice academic thoroughness to make the text practical for the average reader. Each chapter provides an up-to-date examination of the subject, informed by the best in current scholarship.

Second, we sought a volume that was accessible to the student. Technical jargon is kept to a minimum, and explanations are generous for the reader with minimal background. Photographs, charts, and maps each illustrate the argument of the text to enhance understanding.

Third, the text of this book underscores the ancient context of the New Testament (hence the book's title). We believe interpreting the New Testament requires an intimate understanding of its background, culture, and history.

Numerous sidebars point the student to contextual insights and extra-biblical primary sources.

Fourth, we wanted a volume that is responsive to the confessional commitments of the evangelical tradition. Too often academic treatments of the New Testament view faith commitments as passé. We wanted a scholarly text that treated the pages of the New Testament *as Scripture*, which has spoken to the church through the centuries.

These, then, were our goals: academic, accessible, contextual, and confessional.

We represent many years of experience teaching at the undergraduate and graduate levels. We have devoted our careers to understanding and communicating to the alert student. And we have taken those instincts for the classroom and applied them to a text that will serve that audience well. Beginning seminary students will discover this book to be ideal for those just starting their graduate work in theology. And we have learned that the book has wide use in churches where pastors wish to lead an education program through an introduction to the New Testament.

The present volume is a collaborative effort that benefits from countless hours of discussion and consultation. Each contributor brought to the text their own expertise in Pauline studies, Jewish backgrounds, Hellenism, or the Gospels. But in addition, we wanted to take advantage of the best in graphic design and illustration so necessary for the modern reader. Therefore, an ever larger team of artists, editors, photographers, and consultants grew to build *The New Testament in Antiquity*.

HOW THIS BOOK IS BUILT

While the book may be used profitably for personal study, it is ideally suited for classroom instruction. A quick look at the table of contents provides a good outline of its thematic approach. An introductory chapter explains to students why contextual work must be done in order to understand the New Testament effectively. It provides our methodological presuppositions and explains how each chapter is built. We then set out to reconstruct the historical and cultural setting of the New Testament period as concisely as possible. The major eras of intertestamental history run from Alexander to the second Jewish revolt against Rome. This is followed by chapters devoted to the cultural and religious setting of Jesus in Roman Judea and Galilee as well as the setting of Paul in the wider Mediterranean world.

We felt compelled to include a careful study of the sources for reconstructing the life of Jesus and the character of the Gospels. So much technical criticism is now in public debate that students must be abreast of current developments.

We then provide a synthesis of Jesus's life and teachings from these gospels—which is followed by individual analyses of each of the gospels.

A study of Acts (ch. 12) opens our lengthy treatment of Paul and the early church. A summary of Acts' historical and theological method is followed by a synthesis of Paul's life and work. This is then accompanied by a series of chapters on Paul's letters (chs. 14–21), in roughly chronological order. The General Epistles follow, as well as a closing chapter on the Greek text of the New Testament, the development of the canon, and the work of translation. This final chapter is certainly technical, but it is designed for the nonspecialist and answers many of the residual questions about the New Testament that we have heard time and again in class.

A note about sidebars and illustrations: one hallmark of this text is its numerous sidebars. In these we attempt to provide illuminating examples of what contextual study might yield. In many cases, we cite primary sources; in other cases, we use archaeology or cultural anthropology. Above all, we offer insights that will further advance the argument of the chapter.

The same is true of illustrations. Too often textbooks use pictures that are gratuitous, and one wonders why they are there. Or the illustrations are of such poor quality that their impact is severely limited. Our photo researchers worked hard to provide the best illustrations available. The same is true of maps. We sought to build maps that were not only clear but that illustrate for the student how *location* can be critical for understanding most stories.

While an excellent textbook is vital for study of the New Testament, we cannot emphasize strongly enough the need to read the New Testament itself. We have observed a consistent temptation for students: the more thorough the textbook, the less inclined they are to read the original. Our hope is that this book will not replace the New Testament but rather will inspire a passionate and lifelong love for it.

Throughout *The New Testament in Antiquity,* when citing the New Testament, we have used the New International Version. We recognized the great legacy of the NIV (first published in 1973 and 1978) and here have used the 2011 revision that has increased its clarity and power. Where other translations are used, they are noted.

We selected the Bar Kokhba Revolt coin (see the cover) as a unifying thematic image. This is one of the most arresting Jewish silver coins from the early second century AD, showing an image of the Jewish Temple destroyed by the Romans in AD 70. It illustrates richly the hopes for liberation of the Jewish people during the era of Roman imperial domination—a story woven throughout the New Testament as well. The inscription on the reverse reads "For the freedom of Jerusalem," and over the Temple on the obverse (face) of the coin is a star. Simon bar Kokhba, a messianic figure, was known as "Son of the Star," a reference to Numbers 24:17: "A star will come out of Jacob." This text may have also directed the Magi who arrived in Jerusalem, inquiring, "Where is the one who has been born king of the Jews? We saw his star when it rose and have come to worship him" (Matt. 2:2). The coin also bears the image of the Ark of the Covenant between the pillars of the Temple.

ACKNOWLEDGMENTS

A significant number of people contributed to the writing, development, and design of this book. A number of our students provided research and editorial work for the first edition. Among them: John Bonnell, Elizabeth Dias, Esther Giezendanner, Matt Harmon, Christopher Hays, Travis McMaken, and Mary Veeneman. Ben Gladd expertly indexed the first edition.

Colleagues and researchers helped us locate impossible photo targets. Our many ancient coin images have come from the expertise and generosity of Shanna Schmidt, formerly of Harlan Berk, Ltd. (www.hjbltd.com) but currently the owner of Shanna Schmidt Numismatics (www.shannaschmidt.com). The cover image of the Bar Kokhba Revolt coin comes courtesy of Heritage Auctions (HA.com).

Many of our photos come from the expert work of Zev Radovan (Israel), Todd Bolen (USA), and Carl Rasmussen (USA). In the first edition, Hugh Claycombe and Leen Ritmeyer in Jerusalem helped with graphics. In many cases their creative suggestions produced images we did not know existed. And in some cases, they tipped us off about new, interesting discoveries, such as a Roman soldier's sandal print found in a wall at the Greek city of Hippos, Galilee, in August 2007. Few would catch such little details.

At Zondervan, the encouragement for the first edition originally came from Jack Kuhatschek. A team of skilled editors worked with text, photos, layout, and design. Special thanks go to Katya Covrett (editorial), the late Verlyn Verbrugge (copyediting), David Frees and Kim Zeilstra (photos), Sarah Baar, Mark Sheeres, and Rob Monacelli (creative design and layout).

The second edition was worked on by Katya Covrett (editorial), Kim Tanner (copyediting), Dale Williams (photos), and Kait Lamphere (interior design).

Our earnest hope is that this book becomes a beginning for further personal study of the New Testament, its background, and its message. We hope it will become a tool for many classroom explorations of the meaning of our Christian faith and its New Testament legacy.

Gary M. Burge
Gene L. Green

ABBREVIATIONS

AB	Anchor Bible
ABRL	Anchor Bible Reference Library
ANTC	Abington New Testament Commentary
BECNT	Baker Exegetical Commentary on the New Testament
BNTC	Black's New Testament Commentary
BST	The Bible Speaks Today
CBC	Cornerstone Biblical Commentary
EBC	Expositor's Bible Commentary
ESV	English Standard Version
ICC	International Critical Commentary
IVPNTC	InterVarsity Press New Testament Commentary
JETS	*Journal of the Evangelical Theological Society*
KJV	King James Version
LCL	Loeb Classical Library
LEC	Library of Early Christianity
NAC	New American Commentary
NASB	New American Standard Bible
NCB	New Century Bible Commentary
NEB	New English Bible
NICNT	New International Commentary on the New Testament
NIGTC	New International Greek Testament Commentary
NIV	New International Version
NIVAC	NIV Application Commentary
NLT	New Living Translation
NovT	*Novum Testamentum*
NRSV	New Revised Standard Version
NTL	New Testament Library
NTS	New Testament Studies
PNTC	Pillar New Testament Commentary
RSV	Revised Standard Version
RTR	*Reformed Theological Review*
SBLDS	Society of Biblical Literature Dissertation Series
TNIV	Today's New International Version
TNTC	Tyndale New Testament Commentary
WBC	Word Biblical Commentary
ZNW	*Zeitschrift für die neutestamentliche Wissenschaft*

Chapter 1

STUDYING THE NEW TESTAMENT

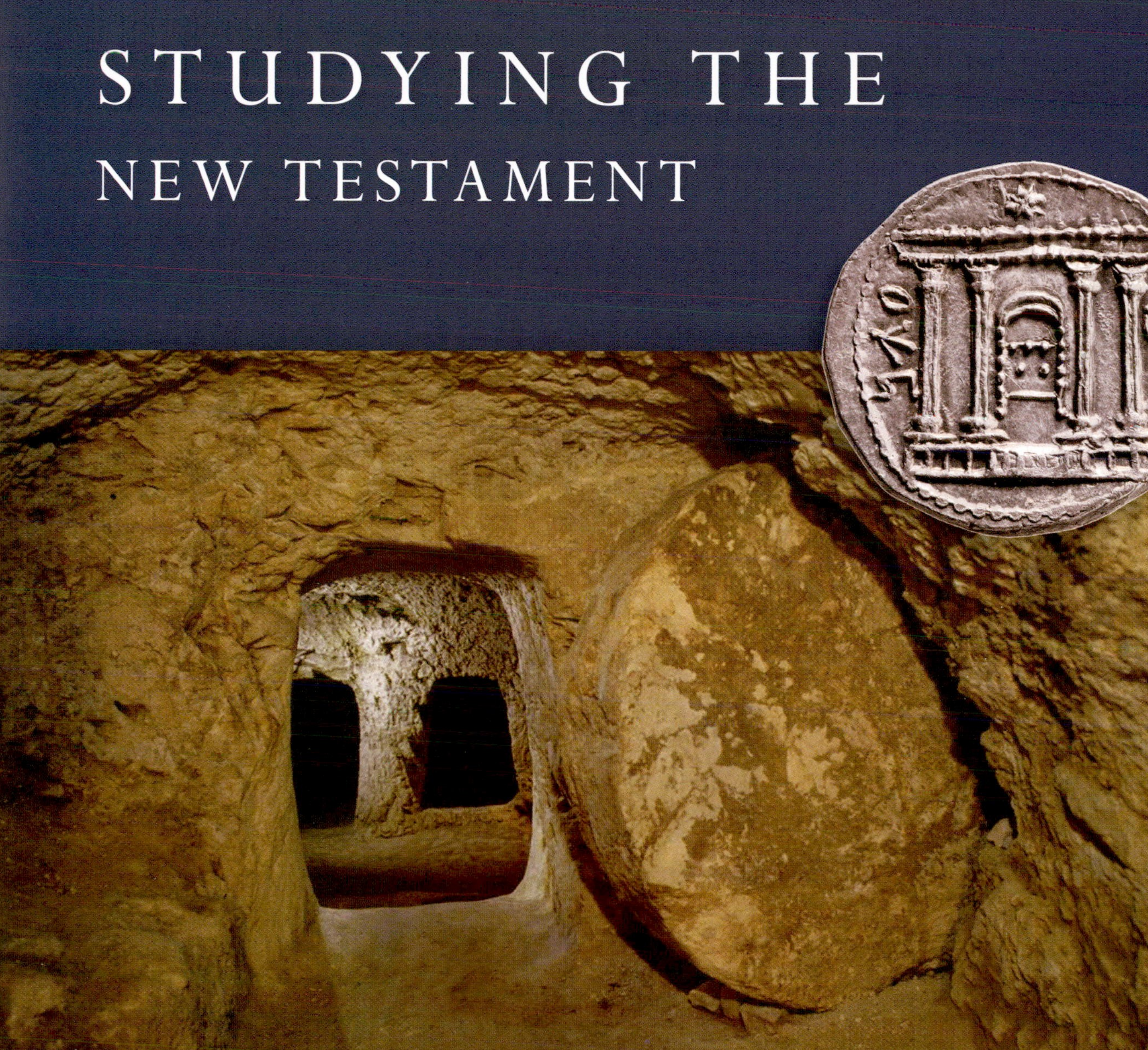

A rolling stone tomb complex from the first century, Nazareth
Alamy Stock Photo

PERSPECTIVE

The New Testament consists of twenty-seven individual "books" written in Greek almost two thousand years ago, and some or all of the New Testament has been translated into 1,168 languages, a characteristic of no other book. Today about 2,500 new translations are underway.[1] But it is not mere curiosity that inspires this study. It is the story contained in these books, a story about a Jewish Messiah and his followers that has led millions in every era to join the ranks of his disciples.

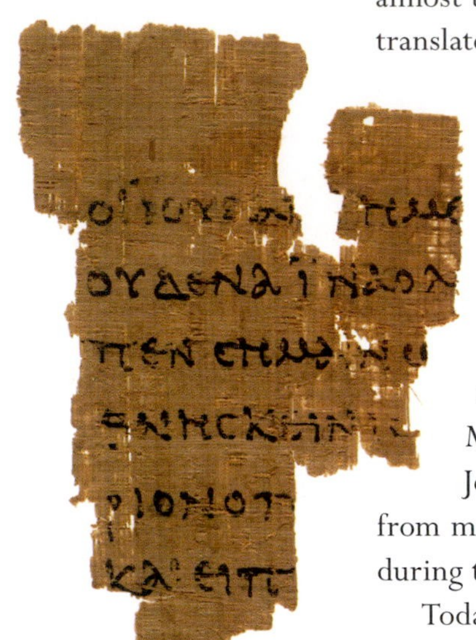

𝔓[52] is the oldest New Testament text that has been discovered (AD 100–150). On one side (the recto) it shows John 18:31–33; on the reverse (the verso) it has John 18:37–38.
© The University of Manchester

The New Testament is first and foremost about Jesus of Nazareth, a man called "Messiah" by his followers, who was killed in Jerusalem and who rose from the grave. His followers were transformed by what they saw and experienced, and they carried the gospel of Jesus to the entire Mediterranean world. The New Testament contains four gospels outlining Jesus's life, a brief history of the early church, and a collection of letters from many of early Christianity's most prominent leaders. They were penned during the fifty years or so following Jesus's death and resurrection.

Today many Christians know the basic elements of this story and enjoy an intimate, deeply personal love for many passages of the New Testament. But few understand the breadth of this story, much less how to interpret each book. Many of us gravitate to familiar texts but lack confidence interpreting more difficult sections. Some know the major characters, such as Jesus, Peter, and Paul, but are vague about the details of their lives or the more complex elements in their teachings.

The aims of this book are simple: to assist students to become alert, capable readers of the New Testament—to guide them through its many books, giving not only essential background information but also a digest of the New Testament's most important teachings.

METHODOLOGICAL PRESUPPOSITIONS

All authors come to the task of writing with presuppositions. For instance, historical optimism—or skepticism—will unwittingly surface in every study of the New Testament. The same is true of this book. Its goals are the same as many other surveys of the New Testament, but some crucial differences will stand out in our approach to reading the New Testament.

Scripture and Study

As Christians we are eager to affirm our commitment that the New Testament is *Scripture*. These words of the Bible are not like other words; God has employed them—indeed, he still employs them—through the work of his Spirit in his church to reveal himself to the world. Therefore, we do not hold merely a historical or antiquarian interest in the New Testament. Rather, God is at work in and through these chapters to bring life and transformation to all who seek him there. Thus, it is appropriate for us to refer to the New Testament (as well as the entire Bible) as *Scripture*, or the divinely inspired Word of God.

This high affirmation of the Bible does not mean that readers in the twenty-first century are capable of understanding the New Testament as if by magic. The message of the Bible may be timeless, but the form of that message is not. To accomplish his self-revelation in history, God necessarily had to embed that revelation in the historical and cultural context of its original readers. When Jesus told a parable, he framed it in ways that made sense to first-century farmers and fishermen. When Paul wrote a letter, he used not only his own personal cultural preferences, but he wrote to be understood, using words and ideas meaningful to a first-century audience. Today we may understand a great deal of that message, but probing its depths requires effort. In many ways, we are foreigners to this story, outsiders looking in and struggling to comprehend it fully. Which means that we will need to become historians and archaeologists as we read these ancient manuscripts.

A Reader's Bias

Meaning can be missed not only by our ignorance of ideas and images presupposed by the New Testament's original audience but also by the cultural framework we ourselves bring to the task of study. Without realizing it, we bring the cultural values and the historical framework of our own world to the text of the New Testament. This is understandable. We only make sense of something we read when the concepts we encounter register with something in our own experience. When we read about the "church" of Corinth, our own images of "church" leap quickly to mind. When Jesus refers to a "sower," our Western notions of farming and seed distribution fill in the picture. Readers bring their own understanding—sometimes called preunderstanding—to any text they encounter.

How do we cope with this? First, we work hard to understand *our own context*. That is, as interpreters of the New Testament we must become increasingly suspicious of our own preferences and ourselves. For example, if we come from a highly individualistic culture (so common in the West) in which the church emphasizes private salvation, we may have difficulty understanding the biblical notion of corporate sin. Or we may be unprepared to see how Jesus's proclamation of "the kingdom of God" had social and economic implications. If we come from a society where religion and politics are strictly separated, it may be impossible to see how Jesus's kingdom bore down on the political structures of his day.

Second, we must embrace the cultural context of the biblical world. If we do not share some of the reflexes of Paul's first readers, if we cannot appreciate the difficulties of gentiles and Jews living side by side in first-century churches, it will be impossible to understand much of the New Testament. This means that the ancient context has precedence because we are interpreting ancient texts. What may seem perfectly obvious to us may not have been obvious to an original ancient reader. This matter of contextual precedence is often behind many disputed passages of the New Testament. When Paul writes, "Does not the very nature of things teach you that if a man has long hair, it is a disgrace to him?" (1 Cor. 11:14) we have to pause and think carefully about Paul's appeal to what is "natural." Natural to whom? And what is "long hair," and why did Paul think it was important? Questions from culture and context pile up quickly around a little text like this.

Context, Context, Context

Words have a certain indeterminacy of meaning. That is, they gain meaning only when they are set firmly in a context. If a modern politician is referred to as "green," it could mean a variety of things. She could be "new" to the field, deeply jealous, an environmentalist, or belong to a party that wears green uniforms. Perhaps she is Irish. For that matter, one of our authors is named "Green." Perhaps that is the politician's surname! We have no idea. In other words, "green" has little meaning unless it is tied to a context. The meaning of the word itself is not "determined" without a context. It must fit its range of meanings, or what is called its *semantic range*. Green cannot mean some things (green cannot mean "red"), but it can mean a lot of other things within limits.

For us to understand the New Testament effectively, therefore, we must rebuild the context of its words as carefully as possible. When John the Baptist introduces Jesus as the "Lamb of God" (John 1:36), does he mean that Jesus is meek? Or helpless? Or does it refer to lambs that are sacrificed at Jerusalem's temple? If this refers to sacrifice, what sacrificial ceremony does John have in mind? The daily sacrifices of temple worship? Or the great annual Passover sacrifices each spring? Knowing the context is the key. But without the context, the phrase "Lamb of God" has little usefulness or meaning. The job of interpretation thus requires humility of the first order because we are admitting that we are reading this story as foreigners and outsiders, not as readers who share its original context.

The title of this book is deliberate: *The New Testament in Antiquity*. Our primary responsibility is to gain the meaning of our Scriptures by understanding not only our own interpretative contexts but also the original context of the New Testament. The *context of antiquity* should control how we understand the New Testament today.

Our earliest picture of Jewish dress comes from the third-century synagogue of Dura-Europos on the Euphrates River, Syria. This fresco shows Samuel anointing David. But note how the dress is strictly Hellenistic and that no fringes are evident on the garments.
Z. Radovan/www.BibleLandPictures.com

RE-CREATING THE CONTEXT

What basic elements are necessary if we are going to be diligent in building this "context of antiquity"? Three important elements contribute to rebuilding the New Testament context: the land, the history, and the culture. Every interpreter of the New Testament must have some mastery of each.

Knowing the Land

When Jesus moved through Galilee or traveled to Judea, he knew where he was. He knew the landscape, the roads, Hellenistic cities such as Scythopolis, and Jewish fishing villages like Capernaum. When Paul organized his missionary journeys, he had a good sense which cities would be strategic for the growth of the church. On his second missionary tour, Paul did not travel north to the region of the Black Sea for good reason. Instead, he headed west to Troas, which was a gateway to the major population centers of the Greek world. These places sound confusing to us. But they were crystal clear to someone like Paul. He could refer to Sardis as easily as we refer to Boston or London.

Such knowledge of geography—landscape, geology, climate, water resources, roads, settlement patterns, and political boundaries—is common among all societies. Most literature simply presupposes that its audience will know these details naturally. The Gospels refer to the Sea of Galilee without telling us its location. They also mention places such as Bethsaida and Cana as if they are familiar to us. The disciples of Jesus are known as "Galileans" when they are in Jerusalem (Acts 2:7), and this word alone carried loads of innuendo and cultural weight. It is the same reason today that Egyptians in Cairo make jokes about other Egyptians "from the south." Everyone knows (supposedly) what an Arab from Al Minya is like!

Our acquaintance with the specifics of biblical geography will play an important role in how we understand the story. When Jesus moves from Judea to Samaria, we must not only know where Samaria is but understand the ethnic differences between Jews and Samaritans. The far north was called "Galilee of the gentiles" because of the rapid Hellenization going on. When Jesus moves around the landscape, sometimes he is in Greek regions; in other cases, in Jewish regions. This setting shapes his teaching and his activity. Therefore, if we cannot locate the city of Tyre or identify the Decapolis (a region known to every Galilean), we will be at a loss.

Geographical questions also follow any reconstruction of Paul's life and work. Paul knows intimately famous cities such as Antioch on the Orontes, Ephesus, Troas, and Philippi. The settlement pattern of Asia Minor played significantly in his plans and likely kept him from traveling to more remote areas. He spent eighteen months founding a strategic church in Corinth, yet it was this city's location as a maritime trading center and transit point that gave the city such value.

Knowing the History

Every culture likewise knows its history, so that allusions to people and events can happen in the subtlest manner. When a student announces he is from Richmond, Virginia, and he is a Southerner, he is saying more than providing geographical information. He is making a comment about history, the American Civil War, and cultural orientation. When students at our college study in a science station in the Black Hills of South Dakota near "Custer State Park" and the "Oglala Lakota Sioux" Native American Reservation, well, every other word is loaded with tension and controversy. But you have to know the history behind these places to understand their cultural power.

The New Testament period also had a history that everyone knew. The coming of Hellenistic culture behind the armies of Alexander the Great impacted Jewish life far more than we can imagine. This was followed by a series of regional Greek kings who sometimes encouraged assimilation but at other times brutally oppressed the Jews. Judaism's successful revolt against the Greeks, and the subsequent Jewish nation formed in the second century BC, inspired stories and writings current in Jesus's day.

No doubt the most important event for the average Jew was Rome's conquest of Israel in 63 BC. The massive armies of Pompey quickly placed it under Roman administration. The reality of this occupation—its tax burden, its Jewish collaborators, its Jewish resistors—shaped the world of Jesus and Paul. Of course, participation in the empire had its benefits. Pompey had also cleansed the Mediterranean of pirates (Plutarch, *Life of Pompey*, 28:2). Suddenly, trade, travel, and communication facilitated and protected by Rome was possible. The early church took advantage of these benefits as it moved its missionaries around the empire.

Therefore, the parameters of our historical enquiry should begin in about 333 BC (Alexander's major defeat of a Persian army at Issus) and end with the second Jewish war with Rome in AD 132–135. Hellenism was changing the cultural landscape while the Roman occupation inspired collaborators like the Herodians as well as fighters like the Zealots. Jewish self-identity was in crisis, and many were asking whether the successful revolts of the second century BC should serve as a model for how to treat the Romans.

Knowing history thus builds the context in which present events can be understood. In John 10, for example, Jesus attends the Festival of Dedication. This celebration was popular since it retold the story of Judaism's guerrilla war against the Greeks and the rededication of the temple (after the Greeks had profaned it with an altar to Zeus). When Paul writes a letter to Philippi, it helps to know something of the history of Macedonia and how Roman soldiers retired in the region. When Mary, Joseph, and the young Jesus return to Judea from Egypt, they bypass Bethlehem and slip into Galilee because a vicious son of Herod the Great is ruling the south (see Matt. 2:19–23). Without a strong grasp of the historical context, we may misunderstand or even misrepresent what is happening in a New Testament passage.

This coin, AR sela, minted during the Bar Kokhba revolt of AD 132–135, shows symbolism that was recognized by every Jew: the four-column entrance to the temple on one side, and on the other side, a *lulav*—a bundle of four branches used at the Feast of Tabernacles ceremonies. *Image courtesy of Heritage Auctions, HA.com*

Knowing the Culture

Every society orchestrates its life with predictable reflexes and rituals. Social habits, religious traditions, political interests, even music and art contribute to values shared by generations. Rarely do they need to be defined overtly since we inherit them. One of the biggest hurdles for foreigners visiting another country is to understand what is going on. They may think they know, but they gradually sense they are missing a great deal. Humor, irony, and sarcasm presuppose much that is unsaid; what may be funny to one person may mean nothing to another. Try watching a film in a foreign theater. Americans will tell you that the British laugh at all the "wrong" places. (The British will say the same about Americans.) A Middle Eastern student was once having lunch with a faculty member who asked him whether he'd like to go back for more. "No thank you," the student said, "I'm all fed up." The idea was perfect if said in Arabic, but in English it created a complete cultural disconnect!

Of course, the New Testament world shared many values that were understood but unspoken. Today these values are being studied. The advent of modern anthropology gave birth to an interdisciplinary effort to bring these academic skills to the study of the New Testament. Scholars look at the literature of the period, the archaeological remains, and even the evidence of rural village cultures for clues of how to understand the social reflexes presupposed in the Bible. For example, women were responsible for the transport and management of well or cistern water. Both the Old and New Testaments attest to this, but so does the culture of Middle East village life, where it has been least disturbed by Western influences.

One key to understanding Luke 11 is seeing that ovens were often shared in a community. This oven, a small dome within a mud-brick chimney, from a village called Qatzrin was used for cooking and heating the house. *Todd Bolen/BiblePlaces.com*

When we look at particular New Testament passages, asking questions about culture may lead us to entirely new levels of understanding. When a young son comes to his father and asks for his inheritance (Luke 15:11–12), what is the expected response? What will his older brother think? What happens when a neighbor awakens a man in the middle of the night asking for bread (Luke 11:5–6)? What leads the sleeping man to arise and share? Or what cultural assumptions drive a shepherd to leave ninety-nine sheep alone in search of one that is lost (Luke 15:4)? We dare not complete the picture with our own cultural assumptions, since our culture is foreign to the story.

One key cultural value in the New Testament is the place given to shame and honor. Life was organized around the accumulation of honor and the avoidance of shame. For example, Jesus once sat in the home of Simon the Pharisee (Luke 7:36–50), having dinner with the village's religious and intellectual elite. When a woman interrupted the party by clutching Jesus's feet, wetting them with tears, kissing them, and drying them with her loosed hair, Simon discredited Jesus because he had violated principles of male/female contact by defending rather than rejecting the woman. *Simon concluded that Jesus was a man who had no honor.* But in addition, cultural values cascade over each other in dizzying swiftness: How did the woman get in? What did she intend? How did Jesus sit so that his feet were accessible to her? Who was there at the meal? Why did Simon see the woman's deeds as sexually inappropriate? Why did Simon not wash Jesus's feet when he greeted him or anoint his head? What did Simon mean by his treatment of Jesus?

The interpreter will always bring cultural values to a story such as this. But the key is to limit the intrusion of our own cultural preconceptions and rebuild the context of the story using first-century values. For example, every culture has "greeting rituals." In the Luke 7 story, Simon has omitted these in front of other guests, shaming Jesus publicly. Without a clear understanding of "public shaming" and "greeting rituals," we are at a loss to understand what energizes this story.

The New Testament, however, represents more than one culture, and we must reconstruct each context accurately. Rural village life in Judea was different from urban life in Ephesus. Hellenistic Jews living throughout the Mediterranean often experienced clashes of culture that made them uncomfortable. Greeks and Romans had different assumptions about culture. We will discuss many of these in the pages that follow.

FEATURES

Sidebars. Throughout this book, sidebars (marked by the blue "ribbons") provide illustrations for how the first-century context can be understood. These notes form illustrations of some of the ideas inherent in the New Testament passages under discussion. Other sidebars explain how to interpret troublesome passages and apply them responsibly to our own setting. These notes provide background data such as archaeological research, anthropological insights, historical notes, or even citations of ancient texts to help us gain greater understanding of the New Testament.

Illustrations. Each chapter also uses a wide array of graphics and photographs, carefully chosen to aid us in reconstructing the world of the New Testament. Museum pieces, landscapes, maps, aerial photos, archaeological sites, and artist reconstructions each contribute to contextual material that will help our interpretation. Note especially the study of coins (numismatics). Coins served a much different purpose in the ancient world.

A Roman silver denarius showing the tools of minting: tongs, dyes, and hammer
Z. Radovan/www.BibleLand Pictures.com

"For instance, ancient coins did not *represent* their value (as modern coins do); their value was directly linked to their weight. A denarius is a measure of weight. A government mint would "strike" a coin with an image to verify its worth—but these images also conveyed political messages. They distributed propaganda for the emperor—or they became an opportunity for dissenting peoples to resist any apparent participation with an occupier. The question given to Jesus in Matthew 22:15–17 about taxes is hardly innocent. It is about politics.

Questions for Discussion

1. Are we giving deeper respect to the Bible when we say that it requires earnest study to unlock its deeper meaning? Why?
2. If the Bible is inspired by God, why should it take so much effort to understand it? Did God intend to make it so difficult?
3. If access to the deeper meaning of the New Testament can come only through thoughtful study, doesn't this exclude those who are unable to study? Are we making a "priesthood" of scholars who alone know the secrets of the New Testament?
4. If each of us brings some bias to our reading of the Scriptures, how can we know whether any interpretation of a New Testament passage is correct?
5. What tools do scholars use to reconstruct the original context of the New Testament? Which do you think are most important?

BIBLIOGRAPHY

Introductory

Bell, A. A., Jr. *Exploring the New Testament World: An Illustrated Guide to the World of Jesus and the First Christians.* Nashville: Thomas Nelson, 1998.

Brown, J. *Scripture as Communication: Introducing Biblical Hermeneutics.* Grand Rapids: Baker, 2007.

Marshall, I. H., ed. *New Testament Interpretation: Essays on Principles and Methods.* Grand Rapids: Eerdmans, 1977.

Stambaugh, J. E., and D. L. Balch. *The New Testament in Its Social Environment.* LEC. Philadelphia: Westminster, 1986.

Tate, W. R. *Biblical Interpretation: An Integrated Approach.* Peabody, MA: Hendrickson, 1991.

Advanced

Ferguson, E. *Backgrounds of Early Christianity.* Grand Rapids: Eerdmans, 2003.

Green, J. B., and L. M. McDonald, eds. *The World of the New Testament: Cultural, Social, and Historical Contexts.* Grand Rapids: Baker, 2013.

Klein, W., C. Blomberg, and H. Hubbard. *Introduction to Biblical Interpretation.* Second edition. Nashville: Nelson, 2003.

Osborne, G. *The Hermeneutical Spiral: A Comprehensive Introduction to Biblical Interpretation.* Revised and expanded. Downers Grove, IL: InterVarsity Press, 2006.

NOTES

1. See https://www.wycliffe.org/about/why.

Chapter 2

THE HISTORICAL SETTING OF THE NEW TESTAMENT

Ancient ruins of the Hellenistic city of Hippos, on the eastern shore of the Sea of Galilee

PERSPECTIVE

Coin from the Persian Achaemenid Empire, ca. 520–505 BC
Savoca Numismatik GmbH & Co. KG, Auction 29, Lot 178

Every culture is influenced by the historical forces that shape it. Events in history change who we are. Thus, it is impossible to understand the world of the New Testament without some grasp of the major political events that shaped its world and culture. Jerusalem's recovery from the Babylonian exile influenced the nature of Israel's priesthood. The cultural conquest of Hellenism changed the way people spoke and thought. Even the Roman Empire affected Judaism by bringing new possibilities of commerce and cultural exchange from the western reaches of the Mediterranean.

THE POST-EXILIC PERIOD, 539–332 BC

The turmoil described at the close of the Old Testament period set the stage for the Jewish faith we meet in the New Testament. Babylonian armies had sacked the walled city of Jerusalem and destroyed its temple in 586 BC. The sacred vessels of the temple and numerous exiles were carried off to Babylon, where the conquering king Nebuchadnezzar presented them as a part of his spoils of war. For a generation Judaism lived in despair, wondering whether they could believe in a God who could be defeated like this. Lamentations reflects this numbing reality for Israel, and Psalm 137 echoes profound despair:

> By the rivers of Babylon we sat and wept
>   when we remembered Zion.
> There on the poplars
>   we hung our harps,
> for there our captors asked us for songs,
>   our tormentors demanded songs of joy;
>   they said, "Sing us one of the songs of Zion!" (vv. 1–3)

Persia's defeat of Babylon in 539 BC changed Israel's fortunes immediately. While Babylon's policy for conquest had included the resettlement of defeated national groups (to disrupt their national identities), the Persians used these frustrated exiles as allies, promising to send them back to their homelands. Cyrus, the Persian monarch, permitted the Jews to begin this emigration soon after Babylon's fall. While many no doubt returned at once, the migration was likely gradual, taking decades to complete. But some Jews chose to remain in Babylon, and by the first century, they enjoyed self-rule. The Jewish Babylonian community grew large, though little evidence remains to help us reconstruct its size or welfare.

Cyrus the Great

Xenophon was a prolific writer who served in the Greek cavalry in the late fifth century BC. Among his many works, the *Cyropaedia* ("Education of Cyrus") survives as a pseudo-historical account of Cyrus the Great's life. In 1.1.5 he describes the character of the Persian king:

> He ruled over these nations, even though they did not speak the same language as he, nor one nation the same as another; for all that, he was able to cover so vast a region with the fear which he inspired, that he struck all men with terror and no one tried to withstand him; and he was able to awaken in all so lively a desire to please him, that they always wished to be guided by his will. Moreover, the tribes that he brought into subjection to himself were so many that it is a difficult matter even to travel to them all, in whatever direction one begins one's journey from the palace, whether toward the east or the west, toward the north or the south.

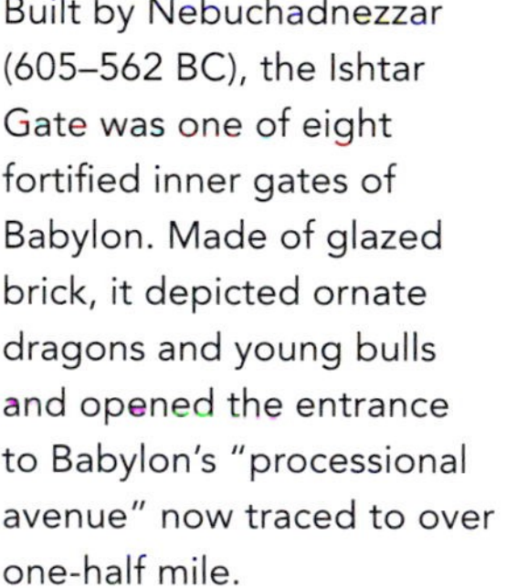

Built by Nebuchadnezzar (605–562 BC), the Ishtar Gate was one of eight fortified inner gates of Babylon. Made of glazed brick, it depicted ornate dragons and young bulls and opened the entrance to Babylon's "processional avenue" now traced to over one-half mile.
© 2008 by Zondervan

The story of Israel's return can be traced in the Old Testament books of Ezra and Nehemiah and in the prophets Ezekiel, Haggai, Zechariah, and Malachi. Some scholars add Daniel and Esther to this list. Since the exile was explained as divine judgment for Israel's covenant failings (Mal. 2:11), the Jewish leadership returned to Jerusalem with a profound desire to keep the law. Religious rigor characterized the call of Ezra, who not only demanded that the law be kept with care but called on Jews to separate themselves from those people living in the surrounding hills. The prophet Malachi reinforced this, prohibiting "mixed marriages" that would compromise faith (2:10–12) and calling for righteousness in everything from temple sacrifices (1:6–8) to wages given to the poor (3:5). This remarkable severity signals how fragile the Jews saw themselves as a culture and as a nation. They were in jeopardy of not surviving and so demanded their tribal exclusivity be maintained.

Haggai reminded Israel that faithfulness to God would return prosperity to the land (Hag. 2:19). And he pronounced a test on the nation's faith by calling for God's house (the temple) to be built before any of the city's neighborhoods (1:4–8). Many of the minor implements for the temple returned with the Jews, but most major items (such as the ark of the covenant) were lost. Work on a new temple began promptly and took about five years to complete (515 BC).

Dating from 539 BC, the Cyrus Cylinder authorized the decree of Cyrus that permitted the Jews to be transferred from Babylon to Judah and rebuild their temple.
© 2013 by Zondervan

But the full restoration of Jerusalem was incomplete until Nehemiah began reconstructing the city's wall system (about thirteen years after Ezra's arrival). He had been a high official of the Persian king, but when he learned about the devastated condition of Jerusalem's infrastructure, he returned to Judea with the king's blessing.

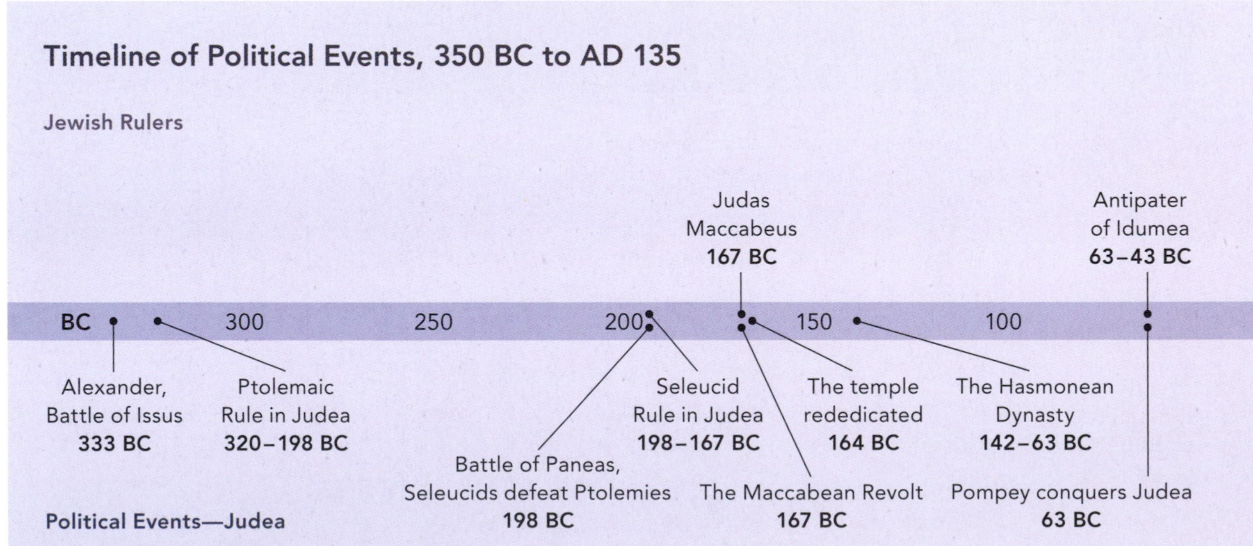

This development, combined with the rebuilding of the temple, signaled something ominous to those non-Jews living in the area. Ezra carried an authorization from the Persian king to resettle the land (Ezra 1:2–4, 6:3–5), Nehemiah had an approval to reconstruct the walls (Neh. 2:1–8), and now the returning refugees were acting on these pledges. To the non-Jewish tribes in the hills north and south of Jerusalem, these efforts would have been viewed as deeply political acts, threatening perhaps to their own security. The Persians were unsure whether the rebuilt Jerusalem would become a regional rival to local Persian rule. So the Jews were prohibited from raising an army or reconstituting their monarchy. Political leadership then fell to the Jerusalem priesthood.

Judaism had changed during the exile. It adopted the popular use of Aramaic, a Semitic language similar to Hebrew. This language had long been the *lingua franca* of the east, and using it linked the Jews to the commercial and political channels of the emerging world. By the first century this was the common language of life in Israel and was likely Jesus's native tongue.

Judaism also had to come to terms with the meaning of faith *without* the temple and sacrifice. Piety was expressed through study, obedience, and prayer. This was likely the origin of the synagogue, which began as a gathering of Jews who debated the Scriptures, prayed, and formed community centers. When the Jews rebuilt the temple, these village-based gathering places continued to flourish.

Persian guards oversaw Jewish independence in Judah. This relief comes from the fifth century BC and was found at Persepolis.
Z. Radovan/www.BibleLand Pictures.com

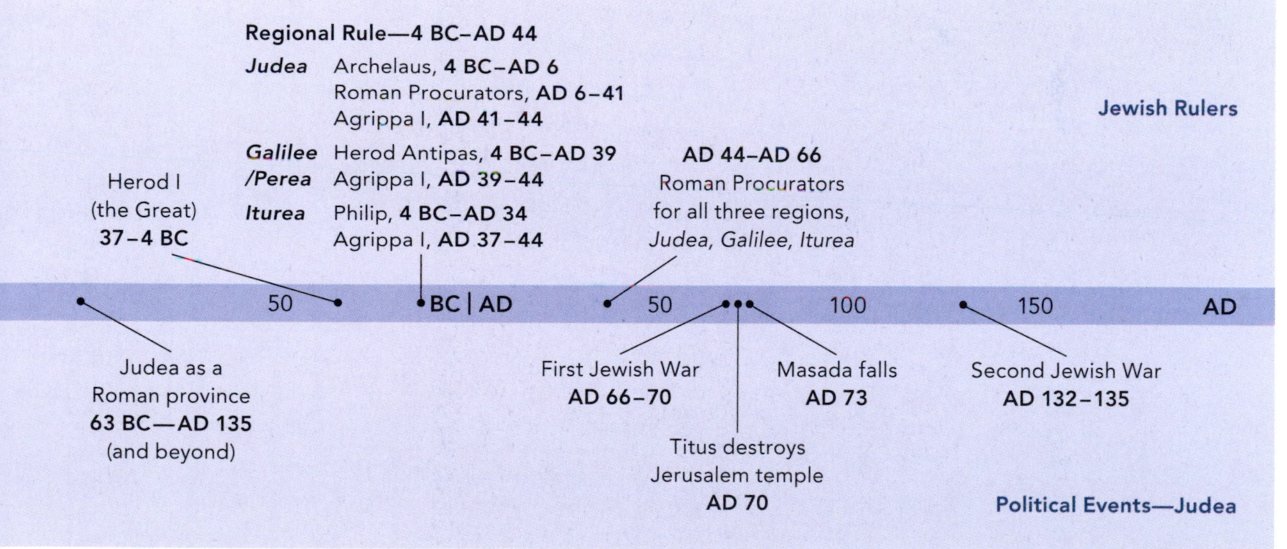

Throughout the Hellenistic era, Alexander's life had become legend. His image, like this one discovered at Pompeii, decorated buildings throughout the Mediterranean.
giannimarchetti/Shutterstock

THE HELLENISTIC PERIOD (332–63 BC)

While the conquering empires of the east permitted the Jews to retain their cultural and religious identity, the coming of Greek culture—or Hellenism—in the fourth century made an indelible mark on Jewish life. Greek culture was missionary by nature, sweeping up new peoples and converting them to a new, "modern" way of life. Judaism soon found itself enticed to join the wider Mediterranean world, and this would both bring enormous opportunities and present subtle threats to the integrity of Jewish life.

Alexander the Great of Macedon

Few figures in the ancient world were as romanticized as Alexander the Great (356–323 BC). Images on coins and sculptures lived alongside biographies and legends, recalling his life for centuries. Rumors reported that he had descended from Zeus, that he read Homer on his campaigns, that he and his officers enjoyed lavish lives filled with finery, expensive food, and wine, and that his military instincts were as brilliant as they were severe.

As a Macedonian (from northern Greece), Alexander's political goal was the defeat of the Persians, who had controlled the eastern Aegean since about 513 BC. Alexander's father, Philip, was a charismatic leader who asserted Macedonian dominance by defeating southern Greece—a region that viewed the Macedonians as hardly more than barbarians. Philip persuaded Aristotle to tutor his young son, which prepared Alexander for early leadership when his father was assassinated in 336 BC.

Alexander was only twenty at the time. But he picked up his father's mantle, won the allegiance of Philip's legendary generals, and reasserted Macedonian

Cutting the Gordian Knot

Many fables followed the story of Alexander. One describes him visiting the town of Gordium, the ancient capital of Phyrgia. Here was a wagon affixed to a pole by a rope with a series of tangled knots. Legend said that anyone who could unravel the knot would possess Asia.

Alexander made clear that his aim was the conquest of the East and so it was impossible not to try his hand at the knot of Gordium. With his army looking on, Alexander worked the knot unsuccessfully. But now there was a propaganda problem: Would his superstitious followers see the failure as an omen of defeat? "What difference does it make how I free it?" Alexander cried. He removed his sword and cut the knot in half—indicating that his tactics did not matter. Asia would be his.

War Elephants in India

Alexander's superior military discipline and strategies found no successful opposition. But in India he encountered something he had never seen. The Indian king Porus had equipped his army with two hundred elephants trained for battle. They were armored with iron blades on their tusks, frequently wore loud bells, and could wreak havoc on a field of infantry and terrorize cavalry. An elephant's master rode in an elevated shelter on its back. Porus himself—all seven feet of him—rode on his own beast, leading the charge against the Greeks. Even Alexander's own armored cavalry were no match for them.

Eventually the notion of using elephants against infantry moved west and was used by various armies in the Mediterranean. But the elephant could be dangerous. It could easily become crazed in battle and turn on its own troops, in which case the master had to kill it immediately.

nationalism. Alexander's first aim was to defeat the Persians, who held Anatolia (Asia Minor). In 334 he visited Troy—the symbolic site of the Greek defeat of Asia—and then engaged the Persian satrap (governor) in his first battle at the Granicus River. This important victory led to the collapse of Persian control in Anatolia. He moved south, freeing Greek cities (such as Ephesus, Sardis, and Miletus) along the Aegean Sea and was cautiously hailed as a liberator.

As the agile Macedonians (thirty thousand strong) moved east, the Persian king, Darius III, knew he had to confront Alexander immediately. He raised an army of one hundred thousand and met his foe in a narrow plain of Issus in 333 BC. The battlefield constricted the Persian army's superior size, and Alexander's swift, armored cavalry quickly breached Darius's line. Darius fled, and the field belonged to the Macedonians.

Alexander continued his victory march south, stopping first to subdue the minor region of Judea. His main goal there was Egypt, which he occupied in 332 BC. Then he led his troops to the Euphrates and followed its course until he entered Mesopotamia. North of Babylon, Darius held a massive army of 200,000

The Judean *prutah* was one of the most popular coins minted in Judea. It shows the influence of Alexander in its display of the Macedonian rosette. *Gene L. Green*

The Empire of Alexander

at an open plain (Gaugamela) and assumed that his ability to outflank the smaller Macedonians would win the day. But he was wrong. Again Alexander drove his armored cavalry through the center of the Persian line and placed his opponent in disarray. Darius' conscripts collapsed; again Darius fled and sought refuge, this time in Bactria (modern Afghanistan), but there he was slain. Alexander (who pursued him) found his body on a roadside in 330 BC.

When Alexander defeated the Indian King Porus in 326 BC, the Macedonians struck a silver coin showing Alexander, Porus, and his war elephants from the Punjab (India).
© The Trustees of the British Museum

Alexander's military successes came from three strategic changes in field warfare. First, ancient war had generally consisted of wide lines of troops, many men deep, rushing at each other in a desperate melee. Philip and Alexander developed the Macedonian phalanx—a highly disciplined square of 256 men (sixteen per side) each armed with a long eighteen-foot spear, the *sarissa*, that could outreach the enemy. The phalanx was heavily armed and disciplined, and could move independently with local commanders. Second, Alexander developed heavy cavalry. These were large horses well-protected with armor and ridden by highly trained, well-armed soldiers. Their high-speed charge could burst through most enemy lines. Finally, Alexander developed the siege train. These were wagons bearing supplies, catapults, ladders, and siege engines. Alexander (and every general) knew that an army's resupply was as important as its war-fighting ability. The Macedonians made such preparation a science.

The swift collapse of the Persian military was unexpected. Suddenly, Alexander viewed the prospect of unraveling the balance of Persia's great empire. He plundered the Persian treasuries, freeing its cities (such as Babylon), and later conquered the great Persian capital of Persepolis, which he burned. He continued to move east, hoping to build the greatest empire in history and see the "great

The Alexandrian Base in Samaria

When the Persians controlled the province of Judea, they chose Samaria as their base. Here were potential allies who hated Jewish rule yet understood local politics. When Samaria fell to Alexander in 332 BC, he made this his base of regional control and stationed some of his Macedonian troops there.

Roman conquest in 63 BC again had a role for Samaria. It was one more vital Roman military outpost keeping an eye on Judea. During the Roman period, Herod the Great rebuilt Samaria splendidly, renaming it Sebaste (the Greek name of Emperor Augustus).

Samaria's use as a staging area for foreign rulers reinforced Judaism's antagonism toward the region and its people. Today remnants of Alexander's fortress, along with numerous Roman remains, can still be seen there.

When Alexander the Great conquered Judea, he fortified towers such as this in Samaria to control his rule of the region.
Phoenix Data Systems

ocean" of the east, which would mark the end of the world. He announced that he would cross the Hindu Kush Mountains and next take India. He defeated the Indian king Porus but had no idea how many kingdoms still lay ahead. His trusted veterans had crossed over eleven thousand miles in eight years of constant campaign, and in western India they compelled Alexander to turn the army around. After two years, they made their way back to Babylon, where Alexander worked hard to build an administrative system for the empire. But in 323 BC, at age thirty-three, he died.

Alexander's death left his empire in the hands of his generals, who struggled for supremacy. Soon the empire was divided into political regions that were defended by powerful officers. Two dynasties affected Judaism's fortunes. In Egypt the Ptolemaic dynasty was founded in 323, with its capital in Alexandria. Ten years later the Seleucid dynasty was formed in Syria, with its capital at Antioch. Judea was ruled from Egypt until 198 BC, when war changed the landscape dramatically.

Tetradrachm depicting Zeus seated facing left and the name of Alexander on the right
© The Trustees of the British Museum

While Alexander was committed to conquest, his legacy was more than that. The lands he conquered were quickly Hellenized. Cities were founded with features that reflected the values of his homeland: theaters, gymnasiums, schools, and municipal government. A universal monetary currency was established. Above all, Greek became the new language of a new world that united the cultures of Mesopotamia, Egypt, and the Mediterranean. Literature, commerce, medicine, religion, philosophy, and mathematics (to name a few) all used Greek.

Greek culture dominated the eastern Mediterranean for almost nine hundred years and ended only with the coming of Islam in the seventh century. Greek also became the language of the early Christian communities and of the New Testament.

Alexander the Great's Tomb

On his deathbed, Alexander appointed his general Perdikkas as regent of the kingdom until his son (Alexander IV) was born. Perdikkas laid Alexander in an anthropoid sarcophagus, which in turn was encased in a gold casket and covered with a purple robe. A gold carriage carried this and all Alexander's armor (Diodorus of Sicily, *The Library of History* 18.26.3). Perdikkas was intent on taking the king to Aegae in Macedonia, the traditional resting place of the Macedonian kings.

With Alexander's body in transit, Ptolemy I decided to travel to Syria to meet the assembly and (presumably) to pay his respects. But Ptolemy attacked the caravan, seized the mummy, and spirited it away to Egypt, where he buried it in his own kingdom. Alexander had once visited the famous Oracle of Ammon in the Egyptian desert in 331 BC, where he was declared "son of god." Soon stories serving Ptolemy's propaganda spread widely that this was Alexander's deathbed wish to return to the Oracle.

Alexander's tomb was finally located in Alexandria, the city named after him. The Ptolemaic kings used his burial to legitimize their rule and even claimed at one point to descend from him personally.

Ptolemaic Rule (320–198 BC)

Ptolemy I Soter (*savior*) had been one of Alexander's most trusted generals, accompanying him throughout Asia. At Alexander's death, Ptolemy became governor of Egypt and with time was designated as king. Despite the turmoil of these years, Ptolemy successfully defended his hold on Egypt, based his capital at Alexandria, and Hellenized the northern cities of the country. With time, Egypt (in its northern reaches) became a spectacularly Hellenized world, and Alexandria became one of the leading cities of the day.

During this era, Judea enjoyed remarkable freedom as the Ptolemies considered it pacified. It was a small kingdom encircling Jerusalem and was viewed as a temple-state ruled by priests who merely had to pay taxes to the local Ptolemaic governor. Many Jews lived elsewhere outside Judea (called the Diaspora or Dispersion), and migration to cities like Alexandria was common. Soon permanent Jewish communities were established in cities like Alexandria.

The greatest threat to Jewish identity was the gradual assimilation of Hellenistic culture. When a culture is threatened by a military enemy, it will close ranks and defend itself. But in times of peace, a culture can be undermined in subtle ways that at first seem innocent. Intertestamental literature records how Jerusalem's priests warned about the encroachment of these foreign Greek values. Theaters offered dramatic arts that were foreign to Jewish life. Gymnasium guilds enlisted young men at eighteen to join their social and athletic centers, where sporting events were practiced nude. (Some young men even sought to reverse the signs of circumcision to avoid shame when they entered the games.) Clothing styles—always a potent symbol for the young—now made outlandish cultural statements. Jewish beards and flowing robes were being replaced with broad-rimmed hats, short togas, and high-laced sandals (2 Macc. 4:10–17). Hellenistic life was eroding traditional Jewish culture and identity.

Jews began to use common Greek (or Koine Greek) as their common language. Thus, the Hebrew Scriptures were no longer understandable in the synagogues. According to the ancient *Letter of Aristeas*, the librarian of Alexandria called for the first-ever translation of the Hebrew Scriptures into Greek.

While Alexander's tomb has never been found, the Istanbul Archaeological Museum has an ornate marble sarcophagus attributed to Alexander that was discovered in 1887 in Sidon, Lebanon. *iStock.com/muharremz*

One of our best sources for reconstructing the Jewish history of this period comes from a man named Josephus. He was a military leader in the Jewish war against Rome (AD 66–70; see p. 59) and following Jerusalem's defeat, he retired to Rome to write a "history" of his Jewish people and in particular, to explain the nature of this war with Rome. His historical works have survived, and in them we can find a wealth of information about Jewish values, beliefs, legends, and many of the main characters of first-century history. In his general history called *The Antiquities of the Jewish People,* we can learn about how legend explained the origin of the Greek translation of the Hebrew Bible (the Old Testament). Josephus tells us (*Ant.* 12.2.1–16 [17–23]) that the high priest chose seventy-two scholars who were fluent in both Hebrew and Greek. They traveled to and worked in Alexandria, Egypt, for a mere seventy-two days, translating the Hebrew Bible. They presented their efforts to the Egyptian king and placed a curse on any who might change anything. This translation was completed in about 250 BC and was sponsored by Ptolemy II Philadelphus (285–246 BC). Among Greek-speaking Jews (such as Paul) this Bible became a standard text, serving both Judaism and the early church for centuries. Of course, most scholars see this story as legendary, but it served one important purpose: it provided an endorsement (a divine endorsement perhaps) for a translation that Hebrew-speaking Jews might find suspect. Today scholars refer to it as the Septuagint (recalling its seventy-two translators).

Seleucid Rule (198–167 BC)

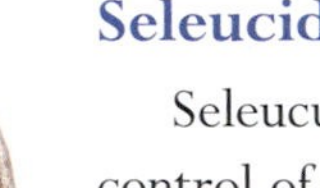

A silver *tetradrachma* minted during the reign of Seleucus I (305–281 BC) in Susa, Persia. Here Seleucus places Alexander's image on the coin as a unifying icon for his empire. On the obverse (front) of this coin appears a portrait of Alexander the Great wearing a panther-skinned helmet adorned with the ears and horns of a bull. The reverse shows a figure of Nike crowning a trophy.
Numismatica Ars Classica NAC AG, Auction 59, lot 658

Seleucus I Nicator (*conqueror*) was also one of Alexander's generals who vied for control of the fragmented empire. Along with Ptolemy I, he became a powerful leader and eventually ruled Babylon, the upper Euphrates valleys, Syria, and Anatolia (or Asia Minor). In order to build a second capital for his western interests, he founded the city of Antioch on the Orontes, with its own Mediterranean seaport named Seleucia. Scholars often refer to this as Syrian Antioch because many cities bear the name "Antioch."

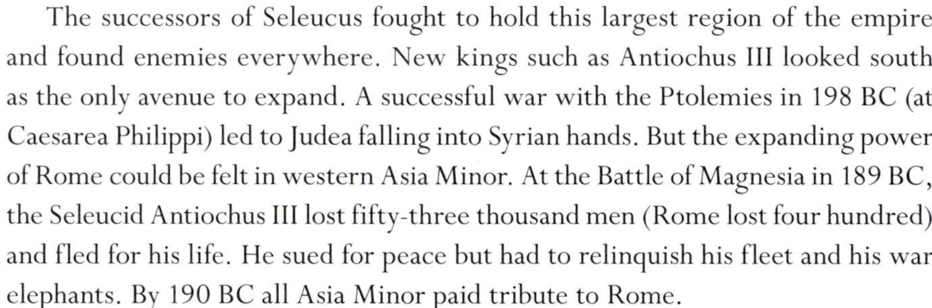

The successors of Seleucus fought to hold this largest region of the empire and found enemies everywhere. New kings such as Antiochus III looked south as the only avenue to expand. A successful war with the Ptolemies in 198 BC (at Caesarea Philippi) led to Judea falling into Syrian hands. But the expanding power of Rome could be felt in western Asia Minor. At the Battle of Magnesia in 189 BC, the Seleucid Antiochus III lost fifty-three thousand men (Rome lost four hundred) and fled for his life. He sued for peace but had to relinquish his fleet and his war elephants. By 190 BC all Asia Minor paid tribute to Rome.

In 175 BC, following the murder of Antiochus III's successor (his son, Seleucus IV), Antiochus III's second son, Antiochus IV, gained the Seleucid throne and worked to consolidate his rule. In Jerusalem he joined the tradition of his predecessors and accepted the bribes of men who desired to be high priest. Soon corrupt Hellenizers, such as Jason and Menelaus, were running the temple to the despair of the priestly families. Antiochus' presumption reached new heights when he assumed the title Epiphanes (*manifestation*, i.e., the revealing of God on earth) and sought to be worshiped. This expectation was not uncommon among ancient rulers. Recall that even Alexander sought to be known as a divine "son of god."

Antiochus Epiphanes (or Antiochus IV; "Epiphanes" means "revealed"—as if Antiochus were a divine revelation of God) worked to increase his hold on Egypt as well, but there he encountered the Romans in 168 BC. Antiochus returned north shaken and humiliated and turned against perceived ethnic minorities that might weaken his slipping position. Jewish leaders witnessed his defeat in Egypt and attempted a rebellion. Antiochus viewed Jerusalem as rebellious, and on his return from Egypt he sacked the city, tore down its walls, and looted the temple treasury. He made decrees prohibiting temple festivals and religious ceremonies such as circumcision, and it became illegal to possess the Jewish Scriptures. The worship of Greek gods became mandatory, and soon festivals for the god Dionysus could be seen in Jerusalem's streets. In the winter of 167 BC, the temple was turned over to the worship of Zeus, and for three years Greeks sacrificed pigs on Israel's holy altar. In Jewish eyes, the temple had been desecrated (1 Macc. 1:41–61). It was a desecration that would forever remain in Jewish memory and is retold even today in the Jewish festival of Hanukkah.

Maccabean War (167–141 BC)

Resistance to Hellenism had been expressed for decades before this famous "abomination of desolation" at the temple. A group of Jews calling themselves the Hasidim (*pious ones*) saw the long-term implications of Hellenistic cultural advances and openly criticized Jews who flirted with Hellenistic ways. Using Greek speech might lead to youth visiting Greek theaters—and then Greek race-tracks and temples. But if some Jewish leaders were ever complacent about the assimilation of Hellenistic culture, much of it stopped in 167 BC with the temple's desecration. This tragedy brought an opportunity that the Hasidim now exploited. Antiochus had gone too far, and his offense to the temple proved to be the catalyst Judaism needed.

The story of the Jews' resistance to their Seleucid oppressors became something legendary, since it was retold every year at the feast of Hanukkah. The apocryphal book 1 Maccabees outlines its history and 2 Maccabees records heroic episodes of suffering and martyrdom. For example, we read about the faithful priest Eleazar, who refused pressure to sacrifice to Zeus and instead chose death (2 Macc. 6:18–31). These stories were well known in Jesus's day and inspired resistance to cultural compromise that would eventually fuel Jewish resistance to Rome.

The passive resistance of the Hasidim quickly shifted to open warfare. Typical was the priest Mattathias, who refused to compromise under pressure and traveled to the

Judas Maccabaeus Cleanses the Temple

The most profound moment in the Maccabean war came in 164 BC, when Judas and his brothers fought their way to Jerusalem and arrived at the temple. "They saw the sanctuary desolate, the altar profaned, and the gates burned. In the courts they saw bushes sprung up as in a thicket . . . [and] they saw the chambers of the priests in ruins" (1 Macc. 4:38).

Judas wept and cried out to heaven. Then he appointed priests to rededicate the temple and restore its offerings and sacrifices.

Antiochus IV used repressive measures to Hellenize Judaism not long after he came to the throne in 175 BC. This gold coin, issued in his kingdom during this period, shows Zeus enthroned, aligning Antiochus with a divine identity.
Z. Radovan/www.BibleLand Pictures.com

village of Modein, a village northwest of Jerusalem. There ambitious young Greek soldiers demanded that he sacrifice to Zeus. Mattathias refused, drew a sword, killed the men, and destroyed their gentile altar. With his sons Judas, Simon, and Jonathan, Mattathias inspired a widespread revolt that stirred the villages of Judea and launched a guerrilla campaign to expel the Greeks from the land of Judea. Mattathias was killed and his son Judas led the war, gaining the nickname "Maccabeus" (*hammer*). Soon the revolt was called the Maccabean Revolt.

The Jewish fighters often won battles since they knew the terrain well and fought against an empire being challenged on every border. In 164 BC Judas gained the temple precincts and cleansed the sanctuary, inaugurating the feast we know as Hanukkah (*dedication*, 1 Macc. 4:36–51; Josephus refers to it as "the festival of lights," *Ant.* 12.7.7 [325]). The balance of the walled city had been planned as a Greek city and renamed Antiochia. Judas built a siege wall around it, defeated it, and razed it; then he built a Jewish palace on its grounds. His brother Jonathan gained a treaty with Rome, thus giving more threatening support to the war. Soon the Seleucids were in full retreat as they pulled back to Antioch and there awaited the coming Roman armies, who would conquer that capital seventy-five years later.

The Hasmonean Dynasty (141–63 BC)

The spoils of war now fell into the hands of the leaders of those campaigns. The family of Mattathias and its heirs formed the first Jewish dynasty in centuries, naming it the Hasmonean Dynasty. Since Judas and Jonathan had both died in battle, a popular assembly in Jerusalem proclaimed Simon a "high priest forever until a trustworthy prophet should arise" (1 Macc. 14:41). A Jewish calendar began with this *theocracy* as year 1. Note in 1 Maccabees 13:42 how documents and contracts were marked: "in the first year of Simon the great high priest and commander and leader of the Jews." For the first time since 586 BC, Jewish coins were minted, and the Jews enjoyed genuine autonomy.

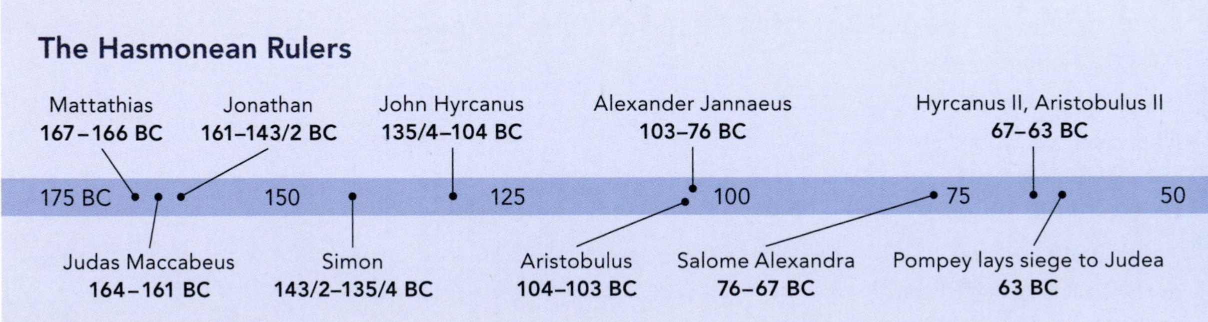

The Hasmoneans consolidated their power and wealth and soon became a small aristocracy ruling Jerusalem. These efforts alienated many who had fought in the war but who now felt marginalized. Those with roots going back to the original Hasidim, whose zeal for the law and the purity of the land inspired the war, now recognized that they had little stake in the new government in Jerusalem. In a generation, Judaism found itself torn three ways: Hellenized Jews, who still embraced Greek culture and life; Hasmoneans, who brokered power and maintained significant wealth in Jerusalem; and Hasidim, a grass-roots movement that called for religious purity and warned of the corrupting dangers of power. Some went so far as to condemn the hereditary priesthood that began with Simon.

These tensions only increased as the Hasmonean princes expanded their borders and prosperity increased. Resistance to their rule focused on the Hasidim (known later as the Pharisees), whose power was localized in the numerous synagogues around the country. The Hasmoneans became an urban autocracy invested in the temple and the religious success of the Jewish nation. Struggle between these two groups intensified throughout the years 100–65 BC. Fearing a civil war, many Hasmonean kings tried to preempt rebellions by destroying any cities sympathetic with Hellenism. Archaeologists have found destruction layers at various Hellenistic cities in the area that were attacked and destroyed by the Hasmoneans in this period (Mount Gerizim, Shechem, Marisa, and Pella). Sometimes they even attacked moderate Jews who challenged their authority. Alexander Jannaeus, for instance, ruled from 103–76 BC and in one year crucified eight hundred Pharisees in order to protect the status quo.

Hasmonean *lepton* or *prutah*, a coin of the smallest value, minted 103–76 BC with upright palm branch surrounded by the inscription "Yehonatan the King."
© The Trustees of the British Museum

THE ROMAN PERIOD (63 BC–AD 135)

Throughout the Seleucid period, the fledgling Roman Empire expanded east. Two prizes were in its sights: Egypt (famous for its wealth, its academies, and its agricultural produce) and Syria (gateway to the Euphrates valley). From the Taurus Mountains to Lebanon, the fertility of the land was unmatched. And control of the Upper Euphrates meant that Rome could halt any threat from its rival Parthia (or Persia). The empire therefore devised a plan. A swift march of legionnaires through Anatolia could capture Antioch, then move down the coast, controlling the corridor that would take them to Egypt. It was a strategy used and proven by Alexander the Great. Rome would retrace his steps.

Pompey's Conquest (63 BC)

Pompey the Great (106–48 BC), one of Rome's most celebrated commanders in the first century BC, had established his reputation through successful wars in Sicily, Africa, and Spain. He also was given command of a naval force and

Pompey enjoyed a reputation as one of the leading military officers in first-century BC Rome. When civil war broke out in Judea between the brothers Hyrcanus and Aristobulus, he exploited it masterfully, turning Judea into a Roman province. *PLRANG ART/Shutterstock*

successfully cleared much of the Mediterranean of pirates that often intercepted Roman merchant ships and impeded Roman communication networks. In 67 BC he was assigned to bring a Roman force to the boundary of the Seleucid domain. In 64 BC Syrian Antioch fell to Pompey. Immediately, he began his march south, where Judea was his next strategic goal.

Pompey's march into Judea has been recorded in some detail by Josephus (*Ant.* 14.4.1–4 [57–71]; *War* 1.7.1–5 [141–151]). Conditions could not have been better for a siege. A civil war had erupted in Jerusalem between factions supporting rival brothers for the Jewish throne. Pompey followed the Orontes River south from Antioch. He liberated Damascus and the many Greek settlements and cities that had lived under merciless Hasmonean rule for a hundred years. There he found auxiliary troops as well as abundant provisions. He promised that under Roman administration, Damascus and the rest of the Decapolis (or League of *Ten Cities*) would never again live under Jewish rule. The Greeks of Syria celebrated and eagerly joined Pompey's legions.

In 63 BC Pompey moved to Jericho and there began receiving peace overtures from a Jerusalem in disarray. He promptly marched west, but when he arrived at Jerusalem's walls, some factions wanted to welcome him while others threatened hostilities. Pledges of peace from the city were evaporating, so Pompey prepared for war. He built a siege wall around the city, broke through the city's western defenses, and finally entered the temple where the priests were slain as they served. According to Josephus (*Ant.* 14.4.4 [69–72]), Pompey entered the temple sanctuaries and demanded to enter the Most Holy Place, something the high priest did only once each year (on the Day of Atonement). For Israel, it was a high sacrilege. He entered and looked around, but he did not touch the temple furniture or its treasures. In this one-day siege, twelve thousand Jewish citizens of Jerusalem died.

The Decapolis

Following his successful conquest of the region, Pompey freed numerous cities from Jewish rule that the Roman governor of Syria administered. The Roman historian Pliny was the first to list them (*Natural History*, 5.16 [74]): Scythopolis, Gadara, Hippos, Dion, Pella, Raphana, Canatha, Damascus, Philadelphia, and Galasa (Gerasa). These cities formed a "league" and controlled important trade routes from Syria. Pompey also created several other autonomous Greek cities, setting them free from Jewish jurisdiction.

Jesus visited the Decapolis during his ministry (Mark 5:20; 7:31). For instance, the Gerasene demoniac was possibly from Gerasa (Mark 5:1–20). When Jesus visited here he entered a strictly Greek world—hence the presence of swine in Mark 5:11–12.

Gerasa was a major Decapolis city located in the mountains of Gilead. This is the main street (or cardo) that was once lined with public buildings. During Pompey's campaign into Judea, he conquered Gerasa and made it a part of his alliance of pro-Roman cities.
Todd Bolen/BiblePlaces.com

Plaza columns are still standing in Gerasa, modern Jordan.
Iuliia Khabibullina/Shutterstock

Pompey laid a heavy tribute (or tax levy) on the city and appointed a high priest of his choosing (Hyrcanus II). Pompey beheaded many of Jerusalem's leaders who resisted him and distributed rewards to those who had rendered support. After his departure, Roman rulers set about administering the new province, rebuilding the freed Decapolis cities and organizing two legions (9,600 troops) to quell any resistance.

Jewish Rulers under Rome

For the next two decades, Jewish leaders engaged a delicate game of political cooperation and passive resistance. Antipater (significant from 63–43 BC) was

The Roman Empire

a wealthy Idumean (from the southern deserts) who Pompey had valued for his political help. Antipater had supported the new high priest Hyrcanus and seemed cooperative. Rome needed him because he understood the local politics of Judea well, but as an Idumean he might not succumb to nationalistic urges. Antipater soon became the power behind Hyrcanus, and because Antipater won Rome's favor, Julius Caesar made him a tax-free Roman citizen and overseer of Judea in 47 BC. Permission to rebuild Jerusalem's walls came next, but in 43 BC he was poisoned by a rival. However, his two sons had already become regional rulers: Phasael led Judea and Herod ran Galilee. Herod had aspirations to lead the entire country. With their father's death, both men were appointed joint rulers of the province.

In 40 BC the Parthian threat that Rome had predicted now broke over Syria. Jerusalem was captured, Hyrcanus exiled, and Phasael killed. Herod fled for his life, running to Bethlehem, to the Dead Sea, then south to Egypt, where he was received in Alexandria by Cleopatra, and took passage to Rome, vowing to return. The Roman Senate declared him "King of the Jews." Fortified with Roman troops, he returned to Jerusalem in 37 BC and attacked the city's defenders. The conflict was short-lived and established Herod on the throne.

Among Herod's greatest engineering achievements, the port city of Caesarea stands out. Here a deep-water artificial harbor welcomed Roman ships from the west. The project began in about 22 BC and took Herod's engineers twelve years to complete. Recently scholars have located a hippodrome, warehouses, and a palace complex as well.
Balage Balogh/www.archaeologyillustrated.com

Herod the Great (37–4 BC)

Herod the Great ruled for thirty-three years and became an expert at placating Roman interests in the region while keeping his Jewish province intact and prosperous. He built a series of fortresses around Judea, which accurately show his political concerns and vulnerabilities. All risks were to the east and south. The Parthians might return through Syria; the independent Arab Nabatean Kingdom was across the Dead Sea; and Cleopatra in Egypt had already gained ownership of Jericho (as well as Phoenicia and parts of Arabia).

The theater at Caesarea has been completely excavated. It was rebuilt after Herod but still conveys something of the city's might. It seated about four thousand people.
volkova natalia/Shutterstock

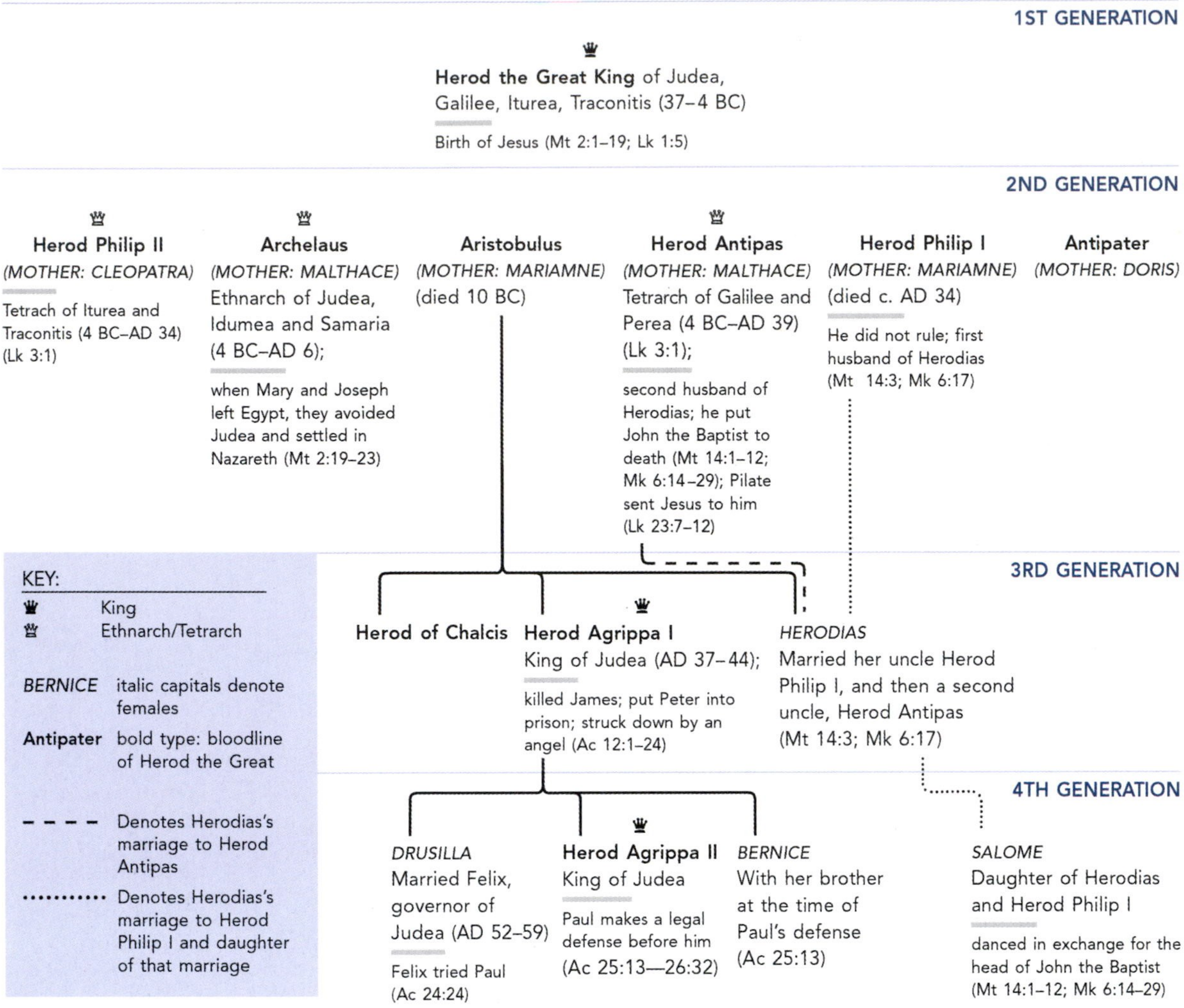

1ST GENERATION

Herod the Great King of Judea, Galilee, Iturea, Traconitis (37–4 BC)

Birth of Jesus (Mt 2:1–19; Lk 1:5)

2ND GENERATION

Herod Philip II
(MOTHER: CLEOPATRA)
Tetrach of Iturea and Traconitis (4 BC–AD 34) (Lk 3:1)

Archelaus
(MOTHER: MALTHACE)
Ethnarch of Judea, Idumea and Samaria (4 BC–AD 6);
when Mary and Joseph left Egypt, they avoided Judea and settled in Nazareth (Mt 2:19–23)

Aristobulus
(MOTHER: MARIAMNE)
(died 10 BC)

Herod Antipas
(MOTHER: MALTHACE)
Tetrarch of Galilee and Perea (4 BC–AD 39) (Lk 3:1);
second husband of Herodias; he put John the Baptist to death (Mt 14:1–12; Mk 6:14–29); Pilate sent Jesus to him (Lk 23:7–12)

Herod Philip I
(MOTHER: MARIAMNE)
(died c. AD 34)
He did not rule; first husband of Herodias (Mt 14:3; Mk 6:17)

Antipater
(MOTHER: DORIS)

3RD GENERATION

Herod of Chalcis

Herod Agrippa I
King of Judea (AD 37–44);
killed James; put Peter into prison; struck down by an angel (Ac 12:1–24)

HERODIAS
Married her uncle Herod Philip I, and then a second uncle, Herod Antipas (Mt 14:3; Mk 6:17)

4TH GENERATION

DRUSILLA
Married Felix, governor of Judea (AD 52–59)
Felix tried Paul (Ac 24:24)

Herod Agrippa II
King of Judea
Paul makes a legal defense before him (Ac 25:13—26:32)

BERNICE
With her brother at the time of Paul's defense (Ac 25:13)

SALOME
Daughter of Herodias and Herod Philip I
danced in exchange for the head of John the Baptist (Mt 14:1–12; Mk 6:14–29)

KEY:
♛ King
♕ Ethnarch/Tetrarch
BERNICE italic capitals denote females
Antipater bold type: bloodline of Herod the Great
– – – – Denotes Herodias's marriage to Herod Antipas
.... Denotes Herodias's marriage to Herod Philip I and daughter of that marriage

A family tree showing the lineage from Herod the Great to Agrippa II

Herod felt additional vulnerabilities as an "outsider" among the Hasmonean families of Jerusalem. Most viewed him as "half Jewish," since his mother was Arab (*Ant.* 14.7.3 [121–122]). He married one of the Hasmonean daughters, Mariamne, hoping to shore up his connections, but throughout his life he was always viewed as an interloper, well-connected to Rome but tenuously supported by leading Jewish families. He felt so suspicious about these families that he arranged to have two of his sons by Mariamne killed "by accident." Altogether he executed forty-five Hasmoneans, fearing conspiracies.

To make Judea into one of Rome's finest provinces, Herod embarked on an ambitious building program. A new fabulous harbor, one of the largest in the Mediterranean, Caesarea Maritima, gave access to ships from the west (*Ant.* 15.9.6 [331–341]). It was dominated by a temple to Augustus. In time it became the center for the Roman

The Herodium was a fortress built by Herod just southeast of Bethlehem. Today Roman baths, a synagogue, defensive walls, and massive sling stones (*ballista*) are among the material remains still in the fort. Pools and palaces graced the foot of the mountain. Later Herod was buried here.
© 2018 by Zondervan

The temple platform built by Herod I is enclosed behind Herod's retaining wall. In this photo, the corner on the right of the platform is Jerusalem's southeast corner.
Z. Radovan/www.BibleLand Pictures.com

provincial administration, where many Roman soldiers were billeted. Cornelius, located at Caesarea, was a typical officer; in Acts 10 he became the first gentile convert to the church.

In addition, Herod began construction projects elsewhere. His most important contribution was in Jerusalem, where he not only refurbished the walls and added theaters, a water system, a racetrack, and an opulent palace, but he reconstructed the temple—a project that began in 20 BC and was not completed until AD 63. The inner sanctuaries

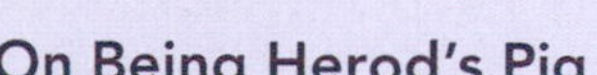

On Being Herod's Pig

Emperor Augustus held little respect for Herod and at one point offered the biting, humorous, and likely apocryphal pun: "I'd rather be Herod's pig [Gk. *hus*] than Herod's son [*huios*]."

alone took eighteen months to decorate and required the training of priests, who alone could labor in the holy places. He added a women's court east of the place of sacrifice, and the court of the gentiles surrounded the temple proper. At the temple complex's northwest corner, Herod rebuilt an old Maccabean fortress so he could keep an eye on all temple activities. He called it the Antonia Fortress (named after Mark Antony, the Roman who appointed Herod king).

Herodian Jerusalem
© 2011 by Zondervan

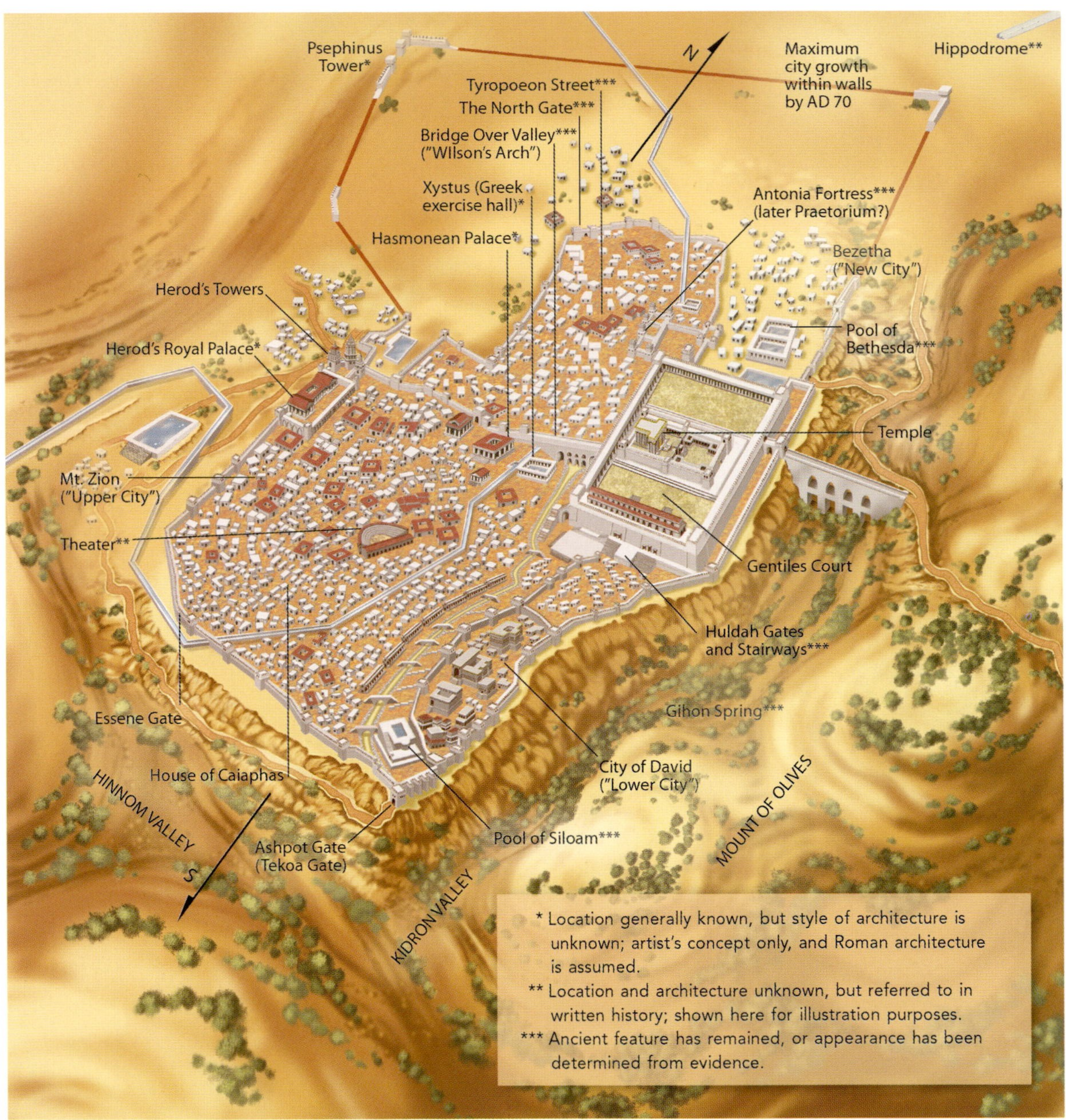

Herod's paranoia was well placed. His successes only embittered the royal families, and such construction projects were financed by taxing the people to their maximum capacity. He was admired by Rome and despised by his own country, which explains why he always watched for conspirators. Jesus was born during his reign, and it comes as no surprise that a report of a "messianic child" in Bethlehem—a child whose story evoked expectations of a messiah and promises of fulfillment—inspired him to send troops to the village on a horrific mission (Matt. 2:16–18).

Herod ordered that he was to be buried at a desert fortress about seven miles south of Jerusalem called the Herodium. However, his actual burial site remained a mystery for centuries. Archaeologists claimed to have found it in 2007, and today much of it is uncovered (see the excavation at the base of the hill). Other scholars have challenged the site's identification, but widespread support for the site remains today.
Bill Schlegel/BiblePlaces.com

When Herod died in 4 BC of incurable diseases, few mourned his death. A funeral train carried him to one of his favorite fortresses, the Herodium—near Bethlehem—where Herod's tomb is thought to be located.
© 2018 by Zondervan

Herod's New Harbor

Excavations of Caesarea—both on land and in the harbor—have continued since 1972. Remarkable discoveries have shown the magnificence of the city. For example, blocks weighing fifty tons have been found in the breakwater. One hundred huge vaults stretched along the coast to store the huge tonnage of goods moving through the port.
Todd Bolen/BiblePlaces.com

Herod built Caesarea to impress its visitors. When his twelve-year project was done, it rivaled Piraeus, the port of Athens. Along a desolate forty-mile stretch of beach, Herod constructed his port on the ruins of an abandoned village (Strato's Tower). Its breakwater used new hydraulic cement and formed a three-and-a-half-acre bay. The city of Caesarea (164 acres) was equally impressive: civic buildings with white marble façades, a theater, a hippodrome, and warehouses. The tides flushed its sewers each day, making the city unprecedented in antiquity. Fresh water came to the city from an aqueduct that carried water from springs in the north.

Above all, Herod wanted the city to signal his allegiance to Rome. A temple dedicated to Caesar Augustus dominated the hill overlooking the harbor. Josephus describes it expansively: "On an eminence facing the harbour-mouth stood Caesar's temple, remarkable for its beauty and grand proportions; it contained a colossal statue of the emperor, not inferior to the Olympian Zeus, which served for its model, and another of Rome, rivalling that of Hera at Argos. The city Herod dedicated to the province, the harbour to navigators in these waters, to Caesar the glory of this new foundation, to which he accordingly gave the name of Caesarea." (*War* 1.21.7 [414]).

The Temple's Gold Facade

Herod used much gold in the design of the temple. The exterior was adorned with massive plates of solid gold and where these were absent, brilliant white limestone blocks stood in contrast (*War* 5.5.6 [222–24]). Along the roof edge, they installed a line of tall golden spikes that prevented birds from resting there and spoiling the roof and walls with their droppings.

Mourning for Herod

Toward the end of his life (about 4 BC), Herod was gravely ill. He moved from Jerusalem to his winter residence in the desert oasis of Jericho. There he had built lavish palaces, swimming pools, and gardens near an outlet of a river canyon above the oasis. (Today visitors refer to it as "New Testament Jericho.")

Herod ordered all the noble Jewish families to come to Jericho to attend to him. When they arrived, he had them herded into Jericho's hippodrome (horseracing track) and told his soldiers to slay them the moment he died. This was to promote national mourning.

While he was on his deathbed, he obtained a letter from Rome giving him permission to slay his too-ambitious son Antipater. He did so immediately. Then he gave his will: Archelaus would be king, Antipas would rule Galilee, and Philip would rule the northeast regions (Gaulanitis, Paneas). Five days later he died.

When Herod was dead, the hippodrome was opened, no one was killed, and the people gathered together in the theater. Herod's will was read, and Archelaus was hailed as king.

Herod's temple looms large in the New Testament. Once, when the disciples arrived at Jerusalem, they were amazed at Herod's efforts: "Look, Teacher! What massive stones!" (Mark 13:1). The temple was an enormous engineering effort (led by Roman architectural skills) that placed a temple-sanctuary on top of a massive level platform. This platform was held up by a retaining wall built with enormous stones each weighing many tons. The so-called "highest point of the temple" where Jesus was tested (Matt. 4:5) likely was this retaining wall's southeast corner. When Jesus cleansed the temple of money changers (21:12–17), this took place in the Court of the gentiles (in the open courts near the sanctuary). When he debated the temple leadership (ch. 23), he did so in the expansive porches surrounding its façade. Finally, when Jesus was arrested, he was taken to the "praetorium," which housed the Roman governor (27:27). Many scholars believe his interrogation with Pilate took place in the Antonia Fortress, which was located on the temple platform's northwest corner.

House of Herod

The Division of Herod's Kingdom

As ruler of Galilee, Herod Antipas struck his own coins. No bust appears on the coin out of deference for the Jewish avoidance of images. *Z. Radovan/www.BibleLandPictures.com*

After Herod's death, three of his sons ruled various parts of the kingdom. **Archelaus's** rule of Judea (4 BC–AD 6) was vicious and feared. He was titled an "ethnarch" (ruler of a nation) because of the size of his rule (Judea, Samaria, and Idumea [Matt. 2:22]). But the country was ready to explode in rebellion. Numerous guerrilla groups revolted but were defeated when the Syrian governor Varus sent as many as three legions (fifteen thousand men) into Judea, as well as numerous auxiliary troops. Over two thousand Jewish captives were crucified. When Mary and Joseph were returning from Egypt with Jesus, they avoided Judea and returned to Galilee because "Archelaus was reigning in Judea in place of his father" (Matt. 2:22). Archelaus's brutality inspired delegations of both Samaritans and Jews to appeal to the Emperor Augustus for his removal. In AD 6 Augustus agreed and banished him to Gaul. Archelaus's territory was then placed under the jurisdiction of Roman governors.

Antipas retained his rule over Galilee and also controlled Perea, the region east of the Jordan River (4 BC–AD 39). Because he ruled a "part" of the kingdom, he was officially called a *tetrarch*, but he was allowed to use his family name of Herod, which enhanced his authority (Luke 3:19). Jesus's ministry began under Antipas's rule. Antipas rebuilt Galilee's ancient capital, Sepphoris, and made it his base. Since it was just north of Nazareth, Jesus and Joseph (who were tradesmen) may have worked there. Later Antipas built a new capital for himself on the western shore of the Sea of Galilee, calling it Tiberius (named after the emperor). The New Testament sometimes refers to the sea as "the Sea of Tiberias" (John 6:1).

Herod Philip II ruled regions northeast of Galilee. His primary capital was Caesarea Philippi, where numerous public buildings are now being uncovered. These are the ruins of the palace of Agrippa II. *Opachevsky Irina/Shutterstock*

Sepphoris: A Window into Hellenized Galilee

The traditional capital of Galilee had always been Sepphoris, a town that sat on a hill as "the ornament of all Galilee" (*Ant.* 18.2.1 [27]). Today the excavations of the Joint Sepphoris Project have uncovered a huge and remarkable Hellenistic city just north of Nazareth.

The theater and mosaics there have offered up evidence of how Hellenized the first-century city had become. In one villa, archaeologists uncovered panels that framed a dining room, depicting a drinking rivalry between Dionysus and Hercules. Dionysus, the Greek god of wine, wins.

In 1987 archaeologists uncovered a significant villa in Sepphoris with a mosaic panel depicting a woman now called the "Mona Lisa of Galilee."
Alexey Stiop/Shutterstock

Philip ruled as tetrarch over the northern regions of the kingdom (4 BC–AD 34): Gaulanitis, Auranitis, Batanea, Trachonitis, Paneas, and Iturea. These areas were chiefly Hellenistic, and he found little difficulty leading them. He built Caesarea Philippi (to distinguish it from Caesarea on the coast) as his capital, near the ancient shrine to Pan on the Jordan River's headwaters. Here Jesus was identified as Son of God and Messiah for the first time (Matt. 16:13–16). Philip also built a southern royal city at the site of Bethsaida and renamed it Bethsaida Julias (honoring Augustus's daughter). Bethsaida was the original home of the disciples Peter, his brother Andrew, and Philip (John 1:44).

When Philip the tetrarch died in AD 34, the region was temporarily given to Syria. But the new emperor Caligula gave these areas, along with Galilee, to Agrippa I in AD 39.

The excavation of ancient Jerusalem since 1967 has uncovered much of the city's material culture from the first century. This finely decorated plate typifies the life of the upper classes in the first century.
© 2018 by Zondervan

Rome Rules Judea

Form	Title	Ruler	Dates	New Testament
Client Kingdom	King	**Herod the Great**	37–4 BC	Matthew 2:1
	Ethnarch	**Archelaus**	4 BC–AD 6	Matthew 2:22
Roman Province	Prefect	Coponius	6–9	
	Prefect	Marcus Ambivius	9–12	
	Prefect	Annius Rufus	12–15	
	Prefect	Valerius Gratus	15–26	
	Prefect	**Pontius Pilate**	26–36	Luke 3:1; 23:1
	Prefect	Marullus	37–41	
Client Kingdom	King	**Herod Agrippa I**	41–44	Acts 12
Roman Province	Procurator	Cuspius Fadus	44–46	
	Procurator	**M. Antonius Felix**	52–59	Acts 23:26–24:27
	Procurator	**Porcius Festus**	59–62	Acts 25
	Procurator	Albinus	62–64	
	Procurator	Gessius Florus	64–66[2]	

Roman Prefects

Rome administered two types of provinces. Senatorial provinces were compliant with Roman rule, paid tribute, were ruled by a proconsul, and did not host a military legion. Gallio of Achaia was one such governor (Acts 18:12). Imperial provinces lived on the frontiers of the empire and were under the direct command of the emperor. If they held a Roman legion, they were governed by a *legate*. If the province was granted significant autonomy—as was the case with Judea—it was governed by *prefects* (after AD 44, called *procurators*). When Archelaus was exiled from Judea in AD 6, the emperor decided to place this important region under the direct control of Rome and thus give birth to the imperial province of Judea. We can reconstruct the names of these Roman governors (see chart above), but only three are mentioned in the New Testament (Pilate, Felix, Festus). For three years (AD 41–44) Judea returned to the status of client kingdom but then in 44 returned to an imperial province.

In AD 26 Tiberius appointed *Pontius Pilatus* or **Pontius Pilate** as the fifth governor of Judea. At the excavation of Caesarea in 1961, an inscription bearing his name was uncovered. As governor, he had full control of the territory of Archelaus. He based himself in Caesarea with a large contingent of Roman soldiers and came to Jerusalem only when necessary, staying, no doubt, at the well-armed

How Pilate Offended the Jews

The attitude of the Roman governors toward Judea is illustrated by an incident recorded by Josephus (*War* 2.9.2–3 [169–174]). The temple leaders prohibited any images in Jerusalem because it violated the second commandment. All previous governors had respected this. But Pilate brought military standards bearing Tiberius's image directly to Jerusalem by stealth at night.

A Jewish delegation went to Pilate's residence in Caesarea and demanded the removal of the standards. For five days they knelt before his house. Pilate's soldiers then surrounded them with weapons, threatening to kill them if they would not relent. The Jews offered their necks, saying they would rather die than see God's holy law profaned in the Holy City.

Pilate was stunned and removed the standards immediately.

Because of this incident (and many others), the Hellenistic Jewish philosopher Philo found little to like in Pilate. He referred to him as by nature rigid and stubbornly harsh—merciless as well as obstinate (*The Embassy to Gaius* 38 [301]). Rome also disliked Pilate's efforts. He was recalled in AD 36, and one of his lieutenants, Marcellus, took his place as overseer until Marullus, the new prefect, replaced him.

Excavators in Caesarea Maritima located a four-line dedicatory inscription with these words:

> TIBERIEUM
> [PO]NTIUS PILATUS
> [PRAEF]ECT US IUDA [EA]
> [FECIT D] E [DICAVIT]][1]

This is likely a building dedication honoring the emperor Tiberius. The *Tiberium* may have been an imperial building dedicated to the emperor. Translation: *Tiberium. Pontius Pilate, Prefect of Judea, has dedicated.* Or it may be: *To Tiberius. Pontius Pilate, Prefect of Judea, has dedicated.*

Antonia Fortress or Herod the Great's palace. The New Testament and Roman historians mention him as the governor who oversaw the trial of Jesus and called for his crucifixion (Tacitus, *Annals* 15:44; Luke 23:1).

Later Jewish Rulers

Following Pilate, a series of governors ruled the province of Judea without event. But there were occasions when Jewish rule returned to Jerusalem, generally as a result of some palace intrigue in Rome. Two Jewish rulers are noted in the New Testament.

Many of the children of the Herodian dynasty—such as all the sons of Herod the Great—were educated in Rome and became friends with the imperial families. Herod's grandson **Herod Agrippa I** was given rule of Philip's tetrarchy by Emperor Caligula in AD 37. But when Caligula died, Agrippa's boyhood friend in Rome, Claudius, ascended to the throne (AD 41). Claudius immediately made Agrippa king over all Judea, thus retiring the system of governors. He even inherited the lands and wealth of Antipas, his uncle, who had ruled Galilee.

Agrippa is mentioned in the New Testament in Acts 12:1–2 as the ruler who executed James, the son of Zebedee, in Jerusalem. He also imprisoned Peter one Passover. When an angel miraculously released Peter, Agrippa ordered Peter's guards killed (12:19). Of all the Herods, Agrippa was the most admired. Josephus records how he honored the temple upon his attainment to kingship. He offered the gift of a golden chain, a replica of one that had once imprisoned him. One of his first deeds was to enter the temple, stand on a platform, and with the high priest read the Law. When he came to Deuteronomy's "law of kingship" (Deut. 17:14–20), he wept. Jewish sources from the Mishnah to the Talmud record his piety.

But kingship also brought liabilities. Both Josephus (*Ant.* 19.8.2 [343–52]) and Acts 12:20–23 record similar accounts of his death in AD 44. He was in Caesarea wearing royal robes made of silver thread, enjoying the flattery of the crowds, some of whom called him divine. An angel of the Lord then struck him dead.

When Agrippa died, his son, **Agrippa II**, was only seventeen and according to some, too young to rule. Thus, Roman governors returned to Caesarea (now called *procurators*). In AD 50 Agrippa II was given Chalcis (today central Lebanon) and in AD 53 obtained the old northeast tetrarchy of Philip. In AD 54 Emperor Nero gave him much of Galilee, and in gratitude he rebuilt Caesarea Philippi, renaming it Neronius (*Ant.* 20.9.4 [211]).

Roman governors commonly called on local rulers for counsel when they prosecuted provincial difficulties. In Acts 25 the governor Festus called on Agrippa II and his sister Bernice to adjudicate the case of Paul (v. 13). Paul met with Agrippa and made his defense (26:1–29), whereupon the king advised Festus to free him.

Agrippa's rule (until AD 93) was without event until the outbreak of war in AD 66. He tried to stop the revolt but failed and throughout the conflict sided openly with Rome.

TWO WARS WITH ROME

Judaism's history of revolt against foreign empires such as the Seleucids was retold every winter at Hanukkah. The Maccabees had proven that revolt could be successful, and aspirations for freedom lay hidden for decades. It only took a catalyst to make it explode.

The First Revolt (AD 66–70)

The burden of rule under the Roman governors shifted with each regime. Gessius Florus (AD 65–70) was unmatched in his personal corruption and contempt for the Jews. Appeals to the legate in Syria fell on deaf ears, and soon Jewish plans to revolt erupted. A riot in Caesarea was followed by conflict in Jerusalem, where Florus crucified 3,600 people. He plundered the temple treasury, which inspired further outrage. Rome worried about a collapse of the eastern frontier, and Emperor Nero ordered Florus to increase severity lest the Parthians exploit Roman weakness.

The Jewish fighters (many of them Zealots) attacked Jerusalem's Antonia Fortress, burned Herod's Palace, and killed the Roman soldiers stationed in Jerusalem (after promising them safe passage from the city). They then occupied three of Judea's desert forts (*Herodium* near Bethlehem, *Masada* adjacent to the Dead Sea,

Titus's siege of Jerusalem took several months. The temple was entered by razing the Antonia fortress on the northwest corner of the temple.
akg-images, London/Peter Connolly

and *Machaerus* on the Nabatean border). Remembering the successes of the Maccabees, they also attacked Greek cities like Sebaste (or Samaria) and Scythopolis. In August AD 66, the temple stopped sacrificing to God on behalf of the emperor, which was, in effect, a declaration of war.

The Syrian legate, Cestius Gallus, decided to march south from Antioch with the Twelfth Roman Legion Fulminata (*thundering one*) and numerous auxiliaries. Even King Agrippa sent troops. Gallus arrived in Caesarea and obtained direction

Evidence of Rome's violent destruction of Jerusalem has been recovered along the south wall of the temple, where columns were hurled from the top of the temple and crashed onto the first-century street below.
Todd Bolen/BiblePlaces.com

The Roman Senate built the triumphal Arch of Titus in AD 81 to commemorate Titus's conquest of Judea over a decade earlier.
Wikimedia Commons/Phillip Capper, CC BY 2.0

for his march east into Judea. Minor attacks were quickly repulsed. But when he saw Jerusalem's fortifications, he decided to retreat for unknown reasons. Gallus turned around and descended the mountain, using a shortcut to Caesarea along the narrow Beth Horon ridge. His men were relaxed, and the legion was out of formation.

Suddenly, Zealot fighters ambushed them, showering the legion with arrows. No Roman defense could be formed, and soon it was a rout. Rome lost 5,300 infantry and 380 cavalry (*War* 2.19.9 [555]) as well as the legionary eagle.

The Fortress of Masada

Masada rests on the top of a dramatic mountain outcropping 1,400 feet above the western shore of the Dead Sea. Herod the Great built a palace and fortress here, guarding an escape route across the sea—one he used in 40 BC when he fled the Parthians.

Defenders saw Masada as impenetrable. Herod surrounded the mountain cliffs with a double wall and 110 defensive towers. Water was brought onto the mountain with an ingenious system that exploited a winter-flooding valley (or wadi) nearby and aqueducts that ran water into twelve cisterns that could hold 1.4 million cubic feet of water (or about 10.5 million gallons). That's enough to supply 1,000 people drinking one gallon per day for about thirty years.

The Zealots captured the fortress and used it as their "last stand" against the Romans. Evidence of their occupation—such as a first-century synagogue and ritual baths—still remain. Titus assigned an officer, Flavius Silva, to lay siege to the mountain. Silva constructed a massive siege ramp over one of the aqueducts and, using Jewish slaves from the Bethlehem region, built his way to the rim. According to Josephus, he found the grain stores burned and the defenders dead by suicide.

The final holdout for the Jewish resistance was on Herod's mountain fortress of Masada. Josephus records the possibly legendary story that the defenders committed suicide rather than surrender (*War* 7.9.1).
Todd Bolen/BiblePlaces.com

The Zealots gained all their equipment. On the ridge of Beth Horon, where Judas Maccabeus had won so many campaigns, the Roman Twelfth Legion was lost—something unprecedented in Roman history. Gallus fled with his officers back to Caesarea, and immediately a messenger was dispatched to the emperor.

The well-known general Vespasian and his son Titus formed a battle plan while the Jews of Galilee and Judea began to fortify the country. Vespasian organized an army with two complete legions (the Tenth and Fifteenth, each of which brought six thousand troops), twenty-three auxiliary cohorts (each bringing six hundred men), six detachments of cavalry, and numerous supplemental troops sent by regional kings. As he moved south, he devastated Galilee in AD 68. That same year, Emperor Nero committed suicide following defeats in Gaul and Spain, and Vespasian returned to Rome eventually to assume the throne. Titus had sailed to Alexandria and formed an army centered on the Fifth Legion and now received orders to complete the war.

Many remains of Masada's defenders have been discovered. A rare sample of clothing and studded sandals provides a glimpse of Jewish life there.
Z. Radovan/www.BibleLand Pictures.com

When Titus arrived in Caesarea, he now had four legions: the Fifth, Tenth, and Fifteenth, which were joined by the defeated and rebuilt Twelfth from Syria. He had at his disposal sixty thousand experienced soldiers and numerous war engines. Titus quickly assembled forces at every access road into Judea from Jericho to Emmaus. The Fifth Legion camped at Emmaus, the western gateway to Judea. The Tenth defeated Jericho and camped on the Mount of Olives, the eastern gateway. Troops controlled all roads north and south. No escape was possible for Jerusalem. Only its siege and destruction remained.

Coins made a political statement. In the Second Revolt (AD 132–135), Simon bar Kokhba's followers struck their own coins with a characteristic Judean palm, indicating their autonomy from Rome. This coin likely dates from AD 132.
Z. Radovan/www.BibleLand Pictures.com

Titus marched into the mountains following a route not dissimilar to that used earlier by Gallus. Following a five-month siege, Jerusalem was sacked, its population killed or enslaved, and the temple—which Titus tried to save—was burned to the ground. Titus's subordinates were then assigned to attack the remaining Zealot forts. Herodium and Machaerus fell in AD 71, and in 74, legend had it that 960 defenders of Masada chose to commit suicide rather than surrender to the Romans who surrounded them (*War* 7.8–9 [252–406]). Titus, meanwhile, began a meandering return to Rome, where he celebrated his triumph with spectacular gladiatorial games and feasts. In AD 71 he joined his father Vespasian in Rome for a joint celebration of their defeat of the Jews.

The fall of Jerusalem and the destruction of the temple devastated Judaism. Before the city's siege, Zealot rebels had taken the city and killed any Jews who whispered suggestions of surrender. At the same time, many of Jerusalem's great religious leaders departed as well, only to rebuild their academies in Galilee. Of greatest consequence were the end of temple sacrifice and the disruption of the legal system and its schools. The Sanhedrin and many leading families fled, first to the western hills (Jamnia), then to Galilee, which became their home for centuries. The early Christian church in Jerusalem likewise fled. They hid in the Decapolis city of Pella (south of the Sea of Galilee) until the war was finished (Eusebius, *Eccl. Hist.*, 3.5.3). Many of them returned to Judea and formed the nucleus of the ancient church that still survives in the region to this day.

The Second Revolt (AD 132–135)

Titus Flavius Vespasianus, the oldest son of Vespasian, led the conquest of Jerusalem and later ruled as emperor from AD 79–81.
Alfredo Dagli Orti/Shutterstock

This bronze statue of Hadrian was found at the Decapolis city of Scythopolis.
Z. Radovan/www.BibleLandPictures.com

Titus left the Tenth Legion behind in Jerusalem to maintain order, and its general became the *de facto* governor of the city. His headquarters remained at Caesarea. Jerusalem had been so completely destroyed that Josephus notes "there was left nothing to make those that came there believe it had ever been inhabited" (*War* 7.1.1 [3]).

Under Emperor Hadrian (AD 117–138) Rome decided to found a Roman colony in Jerusalem and rebuild the city, complete with gentile temples. Hadrian likewise forbade the practice of some Jewish customs, such as circumcision. This provided the catalyst for another revolt. Its religious leader, the influential Rabbi Akiba, generated support from Jewish communities throughout the Diaspora. He recognized the military genius Simon bar Kokhba as the messiah-deliverer who would drive Rome out of Judea. Akiba called him "the son of the star" (bar Kokhba), taken from Numbers 24:17 ("a star will come out of Jacob"), which was generally understood as messianic.

Following the rebels' successful occupation of Jerusalem and the retreat of the Tenth Legion, a four-year war brought Roman control back to Judea with a vengeance. Bar Kokhba and Akiba were killed in AD 135, and their followers fled to caves above En Gedi (near the Dead Sea), where they perished, leaving behind letters and remains recently discovered by archaeologists.

Hadrian now completed his plan for Jerusalem. The city was renamed *Aelia Capitolina*, and Jews were forbidden to step inside its walls. A temple dedicated to Jupiter was erected on the site of the Jewish temple, and even a temple to Aphrodite (Venus) was built on what is now the traditional site of Jesus's tomb. Hadrian laid out the city plan for Jerusalem, which is still in use today within Jerusalem's present Walled City.

Questions for Discussion

1. When did Hellenism first enter Judea and how did Jewish leaders react?
2. Why would some Jews welcome the occupation under Rome following the defeat of the Seleucids?
3. How deeply politicized was the environment in the New Testament period?
4. What features of Jesus's message about the kingdom of God would have resonated with the Jewish rebels fighting Rome?
5. How was Judaism permanently affected following the war of AD 70?

BIBLIOGRAPHY

Introductory

Bruce, F. F. *New Testament History*. New York: Doubleday, 1969.

Carter, W. *Seven Events that Shaped the New Testament World*. Grand Rapids: Baker, 2013.

Jeffers, J. S. *The Greco-Roman World of the New Testament Era*. Downers Grove, IL: InterVarsity Press, 1999.

VanderKam, J. C. *An Introduction to Early Judaism*. Grand Rapids: Eerdmans, 2001.

Advanced

Reicke, B. *The New Testament Era: The World of the Bible from 500 BC to AD 100*. Philadelphia: Fortress, 1968.

Rhoads, D. M. *Israel in Revolution, 6–74 C.E.: A Political History Based on the Writings of Josephus*. Philadelphia: Fortress, 1976.

Schiffman, L. *From Text to Tradition: A History of Second Temple and Rabbinic Judaism*. Jersey City: Ktav, 1991.

Schürer, E. *The History of the Jewish People in the Age of Jesus Christ*. 4 vols., rev. and ed. G. Vermes, F. Millar, and M. Black. Edinburgh: T. & T. Clark, 1973–1987.

NOTES

1. This reconstruction is from K. C. Hanson and D. E. Oakman, *Palestine in the Time of Jesus: Social Structures and Social Conflicts* (Minneapolis: Fortress, 1998), 78.

2. Source is J. S. Jeffers, *The Greco-Roman World of the New Testament Era* (Downers Grove, IL: InterVaristy Press, 1999), 122.

Chapter 3

THE WORLD OF JESUS IN HIS JEWISH HOMELAND

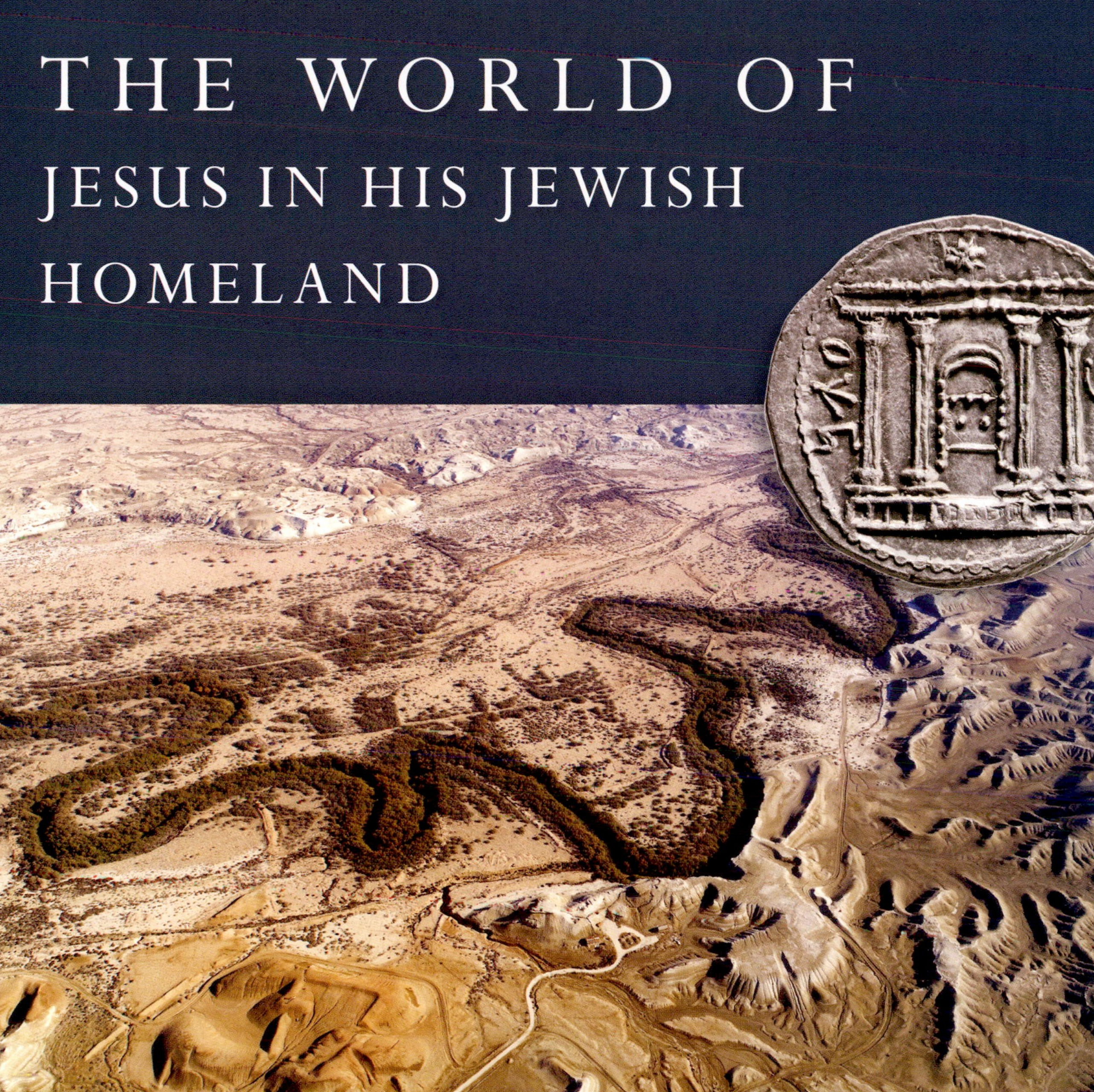

The Jordan River, south of Allenby Bridge
Bill Schlegel/BiblePlaces.com

PERSPECTIVE

Every person understands life through the set of cultural habits shared from generation to generation. This was equally true for Jesus's earliest followers, who lived in a world vastly different from our own. Factors such as religious traditions, social habits, economic and agricultural customs, architecture, historical events, and even geographical features of the landscape each contributed to the "framework" or "lens" through which they saw life.

The cultural forces of the Roman Empire during the first century may be seen at Caesarea Maritima in this *nymphaeum*, the remains of a palace fountain with a partial statue of a Roman emperor.
Roman Yannushevsky/ Shutterstock

Today scholars are keenly aware of the need to reconstruct the social world of first-century eastern Mediterranean society. A number of New Testament researchers have applied the tools of cultural anthropology to the New Testament and offered remarkable insights into first-century Palestine and the events in the Gospels. The same is true for the life of Paul. Everything from the cultural forces of Hellenism to the travel of trade routes influence how we view the apostle and his journeys.

The challenge for modern interpreters of the New Testament is that we read our Scriptures with entirely different cultural assumptions. Humility forces us to recognize that we are *foreigners to the biblical stories*, that they represent a different time and place from our own. When we try to understand them, we miss many cultural cues and may even misrepresent some of their stories.

Thus, for us to understand Jesus, Paul, and the world of the earliest Christians, we need to become cultural anthropologists. What did it mean for a Greek-speaking Jew like Paul to address an audience of philosophers in Athens? How did people travel and why does the New Testament emphasize hospitality? What is the difference between Galilee and Judea? How was gender perceived in this world and what boundaries existed between men and women? This chapter will help us probe the world of Jesus, centered on Galilee, Samaria, and Judea. Chapter 4 will concentrate on the wider Mediterranean world. In each case, we will try to reconstruct what the earliest Christians knew, so that we can read the New Testament in its setting in antiquity.

THE LAND OF ISRAEL

It is difficult to overestimate the importance of the land of Israel to Jesus's contemporaries. Rabbis wrote with longing about life there. They called it a "goodly land" and a "land which is the most precious of all lands." It was viewed as "extensive and beautiful," "pleasant and glorious," and "promised to all those who remained faithful to God."[1] During festivals Jews traveled from great distances to come to Jerusalem (note Acts 2:9–11). Jews argued with each other about the obligation to live there—and many Jews sought at least to be buried there.

Fully 35 percent of the Mishnah was devoted to issues related to life in the land—and this only reflected the emphasis of the Old Testament, where residence in Israel was presupposed. The instruction for agricultural tithes, cities of refuge, and sacrifices assumed one lived in Israel. But it was temple worship and sacrifices that (according to the Mishnah) gave the land its high degree of holiness. The sacrificial altar would only accept animals and produce that had come from Israel itself. One rabbi, writing on Numbers 23:7, insisted that in every prayer after eating, the people should pray: "The Holy One, blessed be He, said, 'The Land of Israel is more precious to me than everything.'"

This fourth-century mosaic from the synagogue at Hammat Tiberius shows four images sacred to early Jewish use: the lulav bundle, the temple candelabra, an incense shovel, and the shofar (ram's horn). The lulav was used in antiquity at every Tabernacles feast.
Z. Radovan/www.BibleLand Pictures.com

This means that Judaism was a "territorial religion." That is, Judaism would always have difficulty understanding itself apart from its life in "the land" promised by God to Abraham. Some scholars even believe "land" is the central theme of all biblical faith.[2] This explains the devastating consequences of the destruction of Jerusalem in both 586 BC and AD 70. Many wondered: How could Israel live its life apart from its land?

This theme will return to us with unexpected force as we read the New Testament. Since the early church understood that in Christ some of the fundamental categories of Judaism were being transformed (such as gentiles being counted among the people of God), so too the territoriality of Judaism would undergo enormous changes in the New Testament. The "holy land" will not exclusively be found in Judea but will include the entire world. But for this we will have to wait for the book of Acts.

The lulav is used today in the Jewish holiday of Tabernacles.
iStock.com/Tova Teitelbaum

Geographical Setting of Israel

Israel is located at the eastern end of the Mediterranean Sea and forms a land bridge that connected great empires in antiquity. Because of the massive deserts of Arabia and Syria, trade and communication between Mesopotamia and Egypt passed through an area known as the Fertile Crescent (the upper Euphrates River, northern Syria, Israel, and Egypt). In times of peace, this brought prosperity; but in times of war, devastation. With the coming of the Greeks and Romans, for the first time, control over Israel was oriented toward western Mediterranean cultures.

The classic boundaries of biblical Israel generally began with the western coastline that ran along the Mediterranean. The natural eastern boundary was the Jordan River (Num. 34:12). The north/south limits were often described as "from Dan to Beersheba" (Judg. 20:1), which simply marked settlements in the rugged north Galilee mountains and the south central deserts (though Israel's rule often went farther south).

Zone One: The Coastal Plain

Look carefully at the map on page 71. It is easiest to divide the country into a series of five longitudinal zones. Note how a major backbone of mountains runs north-south and then in northern Samaria it turns northwest and continues to the sea. This creates the first major zone—the coastal plain—which runs from Mount Carmel in the north to regions south of Gaza.

Caesarea Maritima was built by Herod the Great as the chief gateway into the country from the west. Today the ancient city and its port are being excavated. This racetrack, south of the harbor, stretches along the coastline.
© 2018 by Zondervan

In the New Testament era, this coast had a number of fishing villages, such as Joppa (see Acts 10). It also had coastal cities such as Azotus, Ashkelon, and Caesarea, home to Cornelius (Acts 10:1) and the site of Paul's two-year imprisonment (Acts 23–26). Each period of political rule sought some link to the west. Thanks to Herod the Great's architectural plans, Caesarea became one of the greatest ports in the entire empire. The Roman political administration for the province was located here, and it became a critical harbor for Israel, linking it with the rest of the Roman Empire. Following Herod's death, his son Antipas

The Physical Geography of Israel

From the coast, the hills of Judea begin to rise immediately. Here the Sorek River runs from the hills near Jerusalem to the Mediterranean Sea.
Z. Radovan/www.BibleLand Pictures.com

(who ruled western Galilee) knew that his connection to Caesarea was limited. In this era Ptolemais, built in the natural harbor that today shelters modern Haifa, was developed into a significant commercial center between the Mediterranean and central Galilee.

Zone Two: The Coastal Hills

Traveling east from the coast, we see low coastal hills that begin near Beersheba in the south and continue north just east of Caesarea. Mount Carmel abruptly interrupts these hills and replaces them with dramatic vertical cliffs. The area is remarkably fertile and enjoys the rainfall of the coast without the problems of low-lying sand and swamp.

Various smaller villages from the New Testament era have been discovered in these hills. Perhaps the most famous is Emmaus. Luke 24:13–32 tells us about disciples who made the seven-mile journey from Jerusalem to Emmaus when the resurrected Jesus joined them. They continued to the village, where Jesus ate with them and explained the events of his death.

The coastal hills crest at the top of the Judean hills. This is near the headwaters of the Sorek River.
Z. Radovan/www.BibleLand Pictures.com

Zone Three: The Central Mountains

East of the foothills is the central mountain range that begins south of Hebron and continues north to Samaria (where the mountains turn northwest toward the sea). These mountains rise as high as three thousand feet and are made of hard limestone that is excellent for building. Because limestone is porous, it serves like a sponge, soaking up rainwater and holding it all year. Farther down the mountain or in valleys, the water escapes in a spring or can be tapped by a well. The mountains form deep valleys, and the limestone erodes into a rich soil that is excellent

for agriculture (called *terra rosa*). Villages thus hugged the hillsides, and farming was done either in the valley or along terraces. In Matthew 5:14 Jesus referred to a "a town built on a hill"; he likely had such villages in mind.

In these mountains three great cities were like landmarks: Hebron, Jerusalem, and Shechem. Hebron is the site where Abraham, Sarah, Isaac, Rebekah, Jacob, and Leah were buried (in the cave of Machpelah, Gen. 23:19; 49:29–31). In fact, in Jesus's day Herod the Great built a major shrine over the site, commemorating the burial ground, and the monumental building still stands to this day (it is deeply venerated by both Jews and Muslims). Jerusalem, of course, lay at the heart of Judaism's religious life, and its temple was the site of regular pilgrimage for pious Jews. Jerusalem was therefore a city set in the mountains. It was a "high place," with the temple being its highest point (Micah 1:5). This is both a geographical truth as well as a theological truth, since high places were thought to be places of special spiritual significance in antiquity (see Num. 33:52; 1 Kings 3:2; and Luke 4:5). Therefore, whenever you traveled, you always went "up" to Jerusalem (Matt. 20:17–18).

To Jews in Jesus's day, these central mountains, with Jerusalem at the center, were called Judea and served as the heartland of Jewish life and thought. Even Galilee lived in its shadow. But an ethnic divide almost eight hundred years old still existed north of Judea. Just north of Jerusalem lived the Samaritans, who claimed a separate heritage, denied their Jewish identity, and located their own temple on a mountain above ancient Shechem. Hostilities between the two communities flared regularly, which made it all the more surprising that both Jesus (Luke 9:52; John 4:9) and the early Christians (Acts 8:25) reached out to them.

In addition to these main cities (such as Jerusalem), numerous minor poor villages dotted the hills. Bethlehem is perhaps the most famous of these, located about five miles south of Jerusalem. In Jesus's day Bethlehem looked nothing like the large city of twenty-five thousand we see today. It was a tiny village made up of perhaps a few dozen extended families.

Bury Me in the Holy Land

Throughout the New Testament era, Jews desired to be buried on the Mount of Olives east of Jerusalem, where the Messiah might appear. Ancient tombs still abound on this hill—and today modern Jewish cemeteries cover the western face of the hill.

Following the second Jewish war of AD 135, burial around Jerusalem became impossible, since Hadrian had prohibited it to Jews. The Sanhedrin moved to Galilee, and eventually the village of Beit She'arim became the first choice for burial. The great organizer of the Mishnah, Rabbi Judah ha-Nasi, lived and was buried there.

Evidence of the popular desire of Jews from throughout the Mediterranean region to be buried in the Holy Land can be seen in the magnificent catacombs and architectural remains at Beit She'arim. Rock-cut tombs and sarcophagi abound in tunnel after tunnel. One vast catacomb (number twenty) contains two hundred single-grave wall niches and 125 sarcophagi (free-standing stone burial boxes).

Houses Built on a Rock

Jesus once compared obedient disciples to wise people who built their houses on rock, and disobedient disciples to foolish people who built houses on topsoil (see Matt. 7:24–27). Jesus likely has in mind the person who builds his home by carving its foundation out of mountain bedrock (a practice found everywhere among Palestinian villages). Cut limestone stacked on bedrock cannot be moved. The topsoil of the valley often floods and is subject to instability.

Jerusalem viewed from the Mount of Olives in the east. The limestone wall in the foreground was built during Herod's refurbishing of the city in the first century BC. *Mordechai Meiri/Shutterstock*

The central mountains form the backbone of the country, and a short walk east of their main ridge delivers the traveler into an unexpected rocky wilderness. Small villages hug the upper reaches of this eastern ridge (Bethphage, Bethany), but life here is difficult, since the mountains form a rain shadow, converting Jerusalem's generous twenty-four inches of rainfall to just over eight.

The wilderness ends at the Dead Sea. Nearby were oases such as Jericho and communities such as Qumran. *David Bivin/www.BiblePlaces.com*

Zone Four: The Jordan Valley

From the mountains, the wilderness landscape descends dramatically for almost ten miles, dropping almost 3,500 feet. The chief geographical marker in this desert is the Jordan River, which lies at the base of this deep depression. It is part of a far larger geological fissure that runs for 3,700 miles from Turkey to Africa, making the Dead Sea the lowest point on earth. The Jordan River begins in the far north, in mountains above Galilee (near Mount Hermon) and feeds the Sea of Galilee basin, which is already about seven hundred feet below sea level.

The Wilderness

Proximity to the wilderness defined life in almost every biblical city—Hebron, Bethlehem, Jerusalem, Ramah, Shechem. From Jerusalem it is just behind the Mount of Olives. When Saul was in pursuit of David, David fled east, slipping into the wilderness for safety, making his way eventually to the oasis of En Gedi (1 Sam. 24:1). When travelers in antiquity wanted to walk from Jerusalem to Galilee, they often entered the wilderness on a road (nicely carved by the Romans) and headed to Jericho. From there it was about seventy-five miles north to the great inland Sea of Galilee.

The wilderness is a physical reality and a spiritual motif in biblical life. The wilderness is where faith was forged (see Deut. 6–10). From Abraham to Moses in the Old Testament, even Israel itself, religious identity was shaped in the desert wilderness. In the New Testament, John the Baptist required Jews to enter the wilderness to experience his baptism, Jesus was tested in the wilderness for forty days, and Paul was in the Arabian wilderness for three years after his conversion.

East of Jerusalem, the landscape becomes a wilderness. This Judean Wilderness was the area where Jesus was tempted for forty days.
© 2018 by Zondervan

The Jordan River descends into the desolate wilderness here near the Jabbok River. Viewed from the west facing modern Jordan, it is barely visible and winds its way through the lush river valley seen here.
Todd Bolen/BiblePlaces.com

It then continues its descent, ending in the Dead Sea (about 1,200 feet below sea level). From the Jordan River, the valley climbs back up steep eastern cliffs that ascend as high as 3,600 feet.

Occasional oases, such as Jericho, permitted villages to grow, but without a natural spring or a clever water retention system (such as Qumran), life here was impossible. The wilderness was well known as a place of refuge and testing for everyone from King David to Jesus (1 Sam. 19–24; Matt. 4:1–11). John the Baptist also used this region, and Jesus told stories about travel through this region. Jews coming to Jerusalem from Galilee often used this valley route, stopping at oases along the way. They arrived at Jericho and climbed west, ascending the Judean mountains, passing through Bethany and Bethphage, and arriving at Jerusalem. This desolate road was the setting for Jesus's famous parable of the Good Samaritan (Luke 10:29–37).

Zone Five: The Eastern Plateau

On the east side of the Jordan, a plateau rises precipitously, and its elevation reclaims the rainfall that had been prohibited to the deep Jordan Valley. Here were cities that could grow cereal crops (thanks to fifteen inches of rainfall) and benefited from desert trading routes. Here were the cities of the Decapolis (see ch. 2). The northern region just east of the Jordan River was known as Perea and was under the authority of Herod Antipas (along with Galilee itself). This explains why John the Baptist, who lived in this desert, could be pursued by Antipas. South of that was Nabatea, which had its capital at the famous canyon of Petra. Antipas feared the Nabateans and constructed a fortress on the border called Machaerus. Paul lived in these deserts for a while after his conversion (Gal. 1:17, called Arabia) and was threatened by the governor of Damascus, who served Aretas IV, king of Nabatea (2 Cor. 11:32).

Galilee

The geographical features that defined Judea and Samaria are absent in the northern region of Galilee. The north/south mountains disappear and a wide valley—the Jezreel Valley—separates Galilee from the central mountains. The chief feature of the region is a large (thirteen by eight miles) freshwater lake, the Sea of Galilee, which is fed by the descending Jordan River. This sea was a chief source of fishing. To date, we have discovered the remnants of almost twenty ancient harbors surrounding the lake.

Upper Galilee (the northern part) has mountains that are nearly four thousand feet in elevation. This region is desolate. When Jesus departed into the mountains to be alone, this was his destination.

Jewish fishing villages and Hellenistic cities surrounded Galilee's shores. Here we see two views of the ancient harbor of En Gev. The view from the lake shows a cone-shaped hill. This is the ancient Roman city of Hippos.
Todd Bolen/BiblePlaces.com

Galilee's villages prospered for many centuries. This is Chorazin's fourth-century synagogue.
A. D. Riddle/BiblePlaces.com

Fishing on Galilee's North Shore

Capernaum and other fishing villages were located on Galilee's northwest shore. Jesus told many stories about fishing and boats from this location. This may have been the site of his miraculous catch of fish (Luke 5:3–7; John 21:4–8).

Why Galilee's north shore? Numerous underground springs feed the sea, but many of these are geothermal springs, giving areas of the lake less preferable mineral water. But the northwest corner has an abundance of *freshwater* springs attracting large numbers of fish. This area was called *Heptapegon* (Greek for "seven springs").

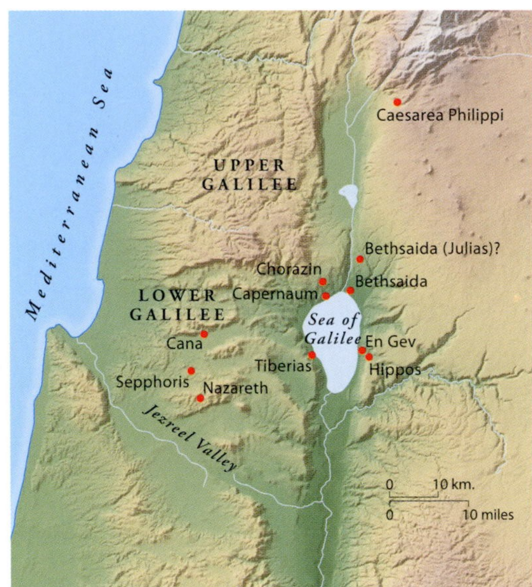

Galilee

Lower Galilee is much more dense in population. Villages like Nazareth (Matt. 2:23) and Cana (John 2:1; 4:46) were typical of conservative Jewish communities that Jesus frequented. Jesus eventually moved from Nazareth to Capernaum (Matt. 4:13) and began to call it his "home" (Mark 2:1). From here he called his disciples and began his ministry, traveling to villages throughout Galilee. Most of his ministry was in a triangle formed by Capernaum, Bethsaida, and Chorazin.

The gentile presence in Galilee grew rapidly, however, and strict Jews referred to it derisively as "Galilee of the gentiles" (Matt. 4:15). The ancient capital of Galilee, Sepphoris, lay in a valley just north of Nazareth, so that Hellenistic culture thrived not far from Jesus's childhood home. Jewish communities linked to Herodian ruling authority were likewise expanding: Bethsaida-Julias, Caesarea Philippi, and Tiberias.

Summary

Recent archaeological work in Galilee has changed how we think about Jesus's background and ministry. Trade moved efficiently between village and city; political consciousness was well developed, making resistance to Roman rule common; and Hellenistic cultural values were spreading quickly. Jesus was exposed to all this. He likely chose Capernaum as his teaching and healing base because the town was on a major trade route that moved north/south from the Mediterranean coastal plain to Damascus. It was no accident that the Romans built a tax station in Capernaum and fortified it with troops (Mark 2:14). Therefore, Jesus was known as a "Galilean"—he had an accent and wore regional clothing styles—and he was labeled critically by those living in Judea who heard him when he traveled south to celebrate the festivals at the Jerusalem temple (John 1:46; 7:52).

JEWISH VOICES IN THE FIRST CENTURY

These massive columns lie where they fell in the Decapolis city of Scythopolis. Such public architecture in one of Rome's largest cities in Judea projected the true power of the empire in Galilee.
Carol Burge

Judaism in the first century proved to be a dynamic and vibrant religious tradition for many. Jewish teachers abundantly promoted values such as prayer, Scripture readings, festival worship, the practice of the law, and temple sacrifice. Like any religious faith, Judaism had a diversity of currents, each competing for the mainstream—and it is impossible to talk about the Jewish faith as if it had one voice any more than we can talk about Christianity as if it has one voice today.

Judaism was well known throughout the Roman Empire. Its native province (known as "Judea") was populated by as many as 1.5 million. The Diaspora may have had as many as four million (or 7 percent of the Roman Empire), making Judaism a significant minority. Around the Mediterranean there may have been close to a thousand synagogues by AD 70.

Within Israel itself the majority of the people had been reduced to near-subsistence living (agriculture, trades, or fishing) because of the financial burden of the Roman occupation. Debt fueled resentment and rebellion—which may explain the power of Jesus's prayer, "forgive us our debts, *as we also have forgiven our debtors*" (Matt. 6:12, emphasis added). This widespread poverty made observance of Jewish law a luxury. In fact, most Jews likely spent most of their lives living in a state of "ritual uncleanness." They were often labeled derisively as the *'am ha-aretz* ("people of the land").

The village of Gamla was located northeast of the Sea of Galilee (present day Golan Heights). Destroyed in the first Jewish war, its remains reflect life in the first century.
Z. Radovan/www.BibleLandPictures.com

The excavated synagogue at Gamla gives a rare glimpse at first-century Jewish religious life. If Jesus visited most of the villages of Galilee (Matt. 4:23), he likely visited Gamla.
Todd Bolen/BiblePlaces.com

They were also the ʿ*anawim* ("the poor"), for whom the burden of life seemed unbearable. Again, Jesus spoke to their condition, "Come to me, all you who are weary and burdened, and I will give you rest" (11:28). These people were Jesus's primary audience.

Josephus outlines three sects among the Jews in the first century: the Pharisees, the Sadducees, and the Essenes (*Ant.* 13.5.9 [171]); there was also a "fourth philosophy," a generic grouping of those who resisted Rome violently (*Ant.* 18.1.6 [23]). But these do not reflect the mainstream of Jewish faith, for they represent barely 5 percent of the Jewish population. Yet we must understand who they are.

The Pharisees

Once the Maccabean revolt had succeeded in overturning Greek rule in the second century BC, the new Jewish dynasty—the powerbrokers of the war—no longer needed the religiously motivated sects that had given ideological support for the revolt. These deeply pious fighters (called "Hasidim") were soon marginalized from the politics of the country and focused instead on creating a world of religious rigor and separation from the corruption that followed the Jewish victory. The name "Pharisee" first surfaces when the Hasmonean ruler John Hyrcanus I (135/4–104 BC) persecuted the Pharisees for resisting the Hasmonean rule. They are often considered the descendants of the Hasidim (but this is uncertain).[3]

Jesus referred to Pharisees who "sit in Moses' seat" (Matt. 23:2). This was a seated position of authority, often in a synagogue. A fourth-century stone "seat" was excavated in the Galilee synagogue of Chorazin. *Z. Radovan/www.BibleLand Pictures.com*

But a hundred years later, the Pharisees (meaning: *separated ones*) were widely known. They chastised those who flirted with Hellenism, promoted a vigorous adherence to the law, demanded ritual purity, and anticipated a coming Messiah who would bring a thoroughgoing righteousness to the land. Josephus, himself a Pharisee, described them as "a certain sect of the Jews that appear more religious than others, and seem to interpret the laws more accurately" (*War* 1.5.2 [110]). Because they flourished in the villages of Judea, they were almost a populist movement, promoting personal righteousness and purity and in some cases living in sharp tension with the less pious leaders of Jerusalem. They not only promoted the law but belonged to a developing tradition of interpretation (the "oral law") that they felt was binding.

One unique factor in their teaching was their call not just to national righteousness but to individual, personal decisions. Ironically, this shift likely came from the individualism of the Hellenistic world (a culture the Pharisees resisted). Individual adherence to the law was one firm way to express Jewish cultural and religious identity. This helps explain the Pharisees' focus on circumcision, tithing, Sabbath observance, the observance of clean/unclean, and food purity laws.

The Pharisees appear with surprising frequency in the gospels as primary opponents of Jesus. He took the Scriptures seriously and was skilled at their use—which gave him and the Pharisees much common ground. But no doubt Jesus's interpretation of the law, his habit of breaking religious traditions to make a point (such as Sabbath rules), his claims of authority, and his popularity made him a lightning rod for the Pharisees' criticisms. While the Pharisees had central theological commitments—such as a strict theological determinism, the resurrection of the dead, and a messianic hope—it was their focus on external formalities that set them apart. But where this emphasis became rigid, they found a debating opponent in Jesus.

It would be wrong to think all Pharisees succumbed to this tendency toward rigidity or that all Pharisees were "legalistic." Many Jews rejoiced in the law and in its adherence found life (see Ps. 119). Paul was a Pharisee, and he did not find his Jewish faith burdensome (see Phil. 3:3–8). In Acts 5:34 the Pharisee Gamaliel spoke up in defense of the apostles before the Sanhedrin (cf. also Acts 21:20).

The Sadducees

As a result of the Maccabean revolt, the Hasmoneans inherited the wealthy estates left by the Greeks and consolidated their power through their control of Jerusalem and the temple. By Jesus's day, they were called the Sadducees—the educated elites, landowners, and members of a Jerusalem urban class who had learned how to profit from the Roman occupation. For this reason, they were suspicious of any religious fanaticism that might upset the status quo; thus, they rejected the messianism common to the Pharisees.

The Jews Burn Jerusalem's Tax Archive

The tax burden on the Jews was so severe that in AD 66 (during the war with Rome), once the Jewish rebels gained control of Jerusalem, they burned the tax record office: "The king's soldiers were overpowered by the multitude.... The others then set fire to the house of Ananias the high priest, and to the palaces of Agrippa and Bernice; after which they carried the fire to the place where the archives were deposited and hurried to burn the contracts belonging to their creditors and thereby to dissolve their obligations for paying their debts.... This was done to persuade the poorer sort to join in their insurrection with safety against the more wealthy." (Josephus, *War*, 2.17.6 [426–427])

Clean and Unclean

Scholars believe that around 150 BC many Jews became concerned—obsessed perhaps—with worries about ritual cleanliness. This has nothing to do with hygiene, but measures contact with things that are religiously irregular. Four principal things were worrisome: contact with gentiles, skin disease, cemeteries (called corpse impurity), and bodily discharges (see Leviticus 11 for a list; see also the 6th division of the Mishna, *Tohoroth*, "Cleanness"). In each case, purity can be regained through various cleansing rituals, generally employing immersion in water. If, for instance, you buried someone, you would then employ a cleansing ritual to restore your religious status. This explains the presence of ritual baths in Jewish villages throughout the first century. But we think these rules were so onerous that most people lived regularly in a state of being "unclean."

Mark 5 shows Jesus's treatment of this topic. He moves from a cemetery (corpse impurity, vv. 1–20), to a village where he is touched by a woman with a flow of blood (discharge impurity, vv. 24–34), and then he touches a dead girl (corpse impurity, vv. 35–43). He is unconcerned and believes that his own purity is unaffected by these things.

While the Pharisees and the Sadducees are often studied, their differences are not easily compared. The Pharisees were committed to purity laws and the religious restoration of the country. The Sadducees were invested in *social position* and the benefits of the political architecture of the country under Rome. Many priests were likely Sadducees, and it is plausible that the Hasmonean rulers shared Sadducean sympathies (some perhaps were Sadducees).

Josephus notes distinguishing marks of their belief. They disputed the notion of the resurrection and argued that "souls die with the bodies" (*Ant.* 18.1.4 [16]). They also debated the Pharisees' commitment to determinism, especially as it referred to an apocalyptic end to time. In the New Testament they only occasionally debated with Jesus. But since their influence was significant in Jerusalem, when they questioned him publicly, they were testing the threat his movement might bring to the city (Matt. 22:23).

The Essenes

Josephus discussed a third Jewish sect called the Essenes, a small ascetic group (about four thousand total) that likely had communities throughout the country. Josephus, intrigued with this group, wrote about them more than any other (*Ant.* 13.5.9 [171–72]; 18.1.4–5 [18–22]; *War* 2.8.2–13 [119–61]). He gives remarkable detail about their lives: their vows of obedience to leaders, their initiation practices, their denial of luxuries and private property, even their dress (white garments), anointing practices, and communal meals. The seriousness of their lives inspired admiration

Many scholars believe the Jewish settlement at Qumran, at the northwest corner of the Dead Sea, was Essene.
Bill Schlegel/BiblePlaces.com

even from Roman writers like Pliny, who made the Essene "way" something known in the empire.

The origin of the movement probably began after the fragmentation of the Maccabean wars. Seeing the political corruption that quickly consumed Jerusalem, these Jews chose to live isolated, separated lives that avoided engagement with the growing gentile population and most Jewish groups. Some members may have been married, others were strictly celibate. As one matured in the sect, personal discipline and purity were measured as tokens of devotion and dedication.

Most scholars think the community at Qumran that produced the Dead Sea Scrolls was likely a branch of the Essenes. It was a rigorously pious monastic commune using Old Testament texts such as Isaiah 40:3 as their vision for life: "In the wilderness prepare the way for the LORD; make straight in the desert a highway for our God." This was an all-male monastic community living in isolation, critical of the temple, promoting regular water baptism, and awaiting God's intervention in history. Since this text was important to John the Baptist, some scholars argue that this group may have influenced him.

The "Fourth Philosophy"

As we have seen, resistance to the Roman occupation or to Hellenistic cultural assimilation took many forms. Some were cooperating with the Romans, hoping to bring about negotiated changes (the Sadducees). Some removed themselves entirely and sought purity in remote locations (the Essenes). Still others worked to preserve the cultural and religious traditions and waited on God's intervention (the Pharisees). Some decided to fight back with the sword. Some, such as the *Sicarii* (see sidebar), used psychological terror tactics, while others organized armed campaigns.

The Dead Sea Scrolls

Throughout the nineteenth century archaeologists were aware of an ancient site located at the northwest corner of the Dead Sea. Many thought it was a fort dating to the Second Temple era. But then in 1947, when parchment and papyrus scrolls were found in a hidden cave, new interest was kindled, and a full excavation began. From 1947 to 1956 eleven caves were found, yielding hundreds of ancient manuscripts. Since then numerous archaeological efforts have uncovered a surprising building complex. A large cemetery, a water system, numerous ritual baths, various rooms, and cisterns were found. Pottery and coins helped date the site to the first century.

Scholars have offered various theories for the site and these are debated today. The strongest theory is that it was the main settlement of the separatist Jewish sect of Essenes. The scrolls describe Jews who lived an austere life, practiced ritual washings regularly, were strongly critical of Jerusalem's leadership, and awaited the eschatological arrival of the Lord. They were led by someone called "The Teacher of Righteousness."

Rome destroyed the settlement sometime during the First Jewish War (likely before the siege of Jerusalem). This is when the scrolls were hidden in the caves for safekeeping—but weren't recovered until the twentieth century.

The Terrorist and the Cross

Each of the men crucified with Jesus, as well as Barabbas, the man released during Jesus's trial, is called a *lestēs* (Mark 15:27; John 18:40). Josephus uses this word for Zealot leaders who either robbed victims (cf. Luke 10:30) or fought in uprisings. Luke says that Barabbas had participated in an "insurrection in the city" (23:19), which suggests that he had engaged in social banditry as a form of revolt. The best modern translation may be that Barabbas was a *terrorist*.

The Sicarii

Outright military conflict with Rome was often devastating to Jewish fighters. The Roman army was well trained, organized, and equipped. After Herod's death, for example, a rebel leader named Simon captured Jericho, plundered it, razed the royal palace by fire, and crowned himself king. A Roman army led by Gratus quickly engaged Simon's troops in battle. Thousands died, and Simon was promptly beheaded (*Ant.* 17.10.6 [273–276]).

The "Sicarii" used a different method of violence. A *sica* is a short dagger that was easily concealed (*Ant.* 20.8.10 [185–187]). These people mingled among the multitude with concealed daggers, stealthily stabbed their enemies, then melted into the crowd. This form of "social terrorism" created an enemy the Romans could not locate.

The excavation at Masada yielded numerous weapons from the first century. The Romans used this type of weapon to quell Jewish rebellions.
Kim Walton

Sirach the Scribe

In the intertestamental period, one of the greatest scribes was Jesus ben Sirach, who lived in Jerusalem in the early part of the second century BC. He trained sons from wealthy Jewish families in his "school" (Sir. 51:23). He taught that wisdom comes from keeping the commandments. He also believed that piety was a true mark of wisdom; it was not enough to simply memorize the commandment, one must also do it. His work is preserved in the Apocyrpha as the Wisdom of Jesus ben Sirach or simply Sirach.

Judaism's commitment to military resistance, forged during the Maccabean campaigns, taught the Jews that guerrilla campaigns could work and that foreigners who occupied them would eventually find control of the country too costly. By the first century, the "politics of violence" was familiar to everyone. Various scriptural models of this type of resistance were celebrated, such as the zeal of Phinehas (see Num. 25:1–13). The Jewish warriors who finally occupied and defended Jerusalem in AD 66–70 took up the name "Zealots" and made their last stand in the famous siege at the mountain fortress of Masada.

We should expect that movements such as these would have tested Jesus's ministry. The question about taxes given in Mark 12:14 is likely a probe about zealotry, which made sense, since one of Jesus's followers was known as a (former) Zealot (3:18).

The Scribes

In addition to the four sects listed by Josephus, there are a number of other groups listed in the New Testament. Some represent professions, others are regional ethnic groups, others reflect political alliances.

In antiquity professionals who could read and write—and interpret the law—were in high demand. They served as secretaries and chroniclers, taught the law in synagogues, or adjudicated legal disagreements in court. Because of their strict devotion to the Scriptures and their role as custodians of Jewish tradition, many of the scribes were Pharisees (though not all Pharisees were scribes). Among the titles used for them, "teacher" and its Hebrew form "rabbi" were common (Matt. 23:7–8). Much of their activity was concentrated in Jerusalem, since it was the seat of Jewish learning and home of the judicial council (the Sanhedrin). Only the scribes who belonged to the Pharisees could enter the Sanhedrin and participate in judicial decisions.

The Samaritans

After the destruction of the northern kingdom of Israel, a remnant population survived around the city

"I Am Not Jewish"

According to Josephus, the Samaritans refused any participation in the Maccabean wars by denying their Jewish heritage (*Ant.* 12.5.5 [257]): "When the Samaritans saw the Jews under these sufferings, they no longer confessed that they were of their family, nor that the temple on Mount Gerizim belonged to Almighty God. This was according to their nature.... And they now said that they were a colony of Medes and Persians—and indeed they were."

To save their temple, the Samaritans sent a letter to the Greek king Antiochus, honoring him with the title of "god" and offering to dedicate their temple on Mount Gerizim to Jupiter Hellenius (*Ant.*12:5.5 [261]).

Ruins of the temple on Mount Gerizim
iStock.com/HisWondrousWorks

Mount Gerizim viewed from Shechem. The Samaritans viewed this mountain as sacred (John 4:20) and built a temple here in the fourth century BC.
Todd Bolen/BiblePlaces.com

of Shechem. When the Jews returned from Babylon to rebuild their temple, these Samaritan people were viewed as deeply compromised. In addition, the Assyrians had moved many Persians into Samaria, who assimilated with the Israelites, and the Jewish leaders with Ezra and Nehemiah wanted nothing to do with them.

These Samaritans "revised" the Hebrew Scriptures (to promote their own place in history) and built a rival temple on Mount Gerizim that towered over Shechem, north of Jerusalem. Hostilities between Samaritans and Jews ran high. In the Maccabean era, Jewish armies razed Samaria in war (*Ant.* 13.10.2 [275–279]).

On another occasion, Samaritans tried to sabotage the Jerusalem temple at Passover by entering in disguise and spreading exhumed human bones throughout its chambers (*Ant.* 18.2.2 [29–30]).

This background makes the presence of Samaritans in the gospels surprising. Jesus told a parable in which he made a Samaritan the hero (Luke 10:25–37). It is crucial not to miss the shock of this choice. Jesus describes a Samaritan exhibiting righteous deeds, while traditional Jewish leaders do nothing. Jesus healed a Samaritan on one occasion and praised him for his gratefulness (17:15–19). At the well of Jacob in Shechem, Jesus held his famous conversation with "the Samaritan woman" (John 4:1–38), whose testimony about Jesus led to the conversion of her village. Early Christian mission likewise came to Samaria (Acts 8:5).

The Great Royal Porch/Portico

Both Romans and Greeks graced their temples and public buildings with elaborate open-air buildings supported by massive columns and a roof (see the entrance to the pantheon in Rome). These could be found as entrances to a temple or a covering for markets. Greeks referred to this as a "stoa," (in Greek a *stylos* is a column). A Roman might refer to it as a "porticus" (hence our "portico" or porch today). Herod had his engineers build a major covered portico at the south end of the temple that formed one perimeter to the Court of the gentiles. It was called the Royal Portico. Here four rows of forty columns (160 total) supported a massive wooden roof. Each column weighed five tons, was twenty-seven feet high, and, according to Josephus, was so wide that "three men might, with their arms extended, reach around it." Each was completed with a Corinthian capital. The Sanhedrin often met here, and teachers such as Jesus commonly conversed with their students in its corridors.

When Titus destroyed Jerusalem in AD 70, this porch collapsed, and most of its columns fell over the south retaining wall. Many were carried away for centuries-later building projects. But others remained buried, unearthed until 1968 in the excavation of the temple's southern wall.

The Herodians

Mark and Matthew refer to opponents of Jesus called "Herodians" (Matt. 22:16; Mark 3:6). Little is known about them, but they were probably political patrons living in the major cities of Galilee and Judea. They were the ones who questioned Jesus about paying taxes (Mark 12:13–14) to assess the threat he might bring to the status quo of Jewish political life. The Herodians had compromised with Rome and only saw the benefits of Jewish life in a Roman province.

Any from these circles who followed Jesus likely kept it secret, since the social costs would be high. Nevertheless, Luke tells us that the financial officer of Herod Antipas was named Chuza and that his wife Joanna helped finance Jesus's ministry (Luke 8:1–3).

THE JERUSALEM TEMPLE

It is difficult to overestimate the importance of the Jewish Temple in first-century Judaism. It was a building of national as well as religious pride. The Babylonians had destroyed Solomon's Temple (586 BC), but it was rebuilt by Ezra following the exile. About 20 BC Herod the Great launched a monumental rebuilding program that promised to make this temple one of the greatest in the ancient world.

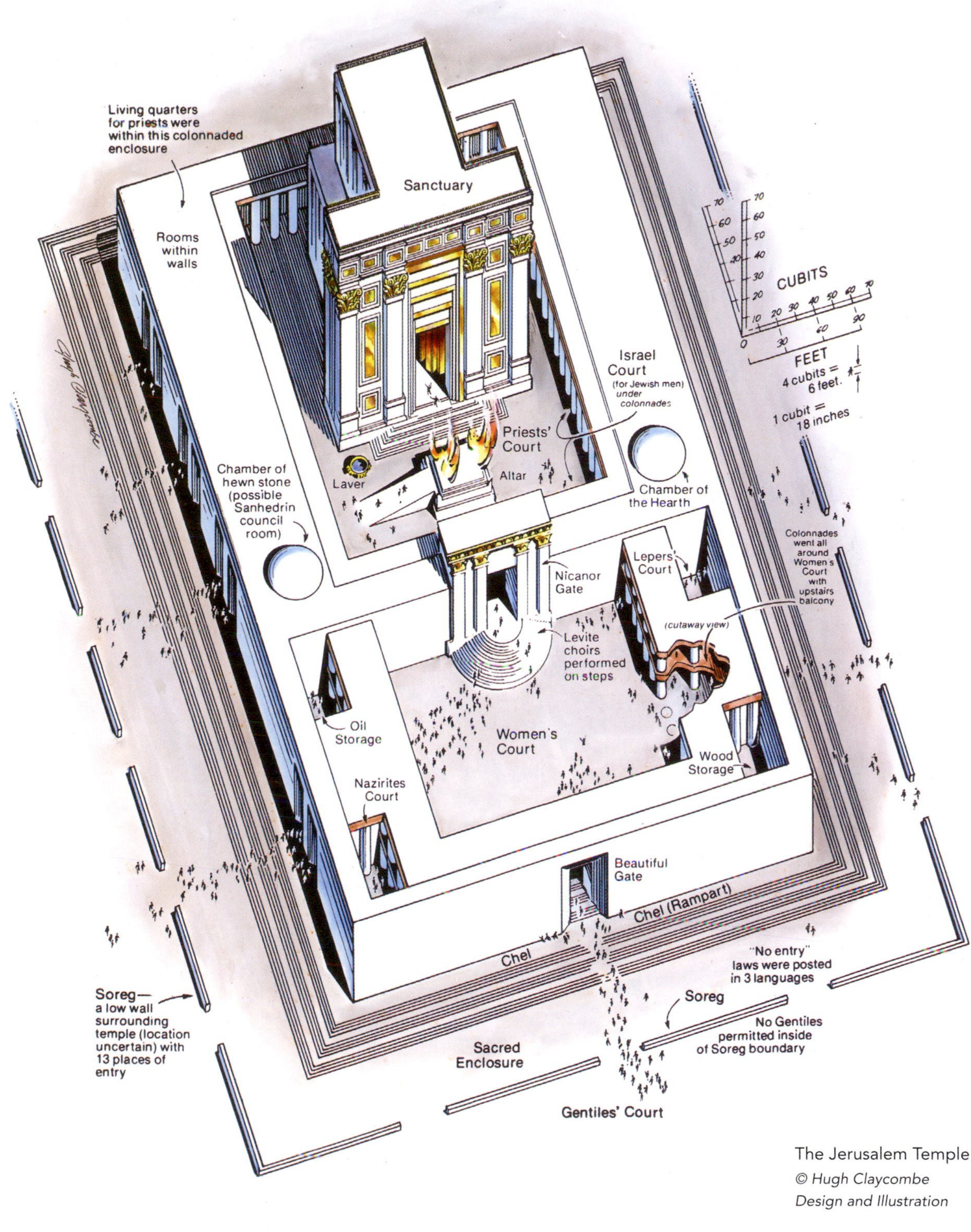

The Jerusalem Temple

Every city in the Mediterranean boasted in the size and beauty of its temple, and Jerusalem was no exception. But this temple, rather than reflecting allegiance to Rome and its pantheon, would be dedicated to the worship of the one God of the Jews.

The project was in full construction during Jesus's life. Herod not only refurbished the inner courts but expanded the building's size so that it measured 360,000 square feet (equivalent to nine football fields). Fifty-ton stones were lifted into place—a process that still today defies explanation. When Titus's armies entered the temple courts in the Jewish war, they were stunned at its beauty and desired to preserve it (*War*, 5.9.2; [360–361]; 7:5:2 [112–113]). Unfortunately, as a result of the war, the temple was set on fire and ultimately destroyed in the Roman campaign of AD 70.

Not only was the size of the temple astounding, but much of the city's economic energies were invested in its functions. Twenty-four priestly families—numbering over seven thousand priests—worked alongside 9,600 Levites in the day-to-day tasks of maintenance, sacrifice, and worship schedules. Tithe money came in regularly, and sacrifice became a major industry, making the temple remarkably wealthy.

Herod knew that the Temple would likely be the site of any revolt against him. Thus, in the northwest corner he built a fortress, named it after Mark Antony, and staffed it with Roman auxiliary troops. This Antonia Fortress loomed over the temple courts below and sent a clear message to zealous pilgrim traffic. The Temple was also the only location where the Romans permitted Jewish troops to be armed. They appeared at Jesus's arrest (Luke 22:52) and frequently did the bidding of the leading priests (Acts 5:26).

Dogs in Jerusalem?

A major controversy surrounded how one should view Jerusalem. Religious sectarians, such as the members of Qumran, viewed Jerusalem as the "camp" of Israel in the Old Testament. This meant that various rules then applied there. Above all, only sacrificial animals could be slaughtered in the city and nonsacrificial animals had to be kept out. Even sacrificial animals (an ox, lamb, or goat) had to be offered to the Lord as a gesture of worship (see Lev. 17:3–4). Some rabbis disagreed, but the debate may have been contentious.

The problem was that dogs were scavengers and would eat the scraps from slaughtering. If Jerusalem was a sacred camp, and if all its meat was sacred, dogs could not be permitted to eat holy sacrificial meals. For this same reason, Qumran viewed its settlement as a holy camp, and no dogs were permitted.

Is this what Jesus meant when he said, "Do not give dogs what is sacred; do not throw your pearls to pigs" (Matt 7:6; cf. G. Thomas, 93)? Jewish literature compared dogs with pigs and viewed them both as representing uncleanness.[4]

THE JEWISH FESTIVALS

The Jerusalem Temple supervised and orchestrated the many details of the Jewish festival calendar. The foremost festival was Sabbath, a weekly event beginning on Friday evening at dusk and continuing to Saturday evening. But there were also annual festivals organized around a twelve-month system (that followed the evolving cycles of the moon). Hence, the Jews held a *lunar calendar* for their worship.

Months were named (Nisan, Elul, Chislev, etc.), and many of them held important festivals that appear in the New Testament. Festivals pointed to events in the agricultural season (first harvest, last harvest) but also remembered the great saving acts of God in Israel's history.

Israel promoted three "pilgrimage festivals," in which Jews were expected to travel to Jerusalem and participate in Temple sacrifices and worship. Few imagine that every Jew in the country came (this would leave whole villages abandoned), but instead, this was the desire and intention of most. In the twelve-month calendar, Passover (Pasach), Pentecost (Shavuot), and Tabernacles (Succoth) were each pilgrimage festivals.

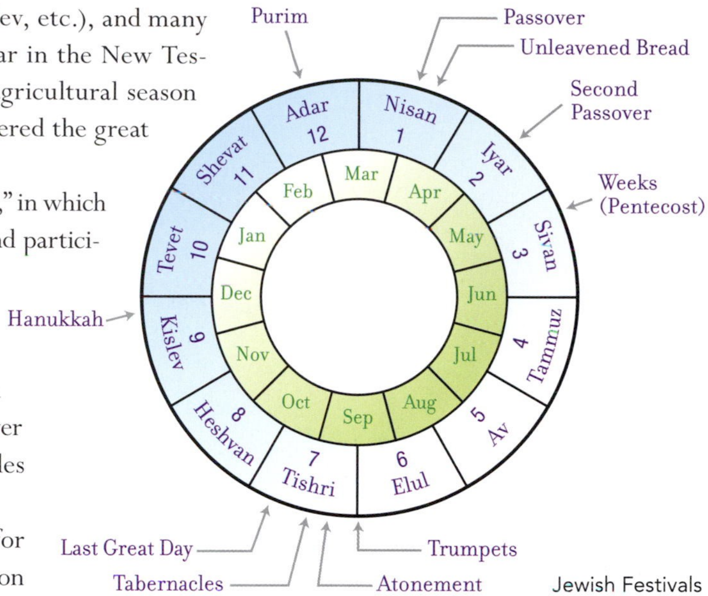

Jewish Festivals

The most significant of these festivals for the New Testament is Passover, celebrated on the fourteenth day of the first month, called Nisan. Here pilgrims would come to Jerusalem to offer to God not only the first harvest of barley (the earliest cereal to ripen in Israel) but also the first "harvest" of their flocks as lambs were born. This sacrifice of a lamb linked to the historical ceremony of the Exodus, when God liberated his people from Egypt. Therefore, Passover ceremonies were filled with themes of gratefulness for the new harvest year and also for salvation (Ex. 12:3–20; Deut. 16:1–8).

Jesus was fully aware of these themes when he came to Jerusalem during his final week. It was Passover, and following the custom, he celebrated it by sharing with his apostles a full "Passover meal" as the festival day began. During the meal he offered bread and wine, symbolizing in them his own sacrifice, because when he went to the cross the next day, he understood—as did his disciples—that his life would be a sacrificial *Passover sacrifice* that would save them (as the Passover lamb had saved the Israelites).

Jesus appeared at various other festivals, and we believe he was deeply committed to the festival calendar. John 7 describes him appearing at Tabernacles. John 10 describes him speaking at the extrabiblical festival of Hanukkah. The calendar even appears in the book of Acts. After Jesus's resurrection and ascension, the disciples wait in Jerusalem for the promised anointing of the Spirit as Jesus had promised. This occurs on Pentecost, the second pilgrimage festival. This feast not only celebrated the end of the cereal harvest but recalled the movement of Israel to Mount Sinai and the birth of Israel's covenant with Moses. In Acts 2 we will witness the birth of the church, now empowered to move toward the world (as Israel was called to move toward the Holy Land).

Jerusalem was a temple with a city wrapped around it. Its walls protected a population of about thirty thousand to fifty thousand, but its economy served the temple and its work.
Balage Balogh/www.archaeology illustrated.com

The festival calendar was known intimately by every major character in the New Testament, no less than we would understand the symbolism and meaning of Christmas or Easter. Each month they were aware of what season they were in, and in many cases, we can find Jesus speaking about a theme or topic that was discussed in the festival. John 6 is an excellent example. It is no accident that Jesus feeds the five thousand during Passover. This alluded to Moses feeding Israel in the wilderness after the exodus.

THE SANHEDRIN

In antiquity every community gathered together its prominent members to bring leadership and order to civic life. This was as true in a Roman city, such as Ephesus, as it was for Jerusalem. Jerusalem had its own lay nobility—men who were keenly invested in the success of Jerusalem and who worked closely with the temple priests to bring order. One example is Joseph of Arimathea, who supplied Jesus's tomb (Mark 15:43; John 19:38–42).

These elders joined together with select members of the priesthood (who were generally Sadducees) and leading Pharisees to form a "high council," called the Sanhedrin. Its tripartite structure gave wide representation to diverse interests and worked hard to give a fair and judicious hearing to legal complaints. It took its structure from the seventy elders Moses appointed (Num. 11:16; Mishnah, *Sanh.* 1:6). Seventy was considered the appropriate number needed to form a council in Judaism. Note how Jesus sent out seventy disciples as his delegates to Galilee (Luke 10:1 NASB).

The Jewish high priest (e.g., Caiaphas during Jesus's trial, Matt. 26:3) led the Jerusalem council. But this did not mean that the council convened for every decision. The Mishnah outlines how smaller groups of elders could decide cases (e.g., theft and personal injury took three judges). A "lower court" made up of twenty elders and the high priest heard intermediate cases (Mishnah, *Sanh.* 1:2–5). The stipulations for the prosecution and defense in trial are clearly laid out and impress even the most casual reader.

VILLAGES AND SYNAGOGUES

During the Babylonian exile, Israel had to rethink its worship in the absence of a temple. Without sacrifice, worship centered on personal study, corporate prayer, and worship. When the Jews returned to Jerusalem, they brought these "assemblies" (Gk. *synagōgē*) with them, and despite the rebuilding of the temple, public meetings with study, discussion, and prayer continued.

Did Women Lead Synagogues?

Synagogue meetings were convened when ten Jewish men gathered. But newly found inscriptions suggest that some women were leaders in their communities. For example, in a second-century inscription from ancient Smyrna, a woman named Rufina was called the head or leader of her synagogue. The text reads: "Rufina, a Jewess, head of the synagogue (*archisynagōgos*), built this tomb for her freed slaves and the slaves raised in her house. No one else has the right to bury anyone [here]. Anyone who dares to do [so], will pay 1500 denaria to the sacred treasury and 1000 denaria to the Jewish people. A copy of this inscription has been placed in the [public] archives."

Rufina, and other women like her, were leaders in their communities, working for the good of others. Paul would have met such women as he traveled throughout the Roman world. Some, such as Phoebe (Rom. 16:1–2) and Lydia (Acts 16:14), became followers of Jesus and joined in Paul's ministry to spread the gospel message.

Since 1968 the excavation of Capernaum's entire fourth-century synagogue has been completed. A first-century village was located around its perimeter, and the foundation of a first-century synagogue was identified beneath the floor of the fourth-century building.

Ancient Synagogue Inscriptions

Synagogues were present throughout Galilee and Judea in Jesus's day. Unlike the temple in Jerusalem, these buildings were not seen as sacred space, though prayer and teaching took place within them. Both literary texts and inscriptions help us understand their role in Jewish life. The following inscription, called the Theodotus Inscription, may have come from first-century Jerusalem: "Theodotus, son of Vettenus and ruler of the synagogue, son of a ruler of the synagogue, and grandson of a ruler of the synagogue, built the synagogue for the reading of the Law and instruction in the commandments; also the strangers' lodgings and dining rooms and water facilities and hostel for the use of those from foreign lands. The foundation of this his fathers and the elders and Simonides laid."[5]

Theodotus Inscription from a Jerusalem synagogue, first century BC
© 2018 by Zondervan

Capernaum was first identified in 1838 by the American scholar E. Robinson. It was rubble with the exception of a ruined building he correctly identified as a synagogue. This picture from 1898 shows how little was there.
Courtesy of Library of Congress

By the first century, synagogues were commonplace in the villages of Israel. These may have been public gatherings to discuss civic issues, or they may have been gatherings for religious debate and prayer. A quorum of ten Jewish men could convene a synagogue meeting at any time, which revolutionized Jewish life. The synagogue was accessible to the average person, compared with the temple's distance and formidable rituals. In this sense, the synagogue *decentralized* Jewish identity by bringing opportunities for religious expression to the village.

Moreover, the synagogues became a network for expressing conservative Judaism. The gospels depict Jesus as performing miracles in synagogues and teaching in many of them (Mark 6:2; Luke 4:15), and it was here that he had his fiercest debates with Pharisees. Through the synagogues, the influence of rabbis (or scribes) grew, and the priesthood in Jerusalem came to be viewed with increased suspicion and cynicism.

The everyday life of a family in a Galilee village, however, did not revolve around temple sacrifice or synagogue attendance. These were vital, but Judaism also underscored the importance of personal purity, study, and observance, expressed in community and shaped by a family who would sustain faith for life. This helps explain why Jesus had his most effective results outside the formal religious structures of the temple and the synagogue. On hillsides or grassy plains, crowds gathered and understood the personal care and grace of God, the importance of the Scriptures, and the pursuit of righteousness.

Archaeologists have found few first-century synagogues in Israel that had not been rebuilt or destroyed over time. We have remnants of them in sites such as Gamla, Jericho, Masada, and Herodium. In 2009, during an excavation to build a retreat center, the synagogue of Magdala was discovered and today is under excavation.
Ferrell Jenkins/BiblePlaces.com

THE GREAT JEWISH DIASPORA

For hundreds of years, Jews had migrated to regions throughout the Mediterranean. This dispersal (the Septuagint refers to it as a *diaspora,* or scattering) of Jewish life into non-Jewish cities in the Roman Empire raised questions about the integrity of Jewish identity outside Judea. Was it legitimate to be a Jew and live in places like Corinth? Were sincere Jews obligated to live in Judea? Abundant evidence makes clear that these Diaspora communities saw themselves as fully Jewish, holding to their culture and faith with integrity.

Jews generally left Judea for one of two reasons. Either they were conquered and taken as slaves, or they moved voluntarily, looking for greater opportunities. Forced removals began with the Babylonian exile in the sixth century BC. Within a few hundred years, the Jewish Diaspora in the east had large and significant Jewish communities in Babylonia, Parthia, Media, and Armenia. The conversion of Queen Helena of Adiabene (on the Tigris River), whose tomb still stands north of Jerusalem's Old City, is further evidence of a lively Jewish life in Mesopotamia.

By the first century, Josephus could refer to the impressive size and importance of the Jewish communities in the east. On the remote stretches of the

Fresco from the Dura-Europos synagogue depicts the scene from Exodus where Moses was found in the river. It also illustrates how Second Temple Jews may have dressed, AD 244–255.
Public Domain

Euphrates River in northern Syria, the Dura-Europos synagogue (third century) illustrates Jewish life near this period and has given to scholarship perhaps the earliest pictorial representation of Second Temple Jews we possess.[6]

Jews were also drawn to Syria. Not only were cities like Damascus and Syrian Antioch (on the Orontes River) nearby, but Syrian kings, such as Seleucus I Nicator (358–281 BC), gave financial incentives for Jews to move north. By the first century, the Jewish community in Syrian Antioch was hundreds of years old, notably large, and successful (Josephus, *Antiquities*, 12.3.1 [119–124]; *Wars*, 7.3.3 [43–53]). A glimpse of their size comes from a grim historical note, however. Josephus says in one passage that during the war of AD 66–70, ten thousand Jews were massacred in Syrian Antioch (*Wars,* 2.20.2 [561]) and in another the count is eighteen thousand (*Wars*, 7.8.7 [368]). Both numbers are no doubt exaggerated, but nevertheless, they point to a significant Jewish population there.

A similar story of Jewish settlement could be told for Egypt, where Philo estimates the number of Jews at one million (*Flaccus*, 43). By the first century, two of Alexandria's five residential sectors were Jewish (Philo, *Flaccus*, 8).

Awareness of the extent of the known world west of Judea and its populations can be found in Jewish writing from the period. Josephus, for example, provides a speech of King Agrippa I at the beginning of his *Jewish Wars* (2.16.4 [345–401]), in which he details how Rome rules the entire earth. He then supplies an impressive table of nations that Rome has defeated, no doubt to dissuade Jewish rebels still holding dreams of revolt.

These sources demonstrate that the size of the western Diaspora was truly impressive. It is impossible to know how many Jews lived there. Some have argued for Rome's Jewish population at forty thousand. Others speculate that the entire Diaspora numbered anywhere from four to six million. Still others think Jews comprised 10 percent of the empire itself. If four million lived in the western Diaspora and one million in Egypt, estimates are that Judea's population was about three million. Remarkably, *more Jews were living outside Judea than were living in it.* This brought major implications to Jewish thinking and perspective.

Paul was a Diaspora Jew (from the city of Tarsus in southern Anatolia). This may well explain his comfort moving throughout the Roman Empire and his impressive fluency in Greek.

Jewish Diaspora

JEWISH LITERATURE

Another window into Jewish thought and life can be found through the literature read during the first century. Jesus (and his followers) would have known a number of these sources in the same way that we can make casual reference to well-known literature today. Of course, some of these sources were limited to scholars, and others were the exclusive domain of isolated communities (e.g., the Dead Sea Scrolls).

The Scriptures

The Bible of the synagogues consisted of our Old Testament. It was called the *Tanak* (from the Hebrew consonants T-N-K) as a shorthand expression for its three chief categories: the law (***T****orah*), the prophets (***N****ebiim*), and the writings (***K****ithubim*). But it was also common to simply refer to any writings from this collection as "the law."

These Scriptures were generally read in Hebrew, but in the second century BC, a Greek translation called the Septuagint (abbreviated LXX) became increasingly popular among Jews for whom Hebrew had become a dead language. Among Diaspora Jews, the LXX was the only "Bible" they knew.

The LXX also collected a series of writings from the intertestamental period, commonly called the "Apocrypha." It contained historical works (such as 1 and 2 Maccabees), works of fiction (Tobit, Judith), and wisdom writing (Sirach, The Wisdom of Solomon). While their inclusion in the LXX gave them an air of authority, still, they were not embraced by Hebrew scholars eager to create an authoritative canon of Scripture in the first century. Nevertheless, these books are important sources when we reconstruct the intellectual life of Judaism in the century immediately preceding the New Testament.

Extracanonical Books

The search for Jewish writings that shed light on the first-century world has netted surprising results. The Old Testament refers to books now lost to us (e.g., *The Book of the Wars of Yahweh*, see Num. 21:14), and Judaism had many others in the Herodian era that we can only imagine. Some were deemed inspired by religious communities; others were rejected. Modern collections of these works often refer to them as "Pseudepigrapha," which means "false signature"—referring to their spurious origins and frequent claim to having been authored by some biblical figure such as Baruch or Enoch.

The current collection, edited by James Charlesworth, includes fifty-two books that date from 200 BC to AD 200.[7] These writings include apocalyptic books that give a vision of the end of history (*Enoch*), historical interpretations (*Jubilees*, *Assumption of Moses*), exhortations staged as blessings of Jacob to his twelve sons (*The Testaments of the Twelve Patriarchs*), and hymnic expressions of frustration and despair as Jews lived under Greek—then Roman—occupation (*Psalms of Solomon*). These writings teach us a great deal about the theological diversity in postexilic Judaism and how completely Hellenistic thought had penetrated the minds of the Jews. Reading their pages sets the intellectual stage for interpreting a variety of New Testament passages.

Another collection, hailed as the most important archaeological find of the twentieth century, is the Dead Sea Scrolls (see sidebar on p. 83). Here we have Jewish writings that precede the Jewish War (the Qumran settlement was destroyed about AD 68). Over nine hundred manuscripts were located in eleven caves and represent everything from manuals of discipline to liturgies and commentaries. The three most cited Old Testament books are Psalms (36x), Deuteronomy (29x), and Isaiah (21x)—the same books cited most frequently in the New Testament.

The Qumran community produced extensive scrolls. This scroll, written in Hebrew, is from the "Community Rule" and outlines how community members should live. *Image courtesy of Library of Congress*

Rabbinic Literature

A flourishing intellectual world came from the synagogues and schools of Israel, where Jewish scholars sought to interpret and apply specific scriptural texts. These writings often help us understand debates that Jesus engaged in with his opponents, such as the debate about the Sabbath in John 5:1–17.

The Judean desert still holds many caves in which additional ancient writings may be found. This is the interior of Qumran Cave 1, where seven scrolls were discovered.

This is the entrance of Qumran Cave 1.
www.HolyLandPhotos.org

Jewish scholars wrote commentaries on their Hebrew Scriptures. In some cases they were an expansive rewriting of the story (*Jubilees*), other times they were only added comments. Collections of these comments are called *midrash* (plur. *midrashim*; Heb., to "inquire"). Catalogs of legal collections exist (*Sipra* on Leviticus, *Mekilta* on Exodus), as well as narrative commentary (*Genesis Rabbah*).

Because many Palestinian Jews spoke Aramaic, the Bible was translated into popular Aramaic paraphrases. These were called *Targums* (Aram. "translation"), and because they were considerably free with their rendering of the Old Testament, they give astounding insight into how Jewish teachers viewed the Bible in their day.

The disruption of the great rabbinic schools in AD 70 compelled leading scholars to formalize the teachings of their time. By the mid-second century, these schools saw a need to catalog their primary laws that until then had been recited from memory. This "oral tradition" became a collection of sixty-three tractates (in six divisions) called *The Mishnah*. Here were rules governing everyday life from agriculture to legal damages. Since the Mishnah was formally compiled in the late second century, we cannot be sure how many of its provisions reflect the Jewish world during the time of Jesus. Therefore, it must be used with a degree of caution. Some rabbinic sayings in the Mishnah record reflections from the era of Jesus (before the war of AD 70), but others are almost 100 years later and do not express life in the first century.

Subsequent rabbis continued to provide guidance to the people as they were living in new situations, and they began to comment on the Mishnah itself. These commentaries were called the *Tosefta* ("supplements"). The final compilation of Jewish commentary is *The Talmud* (from Heb. *lamad*, "to learn"). These volumes gather up scholarly rabbinic work from AD 200 to about AD 600 and helped later generations apply the Mishnah in yet a new context. Two editions of the Talmud exist. The oldest (and less complete) is the *Jerusalem Talmud*, which came from Israel and was organized around AD 400. The more famous is the thirty-six volume *Babylonian Talmud*, coming from the huge Jewish community living in Mesopotamia about AD 600.

Josephus

During the first Jewish war with Rome, a man named Josephus rose to leadership and became the defending general of Galilee. The north quickly fell to the Roman legions, and Josephus recognized that the Jewish revolt could not win and would likely lead to the utter destruction of Jerusalem. He accompanied the Roman general (and next emperor) Vespasian to Judea and then followed Vespasian's son Titus to Jerusalem, trying to persuade his former allies to surrender. After the war Josephus retired to Rome, where he wrote his famous *Antiquities of the Jews* and an account of the war (*The Jewish War*).

Josephus's writings are of crucial importance because he provides a firsthand account of the war, an early Jewish interpretation of Jewish history, and the earliest non-Christian references to Jesus. But we must keep in mind that Josephus is often idiosyncratic and deeply polemical. He writes to bolster his own role in Roman eyes and to demonstrate that the rebels who fought the Roman legions never represented the mainstream of Jewish leadership.

Philo of Alexandria

Among the few Jewish works that have survived from the first-century Jewish Diaspora, the writings of Philo of Alexandria (called Philo Judaeus) are among the most important. Philo lived in Alexandria, Egypt, during the lifetime of Jesus and Paul. His birth is often dated at about 20 BC and his death at about AD 50.

Philo's works give us insight into the mind of a Diaspora Jew precisely where the tensions between Hellenism and Judaism were evident. In this sense, Philo helps us understand some New Testament books that may reflect this same milieu. John's gospel (cf. John 1:1), Paul's letters (e.g., Colossians), and particularly Hebrews may share this setting. Hebrews shares many patterns of thought with Philo and has led some to recommend Apollos, a native of Alexandria, as its author.

The Alexandrian Jewish community (home of Apollos, Acts 18:24) was huge. This mosaic, found at Scythopolis in Israel, shows a voyage down the Nile and names "Alexandria." *A. D. Riddle/BiblePlaces.com*

But there is the danger of reading Philo (or Josephus) and concluding that his words are typical of the Jewish communities of the Mediterranean. His is only one voice, though an important one. The dualism of later Platonic thought deeply influenced Philo, but this was not necessarily the case with Jews in synagogues throughout the Mediterranean.

Philo's Synagogue in Alexandria

Diaspora Jews such as Philo met regularly in buildings they referred to as "places of prayer" (Gk. *proseuchai*). Prayer and the teaching of the law were central. Philo explains his own experience in Alexandria: "Each seventh day there stand wide open in every city thousands of schools of good sense, temperance, courage, justice and the other virtues in which the scholars sit in order quietly with ears alert and with full attention, so much do they thirst for the draught which the teacher's words supply" (*On the Special Laws*, 2:62).

Questions for Discussion

1. Name the villages in Galilee that were most important in Jesus's public ministry. Why did he choose to anchor his efforts in Capernaum?
2. Why did John the Baptist become an opponent of Herod Antipas? What geographical insights are essential in this answer?
3. What did Jesus have in common with the Pharisees and why did they become his foremost opponents?
4. What would be the most faith-shaping experiences of a Jewish child as they grew up in a village like Capernaum?
5. Select some cultural elements from Jesus's ministry that cannot be understood without a background knowledge of the first-century world.

BIBLIOGRAPHY

Introductory

Burge, G. M. *Jesus and the Land: The New Testament Challenge to "Holy Land" Theology*. Grand Rapids: Baker, 2010.
Malina, B. *Windows on the World of Jesus: Time Travel to Ancient Judea*. Louisville: Westminster John Knox, 1993.
Murphy, F. J. *The Religious World of Jesus: An Introduction to Second Temple Judaism*. Nashville: Abingdon, 1991. Revised as: *Early Judaism: The Exile to the Time of Jesus*. Peabody, MA: Hendrickson, 2002.
Stambaugh, J. E., and D. L. Balch. *The New Testament in Its Social Environment*. LEC. Philadelphia: Westminster, 1986.
Vanderkam, J. C. *An Introduction to Early Judaism*. Grand Rapids: Eerdmans, 2001.

Advanced

Bauckham, R. *The Jewish World Around the New Testament*. Grand Rapids: Baker, 2008.
Green, J. B., and L. M. McDonald. *The World of the New Testament: Cultural, Social and Historical Contexts*. Grand Rapids: Baker, 2013.
Hanson, K. C., and D. E. Oakman. *Palestine in the Time of Jesus: Social Structures and Social Conflicts*. Minneapolis: Fortress, 1998.
Magness, J. *Stone and Dung, Oil and Spit: Jewish Daily Life in the Time of Jesus*. Grand Rapids: Eerdmans, 2011.
Safrai, S., and M. Stern. *The Jewish People in the First Century*. 2 vols. Assen/Minneapolis: Van Gorcum/Fortress, 1974, 1976.
Sanders, E. P. *Judaism: Practice and Belief, 63 BCE—66 CE*. Philadelphia: Trinity Press International, 1992.

NOTES

1. W. D. Davies, *The Territorial Dimension of Judaism* (Minneapolis: Fortress, 1991), 19.

2. W. Brueggemann, *The Land: Place as Gift, Promise and Challenge* (Minneapolis: Fortress, 2002), 3.

3. E. Schürer, *The History of the Jewish People in the Age of Jesus Christ*, rev. and ed. by G. Vermes, F. Milar, and M. Black, 4 vols. (Edinburgh: T&T Clark, 1973–1987), 1:212; E. P. Sanders, *Judaism: Practice and Belief, 63 BCE to 66 CE* (Philadelphia: Trinity Press International, 1992), 380–412.

4. J. Magness, *Stone and Dung, Oil and Spit: Jewish Daily Life in the Time of Jesus* (Grand Rapids: Eerdmans, 2001), 44–53.

5. H. C. Kee and L. H. Cohick, eds., *The Evolution of the Synagogue* (Harrisburg, PA: Trinity Press International, 1999), 10; cf. 9–26.

6. These frescoes are now on display in the National Archaeological Museum, Damascus, Syria.

7. J. Charlesworth, ed., *The Old Testament Pseudepigrapha*, 2 vols. (New York: Doubleday, 1983, 1985).

Chapter 4

THE MEDITERRANEAN WORLD OF THE APOSTLE PAUL

The city of Corinth and the Gulf of Corinth
Todd Bolen/BiblePlaces.com

PERSPECTIVE

Paul arrived in the city of Corinth around the middle of the first century AD, having traversed the Roman road system (See map on p. 106.) from Antioch in Syria all the way to Troas on the western coast of Asia Minor. He and his companions crossed the Aegean Sea to Neapolis, the port of Philippi, then walked through the eastern cities of Macedonia. After preaching in Berea, they again paid passage on a ship to Athens. From there it was a short overland trip to Corinth. The roads they walked were paved and filled with pedestrians, horses, mules, and carts.

Throughout the journey Paul spoke Greek and, since he was a Roman citizen, he would have known Latin as well. He also encountered peoples whose language he did not know. While the vast region he and his associates traveled was under Roman rule, the Macedonians of Berea had a distinct cultural heritage from the Greeks in Athens, and the Galatians' history was markedly different from that of the inhabitants of Antioch in Syria. Romans from Italy made their home in many cities, and Corinth itself was a Roman colony on Greek soil. Paul undoubtedly heard the flute during worship in the temples, smelled the meat in the market next to the temple of Apollo, saw orators in the central forum performing before the crowds who praised them, and witnessed the dozens of clients who followed a rich man as he strode toward the public basilica. This was the gentile world where Paul, the Jew from Tarsus, proclaimed the gospel.

Paul took up the issues and debates of his day and constantly pointed people to the new thing God was doing through a crucified and resurrected Jew called Jesus. He engaged the current thinking on the nature of the gods, the world, and the values by which people should live. As an orator in the forum, he proclaimed publicly that only Jesus, not the emperor or any of the gods, was Savior and Lord. The apostle heralded the message of salvation, which offered hope amid the insecurities of life. His words spoke powerfully and pointedly to the peoples of the Mediterranean.

Some cities, such as Thessalonica, had both Latin and Greek speaking inhabitants. This monument has a Greek inscription above the scene and a Latin inscription, which is difficult to see, below the scene.
Gene L. Green

Enlarged Greek inscription.

Aerial view of Corinth
Aerial-motion/Shutterstock

THE GEOGRAPHY, THE JOURNEY, AND THE PEOPLES

The Geography

During the days of the apostles, the Roman Empire extended from southern Britain and Spain in the west to Syria and Judea in the east. North Africa, including Egypt and the Nile River valley, was under Rome's dominion, while the northern boundary followed the Danube basin. The Roman world surrounded the whole Mediterranean Sea, known simply as "Our Sea." Beyond the borders lived many peoples who were often hostile to Roman interests, such as the Parthians to the east and Germanic tribes in the north.

The New Testament story plays out over a large portion of this vast empire. The center of the early Christian mission quickly moved from Jerusalem in Judea north to Antioch, the third largest city in the empire (called "The Pearl of the East") and the city Pompey established in 67 BC as the capital of the eastern part of the empire. By Paul's time, the Romans had organized Asia Minor (modern-day Turkey) into provinces. In three provinces—Cilicia, Galatia, and Asia—Paul established churches.

With Paul being from Tarsus, Cilicia was his home province. The Galatian churches, located in the southern section of Galatia, received one of Paul's earliest letters, while Asia, on the western side of Asia Minor, had the great city of Ephesus as its capital. The seven churches that received the book of Revelation were scattered throughout this Roman province as well (Rev. 1:4; 2:1–3:22).

But the gospel also spread to the northern provinces of Asia Minor (a region sometimes known as Anatolia) early in the church's history. First Peter circulated among the believers in the provinces of "Pontus, Galatia, Cappadocia, Asia and Bithynia" (1 Pet. 1:1). By this time the Romans had united Pontus and Bithynia into a single province bordering the Black Sea and bisected by the Pontus Road. Cappadocia was located south of Pontus and north of Cilicia.

The Roman provinces in Anatolia or Asia Minor

Cenchreae was the port city of Corinth on the Aegean. Excavations of the harbor suggest the port continued to be used through the seventh century. The remains of the sanctuary of Isis are pictured here.
Todd Bolen/BiblePlaces.com

The ancient region of Galatia was also in the north, but when Rome reorganized this former kingdom, it became a province joined with lands to the south. Imperial Rome reorganized the land without full respect to traditional boundaries.

On the other side of the Aegean Sea were the provinces of Macedonia and Achaia. Macedonia spread across present-day northern Greece as well as portions of Macedonia and Albania. The Roman road that cut across the province was known as the Via Egnatia. Paul founded churches in Philippi and Thessalonica, principal metropolitan centers situated along this road. He wrote to the Roman believers that "from Jerusalem all the way around to Illyricum [located northwest of Macedonia], I have fully proclaimed the gospel of Christ" (Rom. 15:19). At some point he must have traveled the length of the Via Egnatia, which reached Illyricum on the coast of the Adriatic Sea.

The provinces of Macedonia and Achaia

The province of Achaia was the land of southern Greece, including the great peninsula known as Peloponnesus. Corinth was situated on the strategic narrow isthmus between the mainland of Greece and the Peloponnese. The only other Achaean city mentioned in the New Testament, apart from the port city of Corinth, called Cenchreae, is the famed Athens (Acts 17:15–34).

The Appian Way was a typical Roman road and linked Rome to the eastern port of Brundisium.
julius fekete/Shutterstock

The Roman Empire extended as far as North Africa.

Midway through the first century AD, there is evidence of Christians in Italy (Acts 18:2). Neither Paul nor Peter was the first to proclaim the gospel there, although both met martyrdom in Rome during Emperor Nero's reign. Paul's vision for his missionary journeys extended even farther to Spain (Rom. 15:24, 28), also a Roman province, and he may have traveled there after his release from imprisonment in Acts 28. Spain stood at the western mouth of the Mediterranean, and the ancient city of Gades (modern Cádiz) was sometimes called "the ends of the earth."

The Journey

A network of all-weather roads that the Romans had constructed facilitated travel throughout the empire. The Via Appia was the "queen of roads," extending from Rome to Brundisium, a city on Italy's southeastern coast. The Via Egnatia traversed the province of Macedonia between Apollonia on the Adriatic Sea and Byzantium (modern Istanbul). The Cilician Road crossed the southern portion of Asia Minor, connecting Ephesus in the province of Asia with the cities of Syria. The roads were signposted with *miliaria* (mile markers) at strategic points and *itineraria* were available, which informed travelers about distances between cities and places to stop. A network of other roads radiated from the main, paved highways. Through these great arteries of the empire flowed the message of salvation.

Travel along these roads was arduous and could be dangerous, especially in isolated places (see 2 Cor. 11:26). Paul traveled in the company of others both for protection and to help carry provisions (Acts 13:5—in travel narratives a "helper" was a servant who carried baggage). Inns for travelers were known for their poor food, bad wine, and worse company, so travelers preferred to stay in private homes of friends and patrons (Acts 16:15; 17:5–7). The virtue of hospitality was highly prized across the Mediterranean world (1 Pet. 4:9).

A *miliarium*, or mile marker, from outside Thessalonica that identifies the Roman proconsul Gnaeus Egnatius as the one responsible for the construction of this highway through Macedonia.
Kim Walton, Archaeological Museum of Thessaloniki

Travel by sea on cargo vessels (no ships carried only passengers) was much quicker than by road, although more precarious. On foot, a band of travelers could cover fifteen to twenty miles a day and in a carriage, twenty-five to thirty miles. But with favorable winds a ship could cover a hundred miles. Contrary winds would slow this pace considerably (cf. the two-day journey from Troas to Neapolis in Acts 16:11 and the five-day return journey in 20:6). Sea travel could be treacherous because of storms and shipwreck (Acts 27; 2 Cor. 11:25–26) and because of pirates, even though Augustus had cleared the sea of many of these brigands. Between October and May the sea lanes were virtually shut down (cf. 2 Tim. 4:21). Seamen were particularly superstitious and would not sail on ill-omened days, such as Friday the thirteenth.

Antipater of Thessalonica on the Dangers of Sea Travel

During the early part of the first century AD, Antipater wrote many epigrams about the dangers of travel by sea. In one he said, "Ill-starred Nicanor, wasted by the grey sea, naked you lie on a foreign shore or by the rocks. . . . Ah pitiable, your life is over, and your labours served only fishes and the sea." Another warned, "Trust not the fatal sea, mariner, not even when at anchor, not even if the beach holds your stern-cables. Ion fell into the harbour, and the sailor's hands, so swift to dive, were fettered by wine. Avoid dances on deck; the sea is the wine-god's enemy."[1]

What motivated early Christians to subject themselves to such adversity? The apostles were responding to Jesus's commission to "be my witnesses in Jerusalem, and in all Judea and Samaria, and to the ends of the earth" (Acts 1:8; cf. Matt. 28:18–20; Luke 24:46–49). In the midst of a pluralistic world, they were also driven by the conviction that there was only one God, who created the first human from whom all people are descended and therefore all peoples are responsible to him (Acts 17:24–31; 1 Cor. 8:4–6). Only through Jesus Christ can humanity approach him (1 Tim. 2:5) since Jesus's death was a sacrifice for everyone's sins (1 John 2:2).

The Peoples

Since the time of Alexander the Great, Greek was the universal tongue that facilitated trade and politics. The Greek spoken during the New Testament era is commonly called *koinē* ("common") Greek. When the Romans conquered a people group, they did not attempt to Latinize them, although they carried out the affairs of government in Latin.

During this era, an educated person would speak both Latin and Greek (Suetonius, the Roman historian, called these "our two languages," *Claudius* 42.1). Greek became so entrenched that Horace could say, "Captured Greece took captive her savage conqueror and brought civilization to rustic Latium" (*Epistles* 2.1.156). Those both within and outside the empire who did not speak Greek were simply known as "barbarians" (Rom. 1:14 KJV). For example, Acts relates Paul's encounter with those who spoke the Lycaonian language in Lystra (Acts 14:6), and he testified of his sojourn among the Nabateans in Arabia, people whom he likely evangelized (Gal. 1:15–17). Paul hints at the evangelization of the uncivilized Scythians, who lived around the Black Sea (Col. 3:11). Since there is one God and Christ's death was for all, the gospel opens the door to all peoples and breaks down the ethnic boundaries between them.

Mosaic from the second century depicting male and female slaves. Found in a Roman settlement near Tunisia, it resides at The National Bardo Museum. *Pascal Radigue/Wikimedia Commons, CC BY 3.0*

THE ORDER OF SOCIETY

Roman society was highly stratified, and the Romans recognized that every person had their place within the established order (Latin *ordo*). A number of factors determined one's position, including whether free or a slave, had wealth or not, and were a citizen or foreigner. Greater honor accrued to those who enjoyed higher status. The world where the gospel was first proclaimed was hierarchical and far from egalitarian.

Slaves, Liberti, and Free

The people of lowest status in society were slaves. Above them were freedmen and freedwomen, who had formerly been slaves, while the highest status was reserved for those born free. Even if a former slave attained great wealth, the stigma of once having been a slave could not be erased.

Slavery was widely practiced throughout the Roman world, and the institution itself was unquestioned. Within Italy there was about one slave for every three free persons, though in other parts of the empire the ratio was not as high. Wealthy people sometimes owned slaves numbering into the hundreds, and this became an indicator of a person's status. But even those of the lower artisan classes who made their living in local trades could own a few slaves.

Some free people became slaves when they were captured as prisoners of war or were kidnapped and sold into slavery (1 Tim. 1:10). Some were slaves because they had been born to slave parents, while others sold themselves or even their children into slavery because they could not repay debts. Unwanted children, especially females, were left either to die or to be found by strangers who, in turn, could raise them and then sell them as slaves. Slaves were human property (called "a living tool") and were bought and sold as any other commodity.

Regulation of the Slave Trade

Slave markets were regulated to protect the buyers. One ancient regulation stated, "Let care be taken that the bill of sale for each slave be written in such a way that it can be known exactly what disease or defect each one had, and which one is a runaway or a wanderer, or not innocent of any offence" (Aulus Gellius, *Attic Nights* 4.2.1).

Slaves on the Farms

In *On Agriculture* 1.17.1–2, Varro makes the following classification: "Now I turn to the means by which land is tilled. Some divide these into ... three parts: the class of instruments which is articulate, the inarticulate, and the mute; the articulate comprising the slaves, the inarticulate comprising all cattle, and the mute comprising the vehicles."

The Value of a Good Mind

"Lucius Voltacilius Pilutus is said to have been a slave and even to have been chained to the doorpost as a doorman until he was manumitted because of his intelligence and interest in education.... Then he became a teacher of rhetoric" (Suetonius, *On Rhetoricians* 27).

Obligations of the *Liberti* and Their Patrons

Roman law as well as social custom underscored a freedman's or freedwoman's obligation to their former master and the duty of the patron to the client. One Roman law stated: "A freedman must provide services and supply his own food and clothing. But if he cannot support himself, food must be provided to him by his patron" (*Digest of Laws* 38.1.18).

They could be rented to others, a convenient way to recoup the cost of purchasing a slave. The master had complete *dominium* over the slaves.

Slaves constructed, cleaned, served as cooks, nurses, beauticians, barbers, midwives, doctors, cleaners, prostitutes, painters, and even pedagogues, who looked after children and, when the children were old enough, conducted them to school (Gal. 3:24–25). Some slaves held responsible positions as managers, while others ended up as gladiators. Those severely ill-treated believed running away was their only recourse. Slaves could be given ID collars, one of which read, "I have run away. Capture me. When you have returned me to my master, Zoninus, you will receive a reward" (*CIL* 15.7194).

Manumission inscriptions covered this wall at the base of the Temple of Apollo in Delphi. Most of the names are female.
www.HolyLandPhotos.org

Manumission inscriptions like the one above from Delphi recorded the freedom granted a slave. The usual formula was: "Date. N.N. sold to the Pythian Apollo a male slave named X.Y. at the price of— minae, for freedom (or 'on condition that he shall be free, etc.'), followed by conditions and the names of witnesses."[2]
Todd Bolen/BiblePlaces.com

Slaves could obtain their freedom (a process called "manumission") and join the ranks of the *liberti*, or freedmen and freedwomen. Sometimes slaves could purchase their freedom by saving up gifts and the small allowance they received, or if their family or friends could supply the funds. Some masters manumitted slaves to impress others with their wealth, while others freed slaves in their wills. At times, a slave master would free a female slave in order to marry her. If the former master was a citizen, the freed slave commonly received citizenship. These freed slaves had continuing obligations to their former masters. The *liberti* were recognized by the freedman's beanie, a cap made out of felt. Paul encouraged slaves to avail themselves of manumission if such an option became available (1 Cor. 7:21). Although slaves were expected to participate in the religion of their masters, Christian slaves broke with custom and consequently faced abuse (1 Pet. 2:18–20). Paul aimed to alter Christian masters' relationships with their slaves by reminding them of their Master in heaven (Col. 4:1).

Seneca's Advice on How to Deal with Newly-Enslaved Captives

Seneca writes in his *Essay about Anger* 3.29.1–2:

> If a captive who has suddenly been reduced to slavery hangs on to remnants of his former freedom and does not run quickly to perform degrading and laborious services, if he does not keep up with the pace of his master's horse or carriage because he is out of shape from previous inactivity, if sleep overwhelms him because he is exhausted by his demanding daily duties, if he refuses to do farm work or does not do it vigorously when he has been transferred to this hard labor from service in the city with its holidays—let us carefully distinguish whether he *cannot* do the work or *will not*.

Those born free within Roman society all shared the common advantage of higher social status than slaves or even freedmen and freedwomen. But not all free people were of the same social class. Some would be loosely classified as the *humiliores*, those of low birth and status, while people of the higher orders of society were the *honestiores*, or those who were given honor in society.

Honestiores

The highest class of aristocrats in the empire was the *senators*. They owned property with a value of at least one million sesterces, a sum equivalent to two hundred fifty thousand denarii (each denarius was equivalent to a day's wage). The wealth of some senators greatly exceeded this amount. The New Testament names some who were senators, such as Sergius Paulus, the proconsul of Cyprus (Acts 13:7), and Gallio, the proconsul of Achaia (Acts 18:12).

Below the senatorial order were the *equestrians*, those born Roman citizens who had accumulated wealth totaling at least four hundred thousand sesterces (one hundred thousand denarii). Some of the governors of Judea, such as Pontius Pilate, Marcus Antonius Felix, and Porcius Festus, were from the equestrian order (Luke 3:1; Acts 24:1–3, 27). Below the equestrian order were the *decurions*, who were freeborn aristocrats whose wealth needed to total at least one hundred thousand sesterces. Erastus, the city treasurer of Corinth (Rom. 16:23), was a decurion, as was Dionysius of Athens, a man who served in the Areopagus (Acts 17:34).

Honestiores had the most honored seats at public events, such as in the stadium in Delphi.
designpicsinc/123rf.com

Juvenal and Persius on Patrons

Juvenal, the Roman satirist, describes the less-than-refined dinner experience of a client invited to his patron's banquet: "When bidden to dinner, you receive payment in full for all your past services.... See with what a grumble another [slave] has handed you a bit of hard bread that you can scarce break in two, or bits of solid dough that have turned mouldy.... See now that large lobster being served to my lord, all garnished with asparagus.... Before you is placed on a tiny plate a shrimp hemmed in by half an egg—a fit banquet for the dead" (*Satire* 5.12–90).

Another Latin author, Perseus, satirizes a patron: "You know how to present a shivering client with a threadbare cloak, and then you say, 'I love the Truth; tell me the truth about myself!'" (1.54–55).

Humiliores

The enormous wealth of the empire was in the hands of the *honestiores* and not the vast majority of the population known as *humiliores*. A middle class did not exist, and the economic gap between the *honestiores* and the people of low birth and status was huge. The *humiliores* were free people (either born free or *liberti*) who owned small farms or businesses or worked as barbers, moneylenders, potters, shippers, tanners, butchers, weavers, wine and oil makers, soldiers, or other kinds of artisans. Because of their low status in society, people did not consider them virtuous. Most people in the early church were *humiliores* and slaves, the very people society considered less virtuous.

Patrons and Clients

Patronage was a central feature of the Roman world. A person would come under the protection and care of a patron, and clients, in turn, would render services for the patron. Clients followed their patrons as they went about their business and supported their cause in public. The number of clients a patron had as well as the social status of the clients greatly enhanced the patron's public honor. The higher the class of clients, the higher the status of the patron. Patrons offered legal protection to their clients, rewarded them with food and presents, and sometimes invited them to banquets.

Cicero and Seneca on Clients

The senator Cicero commented on the services a client would render to a patron:

> Men of the lower class have only one way of either earning or repaying favors from our class, and that is by working on our political campaigns and following us around.... This constant attendance, which we have come to expect for men who are honorable and generous, is an appropriate activity for friends [a euphemism for 'client'] who are of a lower class and not busy.... As they themselves often say, they cannot plead cases for us, or pledge security, or invite us to their homes. Yet they ask all these things from us, and they think that the favors which they receive from us can be repaid by their service (*Speech in Defense of Murena* 70–71).

Seneca is a bit more cynical: "Clients, you say? Not one of them waits upon you, but rather what he can get out of you. Once upon a time, clients sought a politically powerful friend; now they seek loot. If a lonely old man changes his will, his morning visitor goes to someone else's door" (*Letters* 19.4).

A patron could, in turn, be a client of a person of higher social status. Higher status clients were sometimes euphemistically called "friends," a sense that is behind Jesus's statement, "I no longer call you servants . . . I have called you friends" (John 15:15). The greatest patrons were the emperors themselves, who, among their many honorific titles, were called "benefactor" (*euergetēs*). In the New Testament, Jesus is sometimes viewed as the one who is the greatest benefactor of all (see Acts 10:38).

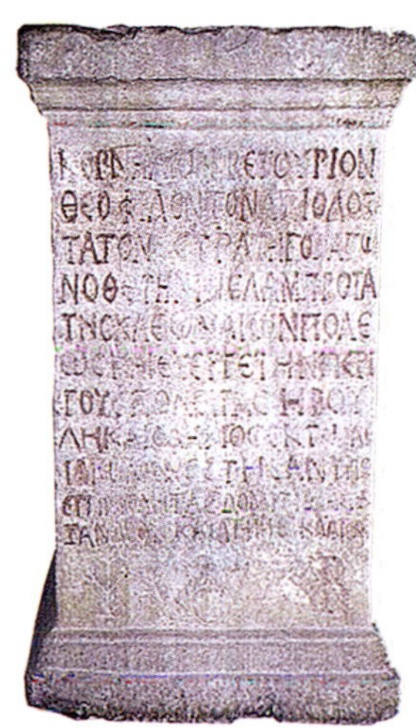

Inscription that honors a benefactor, "one who does good."
Gene L. Green

Citizens and Aliens

Paul was a Roman citizen (Acts 22:25–29) but not because he was born and lived in the Roman Empire. Many within the provinces of the empire, although free persons, did not enjoy the rights of citizenship, which included exemption from humiliating forms of punishment (such as crucifixion) and punishment without trial (16:37–39). While Paul was beheaded when finally condemned in Rome, Peter was crucified, since his legal status was that of an alien. Roman citizens in the provinces could appeal to Caesar if they believed their case was not considered fairly by provincial authorities (25:10–12). And Roman citizens could vote.

Some were born citizens of Rome because their parents were citizens, as was the case with Paul, or one could purchase citizenship (Acts 22:28). Those freed from slavery were often granted citizenship, and those who served in the auxiliary military forces became citizens upon discharge. Citizenship helped ensure loyalty to the imperial power (21:39). The New Testament reflects on the theological meaning of citizenship (Phil. 3:20) and alien status (1 Pet. 2:11).

Cicero on Citizenship

Cicero condemned Verres, a governor in Sicily, for his treatment of a Roman citizen:

> He then ordered the man to be flogged severely all over his body. There in the open marketplace of Messana a Roman citizen, gentlemen, was beaten with rods; and all the while, amid the crack of the falling blows, no groan was heard from the unhappy man, no words came from his lips in his agony except "I am a Roman citizen." By thus proclaiming his citizenship he had been hoping to avert all those blows and shield his body from torture; yet not only did he fail to secure escape from those cruel rods, but when he persisted in his entreaties and his appeals to his citizen rights, a cross was made ready—yes, a cross, for that hapless and broken sufferer, who had never seen such an accursed thing till then. (*Against Verres* 2.162).

The Father's Power of Life and Death

A poignant letter written by Hilarion, away in Alexandria, to his wife, Alis, gives her both warm and dreadful messages: "I beg and entreat you, take care of the little one, and as soon as we receive our pay I will send it up to you. If by chance you bear a child, if it is a boy, let it be, if it is a girl, cast it out" (*Select Papyri* 1.105).

Lesbia

Valerius Catullus wrote about Lesbia, who embodied the image of the new woman:

> Lesbia hurls abuse at me in front of her husband:
> that fatuous person finds it highly amusing!
> Nothing gets through to you, jackass—for silence would signal
> that she'd been cured of me, but her barking and bitching
> show that not only haven't I been forgotten,
> but that this burns her, and so she rants and rages. (Poem 83)0

The Family

The hierarchical social structure within Roman society was also present in the family. The father of the family, known as the *paterfamilias*, had absolute authority (*patria potestas*) over the entire household—spouse, children, extended family, and slaves. He held rights over all the property and financial affairs of the family and could also determine whom his children married. If a child was born to his wife, he had authority to "expose" the child (thus killing it) if it was unwanted. Children continued to be obligated to their father even after they moved out of the family home. The father also directed the religious life of the family.

Marriages were arranged, although there could be genuine affection between husbands and wives. Women were commonly married early in their teens, while men entered marriage much later. Marriages were governed by contracts, which primarily outlined economic matters and inheritance.

Women were under contract to remain faithful to their husbands, while husbands had wide latitude to satisfy their sexual desires outside the family home. Plutarch even wrote, "If therefore a man in private life, who is incontinent and dissolute . . . commit some peccadillo with a paramour or a maidservant, his wedded wife ought not to be indignant or angry, but she should reason that it is respect for her which leads him to share his debauchery, licentiousness, and wantonness with another woman"

(*Advice to Bride and Groom* 140B). Above all, a woman was expected to obey her husband, be faithful, worship only his gods, and manage the household well.

Juno was the goddess of marriage, shown here standing behind the couple. The marriage contract is in the form of a scroll.
© The Trustees of the British Museum

Women passed from being subject to their fathers to being subordinate to their husband. Livy once said, "Never, while their men survive, is feminine subjection shaken off; and they themselves abhor the freedom which the loss of husbands and fathers produces" (*History of Rome* 34.1.12). But during the Roman period, the model of the "new woman" emerged, as many women found themselves with great wealth and less supervision by men who were absent during war and on administrative duty. These women were more socially self-determined in many matters, including financial affairs, political participation, and even sexuality.

New Testament discussions about women developed between the poles of traditional female roles and new emerging definitions. While the gospels and letters are sometimes viewed as advocates for traditional roles, the presence of women in the church who provided significant leadership shows that Christians advocated for models that diverged from the extremes of the surrounding culture (Acts 18:24–26; Rom. 16:1–7; Phil. 4:2–3; Col. 4:15). Women in the church also found freedom to abandon their husbands' religion as they became believers in Christ (1 Pet. 3:1–2).

Society expected children to obey their parents, especially their fathers, and to honor them in a way similar to how a person would honor the gods. Fathers were expected to discipline and be strict with their children as an expression of love, while mothers were more tender.

Fathers taught their sons a trade. Mothers likewise disciplined their children and had their respect. They were solely responsible for the education of their daughters in the skills of domestic life and moral development.

THE GOVERNMENT OF THE EMPIRE

The Emperors

"Caesar" was the family name of Julius Caesar, which Augustus, his adopted son, took and was subsequently used by the succeeding emperors. The title "emperor" comes from the Latin *imperator*, which was originally granted to generals after victory in battle. Julius Caesar adopted it as a permanent title to designate himself as the supreme military authority in Rome.

A child's toy found during archaeological excavations, thought to be from the Imperial era.
Josep/Curtio/Shutterstock

Seneca on Mothers and Fathers

"Don't you see how fathers treat their children one way, and mothers another way? Fathers order their children to be woken up to do their work early. Even on holidays they don't allow them to be idle, and they wring sweat and sometimes tears from them. But mothers want to hold their children in their laps and keep them in the cool shade; they want them never to be made unhappy, never to weep, and never to be in distress" (*Essay about Providence* 2.5).

A model of the imperial temple of Augustus in Ankara, Turkey
Todd Bolen/BiblePlaces.com

Tiberius, for example, said, "I am *dominus* [lord] of my slaves, *imperator* of my troops, and *princeps* [first citizen] of everyone else" (Dio Cassio, *Historia* 57.8.2).

Augustus
Marie-Lan Nguyen/Wikimedia Commons, CC BY 2.5

Augustus wanted to restore the religious traditions of Rome and thus adopted the title *pontifex maximus* as well. He was also called *pater patriae*, "the father of the fatherland," a title that suggested not only his protective care but his unrivaled authority (similar to *paterfamilias*). These titles highlight how exalted the emperor became in the first century. The culmination of this process was the emperor cult, which flourished especially in the East.

When Augustus became emperor, he added to his title *divi filius* ("son of god", i.e., son of the deified Julius Caesar). Augustus became known as "the god and savior, emperor" and Nero was hailed as "the lord of the entire world." The Christian proclamation that Christ was the true Lord and only Savior was a direct challenge to the exalted status of the emperor (Phil. 2:11; Titus 2:13). Only Jesus could be rightly called the "Son of God" (John 3:16; 1 John 5:5).

The tradition of worshiping a ruler as divine was common in the East, as Nebuchadnezzar demanded (Dan. 3) or as the adoration that the pharaoh received in Egypt. This notion gained wider circulation through the conquests of Alexander

The Emperors

Augustus (Octavian)
31 BC–AD 14
Luke 2:1

Tiberius
AD 14–37
Luke 3:1

Caligula (Gaius)
AD 37–41

Claudius
AD 41–54
Acts 11:28; 18:2

Nero
AD 54–68
Acts 25:10; 28:19

Galba
AD 68

Otho
AD 69

Vitellius
AD 69

Vespasian
AD 69–79

Titus
AD 79–81

Domitian
AD 81–96

Nerva
AD 96–98

Trajan
AD 98–117

Hadrian
AD 117–138

Harlan J. Berk, Ltd.

the Great and the cult that flourished in the wake of his own divinization. The ruler cult only slowly spread to Rome itself. These men were considered to have done great deeds that one would expect of the gods.

Augustus had established peace in the empire (*pax Romana*) and earned acclaim as the universal benefactor. His name Augustus (Gk. *Sebastos*) means something like "his reverence" or "his worship" and has divine overtones. Despite such high honors, we should not assume that the imperial cult was simply a religious affair. The emperors were the greatest patrons in the empire, controlling vast wealth to promote their interests. Cities that received imperial patronage returned the favor by honoring such an exalted patron with a temple erected for his veneration, complete with sacrifices and priesthood. This overwhelming act of thanksgiving to the patron helped ensure future benefits.

Augustus was considered as the "son of god" (*divi filius*), that is, the son of the deified Julius Caesar.
Harlan J. Berk, Ltd.

The *Res Gestae* of Augustus

The *Res Gestae* ("notable deeds") of Augustus highlights the great accomplishments of the emperor Augustus, which were foundational for the belief in his divinity. In part it reads:

> The accomplishments of the deified Augustus by which he subjected the whole world to the empire of the Roman People, and the expenses which he incurred for the state and the Roman People.... Wars on land and sea both domestic and foreign throughout the whole world I often waged and as victor I spared all citizens who sought forgiveness.... I was acclaimed twenty-one times imperator.... I pacified the sea, freed it of pirates.... In that war the slaves, who had fled from their masters and had taken up arms against the Republic, I captured about thirty thousand of them and turned them over to their masters for punishment.... As for all those provinces of the Roman People bordered by tribes not subject to our Empire, I increased the frontiers.... I added Egypt to the empire of the Roman People.... I established colonies of soldiers.... To me embassies of kings were often sent from India, not seen before this age in the presence of any commander of the Romans.... To me kings fled as suppliants.... In my sixth and seventh consulships, after I had extinguished the civil wars and by the consent of all had acquired control of everything....[3]

The Imperial Cult in the East

One of the ways citizens of cities in the eastern part of the empire honored the emperor for his generous patronage was to establish a temple and priesthood as part of the imperial cult. A fragmentary inscription from Thessalonica records the construction of such a temple:

> ...proconsul...of Latomia buil[t the] tem[ple] of Caesar. In the time of priest and agon[othete of Im]perator Caesar Augustus son [of god]...-oms son of Neikopol[eoms, priest] of the gods, Dom [... son of ...]-pos, and (priest) of Roma a[nd Roman] benefactors, Neik[... son of] Paramonos. In the term of the Politarchs Diogenems son [of...] Kleomn son of P..., Zompas son of Kal..., Eulandros son of ..., Promtogenems son of ..., and the superin[tendent] of the work, trea[surer of the city] Somsomnos s[on of ...] [In the term of the] architec[t] Dionysiu[s son of ...].[4]

The Senate

During the Roman republic, which lasted until the time of Augustus, the Senate ruled supreme over all affairs, domestic and foreign. This body of about three hundred was composed of men of the highest social class. Only those with the greatest wealth could be members of the Roman Senate, and they held their position for life. But after the assassination of Julius Caesar in 44 BC, the Senate lost its prestige and power, as the emperor, beginning with Augustus, gained supremacy. The Senate was allowed to govern certain of the less problematic provinces of the empire, but in many ways it became more of a club of the Roman aristocracy.

The Cities and the Provinces

We are accustomed to governments that have well-defined structure and boundaries and little variation from region to region. The Roman Empire, however, was characterized by diversity in its governmental institutions. While much of the empire was organized into provinces, there were also vassal states. Governors were prefects, legates, or proconsuls, depending on the type of administrative district they governed and their own status within the empire. Cities were classified in various ways, with some enjoying free city status, while others were Roman colonies. Vassal states could become provinces, and provinces could move from being imperial to senatorial, and then back again. During the New Testament era, Judea was sometimes a vassal kingdom and at other times governed directly by the Romans as a province (see ch. 3).

Corinth was a Roman colony on Greek soil. View looking down the Lechaion Road to the Acrocorinth.

The cities. The Roman Empire was basically a commonwealth of autonomous cities that were the political and economic backbone of the Roman Empire. A city was a social and economic unit that exercised control over a large geographical area—its hinterland or *territorium*. Produce from the country was brought into the city markets. These products were also the source of much of the riches of the aristocracy, who owned most of the arable land. The seat of government over the surrounding area was in the city, similar to our county governments.

Though the Jesus movement began in the rural regions of Galilee, it soon became an urban phenomenon. In fact, when Paul spread the gospel throughout the Roman world, his center of operations were the cities, and via these the surrounding countryside was influenced (see Acts 19:10; 1 Thess. 1:8). He proclaimed that he had filled the whole region from Jerusalem to Illyricum with the gospel (Rom. 15:19), even though he limited his ministry to significant urban centers.

Two types of cities are relevant for our study of the New Testament. The first is the *colony* of Roman citizens (*coloniae civium romanorum*). The program of colonization began with Julius Caesar and continued under succeeding emperors. Colonies were often populated with veterans of the Roman legions, as was Philippi (Acts 16:12), or with members of the proletariat who had no land and lived from the sale of their labor, as was Corinth (which was populated largely with *liberti* from Italy).

The colonies mirrored life in the imperial city of Rome. Except for the excluded classes, such as slaves and foreigners, their populations enjoyed Roman citizenship. They were exempt from taxes paid to Rome and Roman law was their law. The gospel spread through various Roman colonies during the early Christian mission, such as Pisidian Antioch, Lystra, Iconium, Troas, Philippi, Corinth, Ptolemais (Acts 21:7), and Syracuse (28:12).

COLONIAE I
IVLIAE ·
CORINTHIENSI ·
Q · GRANIVS · Q · F ·
BASSVS · S · P · D · D
PROC · AVG ·

Colonies were governed by Roman law. This inscription identifies Corinth as a Roman colony.

The second type of city, which were numerous, were *free cities*, such as Ephesus, Smyrna, Tarsus, Antioch in Syria, and Thessalonica. These cities could govern themselves according to local tradition, could mint their own coins, and were exempt from many of the taxes normally paid to Rome. Here the democratic Greek system of government prevailed, with the highest ruling authority being the *ekklēsia* ("assembly," a word commonly used to describe the "church" in the New Testament) of the *dēmos*, the people or the free citizens of the city (Acts 19:30, 33).

A street from Tarsus, home of the apostle Paul, one of many free cities in the empire.
Todd Bolen/BiblePlaces.com

This assembly had final say in political/legislative as well as judicial matters. Meetings of the *ekklēsia* included prayers and sacrifices to the local deity. Free cities also had a *boulē*, or senate, and frequently we find inscriptions speaking of *hē boulē kai ho dēmos* ("the council and the people"). The Areopagus of Athens was one such body (Acts 17:19, 34); the Sanhedrin in Jerusalem functioned in a similar way. The leading magistrates in some Macedonian cities were called "politarchs" (Acts 17:6, 8) while in other cities they were simply "rulers" (Matt. 20:25; Rom. 13:3; Titus 3:1).

Marble stele with a Greek inscription of the gift of a golden crown to Aurelios Alexandros by the council and people *boulē kai dēmos* of a city, ca. 300–100 BC. *© The Trustees of the British Museum*

The provinces. The Roman Empire was divided into administrative districts called "provinces" (see Acts 23:34; 25:1), which were classified as either imperial or senatorial. Imperial provinces (e.g., Cilicia, Syria, Egypt, Galatia, Cappadocia, and Pamphylia) were the more problematic and came under the direct control of the emperor. Judea was especially problematic for Rome because of the number of its violent uprisings. One or more Roman legions were garrisoned inside an imperial province to maintain order (legions were about six thousand soldiers strong). For Judea, a legion was located both in Egypt and in Syria. These provinces were governed by legates of senatorial rank (*legatus*), although the minor imperial provinces could be administered by a prefect (*praefectus*), who could be an equestrian. Jesus was crucified by Pontius Pilate, the *prefect* of Judea.

Senatorial provinces were those that posed no threat to the empire. These had only a small garrison of troops. Senatorial provinces mentioned in the New Testament are Macedonia, Achaia, Asia, Crete (united with Cyrene in Africa), Bithynia (united with Pontus in 74 BC), and Cyprus. The governor of these provinces was called a proconsul (see "Honestiores," p. 111).

Vassal Kingdoms

The Roman Empire also had vassal kingdoms. Although governed by kings or royalty of lower status, these enjoyed a modicum of freedom under the authority of the emperor and had the liberty to govern their internal affairs as long as they remained loyal to Rome. They could collect taxes and even maintain an army. They could not develop their own foreign relations, and their power to mint their own money was limited. They paid tribute to Rome and had to assure that the frontiers were secure. Galatia was a vassal kingdom until 25 BC; Judea under Herod the Great and his descendants was another.

Thessalonica was a "free city" and not a colony. This coin commemorates the city's grant of freedom. The image is the bust of Eleutheria (Freedom). *Harlan J. Berk, Ltd.*

RELIGION IN THE MEDITERRANEAN WORLD

When the early Christian messengers spread the gospel across the Mediterranean world, every city they entered contained numerous temples, altars, and shrines dedicated to local deities as well as gods worshiped throughout the empire.

In 1 Corinthians, Paul discussed what he called the "so-called gods, whether in heaven or on earth" (1 Cor. 8:5); in Athens he became distressed because "the city was full of idols" (Acts 17:16).

Atheists were not common, and almost everyone believed that there were multiple gods who governed the affairs of humanity and the world. Jews and Christians, by contrast, acknowledged only one God and considered that the fundamental movement of salvation was to forsake the worship of those gods and turn to the one true and living God (1 Thess. 1:9). Ancient Greeks and Latins correctly perceived Christianity as an attack on the worship of idols (Acts 14:11–18; 17:22–31; 19:23–41) since the heralds of the gospel condemned such worship and called people to serve the true and living God (e.g., Rom. 1:22–25; 1 Cor. 5:11; 6:9; 10:14–22; Gal. 5:20–21; 1 John 5:21; Rev 21:8; 22:15). During that era, society was critical of those who abandoned the gods of their community and family, for rejecting the family deities or the gods of the city was seen as an antisocial act, for the gods were regarded as patrons of the community.

The temple housed the image of the deity, as in the Temple of Artemis in Ephesus depicted on this coin.
© The Trustees of the British Museum

Gentiles, Judaism, and Christianity

Christians were not alone in their rejection of common gentile notions about the divine. Judaism too differentiated itself from gentile beliefs and practices. In the first place, the gentiles had various temples in different places to worship their deities and could sacrifice to their gods even if there were no temple. But the Jews only sacrificed in the temple in Jerusalem. For their part, the Christians gathered in any convenient location, although most often in private houses. Worship was not tied to any particular locality, and in some respects, Christian practices mirrored those of the synagogue.

The Temple of Hephaestus was one of many temples and altars that filled the agora in Athens.
Aerial-motion/Shutterstock

Pausanius on the Gods in Athens

Writing in the second century AD, Pausanius describes in great detail the religious environment in Athens, making note of the multiple temples and images, along with the myths that stand behind them. He writes, "Near the statue of Demosthenes [the orator] is a sanctuary of Ares, where are placed two images of Aphrodite, one of Ares made by Alcamenes, and one of Athena made by a Parian of the name of Locrus. There is also an image of Enyo, made by the sons of Praxiteles. About the temple stand images of Heracles, Theseus, Apollo binding his hair with a fillet" (*Description of Greece* 1.8.4). Pausanius even mentions the "altars of the gods named Unknown" (1.1.4), a description strikingly similar to Paul's discovery of the Athenian altar dedicated "To an Unknown God" (Acts 17:23).

Second, the function of a temple in the Roman world was to house the image of the deity. The temple was the dwelling of the deity, not a religious meeting place for worshipers. But in the temple of God in Jerusalem, there was no image (Ex. 20:4–6). The temple was holy since it was dedicated to the worship of the God who lived there (Matt. 23:21; 27:51; Heb. 6:19). Yet early Christian apologetic was critical of the notion that God could be confined to the temple in Jerusalem (Acts 7:48–50), and Paul declared that the gathering of God's people was his temple and his presence dwelt in their midst (1 Cor. 3:16; 2 Cor. 6:16).

Third, the worship of Yahweh was expensive. The priesthood in the Greek and Roman temples was an honorary position, underwritten by those who served as priests. The priests were from the aristocracy, and those who wanted to advance in society sought out a priesthood. But in Judaism the priesthood was hereditary, and Jewish society maintained the priests. While the gods of the Greeks and Romans ended up with little of the sacrifice (normally only the bones, since the meat of public sacrifices was sold in the market, cf. 1 Cor. 10:23–30), the sacrifices in Jerusalem consumed most of the animal (although priests and worshipers received a considerable portion of certain sacrifices). Early Christians looked to Christ as their great high priest (Heb. 3:1; 4:14–15) and did not acknowledge any other person as priest who mediated between humanity and God. Those who did serve as ministers of the gospel could expect to be supported by the churches they served (Luke 10:7; 1 Cor. 9:7–12; 1 Tim. 5:17–18).

Dionysus was the god of wine. Note the grapes strung through his hair. *Marie-Lan Nguyen, Public Domain*

Fourth, a feature that distinguished Judaism from gentile religion was the subjection of the whole life of the worshiper to Yahweh. Among the gentiles, ethics was a subject of philosophy, alongside metaphysics, and was not connected to one's religious allegiances. But within Judaism, religion and ethics were intimately intertwined.

The "pious" gentile was not necessarily a moral person but rather one who faithfully performed the necessary obligations before the gods, as well as family and country.

Todd Bolen/BiblePlaces.com

Temples of the same god were in various cities, such as these temples of Jupiter in Baalbek (left) and Athens (right). To the Romans, Jupiter and Zeus were equivalent.
Guillaume Piolle/Wikimedia Commons, CC BY 3.0

Religion had nothing to do with the morality of the worshipers. In fact, a number of cults promoted lifestyles that Christians viewed as immoral. Dionysus was the god of wine and drunkenness; Aphrodite was the patroness of prostitutes. Christianity shared with Judaism the conviction that faith in God results in an ethical life subject to God's will. Conversion to faith in the living God includes serving him (1 Thess. 1:9) as obedient children who hear God's call, "Be holy, because I am holy" (1 Pet. 1:13–16).

Gentiles and Christians on the Relationship with the Divine

In the Greco-Roman world, the relationship with the gods was transactional: "Do this for me and I'll do that for you." People gave the gods votive offerings in anticipation of receiving some benefit, such as an answer to prayer. Thanksgivings for benefits received were not mere expressions of gratitude. In offering to the gods, the worshiper had to follow the established formulas. If one made a mistake, the ritual had to begin over again. Christians, however, embraced a different approach to God, whom they viewed as their Father (Matt. 6:7–13).

Votive offerings from the Serapeum, the temple of Serapis, in Thessalonica
Gene L. Green

The gods were capricious. The very same god could bring a person tragedy or blessing. Antipater shows how perplexed people could be as they tried to understand the gods' behavior: "Easy-going is Hermes, shepherds, pleased at libations of milk and honey from the oak. Not so Heracles; he demands a whole ram or a fat sheep, or anyway exacts a whole victim. But he keeps the wolves away. But what good is that if what is protected is killed, whether by wolves or by the protector?"[5] Much Roman cult activity was devoted to keeping the gods on your side in the hope of maintaining the *pax deorum* ("peace with the gods"). Keeping the proper relationship with the gods was the essence of *pietas* ("piety"). The unwavering and self-sacrificial love of God, as understood by the Christians, stood in bold relief to these popular notions about the gods (John 3:16; Rom. 8:31–39).

Other Religious Trends in the Mediterranean World

Although the established cults of the cities and the empire were the dominant religious force in the Roman world, from the time of the Roman republic, new religions from the East began to establish their roots. These so-called "mystery religions" promised the worshiper a more personal communion with the divine. Initiation into the cult and its secrets was often a dramatic and emotional event through which the initiate came into union with the deity, obtained salvation, and expected bliss in the afterlife. These religions, such as the worship of Mithra, Isis, Cybele, Demeter, and Dionysus, resonated with the themes of death and rebirth tied with the agricultural cycle of sowing and reaping.

Although some scholars have attempted to understand the rise of Christianity as part of this movement, significant differences exist between the Christian story and that of the mysteries. The death and resurrection of Christ, for example, is not an annual cyclical event but a once-for-all occurrence. Although the Christian faith offers personal communion with God, it does not promise that the deity will absorb the initiate.

Religion in the Mediterranean world was not limited to the temples and public altars. Private religion included such practices as divination, magic, and astrology. In the first century, Antipater of Thessalonica notes the prevalence of astrology in one of his many epigrams: "The experts in astrology tell of an early death for me; though it be so, I care nothing for that, Seleucus.

Josephus on Religion and Ethics

Josephus comments on how religion and ethics go hand in hand in Judaism: "The reason why the constitution of this legislation was even better directed to the utility of all than other legislations were, is this, that Moses did not make religion a part of virtue, but he saw and he ordained other virtues to be parts of religion; I mean, justice, and fortitude, and temperance, and a universal agreement of the members of the community with one another; for all our actions and studies, and all our words [in Moses's settlement], have a reference to piety towards God" (*Against Apion* 2.17 [170–171]).

It's Magic!

While the purpose of religion was to placate the gods, the goal of magic was to control the powers by using prescribed formulas and incantations. Ephesus was known as a center of magic (Acts 19:18–20). If the ritual was performed in the proper way, one could expect the desired results. Cato the Elder described a chant by which one could cure a dislocated limb:

> A dislocation can be remedied with this chant. Take a green reed, about four or five feet long, split it down the middle, and have two men hold it against their hips. Begin to chant: *motas vaeta daries dardares astataries dissunapiter.* Continue until the two halves of the reed come together. Wave an iron knife over the reed. When the halves have joined and are touching one another, take the reed in your hand and cut it on the right and on the left. Fasten it to the dislocation or fracture, which will then heal. Continue to chant every day: *huat hauat huat ista pista sista dannabo dannaustra.* Or: *huat haut haut istasis tarsis ardannabou dannaustra.* (*On Agriculture* 160).

An inscribed lead curse tablet from Roman Britain, which translated reads: "May he who carried off Vilbia from me become as liquid as water. (May) she who obscenely devoured her (become) dumb, whether Velvinna, Exsupereus, Verianus, Severinus, A(u) gustalis, Comitianus, Catus, Minianus, Germanilla, (or) Jovina."[7]

Used by permission from Llyn Llydaw from Crrib Goch by Mike Peel/www.mikepeel.net, CC BY-SA 4.0

All men have the same way down to Hades; if mine is quicker than others', I shall be face to face with Minos the sooner."[6] People understood the gods to speak through dreams, visions, and oracles.

By using curses, often inscribed on lead tablets and thrown into wells or buried, a person could attempt to banish their enemies to the underworld. One such tablet reads: "Spirits of the netherworld, I consecrate and hand over to you, if you have any power, Ticene of Carisius. Whatever she does, may it all turn out wrong. Spirits of the netherworld, I consecrate to you her limbs, her complexion, her figure, her head . . . [and] if I see her wasting away, I swear that I will be delighted to offer a sacrifice to you every year" (*Corpus Inscriptionum Latinarum* 10.8249; cf. Luke 6:28; Rom. 12:14). "Demons" (*daimōn*) filled the gap between the gods and humans, and exorcism for those possessed by spirits was widely known and practiced.

PHILOSOPHY IN THE MEDITERRANEAN WORLD

Philosophy played a central role in ancient Greco-Roman society. Philosophers wrote and gave public lectures throughout the cities of the empire; we meet many of them face-to-face, with characteristic garb and beard, in statues that survive from the period. The Roman philosopher Gellius once quipped, "*Video barbum et pallium, philosophum nondum video*," which translates, "I see the beard and the mantle, but I do not yet see the philosopher."

Athens retained something of its classical flavor as philosophers could be found declaiming in the central agora (Acts 17:17–18). Cicero (first century BC) was largely responsible for mediating Greek philosophical trends to the Roman people, though they were much more reluctant to engage in philosophical speculation, considering it a waste of time.

Philosophy was principally concerned with reason (or how to know the world), metaphysical issues (or how to understand the world), and moral questions (or how one is to live to assure happiness). Common topics were the nature of the gods and practical aspects of daily life. For example, Plutarch's *Moralia* includes essays on "The Delays of the Divine Vengeance" and "Fate" as well as tracts on "The Love of Wealth," "Compliancy," "Envy and Hate," and "Praising Oneself Inoffensively." He also wrote "Advice to Bride and Groom."

The small theater, or "odeon," in Ephesus was used for musical performances or speeches. *Reproduced by permission from Francisco Bini/Wikimedia Commons, CC BY-SA 3.0*

In the encounter with the philosophical trends of the era, we find Christianity co-opting the place of philosophy as it had the place of religion within society. Paul, like the philosophers, makes his case in the marketplace (Acts 17:16–31), and the themes he addressed were part of the current debates. New Testament moral teaching addresses the common topics of philosophical discussion, such as the proper conduct expected of each one according to his or her station (the household codes in Eph. 5:21–6:9; Col. 3:18–4:1). Christians also discussed moral issues, such as the vice and virtue lists in Galatians 5:19–23 (see also Rom. 1:28–32). Yet while the *form* of the teaching is strikingly similar, the understanding of the *sources* of vice and virtue are distinct. Christian ethics find their foundation and motivation in the character of God and his redemptive work (1 Pet. 1:13–16).

Two of the most prominent philosophical schools during the first century were the Epicureans and the Stoics. Paul encountered adherents to both these philosophies in the city of Athens (Acts 17:18). The Epicureans, founded by Epicurus around 300 BC, did not believe in the existence of the gods, or if they did truly exist, they were far distant from the world and did not exert any influence over it. Hence, they denied the notion of divine providence and affirmed that everything happens by chance.

Reconstructed stoa in Athens. The Stoics took their name from this place. *© 2012 by Zondervan*

They therefore rejected all forms of divination and prophecy. They also rejected the notion of a future divine judgment. In the field of ethics, they emphasized the importance of pleasure—not simply the sensual kind but pleasures of the mind—and tranquility, the state of being free from passions and fears.

The Stoics, founded by Zeno also around 300 BC, received their name from the Stoa of Attalos, a building in Athens where they taught. They placed emphasis on "reason," which governed the universe. Theologically they were pantheists, so the relationship between God and the world is like that between the soul and the body. Against the Epicureans, they affirmed divine providence and immanence. They argued that one should live in harmony with nature. In ethics they emphasized the need for acting according to reason, which indwells all things; self-sufficiency; and obedience to one's obligations. Contrary to Epicurean belief, they expected a final destruction of the world by fire, after which a new world would be born (regeneration).

RHETORIC IN THE MEDITERRANEAN WORLD

Epicurus, 341–270 BC
Marie-Lan Nguyen, Public Domain

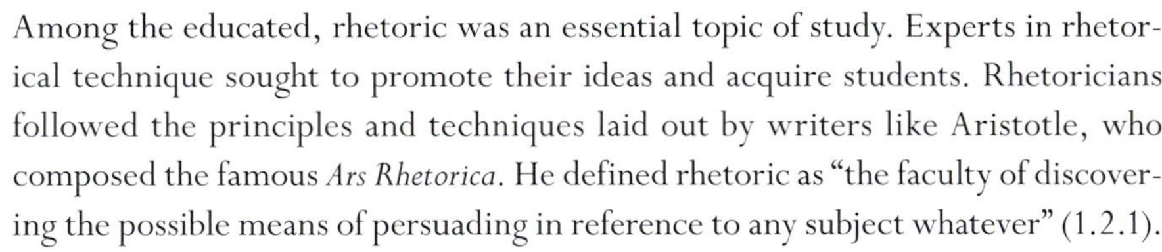

Among the educated, rhetoric was an essential topic of study. Experts in rhetorical technique sought to promote their ideas and acquire students. Rhetoricians followed the principles and techniques laid out by writers like Aristotle, who composed the famous *Ars Rhetorica*. He defined rhetoric as "the faculty of discovering the possible means of persuading in reference to any subject whatever" (1.2.1).

Rhetoricians gave public lectures in various locations in the cities. Those who sought their instruction wanted to enter public office or to become professionals in rhetorical technique. Such people were also equipped to serve as ambassadors or legal counsel.

Aristotle classified public discourse into three categories: deliberative, judicial, and epideictic rhetoric. Deliberative rhetoric was used in discourses that had to do with the future, and its purpose was to exhort or dissuade. Judicial rhetoric was oriented to the past, and its purpose was to accuse or defend. Epideictic rhetoric concerned the present, and its purpose was to praise or blame. Aristotle taught that the epideictic style was especially suited for written compositions, and it

Tacitus on Rhetorical Training

Among our ancestors, a young man was trained for public speaking in the following manner. Once he had been prepared by instruction at home and had been crammed full of worthwhile learning, he was taken by his father or a close relative to an orator who held a prominent position in the state. The young man would then accompany him and follow him about and be present during all his speeches whether in the law courts or the assembly meetings, so that he listened to debates and heard legal disputes and learned to fight battles by being, I think I may say, right in the battle. Under this system, young men acquired, right from the start, a great deal of experience, self-possession, and good judgment because they were studying in broad daylight and in the very middle of the battle.... Therefore young men were immediately imbued with true and perfect eloquence (*A Dialogue on Orators* 34.1–4).

should come as no surprise that the majority of the letters in the New Testament are filled with praise for good behavior and blame for bad conduct (see, e.g., Rev. 2–3). On occasion, Paul had to defend himself because of his lack of refined rhetorical skill (1 Cor. 2:4; 2 Cor. 10:10) and felt compelled to distance himself from those who used their rhetorical finesse for their own self-interest (1 Thess. 2:1–12). Paul did not come to the cities as a rhetor but as a herald who proclaimed the message of Christ crucified in the power of God (1 Cor. 2:1–5).

Questions for Discussion

1. Why is it important for a student of the New Testament to understand the history and culture of the Greco-Roman world, especially considering that Christianity finds its roots within Judaism?
2. How did the Christian proclamation of the "kingdom of God" impact the existing political structures of the day?
3. How did Christians come to support the abolition of slavery when the New Testament calls for slaves to submit to their masters? May the church seek to change social orders?
4. How did Christianity respond to the challenges presented to it by religious pluralism? What guidance can contemporary Christians find in the New Testament as they seek to understand their faith amid a pluralistic world?
5. How does Paul "contextualize" the gospel as he takes the faith that was born in Galilee and Judea and spreads it throughout the Greco-Roman world?

BIBLIOGRAPHY

The Loeb Classical Library. Cambridge: Harvard University Press. (This collection contains original texts and translation of Latin and Greek authors.)

Introductory

Bell, A. A., Jr. *Exploring the New Testament World*. Nashville: Nelson, 1998.

Jeffers, J. S. *The Greco-Roman World of the New Testament*. Downers Grove, IL: InterVaristy Press, 1999.

Keener, C. S. *The IVP Biblical Background Commentary: New Testament*. Downers Grove, IL: InterVaristy Press, 2013.

Advanced

Evans, C. A., and S. E. Porter, eds. *Dictionary of New Testament Backgrounds*. Downers Grove, IL: InterVarsity Press, 2000.

Ferguson, E. *Backgrounds of Early Christianity*. Grand Rapids: Eerdmans, 2003.

Green, J. B., and L. M. McDonald, eds. *The World of the New Testament*. Grand Rapids: Baker Academic, 2013.

Hornblower, S., A. Spawforth, and E. Eidinow, eds. *The Oxford Classical Dictionary*. Oxford: Oxford University Press, 2012.

NOTES

1. A. S. F. Gow and D. L. Page, *The Greek Anthology* (Cambridge: Cambridge University Press, 1965), 2:21–23.
2. A. Deissmann, *Light from the Ancient East*, trans. L. Strachan (New York: Kessinger, 2003), 322.
3. R. K. Sherk, ed. and trans., *The Roman Empire* (Cambridge: Cambridge University Press, 1988), 41–50.
4. H. Hendrix, "Thessalonicans Honor Romans" (ThD diss.; Harvard University, 1984), 107–8.
5. Gow and Page, *Greek Anthology*, 1:73.
6. Ibid., 1:35.
7. Translation from romaninscriptionsofbritain.org/inscriptions/154

Chapter 5

SOURCES FOR THE STORY OF JESUS

The Sea of Galilee from the Mount of Beatitudes

Todd Bolen/BiblePlaces.com

Excavators at Magdala discovered a mosaic depicting a first-century fishing boat, the only image of such a vessel we possess. It is now located on the grounds of Capernaum. *© William D. Mounce*

The central interest of the New Testament is the person of Jesus Christ. His life, death, and resurrection are the focal point of every sermon the New Testament authors recorded. While Paul and other letter writers concentrate on Jesus's death and resurrection, it is the four gospels (Matthew, Mark, Luke, and John) that invite us to study the events of Jesus's earthly life.

For the last two centuries the critical study of the gospels has preoccupied many New Testament scholars. They want to reconstruct the "historical Jesus," and yet they also want to weigh the value of our sources about him. Building on the intellectual tradition of the Enlightenment, biblical scholars in continental Europe, and later in Great Britain and North America, asked difficult questions of the biblical texts. They believed that no text (including the Bible) was above scrutiny and historical analysis. This debate increased sharply toward the end of the twentieth century as book after book sifted the evidence once more. The so-called "Jesus Seminar" (see sidebar p. 145) is only one example of scholars trying to reframe the portrait of Jesus. Some have insisted that for the Bible's historical claims to be considered reliable, those claims would need to be validated with evidence in much the same way as one might demand evidence in the natural sciences. Such research raised questions. Can we determine which gospel is earliest? Can we discover what sources these gospels used? And what about other noncanonical books that refer to Jesus (such as the apocryphal gospels)? Do they supply credible historical evidence for Jesus? Today many scholars have answered yes to each of these questions.

Today it seems that the burden of proof has been flipped in many cases. While the Bible's portrait of Jesus was considered largely reliable for many years, more recently it is often viewed with suspicion. Perhaps one could even say it is guilty until proven innocent. Questions that once seemed irrelevant are now crucial for Christians to consider. Can we be confident that the Jesus described in the gospels represents the "historical Jesus"?

Answers to these and other questions have led scholars to examine two areas of evidence. First, sources outside the gospels could theoretically provide objective data about Jesus's life. As we will see, however, questions of dating, bias, and influence often make these sources difficult to interpret. Second, scholars have looked at the gospel accounts themselves. In attempting to describe the process of the gospels' composition, various theories have been proposed, although many conclusions still lie in the realm of hypothesis.

SOURCES OUTSIDE THE GOSPELS

While we have ample writings informing our general knowledge of the life and culture of the Roman Empire in the first century, the same cannot be said of extrabiblical evidence about Jesus. One might assume that the founder of the largest religious movement in history would have attracted ancient biographers and historians. But the opposite is true. However, this should not surprise us. Jesus lived in a remote corner of the Roman Empire (called Judea), in that province's rural area called Galilee. Historians of his day were interested in epic imperial events, not (in their view) minor prophets from the periphery. To capture a picture of Jesus from nonbiblical authors, we need to rely on incidental historical references, views of skeptics, or references in sources that in some cases may be fifty years later. Although this evidence is often agonizingly limited, we do find confirmation of important historical facts about Jesus as well as the beliefs of his earliest followers.

Gentile Sources

Among the thousands of pages that have survived from the first-century Roman Empire, nothing mentions Jesus. The first reference comes in the early second century, from a Roman governor named Pliny, living somewhere in the Roman province of Bithynia. Pliny wrote to Emperor Trajan about a religious cult made up of "Christians" that was growing in his province and wondered whether he should prosecute them. Pliny mentions that the group worshiped Jesus, but we find no information about Jesus himself.

Suetonius, a Roman historian who wrote during the Imperial era
Jona Lendering/www.livius.org

About the same time, the Roman historian Suetonius wrote about riots that took place during the reign of the Emperor Claudius (AD 41–54) that centered on a man named "Chrestus." This too is an authentic reference to Jesus (misspelling "Christ"), but all it can do is establish the existence of the Christian community in Rome at this time. Perhaps fighting had erupted when followers of Jesus proclaiming his lordship confronted either Jewish or Roman opponents.

A few years later (AD 120), we hear from Tacitus, whose ambition was to record the history of the Roman Empire from roughly AD 14 (the coming to power of Tiberius) to AD 68 (the end of Nero's rule). Our set of his *Annals* is incomplete, and while the section that describes Jesus's time period has not survived, Tacitus does refer to Jesus and his followers in his description of a fire in Rome in AD 64. He thinks of this community as belonging to a superstitious religion, meaning that

Tacitus

As Tacitus describes the great fire that swept through Rome in AD 64, he indicates how Nero blamed it on Christians (even though Nero himself was suspected as the culprit): "To dispel the rumor, Nero substituted as culprits and treated with the most extreme punishments, some people popularly known as Christians whose disgraceful lives (he claimed) were notorious. The source of their name, Christus, had been executed when Tiberius was emperor by order of the procurator Pontius Pilatus. But the deadly cult though checked for a time, was now breaking out again not only in Judea, the birthplace of this evil, but even throughout Rome—where all the nasty and disgusting ideas from all over the world pour in and find a ready following" (*Annals* 15:44).

The Babylonian Talmud

In its section on legal requirements for stoning (*Sanh.* 43a), the Babylonian Talmud discusses the Mishnah's requirement that before a man is killed a call must go out soliciting the public for any additional information that might acquit him. Many scholars believe this is an authentic reference to Jesus: "It was taught: On the Eve of the Passover Yeshu was hanged. For forty days before the execution took place, a herald went forth and cried, 'He is going forth to be stoned because he has practiced sorcery and enticed Israel to apostasy. Anyone who can say anything in his favor, let him come forward and plead on his behalf.' But since nothing was brought forward in his favor he was hanged on the eve of the Passover."

it was dangerously antisocial and decidedly irrational. Even though Tacitus rarely mentions Jesus, he does confirm his execution at the hands of Pontius Pilate during the reign of Tiberius (*Annals* 15:44).

These references are helpful in that they establish Jesus within the first century and validate his death under Pilate, but they do little to provide us with a full or complete profile of Jesus's life.

Jewish Sources

Early Judaism likewise left behind a rich trove of written documents, and some scholars are convinced that we can find references to Jesus in them. But most of these are controversial. Note that we are seeking *independent* information about Jesus that supplements what we have in the gospels.

There is a huge body of other Jewish writings that may be of use to us. But in virtually every case, these documents were penned well into the Christian era and if they refer to Christ, they may be responding to Christian writings already in circulation. Examples of this include the Mishnah (Judaism's oral traditions written down in about AD 200), the Tosefta (later rabbinic commentary), the Targums (Aramaic translations and expansions of the Bible), and the Talmuds (commentary on the Mishnah stemming from about six hundred years after Jesus). No helpful references to Jesus are among these. For instance, the Babylonian Talmud, which was finished about AD 500, offers an example of someone who was killed on the eve of the Passover and tells us his name is "Yeshu." He was a criminal, we learn, because he practiced magic, beguiled people, and led them astray (*Sanh.* 43a).

Far more important is the Jewish historian Josephus, who wrote a history of the Jewish people sometime around AD 80. Josephus was a Galilean commander in the Jewish war against Rome (AD 66–70), was captured by the Romans, and accompanied the commander Vespasian and later his son Titus in their siege of Judea and Jerusalem. When he knew that his fight against

Rome was lost and that Jerusalem would be destroyed completely by the incoming Roman army, he changed sides and tried to dissuade the Jewish resistance. Thanks to his helpful counsel to the Romans, Josephus was rewarded and retired comfortably in Rome, where he wrote both *The Jewish War* (telling the story of the Roman conquest of Judea) as well as the much longer *The Jewish Antiquities* (which begins with Adam and Eve). Both survive in excellent texts to this day (having been preserved by Christian scribes).

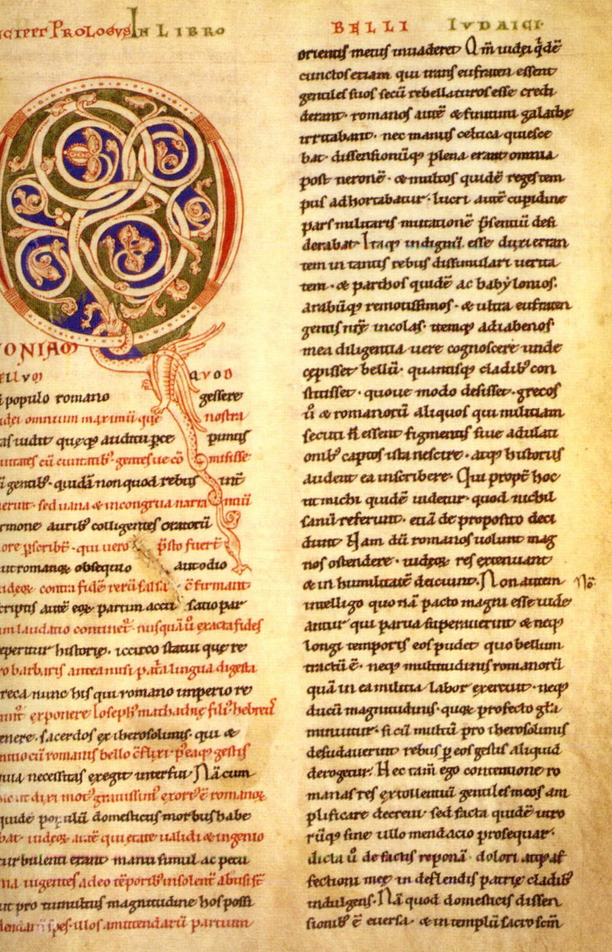
INCIPIT PROLOGUS IN LIBRO BELLI IUDAICI

Latin illuminated manuscript of *The Jewish War* by Josephus, ca. twelfth century
Wikimedia Commons, PD-US

Since Jesus was crucified forty years before the fall of Jerusalem, it is perhaps not surprising that Josephus does not refer to Jesus in the *War*. But in the *Antiquities*, we find two intriguing passages. Josephus describes the transition between two governors of Judea (Festus and Albinus). While Albinus was en route to Judea, the high priest Annas decided to kill criminals in his prisons. Josephus writes: "When, therefore, Annas was of this disposition, he thought he had now a proper opportunity [to exercise his authority]. Festus was now dead, and Albinus was but upon the road; so he assembled the Sanhedrin of judges, and brought before them the brother of Jesus, who was called Christ, whose name was James, and some others [or, some of his companions]; and when had formed an accusation against them as breakers of the law, he delivered them to be stoned" (*Ant.* 20.9.1 [197–203]).

This passage corroborates the New Testament view that Jesus had a brother named James (Mark 6:3; Gal. 1:19), and it points to the priest Annas (John 18:13). But note that Josephus cannot identify James by referring to his family lineage ("James, father of x"). Rather, he notes James's brother Jesus, whom Josephus must believe is easily recognizable to his reader. Of course, the passage offers a cynical view of Jesus (called "the Christ"), but this is what we'd expect since Josephus never became a Christian.

A more perplexing text from Josephus appears in *Ant.* 18.3.3 [63–64]. Since Josephus evidently did not believe Jesus was the Messiah, it is surprising to find the following:

> **The Gospel of Thomas**
>
> *The Gospel of Thomas*, found in 1945 in Southern Egypt, contains 114 sayings of Jesus without any narrative. Some parts echo what we find in the Canonical Gospels. Others are a complete Gnostic reworking of Jesus's original sayings. Today scholars debate whether any of these sayings are authentically from Jesus and thus can be used to build his historical portrait.
>
> Here are some sample sayings of *The Gospel of Thomas*:
>
> 05 Jesus said, "Recognize what is in your sight, and that which is hidden from you will become plain to you."
>
> 07 Jesus said, "Blessed is the lion which becomes man when consumed by man; and cursed is the man whom the lion consumes, and the lion becomes man."
>
> 82 Jesus said, "He who is near me is near the fire, and he who is far from me is far from the kingdom."
>
> 92 Jesus said, "Seek and you will find. Yet, what you asked me about in former times and which I did not tell you then, now I do desire to tell, but you do not inquire after it."
>
> 114 Simon Peter said to them, "Let Mary leave us, for women are not worthy of life." Jesus said, "I myself shall lead her in order to make her male, so that she too may become a living spirit resembling you males. For every woman who will make herself male will enter the kingdom of heaven."

> Now there was about this time Jesus, a wise man, if it be lawful to call him a man; for he was doer of wonderful works, a teacher of such men as receive the truth with pleasure. He drew over many of the Jews and many of the gentiles. He was [the] Christ. And when Pilate, at the suggestion of the principal men among us, had condemned him to the cross, those that loved him at the first did not forsake him; for he appeared to them alive again the third day, as the divine prophets had foretold these and ten thousand other wonderful things concerning him. And the tribe of Christians, so named from him, are not extinct at this day.

This passage is no doubt an insertion into the text of Josephus penned by a Christian scribe. Josephus not only seems to embrace Jesus as the Messiah, but he announces the resurrection! Some scholars believe we should edit the paragraph, removing all the explicitly confessional elements to find a core that may have been written by Josephus himself. If this reconstruction is correct, we may have an important second reference to Jesus:

> At this time there appeared Jesus, a wise man. For he was a doer of startling deeds, a teacher of people who receive the truth with pleasure. And he gained a following both among many Jews and among many of Greek origin. And when Pilate, because of an accusation made by the leading men among us, condemned him to the cross, those who had loved him previously did not cease to do so. And up till this very day, the tribe of Christians (named after him) has not died out.[1]

Even with these passages from Josephus, we have limited new information about Jesus coming from Jewish sources. They refer to Jesus and a group of followers, but that is about all.

Second- and Third-Century Christian Sources

In recent years scholars have revisited a collection of Christian writings produced in the two or three centuries following the writing of the New Testament. An important category of sources is the so-called "apocryphal gospels." These are Christian writings stemming from the centuries following the New Testament, which in some cases record fantastic legends (such as in the *Infancy Gospel of Thomas*) or may simply rebuild and embellish the New Testament gospels themselves (such as the *Gospel of the Nazarenes*).[2] For the most part, this material offers no help with our questions.

But two ancient gospels deserve special mention. In about 1886 French archaeologists in Egypt uncovered a gospel manuscript that would stir controversy a hundred years after its discovery. The second-century apocryphal *Gospel of Peter* is sometimes promoted as the oldest form of the passion story (called "the Cross Gospel"), and Mark supposedly used this story when he wrote his gospel.[3] The weight of scholarly opinion has been severely critical of any suggestion that the *Gospel of Peter* precedes the Canonical Gospels or provides material to them.[4] But such an example is fair warning to beginning students of the New Testament. Suggestions such as this abound, and in each case, the theories must be examined with judicious scholarship before they are accepted. Sensational discoveries will always be exploited, and the student must be careful to follow the lead of specialists who will weigh them in time.[5]

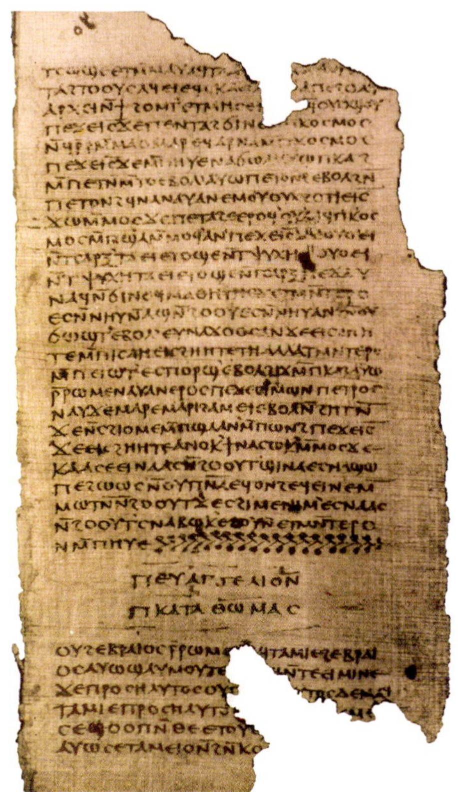
A page from *The Gospel of Thomas*. Fragments of the gospel were discovered at the Egyptian village of Oxyrhynchus in 1897, 1903, and 1905. A Coptic manuscript was found in Nag Hammadi, Egypt, in 1945.

Z. Radovan/www.BibleLandPictures.com

A few years before the discovery of the Dead Sea Scrolls, archaeologists found a library of Christian documents in the ruins of an ancient monastery in the village of Nag Hammadi in southern Egypt, mostly copied in the 300s by Gnostic Christians. While much of the library is of dubious value to research the historical Jesus, some scholars now argue that one book, *The Gospel of Thomas*, provides sayings of Jesus that are authentic and historically reliable. *Thomas* consists of 114 sayings of Jesus (with no narration) that are strung together thematically. Some scholars immediately related this to the sayings source "Q" (see below). The trouble with this view, however, is that *Thomas* was filled with a Gnostic theological outlook that supplies the framework for understanding any of the sayings. While recent studies have argued that *The Gospel of Thomas* depends on the Canonical Gospels, some scholars (such as Helmut Koester) still insist that "nearly all biblical scholars in the United States" agree that Thomas gives authentic sayings of Jesus. Many New Testament scholars would dispute this strongly, arguing that this is a late document (far beyond the Canonical Gospels) coming from a second-or third-century Gnostic milieu.

Summary of Sources

It may be surprising to see how little information we have about Jesus outside the New Testament gospels. But we must keep in mind that the events of Jesus's life occurred in a remote corner of the Roman Empire—much of it in the rural areas of Galilee—and these events would hardly be of interest to professional historians of the era who were charting the epic events of Roman history. Nevertheless, these sources identify Jesus within the first century, they locate him in the province of Judea, and they make clear that a controversy spun around him centered on his religious claims about himself and his movement. And we know that Jesus's followers concluded immediately after Jesus's resurrection that he *continued* to live with God and was worthy of worship and that within decades of his death, public controversies broke out surrounding him. Therefore, these sources tell us that Jesus was truly a historical figure and not an invention of a first-century religious imagination.

For the most part, the Canonical Gospels provided the substance of what the church knew about Jesus, and later writings generally embellished that story in order to make it more compelling to new audiences around the Mediterranean. But in the main, Christian communities (no doubt mentored by their Jewish counterparts) preserved their traditions about Jesus. Communication among the earliest Christians was excellent. Roads and sea lanes were good, and couriers moved regularly among churches, carrying all variety of Christian writings. In other words, *the early Christians were talking to each other.* They could discuss what gospels were important and reliable, and they could weigh the merits of new offerings to their archives of Christian writings.

THE GOSPELS AS SOURCES FOR JESUS'S LIFE

When we turn to a gospel as a source of Jesus's life, a long list of questions immediately confronts us. What sort of literature is this? How would the ancient world classify it? What were the aims of its authors? Why do we have four gospels? Is there a literary relationship among them—and if so, which gospel is oldest? Above all, do these gospels represent the historical Jesus accurately or are they embellishments based on the Jesus worshiped in the early church? New Testament scholarship has wrestled with each of these questions for two centuries, and it is important for us to briefly examine the contours of this contemporary conversation.

The Genre "Gospel"

Every literature fits into its surrounding culture by using recognizable forms of style and composition. It would be interesting to ask how an ancient librarian from the great library of Alexandria might have classified the gospel of Mark. He would notice that Mark opens his text by saying that this is "the beginning of the gospel of Jesus Christ" (KJV). But there a problem emerges. In antiquity "gospel" (Gk. *euangelion*) was not used for a written document. It was a "great announcement" or a proclamation. In non-Christian circles, it might refer to the emperor's birth or a victory in battle, but never a book. Perhaps this hint betrays something about Mark's theological purposes: his writing is indeed a "great announcement" and is penned to announce something unparalleled that God has done in history.

But our librarian has not solved the problem. In the past, scholars tried comparing the gospels with a variety of ancient literature types (from "memoirs" to "miracle working" stories). Many even viewed the gospels as a unique genre, unparalleled in ancient writing. This last option seems unlikely. Writers try to communicate by using forms that readers/hearers will easily understand. Today scholars are inclined to view the gospels as "biographies" (Gk. *bioi*). In antiquity Roman biographies existed in abundance (e.g., Plutarch's *Lives*, Suetonius's *Lives of the Caesars*). These sophisticated writings both chronicled the fascinating events in their subjects' lives and built a profile of them. Plutarch, for example, provides an outline of the work of the biographer in his introduction to his biography of Alexander the Great:

> It is not Histories that I am writing, but Lives; and in the most illustrious deeds there is not always a manifestation of virtue or vice, nay, a slight thing like a phrase or a jest often makes a greater revelation of character than battles where thousands fall, or the greatest armaments, or siege of cities. Accordingly, just as painters get the likenesses in their portraits from the face and the expression of the eyes, wherein the character shows itself, but make very little account of the other parts of the body, so I must be permitted to devote myself rather to the signs of the soul in men, and by means of these to portray the life of each, leaving to others the description of their great contests (Plutarch, *Alexander* 1).

Ancient *bioi* were unlike modern biographies in at least one respect. Rarely did they probe beneath the surface looking for signs of development. This was long before the advent of psychology. Instead, the biographer worked to unveil the true identity of a man or woman and thereby explain his or her great deeds. And this meant they could be selective with their subject. They felt no need to write comprehensively about everything that occurred in the subject's life. This is precisely what we have in the gospels. There is little attention to the early years of Jesus's life, and the full story begins when he is about thirty. In Mark's gospel, almost 60 percent of the narrative focuses on the last week of Jesus's life. These are writing strategies common to a Roman biographer.

The Literary Criticism of the Gospels

A pressing question is the quality of history we can find in the gospels. Can we rely on them as a source to reconstruct the life of Jesus? From the beginning of the nineteenth century, New Testament scholarship recognized that three of four gospels (Matthew, Mark, and Luke) have a great deal in common.

Matthew 8:16–17	Luke 4:40–41	Mark 1:32–34
16 When evening came,	40 At sunset	32 That evening after sunset
many who were demon-possessed were brought to him,	the people brought to Jesus all who had various kinds of sickness,	the people brought to Jesus all the sick and demon-possessed.
and he drove out the spirits with a word and healed the sick.	and laying his hands on each one, he healed them.	33 The whole town gathered at the door, 34 and Jesus healed many who had various diseases.
	41 Moreover, demons came out of many people, shouting, "You are the Son of God!"	He also drove out many demons,
17 This was to fulfill what was spoken through the prophet Isaiah: "He took up our infirmities and bore our diseases."	But he rebuked them and would not allow them to speak, because they knew he was the Messiah.	but he would not let the demons speak because they knew who he was.

A synopsis is a book that prints each gospel in columns so that parallel passages may be compared. For some scholars (see Griesbach below) this text illustrates how Mark combined Matthew and Luke. Notice how items coming from Matthew (in red) appear in Mark. And notice how items coming from Luke (blue) appear in Mark. It appears that Mark is bringing together Matthew and Mark.

They have been termed the "synoptic" gospels. About 93 percent of Mark can be found in Matthew or Luke; 58 percent of Matthew can be found in Mark and Luke; and 41 percent of Luke can be found in Matthew and Mark.[6] Let's put this another way: Of Mark's 661 verses, Matthew holds 606 of them and Luke holds 308; only 31 verses in Mark are not found in either Matthew or Luke. How do we explain this? The parallels among the synoptic gospels are so precise (seen particularly in Greek) that most scholars think there must have been some literary dependency.

One option would be to say each gospel was dependent on some earlier "pregospel." Some point to the remark of the bishop Papias (who lived in Hierapolis in Asia Minor, ca. AD 60–130), who said that Matthew composed the "oracles" (Gk. *logia*) of Jesus in Hebrew and everyone translated them as best they could. Today a number of scholars are intrigued with this view, and while they might not argue that Matthew, Mark, and Luke are independent of each other, they wonder whether a primitive gospel existed that preceded the others. We might diagram this arrangement as in figure 1.

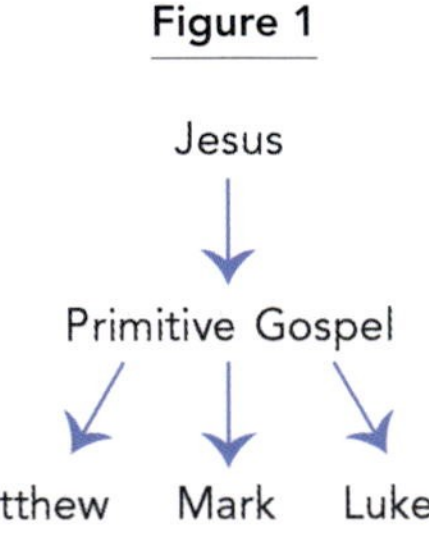

The church fathers recognized this literary puzzle and attempted to find solutions that pointed to one gospel using the other as a literary source. One of the earliest theories (first attributed to Augustine)

understood Matthew as the first gospel, Mark abbreviated Matthew, and Luke used both of them in his gospel. This solution is generally illustrated as in figure 2.

Figure 2

Matthew → Mark → Luke; Matthew → Luke

Figure 3

Matthew → Luke → Mark; Matthew → Mark

Later scholars argued that Mark abbreviated both Matthew and Luke. Note, for example, Matthew 8:16/Mark 1:32/Luke 4:40. Matthew describes Jesus as healing people "in the evening;" Luke says it was "sundown." But Mark conflates the two, saying that it was "in the evening, at sundown." This solution (generally attributed to J. J. Griesbach) can be illustrated as in figure 3.

Other passages, however, point in another direction. For instance, in the story of the paralytic (Matt. 9:1–8/Mark 2:1–12/Luke 5:17–26), Jesus is impressed with the faith of the paralytic's friends because they break open the roof of the house and lower the man to Jesus through the crowd. Matthew tells us that Jesus is "amazed at their faith," but he does not convey the story of the removal of the roof! Matthew assumes you know that detail. This seems to follow a pattern. While Mark's gospel is shorter, each of Mark's narratives is longer, and often details are removed in Matthew (but still assumed). Thus, many scholars today assume that in some manner, Mark must be the earliest gospel written, and Matthew and Luke were expanding on materials that came before them.

On close examination, Mark seems to be the oldest (see sidebar on "Aramaic Words in Mark"). In addition, Matthew seems to make adjustments to Mark. For instance, in Mark 6:14 we are told that Herod Antipas was a "king." Matthew 14:1 amends this to say that Antipas was a "tetrarch." In Mark 6:5 we learn that Jesus "could not do any miracles [in Nazareth]." Matthew appears to supplement this potentially

Headpiece with Christ holding a book, flanked by prophets, and a marginal figure of John the Baptist, at the beginning of Mark, written by the Cretan scribe Ioannes Rhosos at Rome in 1478.

embarrassing admission by saying Jesus did no mighty work there "because of their lack of faith" (Matt. 13:58). As New Testament scholar G. M. Styler once put it, "Given Mark, it is easy to see why Matthew was written. Given Matthew, it is hard to see why Mark was needed."[7] We might illustrate this view as in figure 4.

Figure 4

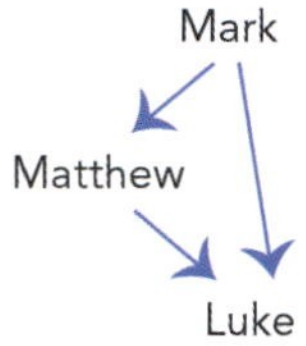

The cumulative evidence has made the majority of scholars affirm what we call "Markan Priority" in the formation of the gospel tradition. But if it is so, the next question is whether Matthew used Luke or Luke used Matthew. Note, for example, that when Matthew and Luke make editorial changes to Mark, none of Matthew's changes show up in Luke and vice versa. If Matthew had known Luke—or if Luke had known Matthew—then surely some of the changes would be apparent. This has led scholars to suggest that Matthew and Luke are each dependent on Mark, but they are not using each other.

But note too that there is a body of verses commonly shared between Matthew and Luke, but these words are not in Mark (about 250 verses). This material is code-named "Q" (from the German *Quelle*, "source"), and scholars suggest that perhaps this is an early "pregospel" collection of Jesus's sayings that stood alongside Mark (but was unknown to Mark). This new diagram of synoptic relationships can be seen in figure 5.

Figure 5

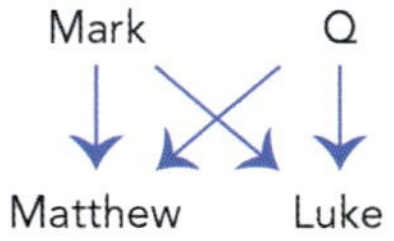

But both Matthew and Luke each made original contributions in the production of their gospels (Matthew has 300 unique verses; Luke, 520 verses). Matthew, for example, has a Christmas story with elements unknown elsewhere (such as the story of Herod and the Magi). Luke has the story of the angel visiting the shepherds of Bethlehem. Matthew has sayings unknown to Luke, and Luke has parables Matthew did not record.

The solution (often credited to a scholar named B. H. Streeter) that is most popular today is the "four source" hypothesis to the synoptic problem; it suggests that each gospel saying and story can be attributed to one of four sources. Note in figure 6 how Matthew and Luke each used three sources.

Figure 6

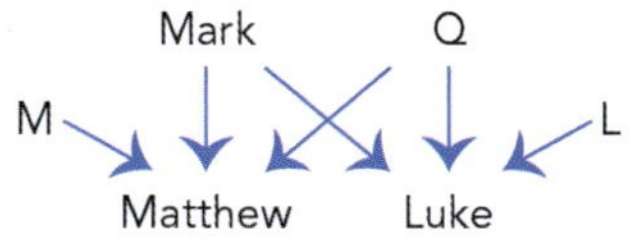

Aramaic Words in Mark

Scholars agree that Jesus spoke in Aramaic (a language like Hebrew) and he *may* have known Greek. The gospels are written in Greek but frequently suggest that their writers were "thinking" in Aramaic. Sometimes they transliterate entire words from Aramaic into Greek. Luke contains none of these and Matthew only has four (in Matt. 27:46). Mark transliterates two Hebrew words (3:17; 15:22) and eight Aramaic words:

5:41	*talitha koum*	"little girl, get up"
7:34	*ephphatha*	"be opened"
14:36	*abba*	"father"
15:34	*Eloi, Eloi, lema sabachthani*	"My God, my God, why have you forsaken me?"

Since the trend of the church was to worship in Greek (not Aramaic), this evidence suggests the antiquity of Mark's sources.

Mark's conflation of MT and LK (following Griesbach)

Matthew 8:16–17	Luke 4:40–41	Mark 1:32–34
That evening they brought to him Ὀψίας δὲ γενομένης many who were possessed with demons; and he cast out the spirits with a word, and healed all who were sick. This was to fulfill what was spoken by the prophet Isaiah, "He took our infirmities and bore our diseases."	Now when the sun was setting, Δύνοντος δὲ τοῦ ἡλίου all those who had any that were sick with various diseases brought them to him; and he laid his hands on every one of them and healed them. And demons also came out of the many, crying: "You are the Son of God!" But he rebuked them, and would not allow them to speak, because they knew that he was the Christ.	The evening, at sundown, they brought to him all who were sick or possessed with demons. And the whole city was gathered together about the door. And he healed many who were sick with various diseases, and cast out many demons; Ὀψίας δὲ γενομένης, ὅτε ἔδυ ὁ ἥλιος and he would not permit the demons to speak, because they knew him.

This view has been so well received that some scholars refer to this result as an "assured finding."[8] Yet today this popular hypothesis is weathering criticism. Just when we thought that at least one historical question could be put to rest, another generation of scholars has argued that it is completely wrong. W. R. Farmer wrote in the 1960s that Mark was the last of the three synoptics to be written and that Matthew was first—and Farmer has a growing following.

Many other scholars see the process of gospel writing as more organic and deny the clean lines of literary dependence shown by these illustrations (above). For them, the "Jesus traditions" were held by those in Jerusalem who served as the custodians of this archive. This was a fixed pool of sayings and stories whose linguistic forms were memorized and preserved. Matthew may have written an early Aramaic gospel (recall the words of Papias above) and drawn on these traditions. Peter may have been one of these custodians and drawn on this pool as well—finally contributing to the composition of Mark. Luke 1:1–4 tells us that Luke did genuine research, depending on eyewitnesses and reading what others had penned. No doubt these earliest Christian leaders were talking with each other, sharing notations, and comparing memorized bodies of material.

When all is said, we must sound a note of caution. We are dealing here with hypotheses. Q particularly is hypothetical, for no such document has ever been found. And many who work in this area are trying to find "the original gospel," with the assumption that such a gospel is more historically reliable to build a portrait of Jesus; they thus ascribe levels of reliability to the existing gospels, and this is a hypothetical process that is filled with conjecture.

In our discussion we have barely touched on John's gospel as a source for Jesus's life. For most of the twentieth century, critical scholars viewed John's gospel as secondary to the synoptics—late, and not reliable historically. But in the last twenty years, we have seen a shift in emphasis. John is increasingly viewed as an independent (and trustworthy) recorder of events from Jesus's life. Scholars who once viewed John as a Hellenistic rewriting of the gospel now recognize that John relies heavily on rabbinic thinking, is accurate when using geography, and is faithful to the Jesus tradition. The best reconstructions of Jesus's life today take seriously John's claim as an eyewitness of that life. In chapter 11 we will examine John's contribution to the story of Jesus in detail.

The Historical Criticism of the Gospels

In addition to the issue of sources, scholars have also asked what happened during that mysterious period between Jesus's death and the composition of the gospels. If Q and Mark are the earliest documents (as some suppose), what sources contributed to them? Were Aramaic stories of Jesus circulating among his followers, and if so, could these be discovered within the texts of the canonical Greek gospels?

In 1919 a young German scholar named Karl Ludwig Schmidt turned the key that opened this door. He noted that the gospels consisted of a series of episodes set in a framework with connecting narrative material that served as "bridges" between episodes. Mark 1:16–45 provides a good example, which is a series of stories with a limited chronological sequence: Jesus calls his disciples, exorcizes a man in Capernaum, heals Simon's mother-in-law, and heals a leper. Each of these episodes is "linked" by narrative that gives the story coherence, but in the end, the stories themselves appeared to Schmidt to be independent. Schmidt imagined that you could almost take scissors and cut this chapter in pieces and there find *independent* episodes that could be taught or preached on their own.

Schmidt argued that these brief episodes circulated orally in the earliest Christian communities and that Mark and the other writers picked these up and "threaded" them together by narrative. This means we can locate the "pregospel" stratum of the gospels as well as the "bridge" material inserted by the gospel writers. In subsequent study, these units of tradition were called "forms" and were classified (miracles, parables, legends, etc.), and their study was soon called "form criticism." Therefore, scholars supposed that there were three loci in this process: sayings that came from Jesus himself, sayings that were formed and shaped in the oral tradition of earliest Christianity, and finally, sayings that were woven into a cohesive narrative (a gospel). Schmidt and others were interested in what transpired within this period of "oral tradition."

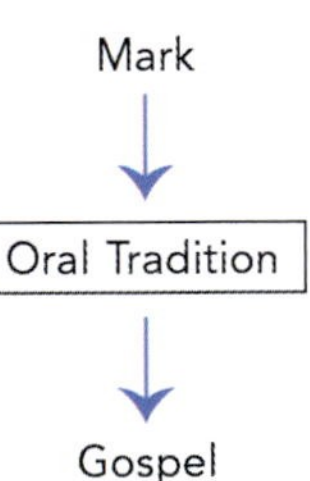

But the aim of form criticism was not merely to classify these events but to make some historical judgment about their value. The passion for gospel research grew rapidly as scholars anticipated that now we were looking under the surface, finding out how the stories of Jesus were formed and preserved. Many viewed this pregospel era skeptically, believing that the early Christians not only shaped the words of Jesus to fit their own circumstances but also created new words of Jesus, generally in the context of worship.

Form critics claimed that the gospel materials were preserved not necessarily because they came from Jesus but because they met some need in the Christian community. Each had a setting in the early church that explained to some degree what was happening at that time. For instance, the early Christians had numerous conflicts with the leadership of Judaism (see 1 Thess. 2:13–16). Thus, stories from Jesus's life that illustrated this persecution were preserved because of their usefulness in preaching. For example, Mark 2:23–28 shows Jesus being criticized for harvesting grain on the Sabbath. The episode does not explore what happened but moves quickly to Jesus's summary comment: "The Sabbath was made for man, not man for the Sabbath" (2:27). These words are an incisive critique for all those who would criticize Jesus's Jewish followers who did not strictly observe Jewish Sabbath regulations. In fact, some felt the early church may have even doctored these stories to fit their situation.

The Jesus Seminar

In 1985 Robert Funk founded the Jesus Seminar along with thirty other scholars. The goal of the seminar—and its many "fellows" (now claiming two hundred)—was to sift the gospels and locate the true historical Jesus, employing the best higher critical methods. Today most scholars see the entire effort as a relic of an era that was highly skeptical of the gospels and that used a method no longer in vogue.

When the committee began, it quickly became a lightning rod of criticism not only because it included sayings of Jesus in the apocryphal gospels (such as *The Gospel of Thomas*), but it urged that many of the materials we have in the gospels are inauthentic. The seminar employed a voting method for its members who could make personal judgments on the authenticity or inauthenticity of a saying or deed of Jesus. And the average vote rendered a value for a saying.

The first major publication assessing the "sayings" of Jesus appeared in 1993: *The Five Gospels: The Search for the Authentic Words of Jesus*. Of Jesus's sayings only 18 percent were deemed authentic. In 1998 a second publication weighed the 176 events in Jesus's life and was published as *The Acts of Jesus: The Search for the Authentic Deeds of Jesus*. In this study, only 16 percent were deemed authentic.

The Authenticity of the Gospels

A highly significant question for Christians today is whether one can be confident that indeed the words of Jesus uttered in first-century Palestine are accurately represented in our gospels. When I read the gospel of Matthew, am I reading what Jesus himself said, or am I reading the musings of Christian prophets and leaders—inspired as they might be—who wrote about Jesus decades after his death? Of course, these questions center directly on our understanding of the authority of our Scriptures.

The *Ipsissima Vox Jesu*

When scholars defend "authentic" words of Jesus in the gospels, they allow for the possibility that the gospel writers may have paraphrased Jesus's words, particularly since he commonly spoke in Aramaic. Hence they distinguish the *ipsissima verba Jesu* ("the very words of Jesus") from the *ipsissima vox Jesu* ("the very voice of Jesus"). An authentic "word" of Jesus may well represent his "voice," though not his exact words.

Paul Feinberg, a conservative evangelical, writes, "Inerrancy does not demand that the sayings of Jesus must contain the *ipsissima verba*, only the *ipsissima vox*. When a New Testament writer cites the sayings of Jesus, it need not be the case that Jesus said those exact words."[9] This careful definition permits variations in parallel gospel accounts of Jesus's sayings. Thus, in Matthew 27:54 the centurion's cry at the cross was, "Surely he was the Son of God." In Luke 23:47 he says, "Surely this was a righteous man." For a Roman—Luke's audience—"Righteous person" was the meaning of "Son of God."[10]

The best way to approach this subject is to be sure we understand the nature of the problem. Historical criticism posits that following the death of Jesus, the "Jesus tradition" was preserved for about thirty or forty years before it was finally written down in the gospels we possess today. The heart of the question is this: Was the church in this earliest era successful in preserving Jesus's sayings and deeds so that the gospel record is accurate?

Our confidence in the success of this process can be helped by keeping various things in mind. Together their cumulative weight gives us confidence that the gospels we read today do indeed point back to the historical Jesus.

(1) The stylistic forms of Jesus's sayings. Many of the sayings of Jesus in the gospels reflect forms that could easily have been retained through these decades. Parables, proverbs, riddles, poignant phrases ("The first will be last—and the last first!"), and catch-phrases ("the kingdom of God") each would aid historical preservation. In addition, we have Aramaic—both transliterated words and grammatical phrases—that hint at the earlier, Aramaic world of Jesus. In other words, the era of the historical Jesus is indeed reflected in the gospels even though the gospels are written later for Greek-speaking audiences.

(2) The terminology of tradition. Paul was a rabbi, trained in the skills of handling religious materials passed down orally (see, e.g., 1 Cor. 11:2, 23; 1 Thess. 2:13; 2 Thess. 2:15; 3:6). This reflects the well-honed Jewish ability to retain vast amounts of material and transmit them to a new generation. The Mishnah (the oral law of Judaism) was preserved this way for generations. Thus, it comes as no surprise that the apostles, living in this Jewish context, knew how to handle sacred stories coming from Jesus. They treated Jesus's words as carefully as any rabbi treated sacred traditions brought to him.

(3) The function of apostles. In the first half of the first century, the apostles were regarded as the custodians and the transmitters of the authoritative traditions about Jesus. This was a stable community, anchored in Jerusalem, to which even leaders like Paul came to confirm the veracity of their teaching (Gal. 1:18; 2:2–10). In one important respect, they behave like the scribes of Judaism, whose teaching was devoted to the recitation of Judaism's great traditions.

(4) The cultural role of memory. Contemporary Westerners depend on the written word and often assume that memorizing large bodies of material is impossible or at least unreliable. But this is a cultural prejudice that has no place in discussions of ancient societies, where the majority of people could not read. First-century Judaism taught through memorization and expected young people to hold secure large portions of Scripture. "Good students are like good cisterns," one saying went, "They never lose a single drop." Leading Jewish teachers spoke orally and were measured by their students and followers who sat at their feet and repeated verbatim what they heard. For some scholars, this explains why we have a limited number of sayings from Jesus. He moved from village to village repeating his parables and sayings with great frequency.

(5) Eyewitnesses and the lapse of time. It is helpful to remember that the same generation who heard Jesus speak in Galilee was also alive during the writing of the gospels. These were eyewitnesses, who could now read the gospel of Mark and make a judgment about its truth. If the gospels had departed significantly from the historical memory of Jesus, objections would have been lodged and quickly corrected.

(6) Written records? We know that following the war of AD 70, rabbinic students frequently took written notes of their teachers' sayings. Today scholars dispute whether this practice occurred during the era before the war. If it did, this opens up the possibility that written records existed during the earliest years of the church—and perhaps even during the ministry of Jesus. And so, it adds to our confidence that these sayings of Jesus were preserved.

(7) Christian prophecy and caution. It is not true that during the earliest era of the church, Christian prophets had free reign to speak whatever they wanted in the name of the Lord and so produce sayings of Jesus. New Testament communities were cautious regarding prophets. In 1 Corinthians 14, for example, Paul warns the Corinthians about giving too much power to prophets and expects that the prophets in their community will confer with one another before speaking. Further, the heresy addressed in 1 John 4:1–6 stemmed from prophets who believed they were anointed with the Spirit and could dismantle

Memory

Today the Middle East still values the role of memory in the preservation of important traditions. Muslim youth, for example, frequently memorize the entire Qur'an—which is about the length of the New Testament. In rural Arab communities among the Bedouin, the great events of Arab history are preserved in stanzas of poetry and repeated communally by men and boys in their large goat-hair tents. Westerners who heard these stories in the eighteenth century wrote them down. When those writings are compared with today's oral traditions, we see a perfect retention of literature and history.

In the early 1970s, an American professor of chemistry taught for one year at the American University of Beirut. After an exam he accused an Arab student from the Arabian Gulf of cheating. "But I memorized the textbook chapter," the student explained. Incredulous, the professor hauled the student before the university's Arab dean—who produced the book, turned to a page in the chapter, and ordered the student to recite. The student was quickly vindicated, and the professor apologized for his error.

orthodox teaching about Jesus. John warns about them and tells the community to be wary of such teachers and prophets (2:18–27).

(8) Respect for the sayings of Jesus. The early church carefully distinguished the sayings of Jesus from its own teachings and did not pretend to invent sayings. Paul, for example, explains when he has a word from the Lord and when he doesn't (1 Cor. 7:8, 10, 12, 25, 40). Also, since Paul wrote before the gospels were penned, we might expect to find some of Paul's sayings in the gospels. There is not one example of this.

(9) Dissimilarity of interests. If the formative era of the church could create sayings of Jesus, we should expect some correlation between what we know to be the concerns of the early church and the primary themes of the gospels. But we do not. For example, important issues in the life of the early church centered on the gentile mission, circumcision, food laws, the Holy Spirit, and even the notion of the church itself. Jesus says little about any of these. The early church did not try to settle a dispute by putting words in his mouth.

The gospels talk a great deal about the kingdom of God and refer to Jesus repeatedly as the Son of Man. Oddly, perhaps, no other literature from this era shows an interest in either of these. What does this mean? Simply that the gospels reflect a context that is *dissimilar* to the context of the early church—and the burning issues that troubled earliest Christianity do not show up in the gospels.

Summary

Each of these points is important because their cumulative effect shifts the burden of proof. It is fully defensible to argue that the works and words of Jesus as recorded in the gospels reliably reflect the Jesus of history; that the gospels are "innocent until proven guilty." Students of the gospels can confidently sustain a reasonable argument that the gospels' portrait of Jesus is accurate and reliable.

Jesus's teaching ministry included the mentoring of a circle of close followers (the apostles) whose task in part was to learn what he taught and to carry that teaching to new places (Mark 6:7). When Jesus died, this community of Galileans took up residence in Jerusalem and from there served as custodians of the traditions that stemmed from Jesus. They preserved these as carefully as anyone would in the Jewish ethos—and more so. They believed that Jesus was not merely an itinerant preacher from Galilee but that he was the Messiah, a messenger from God whose words rivaled those of Moses. Their archive of sayings and stories became a wellspring of resources that quickly took shape and within years provided the gospel writers with their raw materials.

Questions for Discussion

1. Why do scholars not believe that each gospel writer worked independently and that their parallel accounts buttress the authority of the gospel record?
2. Why do scholars work so hard to discern which of the gospels is earliest? What inspires their labor? What do they hope to achieve?
3. How does "Q" disappear if we posit that Matthew and Luke used each other?
4. What safeguarded the "Jesus tradition" from alteration during those formative years between Jesus's death and the writing of the gospels?
5. What are the theological implications if we decided that some of the sayings of Jesus in *The Gospel of Thomas* were authentically from Jesus?

BIBLIOGRAPHY

Introductory

Blomberg, C. *Jesus and the Gospels.* Nashville: Broadman & Holman, 2009.

———. *The Historical Reliability of the Gospels.* Downers Grove, IL: InterVarsity Press, 2007.

Wilkins, M. J., and J. P. Moreland. *Jesus under Fire: Modern Scholarship Reinvents the Historical Jesus.* Grand Rapids: Zondervan, 1995.

Wright, N. T. *The Contemporary Quest for Jesus.* Minneapolis: Fortress, 2002.

Advanced

Bauckham, R., ed. *The Gospels for All Christians: Rethinking the Gospel Audiences.* Grand Rapids: Eerdmans, 1998.

Bird, M., *The Gospel of the Lord: How the Early Church Wrote the Story of Jesus.* Grand Rapids: Eerdmans, 2014.

Borg, M., and N. T. Wright. *The Meaning of Jesus: Two Visions.* San Francisco: HarperSanFrancisco, 2007.

Gerhardsson, B. *The Reliability of the Gospel Tradition.* Peabody, MA: Hendrickson, 2001.

NOTES

1. J. P. Meier, *A Marginal Jew: Rethinking the Historical Jesus* (New York: Doubleday, 1991), 61.

2. For an exhaustive catalog of these, see E. Hennecke and W. Schneemelcher's two-volume study, *The New Testament Apocrypha*, trans. R. M. Wilson (Philadelphia: John Knox, 1991).

3. J. D. Crossan, *The Cross That Spoke: The Origin of the Passion Narrative* (San Francisco: Harper, 1988); H. Koester, *Ancient Christian Gospels* (Valley Forge, PA: Trinity International, 1992), 216–40. For the text of the Gospel of Peter, see www.earlychristianwritings.com or R. E. Brown's translation in *The Death of the Messiah*, 2 vols, ABRL (New York: Doubleday: 1994), 1317–49. See also idem., "The Gospel of Peter and Canonical Gospel Priority," *NTS* 33 (1987): 321–43.

4. J. W. McCant, "The Gospel of Peter: Docetism Reconsidered," *NTS* 30 (1984): 258–73; J. Green, "The Gospel of Peter: Source for a Pre-Canonical Passion Narrative?" *ZNW* 78 (1987): 293–301.

5. Students may one day read about the so-called *Secret Gospel of Mark* discovered in 1958—which supplements Mark with about twenty previously unknown sentences. But today these verses have stirred a whirlwind of controversy. One scholar remarked, "To use such a small fragment of dubious origins to rewrite the history of Jesus and the Gospel tradition is to lean on a reed" (J. P. Meier, *A Marginal Jew*, ABRL [New York: Doubleday, 1991], 121).

6. John, by comparison is utterly different; only 8 percent of John is shared by the other three.

7. G. M. Styler, "The Priority of Mark," in C. F. D. Moule, *The Birth of the New Testament* (New York: Harper and Row, 1982), 285–316.

8. W. Marxsen, *Introduction to the New Testament* (Philadelphia: Fortress, 1968), 118.

9. P. Feinberg, "The Meaning of Inerrancy," in *Inerrancy*, ed. N. L. Geisler (Grand Rapids: Zondervan, 1979), 270, cited in G. Osborne, "Historical Criticism and the Evangelical," *JETS* 42 (March 1999): 193–210.

10. Osborne, "Historical Criticism and the Evangelical," 193–210.

Chapter 6

THE STORY OF JESUS

The northern coast of the sea of Galilee was dotted with numerous fishing villages. Fishing was abundant thanks to fresh-water springs in the area. The site of Heptapegon (*seven springs*) is in the trees along the shoreline.

Bill Schlegel/BiblePlaces.com

Recovering the story of Jesus's life has become one of the great pursuits of our time. Not only have literary and historical analyses of the gospels advanced (see ch. 5), but today our understanding of the cultural environment that shaped Jesus's world has also matured. The disciplines of comparative anthropology and archaeology (to name only two) have given us access to the world of Jesus in ways unimaginable only fifty years ago.

Yet we must be clear about the limitations of our pursuit. Jesus was an itinerant preacher in one of the remote provinces of the Roman Empire. He had no "international" prestige and hence limited public recognition from the great record-keepers of society. Thus, a complete portrait of his life and work may not be possible. But what we do have in our gospels squares nicely with what we are learning about the first century. These discoveries supplement the gospel story, giving us a more accurate view of Jesus's world.

For example, the excavation of Sepphoris (the capital of Galilee, close to Jesus's hometown of Nazareth) informs us about the Hellenization of Galilee. It is also disclosing its secrets about the economic relationships between the rural villages and the urban centers of the region. This city of thirty thousand was in full reconstruction during Jesus's adolescence, and Jesus and his father Joseph may have worked there.

Nazareth was not a prominent village in Galilee, but it was located a mere five kilometers (three miles) from Sepphoris (*Zippori* in Hebrew, a place Josephus called "the ornament of Galilee"), which lay on the intersection of the Via Maris and the Acre-Tiberias roads. Sepphoris, shown here, was the Jewish administrative center in Galilee.
Bill Schlegel/BiblePlaces.com

The theater of Sepphoris was in use during Jesus's day and sat 4,500 in its audience. This may explain Jesus's knowledge of Greek stage names such as "hypocrite," Matt. 6:2, which was the Greek word for "actor."
Reproduced by permission from Carole Raddato.

The first surface survey of Sepphoris began in 1930, but work started in earnest in 1985. Today Sepphoris is a huge archaeological park (Heb. *Zippori*; Arabic, *Safurriya*) that opened in 1992. Archaeological work is ongoing.
David Hendin

CHRONOLOGY

Building a chronology for Jesus's life has always been difficult. In the first century, calendars took their starting point from the founding of the city of Rome (754 BC or year 1 for Rome). But in the sixth century AD, a Christian monk (Dionysius Exiguus of Scythia) proposed instead a "Christian calendar," which started with the birth of Jesus. Unfortunately, he failed to take into account the death of Herod the Great, who was certainly alive during Jesus's infancy (Matt. 2:1). Herod died in 4 BC, which means that Jesus was likely born sometime between 7 and 5 BC on Dionysius's calendar, which we use today.

Genealogies

Both Matthew and Luke provide a genealogy for Jesus (Matt. 1:1–17; Luke 3:23–38). Matthew's forty-two generations begin with Abraham, while Luke's seventy-seven names reach back to Adam. Both lists are basically parallel from Abraham to David, and then they diverge significantly.

Numerous theories have tried to explain the differences in these lists. For instance, Matthew's account gives three blocks of fourteen names, and fourteen is the numeric value of the Hebrew name "David." Luke uses cycles of seven, another sacred Hebrew number. Contrary to common assumptions, it is not likely that Matthew's genealogy traces the line of Joseph and that Luke stems from the family of Mary.

Genealogies were not designed to give an exhaustive lineage. They were stylized and selective, skipping whole generations. They were written to make a theological statement about the person's heritage and thus to interpret their personhood. Matthew lists four gentile women, which is probably significant in the overall theme of his gospel. Luke probably links Jesus to Adam to signal that the Messiah will serve not simply the descendants of Jacob (the Jews) but all people, including gentiles.

The date of the crucifixion, of course, is tied to the duration of Jesus's ministry (determined by counting the number of annual Passover Festivals in his ministry). If he had a three-year ministry that began in AD 26 or 27, his crucifixion may have occurred in the spring of AD 30. Some scholars, on the other hand, believe the date may have been the spring of AD 33.[1] Even though the precise year is unclear, every gospel writer agrees that Jesus was crucified on a Friday afternoon, in spring, during Passover.

BIRTH AND EARLIEST YEARS

Matthew and Luke tell the story of Jesus's birth (during the reign of Emperor Augustus, 43 BC–AD 14). An angel (Gabriel) appeared to the priest Zechariah in Jerusalem and to a young, unmarried woman named Mary in Nazareth. He announced that Zechariah's wife, Elizabeth, would give birth to John, who would become a prophet, and Mary would give birth to Jesus, who would be known as "the Son of the Most High" (Luke 1:32). Since Mary and her fiancé, Joseph, were not married, Mary's pregnancy would be a miracle (Matt. 1:20).

Following their marriage, Mary and Joseph were forced to travel south to Bethlehem, where a Roman census required that each family return to its ancestral or tribal region for registration. The Roman census was an instrument of occupation designed to control and tax (see sidebar); it brought extreme hardship to all. Mary and Joseph's entrance into this scene evokes images of terror and displacement: they are a young, poor couple, pushed into a distant village by the military and forced into a peasant's home to give birth to Mary's first son. We should not understand that Mary and Joseph made this trip alone as so many modern depictions would have it. This sort of travel was dangerous, and it's likely groups of travelers made this journey together. On a subsequent trip, the crowd of travelers is so great that Mary and Joseph lose track of Jesus (Luke 2:41).

Matthew and Luke develop different aspects of the story while agreeing on its essential elements. Matthew records details about Joseph, the star, the visit of the Magi, the attack of Herod's soldiers, and the family's flight into Egypt. For him an important theme is the parallel between the birth of Moses and of Jesus.

Luke includes the story of John the Baptist's family and birth, the visit of the shepherds, the purification of Mary, the naming of Jesus, and hymns from Mary (Luke 1:46–55), Zechariah (1:67–79), and Simeon (2:28–32). Luke is interested in God's unexpected visitation to the "poor" and lowly, who, like models of salvation in the Old Testament, become agents of salvation.

Mary, Joseph, and the Inn

We often use European/American conceptions of the setting of Jesus's birth. Public inns were rare, especially in small villages like Bethlehem. Peasants lived in small one-room houses or caves divided into two parts, one for animals and an elevated area for the family. Occasionally they had extra space on the roof or in a small back room. Mary and Joseph tried to obtain such a space as a guest room (Gk. *katalyma*, Luke 2:7).

Luke knows the word for public inns. In the parable of the good Samaritan, he uses it when describing the inn of Jericho that cared for the injured man (10:34). But Luke does *not* refer to an inn ("no room at the inn") in Luke 2. Instead, Mary and Joseph were offered the small interior section of a peasant's home where animals were kept. The manger was likely a feeding trough carved out of stone in the wall or the floor. Therefore, this is not a grim story of rejection. These hosts were poor Jewish peasants doing what they could for a poor, desperate couple from Galilee.

Stone manger discovered at Megiddo
© 2018 by Zondervan

The "shepherd's" fields outside Bethlehem near the Palestinian Christian village of Beit Sahour.
Ferrell Jenkins/BiblePlaces.com

Mary and Joseph fled to Egypt due to Herod's threat to kill the children of Bethlehem. It is difficult to know how long they remained in Egypt following Jesus's birth. Certainly they waited until Herod's death (4 BC) since when they return, Herod's son Archelaus is ruling Judea (Matt. 2:22). Archelaus was notorious for his ineptitude and arrogance, and the Romans deposed him in AD 6. To avoid Archelaus, Joseph's family bypassed Judea and settled in Galilee (2:22–23).

Jesus grew up in the Galilee village of Nazareth, secluded in the mountains of Lower Galilee but nevertheless near to the expanding city of Sepphoris and the busy trade routes moving through the valleys. Jesus was probably educated in the local synagogue each morning from age five or six and each afternoon worked at

Jesus and the Galilee Caravan

How did Mary and Joseph lose track of Jesus at age twelve (see Luke 2:41–51)? Jewish boys were under the care of their mothers until puberty. At age thirteen they associated with village men, formally became a "son of the law," and were permitted to be a legal witness, lead in prayer, and enjoy a legal independent status.

Cultural anthropologists offer insight into what may have happened. When Mary and Joseph traveled to Jerusalem they probably did so with a large caravan, and the men and women traveled separately. Since Jesus was at a transitional age, it's likely that Mary thought Jesus was with Joseph and Joseph thought he was with the women. At night they discovered their error.

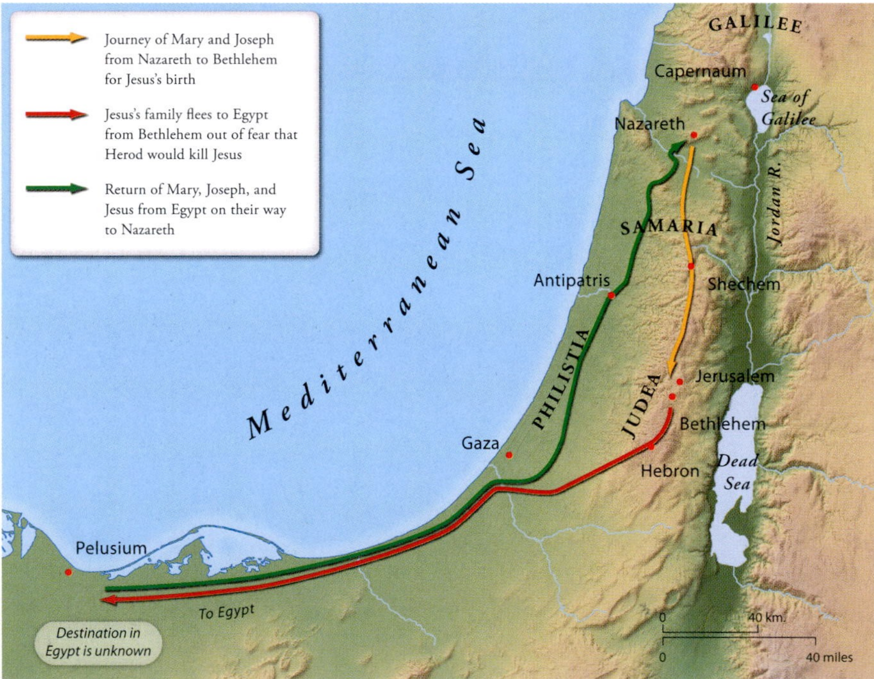

Jesus's birth and early life

his father's trade. Joseph was a *tektōn* (Mark 6:3), which really refers to a "builder" who works in wood, metal, or stone. Such multiskilled workers were needed for construction, particularly for cutting stone, which made up almost all construction in Galilee. Hence, Jesus knew hard labor and probably followed his father to nearby Sepphoris, working there to rebuild the new Greek city.

Like other boys in his village, from the age of six to ten Jesus became literate in Hebrew, through study of the Torah either from his father or in the Nazareth synagogue, and he likely memorized vast quantities of Scripture. From ages ten to twelve he became acquainted with the oral laws under the direction of the synagogue teacher and custodian, the *hazzan*. At this point, he would have ended his schooling and begun working full-time with his father. The only event from this time recorded in the gospels is Jesus's visit to a Passover in Jerusalem at age twelve.

From the age of thirteen until the beginning of his public ministry (about age thirty), Jesus worked in Nazareth and joined the village men at the synagogue for discussion and debate. These exclusively male gatherings sharpened understanding of the law and were as raucous as they were inspiring. Thus, Jesus had almost twenty years' experience debating in his local synagogue before he began teaching in the synagogues of Galilee. By the time he was an adult, he was a skilled craftsman, reasonably literate by first-century standards, knowledgeable in the traditions of his people, and adept at public discourse. Of course, we cannot be certain of these details. But they are reasonable conjectures given what we know about early Judaism's commitment to literacy and education. Many scholars believe the first Jewish schools for children opened as early as the second century BC, and by Jesus's day these were common for students. By the late first century, one later Jewish tradition (The Babylonian Talmud, *Baba Bathra*, 21) says that such schooling was mandatory. All this is vital because it gives us some sense of Jesus's own mastery of his Scriptures and religious traditions. And it implies that the apostles who follow him were likewise surprisingly skilled. This changes the popular view that Jews and his followers had little, if any, education.

Lactantius on the Roman Census

Lactantius was a Roman scholar who converted to Christianity in about AD 300 and soon became the tutor of the Emperor Constantine's son Crispus. As a devout Christian, he was critical of the brutality of Roman public policy. Here he writes about a typical Roman census:

> The census-takers appeared everywhere, and produced a tumult wherever they went. The fields were measured clod by clod; every grapevine and fruit tree counted, every head of livestock of every kind was listed, the exact number of people noted, and in the autonomous cities the urban and rural population were herded together until the market places were filled with the collected families. All came with their whole band of children and slaves. Everywhere was heard the screaming of those who were being interrogated with torture and beatings. Sons were forced to testify against their fathers, the trustiest slaves driven to bear witness against their masters, and wives against their husbands. When all other means had been exhausted, the victims were tortured until they gave evidence against themselves, and when pain had at last conquered, taxable property that did not exist was registered. Neither age nor illness won exemption. The ill and the infirm were dragged before the examiners; age was set down by estimate and the age of [tax-free] minors was raised while that of the old [who were likewise exempt] was lowered. The market places rang with lamentations (*De mortibus persecutorum* 23.1ff.; cf. 26.2ff.).

Mount Precipice, the cliff in Nazareth where people attempted to throw Jesus off (Luke 4:29).
John Theodor/Shutterstock

Fragment of a mezuzah (41Q149) dated to the second to first century BC from Qumran, Cave 4. A fragment like this contained the *shema* and would have been stored on doorposts.
Courtesy of the Leon Levy Dead Sea Scrolls Digital Library, Israel Antiquities Authority, photo: Tsila Sagiv

Records found in rabbinic Judaism in the century after Jesus give us some idea what life was probably like in the first century. As a faithful Jew, Jesus likely traveled to Jerusalem multiple times a year to celebrate the festivals of Passover, Pentecost, and Tabernacles. The "markers" of his Jewish faith surrounded him. The front door of his home had Scriptures (likely Deut. 6:4–9; 11:18–21) nailed to the right upper post (the mezuzah). He also dressed in a long cloak with double tassels on each of the four corners of its hem—but unlike the Greeks, he made one thread at each corner blue, signaling his identity as a Jew. Twice each day he recited the *Shema* (Deut. 6:4–9), which explains how he can readily refer to it when asked in Matthew 22:34–40. He kept a kosher diet, wore his hair and beard long, and observed the many rules regulating the Sabbath. This fidelity to Jewish cultural and religious custom was observed carefully by his world. Which makes it all the more dramatic when he violates some of these customs during the course of his ministry.

BAPTISM AND TEMPTATION

The public ministry of Jesus opens with a preliminary scene describing John the Baptist. John took on the role of a prophet, traveled into the eastern deserts and along the Jordan River, and called the residents of Judea to repentance (Matt. 3:5–10; Luke 3:7–9). Many of the leaders of Jerusalem came to him and pressed him to explain himself (John 1:19–28).

Jesus made his first public appearance at the Jordan River with John. When he entered the water, the Spirit descended on him and God's voice confirmed,

The Judean wilderness lies between Jerusalem and the Jordan River. This was the region of Jesus's forty-day testing.
© 2018 by Zondervan

Jesus was baptized in the Jordan River, which originates near Mount Hermon in the far north, flows into the Sea of Galilee near Bethsaida, and flows out of the south end of the Sea of Galilee to the Dead Sea.
Angon_Ivanov/Shutterstock

"You are my Son, whom I love" (Mark 1:11). John told the crowds that Jesus was "the Lamb of God, who takes away the sin of the world" (John 1:29) and that he would "baptize with the Holy Spirit" (1:33).

Jesus then entered the wilderness alone and was tested for forty days by Satan (Matt. 4:1–11). His triple test evoked memories of Israel in the wilderness—perhaps also the testing of Adam—but Jesus prevailed, citing passages from Deuteronomy 6–8 in response to each provocative offer. Satan weighed in on Jesus's understanding of sonship and the empowering that came at his baptism. Would Jesus exploit his power for self-interest? Would he exchange his divine calling for a secular understanding of power? In each case, Jesus refused.

THE BEGINNING OF THE GALILEAN MINISTRY

Jesus and John worked side by side in the Jordan Valley; gradually some of John's followers changed their allegiance to follow Jesus (John 1:35–42). Jesus moved quietly between the Jordan Valley and Galilee, gaining disciples and establishing his reputation. His first miracle was at Cana in Galilee (John 2).

Machaerus, a Herodian fortress, occupied a defensive position against the Nabatean kingdom but also, according to Josephus, was the location of John the Baptist's death.
dbajurin/123rf.com

These first-century stone jars were discovered in Jerusalem and illustrate the water jars used by Jesus in John 2:6. Unlike pottery jars, these jars could not become "unclean" through common use (Lev. 11:33) and thus could hold purification water.
© 2018 by Zondervan

Jesus's world changed abruptly with the arrest and imprisonment of John the Baptist. The prophet's moral exhortations condemned the illicit marriage of Herod Antipas (the political ruler of that area) to Herodias (his brother's wife, Mark 6:17–18). Josephus tells us the full story (*Ant.* 18.5.1–2 [109–119]). When Antipas decided to marry Herodias, he also shamed his first wife, the daughter of King Aretas of Nabatea (an Arab kingdom encompassing much of present-day Jordan).

Gamla: A First-Century Community Uncovered

In the Golan Heights, northeast of the Sea of Galilee, archaeologists in 1967 discovered a village well-known among Jewish historians. Gamla was destroyed at the beginning of the great war with Rome (AD 66–70) and was never rebuilt.

The excavation of the site is impressive. Over six hundred sickle blades have been found, showing that Gamla was an agricultural center. Likewise, loads of military gear testify to the last fight at the town. Above all, a first-century synagogue has been completely excavated.

If Jesus visited the many villages of Galilee, he certainly came to Gamla. At this remote site we can revisit the world of the first century and an actual synagogue where Jesus preached.

Gamla was one of Galilee's many villages. It occupied a precipitous ridge, here seen with the excavated village's walls and buildings. (See ch. 3 for a photo of Gamla's synagogue.)
Bill Schlegel/BiblePlaces.com

When this princess fled home, her father was enraged, and John's preaching contributed to his fury. Antipas killed John at his fortress of Machaerus, on the Nabatean border, to silence his critic and avoid a possible border war. King Aretas did attack Antipas in AD 36 and destroyed his army. Many Jews saw this defeat as God's judgment on Antipas for killing John (*Ant.* 18.5.2 [116–119]).

With the arrest of John, Jesus moved north, no doubt to escape these political dangers (Mark 1:14). His destination was the familiar hills of Galilee, and soon he became a public figure, moving from village to village, gathering disciples, and establishing his reputation as a healer, exorcist, and skilled teacher.

Cana (Re)Discovered?

Today the visitor to Israel can travel to the Palestinian town of Kana (or Kefr Kenna), a few miles northeast of Nazareth. Here Arab Christian churches keep alive memories of Jesus's dramatic visit—and frequently western Christian tourists rededicate their marriages in the local Orthodox or Catholic churches, remembering how Jesus blessed a wedding in John 2:1–11.

But Arab Kana is likely not the site of this first-century village. In 1997 a field survey located an important ruin eight miles north of Nazareth, and in 1998 excavations began. Today scholars think this is first-century Cana (Khirbet Kana, "ruins of Cana"). Archaeologists have already uncovered impressive Byzantine ruins, a water system, cisterns, buildings, and pottery from as far back as the eighth century BC.

This story about Cana illustrates something important. Historical discoveries are ongoing and what once was considered a "certain discovery" may require revision in subsequent years. Currently the Galilee village of Bethsaida (often visited by tourists) is undergoing a complete scholarly revision. The present site (et-Tell) has few scholarly supporters today, and many think a new site now under exploration near the lake (el-Araj) is correct.

Aerial view of the excavations of this fourth-century synagogue at Capernaum on the Sea of Galilee.
Bill Schlegel/BiblePlaces.com

Nevertheless, Herod Antipas was not amused, and superstitious rumors gathered momentum in Galilee that in fact, Jesus was actually John the Baptist, now returned to life (6:16).

Despite his reputation as a "Nazarene," Jesus never returned to Nazareth permanently and instead moved to the fishing villages on the north end of the Sea of

Galilee. Capernaum became his new home (Mark 2:1), a fishing village that lay on the main highway connecting central Galilee with the mountain villages of the Golan Heights—as well as far-off Damascus. It was also on the border with Philip's territory (Antipas's brother) and thus a tax station for commerce moving down the highway. If Antipas ever pursued Jesus, he could simply slip across the border by boat (6:45). Capernaum even had its own Roman garrison. A centurion from its barracks helped build Capernaum's synagogue (Luke 7:3–5).

GROWING POPULARITY

As Jesus's popularity grew, he was followed by groups of people who hung on his every word. "A large crowd" from both Galilee and Judea followed him (Mark 3:7). He spoke from the coves on Galilee's shores and on some occasions used moored boats as his platform. On one occasion he gathered the crowd on the side of a mountain and delivered his famous Sermon on the Mount (Matt. 5–7), after which the audience was stunned at his authority, contrasting it with the efforts of Jewish teachers of the law.

The term "disciple" (Gk. *mathetes*, "learner") referred to the wider public that followed Jesus. To further advance his work and to develop a circle of uniquely trained disciples, Jesus chose twelve men (called "apostles" or "the Twelve"; see Mark 3:13–19). The Twelve played a role well known in Judaism. They were authorized representatives or agents who carried their patron's authority. They could speak for him and act in his name. These men were entrusted to go into the villages of Galilee, preaching what Jesus taught them and casting out demons, all under the authority of Jesus.

Their efforts moving in twos throughout Galilee (Luke 9:1–6) no doubt spread word about Jesus rapidly. Many people traveled to find him, so that when Jesus arrived in their towns, he found audiences who were expectant and receptive. This strategy was so effective that at one point Jesus appointed seventy-two people to accomplish the same purpose (Luke 10:1–20).

A further index of Jesus's growing fame is the great feeding miracles. Once in Galilee about five thousand men (plus additional women and children) listened to his teaching for so long that they needed to be fed.

Matthew opens the public ministry of Jesus with the Sermon on the Mount, which took place on the hills near Capernaum. Pilgrims have commemorated the proposed site of the sermon with a church structure from as early as the fourth century.
Berthold Werner, Public Domain

Galilee during Jesus's ministry

Jesus repeated this miracle on a separate occasion, where he fed four thousand with seven loaves and a few fish.

One characteristic of Jesus's followers was the unexpected mix of people. Jesus eagerly crossed social boundaries that we might miss when we read the gospels today. For instance, when he visited Tyre and Sidon (Mark 7:24) or moved through the Decapolis (the Greek cities east of Galilee), he was with gentiles (7:31). These were unexpected contacts for a Jewish teacher. He likewise responded to a request for healing from a Roman centurion in Capernaum (Matt. 8:5). Similarly, he had a ministry among the "outcast" Samaritans (John 4) and sent his followers into their villages to preach (Luke 9:52).

Jesus associated with women as well as men (Luke 8:43; 10:38; John 4:7). Some women were deeply troubled, such as Mary Magdalene (Mark 16:9) and the

Where Was Magdala?

Mary Magdalene (Luke 8:2) was from Magdala, a fishing village on the west side of the Sea of Galilee. This town was north of Tiberias about two miles, located at an important junction where the main road west from the sea began through the Mount Arbel pass. Josephus refers to Magdala as Tarichea and remarks that it was famous as a center for the fishing industry (*War* 2.21.8 [632–637]; 3.9.7ff. [443ff.]). The name "Magdala" was preserved in the name of an Arab village on the site, called Majdel.

Today Majdel is gone and the ancient site of Magdala is under rapid development. Archaeologists have discovered one of the oldest synagogues in Israel as well as the first-century fishing community there. Magdala is one of the most anticipated excavations in Galilee today.

Excavations at Magdala with the synagogue shaded by the wood pavilion. *Ferrell Jenkins/BiblePlaces.com*

woman caught in adultery (John 8:3), while others were established leaders in the community who helped pay Jesus's expenses (such as Susannah and Joanna, the wife of Herod's financial minister, likely from the important city of Sepphoris, Luke 8:3).

Jesus also ministered to those who lived on society's margin: tax collectors, lepers, adulterers, and "sinners." Even one of his apostles was a political revolutionary (Matt. 10:4). In this sense Jesus failed to maintain "social boundaries" that promoted the Pharisees' notion of separation and purity, and he incurred criticism for making "misguided" social choices (Mark 2:16).

Cultural anthropologists wonder whether Jesus was labeled a "bad son" by some of his contemporaries. He rejected conventions held deeply in his society (such as diet, Sabbath-keeping, and social boundaries). He did not marry, devote himself to Joseph's trade, or become an established member of Nazareth.

Authorized Agents

The ancient world did not enjoy the ease of communication we see today. Written communication was common, but more importantly, people authorized others to conduct business or convey privileged information. This required a "sender" and an "agent" who could speak and act with binding authority on behalf of the sender. When Jesus selects "apostles" he is assuming this practice. He is authorizing them as his representatives to speak in his name. Twelve of these had a unique relationship with him and their names are listed in each of the Synoptic Gospels. The Twelve were thus set apart—but others (such as Paul, 1 Cor. 9:1) would later be able to assume the title in a more informal sense.

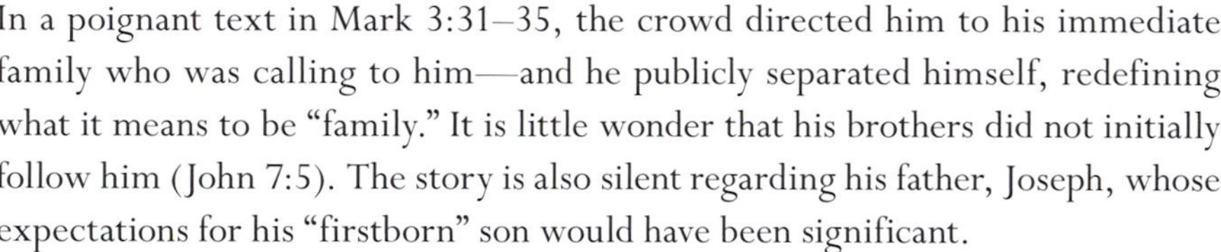

In a poignant text in Mark 3:31–35, the crowd directed him to his immediate family who was calling to him—and he publicly separated himself, redefining what it means to be "family." It is little wonder that his brothers did not initially follow him (John 7:5). The story is also silent regarding his father, Joseph, whose expectations for his "firstborn" son would have been significant.

GROWING OPPOSITION

The source of opposition to Jesus is a critical question among modern researchers. Discovering its source to a large degree discloses what is at the heart of Jesus's self-consciousness and mission. Was he a religious reformer within Judaism who threatened its leadership? Was he challenging the social and political injustices of his day and so jeopardized Israel's uneasy equilibrium with Rome?

Jesus's critics felt they had good grounds to object to him. One of the major components of the gospels is the sheer number of stories of conflict in which different groups—Sadducees, Pharisees, and scribes—expressed resistance to his teaching and behavior. Two areas provoked conflict. First, Jesus was known as someone who "broke the Sabbath." Multiple stories show him openly violating the Pharisaic Sabbath laws and not refraining from work (Matt. 12:1–14; Mark 2:23–28; 3:1–6; Luke 13:10–17; 14:1–5; John 5:1–18). In each of these stories, Jesus's offensive "work" could have waited until the next day. But he saw this activity as prophetic, acting out a message that expressed criticism of intricate Sabbath legislation. His explanation is remembered in the succinct maxim, "The Sabbath was made for man, not man for the Sabbath" (Mark 2:27).

Second, Jesus seemed too relaxed about purity laws. Mark 7:1–5 outlines the Pharisees' concern about washing and utensils and notes their criticism of Jesus: "Why don't your disciples live according to the tradition of the elders instead of eating their food with defiled hands?" On another occasion, Jesus expressed apparent disregard for food laws (kosher) and declared all foods "clean" (Mark 7:15, 19).

Sabbath

The Jewish Sabbath is the seventh day of the week and a required day of rest based on God's completion of creation in Genesis 1. It begins at dusk on Friday evening and concludes at dusk on Saturday. The requirement to observe the Sabbath is the fourth commandment (Ex. 20:8) and by Jesus's day extensive legislation stipulated how this obedience worked. The Romans viewed this practice, along with circumcision, as characteristic of Jewish culture.

Keeping the Sabbath meant cessation from all work. Exterior jobs (farming, trading) and interior jobs (cooking, cleaning, lighting lamps) were prohibited. In the Jewish oral laws, thirty-nine classifications of prohibited activity are listed, from grinding to sewing (Mishna, Shabbath, 7.2). But debates among the rabbis were fierce: When was moving an object work? Could a ladder be moved a few inches or a few feet? How far could one walk before it was "work"? This is a critical issue when Jesus heals a man on the Sabbath and then tells him to take up his mat and walk (John 5:8). Jesus is accused of breaking the Sabbath, but he has also directed someone else to do so.

Dietary rules and Sabbath observance were principal markers in Judaism that set Jews apart from gentiles. Jesus failed to hold to these boundaries.

Other controversies followed Jesus (such as his treatment of divorce law, Mark 10:1–12), but in each of them Jesus expressed himself as having an authority not subject to human tradition or rule. He might quote from the Torah, but then follow it with an authoritative "I" statement: "You have heard that it was said . . . but I tell you. . . ." He reinforced this with the odd prelude to many of his sayings, "Truly I tell you . . ." (Matt. 5:18; cf. John 3:3). He defended his commitment to the law (Matt. 5:17) but delivered a severe prophetic critique to its practitioners: they practiced outward forms of religion for public viewing but failed to pursue the inner values the law promoted. He claimed that such people were "hypocrites" (6:5). The implication of this language seemed clear: Jesus spoke with a voice authorized by God.

Jesus's teachings could provoke. It would be better to have one of these heavy millstones tied around your neck and be cast into the sea than to lead a little one to sin. The millstone mentioned in Matthew 18:6 was one turned by a donkey to grind grain. These were far heavier and larger than the small millstones used by women. *Todd Bolen/BiblePlaces.com*

Jesus deemed that obedience to his personal words affected a person's relationship with God (Matt. 7:21–27; John 5:23). Jesus explained that his own efforts and words actually represented the work of God in the world. These concerns coalesced one Sabbath in Jerusalem. Jesus "worked" on the Sabbath by healing a lame man but defended himself with an argument based on the rabbinic opinion that God *alone* could work on the Sabbath (John 5:16–18). As Jesus's ministry matured, his audiences increasingly perceived that he bore a presence and power that were unique. He performed healings, raised the dead, exorcized demons, forgave sins, and silenced storms. It's no wonder that they occasionally looked at him in amazement and were filled with fear (Mark 6:50).

JESUS "SETS HIS FACE" TOWARD JERUSALEM

A turning point came at the apex of Jesus's ministry in Galilee. At Caesarea Philippi, Jesus turned toward his followers and asked them to identify him. They explained the public's many incorrect views of him, but then Peter gave the correct answer: "You are the Messiah, the Son of the living God" (Matt. 16:16). This judgment was confirmed the next week when Jesus took Peter, James, and John with him to a high mountain (likely Mount Hermon) and there was "transfigured," showing his radiant glory alongside Elijah and Moses (Mark 9:2–13).

Following these remarkable events, Jesus (lit.) "set his face" to go to Jerusalem for the last time (Luke 9:51). The gospel writers note that during the trip, Jesus made three explicit predictions of his coming betrayal and death: at Caesarea Philippi (Mark 8:31–33), in Galilee near Capernaum (9:30–32), and near Jericho (10:32–34). Each time he became increasingly specific about what would happen in Jerusalem. As they heard these predictions, the disciples' responses changed: initially they rebuked him and were confused (8:32); later they were afraid to ask him what he meant (9:32); and finally they were filled with fear (10:32). As he moved south, even sympathetic Pharisees warned him about what lay ahead (Luke 13:31).

At the base of Mount Hermon near Caesarea Philippi. Springs feed river systems that give birth to the Jordan River.
© 2018 by Zondervan

Why Caesarea Philippi?

Caesarea Philippi began its Roman life when Emperor Augustus gave it to Herod the Great to rule in 20 BC. As a tribute of thanks, Herod built a pure white marble temple in honor of Augustus. After Herod's death, the city passed on to his son Philip, who rebuilt it and made it the capital of Batanea, the region northeast of the Sea of Galilee.

Philip also chose this site because of its sacred traditions. One of the sources of the Jordan River flowed from a cave here, and shrines and temples to the Roman nature god Pan had been built (its most ancient name is Paneas). Soon the city was called "Caesarea of Philip" (Caesarea Philippi) to distinguish it from Caesarea "on the sea." But for most ancient historians, the traditional link to Pan remained. Pliny referred to the city as Caesarea Panias (*Natural History*, 5.71, 74).

Today people can visit Caesarea Philippi. This is where Peter identified Jesus as the Messiah (Matt. 16:16).
Public Domain

THE FINAL WEEK

Jesus's arrival in Jerusalem begins the story of the last week of his earthly life. It was springtime, the season of Passover, and pilgrims from everywhere were pouring into the city. Jerusalem had become for Jesus a theological symbol representing the city that resisted God's messengers (Luke 13:34–35).

Jesus's journey took him to Jericho, and from this oasis he climbed the Roman road west into the desert. Here in the Judean mountains, a short walk from Jerusalem, he stayed with friends in the village of Bethany (home of Mary and Martha);

Ancient travelers would use this Roman road to move between Jericho and Jerusalem.
Todd Bolen/BiblePlaces.com

This scale model of first-century Jerusalem shows the details of Herod's magnificent city. The model is on the grounds of the Israel Museum, Jerusalem.
© 2018 by Zondervan

Jesus found an olive orchard where he prayed and was later betrayed. The name Gethsemane comes from the Aramaic *gat semen*, or "olive press."
© 2015 by Zondervan

The fig was symbolic of Israel and the judgment that would come on Jerusalem (Mark 11:12–14).
Natalija Sahraj/Shutterstock

This artist's reconstruction depicts Herod's refurbished and expanded city of Jerusalem during Jesus's lifetime. Note the temple compound on the east side of the city.

© Hugh Claycombe Design and Illustration

when he first arrived, he electrified the village by raising Lazarus from the dead (John 11:1–45). Upon entering Jerusalem, crowds of residents and Passover pilgrims greeted him as a great messianic figure. Most wanted to see him—others wanted to see Lazarus and confirm the story of his resurrection (12:9–11). Some were deeply devoted to Jesus's teaching, while others were caught up in political dreams of Jesus's talk about "the kingdom of God" (Luke 19:11). Soon palms were waving, and shouts of Jewish nationalism could be heard: "Blessed is he who comes in the name of the Lord!" "Blessed is the coming kingdom of our father David!" (Mark 11:9–10). Jesus rode a donkey, evoking memories of Zechariah's prophecies (Matt. 21:5; cf. Zech. 9:9).

A common Old Testament theme is that God's prophets would bring judgment first to God's house, the temple (Jer. 7:1–15; 26:1–15; Mal. 3:1–5). When Jesus entered Jerusalem, he astonished even his disciples.

Nard

Nard was extremely precious and imported from northern India. Nard is a shrub whose leaves and shoots were harvested and taken by caravan to the west. Sometimes it was mixed with its own root to increase its weight. Note that Mary's gift is called "pure," meaning that it had no additives. Nard smelled like *gladiolus* perfume and had a red color. It was used as medicine, as an aromatic wine, as a breath scent, and as perfume (see Pliny, *Natural History* 12:24–26 [41–46]).

A pound was huge and lavish. Its value of three hundred denarii represents a year's wages for a day laborer. Cheaper nard from Gaul, Crete, or Syria cost a hundred denarii per pound, but Mary owned the best.

wasanajai/Shutterstock

Today's Jerusalem not only has a thriving modern population of Arabs and Jews but has been the site of intensive archaeological work. This view is from the east, showing the Temple Mount.
ventdusud/Shutterstock

The following day, crossing the Kidron Valley, Jesus cursed a fig tree because it had no fruit (Mark 11:12–14). In the Old Testament the fig was a common symbol of Israel itself (Jer. 8:13; 29:17; Hos. 9:10; Joel 1:7), and figs' destruction symbolized the judgment on the nation (Isa. 34:4; Hos. 2:12; Luke 13:6–9).

Jesus then entered the temple courts, expressed outrage at its commercial activities, disrupted the money changers, and interrupted the sacrifices—an act of civil disobedience that confirmed the authorities' commitment to have him arrested. For the remainder of the week, Jesus entered into a sustained critique of Jerusalem's leadership and daily debated them inside the spacious courtyards of the temple (Matt. 23; Mark 12). He even climbed the Mount of Olives just east of the city and prophesied not only the demise of Jerusalem and its temple but the judgment of the world (Matt. 24; Mark 13; Luke 21).

The Roman *Triclinium* and the Passover

Every culture has rules for festival meals. At Judaism's Passover festival, participants dined reclining on cushions at low tables, reaching for common bowls. First-century Jews had adopted the Roman *triclinium* table, a low three-sided table shaped like a *U*. Guests reclined on cushions while the interior of the *U* provided access for servers. The body was supported with the left arm (or elbow), the right hand was used for eating, and the feet were extended away from the table.

This explains why "the beloved disciple" (John) can lean his head back, rest it on Jesus's chest, and ask him a question (John 13:23–25). They were reclining side by side, John to the right, Jesus to the left.

Triclinium in the House of the Ephebe, Pompeii, ca. end of the first century AD.
Todd Bolen/BiblePlaces.com

The Jerusalem leadership started talking about stopping Jesus; some underscored the threat he posed to the security of the nation, in that a popular uprising could lead to a Roman military response (John 11:48). The high priest Caiaphas easily concluded that Jesus should die, since it would be a sacrifice for the whole nation's well-being (11:50). In this context, Jesus's good friend Mary (the sister of Lazarus and Martha) took an alabaster jar of pure nard and anointed him generously. It was as much a disturbing symbol as a luxurious gift. Mary was saying goodbye and readying his body for burial (Matt. 26:6–13; Mark 14:3–9; John 12:1–8).

In antiquity all Jews celebrated the Passover with the ritual slaughter of a lamb. Today this practice continues only among the Samaritans.
Todd Bolen/BiblePlaces.com

Each Passover season anticipated the ritual slaughter of lambs, which was followed after sundown by a Passover meal. This year, the Passover meal began on a Thursday evening. Following Jewish tradition, Jesus secured a room within the walled city, sent two disciples to prepare the tables and the food (Luke 22:8), and hosted his final meal with the Twelve. This ritual meal recalled the exodus from Egypt, God's redemption of his people, and the sacrificed lambs whose blood covered their homes (see Ex. 12–13).

But during the middle of the meal, Jesus interrupted the festivities, broke a loaf of bread, poured a cup of wine, and announced that these would now represent his broken body and shed blood (Matt. 26:26–28). In the Old Testament each covenant was sealed with sacrifice (Gen. 15:9–18; Ex. 24:3–8). Jesus is doing the same here: "This is my blood of the [new] covenant, which is poured out for many for the forgiveness of sins" (Matt. 26:28).

Jesus's crown of thorns may have come from a palm. The fronds were trimmed away on one side and the longer fronds stood upright creating a halo of palms radiating like the sun. This imitated the god Helios (the sun god) and was used widely by Roman rulers. Jesus was thus mocked with an imitation royal crown whose palms were not trimmed, leaving sharp thorns. Pictured here is a Hadrian tetradrachm of Alexandria, Egypt, AD 129–30.
Courtesy of VCoins.com

ARREST, TRIAL, AND CRUCIFIXION

Jesus then left the city and entered an olive orchard not far from the road that would take him back to Bethany. Here he prayed fervently and was burdened by the dread of his coming suffering (Mark 14:32–42). The evening was interrupted when Judas, who had received thirty silver pieces (Matt. 26:14–16), led a determined band of men to arrest Jesus. Priests, temple police (Luke 22:52), and even a detachment of Roman soldiers (John 18:3, 12) arrived with weapons and torches. With the signal of a kiss, Judas identified Jesus, and he was arrested.

Jesus's trial was quickly carried out since the authorities feared a furious reaction from the masses, many of whom came from Galilee (Luke 22:2). The high priest Caiaphas gathered a cadre of leaders at his residence, and his father-in-law, the now-retired high priest Annas, began the interrogation (John 18:13). This was followed by witnesses who made unsuccessful charges against Jesus (Matt. 26:60).

Because the witnesses contradicted themselves about details (Mark 14:56), Caiaphas himself entered the fray. He first prodded Jesus to speak in his own self-defense, hoping to find some incriminating evidence on his own lips. Finally, he asked him forthrightly: "Tell us if you are the Messiah, the Son of God" (Matt. 26:63). It was considered blasphemy to claim divine honors for oneself. Jesus answered by describing himself as an apocalyptic judge who would possess a heavenly role with God (Mark 14:62). This was enough. After calling for a test vote, Caiaphas handed Jesus over to the temple police to be guarded until morning.

For each gospel writer, the scene is tragic. Jesus was alone, and even his leading disciple, Peter, who had followed and stood outside the priest's house and was known for his bravado, denied knowing Jesus three times. Early on Friday

A scale model of first-century Jerusalem at the Israel Museum (Jerusalem) reconstructs the four-tower Antonia Fortress, the likely site of Jesus's interrogation before Pilate.
© 2018 by Zondervan

Pilate's Political Anxieties

When the crowd outside the Antonia Fortress called for Jesus's crucifixion, it also threatened Pilate's career. "If you let this man go, you are *no friend of Caesar.* Anyone who claims to be a king opposes Caesar" (John 19:12, italics added). The title *amicus caesaris* was an administrative label for any ally of Caesar and assured its owner of a brilliant career. The loss of the title had been seen in Pilate's own day. Cornelius Gallus was the governor of Egypt. Augustus stripped him of the title *amicus* on the grounds of ingratitude. He was forbidden admission to the imperial court, expelled from the equestrian order, and banned from imperial provinces. In AD 26 Gallus committed suicide.

The Antonia Fortress was destroyed when Titus sacked Jerusalem in AD 70. Today its courtyard paving stones can be found in the lower levels of the streets of Jerusalem (seen here inside the Sisters of Zion convent).
Z. Radovan/www.BibleLandPictures.com

morning Caiaphas called for a plenary meeting of the Sanhedrin to formalize the decision (Mark 15:1). Because the Jews had lost the privilege to execute a criminal (John 18:31), Caiaphas had to defer to the Roman governor (Pontius Pilate), who was in Jerusalem because of Passover. Pilate's interrogation of Jesus likely took place at the Antonia Fortress.

The Sanhedrin's charges of blasphemy would make little impact on Pilate. Thus, Caiaphas reframed the charges against Jesus, implying that he was guilty of political sedition: "We have found this man subverting our nation. He opposes payment of taxes to Caesar and claims to be Messiah, a king" (Luke 23:2). At which point Pilate probed Jesus's understanding of politics: "Are you the king of the Jews?" (Matt. 27:11). Jesus agreed but was wary of Pilate's meaning and reinterpreted the title: "My kingdom is not of this world" (John 18:36). But the Sanhedrin voices returned, claiming Jesus had disturbed the peace, made trouble in Galilee, and now was bringing unrest to Jerusalem.

When Pilate heard that Jesus was from Galilee, he decided to send him to the Jewish ruler of Galilee, Herod Antipas, who was in Jerusalem. This was a stroke of genius. Pilate could still get Jesus condemned, but shift the blame to a Jewish ruler. But Jesus refused to talk to Herod. Because Antipas had killed John the Baptist, Jesus had little respect for him (Luke 23:6–16).

A Crucified Man Found in 1968

In 1968 at Giv'at ha-Mivtar in Jerusalem, a first-century bone box (or ossuary) was discovered containing the skeleton of a man who had been crucified. His heel bones were still fastened together by a single iron nail 5.5 inches long. The man's ankles had been placed sideways and on top of each other, and the nail was driven through a piece of acacia wood (that functioned like a washer), and the ankles into the olivewood cross. When he was taken down, the nail could not be removed, and he was buried with the nail, the acacia wood, and a fragment of olivewood.

The ankle bone of a crucified man from the first century still shows the nail used in his death. The model foot next to it shows how the original nailing would have looked.
Z. Radovan/www.BibleLandPictures.com

Jesus's case returned to Pilate, and the governor appealed to a Passover amnesty tradition of releasing a prisoner (John 18:38–40). But the crowd outside his fortress called instead for the release of Barabbas, a man described in Greek as a *lestes*. This term should be translated as "bandit patriot" (today we would call him a "terrorist"), describing someone who fought against the Roman occupation. This turn of events troubled Pilate. He handed Jesus to some of his troops, had him thoroughly whipped, and presented him to the crowd, hoping to evoke pity (19:1–11). But this was met only with a cry for Jesus's death.

Following considerable pressure from the Sanhedrin leaders (John 19:12–15) and concerned about his own fate, Pilate handed Jesus over to his troops to commence the crucifixion. Jewish executions generally practiced stoning. But in the ancient world, various rulers began to use public crucifixion as a deterrent (cf. Josh. 10:26). Antiochus Epiphanes used crucifixion against his enemies in 167–166 BC (*Ant.* 12.5.4 [255–256]). The Maccabean ruler Alexander Jannaeus crucified eight hundred Pharisees who opposed him (*Ant.* 13.14.2 [379–380]). In 4 BC the Roman general Varus crucified two thousand Jewish rebels in Judea (*Ant.* 17.10.10 [295]). Jews detested the practice and, in Jesus's day, viewed it as a sign of the Roman occupation.

A victim was thoroughly beaten with a special bone- or metal-tipped whip, cutting the back to promote copious bleeding. He was then forced to carry the horizontal crossbeam to the crucifixion site. After Jesus was beaten (Mark 15:15), he was also mocked with a crown of thorns and robe, poking fun at his claim to be the Jewish king. As he walked to his crucifixion outside the city walls (called

Golgotha, "the place of the skull"), he became so weak that he could not carry the beam. A visitor to Jerusalem, Simon from Cyrene, was forced to carry it for him (15:21). Women wailed as they watched Jesus walking through Jerusalem's streets leaving a heavy trail of blood.

Soldiers oversaw the final execution. Crosses were not tall, and victims were roped or nailed to them with their feet not far from the ground. Victims were also crucified naked, increasing the shame and dread of the method. (This is why the soldiers gambled for Jesus's garments, John 19:23–24.) From their crosses men might dictate their will or hold conversations with their families. Jesus thus speaks from the cross since he is surrounded by his closest friends, his mother, and a circle of Jewish women.

This artist's model gives a credible option for understanding how Jesus was crucified. Note the seat for the victim to rest called the *sedile*. Josephus called this "the most wretched of deaths" (*War* 7.6.4 [203]). *Illustration by Michael J. Williams, reconstructed from the original art of Nicu Haas. Used by permission from the Israel Exploration Society, Jerusalem.*

BURIAL AND RESURRECTION

As a crucified criminal, Jesus should have been buried in a field adjacent to Jerusalem (*Ant.* 5.1.14 [43–44]). This is what happened to Judas Iscariot when he regretted his deed, committed suicide, and was buried in a field the priests purchased with his bribe money (Matt. 27:3–10).

In Jesus's case, a wealthy member of the Sanhedrin named Joseph from the village of Arimathea came forward. Joseph believed in Christ secretly and did not agree with the Sanhedrin's decision (Matt. 27:57; John 19:38). Together with Nicodemus (see John 3:1–21; 7:50), he asked for Jesus's body. It was a custom of respect in Judaism to bury bodies before sundown (John 19:31).

Rolling stone tombs, such as this one at Khirbet Midras, were well-known in the hills of Judea.
Todd Bolen/BiblePlaces.com

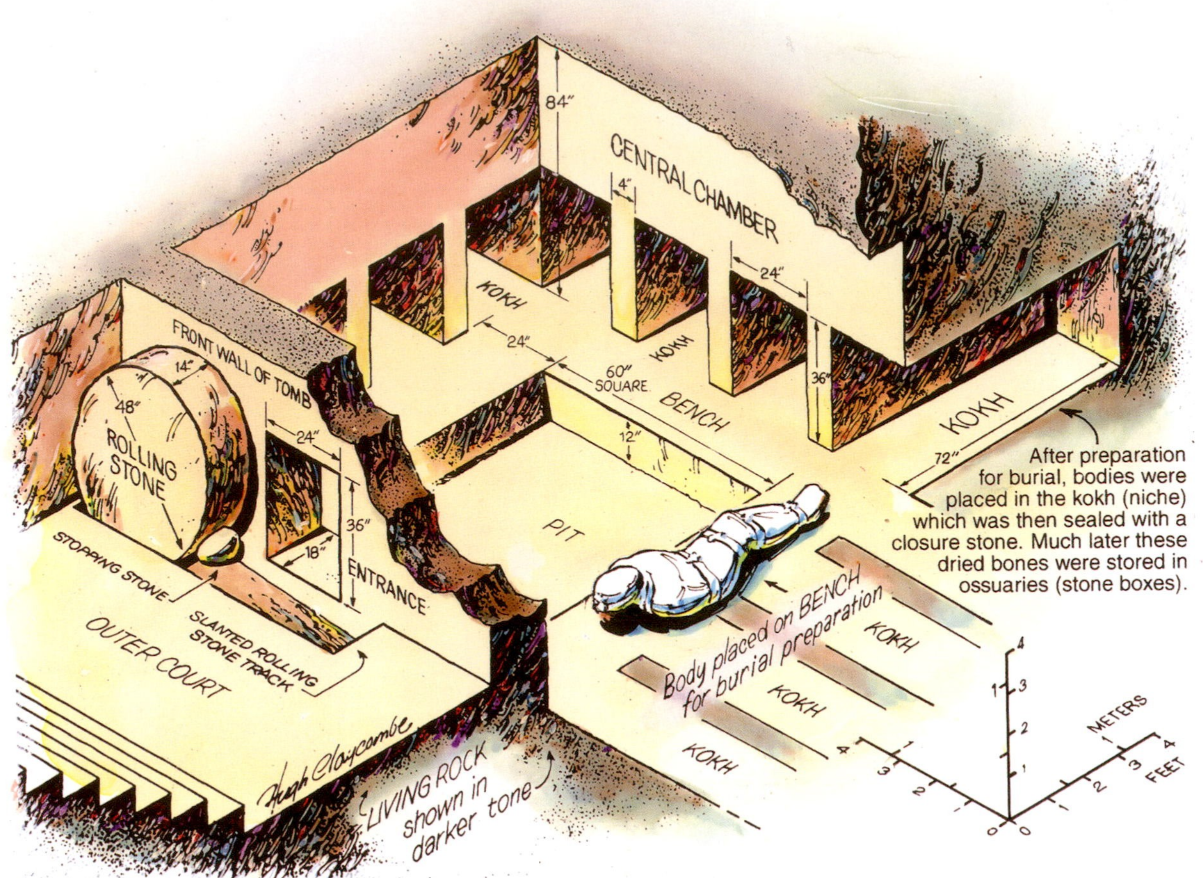

Some first-century tombs had characteristic designs. This tomb (based on a variety that have been found) shows a rolling stone, an interior reception area, a burial bench for anointing and preparation, and burial niches called *kokhim*. Bodies were covered with spices, wrapped and then slipped into the *kokh*, where they would decompose. *© Hugh Claycombe Design and Illustration*

Joseph possessed a new tomb that was unused and offered it immediately. Certainly the authorities had to assess if Jesus was already dead. Using a mallet, they crushed the legs of the two men crucified with Jesus (19:32) but they did not hit him. Instead, one soldier took his spear and stabbed him in the side. But Jesus's life had already expired.

Joseph and Nicodemus—no doubt aided by the women at the cross—removed Jesus's body and carried it to Joseph's tomb not far away. Archaeologists have found about nine hundred tombs from this period, so we have a good idea how this one was built. In one type, Jews carved cave tombs into the limestone hills outside Jerusalem's walls. A low door led to a square burial chamber (or receiving room) inside, which was encircled by a stone bench running along the room's perimeter. Six-foot shafts (or niches, Heb. *kokhim*) could be seen above the bench for final placement of the body. Many of these tombs were sealed with a movable "rolling" stone door.

Jesus was laid on the stone bench and wrapped loosely in linens dusted with spices; his head was given a burial napkin, and he was surrounded by seventy-five pounds of myrrh and aloe—an expensive gift from Nicodemus (John 19:39). Because Sabbath was beginning, no doubt they thought they would return to place Jesus in a wall niche and complete the burial later. Therefore, the rolling stone was closed. Fearing that his body might be stolen, the priests requested a guard at the tomb, sealing it for the duration of the Sabbath.

Early on Sunday morning, a group of women arrived at the tomb prepared to complete Jesus's burial (Mark 16:1–2). They worried about moving the heavy stone at the cave's entrance. But when they arrived, what looked at first like a disaster—the tomb was open, the body was gone—turned their sorrow into joy. Angels appeared, telling them that Jesus was alive and that they should tell the others. Then Jesus surprised them by appearing himself, telling them how his promises had been fulfilled. Soon the disciples were rushing to see for themselves.

Jesus met with his disciples that evening, showing them his wounds and fulfilling his promise that he would never abandon them (John 14:18). He also surprised some disciples on the road to Emmaus, west of Jerusalem (Luke 24:13–27). He continued to appear to them in Jerusalem (Luke 24:36–49) and in Galilee (Matt. 28:16–20) for forty days (Acts 1:3). On one occasion he appeared to five hundred people (1 Cor. 15:6).

The gospel writers are remarkably modest in their presentation of "proofs" for the resurrection. On occasion, the details of their stories collide as if written by independent and excited witnesses. But they stand in firm agreement that this event, this divine vindication of the truth of Jesus's life and message, lies at the center of Christian faith and experience.

Questions for Discussion

1. Explain some of the chief reasons Jesus was successful in his public ministry.
2. In what ways was Jesus's behavior different from that of the scribes and Pharisees in his day?
3. Did political issues affect Jesus? How did he embrace them or avoid them?
4. What was the Sanhedrin's chief complaint against Jesus? Why were its members persuaded that he had to die?
5. What are the literary and theological connections between the Old Testament Passover traditions and Jesus's death in the gospels?

BIBLIOGRAPHY

Introductory

Barnett, P. *Jesus and the Rise of Early Christianity*. Downers Grove, IL: InterVarsity Press, 1999.

France, R. T. *The Man They Crucified: A Portrait of Jesus*. Downers Grove, IL: InterVarsity Press, 1975.

Gibson, S. *The Final Days of Jesus: The Archaeological Evidence*. New York: HarperOne, 2009.

Harrison, E. F. *A Short Life of Christ*. Grand Rapids: Eerdmans, 1968.

Advanced

Bock, D. L. *Jesus according to Scripture: Restoring the Portraits of the Gospels*. Grand Rapids: Baker, 2002.

Charlesworth, J. H., ed. *Jesus and Archaeology*. Grand Rapids: Eerdmans, 2006.

Dunn, J. D. G. *Jesus Remembered*. Grand Rapids: Eerdmans, 2003.

Keener, C. S. *The Historical Jesus of the Gospels*. Grand Rapids: Eerdmans, 2009.

Meier, J. P. *A Marginal Jew: Rethinking the Historical Jesus*. 5 vols. ABRL. New York: Doubleday, 1991, 1994, 2002, 2009, 2016.

NOTES

1. A. Kostenberger, *The Final Days of Jesus: The Most Important Week of the Most Important Person Who Ever Lived* (Wheaton: Crossway, 2014).

Chapter 7

THE TEACHINGS OF JESUS

A first-century Jewish ritual bath (*mikveh*) from the Galilean village of Gamla, taken from overhead. Notice the steps entering the bath.
Todd Bolen/BiblePlaces.com

Why Didn't Jesus Write a Gospel?

We have no evidence that Jesus wrote down any of his own sayings—much less that he wrote a book. The great scholars of Jesus's day were recognized by the number of students (*talmid*) they could attract, not the books they wrote. Communication was verbal and memorization was commonplace. Thus, like Jesus, the rabbinic scholars Johannan ben Zakkai, Gamaliel, Hillel, and Shammai did not leave their own writings behind, but rather their followers collected and preserved their teachings.

This also explains the repeated mention of the great crowds that followed Jesus. He began with twelve disciples, and at one point more than five thousand flocked around him. By every first-century measure, Jesus was a respected teacher and speaker.

Jews practiced "secondary burial" in which the decomposed body's bones were placed in ornately carved limestone boxes. Jesus compared these to the Pharisees (Matt. 23:27). This Jewish burial box (or "ossuary") is from the New Testament era.
Walters Art Museum

Throughout the gospels, Jesus is recognized as a great teacher. The Greek term for "teacher" (*didaskalos*) translates the Hebrew word *rabbi* ("my great one," Matt. 23:8; John 1:38) and was used as an exalted title for teachers of the Jewish law. When Jesus moved from village to village, particularly in Galilee, the crowds immediately recognized a skill and an authority that surpassed what they met in the synagogues. Note Matthew 7:28–29: "When Jesus had finished saying these things, the crowds were amazed at his teaching, because he taught as one who had authority, and not as their teachers of the law."

When we imagine Jesus's teaching in his own time and place, we cannot use profiles of teachers from our own world to understand the nature of his work. Our culture is heir to the Greek tradition, where abstract reasoning and verbal prowess are the measure of the teacher. Jesus's world was different. He communicated through word pictures, dramatic actions, metaphors, and stories. Rather than lecture about religious corruption, Jesus referred to the Pharisees as "whitewashed tombs." Rather than outline the failings of the temple, he cursed a fig tree. This means that we should think of Jesus as a "metaphorical theologian" for whom drama, humor, and storytelling were all a part of his method.[1]

But was Jesus a *sophisticated* teacher? Some scholars have a romantic view of him as a rural village carpenter who offered pithy and simple insights about God. Jesus was indeed a craftsman, but rabbis commonly held such practical jobs. Paul was a tentmaker, and the famous rabbi Shammai was a stonemason. The Mishnah described the law as a "crown" worn by the teacher, but it could not be used to glorify oneself or to gain profit. Instead, the rabbi was to have an occupation through which God granted the means to teach (Mishnah, *Aboth* 4:5).

Jesus's teaching ministry focused on the villages of Galilee, many of which could be found by the Sea of Galilee. This aerial view from the southeast overlooks Magdala, which sits at the base of Mount Arbel.
Bill Schlegel/BiblePlaces.com

Jesus's most famous teachings, such as the Sermon on the Mount, took place in the hills on the Sea of Galilee's northwest shore. This region was known as the Plain of Gennesaret (Matt. 14:34; Mark 6:53). This aerial view from the southwest looks over Tabgha, the traditional location for the calling of the disciples.
Bill Schlegel/BiblePlaces.com

As noted in Chapter 6, Jesus and other young men his age would have regularly met with men who studied and debated the Jewish law over communal meals. Such men called themselves *haberim* ("friends") and took their mandate from Psalm 119:63, "I am a friend [*haber*] to all who fear you."[2] The Jews at Qumran did this regularly (*Damascus Document*, Geniza A, Col. 6:2–10). Jesus had honed debating skills for many years and was adept at theological discourse.

JESUS'S AUTHORITY

Jesus's audiences frequently recognized that he had "authority." For example, Mark writes that after Jesus taught at the synagogue in Capernaum: "The people were

Discovering a "Moses Seat"

When Jesus criticized the Jewish leaders in the temple, he said, "The teachers of the law and the Pharisees sit *in Moses' seat*. So you must be careful to do everything they tell you. But do not do what they do, for they do not practice what they preach" (Matt. 23:2–3, italics added). In Jesus's culture, teachers sat when they taught, and because the rabbi represented the authority of Moses, that chair was called "the Moses seat."

Such stone seats have been discovered in the excavations of fourth-century synagogues at Hammath Tiberias and at Chorazin. The most prominent elder sat on this stone seat, on a raised platform adjacent to the box (or ark) containing the Scripture scrolls; from here he interpreted the teachings of Moses.

This seat is from a synagogue on the Greek island of Delos that dates to the second half of the second century BC, making it the oldest synagogue discovered.
www.HolyLandPhotos.org

amazed at his teaching, because he taught them as one who had authority, not as the teachers of the law" (Mark 1:22). "Authority" is one of the most frequent descriptors for Jesus. Sometimes it was linked to his power (Luke 4:36). At other times the Jewish religious leaders recognized it (Mark 11:27–33). Even a Roman centurion saw it (Matt. 8:5–13).

Among religious teachers, *authority* rarely referred to inherent authority or something tied to personality or formal study. A rabbi *conveyed* authority (Heb. *reshuth*) through a solemn rite performed from Jesus's day up to the third century AD. A rabbi conveying authority "leaned" (*samakh*) on his disciple, placing his hands on the disciple's head. This ritual of ordination was called Semikah, or "leaning," and through it a rabbi "communicated his personality [and] his status to the disciple."[3] Within Jewish tradition, Moses's commissioning of Joshua provided a model for subsequent leaders (Deut. 34:9; cf. Num. 11:25).

Judaism viewed itself as living within a "stream of tradition." That stream carried the Scriptures, as well as traditions, to each new generation. But the capacity to bear those traditions forward required that one be authorized to do so. This was one of the chief functions of "rabbinic authority." If this chain of *reshuth* was broken, Jewish survival might be at risk. In the war of AD 132–135 Hadrian hoped to defeat Judaism by forbidding this ordination, but rabbi Judah ben Baba laid hands on numerous disciples of the deceased Rabbi Akiba and was killed for sabotaging Hadrian's plan.

How did *reshuth* begin? The headwaters of this stream of tradition began with Moses, who was the only man ordained directly by God. Since rabbinic authority was secondary and indirect, the rabbi taught the sacred teachings found inside the stream, teachings that began with Moses. Thus, when a rabbi taught in a synagogue, he would sit in "Moses's seat" (see sidebar).

But if this was the nature of authority, how did Jesus gain his? This question recurs with surprising frequency in the gospels (Matt. 21:23). Jesus not only behaves like a rabbi but has disciples and extends his own authority to them (Mark 6:7). He even interprets the traditions, contrasting his own views with Moses, and he breaks traditions (such as work rules for the Sabbath). Such behavior led to an inevitable deduction: Jesus claimed an ordination not by human hands but by God, *just like Moses*. Thus, he stood outside the stream of Jewish tradition and claimed an entirely new trajectory of tradition. His teaching was thus like new wine that broke old wineskins (Mark 2:22). He equated obeying him to obeying God (Matt. 7:21–23).

Such suggestions of authority made conflict with the Jewish leaders inevitable. Among his followers, it led to reflection about Jesus's true identity. His authority implied something important about his identity in relation to God.

JESUS'S TEACHING STYLE

According to the gospels, crowds were impressed not only by his authority but also by his teaching skill. Simplicity was one of his hallmarks. He rarely used technical theological speech. Jesus also liked to tell stories. But here we need a word of cultural warning: *Simplicity and storytelling do not betray a lack of profundity.*

The effectiveness of Jesus's work stemmed from *how* he communicated. If we recognize these verbal strategies, we will not misinterpret his words. For example, Jesus (and his culture) enjoyed overstatement and gross exaggeration. In Mark 9:43–47 Jesus does not ask his disciples to mutilate themselves but wants to underscore *dramatically* the importance of sin. "If your hand causes you to stumble, cut it off." The truest meaning of such verses is found in their figurative sense. The image is dramatic and shocking to make a point of the seriousness of sin. In a similar way, Jesus talks about straining out gnats and swallowing camels. He describes how we see specks in another's eye but miss the log in our own. These are a few examples of humorous and dramatic exaggerations meant to rivet audiences.

Jesus also used puns where wordplay in the original language created intriguing and amusing meanings. Some of these are in Greek: in Matthew 16:18 Jesus says, "And I tell you that you are Peter [*petros*], and on this rock [*petra*] I will build my church, and the gates of Hades will not overcome it." The Aramaic word for

Jesus commonly used images drawn from his own culture, such as camels (Matt. 23:24).
Pixabay.com

Was Jesus Trilingual?

Four languages were known in the first-century Roman province where Jesus lived (called Judea): Latin, Greek, Hebrew, and Aramaic. Since the New Testament was written in Greek for Greek readers, what we read today in our New Testament is a translation of Jesus's words. However, the gospels betray hints of another language that was likely native to Jesus—Aramaic.

Aramaic (a language related to Hebrew) was used in the villages of Jesus's day. That Jesus spoke Aramaic seems assured (see sidebar on "Aramaic Words in Mark" in ch. 5). Some scholars also believe Jesus knew Hebrew (the language of the Old Testament), for he read from the Hebrew Scriptures when invited (Luke 4). But this was probably not the language he used regularly in rural villages. Aramaic was the commonly spoken language of everyday life.

Jesus likely did not know Latin, the language of Rome. This would have been spoken by the Roman military and government leadership, who also knew Greek. But some scholars argue that Jesus knew Greek, thanks to its common use throughout the country. Yet Jews used it less than we think. Josephus admitted to his lack of ability in Greek and probably had translators render his Aramaic into Greek (*Against Apion* 1.9 [50]). When Titus laid siege to Jerusalem in AD 70, he was unable to talk to the defenders in Greek but sent Josephus to speak to them "in their own language" (*War* 5.9.2 [361]).

rock was *kepha* (English: Cephas; cf. John 1:42; 1 Cor. 3:22) so because Simon Peter was a "rock," he would become a rock *for the church*. Other puns are in Aramaic: in Matthew 23:24 Jesus contrasts a gnat and a camel chiefly because in Aramaic they sound similar (gnat, *galma*; camel, *gamla*).

The mustard seed (*sinapis alba*) was used medicinally in antiquity and as a metaphor for faith in Jesus's teaching.
Gordon Franz

Similes and metaphors provided colorful illustrations of his message. Disciples should be shrewd as snakes and as innocent as doves (Matt. 10:16). Faith should be like a mustard seed (Luke 17:6). The Pharisees were like whitewashed tombs (Matt. 23:27). Disciples should both be the salt of the earth and the light of the world (5:13–16).

Other techniques included proverbs, which expressed wisdom in a memorable or pithy form. "Where your treasure is, there your heart will be also" (Matt. 6:21). Paradoxes created intriguing contradictions that needed unraveling to be understood. How can a widow who contributes two tiny copper coins to the treasury be credited with the largest gift (Mark 12:41–44)? How can the first be last and the last first (10:31)? And how can someone gain life only by losing it (Luke 17:33)?

Jesus stood in the tradition of the Old Testament prophets when he used parabolic acts to demonstrate the meaning of his message. Instead of merely lecturing about God's love for the outcast, he ate meals with tax collectors and sinners

(Luke 19:1–6). He underscored his criticism of Judaism's many Sabbath rules by breaking them (Mark 2:23–27). Rather than lecturing about corruption in the Jerusalem temple, he caused a public disturbance by upending tables and scattering coins (Mark 11:15–19).

This activity helps explain Jesus's many miracles and exorcisms. These were not only acts of compassion, for they also signaled how God's power was at work in Jesus and how his messianic kingdom was entering the world. Curiously, in Mark 1:27 after Jesus's first exorcism in Capernaum, the crowd shouts, "What is this? A new teaching—and with authority! He even gives orders to impure spirits and they obey him."

JESUS'S PARABLES

Almost a third of Jesus's teaching comes in the form of parables. The background of Jesus's parables can be found in the old Hebrew custom of figurative speech, the *mashal*. A *mashal* could be any figurative saying—a proverb, a riddle, even an allegorical story. This explains why so many of Jesus's different teachings are figurative. Proverbs (Luke 4:23), similes (Matt. 10:16), brief stories (Luke 15:1–10), and even longer narratives (Luke 15:11–32) are all called "parables."

The characteristic form of Jesus's parables was the brief, clever word picture, and little has been found among Jesus's contemporaries to parallel it (although almost two thousand parables have been discovered for rabbis in the period following Jesus). Jesus used commonplace themes from his world to catch the attention of his audience and help them understand his message. But while the parables strove to make things clearer, they also had an enigmatic quality that could make the hearer puzzled. Parables both exclude listeners as well as invite them in. Following some of Jesus's sayings, he had to take his disciples aside to explain it to them (Mark 4:33–34). In this sense, parables *provoke a response* and lead us to probe deeper, to react in frustration, to depart perplexed, or to step nearer, seeking answers.

In recent years, new literary analysis has enriched our understanding of the parables. Scholars have shown that the parables not only use images and metaphors unique to the biblical period but also employ a *poetic form* that made them poignant to hear and easy to retain. Some refer to the symmetry of the parables and how they provide repetitive structures that enhance the parable's interest and memorization. In some cases it is a simple reversal, such as we find in Mark 2:27. Note how the terms "Sabbath" and "man" reverse order, forming an X, like a Greek letter *chi* (giving this form the title, *chiasmus*).

> The *Sabbath* was made for *man*,
> not *man* for the *Sabbath*.

The Parabolic Sayings of Jesus

Jesus's use of parables and imagery characterized his ministry. The following list sets out the synoptic parables, organized by the periods of Jesus's ministry. In John's gospel Jesus does employ imagery and metaphor (4:1–42; 10:1–42; 15:1–16) but nothing similar to the Synoptic parables.[4] (Where available, parables in the *Gospel of Thomas* are listed for comparison.)

The Sermon on the Mount (Matthew)

The salt of the earth (Matt. 5:13; Mark 9:49–50; Luke 14:34–35)
The light of the world (Matt. 5:14–15; Mark 4:21; Luke 8:16; cf. 11:33; John 8:12)
On treasures (Matt. 6:19–21; Luke 12:33–34; cf. 16:9)
The sound eye (Matt. 6:22–23; Luke 11:34–36)
On serving two masters (Matt. 6:24; Luke 16:13)
The birds of the air and the lilies of the field (Matt. 6:26–30; Luke 12:24–28)
The speck in the eye (Matt. 7:3, 5; Luke 6:41–42; cf. *Thomas* 27)
On profaning the holy (Matt. 7:6)
The two ways (Matt. 7:13–14; Luke 13:23–24)
The wolves in sheep's clothing (Matt. 7:15–20; cf. 3:10; Luke 6:43–45; cf. 3:9)
The house built on the rock (Matt. 7:24–27; Luke 6:47–49)

Galilean Ministry

The harvest is great (Matt. 9:35–38; cf. 4:23; 14:14; Mark 6:6, 34; Luke 8:1; 10:2; John 4:35)
The two debtors (Luke 7:41–43)
He who has ears to hear, let him hear (Matt. 11:15; 13:9, 43; Mark 4:9, 23; Luke 8:8; 14:35)
The sign of Jonah (Matt. 12:38–42; 16:1–4; Mark 8:11–12; Luke 11:16, 19–32; John 6:30)
The parable of the sower (Matt. 13:1–9; Mark 4:1–9; Luke 8:4–8; cf. *Thomas* 8)
The reason for speaking in parables (Matt. 13:10–17; Mark 4:10–20, 25; Luke 8:9–16, 18; John 9:39)
The interpretation of the parable of the sower (Matt. 13:18–23; Mark 4:13–20; Luke 8:11–15)
Jesus's true family (Matt. 12:46–50; cf. 7:21; Mark 3:20–21, 31–35; Luke 8:19–21; John 15:14)
The seed growing secretly (Mark 4:26–29)
The wheat and the weeds (Matt. 13:24–30)
The mustard seed (Matt. 13:31–32.; Mark 4:30–32; Luke 13:18–19; cf. *Thomas* 20)
The leaven (Matt. 13:33; Luke 13:20–21)
Jesus's use of parables (Matt. 13:34–35; Mark 4:33–34)
The interpretation of the parable of the weeds (Matt. 13:36–43)
The hidden treasure and the pearl of great price (Matt. 13:44–46)
The fish net (Matt. 13:47–50)
Treasures old and new (Matt. 13:51–52)
The unforgiving servant (Matt. 18:23–35)

On the Way to Jerusalem (Luke)

The good Samaritan (Luke 10:29–37)
The friend at midnight (Luke 11:5–8)
Light (Luke 11:33; cf. 8:16; Matt. 5:15; Mark 4:21)
The sound eye (Luke 11:34–36; Matt. 6:22–23)
The rich fool (Luke 12:16–21; cf. *Thomas* 64)
On treasures (Luke 12:33–34)
The barren fig tree (Luke 13:1–9; cf. Matt. 21:18–19; Mark 11:12–14)
The mustard seed (Luke 13:18–19; Matt. 13:31–32; Mark 4:30–32)
The leaven (Luke 13:20–21; Matt. 13:33)
The great supper (Luke 14:15–24; cf. Matt. 22:1–14)

The cost of building a tower and going to war (Luke 14:28–33)
Salt (Luke 14:34–35; Matt. 5:13; Mark 9:49–50)
The lost sheep (Luke 15:1–7)
The lost coin (Luke 15:8–10)
The lost (prodigal) son (Luke 15:11–32)
The unjust steward (Luke 16:1–9)
On serving two masters (Luke 16:13; Matt. 6:24)
The rich man and Lazarus (Luke 16:19–31)
On being unprofitable servants (Luke 17:7–10)
The unjust judge (Luke 18:1–8)
The Pharisee and the tax collector (Luke 18:9–14)

Ministry in Judea

On riches (Matt. 19:23–30; Mark 10:23–31; Luke 18:24–30)
The laborers in the vineyard (Matt. 20:1–16)
The pounds (Luke 19:11–27; cf. Matt. 25:14–40; Mark 13:34)

Final Ministry in Jerusalem

The two sons (Matt. 21:28–32)
The vineyard and the laborers (Matt. 21:33–46; Mark 12:1–12; Luke 20:9–19; *Thomas* 66)
The great supper (Matt. 22:1–14)
The poor widow (Mark 12:41–44; Luke 21:1–4)
The fig tree (Matt. 24:32–36; Mark 13:28–32; Luke 21:29–33)
The exhortation to watch (Mark 13:33–37; cf. Matt. 25:13–15; 21:34–36)
The flood, watching, and the thief in the night (Matt. 24:37–44; Luke 17:26–36; 12:39–40; cf. Mark 13:35)
The good and wicked servants (Matt. 24:45–51; cf. 25:21; Luke 12:41–46; cf. 19:17)
The ten virgins (Matt. 25:1–13; cf. Mark 13:33–37; Luke 12:35–38; 13:25–28)
The talents (Matt. 25:14–30; cf. Mark 13:34; Luke 19:11–27)
The sheep and the goats (Matt. 25:31–46)

Another form can be found in Luke 11:9–10. In each paragraph, the words "ask," "seek," and "knock" provide an artful symmetry:

1 *Ask* and it will be given to you;
2 *seek* and you will find;
3 *knock* and the door will be opened to you.
1' For everyone who *asks* receives;
2' the one who *seeks* finds;
3' and to the one who *knocks*, the door will be opened.

In the parable of the lost sheep (Luke 15:4–7) three lines frame a series that invert their themes. As generally happens, the central idea of the structure is found in the turning point: God's celebration of the one who is lost.[5]

A Suppose one of you has a hundred sheep
B and loses one of them.
C Doesn't he leave the ninety-nine in the open country
1 and go after the *lost* sheep

2 until he *finds* it? And when he *finds* it,

3 he *joyfully* puts it on his shoulders

4 and *goes home.*

4' Then he calls his *friends* and neighbors together

3' and says, "*Rejoice* with me;

2' I have *found*

1' my *lost* sheep."

A' I tell you that in the same way there will be more rejoicing in heaven

B' over one sinner who repents

C' than over ninety-nine righteous persons who do not need to repent.

There is considerable discussion among scholars on how to interpret the parables. Our instinct to allegorize each of them down to the smallest detail has now been rejected. Many recent scholars have emphasized that at the heart of each parable we find a crisis—a point or points of stark contrast that shock us, forcing us to make a value judgment on a theme or character. For instance, the foolish barn builder seems to be living with God's blessing, evidenced by his material wealth, until suddenly he hears God's voice, "You fool! This very night your life will be demanded from you" (Luke 12:20). Suddenly we are surprised, forced to realign our thinking.

Some of the parables do have allegorical elements (e.g., the parable of the sower), but this is secondary to the crisis of decision. And the most important issue is to understand the cultural elements at work in each parable. These are stories told from another culture and time, and we read them as foreigners.

In northern Israel (Qatzrin), scholars have created models of residential life in fourth-century Israel (a period culturally similar to the first century). Here a plow and other tools are stored inside a Jewish home. These are the types of cultural elements that would be easily understood by Jesus's listeners.
Todd Bolen/BiblePlaces.com

What does it mean when a young son asks for his inheritance? Or when a coin is lost? Reading the parables is like listening to the musical rhythms of another world. If we cannot recognize this music—or worse yet, if we fail even to admit our own foreignness to its sounds—we will miss the parables' deeper meanings and misrepresent what Jesus intended to teach. A parable in this sense is like a box that we open carefully, wondering what is inside. What we don't expect is that inside this box is a spring that surprises us and shocks us. The key to experiencing this shock is found in unlocking the cultural assumptions embedded in the parable. Irony, humor, drama, and surprise are each culturally embedded elements that foreign readers will miss.

THEMES IN JESUS'S TEACHING

The Kingdom of God

The primary theme of Jesus's teaching was his announcement of the arrival of God's kingdom (Mark 1:15). This topic was at the center of his teaching (Matt. 4:17, 23; Mark 1:15; Luke 9:11; Acts 1:3). The phrases "kingdom of God" and "kingdom of heaven" (which are synonyms) occur with marked frequency in each gospel (Matthew 55x, Mark 20x, Luke 46x, John 5x). If we account for parallel sayings, we have about eighty separate sayings where Jesus teaches about God's kingdom.

But what was this kingdom? Was it a political entity that might compete with Roman rule? Did it imply a revolution? Roman bureaucrats were familiar with provincial kingdoms, and if Jesus's kingdom was tied to nationalism and political resistance, it would be immediately suppressed. Or was this kingdom a heavenly

Many of Jesus's most dramatic teachings took place when he arrived in Jerusalem and entered the temple. The excavation of Herodian Jerusalem uncovered these first-century stairs on the south side of the temple that were in heavy use during Jesus's lifetime.
Public Domain

God's War Plans

The Dead Sea Scrolls provided battle plans to help inaugurate God's kingdom on earth. Here Qumran's "sons of light" will be readied to fight the "sons of darkness" in the apocalyptic battle that will end human history.

The first division shall be armed with a spear and a shield, and the second division will be equipped with a shield and a sword, to bring down the slain by the judgment of God, and to bend the enemy formation by the power of God, to pay the reward of their wickedness to all the nations of vanity. And sovereignty shall be to the God of Israel, and he shall accomplish mighty deeds by the saints of his people (1QM [The War Scroll], 6:5–6. Dupont-Sommer, *The Essene Writings from Qumran*, trans. Vermes, G., Gloucester, Ma.: Peter Smith, 1973).

Jesus's Politics Are Tested

Jesus's frequent discussion about a "kingdom" led some to worry about his political aspirations. After he fed five thousand people in Mark 6, even Herod Antipas began making worried inquiries about him.

On his last visit to Jerusalem, assistants to the temple leadership disguised themselves as disciples and approached Jesus in public, asking him: "What is your opinion? Is it right to pay the imperial tax to Caesar or not" (Matt. 22:17)? This question was not simply about tax revenue. It was a veiled political probe. One of the earliest revolts against Roman rule used the refusal to pay taxes as a form of resistance. Thus, we can reframe the question: "Teacher, do you support the Jewish resistance against Rome?" Read Matthew 22:18–22 to see how artfully Jesus frames his answer.

reality whose benefits were only spiritually available—either now or sometime after death?

The notion that God ruled and sustained the universe *like a king* was commonplace in Jewish thinking (Ps. 22:28). He was deemed the only rightful king of his people (Ps. 47), whose throne was located in Jerusalem (Ps. 48). But the Old Testament prophets also looked forward to a future period when God's kingdom would be asserted with determination—when Israel's enemies would be vanquished (Isa. 34:12), exiles would come home (Isa. 52:7–12), and an everlasting kingdom would be established in Jerusalem (Zech. 14:9–17).

This *eschatological* (or "climactic") coming of God's kingdom was felt fervently in Jesus's day and gave birth to an entire literature devoted to explaining it. Such *apocalyptic* literature (e.g., *Jubilees*, *1 Enoch*, *Psalms of Solomon*) announced the *imminent* conclusion to commonplace human history and a dramatic in-breaking of God's rule. The sectarian Jews in the deserts of Qumran, for example, anticipated that God would soon come in power to lead them in victory (see sidebar on "God's War Plans").

Jesus's affirmation of God's sustaining care of the universe came as no surprise to his Jewish audiences (Matt. 6:25–34). Nor did it surprise them when he spoke about the kingdom as an experience in heaven, meant for those who would banquet after death with God's people of old (Matt. 8:11–12; Mark 10:17–30). Even Jesus looked forward to this time (Luke 22:16, 18). When he arrived in Jerusalem on his final visit, the crowds thought that his coming would be a catalyst for the birth of this kingdom (Mark 11:10; Luke 19:11). But they were wrong. Jesus believed that a final judgment would only come with his own second coming in power (Mark 8:38; 13:26; 14:62; Luke 17:24–30).

What set Jesus apart from other teachers in Judaism was his announcement that something dramatic and epic was happening *in the present*, that in some way not foreseen, the rule of God's kingdom was *now*

Messianic Zeal

Some Jewish groups held a fervent expectation that God would send an anointed (Heb. "messiah") messenger who would be a catalyst for the arrival of God's rule on earth. He would end the gentile occupation of Judea and bring about the resumption of the great kingdom of David (2 Sam. 7). The most explicit outline of this expectation can be found in the *Psalms of Solomon*, written within seventy-five years of Jesus's ministry:

> See, Lord, and raise up for them their king, the son of David, to rule over your servant Israel.... Undergird him with the strength to destroy the unrighteous rulers, to purge Jerusalem from gentiles. He will gather a holy people whom he will lead in righteousness.... He will distribute them upon the land according to their tribes; the alien and the foreigner will no longer live near them.... And he will have gentile nations serving him under his yoke, and he will glorify the Lord in (a place) prominent (above) the whole earth.... And he will be a righteous king over them, taught by God.... There will be no unrighteousness among them in his days, for all shall be holy, and their king shall be the Lord Messiah (*Psalms of Solomon* 17:21–32).[6]

While Jesus compares kingdom growth to yeast that spreads mysteriously through dough, here a woman bakes traditional flatbread, made without yeast, that likely reflects traditions reaching back to antiquity.
Inna Reznik/Shutterstock

taking hold of the world. He told his followers that the kingdom is something that can be entered (Matt. 5:20; 7:21), that people can now be "in" the kingdom (13:41, 43), and that it is a gift to people (Luke 12:32). This kingdom was presently appearing (Luke 19:11).

Note, for example, in Matthew 12:28 (also Luke 11:20) how Jesus indicated that his defeat of a demon through an exorcism signaled far more than a healing miracle; it unveiled the power of his kingdom overturning Satan's power and breaking his grip on the world. A page had been turned; and the relationship between God and the world would never be the same.

Jesus described this kingdom as experiencing resistance and hostility (Matt. 11:12). When he sent his followers out to preach, the arrival of this new order was at the heart of their message (Matt. 10:5–7). In Luke 17:20–21, when Jesus fielded a question about the coming kingdom and the end of the world, he gave an unexpected response: "The coming of the kingdom of God is not something that can be observed, nor will people say, 'Here it is,' or 'There it is,' because the kingdom of God is in your midst."

The advancement of this kingdom can best be seen in Jesus's so-called "parables of growth." Jesus compared kingdom growth to seed scattered on the ground that grows unexpectedly (Mark 4:26–29), to a mustard seed that begins small only to become a tremendous bush (4:30–32), or to yeast that spreads mysteriously through dough (Matt. 13:33). Since this kingdom has now made its arrival, judgment of the world has become inevitable. Weeds grow along with the wheat (Matt. 13:24–30), but at the climax of history, there will be a great "sorting out," when useless weeds are removed and judged.

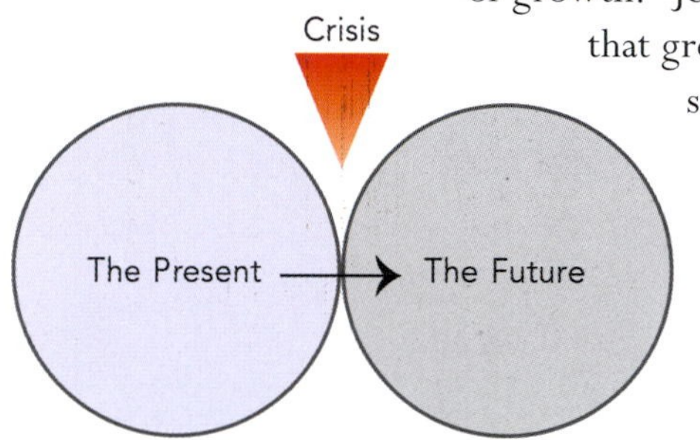

Jewish Eschatology: God's singular intervention.

Therefore, every person *must make a decision* whether or not to belong to this kingdom. Jesus is like a sower, and the only pertinent question is whether we permit this seed to germinate (Matt. 13:1–9). Have we discovered this kingdom as the most precious thing we own, like a precious pearl sought for a lifetime or a treasure discovered by surprise (Matt. 13:44–46)?

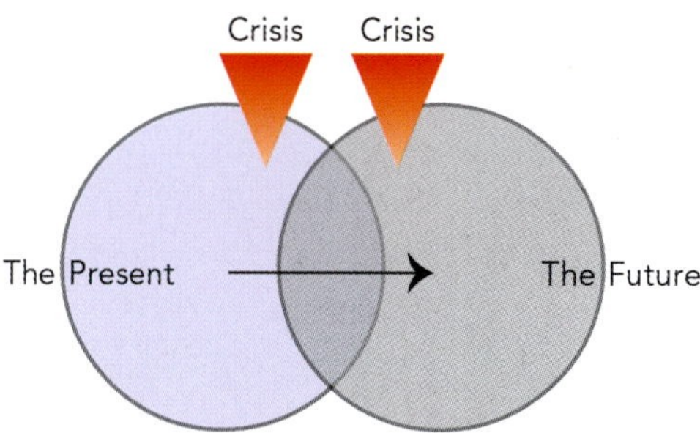

Christian Eschatology: An interim reality inaugurated by Jesus at his birth and concluded by Jesus at his second coming.

In sum, Jesus altered the basic framework of Jewish eschatology. Rather than seeing the kingdom arrive in a climactic, definitive event, Jesus spoke of an interim state—the time of the church—when God's power would be active through the Spirit. The church still awaits its final redemption in Christ's second coming.

In summary, this *eschatological adjustment* can be illustrated helpfully in the diagrams to the left. Jewish expectation understood that the current world and its affairs (the "present") would find their conclusion when God intervened (the "crisis") and established the national life of biblical Israel. This would bring judgment on the gentiles, purify Jerusalem, and bring about a degree of faithfulness to the law not seen before. This would inaugurate a kingdom centered on Jewish ethnicity but bring blessing to the entire world.

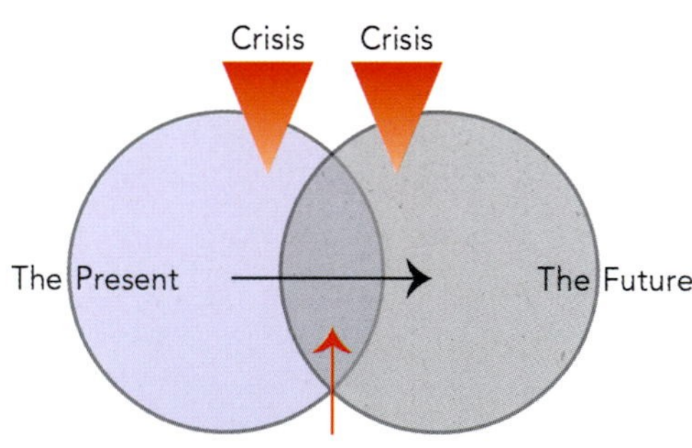

Jesus's followers: life between two realities.

Jesus's understanding of the kingdom differed. His arrival inaugurated a reality of the kingdom of God that had never been seen before. Jesus understood that the Spirit of God that was expected in the Jewish future kingdom was now at work in his own ministry. This was unprecedented. This new reality began with his arrival (the first "crisis") and would culminate with his second coming (the second "crisis"), making an interim period of life-in-the-Spirit that his followers could experience. Jesus's followers announced not simply that the Messiah had come but that the *messianic era* had arrived and that they were experiencing a foretaste of what would be fully realized in the future.

This notion of an interim reality (or technically, a "realized eschatology") is a uniquely Christian concept. It began with the teaching and experience of Jesus and was continued in the life of the early church. This notion forms the backdrop of Christian experience described in the book of Acts and is presupposed in the teaching of Paul.

Discipleship in the Kingdom

In establishing his kingdom, Jesus formed around himself "disciples," whose main task was to obey him and his words. Jesus did not simply recall Jews to their traditions, admonishing them to greater faithfulness to Moses (though this was important, Matt. 5:17–18). Nor did he only promote a revival of wisdom or ethics (though this was important too, 5:19–20). He called men and women *to himself*. This is one of the distinct features that set Jesus apart from other rabbis of his day. People left their trades to become his followers (Mark 1:16–20) and were told that personal obedience to him and his words meant everything (Luke 6:46–49). Jesus formed a self-conscious messianic community, where they would find qualities of forgiveness, generosity, love, and devotion absent in the rest of the world. And with these messianic qualities they would transform the world.

Jesus formed this circle of followers from those who lived on the margins of society: tax collectors, sinners, and prostitutes. He was willing to have direct contact with lepers and risk defilement (Mark 1:40–41). He would have contact with women who were deeply ill, even if contact with that illness put his entire ministry in jeopardy (Luke 8:43–48). He sometimes answered his critics with parables, reminding them that God was like a shepherd in search of a lost sheep or a woman in search of a lost coin (15:1–10)—or more powerfully, like a father scanning the horizon for his lost son (15:11–32). At other times he answered his critics with a proverb: "It is not the healthy who need a doctor, but the sick. I have not come to call the righteous, but sinners" (Mark 2:17). This was clearly an unprecedented kingdom since it was populated by many who lived on the margins of society.

Jesus's unique vision of God as Father of everyone shaped his compassion for humanity—sinner and pious, Jew, Samaritan, and gentile. God is referred to as "Father" fifteen times in the Old Testament (e.g., Isa. 63:16), though these lacked a personal element. But this was Jesus's typical way of referring to God. In Mark 14:36 we even have the Aramaic term "*Abba*." *Abba* was an informal word used

Jesus taught that God is like a shepherd searching for and protecting his sheep (Luke 15:3–7; John 10:1–18). Here a Palestinian shepherd is living a shepherd's life that has not changed for centuries.
Wikimedia Commons, Public Domain

Jesus's call to discipleship demanded a serious commitment. "No one who puts a hand to the plow and looks back is fit for service in the kingdom of God" (Luke 9:62). This minimally decorated sarcophagus from the Antalya Museum shows a farmer plowing with an ox goad.
www.HolyLandPhotos.org

generally by children for their fathers. Jesus's habit was so well known that even Greek-speaking Christians used *Abba* (Rom. 8:15–16; Gal. 4:6).

Jewish disciples who had prayed their entire lives listened to Jesus and asked him to teach them to pray (Luke 11:1). His prayers were different. He did not pray in Hebrew or use the stock liturgical phrases. His model prayer was an outline of intimate conversation with God (the Lord's Prayer; Matt. 6:7–15; Luke 11:2–4).

Similarly, he told parables about prayer that emphasized God's eagerness to respond to our need (Luke 11:5–13); our only requirement is to come to him with humility (18:9–14). In a world where religious symbols were often on public display, Jesus called for profound authenticity in every spiritual endeavor. Public things like fasting and tithing should be hidden (Matt. 6:1–6, 16–18), while more difficult signs of faith, like reconciliation and love (5:23–24, 43–46), should be hallmarks of his community.

The Ethics of the Kingdom

It would be a mistake to think that discipleship in this kingdom is only a matter of spiritual renewal and private devotion to Jesus. Jesus also sought a transformation in his followers' lives. Jesus taught that the reign of God, now empowered by the Spirit, would open new possibilities to human righteousness. Men and women are placed under the ethics of the kingdom and can live out those ethics through his Son. The seemingly impossible standards of the Sermon on the Mount can only portray "the ideal of the person in whose life the reign of God is absolutely realized."[7]

The starting point for these ethics is the righteousness of the inner life—a righteousness that ought to exceed that of the Pharisees (Matt. 5:20). Or more precisely, the starting point consists of a "renewed heart." Thus, while adultery remains a sin, Jesus calls us to curb lust (5:27–30). And while murder is condemned, anger must likewise be resolved (5:21–26). Love must be exhaustive, shown even to those who are enemies. Jesus said, "Love your enemies, do good to them, and lend to them without expecting to get anything back. Then your reward will be great, and you will be children of the Most High, because he is kind to the ungrateful and wicked" (Luke 6:35). How else could such courageous decisions be lived except through a transforming encounter with God?

This is why at the heart of Jesus's teaching is a demand that his hearers make a critical decision—that they repent, turn, and become a disciple (Matt. 13:45–46). Any commitment that stands in the way must be jettisoned at once. The rich young ruler must give up his wealth (Mark 10:17–22). Suddenly, Jesus's paradoxical statements become clear: unless you lose your life, you cannot find it (Matt. 10:39).

The first ethical demand of the kingdom is to love God wholly (Matt. 22:37–38). And the second follows it quickly: "'Love your neighbor as yourself.' All the Law and the Prophets hang on these two commandments" (22:39–40). The ethics of Jesus thus spring from this encounter, and what one learns about God's affection, grace, and forgiveness must then be borne to others. To do otherwise will falsify one's claim to kingdom membership; it will fulfill the role of "hypocrite" (Luke 6:42).

When asked about the most important law, Jesus recited the great *Shema*, recited twice each day and taken from Deuteronomy 6 (see Matt. 22:37–38). Shown here is the Nash Papyrus, a second-century AD Hebrew fragment that begins with the commandments and ends with the *Shema*. *Wikimedia Commons, PD-US*

But to integrate religious experience into life means rethinking major questions of life: Who are my neighbors and what are my obligations to them (Luke 10:30–35)? How many times must I forgive (Matt. 18:21–22)? How much wealth may I collect (Luke 12:16–20)? These questions signal the dawning of the kingdom in the world. Lives lived under such discipleship will become "a light on a hill" that is visible for the entire world to see (cf. Matt. 5:14–16).

The Cross and the Kingdom

Once Jesus's public identity was confirmed among his disciples at Caesarea Philippi (Mark 8:27–30), the gospels indicate that he chose to reframe his messiahship as a "way of the cross": "Whoever wants to be my disciple must deny themselves and take up their cross and follow me" (Matt. 16:24). Three times

Grape production was common in the first century. Using the imagery from Isaiah 5, Jesus compared Israel to a tended vineyard (Mark 12:1–12).
© 2012 by Zondervan

Jesus made predictions about dying, and each gained greater and greater specificity. As he moved toward his final Jerusalem visit, his death became a prominent theme in his teaching, and the disciples became increasingly wary (Mark 10:32–33).

This expectation of death appeared early in Jesus's ministry. He once described himself as a bridegroom whose presence at his wedding banquet naturally led to feasting and celebration. But then, he added, "the time will come when the bridegroom will be *taken* from them, and on that day they will fast" (Mark 2:20, italics added). This verb "taken" (Gk. *apairo*) is a term for violent removal (such as kidnapping; cf. Isa. 53:8). Not long after saying this, Jesus found himself in conflict with some of the Pharisees who were dismayed at his violation of Sabbath law. In an exquisite example of foreshadowing, Mark tells us that immediately these men went out and plotted how they might kill him (Mark 3:6).

Once in Jerusalem during his final week, Jesus offered one of his most important parables to explain his approaching death (Matt. 21:33–46; Mark 12:1–12; Luke 20:9–19). This story describes a vineyard whose tenants refuse to give its owner the rightful portion of the vineyard's yield. The owner sends couriers to the tenants, but they are rejected. Then he sends his son. Thinking that if they kill the owner's heir they might gain the vineyard for themselves, the son is expelled from the vineyard and murdered. The imagery of a vineyard and frustrated expectation comes directly from Isaiah 5:1–7. God had sent his prophets repeatedly to call for "fruit" from his people, and now judgment must result. Here Jesus poignantly shows that his own mission is like that of the son, and his death brings tremendous offense to God himself.

Ancient Roman pottery such as this cup, discovered in a first-century home in Jerusalem, may have been the type used during the final Passover of Jesus. "After taking the cup, he gave thanks and said, 'Take this . . .'" (Luke 22:17).
© 2018 by Zondervan

But Jesus's death in the gospels is not an accident. Jesus was not a martyr. He knew he was accomplishing something purposeful for the kingdom he was establishing. We hear this first from John the Baptist, who introduces Jesus publicly with the words: "Look, the Lamb of God, who takes away the sin of the world!" (John 1:29). Jesus's life would end with a voluntary death, a sacrificial death, no different from the lamb sacrificed each day at the temple.

Following his third and final prediction of the cross (Mark 10:33–34), a quarrel broke out about greatness in the kingdom. James and John wanted places of honor among the twelve apostles. Jesus corrected their presumptuous quest for prestige: "The Son of Man did not come to be served, but to serve, and to give his life *as a ransom* for many" (Mark 10:45, italics added; cf. John 6:51). Here Jesus is explaining the meaning of his death as a "ransom" (Gk. *lytron*). This was a payment that in some manner freed a captive. Jesus here suggests that his death will supply some substitution, some exchange for others in jeopardy. Jesus may well have had in mind the poignant image of the Suffering Servant of Isaiah 53:11.

Scholars at the Tantur Ecumenical Institute near Bethlehem here attempt to reconstruct the cross as it may have been seen in antiquity.
Todd Bolen/BiblePlaces.com

Perhaps the most profound hours of teaching came when Jesus gathered with his apostles for a last Passover meal. Despite the distress of this crisis, he taught them carefully about his own return (John 16:16–24); the promise of the Holy Spirit, who would comfort and equip them (14:16, 26; 15:26; 16:13); the impending persecution that would follow (15:18–27); and the quality of love that should characterize the community of believers (13:34–35; 15:12–17). During this meal, he picked up a loaf of bread, broke it, and ceremonially named it as representing his body: "'This is my body given for you; do this in remembrance of me.' In the same way, after the supper he took the cup, saying, 'This cup is the new covenant in my blood'" (Luke 22:19–20).

Ordinarily, ancient covenants were established with the shedding of blood (Gen. 15:7–11; Ex. 24:1–10). Even the exodus required the sacrificial death of a lamb (12:22–23). Now Jesus intimated that his death was such a sacrifice and that it would establish a new covenant for this new kingdom. The earliest Christians saw profound symbolism in Jesus's crucifixion: *he was a Passover lamb slain for God's people.* John reports that when Jesus was on the cross, his legs were not broken, just as the Passover lamb could not have broken bones (John 19:36; cf. Num. 9:12). When Jesus was cut with a spear (John 19:34), blood flowed freely from his side, fulfilling yet another requirement of slain lambs, that their blood flow freely (Mishnah, *Hullin* 2:6).

Christology

The accelerating revelation of who Jesus was in his earthly ministry climaxed with the resurrection. At once his followers needed new categories to understand him. In John's language, Jesus had been "glorified" (John 12:23; 7:39), and the cross, rather than a place of abandonment and shame, could be seen as a "lifting up" as he began his movement back to the Father (John 8:28; 12:32, 34). This reflection no doubt prompted the earliest Christians to think about the events in Jesus's life from a new point of view.

In this sense, the resurrection forced the question of Christology. Christology (or the doctrine of Christ) refers to theological meaning or assessment of the person of Jesus. What was his relation to God the Father? What was the nature of his own humanity and divine identity? Even though these questions would be definitively answered in church councils centuries later, still, the New Testament provides evidence that the earliest Christians were probing these questions from the beginning. What did Jesus's birth signify? How do we interpret his earthly life (his miracles, his sayings, his deeds)? And how do we understand the deeper meanings of his death and resurrection? In other words, what was Jesus's truest identity?

For example, Jesus once prayed the following: "I praise you, Father, Lord of heaven and earth, because you have hidden these things from the wise and learned, and revealed them to little children. Yes, Father, for this is what you were pleased to do. All things have been committed to me by my Father. No one knows the Son except the Father, and no one knows the Father except the Son and those to whom the Son chooses to reveal him" (Matt. 11:25–27).

Jesus's own self-understanding thus included a keen awareness of his unique place with God, a place no other human shared. Suddenly, Jesus's uncanny authority began to move into focus, as did his uncompromising victory over Satan. The people then understood that in him was something far greater than they ever imagined possible.

How did Jesus exhibit this understanding of his role with God? For one, he often assumed divine prerogatives. For example, when he forgave the sins of a paralytic, the scribes immediately took offense: "Who can forgive sins but God alone?" (Mark 2:7). He repeated this with a marginalized woman who tried to rescue him at a hostile banquet, and again the Jewish leaders became angry (Luke 7:49). Jesus also viewed himself fulfilling roles reserved for God. He saw himself as God seeking out lost sheep (Luke 15:3–7). After breaking the Sabbath by healing a man, he defended his actions by arguing that God himself was working through him (John 5:1–24).

Jesus even cited the Old Testament law and followed such citations with a predictable formula: "You have heard that it was said . . . but I tell you . . ." (Matt. 5:22, 28, 32, 34, 39, 44). When he taught, he reinforced his sayings with a finality that had no parallel in Judaism. He prefaced them with a phrase, "I tell you the truth" (NIV) or "truly" (RSV, NRSV). This translates the word *amen*, a Hebrew term that means "surely" or "firmly."

Was it not enough to follow and obey Jesus? Was it necessary to embrace some commitment to *who he was*? Matthew and Luke offer nativity stories that give us important hints that in the virgin birth we have evidence of a person who exceeds the role of the average child. God was at work in Jesus's birth in unprecedented ways. Mark begins his written gospel with an affirmation that his record tells not simply *the gospel*, but the "good news about Jesus the Messiah" (Mark 1:1). Of course, this is Mark's own confession of faith, but it signals to his readers that the story he is about to tell us is about a man whose identity rests with God.

Thirteenth-century illuminated manuscript depicting Jesus surrounded by the symbols for the four evangelists
Wikimedia Commons, PD-US

What the Synoptic Gospels record with subtlety, John's gospel makes explicit. Not only does John's Jesus evoke all the synoptic hints of unique identity, but Jesus himself explains how his person and work stem directly from God. Jesus once said, "The words I say to you I do not speak on my own authority. Rather, it is the Father, living in me, who is doing his work" (John 14:10).

The gospel writers give us clues to Jesus's identity through the list of titles that appear throughout their stories. For us to understand him, we must understand these carefully in their own original context. (1) *Messiah* is a transliteration of the Hebrew *mashiach* and refers to "the anointed one," a title used in the Old Testament to describe kings and prophets. In the intertestamental period, it referred to an "anointed king" who would usher in the eschatological kingdom of Israel. This term was translated into Greek as "Christ."

(2) *Son of God* (or Son) was another Old Testament title used for Israel's kings as well as heavenly beings such as angels. It was associated with the coming Messiah, and in the gospels it lays claim to Jesus's intimate and unparalleled relationship with the Father.

(3) Jesus's favorite self-designation was *Son of Man* (found 69x in the Synoptic Gospels and 13x in John). In Hebrew the phrase simply meant "man," but in Daniel 7:13 and elsewhere in early Judaism, it likely took on a specialized use for a celestial figure (e.g., *1 Enoch* 46:4; 48:2; 62:9, 11; 71:17).

Each of these titles have been studied at length. They help clarify Jesus's identity. Each gospel writer sought to explain who Jesus was. And in some cases, Jesus's true self exceeded their ability to describe him.

SUMMARY

Although Jesus's birth, death, resurrection, and ability to perform miracles are often the subjects of considerable disagreement, there remains a remarkable consensus that Jesus was a great teacher. His authority was immediately recognizable to those who listened, and his strategy of teaching in parables was provocative as well as innovative. The power and occasional ambiguity of Jesus's teaching are demonstrated by the wide variety of responses it provoked. While some merely marveled at his words, others, after hearing him teach, left everything behind to follow him, while still others plotted to violently take his life. By announcing the arrival of the kingdom of God, Jesus reoriented his audience's expectations and priorities. A longing for political reversal was replaced with the reversal of a new ethical system where the one who serves will be the greatest and the arrogant and powerful will be the least. Such humility through service, however, was only a taste of what Jesus required of his followers. Just as his own ministry would end in suffering and death, so Jesus warned that all who responded to his teaching by becoming his disciples would be called to take up their crosses daily and follow him.

Questions for Discussion

1. What are the essential elements in Jesus's conflict with the Pharisees and the scribes? What fundamental theological ideas did they find in him that were unnerving?
2. What is the relationship between the kingdom Jesus announced and the church that we experience from day to day?
3. What are some guidelines that will assure us that when we interpret a parable, we will not misrepresent Jesus's intention?
4. Why are Jesus's ethical teachings so popular—even among those who profess no faith in Christ?
5. Jesus's serious ethical demands are sometimes sharply contrasted with Paul's emphasis on grace. Is there a way to synthesize these emphases?

BIBLIOGRAPHY

Introductory

Bailey, K. E. *Poet and Peasant and Through Peasant Eyes: A Literary Cultural Approach to the Parables in Luke*. Combined ed. Grand Rapids: Eerdmans, 1983.

Blomberg, C. *Interpreting the Parables*. Downers Grove, IL: InterVarsity Press, 2012.

Green, J., S. McKnight, and I. H. Marshall. *Dictionary of Jesus and the Gospels*. Downers Grove, IL: InterVarsity Press, 2013.

Advanced

Dunn, J. D. G. *Jesus Remembered*. Grand Rapids: Eerdmans, 2003.

Ladd, G. E. *A Theology of the New Testament*. Grand Rapids: Eerdmans, 1974, 1993.

Wright, N. T. *Jesus and the Victory of God*. Minneapolis: Fortress, 1996.

NOTES

1. K. E. Bailey, "Jesus the Metaphorical Theologian and the Rabbinic World," in *Jacob and the Prodigal: How Jesus Retold Israel's Story* (Downers Grove, IL: InterVarsity Press, 2003), 21–22.

2. S. Safrai, "Religion in Everyday Life," in S. Safrai and M. Stern, eds., *The Jewish People in the First Century* (Philadelphia: Fortress, 1976), 2:803–4.

3. D. Daube, "Rabbinic Authority," in *The New Testament and Rabbinic Judaism* (London: Athone, 1956), 207.

4. C. Brown, ed., *The New International Dictionary of New Testament Theology* (Grand Rapids: Zondervan, 1976), 2:749–51.

5. K. E. Bailey, *Finding the Lost: Cultural Keys to Luke 15* (St. Louis: Concordia, 1989). Bailey also does this for the parable of the lost son. The translation here is formal.

6. J. H. Charlesworth, ed., *The Old Testament Pseudepigrapha* (Garden City, NY: Doubleday, 1983), 2:667.

7. G. Ladd, *A Theology of the New Testament* (Grand Rapids: Eerdmans, 1993), 127; N. T. Wright, *Jesus and the Victory of God* (Minneapolis: Fortress, 1996), 282–87.

Chapter 8

THE GOSPEL ACCORDING TO MATTHEW

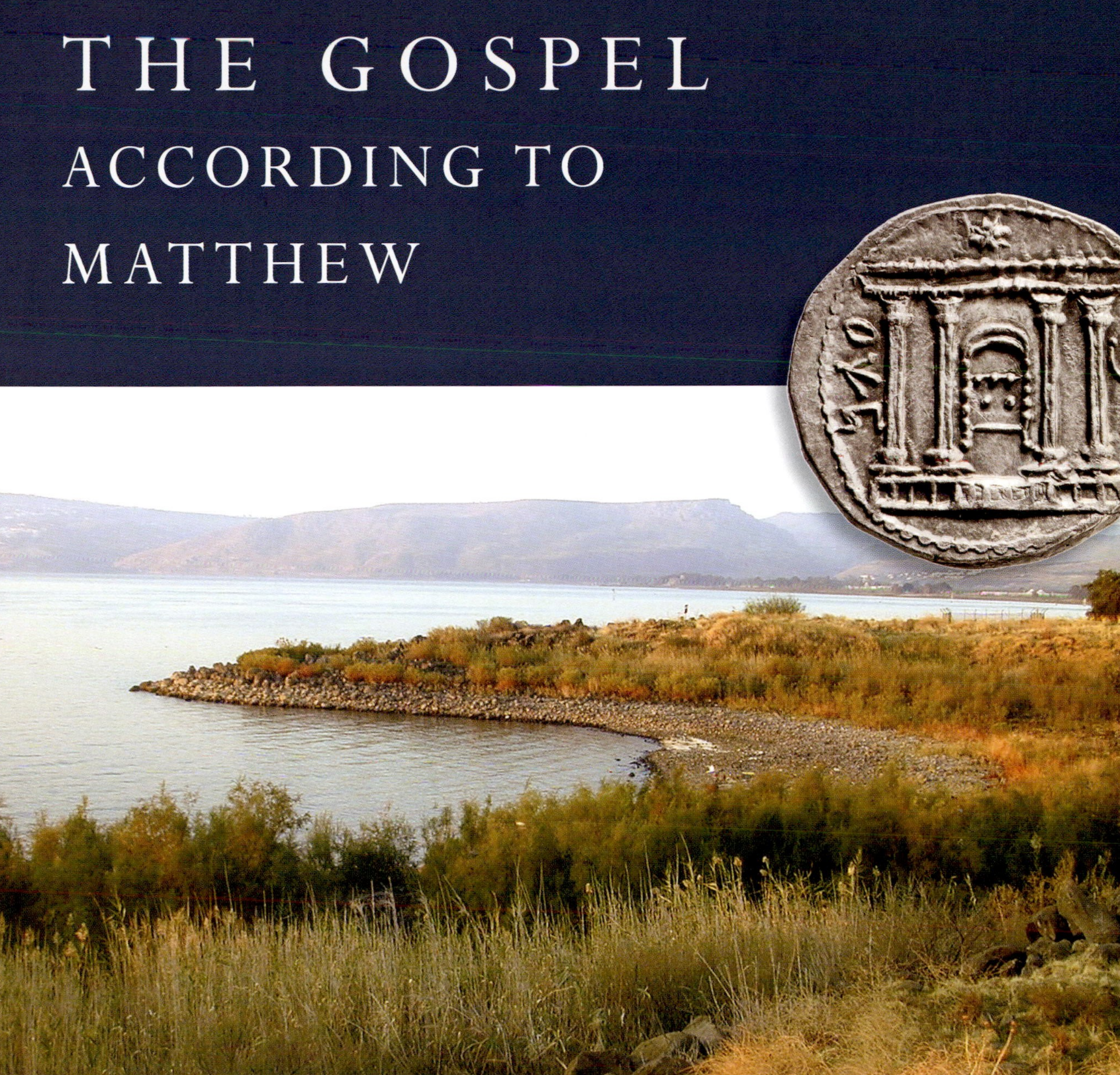

Jesus taught in coves such as this on Galilee's north shore. On occasion he taught from a boat, using the cove as a natural theater (Matt. 13:2).
Todd Bolen/BiblePlaces.com

The Gospel According to Matthew opens the New Testament. While Matthew may not have been the oldest gospel (see ch. 5), it commonly stands first among the four gospels in the ancient church's lists of canonical books. Contrary to contemporary arguments that Mark was the first gospel penned, early Christian authors said that "first was written that according to Matthew . . . who published it for those who from Judaism came to believe" (quoted in Eusebius, *Hist. eccl.* 6.25.3). The high regard for its contents, coupled with the belief that it was the first gospel written, secured its place at the head of the New Testament canon.

THE ORIGINAL AUDIENCE OF MATTHEW

Although Matthew does not name the recipient of his gospel as Luke does (Luke 1:1–4), evidence from within the book itself suggests that he told Jesus's story for a Jewish-Christian audience. The gospel contains Aramaic terms transliterated into Greek but left untranslated (Matt. 5:22; 27:6). The audience was familiar with these terms but not entirely fluent in that language (1:23; 27:46). The author leaves Jewish customs unexplained (15:2; 23:5), since he assumes his readers understand their meaning. In contrast, Mark and Luke wrote their gospels for gentile readers who consistently required interpretations of such terms and customs (Mark 3:17; 5:41; 7:1–4, 34; 14:36; 15:34; Luke 22:1, 7).

Matthew's genealogy looks back to David and to Abraham, connecting Jesus with the promises made to these key figures in Jewish history (1:1–2), again suggesting a Jewish audience. Luke, on the other hand, traces his lineage through Adam to show his gentile audience that Jesus is related to all humanity (Luke 3:38). Matthew pays particular attention to the inaugural mission to Israel (10:5–6; 15:24) and underscores the Lord's interaction with Jewish practices such as Sabbath keeping (12:1–14), temple obligations (5:23–26; 17:24–27), and fasting (6:16–18; 9:14–17). This gospel also focuses on Jesus's interpretation of the Mosaic Law (5:17–48; 15:1–9; 23:1–7, 23–26). Matthew's gospel has roots deep in Jewish soil.

Matthew is particularly concerned with the way Jesus fulfills the Old Testament. The Lord says, "Do not think that I have come to abolish

The Kingdom of Heaven

Matthew's Jewish orientation is evident in his preference for the phrase "kingdom of heaven" over "kingdom of God," as in the other gospels. Jesus spoke Aramaic, so each of his recorded sayings is a translation and interpretation of his ideas. Where Matthew translates his words as "kingdom of heaven," Mark and Luke render them as "kingdom of God" (e.g., compare Matt. 4:17 with Mark 1:15; Matt. 13:11 with Mark 4:11 and Luke 8:10; Matt. 13:31 with Mark 4:30 and Luke 13:18; Matt. 13:33 with Luke 13:20–21). There is no difference between the "kingdom of heaven" and the "kingdom of God." Matthew's choice of "heaven" is a periphrasis for "God" that avoids using the divine name (see Ex. 20:7). "Kingdom of heaven" was a common way to speak of God's reign within Judaism. For example, the Mishnah recalls Rabban Gamaliel's response when questioned why he repeated the *Shema* on his wedding night: "I cannot heed you to suspend from myself the kingdom of heaven even for one hour" (*m. Ber.* 2.5).

Ancient Travel and the Gospels

Ancient Christians took to the roads and sea-lanes of the Roman Empire to spread the gospel, care for newly founded churches, and send communications. Messengers served to carry documents from one congregation to another (Col. 4:16). Early Christian churches and their leaders were not isolated from each other but connected via this "holy internet."[1] You can calculate the distance and travel times between towns in the Roman Empire using this website: http://orbis.stanford.edu/#top.

This Roman road connected Antioch in Syria with the city of Chalcis.
Bernard Gagnon/Wikimedia Commons, GNU Free Documentary License

the Law or the Prophets; I have not come to abolish them but to fulfill them" (5:17). Matthew introduces Old Testament texts with phrases like, "All this took place to fulfill what the Lord had said through the prophet" (1:22; 2:15, 17, 23; 4:14; 8:17; 12:17; 13:14, 35; 21:4; 26:54, 56; 27:9) and cites the Old Testament over forty times. What God promised is now coming to pass, marking Jesus's coming as the inauguration of God's reign (4:17).

The Jewish-Christian community Matthew addresses had a tense relationship with the synagogues. The gospel came first to the Jewish people (Rom. 1:16), and Jesus taught within the synagogues (Matt. 9:35; 12:9–14; 13:54–58). The Jews who came to believe that Jesus was the anticipated Messiah continued to meet in synagogues until conflict arose between them and those who did not become disciples (see James 2:2; Acts 18:5–8; 19:8–10). Most likely Matthew's community had recently separated from the synagogue, since he speaks about "their synagogue" (Matt. 12:9; 13:54) and "their teachers" (7:29), warning about the opposition from the synagogues (10:17; 23:34) and critiquing synagogue practices (6:2, 5; 23:6) and leaders (23:1–36).

Matthew also inserts statements about the inclusion of gentiles in Jesus's ministry (12:15–21; 15:21–28). The Jewish-Christian community Matthew addresses may well have been watching the influx of gentiles into their midst, and Matthew, in response, points out Jesus's affirmation of the astonishing reality that the gospel is for gentiles also. The gospel opens with the genealogy of Jesus and highlights the key place of gentile women in Jesus's lineage (1:3, 5, 6), all whom had irregular unions (cf. 1:18). The gentile Magi come to pay Jesus homage, recognizing that he is the "king of the Jews" (2:1–12). Jesus especially commends a Roman centurion and a Canaanite woman for their faith (8:5–13; 15:21–28), and the parable of the wedding banquet points to gentile inclusion (21:33–44; 22:1–10). Matthew then ends his gospel with Jesus's call to "make disciples of all nations" (28:18–20). The universal inclusion of all peoples, regardless of their ethnicity, race, or nationality, is a hallmark of the gospel of Christ (Acts 1:8; Rev. 5:9).

We do not know Matthew's location when he wrote this book, nor can we say for sure where the recipients lived. While some would suggest Jerusalem or Palestine, most contemporary scholars point to Antioch in Syria as the location of the gospel's first readers. But we also know that this and the other gospels circulated quickly and widely. The whole church knew Matthew's value, both then as now.

Regardless of the first readers' location, Matthew wrote for a community or communities of disciples. Matthew is the only gospel that uses the word *church.* Jesus declared to Peter, "I tell you that you are Peter, and on this rock I will build my church, and the gates of Hades will not overcome it" (16:18). Jesus taught about dealing with sins in the community, instructing the disciples to "tell it to the church" if the person does not respond to initial calls to repentance (18:15–17). Jesus likely used the Semitic term *qāhāl*, meaning "assembly" or "community," as in the "assembly of YHWH" (Num. 20:4; 1 Chron. 28:8; Micah 2:5). Matthew points out that Jesus established this community: "I will build my church." His talk about "building" the church echoes Old Testament texts that speak of the way God builds his community (Jer. 31:4; 33:7; Amos 9:11–12). While Jesus called his disciples to spread the good news (28:18–20), Matthew sought to orient the church in its life together and service to Christ.

Writing "Lives" and Matthew's Gospel

Plutarch wanted to show what was exemplary in the character of the people he wrote about. He and others who wrote "lives" (*bioi*) did not attempt to give a comprehensive history but selected representative examples of a person's deeds and words (see John 20:30–31; 21:25). Plutarch began his *Life of Timoleon* saying, "I receive and welcome each subject of my history in turn as my guest, so to speak, and observe carefully 'how large he was and of what mien' and select from his career what is most important and most beautiful to know" (1.2).

When the Roman historian Suetonius wrote his *Life of Augustus*, he explained why he arranged his material topically rather than chronologically: "Having given as it were a summary of his life, I shall now take up the various phases one by one, not in chronological order but by categories, to make the account clearer and more intelligible" (9).

Matthew, as a historian of his time, carefully selected and artfully arranged Jesus's words and deeds in a way that underscored his exemplary character and work. He did not follow the exact chronology of Jesus's life but grouped together his deeds and teaching thematically.

MATTHEW'S STORY ABOUT JESUS

The "Life" of Jesus

Like the other gospel authors, Matthew wrote a *bios*, or "life," of Jesus. This literary genre was common in the ancient world. Plutarch wrote his *Lives*, Suetonius penned *The Lives of the Twelve Caesars*, and Diogenes Laërtius composed *The Lives of Eminent Philosophers* (see ch. 5 on "The Genre 'Gospel'"). "Lives" were not comprehensive accounts of all the events in a notable person's life but were more like cameo portraits that demonstrated the character of a person and showed both what was honorable and dishonorable in a person's actions. It was not uncommon for those who wrote "lives" to structure their books topically rather than strictly following chronology.

The Structure of the Gospel

Matthew's gospel opens with the genealogy of Jesus (1:1–17), the story of his birth, and his early childhood (1:18–2:23). "Lives" would often include brief stories about a person's ancestry, birth, and youth (see Suetonius' *Life of Augustus* 2–8). After this opening, Matthew arranges the life of Jesus around a series of narratives—five blocks of deeds and five blocks of teaching (3:1–26:2). Matthew marks the end of each discourse section with a phrase like "When Jesus had finished saying these things" (7:28; 11:1; 13:53; 19:1; 26:1). Ancient "lives" were always concerned with the person's *praxis* (deeds) and *logoi* (words) because these would reveal their virtues (see Acts 1:1). At the conclusion, Matthew recounts the events immediately leading up to Jesus's death (26:3–46), his arrest and trials (26:47–27:26), and his crucifixion and burial (27:27–66). The gospel ends with his resurrection from the dead (28:1–15) and Jesus's call to make disciples throughout the nations (28:16–20).

Outline of Matthew

I. Jesus and His Ancestors (1:1–17)
II. Jesus's Birth and Infancy (1:18–2:23)
III. Jesus's Deeds and Words (3:1–26:2)
  1. John the Baptist and Jesus's Preparation for Proclamation (3:1–4:25)
  2. Jesus's Sermon on Discipleship (5:1–7:29)
  3. Miracles and the Good News of the Kingdom of Heaven (8:1–9:38)
  4. Jesus's Directives to His Apostles (10:1–11:1)
  5. Initial Responses to the Proclamation of the Kingdom (11:2–12:50)
  6. Jesus's Parables of the Kingdom (13:1–52)
  7. Further Responses to Jesus's Words and Deeds (13:53–17:27)
  8. Jesus's Teaching on Community Relationships (18:1–19:2)
  9. The Journey to Judea and the Final Controversies (19:3–23:39)
  10. Jesus's Discourse on the Last Days (24:1–26:2)
IV. Jesus's Death and Resurrection (26:3–28:20)
  1. The Prelude to Jesus's Death (26:3–46)
  2. Jesus's Arrest and Trials (26:47–27:26)
  3. Jesus's Crucifixion and Burial (27:27–66)
  4. Jesus's Resurrection (28:1–15)
  5. Jesus's Authority and the Disciple's Ministry (28:16–20)

The Son of David in the *Psalms of Solomon*

The *Psalms of Solomon* is a pseudepigraphical text that dates from the first century BC. It reflects Jewish hopes around the time of Jesus. Chapters 17–18 focus on the messianic age, with prayers such as, "Lord, you chose David to be king over Israel, and swore to him about his descendants forever, that his kingdom should not fail before you" (17:4) and "See, Lord, and raise up for them their king, the son of David, to rule over your servant Israel in the time known to you, O God" (17:21). The expectation was that the son of David would "purge Jerusalem from gentiles who trample her to destruction" (17:22). In contrast, Jesus called his followers to "go and make disciples of all nations" (Matt. 28:19).

Jesus and His Ancestors (1:1–17)

Matthew opens with: "This is the genealogy of Jesus the Messiah the son of David, the son of Abraham" (1:1). The first words echo the Septuagint (LXX) of Genesis 2:4 and 5:1: "the book of the origin of heaven and earth" and "the book of the origin of human beings." Matthew sees Jesus Christ as the beginning of God's new creation. The first verse frames the whole gospel as an origins story, one no less important than Genesis.

Matthew connects his founding epic with the promises God gave to David and Abraham. As the "son of David," Jesus is the rightful heir of David's throne as king of Israel. One of the most important texts of the OT is 2 Samuel 7:11–16, where God promises David that he will raise up his offspring and "establish the throne of his kingdom forever." This promise, repeated in Scripture (Jer. 23:5; 33:15; Zech. 3:8; 6:12) and Jewish literature, is now fulfilled in Jesus Christ (Matt. 1:6, 17, 20; 21:9; Rom. 1:3).

Matthew also introduces Jesus as the "son of Abraham" (1:1). The covenant God made with Abraham included the promise that "all peoples on earth will be blessed through you" (Gen. 12:1–3; 18:18; 22:18). Jesus's authority is over all, and his good news is for people of every nation (28:18–20; see Rom. 4:1–25; Gal. 3:6–29).

Matthew's genealogy is deeply embedded in Israel's history, highlighted by the fourteen generations between Abraham, David,

Matthew and Luke's Genealogies

Both Matthew and Luke include genealogies of Jesus (Matt. 1:2–16; Luke 3:23–38), a feature absent from Mark and John. While both genealogies include Abraham, David, and Joseph, the husband of Mary, they differ in significant ways. As noted, Luke's genealogy traces Jesus's ancestry back through Adam (3:38), connecting Jesus with all humanity. Matthew's only goes as far as Abraham (1:2) and focuses on the generations between Abraham, David, the Babylonian exile, and Jesus, thus tightly connecting with Israel's history. Both authors hold deep theological concerns reflected in their respective genealogies.

The names in the genealogies are quite different from David onward (Matt. 1:6–16; Luke 3:23–31), with Matthew going through his son Solomon and Luke tracing through another of David's sons named Nathan (2 Sam. 5:13–16). Some have suggested that Luke's genealogy is that of Mary, but tracing lineage through the mother was not the normal practice. More likely Matthew's genealogy traces the line of succession for kingship, one of his main theological concerns. Royal lineage did not always follow biological lineage. Luke, on the other hand, appears to focus on biological descent. Such genealogies were rarely complete and commonly had variations.

the Babylonian captivity, and Jesus (1:17 with 1:2, 6, 11–12, 16). While that history was filled with promise, as the first two names indicate, it was also marked by deep sin and pain, signified by the exile in Babylon. God's promise also includes gentiles, as the naming of the gentile women suggests (1:3, 5–6). The promise given to Abraham in Genesis 12 embraces the gentiles as well.

Jesus's Birth and Infancy (1:18–2:23)

Matthew's account of Jesus's life begins with the story of his conception (1:18–25). Mary and Joseph had entered into a contract to be married, a relationship with greater obligations than contemporary engagement but less than a consummated marriage (1:18). Marriage would occur a year later. The betrothal could only be dissolved through divorce, and sexual violation of the vow was considered adultery.

How Old Was Mary?

The regulations governing the marriage union are laid out in the Mishnah tractate entitled *Ketubot*. Mary, according to custom, could have been as young as twelve and a half. Roman law similarly set the minimum age for women to marry at twelve.

Mary became pregnant through the Holy Spirit, a statement made by both Matthew (1:18, 20) and Luke (1:35). Matthew regards this miraculous conception as the fulfilment of the prophecy in Isaiah 7:14: "'The virgin will conceive and give birth to a son, and they will call him Immanuel' (which means 'God with us')" (Matt. 1:22–23). The child was named Jesus, meaning "Yahweh saves" (1:21). God's presence and salvation were embodied in Jesus.

Matthew also recounts the visit of the Magi (2:1–12) and Jesus's family's escape to Egypt and return to Nazareth in Galilee (2:13–23). The Magi were Persian astrologers who saw an unusual star and concluded that a king had been born for the Jewish people and came to kneel and pay him homage (2:1–2), perhaps reflecting their knowledge of Numbers 24:17: "A star will come out of Jacob; a scepter will rise out of Israel." Many attempts have been made to identify the "star," but Matthew's sole concern is to show that Jesus was recognized as king even by these gentiles. We do not know how many Magi there were, only that they were the first to honor or worship him, bringing three royal gifts of "gold, frankincense and myrrh" (2:11; 1 Kings 10:1–2, 25). They found Jesus in Bethlehem as predicted by the prophecy in Micah 5:2 and 4 (Matt. 2:6), another indication of his royal lineage.

The counterpoint to the Magi's homage was Herod the Great's violence (see ch. 2 on Herod the Great). Seeing Jesus as a threat to his own power, Herod unleashed his wrath against the male children of Bethlehem under the age of two (2:16). Matthew describes the horror in the words of Jeremiah 31:15: "mourning and great weeping, Rachel weeping for her children" (2:18). This massacre reflected Herod's cruelty, a man who had even slaughtered members of his own family. Josephus remarks that "he was a man who was cruel to all alike and one who easily gave in to anger and was contemptuous of justice" (Josephus *Ant.* 17.7.1 [191]).

"We saw his star when it rose" (Matt. 2:2). Celestial events such as comets or novae were regarded as divine signs. This coin, minted during the reign of Augustus, shows a comet as a "star" and is inscribed DIVVS IVLIV, "divine Julius."
Wikimedia Commons, PD-US

An angel warned Joseph in a dream to flee to Egypt (2:13–18), which Matthew regards as a fulfilment of Hosea 11:1: "Out of Egypt I called my son." As God brought Israel out of captivity in Egypt, so Jesus goes there in exile, and returns, thus embodying God's promise of a new exodus. Jesus Christ was born into a spiral of violence and came to a violent end on the cross. But violence did not have the final word.

Jesus's Deeds and Words (3:1–26:2)

John the Baptist and Jesus's Preparation for Proclamation (3:1–4:25)

In the first narrative section (3:1–4:25), Matthew introduces John the Baptist and his baptism of Jesus (3:1–17). John announces the main theme of the gospel as he cries out, "Repent, for the kingdom of heaven has come near" (3:2), the very message Jesus himself would soon proclaim (4:17). John dressed like Elijah, who, according to Malachi, was to come as the harbinger of "the day of the Lord" (3:3–4; 2 Kings 1:8; Mal. 4:5–6; Matt. 11:7–15; 17:9–13). The Jewish people expected Elijah's appearance before the end "to turn the hearts of parents to their children, and to restore the tribes of Jacob" (Sir. 48:10), leading Israel to repentance.

John predicted the coming of "one who is more powerful than I," proclaiming that "he will baptize you with the Holy Spirit and fire" and so bring both blessing and judgment (3:10–12). Consequently, when Jesus came to be baptized, John refused, but Jesus insisted that baptism was necessary "to fulfill all righteousness" (3:15). The response suggests that Jesus came to live in full acceptance of what God required of him as revealed in Scripture (5:17–20). When Jesus was baptized, the Holy Spirit descended on him, empowering him for ministry (3:16; 12:18; and Isa. 11:1–2; 1 Sam. 16:13). Just as important was God's declaration: "This is my Son, whom I love; with him I am well pleased" (3:17). The words echo Psalm 2:7, a royal enthronement Psalm, and Isaiah 42:1, which identifies Jesus as the Suffering Servant of Isaiah 42–53. Jesus was the Spirit-anointed king who would suffer and die (cf. Matt. 16:13–21).

Matthew continues to reveal Jesus's qualifications as the Messiah in the story of his temptation (4:1–11). Jesus was the model Israelite who not only came out of Egypt but was tempted in the wilderness. While Satan tempted Jesus to use his power for his own ends, Jesus repeatedly aligned himself with God's will.

The Disciples

In Matthew 5:1 we first learn that Jesus's followers are called "disciples." He had already called his first followers: Simon Peter, Andrew, James, and John (4:18–22). A "disciple" (*mathētēs*, or in Aramaic a *talmîdh*) was more than a learner; it was an adherent of a teacher or master. Josephus, for example, called Joshua the "disciple" of Moses, and Elisha the "disciple and attendant" (*diakonos*) of Elijah (*Ant.* 6.5.4 [84]; 8.13.7 [354]). This commitment to the master is embodied in Jesus's call to Peter and Andrew: "Come, follow me" (cf. John 6:66). True discipleship includes identification with the lifestyle of the master, including embracing the rejection he endured (Matt. 10:24–25). Sometime later Jesus's followers became known as "Christians" (Acts 11:26).

This section (3:1–4:11) lays out Jesus's full qualifications, then follows Jesus as he embarks on his public ministry in Galilee (4:12–17). Jesus came to proclaim the advent of the kingdom of heaven and call people to repentance (4:17). He also summoned disciples to follow him (4:18–22) as he launched out in his ministry of the kingdom in both word and deed (4:23–25).

Wall painting of Moses and the burning bush from the synagogue in Dura-Europos, ca. AD 245.

Z. Radovan/www.BibleLand Photos.com

Jesus's Sermon on Discipleship (5:1–7:29)

Matthew regards Jesus as a new Moses. As Moses had gone up Mount Sinai to receive the law (Deut. 9:9; cf. Matt. 4:2), so Jesus went to address his disciples "up on a mountainside" (5:1). Having announced the kingdom of heaven and called the first disciples, Jesus now teaches his disciples how to live. The sermon begins with the Beatitudes (5:3–12), where Jesus lays out the character of true "blessedness." The term translated "blessed" (*makarios*) may refer to true and profound happiness but more likely suggests being honorable. What constitutes an honorable life, according to Jesus, are not possessions, power, or public acclaim. In contrast with the opinion of his day, he considered the poor, along with those who mourn and are rejected, as having honor. The "poor in spirit" are those crushed by economic adversity, oppressed, and without social standing or power (cf. Luke 6:20). Jesus also linked the honorable life with the character of a person's life and deeds. True honor is in righteousness, mercy, purity, and peacemaking, especially in the face of social rejection. God is the one who grants such honor (Pss. 46:6; 1:1–2). Unfortunately, what God deems honorable, society does not always value.

The ethics of the kingdom taught in the sermon transcend those of the law of Moses since they reach to the very motivations of people's actions (5:21–22, 27–30) and call for a higher standard of righteousness than the law demanded (5:31–48). Jesus did not come to abolish the law but to fulfill it (5:17–18).

The Honorable Life

The society in which Jesus lived was an honor/shame culture, where the highest virtue was honor and the thing to avoid above all else was shame. Aristotle said that "honor and dishonour then are the objects with which the great-souled man is especially concerned" (*Eth. Nic.* 4.3.17). Reflections on honor and shame appear throughout the New Testament (Mark 8:38; Rom. 1:16; 2 Cor. 6:8; 2 Tim. 1:8; Heb. 12:2; 1 Pet. 1:7; 2 Pet. 1:17). Matthew seeks to establish that Jesus is honorable given his ancestry, birth, character, and deeds. But in the Beatitudes Jesus flips the conception of what constitutes an honorable life. He even dies the most shameful way—on the cross—and turns it into something of honor through his resurrection.

The law and prophets pointed to him, and he now fulfills them (cf. 2:17, 23; 4:14). Jesus's statement about the law also suggests that he came to bring out the law's full and true meaning. Jewish expectation was that the Messiah would come to give the true interpretation of Torah, which Jesus did. Indeed, his authority transcended that of the rabbis and even Moses himself. Consequently, Jesus called his disciples to put his teaching fully into practice (5:19–20; 7:13–27).

The Sermon on the Mount also reconfigures how Jesus's disciples should practice their piety. Their prayers, fasting, and generosity to the poor must be done with pure motives and not simply to gain public honor (6:1–18). They must live fully oriented to God and dependent on him (6:19–34; 7:7–12). Disciples of Jesus seek God and his kingdom above all else (6:9–13, 33). The demands of Jesus's teaching are summarized in 7:12: "In everything, do to others what you would have them do to you, for this sums up the Law and the Prophets."

Miracles and the Good News of the Kingdom of Heaven (8:1–9:38)

In the second block of narrative, Matthew focuses in on Jesus—his miracles and his power over disease (8:1–17; 9:2–8, 20–22, 27–31), demons (8:16, 28–34; 9:32–34), nature (8:23–27), and even death itself (9:18, 23–26). Through these he demonstrates the presence and power of the kingdom that is now breaking in (9:35; 12:28).

But amid his preaching and miracles, Jesus talks about the radical cost of being a disciple (8:18–22). Commitment to Jesus must come before personal comfort and even family obligation. Matthew shows that some of Jesus's disciples came from among the most despised in society (9:9–13), so the question came, "Why does your teacher eat with tax collectors and sinners?" (9:11). Jesus's benefaction extends even to those who have broken covenant with God: "I have not come to call the righteous, but sinners" (9:13).

Mosaic from the Orpheus house in Sepphoris, depicting a banquet, ca. second century AD.
Reproduced by permission from Carole Raddato

Jesus's Directives to His Apostles (10:1–11:1)

Up to this point Matthew has demonstrated Jesus's authority as the Messiah who heralds the kingdom through words and deeds. In this second section of teaching, Jesus delegates his authority. He previously stated that the harvest was great and that the workers were sorely needed (9:35–38). Therefore, he calls twelve of his disciples, designating them as his authoritative messengers, or apostles, and bestowing on them his own message, mission, and authority so that they might proclaim the kingdom in power (10:1–8).

Jesus not only commissions his apostles but warns them that they will face opposition as he did (9:16–31). But those who reject them and their message will suffer dire consequences, while those who receive them will receive a great reward (10:12–15, 40–42).

Initial Responses to the Proclamation of the Kingdom (11:2–12:50)

While in prison John the Baptist enquires whether Jesus is truly the Messiah (11:2–6), likely because the Messiah was expected to liberate Israel (cf. Luke 4:18–19). And Jesus did not appear to be executing judgment as John's own preaching had predicted (Matt. 2:10–12). In response, Jesus recounts his miraculous ministry, echoing the words of Isaiah 35:5–6: "Then will the eyes of the blind be opened and the ears of the deaf unstopped. Then will the lame leap like a deer, and the mute tongue shout for joy." Jesus affirms that he is indeed the expected Messiah.

After explaining the role of John the Baptist (11:7–19; cf. Mal. 3:1), Jesus denounces the spiritual blindness in the cities that did not respond to his miracles and teaching (11:20–30). He faces controversy over Sabbath observance (12:1–14) and is accused of being under the influence of "Beelzebul, the prince of demons," or Satan (12:22–37). Matthew contrasts these stinging critiques with Jesus's miraculous healing ministry, which he regards as the fulfilment of the prophecy about the Servant of the Lord in Isaiah 42:1–4 (Matt. 12:15–21). So while Jesus faces rejection, he continues to offer tender care to those in need and who respond to him in faith (11:28–29; 12:19–21), accomplishing his Messianic mission in the power of the Spirit (12:18, 28). The kingdom of heaven was breaking in, but the ultimate sign of the kingdom would be Jesus's resurrection (12:38–42).

Tax Collectors and Sinners

"Tax collectors" were rightfully despised in Palestine since they gathered taxes for the Roman imperial power, abused people who did not pay, and taxed people beyond what was required (Luke 3:12–14; 19:1–10). Matthew himself may have collected excessive custom charges. Their corruption lumped them in with other "sinners" who engaged in various kinds of socially unacceptable and ritually defiling behavior. They had violated the law of God and his covenant. Yet Jesus ate with them, foreshadowing the great banquet of the kingdom of heaven (22:1–14; 8:11).

Apostle

An apostle (10:2) was not only a disciple but was also sent with the authority of the one who sent him. The office has roots in the rabbinic concept of a *šālîaḥ*, a person commissioned to go, speak, and act in the name of the one who sent him. The Mishnah says, "a man's agent (*šālîaḥ*) is like to himself" (*m. Ber.* 5.5).

Jesus and the Sabbath

One of the fundamental religious observances in Judaism was Sabbath-keeping. The law of Moses enjoined the Jewish people to "remember the Sabbath day by keeping it holy" (Ex. 20:8–11). Work was not permitted on the seventh day of the week, beginning at sundown on Friday and ending at sundown on Saturday. Since God created the world in six days and rested on the seventh, Israel was called to rest on the seventh day as well (Ex. 31:12–17). The Sabbath was considered a "lasting covenant" and a day "holy to the Lord." Mishnah Shabbat outlined thirty-nine types of labor prohibited on the Sabbath, including sewing, ploughing, reaping, binding sheaves, shearing wool, making two loops, sewing two stitches, building, tearing down, and putting out or kindling a fire (*m. Šabb.* 7.2). A small act like picking grapes could be considered as harvesting. The Pharisees believed that when the disciples plucked grain to eat on the Sabbath they violated the rule against reaping (Matt. 12:2). Jesus, however, placed human need above Sabbath restrictions and declared himself "Lord of the Sabbath" (12:1–14).

What Are Parables?

The word *parable* could be used of riddles, proverbs, or wisdom sayings. Jesus uses the term (Heb. *māšāl*) to talk about deep truths using illustrations and stories from daily life. Parables were commonplace among the rabbis in Jesus's day. A philosopher once asked Rabban Gamaliel (Acts 5:34; 22:3) why God's anger was against idolaters but not the idols themselves. He responded with a parable: "A king had a son who raised a dog which he named after his royal father; and whenever he was about to swear he said, 'By the life of the dog, the father.' When the king heard of this, against whom did his anger turn, against the dog or against the son? Surely only against the son" (*'Abod. Zar.* 54b).

Jesus's Parables of the Kingdom (13:1–52)

Matthew inserts the parables of the kingdom at this point. The parables of the sower (13:1–9, 18–23), the weeds (13:24–30, 36–42), and the net (13:47–50) all speak about the ways people either accept Jesus's message of the kingdom or reject it, and the resulting consequences. The parables of the mustard seed (13:31–32), yeast (13:33), hidden treasure (13:44), and the pearl (13:45) all illustrate positive responses to the gospel and the benefits to those who accept Jesus's message. Both the mustard seed and yeast parables explain the dramatic growth of the kingdom. Small beginnings can lead to large outcomes.

Jesus uses parables to teach the crowds (13:2–3, 10, 34) but leaves the interpretation of the parables to the disciples (13:11, 18, 36, 51). Jesus offers them an explanation of the parables but then expects them to be able to interpret the parables themselves. The parables utilized common pieces of rural life to teach the truths of the kingdom. Seeds and soil and weeds, yeast and hidden treasure, fishing and nets all made an appearance.

The parables were accessible due to these illustrations from daily life but conveyed deeper truths of the kingdom of heaven. Matthew presents Jesus's explanation for the parables: "This is why I speak to them in parables: 'Though seeing, they do not see; though hearing, they do not hear or understand'" (13:11–17, citing Isa. 6:9–10). Surprisingly, these easily understood stories both revealed and obscured. If one was a disciple and understood the character of the kingdom of heaven, the parables disclosed dimensions of the kingdom. For others, the parables were riddles and mere stories about seeds and soil, nets and fish. The capacity to understand the parable depended on one's response to Jesus and his proclamation.

Parables sometimes utilize allegorical elements, where an object in the parable stands for a particular truth. For example, in the parable of the sower, the seed and the soil refer to ways people receive the message of the kingdom (Matt. 13:18). Other elements in the parables have no symbolic meaning and serve only to move the story along. Jesus uses parables to tell the story of the kingdom of heaven. Some will respond to the message and bear fruit, while others will not (the parable of the sower). The kingdom is present and grows dramatically (the parables of the mustard seed and the yeast) and is exceedingly valuable (the parables of the hidden treasure and the pearl). There will be a final judgment (the parables of the weeds and the net).

A hoard of coins buried in a jar (Matt. 13:44).
The Portable Antiquities Scheme/The Trustees of the British Museum, CC BY 4.0

Further Responses to Jesus's Words and Deeds (13:53–17:27)

The fourth narrative block again takes up the varied responses to Jesus's ministry, starting with his rejection in Nazareth (13:53–58). Matthew frames the story of John's beheading by Herod Antipas within the deep concerns that Herod held about Jesus's miraculous ministry (14:1–12). Pharisees and the teachers of the law question Jesus about why the disciples do not keep the traditions of the elders (15:1–19). The Pharisees and Sadducees seek a sign from him, while he warns about their teaching (16:1–12). Jesus's ministry continues to generate controversy and opposition.

Amid the conflict Jesus feeds five thousand men, with likely an equal number of women and children (14:13–21), and then again feeds an almost equally large number of men, women, and children (15:29–39). His miraculous ministry continues as he walks on water (14:22–36) and heals a Canaanite woman's daughter, commending this gentile woman's faith (15:21–28). He also liberates a man's son from demonic powers (17:14–21). The mounting opposition does not curtail Jesus's ministry of healing, liberation from demons, and providing the necessities of life.

Peter, the Rock

After Peter's confession that Jesus was the Messiah, the Son of the living God, Jesus said to him, "I tell you that you are Peter, and on this rock I will build my church, and the gates of Hades will not overcome it" (Matt. 16:16–20). Is the "rock" on which Jesus builds his church Peter or his confession about Jesus? Jesus tropicalizes Peter's name ("you are Peter") and we have a play on words with "rock" (Gk. *petra*) and "Peter" (Gk. *Petros*). In Aramaic, "rock" and "Peter" are the same word (*kepha*). Many contemporary scholars believe Peter is indeed the Rock, but do not hold that Jesus established a line of apostolic succession from him.

In this section Matthew presents two of the most important events in this gospel. The first occurred at Caesarea Philippi: Peter's confession and Jesus's announcement of his sufferings and those the disciples would endure (16:13–28). Popular opinion varies widely about who Jesus is (16:13–14). When asked, "Who do you say I am?" Peter responds, "You are the Messiah, the Son of the living God" (16:15–16). Peter is a creative theologian who is open to God's leading (16:17; Acts 10). His confession indicates that he regards Jesus as the Messiah or Christ, the "Anointed One." The title, found previously in 1:1 and elsewhere, identifies Jesus as the anticipated king descended from David. Psalm 2:2 says, "The kings of the earth rise up and the rulers band together against the Lord and against his anointed." The "anointed" son is the king and God's Son according to 2:6:

> "I have installed my king
>   on Zion, my holy mountain."

I will proclaim the Lord's decree:

> He said to me, "You are my son;
>   today I have become your father."

"Son of God" was a royal title as well, derived from the promise given to David regarding his descendant whose kingdom God would establish forever: "I will be his father, and he will be my son" (2 Sam. 7:14). Peter recognizes that Jesus is truly the fulfilment of the prophetic hope that God would establish his king to rule forever (Matt. 28:19).

People expected the Messiah King to rule over Israel and judge the gentiles who oppressed the nation. In contrast, Jesus announces that he will suffer, be killed, and rise from the dead on the third day (16:21). The idea that the Messiah would suffer and die was antithetical to everything expected of the coming king. Peter's rebuke, then, hardly comes as a surprise (16:22), but Jesus rejects the rebuke (16:23). Indeed, those who follow Jesus as his disciples must themselves follow him in the way of suffering, even to the point of death (16:24–28).

The second foundational event in this section is the transfiguration (17:1–13). Jesus takes the inner circle of three apostles, Peter, James, and John, up to a mountain where he becomes radiant before them. Jesus is not only the Messiah who will die and be raised but is also the glorious Son of Man (17:9) spoken of in Daniel 7:13–14 (Matt. 16:27; 17:9; 24:30), who here shines with divine radiance (Isa. 60:19; Dan. 7:9). The apostles witness the full majesty of Jesus here (2 Pet. 1:16–15), and his appearance suggests his divinity (Ps. 104:2). Moses and Elijah appear on the mountain with Jesus, both of whom were expected on the day of the Lord (Deut. 18:15–19; Mal. 4:4–5). Jesus radiantly shines as Moses had when he came down from Mount Sinai (Ex. 34:29–35). But God's voice from heaven

Mount Tabor, the traditional site of the transfiguration. Most scholars today point to Mount Hermon as the site of the transfiguration. *irisphoto1/Shutterstock*

indicates Jesus's higher status: "This is my Son, whom I love; with him I am well pleased. Listen to him!" (Matt. 17:5). The words echo Psalm 2:7, Isaiah 42:1, and Deuteronomy 18:15, indicating again that Jesus is the Messiah King, the Suffering Servant of God, and the prophet that Moses predicted.

Jesus's Teaching on Community Relationships (18:1–19:2)

The fourth discourse section focuses on relationships within the community of disciples. The section begins with the topic of honor (18:1–5). The one with greatest honor was to be like a child. Society did not honor children in ancient society and often lumped them together with slaves. Jesus holds up these who are the least significant in society's eyes as the greatest, a lesson for all disciples.

In 18:6–9 and 18:15–35 Jesus addresses the problem of sin in the community. Members of the community are not to provoke or lead others to stumble or sin. The "little ones" here are not simply children (18:6) but all believers. Instead, each disciple must take care to deal with sin radically in their own life (18:8–9). Should there be sin, however, the community should respond by restoring the person who has lapsed into disobedience (18:15–35). Forgiveness is the hallmark of true Christian community (18:21–35). In this section is the parable of the lost sheep, which speaks graphically about God's care for each of the "little ones" (18:10–14), implying that disciples should have the same care for one another.

Shammai, Hillel, and Jesus on Divorce

The Pharisees asked Jesus, "Is it lawful for a man to divorce his wife for any and every reason?" (Matt. 19:3). The question was part of the debate about the legal grounds for divorce based on Deuteronomy 24:1: "If a man marries a woman who becomes displeasing to him because he finds something indecent about her, and he writes her a certificate of divorce . . ." Mishnah Gittin 9.10 indicates that two interpretations of this passage were in circulation at the time of Jesus: "The School of Shammai say, A man may not divorce his wife unless he has found unchastity in her. . . . And the School of Hillel say: He may divorce her even if she spoiled a dish for him." The Pharisees' question reflects this latter position.

In both Matthew and Mark, Jesus opposes Hillel's position that favored easy divorce. Jesus turns to Genesis 1:27 and God's design for marriage (Matt. 19:4–8), although allowing divorce for sexual infidelity (19:9).

Judaism in Jesus's day recognized other grounds for divorce based on Exodus 21:10–11. These included both material and social neglect, as well as sexual unfaithfulness. Jesus did not address the first two issues, although Paul touches on them in 1 Corinthians 7:3–5 and 7:33–34.[2]

While Palestinian Judaism placed the power to divorce solely in the hands of men, Philo of Alexandria assumed that a woman could divorce her husband (*Spec. Leg.* 3.30), as was the case in the wider Greco-Roman culture and Mark 10:10–12.

The Journey to Judea and the Final Controversies (19:3–23:39)

The fifth narrative section describes the events leading up to the final conflict that Jesus had with the leaders of the nation and the people, ending with the denunciation of the scribes and the Pharisees in 23:1–36. The section is not entirely about conflict, however. Also included are his teachings about marriage and divorce (19:3–12; cf. 5:31–32), his blessing of the children (19:13–15; cf. 18:1–5), and his words about the rich and the kingdom of heaven (19:16–30).

The conflict with the authorities in Israel is coming to a head. Jesus predicts his passion for the third time (20:17–19) and again reiterates that following him as a disciple will entail suffering (20:20–28). His triumphal entry to Jerusalem and the cleansing of the temple (21:1–17) contrast the popular acclaim Jesus enjoys among the people with the indignation of the priests and scribes (21:14–15). Jesus came as the triumphant king (21:1–9; cf. Isa. 62:11; Zech. 9:9) and showes his authority even over the temple.

Unsurprisingly, the chief priests and the elders question him as he teaches in the temple (21:23–27), and his parable of the tenants sparks the leaders into action against him (21:33–46). The controversies rage with the Pharisees, Herodians (22:15–22), and the Sadducees (22:23–33). Jesus silences both the Sadducees (22:34) and Pharisees (22:41–46), but the people continue to hold Jesus in high regard (21:11, 46; 22:33). Jesus's parable of the wedding banquet lay out the dire consequences of not responding to the invitation to the kingdom of heaven (22:1–14). He then pronounces woes against the scribes and the Pharisees (22:41–46; 23:1–29), leaders who had enjoyed great acclaim among the people but abused their privilege. Popular support for Jesus rises, while the leaders become increasingly disturbed at his actions and teaching. The end is inevitable (21:38, 45–46).

Jesus's Discourse on the Last Days (24:1–26:2)

The fifth and final discourse section focuses on the last days. The interpretation of this section is fraught with difficulties since many have used the passage to speculate about the end times. Jesus teaches that a delay will occur before the final consummation, and persecution and tribulation for the disciples will mark this intervening time (24:4–28). Jesus also predicts the fall of Jerusalem and the destruction of the temple (24:15–21).

Jewish expectation was that before the coming of the Messiah there would be a time of great distress, a period known as the "labor pains" of the Messiah (24:8; 1 Thess. 5:3; 1 Enoch 62:4). The dreadful events described here—wars, conflict between nations, famines, and earthquakes (24:6–7)—are only the prelude to the end, as labor pains anticipate birth. Afterward the end will come (24:29–31; cf. Dan. 7:13–14).

The purpose of this passage, along with the other NT reflections on the final events of history, was not to speculate about the date when the end would occur but to instruct the church to stand ready for Christ's advent (24:36–25:46). True vigilance means being engaged in the work of the kingdom and seeking people's welfare. We cannot know when the end will come (24:36, 42, 44, 45–51; cf. 1 Thess. 5:1–11). God's final judgment will occur as God evaluates the care people have shown for the neediest (25:31–46). The sheep are people who have put Jesus's teaching into practice, while the goats have not (cf. 7:21–27).

"Truly I tell you, not one stone here will be left on another; every one will be thrown down" (Matt. 24:2). These huge stones (ashlars) were thrown down from the Temple at the time of its destruction in AD 70.
© 2018 by Zondervan

Jesus's Death and Resurrection (26:3–28:20)

The Prelude to Jesus's Death (26:3–46)

The gospel of Matthew ends with the trials, crucifixion, and resurrection of Jesus. The scene is set as the "chief priests and the elders of the people" gather with the high priest Caiaphas to plot Jesus's arrest and death (26:3–5).

A woman anoints Jesus with costly ointment while at Simon the Leper's house in Bethany near Jerusalem (26:6–13). The woman's love for Jesus contrasts starkly with Judas Iscariot, who for "thirty pieces of silver" seeks to betray him (26:14–16). Jesus knows what Judas is going to do (26:20–25).

Both these events and the Passover meal point to Jesus's death (26:17–30). During this meal Jesus takes the bread and the cup and institutes what we know as the Lord's Supper (1 Cor. 1:23–26). The bread stands for his body. The cup of wine stands for his blood: "This is my blood of the covenant, which is poured out for many for the forgiveness of sins" (26:26–29). The bread and wine point to his atoning death and the new covenant established by God (Jer. 31:31–34). Jesus's words also echo Isaiah 53:12: "He poured out his life unto death, and was numbered with the transgressors. For he bore the sin of many, and made intercession for the transgressors." After the Passover meal, Jesus goes to the Mount of Olives where he is in agony (26:36–46), knowing that his death is coming, the disciples will forsake him, and Peter will deny him (26:31–34). Being overwhelmed with anguish, Jesus would rather not take this road. Nevertheless, he submitts to the Father's will. His resolve contrasts sharply with the disciples' failures.

This ossuary, used to bury the skeletal remains of a person, bears the name "Caiaphas." Many believe the bones in this stone box were those of the high priest Caiaphas, although some doubt this identification (Matt. 23:6, 57).
BRBurton/Wikimedia Commons, Public Domain

Money corrupted Judas, a vivid example of Paul's caution in 1 Timothy 6:10, "For the love of money is the root of all kinds of evil." The coins may be denarii (wages for thirty days) but may be Tyrian shekels, about 120 drachmas. The price for this life was extremely low in either case (Matt. 26:15; 27:9–10; and compare Zech. 11:12–13 and Ex. 21:32).
Used by permission from Hana Yariv, CC BY-SA 3.0

Jesus's Arrest and Trials (26:47–27:26)

Jesus is arrested, betrayed with a kiss by Judas, then led away to be tried before the highest governing body in Israel, the Sanhedrin (26:47–68). The trial is compromised since witnesses bring false testimony against him, saying that he had claimed he was going to destroy the Temple (26:61; cf. John 2:19). When asked whether he is the Son of God, he replies by identifying himself with the heavenly Son of Man of Daniel 7:13 and adding a reference to Psalm 110:1: "You will see the Son of Man sitting at the right hand of the Mighty One and coming on the clouds of heaven" (Matt. 26:63–64). They condemn him to death on the charge of blasphemy (26:65–66).

As predicted, Peter denies Christ three times but then repents (26:69–75 and 33–35). On the other hand, Judas, the betrayer, goes out and hangs himself (27:3–10). Peter, the Rock, showed human weakness and grief for his denial (26:75). Judas acted out of greed and, while having regret and recognizing his sin (27:3–4), Matthew's account appears to suggest that Judas did not truly repent and turn to God. He acted as his own jury and executioner.

Pilate is the other party who, through weakness of conviction, yields to the pressure of the chief priests and elders who stir up the crowd to call for Jesus's execution (27:20). Throughout these narratives Matthew is intent on communicating that Jesus was innocent and did nothing worthy of death (27:23).

Matthew carefully notes that Jesus was the King, even though soldiers mocked him (27:27–31) and he was crucified (27:32–56). Matthew does not describe the act of crucifixion but only says, "When they had crucified him . . ." (27:35). Everyone in those days understood the horrors of this Roman form of torture

Cicero on Crucifixion

So horrific and shameful was crucifixion that the Roman senator and philosopher Cicero commented on it in his *Against Verres*. He speaks of "the lash, the fire, and that final stage in the punishment of the guilty and the intimidation of the rest, the torments of crucifixion" (2.5.6), and was aghast at the thought of inflicting this on a citizen: "You dared to crucify any living man who claimed to be a Roman citizen?" (2.5.63). It was for condemned slaves (2.5.6). He called it a "cruel and disgusting penalty" (2.5.64) and said even mentioning crucifixion was unworthy of Roman citizens: "But the executioner, the veiling of the head, and the very word 'cross' should be far removed not only from the person of a Roman citizen but from his thoughts, his eyes and his ears. For it is not only the actual occurrence of these things or the endurance of them, but liability to them, the expectation, nay, the mere mention of them, that is unworthy of a Roman citizen and a free" (*Rab. Perd.* 5.16; cf. 1 Cor. 1:23). Crucifixion was common enough, however. After the death of Herod the Great, a rebellion arose, and the Romans crucified two thousand people (Josephus, *Ant.* 17.10.10 [295]). Jesus met the same fate, but for him the cross was not the end.

and execution. Crucifixion was one of the ways Rome maintained control over subject peoples. Roman citizens could not be sentenced to death by crucifixion. This horrendous death was reserved for criminals and especially slaves.

When Jesus dies, he gives up his life and entrusts himself to the care of the Father. "He gave up his spirit" (27:50).

Rolling stone tombs with burial chambers were common in Israel.
© 2018 by Zondervan

Some have suggested that Jesus's tomb was sealed with a stone that looked more like a mushroom.
Tom Powers/BiblePlaces.com

Jesus is taken down from the cross and placed in the tomb of Joseph of Arimathea, and a guard is placed before the entrance (27:57–66). The tomb was hewn out of rock and a rolling stone covered the entrance. Common Jewish practice was to leave the body in the tomb for a period to allow the flesh to decompose. The bones would later be gathered and placed in an ossuary for a secondary burial. But Jesus did not remain in the tomb.

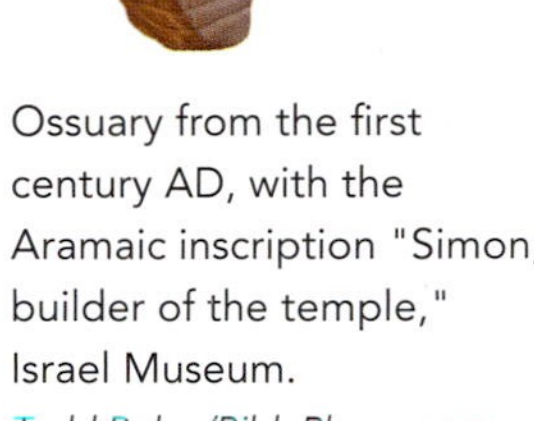

Ossuary from the first century AD, with the Aramaic inscription "Simon, builder of the temple," Israel Museum.
Todd Bolen/BiblePlaces.com

Jesus's Resurrection (28:1–15)

The climax of Matthew's gospel is Jesus's resurrection from the dead. The event was so important that the earliest Christian confession preserved it as the foundation of the Christian faith (1 Cor. 15:3–8). Matthew's account shows that Mary Magdalene and Mary the mother of James (Matt. 27:56) went to the tomb, found the stone removed from the entrance, heard the testimony of an angel that Jesus was risen, and saw the empty tomb (28:5–7). Though the early church recorded the appearance of Jesus to Peter, the apostles, and five hundred disciples (1 Cor. 15:5), these women were the first to hear about the resurrection from the angel, see the empty tomb (28:5–7), and then meet and touch the resurrected Jesus (28:8–10). Matthew also comments that they were the first to proclaim his resurrection (28:7, 10). Being bribed, the soldiers testified that his body was stolen (28:11–15).

Jesus's Authority and the Disciple's Ministry (28:16–20)

Matthew's gospel ends abruptly with the appearance of Jesus to the eleven apostles. While some worship him, others doubted what they saw, so extraordinary was it to see him after his crucifixion. Jesus declares his sovereign authority over all things in heaven and earth (28:18; cf. Col. 1:15–20; Dan. 7:13–14). Unlike Luke, Matthew does not record his ascension (Luke 24:50–53) but rather his command to go and make disciples of all nations (28:19–20), pointing to the mission beyond Israel to the gentiles. Jesus's sovereignty over everything in heaven and earth opens the way to the universal proclamation of the gospel.

The sign of discipleship would be baptism and obedience to Jesus's teaching. Although these new disciples and the apostles cannot follow Jesus physically, they are given the assurance, "And surely I am with you always, to the very end of the age" (28:20).

AUTHOR AND DATE

The author of this gospel did not identify himself, although the book itself yields some information about the author. The person was adept at Greek, but the author's use of the OT suggests that he knew that text in Hebrew and not only in translation. He understood debates among the rabbis. The evidence strongly points to an author who was a Hellenistic Jew and not a gentile.[3]

The evidence from the church fathers points to Matthew, the apostle, as the author (Matt. 9:9; 10:3; also known as Levi in Mark 2:14; Luke 5:27–29). Papias (ca. AD 60–155) ascribed the book to Matthew, saying, "Matthew collected the oracles in the Hebrew language, and each interpreted them as best he could" (recorded in Eusbebius, *Hist. eccl.* 3.39.16). Irenaeus (ca. AD 130–202) says the same: "Now Matthew published among the Hebrews a written gospel also in their own tongue" (Eusebius, *Hist. eccl.* 5.8.2; Irenaeus, *Haer.* 3.1.1). Eusebius mentions that Pantaenus (the teacher of Clement of Alexandria, ca. AD 150–215) went to India and noted the tradition there that Bartholomew, one of the apostles, "had preached to them and had left them the writing of Matthew in Hebrew letters, which was preserved until the time mentioned" (*Hist. eccl.* 5.10.3). Some have suggested that these statements mean it was written in a Semitic style, but these witnesses appear to point to Hebrew or Aramaic as the language Matthew used in composition. What, then, might be the relationship between the gospel we have and these testimonies? Irenaeus also knows about a Greek gospel that he attributes to Matthew (*Haer.* 3.11.8; 3.21.3–4; 3.16.2) as does Origen (AD 184/185–253/254; *Or.* 17). The canonical lists of the early church included the Greek gospel of Matthew. Our best evidence points to Matthew, the apostle, as the author of this book, even though we cannot fully explain the relationship between the gospel we possess and the testimony about a Hebrew edition.

The date of composition was during the first century AD. Both Ignatius and the Didache appear to use it, and the book was well-known in the second century. Some date it in the 80s or 90s, but others believe it was written before the destruction of Jerusalem in AD 70. The question is whether the prediction about the destruction of the Temple in Matthew 24:1–2 spoke prophetically about an event yet to come or whether it recalled the event after the fact. A date before AD 70 is more likely if, indeed, the apostle Matthew was the author.

SUMMARY

The gospel of Matthew records the life of Jesus but also addresses the question of the influx of gentiles into the community of disciples. Some suggest Matthew penned the gospel for the church in Antioch of Syria, a town with a sizable Jewish population but also a place where early on, gentiles integrated into the church (Acts 11:19–21). One of the early witnesses to the existence of this gospel was Ignatius (ca. AD 35–107), who was from Antioch. But this and other gospels circulated quickly throughout the empire. This was a gospel for all Christians, and remains so to this very day.[4]

Questions for Discussion

1. How are Jesus's teaching on ethics in the Sermon on the Mount (Matt. 5–7) relevant today? Can you apply them to concrete situations?
2. What does the gospel of Matthew say about Christian community and the way that Jesus's disciples relate to one another? Be sure to include Jesus's teaching in Matthew 18.
3. Discuss the principle elements of Jesus's teaching on the kingdom of heaven.
4. In what ways does Matthew address the issue of multiculturalism and the church?
5. What significance does the cross and resurrection of Jesus have for understanding salvation and Christian mission?

BIBLIOGRAPHY

Introductory

Blomberg, C. L. *Matthew.* NAC. Nashville: Broadman, 1992.

Brown, J. K. *Matthew.* TTC. Grand Rapids: Baker, 2015.

Carson, D. A. "Matthew." Pages 23–670 in *Expositors Bible Commentary. Edited by Tremper Longman III and David E. Garland. Vol. 9.* Grand Rapids: Zondervan, 2010.

Evans, C. A. *Matthew.* NCBC. Cambridge: Cambridge University Press, 2012.

Keener, C. S. *Matthew.* NTC. Downers Grove, IL: InterVarsity Press, 1997.

Wilkins, Michael J. *Matthew.* NIVAC. Grand Rapids: Zondervan, 2004.

Advanced

Davies, W. D., and D. C. Allison, Jr. *A Critical and Exegetical Commentary on the Gospel according to St. Matthew.* 3 vols. ICC. Edinburgh: T & T Clark, 1988–1997.

France, R. T. *The Gospel of Matthew.* NICNT. Grand Rapids: Eerdmans, 2007.

Hagner, D. A. *Matthew.* 2 vols. WBC. Dallas: Word, 1993–1995.

Keener, C. S. *The Gospel of Matthew: A Socio-Rhetorical Commentary.* Grand Rapids: Eerdmans, 2009

Luz, U. *Matthew.* 3 vols. Hermeneia. Minneapolis: Fortress, 2001–2007.

Nolland, J. *The Gospel of Matthew.* NIGTC. Grand Rapids: Eerdmans, 2005.

Osborne, G. R. *Matthew.* ZECNT. Grand Rapids: Zondervan, 2010.

NOTES

1. M. B. Thompson, "The Holy Internet: Communication Between Churches in the First Christian Generation," in R. Bauckham, ed., *The Gospel for All Christians. Rethinking the Gospel Audiences* (Grand Rapids: Eerdmans, 1998), 49–70.

2. See D. Instone-Brewer, *Divorce and Remarriage in the Bible. The Social and Literary Context* (Grand Rapids: Eerdmans, 2002), ch. 5.

3. W. D. Davies and Dale C. Allison, *A Critical and Exegetical Commentary on The Gospel According to Saint Matthew* (3 vols.; Edinburgh: T&T Clark, 1988–1997), 1.57–58.

4. See Bauckham, ed. *The Gospel for All Christians.*

THE GOSPEL
ACCORDING TO MARK

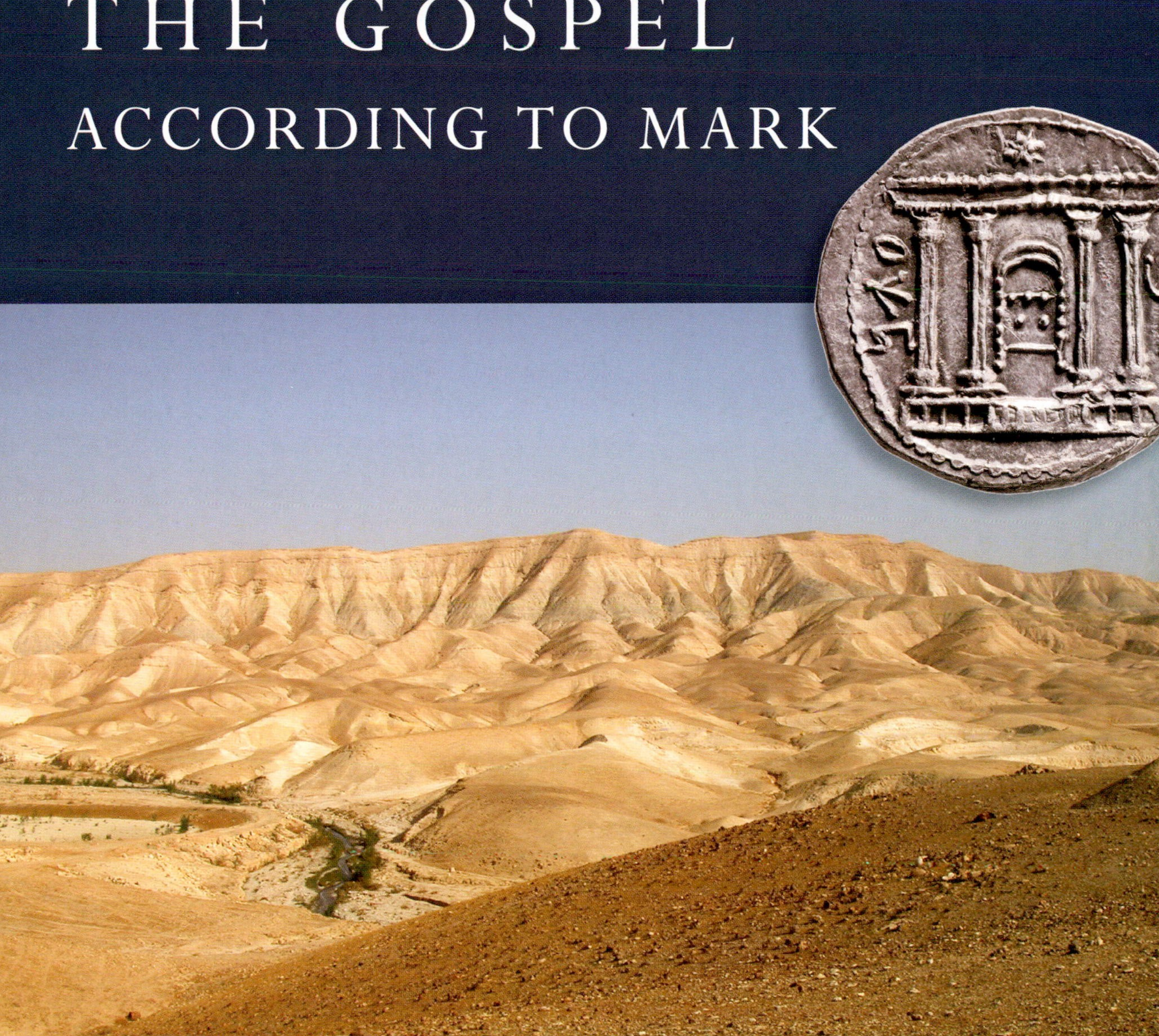

Mark's opening scene finds John the Baptist in the wilderness, calling Israel to repentance.
Todd Bolen/BiblePlaces.com

Mark organizes Jesus's ministry into two simple locales: first Galilee and then Judea. The Sea of Galilee with its many villages saw the bulk of Jesus's ministry. Sunset looking west toward Tiberias.
Todd Bolen/BiblePlaces.com

Mark's story of Jesus is well-known for being quick-paced and dramatic. In fact, its story is so compelling when read aloud and reflects many of the dramatic features of Hellenistic theater that many scholars are convinced that this gospel was originally intended for oral presentation. In Mark 1–3 exorcisms, miracles, and conflict stories appear in rapid succession as Jesus launches his ministry in Galilee. Immediately his authority is established as he demonstrates his power over disease, demons, and even nature. Jesus's authority even encompasses privileges normally reserved for God: the ability to forgive sin and working on the Sabbath. This inspires harsh criticism from his opponents.

As we read Mark's drama we wonder: Who will understand that this is the Son of God (cf. 1:1)? Mark's technique is not unlike watching a film (like a thriller) when you know more than the characters in the story ("Don't go down into that basement with only a flashlight!"). Mark "privileges" his readers in a similar way. We know things that even the apostles have to figure out. If this is the Jewish Messiah, who will embrace and promote his emerging kingdom? In the first half, Mark shows Jesus's public successes in Galilee and in adjacent Hellenistic areas north and east of Galilee (both climaxed by a feeding miracle). Suddenly—at a

During a renovation of Jerusalem in the 1940s, the Syrian Orthodox Church found a sixth-century Aramaic inscription here that referred to Saint Mark. Today it is a chapel commemorating his residence in Jerusalem.
momo/Wikimedia Commons, CC BY 2.0

critical turning point in the story—Jesus turns to his followers near a mountain in the far north and asks them what they think about him (8:27). After two wrong answers, Peter says, "You are the Messiah" (8:29). As readers we almost breathe a sigh of relief that Peter gets it right.

Mark then abruptly shifts the direction of his story. Jesus moves south, toward Judea, toward his fate at the hands of the Jerusalem Temple hierarchy. He predicts his own death three times, and each time Mark explains how Jesus is misunderstood. Finally, Jesus arrives at Jerusalem during Passover, in the midst of crowds of cheering Galilean pilgrims who have celebrated his message in the north. But as his popularity swells, so does his opposition. The religious leadership of Jerusalem moves quickly to check Jesus's growing celebrity status. He confronts them with courage, prophesies God's judgment on their world, and is promptly taken into custody. He is crucified but not defeated. Mark ends his story with an empty tomb, dazed followers, and angels proclaiming his resurrection. In crisp dramatic form, Mark closes the story, telling us that the women are silenced in their astonishment and filled with fear (16:8).

THE ORIGINAL AUDIENCE OF MARK

Some scholars see hidden in Mark's narrative hints of the gospel's intended audience. By the end of the second century, Clement of Alexandria said with confidence that Mark wrote his gospel from Rome. This is no doubt linked to the widely held tradition of Peter's martyrdom in Rome and Mark's connection with him as the recorder of his memoirs. The earliest clear witness to this comes from a prologue (*The Anti-Marcionite Prologue*), written in about AD 175. It says, "Mark declared, who is called the 'stump fingered,' because he had small fingers in comparison with the stature of the rest of his body. He was the interpreter of Peter. After the death of Peter himself he wrote down this same gospel in the regions of Italy."[1]

We can also reconstruct some features of Mark's audience by reading between the lines. Most of Mark's readers/hearers spoke Greek and did not know Hebrew or Aramaic. Hebrew names and Aramaic words are translated (3:17; 7:34; 15:22, 34). In 7:1–4 Mark outlines Jewish purification rituals for those who do not understand Judaism. But this audience does know some of the rudiments of the Christian message. In 15:1 he does not have to explain who Pilate is, nor does he have to explain the Pharisees or the high priest. Words like *rabbi*, *Gehenna*, and *amen* are used without explanation. In 15:21 Mark refers to Simon of Cyrene as the father of "Alexander and Rufus." These two men are likely Christians known to Mark's audience; if we could place them, we could fix the locale of the gospel.

But Mark also shows a casual ease with Latin. He also uses Latin technical terms particularly for items connected to the army (legion, 5:9; *praetorium*,

15:16; centurion, 15:39; *speculator* (or guard), 6:27; *flagellare*, 15:15). He also uses Latin to explain common Greek terms (two copper coins, Gk. *lepta*, also a Latin *quadrans*, 12:42; the fortress, Gk. *aules*, means *praetorium* in Latin, 15:16). All this points to a Roman origin or at least to a setting immersed in Roman culture.

We should note that a strong and lasting tradition attaches Mark with Egypt perhaps before he came to Rome. In the earliest church historian, Eusebius (*Church History*, Book 1, 15–16), we read that Mark founded the church in Alexandria in Egypt. Today the ancient Egyptian Coptic Church claims him as their patriarch.

MARK'S LITERARY FORM

Most agree that a decisive turning point in this gospel occurs when Peter confesses the true identity of Jesus at Caesarea Philippi (8:29). But this confession is also mirrored by two other announcements that frame the ends of the gospel. In 1:1 the gospel begins with Mark's own personal testimony of faith: "The beginning of the good news about Jesus the Messiah, the Son of God" [note: some manuscripts omit "Son of God"]. At the close of the gospel we hear a Roman centurion at the cross proclaim, "Surely this man was the Son of God!" (15:39). Hence three confessions—by the author, the leading Jewish apostle, and a gentile—frame the gospel, hinting at Mark's purposes. This structure plants three literary "flags" in the gospel that confess Jesus's identity, and as they do this they divide the gospel into two discrete sections. To readers, Mark's purpose is clear: he wants to persuade us to see Jesus as the Messiah embraced by all the world.

To accomplish this evangelistic goal, Mark builds his case for Jesus by writing his story in two major divisions. First, Jesus is introduced *in public* to the communities of Galilee. Evidence for his messiahship mounts with each new miracle, exorcism, and parable. When Jesus is farthest from Jerusalem (Caesarea Philippi), he challenges his followers to identify him accurately.

Peter does this, and immediately (this is the second half) Jesus heads toward Jerusalem and teaches the apostles *privately* how he must die when he arrives. Jesus's successes in Galilee suddenly reverse themselves. Though crowds cheer Jesus's arrival, authorities plot his demise. Within three chapters, Jesus is dead. When Mark's audience is at its lowest ebb, a handful of women arrive at the tomb carrying burial spices. Suddenly, the story reverses again. The tomb is empty, and angels proclaim that even death cannot defeat Jesus.

Outline of Mark

I. The Ministry of Jesus in Galilee (1:1–8:26)
   1. Prologue (1:1–13)
   2. The First Phase of the Galilean Ministry (1:14–3:6)

3. The Second Phase of the Galilean Ministry (3:7–7:23)
4. The Third Phase of the Galilean Ministry (7:24–8:26)

II. The Suffering of Jesus in Jerusalem (8:27–16:8)
1. Jesus Travels to Jerusalem (8:27–10:52)
2. Jesus Enters Jerusalem (11:1–13:37)
3. Jesus Dies in Jerusalem (14:1–16:8)

THE MINISTRY OF JESUS IN GALILEE (1:1–8:26)

The first half of Mark's gospel demonstrates how Jesus's power and authority validate his claim to be Judaism's Messiah. Fifteen miracle stories reinforce how Jesus is uniquely equipped to bring the power of his kingdom to bear on the forces of this world. Nevertheless, no one understands him or recognizes his identity except demons, whom he defeats. In both divisions of the gospel we find a lengthy "anchor" parable that summarizes the purpose of the section. In the first half, Jesus is a sower casting seed among a variety of soils, watching for their growth or response.

Prologue (1:1–13)

Mark opens by introducing us to John the Baptist, a prophet who is fulfilling the call of Malachi 3:1 and Isaiah 40:3. His appearance evokes strong memories of Elijah, who likewise stood outside Israel, calling the nation to repentance. But John is not merely calling Israel to repent; he is "on stage" to announce the messianic age soon to be inaugurated by the arrival of Jesus. This Messiah will usher in the messianic kingdom and baptize his followers with the Holy Spirit, empowering them in a manner reminiscent of his own anointing by the Spirit.

Jesus arrives at the Jordan River; when he is baptized, a heavenly voice confirms his identity, and the Spirit descends on him. At once we know we have met the hero of Mark's drama. Endowed with the power of the Spirit, Jesus is sent deeper into the desert to see if his faithfulness to God is greater than the tests of Satan. This test recalls the testing of Israel in the desert (forty years, forty days), but we see the true valor and success of Israel's Messiah.

Herod Antipas ruled in Galilee. These rare coins stem from his rule (4 BC–AD 39). One side shows an upright palm with "Herod the Tetrarch." The reverse: a wreath with the name of Tiberias, where it was minted.
Z. Radovan/www.BibleLandPictures.com

The First Phase of the Galilean Ministry (1:14–3:6)

The opening verses of Jesus's public ministry must be read with care. John has been arrested, yet Mark gives no hint at any opposition. Why? Who has been angered? This is a sign foreshadowing what will come.

Mark next distills the essence of Jesus's public announcement, "The time has come. . . . The kingdom of God has come near. Repent and believe the good news!" (1:15). John was preparing Israel for the inbreaking of God's salvation in history;

John the Baptist was likely killed at Herod's fortress called Machaerus. This is located in Jordan, on the east side of the Dead Sea. *Reproduced by permission from Carole Raddato*

Why Was John the Baptist Arrested?

The region of the Jordan where John worked was called Perea, which shared a border with Nabatea. Mark explains that John was arrested because of his prophetic critique of the wrongful marriage of Herod Antipas to his brother's wife Herodias (6:14–29). Before Antipas married Herodias, he was married to the daughter of the Nabatean king in Petra (now in South Jordan). The princess returned to her father in shame. John the Baptist condemned this well-known scandal, inflaming a possible war. Herod's arrest of John was thus a political move designed to silence this critic. Josephus tells us that John was imprisoned in the fortress of Machaerus, which guarded the Nabatean border.

Today followers of John the Baptist still venerate him as the one true messenger of God. This community (called the Mandeans) lives along the Tigris River in Iraq, practices river baptisms, and follows a secret religion preserved by a handful of Mandean priests.

On one occasion Jesus demonstrated his authority over the Sabbath by letting his followers "harvest" grain on the Sabbath (Mark 2:23). This led to an immediate controversy. *DreamyPixel*

Jesus is the catalyst of this new kingdom. But its announcement must first take place in Galilee. Because of the violent removal and imprisonment of John from the Jordan, Jesus moves north. (In 6:14–29 Mark relates the full story of John's arrest and the fears of Herod Antipas.)

The exciting opening Galilean stories of Mark serve to reinforce the importance of what is happening in Israel. This new kingdom is a realm of power, whose king bears unique authority to challenge the powers of the world. Jesus calls people from their careers—and they respond immediately. He teaches with authority, and the crowds give him undivided attention. With authority he casts out demons, heals Simon Peter's mother-in-law, cures a leper, and restores the legs of a paralytic. He even forgives the sins of a man. Each of these stories underscores that defeating human affliction, sin, suffering, and the demonic are the necessary work of the kingdom of God. But these do not stand alone. Jesus's teaching is intimately linked to these powerful works.

From these earliest days, Jesus's popularity grows swiftly. Crowds from everywhere press about him, whole cities gather in their synagogues, and even the religious leadership begins to question him. Mark builds a picture of Jesus's fame as he moves through the villages of Galilee.

Jesus in Capernaum

Mark tells us that Jesus anchored his ministry in the village of Capernaum. Jesus's move here was a strategic decision. He could have based himself at Sepphoris (Galilee's historic political capital) or Herod Antipas's new seaside town of Tiberias. Magdala, on Galilee's west shore, had a population of about forty thousand (according to Josephus, who surely exaggerates), where one of Jesus's followers named Mary lived (Mark 15:40; Luke 8:2). Or he could have used a hillside village like Cana, Gamla, or Arbela. Galilee was filled with Jewish towns, and archaeologists have located countless synagogues throughout the region. Instead, Jesus chose Capernaum, one of several small fishing anchorages along the Galilee seacoast.

Capernaum had advantages. Located on the northwest shore of the sea, it lay on the main north/south road that cut through the country. Military units and caravans moved north through a variety of valleys until they came to the Sea of Galilee. They then traveled north and entered Capernaum before continuing north. This is why Capernaum was a tax station and also hosted a contingent of Roman soldiers.

The Second Phase of the Galilean Ministry (3:7–7:23)

Jesus's popularity continues to grow, his authority and power are demonstrated in more dramatic scenes, and opposition continues to test him. Jesus's following takes a form that can be measured. Twelve leaders are appointed and assist not only in representing the kingdom throughout Galilee's villages but in managing the crowds, who now number in the thousands.

Mark lists the twelve men (3:13–19)—a symbolic echo of the twelve tribes of Israel. Jesus is like a new Moses, tested in the desert, now leading twelve new tribes into a new kingdom. These twelve "apostles" (6:30) receive unique privileges. They leave their occupations and join Jesus in his itinerant ministry in Galilee. They not only learn by observing his life of faith, but they are given inside teaching unavailable to the masses (4:34). Jesus even invites three among them (Peter, James, John) to observe breathtaking scenes: the raising up of a little girl (5:37) and his transfiguration (9:2). These three will later ask him privately about his teachings (13:3) and accompany him in the night of prayer before his arrest (14:33).

But Jesus also has a mission for his disciples. He sends them out to preach and to have authority over demons. At one point, they strike out on their own in pairs, visiting villages and trusting God for provisions (6:7–13). They discover they are agents of Jesus's kingdom, extending its reach in ways they never imagined. They *can* heal. They *can* defeat Satan. And they *can* explain in public venues what is happening in the land. In a word, they not only represent Jesus, but they now bear his kingdom power.

Mark includes a representative selection of Jesus's parables, whose central aim is to interpret the meaning of this new kingdom. The kingdom reminds Jesus of scattered seed (4:26) or a grain of mustard seed (4:31). But the most significant parable is the parable of the sower (4:1–20), which represents everything happening in the public ministry: Jesus is a farmer casting seed onto a variety of soils. Most receive the seed and it takes root, but only a few seeds find "good soil" that permits the seed to produce a generous yield. This parable thus *interprets* the

Jesus returned frequently to Capernaum and used it as his ministry base in Galilee. A modern Catholic church, supported by pillars, protects what is believed to have been the house of Peter.
Bill Schlegel/BiblePlaces.com

Some scholars believe we may have found the residential area of Capernaum (Mark 1:30). Note the small size of the rooms and their black basalt construction.
vblinov/Shutterstock

nature of Jesus's work in Galilee, casting among the public the good news of the gospel. Such parables are typical of Jesus's teaching style (4:2, 33–34), veiling to many the true secrets of the kingdom (4:11–12).

Since a number of Jesus's apostles are fishermen, we often find him using boats either to teach in (4:1) or to cross the Sea of Galilee. On two occasions storms arise, placing the crew in jeopardy (4:35–41; 6:45–52). On each occasion, Jesus rescues the boat by silencing the storm. Jesus can control the primeval forces of chaos that reside in the seas.

Jesus's first miracle in Mark was an exorcism that took place in Capernaum's synagogue. The white limestone structure seen today is from the fourth century.
© 2018 by Zondervan

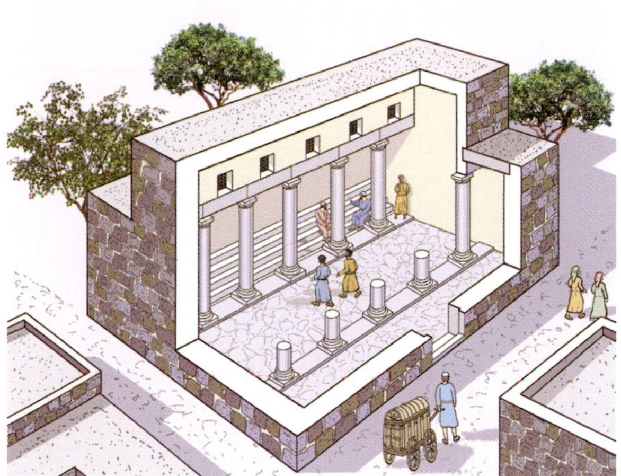

This is an artist's reconstruction of the synagogue that stood in Capernaum in the fourth century.
A reconstruction by Dr. Leen Ritmeyer

The excavation of Capernaum's fourth-century white limestone synagogue revealed that it rests on the foundation of a first-century black basalt synagogue.
Robert Hoetink/123RF.com

Jesus's more assertive posture in Galilee is noticed. In chapter 6 Mark recounts what actually happened during John's arrest and death—not simply to complete the story, but to interpret the political atmosphere of Herod's Galilean tetrarchy. Herod Antipas is now wondering about Jesus. But Herod knows that Jesus had been with John and is disturbed by the prospect that now John the Baptist has returned from the grave to haunt him. Mark's implications are clear.

Along the Sea of Galilee, a man demonstrates the ancient art of throwing a cast net.
Library of Congress, LC-matpc-00691/ www.LifeintheHolyLand.com

Fishing on the Sea of Galilee

Net fishing was the typical method of fishing for those who lived on the sea; the gospels point to Jesus's knowledge of fishing.[2] Hook-and-line fishing was known but used far less since it yielded fewer fish. Three net systems were in use.

The *drag net* (cf. Matt. 13:47–48) was the most ancient form and is attested early in Egypt. A wall-like net with weights on the bottom and cork on the top is pulled along the coast. Then the lead rope is swept across the sea by boat and pulled back to shore, pulling in fish as it comes. The fish are then sorted and distributed to the workers.

The *cast net* (cf. Mark 1:16–17) is circular. It has lead sinkers attached to its edges and is tossed into the sea by a lone fisherman. It lands on the water like a parachute, sinking and catching unwary fish. The fisherman either dives into the water and pulls the fish out individually, or dives down, gathers the weights together, and lifts the net into his boat.

The *trammel net* (cf. Mark 1:19–20) has three "layers" of net connected at the top by a head rope (with cork) and a foot rope (with lead weights). The outer nets have wide openings, while the inner net is finely meshed and loose, flowing easily in and out of the outer nets. The net is spread in the water generally at night in a long line and held while other fishermen scare the fish toward it (with splashing). The fish enter the first net easily, push against the fine mesh net, and then carry the fine net into the third outer net, entangling themselves hopelessly. The fishermen haul the net ashore, disentangle the fish, and repair the many breaks. In the story of the miraculous catch of fish (Luke 5:1–7), the men have already fished all night and now are repairing their trammel nets. Jesus tells them to set sail again and drop the net once more. This was a genuine act of faith! In John 21:1–8 Jesus also meets them after a night of fruitless work and this time tells them to toss a cast net into the sea. This yields a catch of 153 fish.

While net fishing was the most common practice, fish hooks were also in use. Jesus referred to them in Matthew 17:27.
Image courtesy of Marc Breitsprecher, www.Ancient Imports.com

Jesus must be wary of the political forces in Galilee that could execute him on a whim. Thus, Jesus moves away to "a quiet place" (6:31), possibly beyond Herod's reach.

But word of Jesus's movement has also reached Jerusalem's leadership, and they send emissaries to interrogate him (7:1). Jesus uses their questions as an opportunity to unmask their true spiritual jeopardy. He cites harsh words from Isaiah 29 ("They worship me in vain"), then illustrates by citing two examples of the misuse of God's law. The razor edge of his prophetic rebuke comes in Mark 7:9, "You have a fine way of setting aside the commands of God in order to observe your own traditions!"

Fishing was a major industry in Galilee. Fish were used for local consumption and exported throughout the province. These fish (tilapia) are common in the Sea of Galilee.
Z. Radovan/www.BibleLand Pictures.com

The Third Phase of the Galilean Ministry (7:24–8:26)

The Jordan River inlet to the Sea of Galilee (on its north shore) served as a political and cultural boundary in Galilee. The Greek culture influenced the Decapolis to the east; the regions to the west were Jewish. Politically, this line also marked the boundary between Philip (east) and Herod Antipas (west). Thus, when Jesus moves into Bethsaida (6:45), he is moving into a different world, free of Herod's threats. When he exorcises demons from the man in the region of the Gerasenes (5:1), he is in gentile territory (cf. the pigs that become host to the demons, 5:11).

In 1986 two men from the Israeli kibbutz Nof Ginosar discovered a sunken fishing boat from the first century at the bottom of the Sea of Galilee. Today it has been restored and rests in the Nof Ginosar kibbutz museum.
Logan Bash/Shutterstock

Jesus's transition into gentile territory now takes on a more deliberate form. He travels to the far north, beyond Galilee, and enters the gentile cities of Tyre and Sidon, where he meets a Greek woman who exhibits a devotion he had sought among the Jews. He moves directly into the Decapolis (7:31) and following a healing, the Greeks there compliment him. He feeds four thousand people, showing his growing popularity even in this region. Jesus's eating practices are criticized in 7:1–5, and in 7:14–23 Jesus argues against such rules, declaring all foods "clean." He is now signaling a key aspect of his new kingdom where division of "clean" and "unclean" no longer applies.

Jesus moves back and forth between the two political sections. Then he returns to Bethsaida, healing a blind man (8:22–26). This story is as much parable as it is miracle story. After his eyes are anointed the first time, the blind man can only see partially. Jesus must anoint him again, and this restores his sight perfectly. Partial (spiritual) sight is exactly the condition of the apostles (8:21), who now must be given clear vision.

Jesus's decision to move east of Galilee brought him into contact with gentiles from the Decapolis. This site across the water on the eastern side of the lake is Kursi. It held a Greek fishing village and recalls the location of Jesus driving demons into a herd of pigs.
Jennifer Kintner/BiblePlaces.com

THE SUFFERING OF JESUS IN JERUSALEM (8:27–16:8)

The second half of Mark follows Jesus's movement from Caesarea Philippi to Jerusalem during the season of Passover. Once Peter accurately identifies Jesus, Jesus begins the first of his three predictions of the cross (8:31; 9:31; 10:33). Each prediction increases in specificity and is surrounded by ironic responses among the apostles. When Jesus reaches Jerusalem, the confrontation hinted at throughout the gospel comes to a climax.

Jesus Travels to Jerusalem (8:27–10:52)

Caesarea Philippi, in the foothills of Mount Hermon, was the capital of this northeastern region ruled by Philip. Here Jesus probes his followers' understanding of his identity. They report the rumors that are swirling around them; then Peter offers what we have not heard yet in this gospel: "You are the Messiah." It is no accident that this confession occurs far from Jerusalem. In Mark's mind, faith has been discovered far from the epicenter of Jewish practice—among the gentiles no less—and when Jesus moves toward Jerusalem, faith will seem faint, and cynicism and hostility will grow.

Immediately following Peter's confession, Jesus must redefine what it means to be the Messiah as he heads south. In 8:32 Peter tries to correct Jesus's statement but is rebuked. When Jesus is transformed on the peak of a mountain (likely Mount Hermon), Peter offers the foolish suggestion to stay there and bask in the glory and power of the moment. But Jesus leads them down the mountain to a scene of chaos and service, where his truer mission is realized.

The Messianic Secret

One peculiar feature of Mark's presentation of Jesus is that Jesus frequently conceals his true identity. For instance, he tells demonic spirits to be silent as they are expelled (1:25, 34; 3:11–12), and he orders people who have been healed to keep their experience a secret (1:44; 5:43; 7:36; 8:26). After Peter's confession at Caesarea Philippi, Jesus even tells him to be silent (8:30), and when Peter, James, and John return with Jesus from his transfiguration, he charges them not to report what they have seen (9:9). Jesus clearly wants people to know who he is. So why does he refuse to let them speak openly about it?

The best explanation for Mark's "messianic secret" is found in the underlying political forces that shaped messianic expectation in Jesus's day. He does not want to become a pawn serving the agenda of militant Jewish groups, nor does he want to incite a violent revolt against Rome. Some of his actions (such as the cleansing of the temple, the feeding miracles) could lend themselves to this interpretation, and he needs to control the true nature of his mission. Power is not the gateway to understanding Jesus—it is the cross. Thus, Mark presents a Roman centurion (a man of war) who recognizes Jesus only as he stands at the foot of the cross (15:39).

In chapter 9 Jesus again predicts his Passion, and this is followed by an argument concerning which of his disciples is greatest (9:33–37). If Jesus is going to die, they are already positioning themselves for his succession. As he nears Jerusalem, the dreaded reality of this mission hangs over them, and they walk behind him, fearful and amazed (10:32). Following the third prediction (10:33) there is another ironic dispute. If Jesus dies, then James and John want to be sure they have privileges in heaven. In these carefully written stories, Mark is signaling to us the severity of Jesus's prediction and the inability of his followers to embrace it. The "way of the cross" is something they cannot understand or champion.

Caesarea Philippi was the capital of the northeastern region ruled by Philip. Today ancient ruins can still be found, such as this Roman arch used as a bridge over a small river.
Todd Bolen/BiblePlaces.com

These teachings on the road to Jerusalem bridge the mission of Jesus with the call to discipleship. "Whoever wants to be my disciple must deny themselves and take up their cross and follow me" (8:34). "Whoever wants to be first must be slave of all" (10:44). Sacrifice is the first hallmark of membership in this kingdom: "For even the Son of Man did not come to be served, but to serve, and to give his life as a ransom for many" (10:45). Models of true discipleship can be found in children (9:36; 10:14). They can also be found in the blind, such as the man in Jericho, whose request stands in contrast to that of James and John. He cries for mercy and a gift; they demand privilege and power.

Evidence of the Roman occupation of Judea can be seen in the many artifacts of material culture that have been discovered from the New Testament era. This hammered gold-leaf jewelry from the late Roman period is on display at the Israel Museum (Jerusalem).

Jesus Enters Jerusalem (11:1–13:37)

When Mark mentions Jericho, Jesus has almost reached his destination. Pilgrims and merchants often followed the road from Galilee to Jerusalem that went south down the Jordan Valley. At the oasis of Jericho, it climbed the mountain, heading west, following switchbacks for its 3,500-foot ascent. Jesus passes through two villages on the east side of the crest (Bethany and Bethphage) without stopping.

Here Mark's story accelerates. Jesus arrives in the city in triumph, cheered by pilgrims from Galilee who recognize him and have also come for Passover. His confrontation with the Temple now is overt. He expresses outrage at the commercial industries of the Temple's courts, and with the fury of a prophet, judges what he sees. As he crosses back and forth between Bethany (where he stays, 11:11) and Jerusalem, he curses a fig tree—a symbol of Israel and its Temple—because it provides no fruit, and the tree dies. This too is a prophetic gesture.

The leading figures in Jerusalem society now interrogate Jesus: Pharisees, Herodians, Sadducees, and scribes (12:13, 18, 28). In his debates Jesus offers his second major narrative parable that anchors the deeper meaning of the second half of this gospel. The parable of the vineyard and the tenants (12:1–11) echoes Isaiah's song of the vineyard (Isa. 5:1–7), expressing despair for Israel's failure to produce a nation pleasing to God. Then Jesus applies the story to himself: he is the son of the vineyard owner. But the hubris of the tenants prevails. They murder the son, cast him from the vineyard, and hope to claim the destiny of the vineyard for themselves. Instead, the vineyard's tenants will be judged. From the Mount of Olives, Jesus scans the city of Jerusalem and announces its downfall.

Jesus Dies in Jerusalem (14:1–16:8)

The authorities now determine to kill Jesus (12:12), but are unable, thanks to his popularity among the pilgrims. But death looms over the story. Jesus is anointed for burial in Bethany, one of his disciples chooses to betray him, and Jesus reinterprets his final Passover as a meal recognizing his imminent death. As Jesus prays in an olive grove beneath the Mount of Olives, his captors come and spirit him away to the high priest Caiaphas. Here Jesus openly acknowledges his identity and is condemned, sent to the Roman governor Pilate, and beaten in preparation for crucifixion.

Mark's crucifixion scene is deeply ironic since six times Jesus is referred to as "king" (15:2, 9, 12, 18, 26, 32) and three times is mocked on the cross. But he is a king, bringing a kingdom to Israel that Caiaphas and Pilate cannot recognize. He is buried by a rich man and tended by female disciples. They represent the polar opposites of Israel: the pious leadership of the nation and the poor from Galilee.

When the women arrive at the tomb on Sunday morning, a heavenly messenger greets them, announcing that Jesus is alive, fulfilling his threefold promise of resurrection (8:31; 9:31; 10:34). But instead of obeying the angel and reporting back to the others, they flee in fear, awestruck by what they have seen. Most scholars are convinced that Mark's gospel ends at 16:8, giving a poignant ending to the drama (see sidebar). The readers or hearers of this gospel wonder: What happened? Where is Jesus? Where do the women go? The climax of Mark's gospel is taut with mystery and intrigue, and it prods us to complete the drama with our own belief. Imagine this performed as a theatrical drama. Mark's ending is ideal: the empty tomb and the awestruck disciples stand before the audience as a challenge.

Mark's Longer Ending

Mark's gospel ends dramatically at 16:8, with a circle of women exploring the empty tomb and fleeing in fear. But some translations add verses 9–20, which describe personal appearances of Jesus and his commission to the disciples. Later scribes wanted to give Mark a more satisfying and obvious finale.

These verses are undoubtedly a later addition to Mark; our best Greek manuscripts know nothing of them. Their style is strikingly different, and most of their elements are taken from other parts of the New Testament (cf. 16:9–11 with John 20:14–18; 16:12–13 with Luke 24:13–35).

These verses do serve us, however, as a window into a Christian world somewhere in antiquity. They help us glimpse one stream of Christian experience that *someone* thought was normative. The verses show Jesus describing some of the marks of a believer's life: preaching, tongues, exorcism, protection from snakes and poison, and healing.

AUTHOR AND DATE

Unlike most Hellenistic biographies, no gospel bears reference to its author. But such anonymous writing was not unusual for books not being written for the "book trade." The prolific writer Galen (AD 129–c. 199), court physician to Marcus Aurelius, tells us in his essay "On My Own Books" that he gave his works "without a title to my friends or pupils," since he did not have publication in mind. When these things were published for public consumption, "everyone gave them a different title." It is clear that in the world of antiquity, publishing was conceptualized much differently than it is today.[3]

The gospels were likely personal documents, written within the communities they served. Thanks to effective travel and trade routes, Christians began reading each other's texts regularly. Sometime in the second century, the phrase "According to Mark" was attached either to the end or the beginning of this gospel (or even in the margin). Can this later scribal identification be trusted? Who was this "Mark"?

The most important early church record of the tradition that associates Mark with our gospel comes from Papias, bishop of Hierapolis in Phrygia in the early second century (in words recorded by Eusebius):

> The elder used to say this, "Mark became the interpreter of Peter and wrote down accurately (though not in order) all that he remembered of what was said or done by the Lord. For he had neither heard nor followed the Lord; but later (as I said) he followed Peter, who used to give teaching as necessity demanded—but he [Peter] did not make an orderly account of the Lord's sayings. So Mark did no wrong in writing down some things as he recalled them. For he made it his aim to leave out nothing he had heard and to state nothing falsely" (*Eccl. Hist.*, 3.39.15).

Mark is clearly linked with Peter, and his aim is to write an accurate (not necessarily chronological) account of Jesus's life. One argument in support of the accuracy of this tradition is how unlikely it would be for someone to choose the name "Mark" as a pseudonym. "Mark" was one of the most popular names in the Roman world and would hardly distinguish the gospel. A better pseudonym would be the name of an apostle to give the gospel more credibility. We have an ample supply of these pseudonyms in the New Testament apocrypha (*The Gospel of Peter*, *Thomas*, etc.).

In the New Testament only one person named Mark is mentioned. Philemon 24 and 2 Timothy 4:11 refer to an associate of Paul's named Mark, and Colossians 4:10 adds that he was the cousin of Barnabas. Acts refers to someone named Mark once (Acts 15:39), but three times mentions "John, also called Mark" whose mother owned a home in Jerusalem (12:12, 25; 15:37). First Peter may have originated from Rome and refers to Mark as Peter's spiritual son (1 Pet. 5:13).

Many scholars see these references as the same person, whose composite profile may be simply reconstructed: Mark was a Greek-speaking convert who knew some Aramaic, became a Christian, and worked closely with Peter. He joined Paul in his first journey and in later years served both Peter and Paul before their deaths in Rome.

But is this New Testament figure the same as the one Papias attaches to the second gospel? Nothing prohibits it. In the gospel itself, there is indirect evidence that indeed Peter is closely linked to the author. Peter is the most significant leader among the apostles but, ironically, also the object of much criticism, leading out with bravado and failing miserably. When Papias says that Mark "interpreted" Peter, this probably means that Mark made a composite sketch of stories from the reservoir of Peter's preaching.

Is it possible to indicate *when* Mark wrote? Early church traditions tell us that Mark either wrote just before (Clement of Alexandria) or just after Peter's death (Irenaeus). Peter likely lived in Rome during the 50s and 60s and was martyred sometime later in Nero's reign (54–68). This dates the writing of Mark to sometime in the 60s.

A watershed event for dating the gospels is undoubtedly the catastrophic destruction of Jerusalem in AD 66–70. Mark writes as if the Temple is still standing and says nothing about a revolt. His references to the Temple's future destruction (13:2) and to the "abomination that causes desolation" (13:14) make little sense if the temple was already in ruins.

If Mark served as a source for Matthew and Luke (see ch. 5), there is wide consensus that these two gospels stem from the 70s or 80s. If so, Mark had to circulate for some time to gain recognition, which again urges for a date before 70. But if Mark was penned *before* the great war, he may even have written earlier, perhaps in the 50s. Some scholars have even suggested a first draft in the late 40s.

Jesus predicted the destruction of Jerusalem (Mark 13:2), and it was fulfilled in AD 66–70. The heat of fire was so intense that burning shops along the temple's west wall have left a scorched shadow.
Todd Bolen/BiblePlaces.com

Questions for Discussion

1. What literary features of Mark's gospel make it a compelling dramatic presentation?
2. Why does Jesus choose Capernaum as an ideal base from which to work in Galilee?
3. Is Mark using a geographical motif in his gospel? Is Jesus treated differently in Judea, Galilee, and the Diaspora?
4. If people cannot comprehend Jesus when they encounter him (as in the first half of Mark), what are the practical implications of this for evangelism today?
5. The disciples frame Jesus's messiahship in their own terms, and Jesus has to correct them. Does this happen today? What political, social, or religious agendas from our culture have shaped how we understand Jesus's kingdom?

BIBLIOGRAPHY

Introductory

Garland, D. *Mark*. NIVAC. Grand Rapids: Zondervan, 1996.
Lane, W. *Mark*. NICNT. Grand Rapids: Eerdmans, 1974.
Strauss, *Mark*. ZECNT. Grand Rapids: Zondervan, 2014.

Advanced

Edwards, J. *The Gospel According to Mark*. Pillar. Grand Rapids: Eerdmans, 2001.
Evans, C. *Mark 8:27–16:20*. WBC. Dallas: Word, 2001.
France, R. T. *The Gospel of Mark*. NIGTC. Grand Rapids: Eerdmans, 2002.
Guelich, R. A. *Mark 1:1–8:26*. WBC. Dallas: Word, 1989.
Marcus, J. *Mark 1–8*. AB. New York: Doubleday, 2000.
———. *Mark 9–16*. AB. New York: Doubleday, 2009.

NOTES

1. See W. Lane, *Commentary on the Gospel of Mark* (Grand Rapids, Eerdmans, 1974), 9.

2. See M. Nun, *The Sea of Galilee and Its Fishermen in the New Testament* (Ein Gev: Sea of Galilee Fishing Museum, 1989).

3. Galen, "On My Own Books," *Selected Works*, ed. and trans. by P. N. Singer (Oxford: Oxford University Press, 1997), 3.

Chapter 10

THE GOSPEL ACCORDING TO LUKE

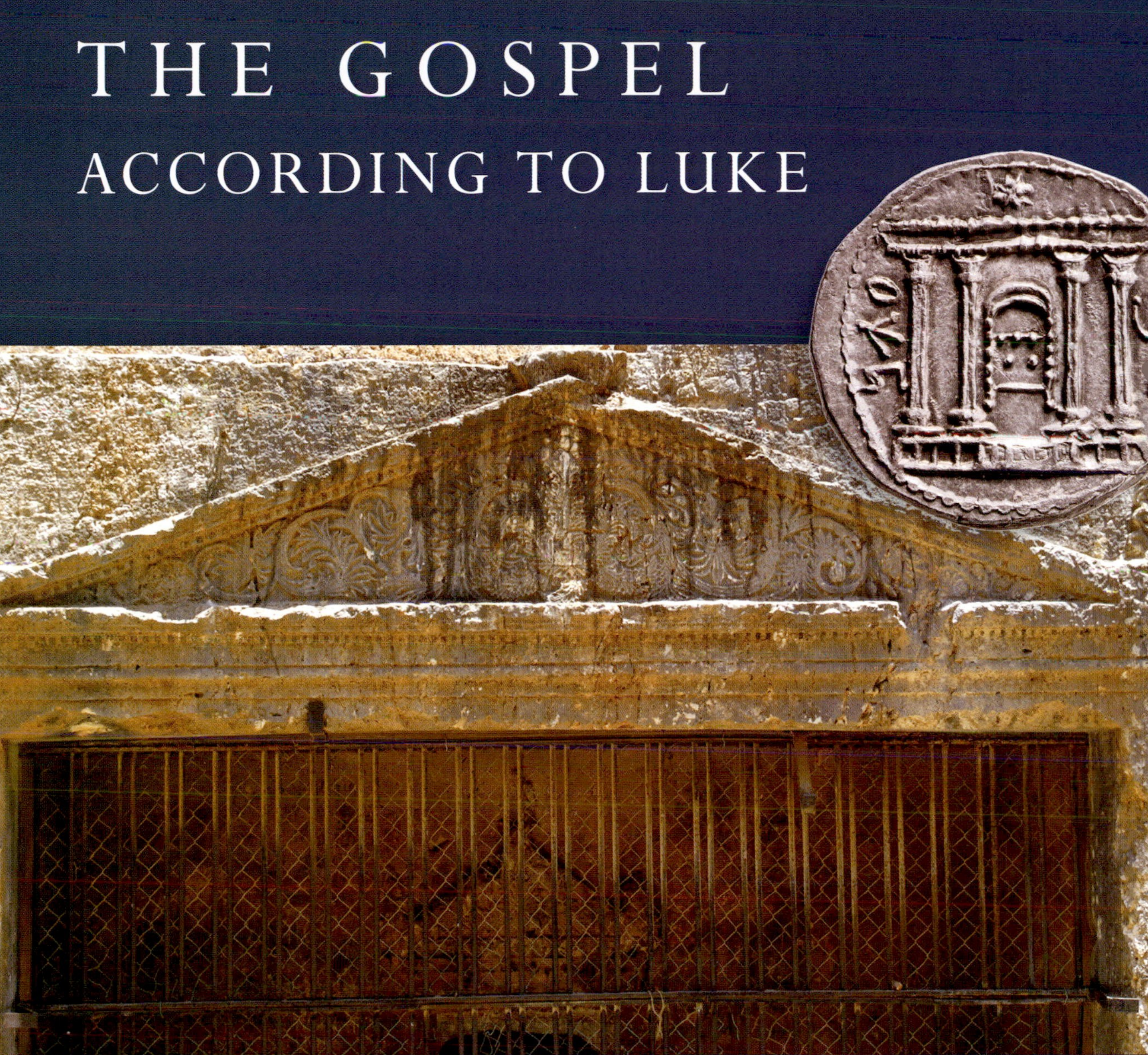

Judaism in the first century assimilated Hellenistic cultural elements, as seen here in the decorated facade to the Sanhedrin Tombs, Jerusalem.
Todd Bolen/BiblePlaces.com

Luke called all the land where the Jews resided, including Galilee, "Judea."

Luke's gospel was originally the first book of a two-volume work (the second being Acts). These volumes comprise about one quarter of the New Testament, making Luke-Acts together the largest New Testament document. Contemporary readers can easily miss that these two volumes tell one continuous story, since John's gospel now separates them. But when originally composed and sent to Theophilus (Luke 1:1–4; Acts 1:1–2), they were read as a single narrative about Jesus and his disciples.

Luke's account speaks eloquently of God's salvation sent first to the Jewish people and then to the gentiles throughout the Mediterranean world. Luke-Acts tells the story of the empire-wide spread of the gospel in a way that also emphasizes how God offers salvation to all people, including those who are "far off" (Acts 2:39), regardless of ethnicity, nationality, social class, gender, or age. Here we watch the church proclaim the message not only to Jews but also to Samaritans, an Ethiopian official, Romans, Macedonians, Greeks, and "barbarians" as the gospel spreads "to the ends of the earth" (Acts 1:8). In Luke, the gospel is preached to the poor, women become full participants in God's salvation, and even children receive Jesus's welcome. People who are social pariahs (e.g., tax collectors and those classified as "sinners") enter into God's kingdom. Luke's story is about the offer of salvation to those who are on the outside, to those marginalized by society, both in the author's time and in ours.

THE SETTING OF LUKE'S GOSPEL

Luke is the only gospel that names its recipient—"most excellent Theophilus" (Luke 1:3; Acts 1:1). This name means "beloved by God," and some suggest he received this name after being baptized as a Christian. However, before the Christian era "Theophilus" appeared in inscriptions and ancient documents referring to both Jews and gentiles. Theophilus is most likely the person's given name.

Theophilus enjoys high social status, since Luke calls him "*most excellent* Theophilus" (cf. Acts 23:26; 24:3; 26:25 where Roman procurators Felix and Festus are similarly addressed). This title identifies him as someone of higher social rank than Luke, possibly a member of the equestrian order. Theophilus possesses considerable economic means and is likely the literary patron who financed the copying of these books, both for Theophilus and for others.

We do not know where Theophilus and other readers were located, although some have suggested Rome or Greece. Perhaps these books circulated among Paul's churches. The readers are likely gentiles, for when Luke presents Jewish customs, he includes explanatory phrases that help his readers understand their meaning. For example, in 22:1 Luke says, "The Festival of Unleavened Bread, called the Passover, was approaching." A Jewish audience would hardly need this explanation about the Passover (cf. also 22:7). The people Matthew calls "teachers of the law" (Matt. 23:13), Luke calls "lawyers" (Luke 11:52 NASB), a term more understandable to gentiles. The way Luke traces Jesus's genealogy back to Adam instead of Abraham (Luke 3:38; cf. Matt. 1:2) underscores that salvation is for the gentiles (e.g., Luke 2:29–32).

Theophilus is likely a believer. The events surrounding the opening of the gospel "have been fulfilled *among us*," and Theophilus is someone who has already been "taught" the gospel (1:1, 4; this verb denotes instruction in Acts 18:25; Rom. 2:18; 1 Cor. 14:9; Gal. 6:6). As new believers living in a world that held hostile attitudes toward Christians (see Acts 17:6; 21:21, 24; 28:22), Theophilus and the others needed to "know the certainty of the things" they have been taught (1:4).

Josephus Writes *Against Apion*

When Josephus wrote *Against Apion*, he began both volumes similar to Luke-Acts. They were written for a man named Epaphroditus, addressed with the honorific title "most excellent." Compare Luke 1:1–4 and Acts 1:1–2 with the following:

Against Apion 1.1 [1]: "In my history of our *Antiquities*, most excellent Epaphroditus, I have, I think, made sufficiently clear to any who may peruse that work the extreme antiquity of our Jewish race, the purity of the original stock, and the manner in which it established itself in the country which we occupy to-day."

Against Apion 2.1 [1–2]: "In the first volume of this work, my most excellent Epaphroditus, I demonstrated the antiquity of our race, corroborating my statements by the writings of Phoenicians, Chaldaeans, and Egyptians, besides citing as witnesses numerous Greek historians; I also challenged the statements of Manetho, Chaeremon, and some others. I shall now proceed to refute the rest of the authors who have attacked us."

LUKE'S STORY ABOUT JESUS

The author's main interest lies in the presentation of God's salvation as revealed in Jesus Christ. I. Howard Marshall notes, "But whereas the stress in Mark is on the person of Jesus, in Matthew on the teaching of Jesus, and in John on the manifestation of eternal life in Him, Luke's stress is on the blessings of salvation which he brings."[1] This "salvation" has numerous nuances, such as healing from disease (17:19; 18:41–42), liberation from demonic control (8:36), restoration of life to the dead (8:50), and rescue from disaster (6:9). But salvation is also tied to the forgiveness of sins (7:49–50) and is a response to faith (7:50; 8:48). Yet the realities of forgiveness, liberation, and healing are not separate and distinct but are aspects of the total salvation that Jesus Christ brings.

Various deities, such as Asclepius (the god of healing, pictured here), Isis, and Sarapis, along with various deified rulers, such as emperors, were called "savior." Luke presents Jesus as the only true Savior. *Marie-Lan Nguyen/Wikimedia Commons, Public Domain*

The combined volumes of Luke-Acts emphasize the significance of this salvation on a broader scale. Stephen spoke of the deliverance of Israel from Egypt (Acts 7:25), an event that prefigured the salvation God offers to all humanity (13:47, quoting Isa. 49:6). Salvation for Luke is the deliverance God brings in the age to come, which has already dawned (Acts 2:16–17, 21). Jesus proclaims to Zacchaeus, "For the Son of Man came to seek and to save the lost" (Luke 19:10). God is the ultimate source of salvation, which he accomplishes through his Son.

The two volumes of Luke-Acts narrate a single continuous story. The author structured these books in similar ways and develops common themes in both volumes, such as the role of the Holy Spirit (Luke 4; Acts 2) and the theme of salvation. The presentation of the history of Jesus and the early church is symmetrical (see chart of "Luke and Acts Compared").[2]

Luke and Acts Compared

Luke	Acts	Theme
3:21–22	2:1–13	Prayer and reception of the Holy Spirit
4:14–21	2:14–39; 13:16–41	Proclamation which focuses on fulfillment and rejection
4:40	28:9	Healing
5:17–26	3:1–10; 14:8–11	Healing of paralytic
8:40–56	9:36–41; 20:9–10	Raising the dead
21:15	6:10	Wisdom
22:69	7:56	Jesus as the exalted Son of Man
23:34, 46	7:59–60	Prayer for forgiveness

The unity of the two books appears in the way that Acts presents the fulfillment of events predicted in Luke, such as the witness of the disciples (Luke 24:48; Acts 1:8) and the persecutions they will suffer (Luke 21:12–23; Acts 4:3; 5:18–25, etc.). The disciples proclaim the same message of the kingdom of God that Jesus announces.

We can understand Luke's literary structure by identifying its four principal sections.

1. After the introductory prologue (1:1–4), Luke describes Jesus's infancy (1:5–2:52) and John the Baptist's ministry (3:1–4:15).
2. Luke follows Mark closely as he tells of Jesus's ministry in Galilee (4:14–9:50). The response of the people is favorable.

3. Next is Luke's "travel narrative," where Jesus travels from Galilee to Jerusalem (9:51–19:27; note 9:51, 53; 13:22; 17:11; 18:31–34; 19:28). The central theme is the rejection of Jesus and the seeming failure of his ministry. It begins with the Samaritans' rejection of Jesus (9:51–56) and ends with Jesus's lament over unresponsive Jerusalem (19:41–44).
4. Luke returns to Mark's outline as he describes Jesus's work in and around Jerusalem (19:45–21:38), his passion (22:1–23:56), and finally his resurrection and ascension (24:1–53).

Outline of Luke

I. Prologue (1:1–4)
II. The Infancy Narrative (1:5–2:52)
III. The Beginnings: John and Jesus (3:1–4:13)
  1. The Ministry of John the Baptist (3:1–20)
  2. Jesus's Baptism and Temptation (3:21–4:13)
IV. The Galilean Ministry (4:14–9:50)
  1. The Proclamation in and around the Synagogues of Galilee (4:14–44)
  2. Calling and Teaching the Disciples (5:1–6:49)
  3. The Authority of Jesus (7:1–50)
  4. The Proclamation of the Kingdom (8:1–9:17)
  5. Jesus: The Messiah Who Will Die and Rise Again (9:18–50)
V. The Journey to Jerusalem (9:51–19:44)
  1. The First Announcement of the Journey to Jerusalem (9:51–13:21)
  2. The Second Announcement of the Journey to Jerusalem (13:22–17:10)
  3. The Third Announcement of the Journey to Jerusalem (17:11–19:27)
  4. Jesus's Arrival in Jerusalem (19:28–44)
VI. The Jerusalem Ministry (19:45–21:38)
VII. The Crucifixion of Jesus (22:1–23:56)
VIII. The Resurrection and Ascension (24:1–53)

THE PROLOGUE (1:1–4)

Luke's prologue outlines his methodology in composing Luke-Acts and reveals his purpose in writing. He is not the first to attempt to give an account of the life of Jesus. "Many" have written about "the things that have been fulfilled among us." "Fulfilled" reflects Luke's emphasis on the fulfillment of God's plan (1:20; 4:21; 9:31; 21:22, 24; 24:44–47). Luke's sources are the "eyewitnesses and servants of the word" (1:2), that is, persons committed to the realities they proclaimed and who handed down the story as a sacred tradition (cf. 1 Cor. 11:23; 15:3–4).

Josephus on Writing History

Josephus makes a spirited defense of his method of writing history that is similar to Luke's opening prologue. He claims he did not make up the account of the things he recorded but thoroughly investigated what had actually occurred, as he sought understanding: "Nevertheless, certain despicable persons have essayed to malign my history, taking it for a prize composition such as is set to boys at school. What an extraordinary accusation and calumny! Surely they ought to recognize that it is the duty of one who promises to present his readers with actual facts first to obtain an exact knowledge of them himself, either through having been in close touch with the events, or by inquiry from those who knew them. That duty I consider myself to have amply fulfilled in both my works" (*Against Apion* 1.10 [53–54]).

Josephus carefully lays out his qualifications as a historian, including that he had not only used sources well but also was present during some of the events he describes: "My qualification as historian of the war was that I had been an actor in many, and an eyewitness of most, of the events; in short, nothing whatever was said or done of which I was ignorant. Surely, then, one cannot but regard as audacious the attempt of these critics to challenge my veracity" (Ibid., 1.10 [55–56]). Luke too is well aware of the challenges to the Christian story in his day and seeks to deflect the critics.

Elijah Will Come

The expectation that Elijah would come to reform Israel before the day of the Lord appears in Jewish literature. Sirach 48:9–10 says of Elijah, "You were taken up by a whirlwind of fire, in a chariot with horses of fire. At the appointed time, it is written, you are destined to calm the wrath of God before it breaks out in fury, to turn the hearts of parents to their children, and to restore the tribes of Jacob." Later Jewish tradition ascribed other roles to him, such as settling disputes (Mishnah, *Baba Mesia* 3:3–4; *Eduyyot* 8:7) and even raising the dead (Mishnah, *Sotah* 9:15). Apparently during Jesus's day it was common belief among the scribes (Matt. 17:10; Mark 9:11–13), the Jewish populace (Matt. 16:14), and Jesus himself (Matt. 17:10–13) that Elijah would appear to inaugurate the new age.

In 1:3–4 Luke adds a comment about his own contribution, stating that he has "investigated" everything, which implies something more than merely "investigated." Josephus uses this word to suggest the idea of following "an account or events so as to understand them."[3] Luke has exercised great care in his quest for accuracy. Thus, he can offer Theophilus this "orderly account" to confirm his faith.

THE INFANCY NARRATIVE (1:5–2:52)

Before telling the story of Jesus's birth, Luke recounts the announcement of the birth of John the Baptist, the harbinger of the Messiah (1:5–25). The account begins with the tragic situation of Zechariah and Elizabeth, who are childless (1:5–7). Luke notes their lineage and character and, since childlessness was considered a reproach (Lev. 20:20–21; Jer. 22:30), he informs the reader that their childlessness is not due to any moral fault.

The focus of the story is on John's special place in preparing Israel for the coming day of the Lord. According to 1:15–17, John will be filled with the Spirit of God, which means the prophetic voice will return to Israel after centuries

The Coming King of the Line of David

Alongside others within Israel during Jesus's day, the Qumran community anticipated the coming of the Messiah who would be a descendant of King David. They also believed in a Messiah descended from Aaron. The Dead Sea Scrolls text 4QFlorilegium quotes and interprets 2 Samuel 7:12–14 and Amos 9:11 saying, "'YHWH declares to you that he will build you a house. I will raise up your seed after you and establish the throne of his kingdom for ever. I will be a father to him and he will be a son to me.' This refers to the 'branch of David', who will arise with the Interpreter of the law who will rise up in Zion in the last days, as it is written: 'I will raise up the hut of David which has fallen', This refers to 'the hut of David which has fallen', who will arise to save Israel" (1.10–13). The Qumran community expected the Davidic Messiah to be a warrior (1.7–9). The Damascus Document speaks of the two Messiahs and emphasizes the militaristic side of the messianic labors: "Those who are faithful to him are the poor ones of the flock. These shall escape in the age of visitation; but those that remain shall be delivered up to the sword when there comes the messiah of Aaron and Israel" (19.9–11).

of prophetic silence. But John is more than a prophet (see 7:26–27; Mal. 3:1) since he fulfills the prophetic hope of Malachi 4:5–6 that Elijah would return before the day of the Lord (see also Matt. 17:10–13).

The scene shifts to the private meeting of Gabriel with Mary in Nazareth (Luke 1:26), which begins Luke's account of Jesus's birth (1:26–2:21). Mary and Joseph are betrothed when the angel arrives. Jewish marriage was a two-stage event. The engagement (1:27) consisted of a formal witnessed agreement to marry, and the payment of the bride price to the bride's father. The marriage ceremony and celebration took place about a year later. Gabriel's announcement includes the proclamation that Mary will have a son who should receive the name "Jesus" (1:31). He will be called the Son of the Most High (1:32), which in Israel was a royal title (2 Sam. 7:14; Ps. 2:7) but in the Roman world was associated with the ruler cult. Jesus's birth is a direct challenge to the imperial claims of Augustus Caesar.

Zechariah, the father of John the Baptist, received a revelation from an angel while offering incense in the temple (Luke 1:8–20). This is an illustration of an altar of incense.

For Luke, the title "Son of the Most High" is also linked with Adam (3:38). Jesus is the second Adam. Gabriel also announces that he will be an heir to the Davidic dynasty in fulfillment of the ancient promise made to David (1:32–33; 2 Sam. 7:12–17), held dear by the Jewish people.

Instead of seeking some sign as Zechariah did (1:18), Mary asks a simple and practical question about how she can conceive without ever having had sexual relations (1:34). Gabriel answers (1:35) that Jesus's conception will be due to direct divine intervention.

The Census Under Quirinius

According to ancient records, Quirinius was the governor of Syria from AD 6–7, sometime after the birth of Jesus Christ (see Luke 2:2; Josephus comments on a census under Quirinius when Archelaus was banished; *Ant.* 17.13.5 [355]; 18.1.1 [1–10]). Luke, however, places the birth of Jesus during his administration although Jesus was born before the death of Herod the Great in 4 BC. This tension between Luke's account and that of ancient records has generated several attempts to resolve the problem.

Sherwin-White[4] mentions a gap in the historical records with regard to the Syrian legates and suggests that Quirinius filled the gap between 4 BC and 1 BC. Another proposal is that "governor" means simply "administrator" here, allowing that Quirinius may have administered the census under the rule of the legate Saturnius (6–4 BC). Luke seems aware of a later census under Quirinius since he notes that this one was the "first." Despite these considerations, to date we do not have a fully satisfactory solution.[5]

Probable tombstone of Publius Sulpicius Quirinius, proconsul of Asia.
Todd Bolen/BiblePlaces.com

The emperor Augustus was the adopted son of the deified Julius Caesar and was therefore known as "the son of god." This inscription from Ephesus begins: Imp(erator) Caesar Divi f(ilius) Aug(ustus) co(n)s(ul) XII tr(ibunicia) pot(estate) XVIII pontifex maximus ("The Emperor Caesar Augustus, son of god, Consul for the twelfth time, with tribunitian power for the eighteenth time, chief Pontifex")
Olga Liubimova/ancientrome.ru/art/artworken/img.htm?id=6813

Luke juxtaposes the birth of Christ with political history (2:1–2). The Roman census, which compelled Joseph and Mary to travel to Bethlehem, was part of the administrative reform of Augustus as he attempted to establish more firmly the tax base in the empire. Augustus himself was considered to have inaugurated a new era of peace, but in Luke's view he is simply one whom God uses to accomplish his plan.

While in Bethlehem Mary's time comes to give birth (2:6–7). There is no guest room, so Mary and Joseph lay Jesus in a manger. The houses there used many caves as part of the house, with stables usually attached to the dwelling.

An angel announces Jesus's birth to shepherds, who represent the lowly and the

Bethlehem's Church of the Nativity can be seen in the bottom right, with the Herodium, the volcano-shaped hill, in the top left. See a picture of the Herodium on p. 51.
Bill Schlegel/BiblePlaces.com

humble to whom God offers salvation through his Son (2:10–11). The announcement is replete with divine and royal titles as the angel calls the infant Jesus Savior, Christ, and Lord. Angels break into a chorus of praise to God for his act and proclaim divine peace, which rests on those who receive his favor (2:14).

THE BEGINNINGS: JOHN AND JESUS (3:1–4:13)

As in 2:1, Luke locates the beginning of John and Jesus's ministry within the political and religious history of the era (3:1–2a). John's ministry fulfills the Old Testament expectation of a harbinger to precede the coming of the Lord (Isa. 40:3–5 in Luke 3:2b–6). The coming one is none other than the Lord himself, who will usher in God's salvation (3:6). John's message in 3:7–14 is that judgment is near (3:7–9), and he therefore calls people to true repentance (3:8). Conversion results in treating others with compassion and justice (3:10–14). John baptizes in the Jordan River, a rite that is a sign of conversion.

John points to one mightier than him, who will bring both salvation and judgment (3:15–17). Luke's presentation of the baptism of Jesus (3:21–22) does not emphasize the theme of fulfillment (cf. Matt. 3:13–17) but rather the divine testimony with regard to his person. The Spirit comes on Jesus, endowing him with power for ministry (4:18; Acts 10:36–38). A voice comes from heaven that includes an affirmation of Jesus's Sonship, echoing the Old Testament (Ps. 2:7; Isa. 41:8; 42:1) and revealing Jesus's kingly rule, his intimate relationship with the Father, and his identification with the Suffering Servant of Isaiah.

In December 2009 an archaeological excavation in front of the Church of the Annunciation discovered a house from the first century AD.
David Silverman/Getty Images

This immersion pool, or *mikveh*, from Masada was used for ritual washing. Religious baths were common within both the Jewish and gentile worlds. John's "pool" was the Jordan River. *Matt Floreen/BiblePlaces.com*

Ritual Washing and the Baptism of John

Ritual washing was common among both the Jews and the gentiles. Initiates into the mysteries of the Egyptian deity Isis underwent a form of baptism. Apuleius tells the story of one such initiation in *Metamorphoses* 11.23: "When I had taken the customary bath, he began by asking the gods' favour and then cleansed me with purificatory sprinkling." Within Judaism, ritual washing was well known (Lev. 13–17; Num. 19; see sidebar on "Ritual Baths" in ch. 8).

Later Jewish theology prescribed ritual washing for gentiles who wished to become Jewish proselytes (*b. Yebah* 46a; 71a), though scholars debate whether this practice was observed during the first century. Josephus provides further testimony that John linked baptism with the call to righteous behavior: "That the washing [with water] would be acceptable to him, if they made use of it, not in order to the putting away [or the remission] of some sins [only], but for the purification of the body; supposing still that the soul was thoroughly purified beforehand by righteousness" (*Ant.* 18.5.2 [117]).

The face of Tiberius Caesar, who was the Roman emperor during Jesus's ministry. *Luis Garcia/Wikimedia Commons, GNU Free Documentation License*

Like Matthew, Luke recounts both the genealogy and temptation of Jesus (3:23–4:13; see ch. 8), after which Jesus begins his public ministry in Galilee in the power of the Spirit (4:14–15). In his genealogy, Luke, a gentile, underscores the universality of Christ as Savior and Lord of all human beings.

THE GALILEAN MINISTRY (4:14–9:50)

Luke introduces Jesus's Galilean ministry with a summary statement (4:14–15), which highlights characteristic themes in Luke: Jesus carries out his ministry in the power of the Spirit (4:14), he engages in a vigorous teaching ministry (4:15a; cf. 6:17–49), and "everyone praised" his ministry (4:15b).

The first full picture of Jesus's teaching takes place in the synagogue in Jesus's hometown, Nazareth (4:16–29). The reading of Scripture and an exposition were common components of a synagogue service.

Jesus presents himself as the Spirit-anointed prophet who fulfills Isaiah 61:1–2 and 58:6. After the reading he proclaims that the time of fulfillment has come (4:21). The blessings described are the signs of the messianic age—the Spirit has returned and is upon him, the good news has come, and the liberation of Israel is breaking in. But the recipients of these blessings are those whom society rejects: the poor, the prisoners, the blind, and the oppressed. In his exposition, Jesus stresses that the gospel is also for those outside Israel, as in the past (4:24–27). The hostile reaction to this declaration is the first sign of Jesus's rejection by his own people (4:22, 29). Luke's gospel foreshadows the cross from the beginning.

As in Matthew, Luke marks the opening phase of Jesus's ministry by the call and teaching of the first disciples (5:1–6:49), the demonstration of his authority to heal and forgive (7:1–50), and his proclamation of the message of the kingdom (8:1–9:17), a ministry that the apostles are commissioned to share (9:1–6). The lifestyle prescribed for these missioners is distinct from that of other traveling orators in the ancient world. They are not to have great entrances and seek fine receptions but to be content with basic provisions. The climax of the revelation of Jesus's teaching and power is Peter's confession, in which he recognizes Jesus as the promised Messiah (9:18–20).

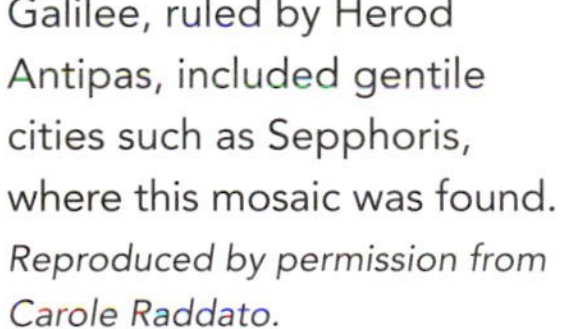

Galilee, ruled by Herod Antipas, included gentile cities such as Sepphoris, where this mosaic was found. *Reproduced by permission from Carole Raddato.*

Quickly following this revelation, Jesus declares that he will not come in power to triumph over the Roman oppressors but will suffer, be killed, and be raised on the third day (9:21–22). The sufferings are a necessary part of God's plan for the Messiah (9:22), a concept unheard of in Jewish theology. This is a new messianic vision—the apocalyptic and royal Son of Man (9:22a; cf. Dan. 7:13–14) who comes in power and glory is identified with the Servant of the Lord of Isaiah 53, who suffers for the sins of the people. His disciples likewise will suffer for the kingdom (Luke 9:23–27).

The design of the synagogue in Nazareth would have been similar to this synagogue in Gamla, located in the Golan Heights, northeast of the Sea of Galilee. *Phoenix Data Systems*

Reading Scripture in a Synagogue Service

The tractate *Megilla* (3–6) of the Mishnah presents guidelines for a synagogue service for a period after the writing of the New Testament. But many of these aspects seem to have been practiced earlier. On reading Scripture, *Megilla* 4:4 instructs: "He that reads in the Torah should read no fewer than three verses. He may not read to the translator [who would translate from Hebrew to Aramaic] more than a single verse [at a time, so the translator will not err], and, in the case of the prophetic lection [a reading from the Prophets], three. If the three constitute three distinct pericopae, they read them one by one. They skip [from place to place] in the prophetic lections but not in the Torah lections."

Translation and interpretation of the Law were standard practices.

The Messiah of God

When Jesus asks Peter who the disciples think Jesus is, Peter responds, "God's Messiah [*christos*]" (9:20). "Christ" or "Messiah" means "Anointed One," a title that marked the bearer as the king (Ps. 2:2, 6). The Jewish people expected God to raise up a ruler from the line of David (2 Sam. 7:4–17). His coming would be a day of mercy: "May God cleanse Israel for the day of mercy in blessing, for the appointed day when his Messiah will reign" (*Psalms of Solomon* 18:5). Peter and the disciples understand that the day has begun.

THE JOURNEY TO JERUSALEM (9:51–19:44)

The journey to Jerusalem dominates the middle section of the gospel and contains most of the information about Jesus's ministry that is unique in Luke. At various points in this section of the narrative, Luke notes that Jesus and his disciples are on their way to Jerusalem (9:51; 13:22; 17:11; 18:31; see also 9:57; 10:38; 14:25; 18:35).

Scholars have debated about the overall purpose of this central section. We suggest it deals with the problems that revolve around the conflict with the Jewish leadership and the question of the nature of discipleship. Jesus, on the one hand, denounces the leadership of the Pharisees and the scribes (11:37–54). Conflict with them widens, and Jesus anticipates his rejection by the whole of the nation (13:31–35). On the other hand, Jesus also focuses in on discipleship (14:25–35), with chapters 15–18 largely addressing the theme of discipleship in the face of rejection. At the end, the Davidic kingship of Jesus comes to the fore again as Jesus comes near Jerusalem (Jericho) and is recognized as "Son of David" (18:38).

As the journey to Jerusalem comes to an end, Jesus heads into the city from the east, coming through Bethphage and Bethany, over the Mount of Olives (19:28).

As Jesus begins his ministry in the holy city, Luke shows that Jesus is in control of the situation. In 19:28–44 he tells the disciples how to procure a colt for his entry.

Jesus's journey from Galilee to Jerusalem is a noted feature of Luke's gospel. After the Transfiguration, Jesus headed south, eventually going through Jericho before entering Jerusalem from the east.

As he enters the city, the crowd hails him as the coming king anticipated in Psalm 118:26 (Luke 19:38). The disciples lead the cheers, and the atmosphere is charged as they praise God for the mighty deeds Jesus has done (19:37). At this point the opposition to Jesus raises the first objection (19:39), but Jesus will not silence the praise (19:40). In 19:41–44 Jesus weeps over Jerusalem and announces her judgment.

A Challenge to Honor

Jesus and his opponents engage in a type of debate well-known in the ancient world. This "challenge-riposte" was a kind of "social tug of war, a game of social push and shove." Such interchanges usually have three parts: "(a) *challenge* in terms of some action (word, deed, or both) on the part of the challenger; (b) *perception* of the message by both the individual to whom it is directed and the public at large; and (c) the *reaction* of the receiving individual and the evaluation of the reaction on the part of the public."[6]

Jesus makes the first claim by entering the social space of the leadership—the Temple—and challenges their authority (19:45–46). The leaders then counter him (20:1–2) by questioning his authority. The concern for honor is central in this social push and shove. Such honor challenges only took place among equals, and therefore the question of Jesus's status comes to the fore. Luke shows how Jesus is on equal footing with the religious leaders. He responds to each challenge and then goes on the offensive. In other words, Jesus is the one who has higher honor and status. He has a rightful claim to authority, demonstrated by his cleansing of the Temple.

The gospel frames this coming cataclysmic event as judgment for not receiving the Lord, "because you did not recognize the time of your visitation from God" (19:44 NRSV). "Visitation" means that God comes to his people, either for blessing or judgment. He had come to bless them (Gen. 50:24–25; Job 10:12; Isa. 23:17), but they did not recognize his hand. What is left is severe destruction.

THE JERUSALEM MINISTRY (19:45–21:38)

Luke highlights the conflict between Jesus and the leaders of the nation. They try to trap him, especially in reaction to his dramatic move of cleansing the temple. When his authority is under question, he responds with a series of rebuttals, including questions concerning the source of John's and his own authority (20:1–8), a parable that shows that the present Jewish leadership is on the way out (20:9–19), a teaching about paying taxes (20:20–26), and another about the resurrection (20:27–40). In these controversies Jesus responds with wisdom that silences the opposition (20:7, 19, 26, 40, 44).

THE CRUCIFIXION, RESURRECTION, AND ASCENSION OF JESUS (22:1–24:53)

After Jesus's final Jerusalem ministry, Luke recounts the crucifixion and triumph of Christ. After the Last Supper (22:1–38), Jesus is arrested and tried. A central point is the absolute innocence of the Lord. Both Pilate (23:1–5) and Herod (23:6–12) examine him and find him innocent (23:4, 14–15; cf. 23:47). This message is important for Theophilus and other Christians who need to understand why the Savior was crucified. The only reason why Pilate yields is the pressure of the crowd. Luke's narrative makes the point that the crucifixion was a travesty of justice.

Cicero called crucifixion the *crudelissimum taeterrimique supplicii* ("that cruel and disgusting penalty"; *Against Verres* 2.5.165) and the *summo supplicio* ("the extreme penalty"; 2.5.168). Everyone considered it the most wretched kind of death.

The traditional site of Jesus's death and burial, the Church of the Holy Sepulcher, Jerusalem.
Todd Bolen/BiblePlaces.com

Inside the church of the Holy Sepulcher (Jerusalem), two burial niches in a first-century tomb.
Todd Bolen/BiblePlaces.com

Cicero on Roman Citizens and Crucifixion

Cicero writes in *Pro Rabirio* 16:

> How grievous a thing it is to be disgraced by a public court; how grievous to suffer a fine, how grievous to suffer banishment; and yet in the midst of any such disaster some trace of liberty is left to us. Even if we are threatened with death, we may die free men. But the executioner, the veiling of the head and the very word "cross" should be far removed not only from the person of a Roman citizen but from his thoughts, his eyes and his ears. For it is not only the actual occurrence of these things or the endurance of them, but liability to them, the expectation, nay, the mere mention of them, that is unworthy of a Roman citizen and a free man.

Roman citizens and, in particular, members of the upper class were exempt from this form of execution. Death on a cross was limited to foreigners and people of the lower class, especially slaves.

The crucified Jesus, however, is raised from the dead. The first witnesses are women (24:1–12) without whose testimony the other disciples would not have known about the resurrection. They hear the witness of the two angels and remember Jesus's words (24:7–8). The implication is that they believe, a point evidenced by their witness (24:9–10). They keep repeating these things to the apostles (24:10), who consider their words to be only "like nonsense."

Luke's gospel ends with Jesus's encounter with the disciples on the road to Emmaus (24:13–35) and his appearance to the disciples, in which he gives them tangible evidence that he is no mere phantasm (24:36–43). Luke's final account is the ascension of Jesus (24:50–53), which stitches this volume together with his second book, Acts (Acts 1:1–11).

Luke comments that the place of the ascension was in "the vicinity of Bethany" (24:50). The Church of the Ascension on the Mount of Olives near Bethany marks the traditional location of the ascension. The church was constructed by Helena, the mother of Constantine, in AD 392.
Todd Bolen/BiblePlaces.com

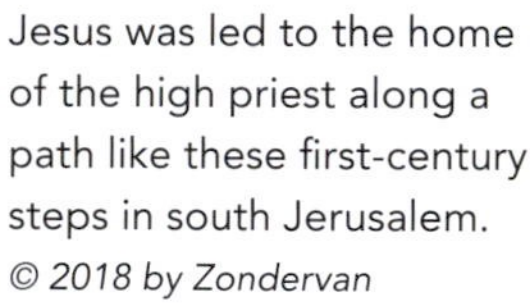

Jesus was led to the home of the high priest along a path like these first-century steps in south Jerusalem.
© 2018 by Zondervan

AUTHOR AND DATE

While Luke-Acts supplies evidence about the identity of the first reader(s), the authorship of these two volumes is a more elusive question. The book does not name its author, but external evidence points to Luke, the travel companion of the apostle Paul, as the person who composed these volumes. If this identification is correct, then Luke-Acts is the only book in the New Testament written by a gentile.

The person who wrote Luke and Acts was a well-educated person who could write fine literary Greek. He was also highly influenced by the Septuagint (LXX), especially in the speeches of Acts, yet he does not betray any direct knowledge of Hebrew Scripture. These evidences suggest that the author was either a Greek or a Hellenistic Jew. He was not an eyewitness of the life of Jesus (Luke 1:2), though he identifies himself as a participant in the gospel (1:1).

In certain sections of Acts, the narrative shifts from the third to the first person plural. These so-called "we" sections indicate that the author is an eyewitness of some of the events in early Christian history. For instance, this person was with Paul in Troas and Philippi during Paul's second missionary journey

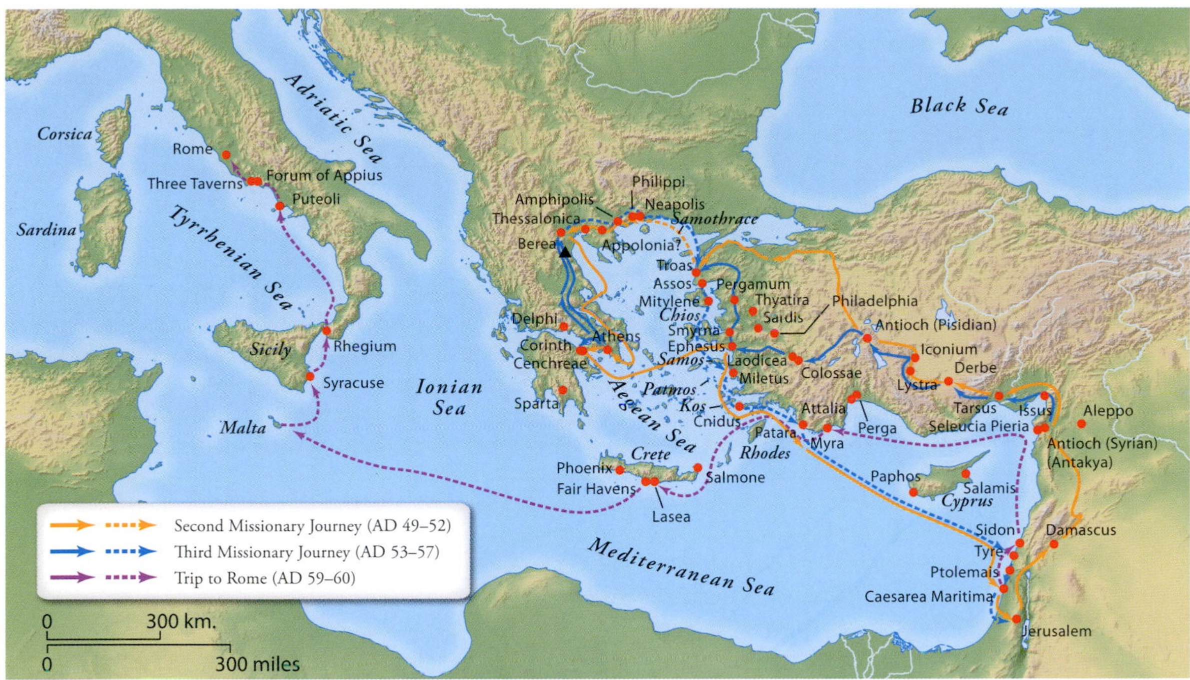

The narrative in Acts occasionally shifts to the first-person plural, and from these "we" sections in Acts, we can trace some of the movements of the author of Luke-Acts (indicated here by the use of dashed lines). The author accompanied Paul for parts of his second and third missionary journeys and his trip to Rome.

(Acts 16:8–10). He apparently remained behind in Philippi during that trip (16:17, 40). Later he rejoined Paul during the third tour when the apostle returned to Macedonia (20:3–5), and he even accompanied him to Jerusalem (21:17). He also traveled with Paul on his imprisonment journey to Rome (27:1–28:16) and remained with him there.

Some scholars have suggested that these "we" sections are an artistic invention or that sources the author used were written in the first person plural but were not changed to "they." But the simplest solution is probably the correct one. The author of Luke-Acts was someone who traveled with Paul and ended up with him at Rome, but whom Acts does not mention by name. Silas and Timothy are excluded as authors since they are mentioned in the third person (Acts 16:6–8; 15:40; 16:1–3), as are Mark, Barnabas, Apollos, and numerous others (20:4). Among the companions who appear with Paul in Rome, known through the letters he wrote from that city, we encounter Luke (Col. 4:14; Philem. 24)—though Luke was not Paul's only unnamed companion. Based on this evidence, it is plausible that Luke was the author, but we cannot prove it either.

The church was unanimous in crediting this book to Luke. Clement of Alexandria (AD 150–ca. 215) quoted the gospel frequently and attributed it to Luke, as did Tertullian (AD 190–220). The Muratorian Fragment (AD 170–200), an early canonical list, refers to the gospel and associates Luke the *medicus* ("physician") with it. Jerome (AD c. 345–c. 419) sums up ancient opinion: "Luke, a physician of

Luke and Suetonius

When the Roman historian Suetonius wrote about the life of Augustus, he explained how he handled his material: "Having given as it were a summary of his life, I shall now take up the various phases one by one, not in chronological order but by categories, to make the account clearer and more intelligible" (*Augustus* 9). Luke, as a historian of his time, selected and arranged the events in the life of Jesus in a way that underscored his portrait of the character and work of Jesus.

Luke and Plutarch

Luke does not present a comprehensive account of every event in the life of Jesus. John, at the end of his gospel, notes that "Jesus did many other things as well. If every one of them were written down, I suppose that even the whole world would not have room for the books that would be written" (John 21:25). Ancient biographers selected significant aspects of their subjects' lives and arranged them in a thematic way to illustrate the character of the person they described. Plutarch, for example, describes his method:

> And in the most illustrious deeds there is not always a manifestation of virtue or vice, nay, a slight thing like a phrase or a jest often makes a greater revelation of character than battles where thousands fall, or the greatest armaments, or sieges of cities. Accordingly, just as painters get the likenesses in their portraits from the face and the expression of the eyes, wherein the character shows itself, but make very little account of the other parts of the body, so I must be permitted to devote myself rather to the signs of the soul in men, and by means of these to portray the life of each, leaving to others the description of their great contests (*Life of Alexander* 1:2).

Antioch as his writings indicate, was not unskilled in the Greek language. An adherent of the apostle Paul, and companion of all his journeying, he wrote a Gospel" (*De viris illustribus* 7).

The earliest date for Luke-Acts is two years after Paul's arrival in Rome as a prisoner (Acts 28:30), or around AD 62. Acts ending so abruptly suggests that this is the time of its composition. Since Luke is deeply concerned with central figures in the early church, such as James (Jesus's brother), Peter, and Paul and the death of none of these is mentioned (James died in 62, Peter in 64/65, and Paul in the late 60s), an early date—in the early 60s, perhaps even AD 62—appears a likely time of composition.

On the other hand, some scholars have underplayed the importance of Luke's final statement, underscoring that the author's concern is to show how the gospel arrived at Rome and not to give a full account of Paul's life and ministry. Also, if Mark was the first canonical gospel written and if Luke used Mark, then the date of the book is likely later than the early 60s. Those who hold to a later date suggest a time after the fall of Jerusalem and the destruction of the temple (AD 70).

LUKE AS HISTORIAN

Luke writes as a participant in the early history of the church. His presence during Paul's journeys added credibility to his work in the eyes of ancient readers. As a gentile convert he relies on sources to garner information about the life of Christ and even admits this in his prologue (Luke 1:1–4). Luke is aware of the existence of other gospels, perhaps including Mark and a collection of Jesus's sayings such as "Q" (see ch. 5). Some of the events he describes were handed down to him as sacred tradition (1:2) by those who observed Jesus's life, likely including Mary (1:5–2:52).

SUMMARY

Luke has used great care in his research. In 1:3–4 he notes how he followed, or "investigated," everything, suggesting that he not only knows his sources well but faithfully hands on what he has found. With this diligent research, he can offer Theophilus this orderly account in order to confirm his faith. This book is not for those inside the church but for those who need to "know the certainty" of the teaching they have received, given the hostility leveled against the Christian faith during this era (17:6; 28:22). The word "certainty" was a favorite term in antiquity to denote a true philosophy as opposed to a superstition. Concern for certainty is also reflected in Acts 1:3, in which Luke tells Theophilus that, after his resurrection, Jesus gave the apostles "many convincing proofs that he was alive."

Questions for Discussion

1. How would you compare Luke's telling of the nativity story with that of Matthew? What are the prominent differences in their accounts of the life of Jesus?
2. Some scholars believe Luke's "opening story" of Jesus in the Nazareth synagogue foretells the entire gospel (see Luke 4). Do you agree?
3. If we say Luke presents theological themes in this gospel, does this present a difficulty for understanding the gospels as historical records of Jesus's life?
4. Examine how Luke underscores Jesus's inclusion of those on society's margin as recipients of God's salvation. Should Jesus's inclusion of women shape our understanding of gender roles in the church today?
5. Do you agree with those liberation theologians who contend that this gospel presents a "preferential option for the poor"? Why or why not? Frame your response in light of Luke's presentation of the gospel.
6. What does the message of salvation mean for contemporary people? How can we proclaim this message while being both faithful to the gospel and relevant to society?

BIBLIOGRAPHY

Introductory

Bock, D. L. *Luke*. IVPNTC. Downers Grove, IL: InterVarsity Press, 1994.
Ellis, E. E. *The Gospel of Luke*. NCB. Grand Rapids: Eerdmans, 1974.
France, R. T. *Luke*. TTC. Grand Rapids: Baker, 2013.
Morris, L. *The Gospel According to St. Luke*. TNTC. Grand Rapids: Eerdmans, 1988.
Stein, R. H. *Luke*. NAC. Nashville: Broadman & Holman, 1993.

Advanced

Bock, D. L. *Luke*. BECNT. 2 vols. Grand Rapids: Baker, 1994, 1995.
Edwards, J. R. *The Gospel according to Luke*. PNTC. Grand Rapids: Eerdmans, 2015.
Fitzmyer, J. A. *The Gospel According to Luke*. AB. 2 vols. Garden City, NY: Doubleday, 1981, 1985.
Green, J. B. *The Gospel of Luke*. NICNT. Grand Rapids: Eerdmans, 1997.
Marshall, I. H. *The Gospel of Luke*. NIGTC. Grand Rapids: Eerdmans, 1978.
Nolland, J. *Luke*. 3 vols. WBC. Dallas: Word, 1989, 1993.

NOTES

1. I. H. Marshall, *Luke: Historian and Theologian* (Exeter: Paternoster, 1970), 117.

2. Based on J. D. G. Dunn, *The Acts of the Apostles* (Harrisburg, PA: Trinity International, 1996), xiv.

3. D. L. Bock, *Luke*, 2 vols. (Grand Rapids: Baker, 1994–1995), 1:60. See Josephus, *Contra Apion* 1.53 [1.10]; 1.218 [1.23].

4. A. N. Sherwin-White, *Roman Society and Roman Law in the New Testament* (Oxford: Clarendon, 1963), 162–71.

5. For a full discussion of the problem, see Bock, *Luke*, 1:903–9.

6. See B. J. Malina and J. H. Neyrey, "Honor and Shame in Luke-Acts: Pivotal Values of the Mediterranean World," in *The Social World of Luke-Acts*, ed. J. H. Neyrey (Peabody, MA: Hendrickson, 1991), 29.

Chapter 11

THE GOSPEL ACCORDING TO JOHN

Ephesus, the traditional location of John's community
iStock.com/sevendeman

The *I Am* Sayings in John's Gospel

One of the unusual features of John's gospel is the number of times Jesus uses the form "I am" in his sentences. Often these have explicit predicates telling us who or what "he is" (all emphases added).

I am the bread of life. (6:35, 51)

I am the light of the world. (8:12; 9:5)

I am the gate for the sheep. (10:7, 9)

I am the good shepherd. (10:11)

I am the resurrection and the life. (11:25)

I am the way and the truth and the life. (14:6)

I am the true vine. (15:1, 5)

Jesus also uses the so-called "absolute" *I am*. Here the grammar defies logic. In the following examples, translators have supplied English words to make the sentences comprehendible. In the following, 8:24 is literally, "Unless you believe *I am*, you will surely die in your sins." The best explanation is to see these as an allusion to the use of I AM when God reveals himself to Moses on Mount Sinai.

Unless you believe that *I am*, you will surely die in your sins. (8:24)

When you lift up the Son of Man, then you will realize that *I am.* (8:28)

Before Abraham was born, *I am.* (8:58)

When it does happen you will believe that *I am.* (13:19)

Sometimes the use is ambiguous. In some cases Jesus is simply identifying himself; in others, he is alluding to God:

I am [or, It is I], don't be afraid. (6:20)

Jesus said to them, *I am* [he]. (18:5)

The gospel of John is a careful retelling of Jesus's life that takes us deeper into the meaning of his life and work. John likely assumes that we understand the basic outline of the Synoptic Gospels and therefore probes beneath the surface, supplying numerous stories untold elsewhere. Using irony, drama, and subtle theological nuance, John illustrates how Jesus's arrival fulfills and upends major Jewish festivals and institutions of worship.

Many unforgettable sayings of Jesus come from this gospel. Note, for example, the "I am" sayings (see sidebar, above). John also provides astounding affirmations of Jesus's divine nature and origin: "Before Abraham was born, I am" (8:58); "I and the Father are one" (10:30). It is John who takes the most creative step of describing Jesus as the Word of God through whom all creation came into being (1:3). His most dramatic turn comes in 1:14, when he tells us that this Word, which shares every feature with the Father, has become flesh, living among us.

In chapters 1–12 John describes Jesus's entry into the world and how Jesus offers "signs" as evidence of his identity. Jesus's "trial" begins the moment he is examined by the world, and throughout these chapters, witnesses are brought forward demonstrating Jesus's truth and innocence. In chapters 13–21 John describes Jesus's movement toward his "glorification" on the cross: his arrest, trial, crucifixion, and burial. This is no tragedy, but rather a further opportunity to unveil Jesus's true mission from God. With unexpected irony, John views the cross as Jesus's royal coronation, as a place of glory from which new life will flow to everyone who believes.

THE SETTING OF JOHN'S GOSPEL

A strong early church tradition places the location of John's ministry in Ephesus. According to fourth-century historian Eusebius and the theologian Irenaeus, John lived in Ephesus. A generation after John, Ignatius of Antioch writes of the faithfulness and strength of the Ephesian church (*Ign. Eph.* 8–9).

If the traditions of early Christianity are correct, John became a leader in this region of Asia Minor. Ephesus may have been his base of ministry if he had jurisdiction over the seven leading churches of Asia (Rev. 1–3). John no doubt traveled to places such as Pergamum, Sardis, and Thyatira. He was the historian and theologian who brought to them the story of Jesus. He was a valued eyewitness to the life of Jesus (John 19:35).

Jesus visited numerous rural villages throughout Galilee. This rural village near Hebron (Der-Samet) reflects many of the architectural features of first-century villages. Therefore, when we think of Jesus in Cana (John 2), we can imagine settings such as this.
Z. Radovan/www.BibleLand Pictures.com

The setting of John's gospel was likely in a Hellenistic city where Jewish and Hellenistic culture met. This Greek tomb from Ephesus depicts the female monster of Greek mythology, Medusa. *Z. Radovan/www.BibleLand Pictures.com*

In later years John stood with the church in times of persecution and conflict. When it seemed that the fledgling community's struggle with the prestigious synagogue community would overwhelm them, John held to a courageous witness of Jesus Christ. When internal conflict later came to the church, John again was the community's strength, writing letters (1–3 John) to encourage them (see ch. 25).

THE LITERARY FORM OF JOHN'S GOSPEL

This gospel betrays evidence of its literary history. If we read the entire gospel without regard for its chapter divisions, we notice its natural literary divisions. In chapters 1–12 Jesus is at work in public, showing signs and teaching diverse public audiences. In chapters 13–17 he is in private, speaking to his followers, almost saying "farewell" to them. The story ends with a detailed passion/resurrection account (chs. 18–21).

Chapter 12 is therefore the climax to Jesus's public ministry. It ends with a "summing up" of Jesus's efforts, a cry of despair concerning disbelief, and a final reaffirmation of the divine origins of Jesus's words. John 13:1 moves to the Passover, remarks that Jesus is now departing from the world, and narrows the stage to those who have followed him. Chapter 17 ends a lengthy prayer. A shift to the Kidron Valley (ch. 18) moves us to Jesus's arrest, trial, and death.

These natural divisions are often labeled the "Book of Signs" (chs. 1–12), since they record Jesus's revelatory miracles, and the "Book of Glory" (chs. 13–21), since John interprets the cross as a place of Jesus's glorification (13:31).

John alone tells us about the healing of a paraplegic man in Jerusalem at the five-porch pool of Bethesda (John 5:2). The pool is also mentioned at Qumran on the *Copper Scroll* (3Q15 11:12–13). This model reconstruction in Jerusalem (at the Israel Museum) shows its probable design. *© 2018 by Zondervan*

The Book of Signs (John 1–12)

The Book of Signs begins with a prelude serving like an overture, a curtain-raiser to the drama that begins at verse 19. This is followed by a unit centered on John the Baptist and his disciples (and their earliest contacts with Jesus). Then the story moves quickly from scene to scene: a miracle at Cana, cleansing the temple, Nicodemus, and so on.

Clearly, these sections are *topically arranged*. From chapters 2–4 Jesus is working miracles on institutions in Judaism; from chapters 5–10 he is making appearances at a series of Jewish festivals (each festival is named). In other words, Jesus is replacing Jewish symbols with abundance, messianic abundance. For instance, at a Passover (ch. 6), which recalls the exodus and God's provision of manna, Jesus feeds the crowd bread and then announces that he is the true bread from heaven (6:41)!

John repeatedly refers to "hour" (Gk. *hora*; e.g., 1:39; 2:4; 5:25; 7:30; 8:20; 12:23). In Greek, *hora* usually refers to an hour of the day, but John frequently uses it to signal a specific period in Jesus's life. For example, at Cana when Mary tells Jesus that the wedding is out of wine, he responds, "My hour [*hora*] has not yet come" (2:4). He tells the Samaritan woman that "a time [*hora*] . . . has now come" for true worshipers to worship the Father in spirit and truth (4:23).

This phrase provides a rhythm for the entire gospel and indicates that Jesus's life was oriented toward one event: his glorification and return to the Father through the cross. Once Jesus returns to Jerusalem for the last time (ch. 12) and is betrayed and arrested (ch. 13), the "hour" of glory is underway, to be completed when he is raised from the dead. In this "hour" many great things happen. His sacrificial work on the cross is completed (19:30), he gives the Spirit (20:22), and he begins his return to glory (17:5, 24).

Outline of the Book of Signs (John 1–12)

I. The Prologue (1:1–18)
II. Jesus and the Baptist (1:19–51)
III. Jesus and the Jewish Institutions (2:1–4:54)
    1. At Cana, Purification Vessels (2:1–12)
    2. In Jerusalem, the Temple (2:13–25)
    3. In Jerusalem, a Rabbi (3:1–21)
       {An additional excursus on the Baptist (3:22–36)}
    4. In Samaria, a Sacred Well (4:1–42)
    5. Return to Cana (4:43–54)
IV. Jesus and Jewish Festivals (5:1–10:42)
    1. Sabbath (5:1–47)
    2. Passover (6:1–71)
    3. Tabernacles (7:1–9:41)

4. Rededication [Hanukkah] (10:1–39)
5. Return to John the Baptist (10:40–42)

V. Foreshadowing Jesus's Death and Resurrection (11:1–12:50)
1. Lazarus: A Paradigm of Death and Life (11:1–57)
2. Jesus Anointed for Death Enters Jerusalem to Die (12:1–50)

A careful examination of the Book of Signs reveals *internal markers* that subdivide each section. For example, stories in Cana frame the section on Jewish institutions. The festival section clearly refers to each respective festival, exploits a major symbol in the festival (Sabbath/work, Passover/bread, Tabernacles/water and light, Rededication/Jesus's consecration), and generally offers a discourse expanding the meaning of the symbols (see 6:15–35 as a comment on Passover). The final reference to John the Baptist (10:40–42) refers back to the beginning of the entire sequence of signs (1:19ff.), making another closing frame and reiterating the value of Jesus's signs. The closing two chapters serve as a sobering warning of what is to come. In chapter 11, the death and raising of Lazarus foreshadows the death and raising of Jesus, and in chapter 12, Jesus is prepared for burial by his friends in Bethany, and he cries out about Jewish unbelief while Greeks eagerly come to the disciples to see Jesus.

In John 4 Jesus's offer of living water referred to ritual water used for purification. This Jewish ritual bath (*mikveh*) at Qumran was "purified" by running ("living") water brought down by channels from cliffs west of the site.
Robert Hoetink/Shutterstock

Living Water in First-Century Judaism

In a land that frequently experienced drought, Israel was keenly aware of water sources and water quality. Springs and rivers that ran all year were few, so people used systems to catch the winter rains and store them (cisterns) or dug wells. In Jewish culture, "dead water" was standing, stored water. "Living water" was moving water (e.g., rivers, springs, and rainfall); such water came directly from God and did not have to be transported by human hands (up a well or cistern). Only living water could serve as water for ritual washings.

This distinction explains why the woman of Samaria is so amused when Jesus claims to know where living water is. Samaria has no river. If Jacob had to cut a well here, how can Jesus be superior?

Jesus mentions living water again at Jerusalem's autumn Feast of Tabernacles (7:37–39). In this period of drought, everyone prayed for renewing rains to end the dry summer. At the festival Jesus makes an extravagant claim: anyone looking for living water should come to him and drink, for he is the source of renewal.

In John 9 Jesus directs the blind man to go wash in the "Pool of Siloam." This pool, south of the Temple, was used daily during the Festival of Tabernacles.
Todd Bolen/BiblePlaces.com

As we examine this structure, we see the topical arrangement (at least in chs. 1–12), even though the stories themselves have a clear historical character. Foremost on John's agenda is the theological meaning of Jesus Christ and his impact on Judaism. As readers who watch the drama unfold, we come away with a clear understanding of Jesus's identity; in light of his coming, every religious position has been called into question.

The Book of Glory (John 13–21)

The same theological agenda can be found in the Book of Glory. Jesus turns in private to his disciples during his final Passover. He teaches them about servanthood, washes their feet, explains the coming Holy Spirit in terms of personal revelation and persecution, and prays at length for his followers and their disciples.

Chapter 18 opens the story of the trial and death of Jesus. It reads much like the Synoptics, moving quickly from scene to scene. The cross is followed by a detailed resurrection account in which Jesus anoints his followers with the Spirit. Chapter 21 is likely an addition about resurrection stories in Galilee and Jesus's lengthy discussion with Peter.

It is important to see that the cross is carefully reinterpreted in John's gospel. The anguish in Gethsemane described by the Synoptics does not appear here. Jesus moves confidently toward "the hour." At his arrest he steps forward and gives orders. At his trial he asks the questions. He is robed like a king and "lifted up" on the cross under a sign announcing in the languages of the world that he is "the king of the Jews."

The Cross and Passover

In 1:29, 36, John the Baptist introduces Jesus as the "Lamb of God." This title may refer to the sacrificial lamb that was killed daily in the temple (Ex. 29:38–46) or the lamb of Isaiah 53:7. But more likely John sees Jesus as the Passover lamb, whose death marked the central event of the Passover—the blood of a lamb that covered the doors of the Israelites in Egypt and saved them (Ex. 12).

Jews coming to Jerusalem to celebrate the Passover had to supply (or purchase) a perfect young lamb for sacrifice. No bones could be broken. No disease could be present. The Levite watched for running blood when the lamb was sacrificed to verify that the lamb was alive.

At his final Passover, Jesus uses the meal to show that his death is a sacrifice (Mark 14:17–31). In John the cross becomes an altar where Christ, the Passover lamb, is slain. The hyssop used at the cross was also used at Passover (cf. John 19:29; Ex. 12:22). Jesus's legs are not broken (19:33), which fulfills a Passover rule (John 19:36; Ex. 12:46). Blood runs freely from his wound (19:34), showing that his life is being exchanged for others.

John tells us that when Jesus was on the cross, hyssop was used to extend a drink of wine to him (19:29). Hyssop was also used by the Israelites in Egypt at Passover to cover their homes in lamb's blood (Ex. 12:22)—a symbol John no doubt valued.
Gloria Suess/BiblePlaces.com

Outline of the Book of Glory (John 13–21)

I. The Passover Meal (13:1–30)
   1. The Foot Washing (13:1–20)
   2. The Betrayal of Judas (13:21–30)

II. The Farewell Discourse (13:31–17:26)
   1. Jesus's Departure and Provision (13:31–14:31)
   2. The True Vine (15:1–17)
   3. The Disciples and the World (15:18–16:33)
   4. The Priestly Prayer of Jesus (17:1–26)

III. The Suffering and Death of Jesus (18:1–19:42)
   1. Arrest and Interrogation (18:1–19:16)
   2. Crucifixion and Burial (19:17–42)

IV. The Resurrection (20:1–31)

V. Epilogue (21:1–25)

THEOLOGICAL THEMES IN JOHN'S GOSPEL

John's stories contribute to a theological portrait that has been deeply valued in the history of the church. In each of the major theological councils of the church when important doctrines about Jesus were being resolved, John's gospel played an essential role. The themes weave themselves throughout the gospel.

John's Central Affirmation

The most important affirmation of this gospel is that God has appeared in human history in the man Jesus Christ. In him we see the glory of God (1:14). Despite the unrelenting darkness of this world, God has entered our world, which stands in enmity with him. But he does so through human flesh, embracing our own creatureliness. This revelation is so potent that darkness cannot defeat it. Even though Jesus is persecuted, tried, and crucified, John affirms that the light cannot be extinguished (see 1:5).

But Christ's gift is not simply his revelation of

the Father (14:9). "In him was life, and the life was the light of all people" (1:4 NRSV). There is hope for the world. John's message is also one of sacrifice and redemption. Those who embrace this revelation by identifying with the light will gain eternal life. The life of the Son is poured out in sacrifice, thereby creating the community of the redeemed (17:6–12, 20–26). They bear Christ's Spirit, which sustains them.

Thus, John writes to explain this revelation and redemption and all their possibilities. In 20:31 he makes clear this aim, "These are written that you may believe that Jesus is the Messiah, the Son of God, and that by believing you may have life in his name." Here all John's major themes converge: belief, acknowledgment of Jesus's sonship, and the promise of life.

Circumstances John Must Address

John is likely written for Christians who, already knowing the rudiments of Christ's life and Christian truth, now wish to go further. Not only is there an uncompromising maturity of thought in this gospel, but also its narratives imply that it is written to address certain practical circumstances in the church. John asserts Christian truth amid unsympathetic forces and clarifies Christian doctrines at an early stage of church development.

The Miraculous Signs in John's Gospel

In John's gospel seven miracles ("signs") are recorded.

1. Jesus changes water into wine. (2:1–11)
2. Jesus heals the official's son. (4:46–54)
3. Jesus heals the man at the pool of Bethesda. (5:1–9)
4. Jesus feeds the five thousand. (6:1–13)
5. Jesus walks on water. (6:16–21)
6. Jesus heals the man born blind. (9:1–12)
7. Jesus raises Lazarus. (11:1–44)

In each case, a sign is divinely given as evidence that justifies faith in Christ. But some scholars question whether this list is absolute. Perhaps the greatest sign of all in this gospel is the cross, where those who crucify Jesus cannot understand the deeper meaning of what is transpiring. If this is true, multiple signs punctuate Jesus's public ministry (1–12) and one sign, one great sign, dominates the Book of Glory. (Some would add the miraculous catch of fish in chapter 21 to this list, but this chapter is likely an addendum and not a part of the gospel's original plan.

Miraculous Signs in John

John does not use the term *dynamis* ("wonder, miracle") in his gospel. Instead, he labels each miracle as a *semeion* ("sign"), an event with a deeper meaning than one sees at first glance. In the Synoptic Gospels, the audience reacts with amazement and excitement at Jesus's miracles. In John, this feature is absent. Usually, the "sign" is met with belief (2:11; 4:48, 54; 11:45). After Jesus raises Lazarus, the authorities remark, "Here is this man performing many signs. If we let him go on like this, everyone will believe in him" (11:47–48).

A miracle (*dynamis*) points to the source of power and fills us with fear and wonder. A sign (*semeion*) points to a deeper underlying meaning that evokes a response. When Jesus fed the five thousand, many only saw the distribution of bread. But Jesus wanted them to see beneath the deed, to see him as the bread of life (6:35) that will be given when he dies on the cross (6:51). Jesus presses his audience to see the deeper purposes of God's work in the world.

Anti-Semitism and John's Gospel

For some scholars, the gospel of John has contributed directly to the anti-Judaism of the past two thousand years. Seventy-one times the phrase "the Jews" appears in this gospel. Matthew and Luke, by comparison, only use the term five times each.

Anti-Semitism has been the dark heritage of the church. But those who interpret John as endorsing anti-Semitism deeply misread it. Jesus and the apostles are Jewish. So are his opponents. Jesus does not wrestle with "the Jews"—he is a Jew! He is not condemned by "the Jews"—he is condemned by the brokers of religious power in first-century Jerusalem. In most cases "the Jews" refers either to the "Judeans" (7:1) or to Jewish leaders.

For instance, John gives attention to the relationship between Jesus's followers and Judaism. The Synoptic Gospels contain many conflict stories between Jesus and the Pharisees. John not only deepens the conflict but explains it (cf. 8:31–59; 10:19–39). The "Jews" virtually becomes a technical term in John for those who reject Jesus. His messiahship and his relationship to the festivals and institutions of Judaism are emphasized. Jesus has come to replace what is offered in the Jewish institutions. Such an emphasis likely springs from a Christian community that is experiencing marked conflict with the synagogue.

John's gospel also emphasizes themes important to the development of Christian life and thought throughout the first century. At the time the gospel was circulating publicly, the early Christian church had grown and diversified considerably. Thus, John includes historic materials relevant to Christian needs in his generation. But we must not think these needs became the controlling force in John's literary design.

When Jesus visited Samaria (John 4), the region had developed its own distinct history, culture, and religious traditions. Mount Gerizim was the site of the Samaritan temple (4:20), which was destroyed in 128 BC. That temple is here depicted (with steps) on a fourth-century Samaritan oil lamp. *Z. Radovan/www.BibleLand Pictures.com*

(1) John the Baptist. Did John the Baptist have followers who refused to follow Jesus? Luke 3:15 and Acts 19:1–7 suggest this and later writings confirm it. This gospel affirms, however, that the Baptist was not the Messiah (John 1:20; 3:28) or the light (1:8–9), and that Jesus is superior (1:30; 3:29–30; 10:41). We even witness certain disciples of John becoming Jesus's first converts (1:35–42).

(2) The person of Christ. In a fashion unparalleled by the Synoptics, John affirms the oneness of Jesus and the Father (10:30; 14:9–10), their distinction from each other (14:28; 17:1–5), and their unity of purpose (5:17–18; 8:42). In the formation of later Trinitarian doctrine, John played a notable role. This was particularly true at the Council of Nicea (AD 325), when Arius denied the eternal nature of the Son and Athanasius affirmed Jesus as the eternal Logos (1:1). Both Greek and Jewish listeners would immediately recognize in this title a profound statement. Greeks would think of the seminal forces that sustain the universe; Jewish minds would think back to Genesis 1, where the word of God was the means of creation.

In Jesus's day the word of God took on personal creative attributes (Ps. 33:6, 9) and was viewed as an apt description for divine Wisdom. In Proverbs 8 Wisdom coexisted with God from the beginning. Through Wisdom—the Logos—God extended himself into the cosmos, creating the world. Jesus shares the very same essence as God: he existed before time and was the agent of all creation. In perhaps

John's gospel ends with Peter meeting Jesus on Galilee's north shore. This site, today called Saint Peter's Primacy, has been venerated by Christian pilgrims at least since the fourth century.
Berthold Werner/Wikimedia Commons, Public Domain

the most surprising verse penned by an apostle, John writes that this Logos, this Wisdom, became flesh and lived among us as a human being (1:14).

For Jews who might have struggled with the divinity of Christ, this category of Wisdom gave a ready-made explanation. No rabbi would doubt that divine Wisdom came from God since the beginning of time. No rabbi doubted the personal coexistence of Wisdom with God. John echoes this conviction: What God is, so the Logos is. And the Logos is Christ (cf. 1:1–2).

To be sure, John's emphasis is on the divinity of Jesus, and for Jewish readers this would have been the most arresting feature of the gospel. But for his Hellenistic readers the emphasis on Jesus's humanity would have been equally disturbing. If a first-generation Christian were inclined toward *adoptionism* (that Jesus was merely a divinely inspired man), the gospel gives an unrelenting rebuttal. But the Greek world was comfortable with divinities and, if anything, hesitated to affirm Jesus's "full humanity." For these followers of Jesus, the Lord only "appeared" (Gk. *dokeo*) human (hence, the theological teaching of *docetism*). John affirms both and wants to keep them in a delicate balance: Jesus was eternally divine and fully incarnate—fully God and fully human.

However, the emphasis on Jesus's divine identity is consistently applied throughout the gospel. And it may be that Hellenistic Christians overlooked the incarnational features of the gospel and promoted Jesus's divinity exclusively. This unbalanced view based on the fourth gospel likely inspired the controversy that later John must address in his letters that we find at the end of the New Testament (see ch. 25).

(3) The Holy Spirit. Unlike the other three gospels, John provides us with a wealth of information concerning the Spirit. His treatment moves in two directions. (1) John emphasizes how the Spirit is an integral feature of Jesus's experience of God. During Jesus's baptism, for instance, the Spirit *remains* on Jesus (1:32–33), underscoring the permanence of God's indwelling. God has given

The Spirit Paraclete in John

Four times Jesus uses the Greek noun *paraklētos* to describe the promised Holy Spirit (14:16, 26; 15:26; 16:7; cf. also 1 John 2:1). This word comes from a verb that refers to someone "called alongside"; it occurs in Greek literature for an advocate in a court of law who comes "alongside" a person to speak in his or her defense and provide counsel. Its basic meaning is someone who counsels, advises, or exhorts. "Counselor" is a popular translation, but one must think of a legal counselor. "Comforter" is another popular translation, but this can be misleading. Some translations prefer to leave it untranslated as *Paraclete*.

Jesus describes the Spirit as *another* Paraclete (14:16). This implies that John views Jesus himself as a Paraclete on our behalf (this is explicit in 1 John 2:1). Jesus is thus a Paraclete, who is now sending a second Paraclete. In other words, the ongoing work of the Spirit continues the work of Jesus. Remarkably, every task of the promised Paraclete in John 14–16 is a task that Jesus does elsewhere in the gospel. The Spirit sustains the work of Jesus in the life of the believer.

him the Spirit without measure (3:34). The Spirit is a source of living water (4:10), which later we learn flows from within Jesus himself (7:37–39). The release of the Spirit is dependent on Jesus's death (7:39): "Unless I go away, the Advocate [Paraclete] will not come to you" (16:7). This imagery that joins Spirit and Christ may be at work in the cross when Jesus is wounded and water (along with blood) flows from him (19:34).

(2) John promises the Spirit to believers. He records Jesus's nighttime conversation with Nicodemus in which he challenges the rabbi to be born again (3:1–10). This is a work not of intellectual or moral conversion, but of spiritual activity. The same is true for the Samaritan woman, a character who stands theologically and socially opposite Nicodemus. The living water she seeks (4:15) is later defined as the Spirit (7:37–38), and Jesus takes advantage of Samaria's cultural rift with Judaism to talk about true worship that engages the Spirit (4:24). The work of the Spirit culminates in Jesus's lengthy farewell discourse (chs. 14–16), where the Spirit is described and promised for all believers. John even records Jesus's giving the Spirit to his disciples on Easter day as a final gift before his departure (20:22). To be united with Jesus is to experience his Spirit, which is set free for the world at the cross.

(4) The sacraments. John has a "sacramental" view of history since the incarnation of Christ for him means the genuine appearance of God in history. And if this is true (that God employs the artifacts of history to reach us) then the objects and forms of worship we use in worship may likewise be used by God. Worship can affirm such genuine appearances when worship symbols (baptism, the Lord's Supper) take on the real properties of that which they depict. Hence, they are called "sacraments." While scholars debate the role of the sacraments in this gospel, John's main message about each (found in 3:1–21 and 6:52–65) is corrective: without the Holy Spirit these expressions of worship become powerless rituals void of their original purpose. John 4:21–24 likewise adds a valuable commentary. God desires above all to be worshipped in spirit and in truth, that is: the Spirit of God and the presence of Jesus who is the Truth must shape our worship. The forms and locations of worship are less important than these two realities.

(5) Our future hope: eschatology. Many early Christians longed for the second coming of Christ and anticipated an imminent end to history. This explains the cherished sayings of Jesus about his second coming in the Synoptics (see Matt. 24; Mark 13; Luke 21). How did they cope when this hope was frustrated (cf. 2 Peter 3:1–12)? John, while maintaining this hope (John 5:25–30; 1 John 2:28), introduces a fresh emphasis: the longed-for presence of Jesus is mediated to us *now* in the Spirit. Jesus has come back and is with us already in the Spirit. In technical terms, John emphasizes a *realized eschatology* in contrast to the apocalyptic hope of the Synoptics.

(6) Irony. John invites us to explore a theme that has troubled interpreters. Is it possible for us to comprehend Jesus's words and actions, or do we always filter them through our own experiences? If the original audience of Jesus had difficulty understanding him, will it be difficult for us who now read his words in English centuries later?

John's gospel creates a drama on a stage. We sit in the audience watching characters move in and out, making contact with Jesus. Remarkably, many misunderstand what is happening and either race to the wrong conclusion (6:15), reject him outright (7:43–44), or debate among themselves (7:12–13).

For instance, Jesus tells Nicodemus that he must be born again, and he wonders if he must return to his mother's womb (3:4). Jesus offers the Samaritan woman living water, and she promptly wonders how he can offer her water when he has no bucket and there are no streams nearby (4:11). Later, Jesus's disciples bring him food and encourage him to eat, but he says he has other food they don't know about. Immediately they wonder, "Could someone have brought him food?" (4:33). Jesus even tells the Pharisees that he is going someplace where they cannot follow (heaven), but they speculate that he must be making a trip to visit Greeks (7:35)! Sometimes

Lazarus's Burial

The death, burial, and resurrection of Lazarus in John 11 are an ironic foreshadowing of Jesus's passion in the fourth gospel. In Jewish custom a person should be buried on the day he or she dies. The body was washed, perfumed, and wrapped, and mourning continued for one week. Visitors came to the tomb to pray and recite Scripture. Emotion was public in this culture, so wailing was loud and raucous. Some believed that a person's soul remained near the body for three days and so it is no accident that here (and in the story of Jesus's death) three days elapse before evidence of raising appears.

This explains Martha's grief in John 11:39. Four days have passed since Lazarus's death, and all hope is lost. Jesus's power, however, can overcome even this obstacle. This also explains Jesus's burial for three days. The women are distraught because if Jesus's body cannot be found immediately, he may not be recognizable. Jesus's return before Monday puts their concerns to rest.

a person makes an ironic, misunderstanding statement and does not even know its significance. In 11:50 Caiaphas is plotting politics when he says that it is good that one man should die for the sake of the nation; no truer words were ever uttered.

What is going on here? Following many of Jesus's speeches, the audience argues over the meaning of his identity. In some cases, when they perceive who he really is, some want to arrest him, while others want to become his disciples (7:43–44). In 9:35–41 Jesus announces that a blind man now can see—and the sighted Pharisees have become blind!

Jesus frequently came to Jerusalem by climbing the mountains of Judea. Here a Roman aqueduct remains from that road between Jericho and Jerusalem.
Todd Bolen/BiblePlaces.com

In 11:2 and 12:3 John identifies Mary of Bethany as the one who anointed Jesus the week prior to his burial with perfume from bottles such as these. These are glass Roman vessels that may have been at her disposal.
Z. Radovan/www.BibleLandPictures.com

When Jesus referred to the vine (John 15), he took advantage of one of Israel's most familiar images. Note how the lintel on this Jewish tomb near Jerusalem uses the images of the vine.
Z. Radovan/www.BibleLandPictures.com

The secret is found in 1:5 and 3:19–21. John understands that the world lives in darkness and so cannot understand the reality of things around it. *Divine revelation is inaccessible to the world.* In fact, when God's light penetrates that darkness, exposing the unreality of the world's life, many flee deeper into the darkness because they prefer it. The darkness hates the light. Only the transforming power of God's Spirit can reverse our incomprehension and make us children of God who are able to see things clearly. Only later do the disciples understand the meaning of Jesus (2:22). Only when they gain the Spirit do they understand (16:12–13).

(7) The world. One of the most frequently used words in John's gospel is "the world" (*kosmos*). The term appears seventy-eight times in his gospel (and twenty-four times in his letters). No other gospel has anything similar. In Greek-speaking Jewish thought, *kosmos* refers to creation, including the heavens and the earth God creates in Genesis 1. John shares this thought (1:3, 10; 17:5, 24) but takes the concept further. The "world" is more specifically the "universe" of humanity. For example, see John 1:10, "Though the world was made through him, the world did not recognize him" when he came. The second "world" refers to humanity.

John understands that this world—though good—is hostile to the things of God. It is controlled by a darkness that cannot comprehend the light and resists it (3:19). It is dead and needs life (6:33, 51), yet it hates the very One who can save it (7:7). The root problem is that the world is under the dominion of Satan (12:31), who will one day be judged.

If Jesus and Nicodemus met in the temple courts (John 3), Jesus may have entered the temple via these southern steps. This area from the first century has now been excavated, showing part of an arch of the Double Gate.
© 2018 by Zondervan

Another gate, the Triple Gate, 70 meters east of the Double Gate, shares the southern steps. There is a debate over which gate was used for entering or exiting the temple courts.
© 2018 by Zondervan

Nevertheless, God loves the world (3:16), that is, sinful humanity arrayed against him. Jesus thus dies to take away the sin of the world (1:29) and bring it the only prospect for life.

Christ wants his disciples to have an honest assessment of the world. They too will be despised (15:18; 17:14), and the Spirit within them will engage the world in its errors (16:7–11). Above all, Jesus gives his followers a word of assurance: "In this world you will have trouble. But take heart! I have overcome the world" (16:33).

AUTHOR AND DATE

John's gospel, like the others, provides no explicit internal evidence concerning its author. It may, however, provide us with clues concealed in the enigmatic figure of the "disciple whom Jesus loved" (the "beloved disciple"). This title occurs in six passages in John (13:23; 19:26–27; 20:2–10; 21:7, 20, 24). This last passage describes him as the one "who testifies to these things and who wrote them down." Therefore, the origin of the gospel must in some way be connected to this person.

But who is he? Some have suggested he is an idealized literary figure. To a degree this is true (he is faithful and intimate in his knowledge of Jesus). But this hardly excludes the possibility of a genuine historical person. Lazarus is sometimes nominated. He is the only figure of whom it is said that Jesus loved him (11:3, 11, 36). Furthermore, these texts occur only after Lazarus is introduced in chapter 11. But this solution is unlikely. Why would Lazarus's name be mentioned in chapters 11–12 but then left shrouded in subsequent accounts?

Some have suggested *John* Mark as the author. We do know that a man named John Mark was a part of the early church (Acts 12:12) and that he was associated with Peter. This may explain the mild rivalry between Peter and the beloved disciple in this gospel (cf. 20:2–8; 21:7–14); further, if Mark was related to the Levite Barnabas (Col 4:10), this would also explain how the beloved disciple knows the high priest in 18:15. But there is a strong patristic tradition that Mark authored the second gospel, not this one; besides, the beloved disciple is certainly one of the Twelve (13:23), which Mark was not.

The most recent suggestion points to Thomas as the beloved disciple. Throughout the gospel Thomas is presented as a person of leadership (11:16). His story with Jesus even concludes the gospel (assuming that ch. 20 originally

Stone jars such as these were used in Jewish homes in the first century. They were made of stone (not pottery) because stone did not take on the properties of ritual impurity. When Jesus turns water into wine at Cana (John 2), he likely used large stone water jars.
© 2018 by Zondervan

ended the book). Above all, Thomas asked to see the wound in Jesus's side, and the beloved disciple was the only one who saw the piercing of Jesus (19:35).

But the best solution is the traditional one: John son of Zebedee (Mark 3:17; Acts 1:13). This man was one of the Twelve, and along with James and Peter formed an inner circle around Jesus. This is the origin of his eyewitness testimony and penetrating insight. In the Synoptics, John appears with Peter more than with any other, and in Acts they are companions in Jerusalem (Acts 3–4) as well as in Samaria (8:14). In fact, John and Jesus may have been cousins. (A careful comparison of the names of the women at the cross suggests that Jesus's and John's mothers may have been sisters.) This explains two things. In John 19:25–27 Jesus entrusts Mary to John because of a natural family relation, and in 18:15–16 John is known by the high priest through Mary's priestly relatives (Luke 1:5, 36).

The Egerton Gospel, or Egerton Papyrus 2, contains fragments of an unknown gospel, dating to the mid-second century.
© The British Library Board

Later patristic evidence also points to the apostle John. Irenaeus was the bishop of Lyons (in modern France) in the late second century. In an important writing quoted by the fourth-century historian Eusebius, Irenaeus gives a full description of John's relation to this gospel. He says that the beloved disciple was John and that John wrote the gospel at Ephesus. But what is the source of Irenaeus's testimony? Irenaeus refers to Polycarp who was the bishop of Smyrna (modern W. Turkey), who was born about AD 70 and who claimed to have been tutored by John the Apostle himself. Eusebius, the first and earliest chronicler of church history (he died in about AD 340), records this John/Polycarp/Irenaeus connection to shore up Christians' understanding of the origin of their gospels. But there is more.

A basilica from the sixth century dedicated to John commemorates his death in Ephesus. Excavations beneath it show a third-century mausoleum that may point to the authenticity of the tradition about John's death in this city.
Gary M. Burge

Eusebius also cites a man named Florinus, who is in Rome and backs up what Irenaeus says. Eusebius cites the bishop of Ephesus named Polycrates, who links John the Apostle with the Fourth Gospel and his burial in Ephesus. All this can be added to other writers such as Clement of Alexandria (who died in about AD 220) and gave the gospel its famous title "the spiritual gospel." Each of these sources explain why there has been a strong church tradition associating this gospel, the Fourth Gospel, with John the Apostle.

If John son of Zebedee wrote this gospel, we can propose a possible date. The sources of John must be early and have their roots in first-generation Christianity. But fixing a certain date for the publication of the gospel is difficult because objective data are slim. Recently in Egypt two papyrus fragments of John (Rylands Papyrus 457 [$\mathfrak{P}^{52}$, see p. 570] and Egerton Papyrus 2) have been dated to the first half of the second century. Allowing time for John to circulate, we can say John could not have been completed after 110.

The earliest possible date for the gospel is more difficult. If John knows and uses the Synoptics (and this is disputed), then AD 70 or 80 is appropriate. In John 9:22; 12:42; and 16:2, we read about Jewish believers being excommunicated from the synagogues. In AD 85 the rabbis of Palestine instituted such expulsions for Christians. Therefore, we find a remarkable consensus of scholarly opinion that John was published somewhere between AD 80 and 100.

Nevertheless, an earlier date may be possible. Current research has challenged John's literary dependence on the Synoptics (esp. Mark and Luke). If anything, John may know pre-Synoptic traditions. Above all, the way in which John describes Jerusalem, his knowledge of the geographical and political divisions in Judaism, and his use of metaphors all point to a date approximating that of the Synoptic writers. The great watershed date of AD 70 is critical: John presupposes a Judaism before this war. With his critical disposition toward the Temple (John 2:13–25; 4:21–25) and severe conflicts with Jewish leadership (cf. chs. 5, 8, 10), we are surprised to find no hint of this catastrophic event.

Questions for Discussion

1. What are the chief differences between John's gospel and the Synoptics?
2. Why does John describe each of Jesus's miracles as a "sign"?
3. How many times in this gospel does Jesus's audience "divide"—some people believe, others become antagonistic? What does this say about the "world"?
4. In some stories in John (e.g., chs. 1, 4, 9) the narrative itself parades before us a catalog of theological names for Jesus. What does John want us to understand about the chief character in the story?
5. What is the relationship between signs and faith in John's gospel? Does John view miraculous signs as genuine avenues to a strong faith? Examine the story of Thomas in chapter 20 as a test case.

BIBLIOGRAPHY

Introductory

Blomberg, C. *The Historical Reliability of John's Gospel*. Downers Grove, IL: InterVarsity Press, 2002.
Burge, G. M. *John*. NIVAC. Grand Rapids: Zondervan, 2000.
Kruse, C. *John*. Tyndale New Testament Commentaries. Downers Grove, IL: IVP Academic, 2008.
Morris, L. *The Gospel according to St. John*. Rev. ed. NICNT. Grand Rapids: Eerdmans, 1995.
Thompson, M. M. *John: A Commentary*. NTLibrary. Louisville: Westminster/John Knox, 2016.

Advanced

Ashton, J. *Understanding the Fourth Gospel*. Rev. ed. Oxford: Oxford University Press, 2007.
Brown, R. E. *The Gospel according to John*. AB. 2 vols. New York: Doubleday, 1966, 1970.
Burge, G. M. *Interpreting the Gospel of John: A Practical Guide*. Grand Rapids: Baker, 2013.
Keener, C. *The Gospel of John: A Commentary*. 2 vols. Peabody, MA: Hendrickson, 2003.
Köstenberger, A. *John*. BECNT. Grand Rapids: Baker, 2003.

Chapter 12

THE ACTS OF THE APOSTLES

Paul was accused before Gallio, the Roman proconsul of Achaia, at the *bēma* (latin: *rostrum*) in Corinth (Acts 18:12–17).
Phoenix Data Systems

Acts serves as a "bridge document" that links the gospels to the New Testament letters. Here we learn about the fate of Christ's earliest followers—how they consolidate the early church in Jerusalem and envision a mission that will send the gospel all the way to the imperial city of Rome.

Luke recounts the compelling story of the establishment of the first churches throughout the empire, although his history does not comprehensively describe all the activities of all the apostles. He traces the spread of Christianity to Jews and gentiles from every social stratum throughout the empire. His subject is God's salvation in Jesus Christ, intended for all people, regardless of class or ethnicity (cf. Rom. 1:16). While Luke writes this history for Theophilus and others (1:1), we find ourselves in this narrative since, in Peter's words, God's promise is "for all who are far off—for all whom the Lord our God will call" (2:39).

THE SETTING OF ACTS IN THE NEW TESTAMENT

The placement of Acts after John rather than Luke is somewhat confusing since Luke composed this story as the second volume of a book written to Theophilus (cf. 1:1–2 and Luke 1:1–4). These two scrolls should be read and understood together as one continuous narrative (see ch. 10 for a comparison of Luke and Acts).

Luke-Acts traces the geographic progress of the gospel. This life of Jesus begins in Jerusalem when John the Baptist's father, Zechariah, goes to fulfill his priestly duty in the temple (Luke 1:9). Jesus is circumcised and presented in the temple as an infant (2:22) and, at the age of twelve, goes with Mary and Joseph to Jerusalem (2:41–51). While his public ministry centers on Galilee (4:14–15), Jerusalem is the place of Jesus's crucifixion, resurrection, and ascension.

The Ends of the Earth

Ancient authors identified the "ends of the earth" with various distant points. First-century geographer Strabo, for example, links the phrase to Gades in Spain (near modern Cadiz; see *Geography* 3.1.8). This may be why Paul is so concerned to bring the gospel to Spain (Rom. 15:24, 28).

But Strabo also views the world as an island, so any distant place that borders the sea can be identified this way. He notes how Homer viewed Ethiopia as the "ends of the earth" (*Geography* 1.1.6). The unknown author of the *Psalms of Solomon* speaks of the Roman general Pompey (who conquered Jerusalem in 63 BC) as having come "from the end of the earth" (*Pss. Sol.* 8:15). Thus, Acts 1:8 may refer to extending the gospel to the imperial city.

But this phrase also has ethnic associations. In Isaiah 49:6, God commissions the Servant of the Lord: "I will also make you a light for the Gentiles, that my salvation may reach to the ends of the earth" (cf. Acts 13:47). Acts 1:8 may therefore refer not only to the geographic but also the ethnic expansion of the Christian faith.

Both Hispania and Ethiopia, as well as Rome, were sometimes called "the ends of the earth."

Just before his ascension, Jesus commands his disciples to spread the gospel from Jerusalem out to the wider world (Luke 24:44–47). Acts begins with this command and expands on it: "You will be my witnesses in Jerusalem, and in all Judea and Samaria, and to the ends of the earth" (Acts 1:8). Acts tells how this command is fulfilled in Jerusalem (2:14–36), around Judea and Samaria (8:1), then all the way to Rome (23:11; 28:11–16).

Luke also wants to demonstrate the place of the gospel within Roman history. Jesus was born during the reign of Caesar Augustus and the rule of Quirinius, governor of Syria (Luke 2:1–2). Jesus's public ministry and crucifixion occurred when Pontius Pilate was prefect of Judea (Luke 3:1). Luke mentions a famine in Jerusalem (Acts 11:28) and expulsion of Jews from Rome (18:1–2) during the reign of Claudius. Paul stood on trial before two governors of Judea, Felix (24:1–2) and Porcius Festus (25:1–7).

Luke is also interested in theology, seen especially in the speeches in Acts. As Martin Hengel observes, "We only do justice to the significance of Luke as the first theological 'historian' of Christianity if we take his work seriously as a source, i.e., if we attempt to examine it critically, reconstructing the story he tells by adding and comparing other sources. . . . He does not set out primarily to present his own 'theology.'"[1]

LUKE'S HISTORY OF THE EARLY CHURCH

Many commentators understand Jesus's commission in 1:8 as a synopsis of the book: "You will be my witnesses in Jerusalem, and in all Judea and Samaria, and to the ends of the earth." Acts is about the spread of the gospel in Jerusalem and Judea (chs. 1–7), then to Samaria and to Antioch (chs. 8–12), culminating with Paul's three missionary journeys throughout the empire (chs. 13–28).

But the story in Acts also revolves around people. Peter is the main protagonist in the first part of the book (chs. 1–12), while Paul becomes the central figure in the second part (chs. 13–28). Luke repeatedly parallels the lives of these two apostles.

Parallels of Peter and Paul in Acts

Peter	Paul
Sermon in Jerusalem (2:22–36)	Sermon in Pisidian Antioch (13:26–41)
Lame man healed (3:1–10)	Lame man healed (14:8–11)
Filled with Spirit (4:8)	Filled with Spirit (13:9)
Extraordinary healings (5:15)	Extraordinary healings (19:12)
Laying on hands to receive Spirit (8:17)	Laying on hands to receive Spirit (19:6)
Conflict with magician (8:18–24)	Conflict with magician (13:6–11)
Tabitha raised from the dead (9:36–41)	Eutychus raised from the dead (20:9–12)
Miraculously released from jail (12:6–11)	Miraculously released from jail (16:25–41)

Luke shows the spread of the gospel throughout the northern Mediterranean, reaching as far west as Rome, where the temple of Divus Romulus, the founder of Rome, is located.
Leonid Andronov/Shutterstock

Another prominent structural element in the book is Luke's summary statements, which stitch his narrative together around the growth of the church and the expansion of the gospel (6:7; 9:31; 12:24; 16:5; 19:20), with a final summary statement at the end (28:30–31). These summaries divide the text into six sections, or panels.

These various structural elements make deciding how best to outline the story of Acts difficult. Ancient ideals about writing history apparently move Luke to bind the various incidents together into a cohesive unit. The "common matter and overlap" in Acts (see sidebar on "The Historian's Task") helps the reader understand the story as a cohesive unit and not as a simple collection of historical vignettes, but it does make outlining the book problematic. But Acts 1:8 is still a useful way to help us see the geographical and ethnic framework of Acts (see outline).

The Historian's Task

Commenting on the historian's task, Lucian writes in *How to Write History* 55: "After the preface ... let the transition to the narrative be gentle and easy. For all the body of the history is simply a long narrative.... [The historian] will make everything distinct and complete, and when he has finished the first topic he will introduce the second, fastened to it and linked with it like a chain, to avoid breaks and a multiplicity of disjointed narratives; no, always the first and the second topics must not merely be neighbors but have common matter and overlap."

Outline of Acts

I. Beginnings in Jerusalem (1:1–26)
II. Mission in Jerusalem (2:1–8:3)
    1. Early Witness to the Jewish Populace in Jerusalem (2:1–3:26)
    2. Early Persecution and Life of the Church (4:1–8:3)
III. Mission in Judea, Samaria, and the Surrounding Regions (8:4–12:25)
    1. Peter's Testimony to the Samaritans (8:4–40)
    2. Call of Saul (9:1–31)
    3. Peter's Miracles and Mission to Gentiles in Caesarea (9:32–11:18)
    4. Spread of the Gospel to Gentiles in Antioch (11:19–30)
    5. Death of Herod Agrippa I (12:1–25)
IV. Mission to the Ends of the Earth (13:1–28:31)
    1. Paul's First Missionary Journey and the Jerusalem Council (13:1–15:35)
        a. Mission to Cyprus and Southern Galatia (13:1–14:28)
        b. Jerusalem Council (15:1–35)
    2. Paul's Second Missionary Journey (15:36–18:22)
        a. Return to the Galatian Churches (15:36–16:5)
        b. Mission to Macedonia and Achaia (16:6–18:22)
    3. Paul's Third Missionary Journey (18:23–20:38)
        a. The Mission to Ephesus (18:23–19:41)
        b. The Return to Macedonia, Achaia, and Troas (20:1–12)
        c. Address to the Ephesian Elders (20:13–38)
    4. Paul's Return to Jerusalem (21:1–22:21)

5. Paul's Imprisonment in Jerusalem, Caesarea, and Rome (22:22–28:31)
    a. Imprisonment and Witness in Jerusalem (22:22–23:22)
    b. Imprisonment and Witness in Caesarea (23:23–26:32)
    c. Journey to Rome and Witness (27:1–28:31)

THE BEGINNINGS IN JERUSALEM (1:1–26)

Before his ascension (1:9–11) Jesus commissions the apostles in response to their question, "Lord, are you at this time going to restore the kingdom to Israel?" (1:6). During the first century, most Jews longed for liberation from Rome and the reestablishment of the Davidic monarchy. Some even attempted to bring about this liberation through armed conflict (5:36–37; 21:38).

The burning hope was for reestablishment of the twelve tribes, the conquest or conversion of the gentiles, a purified and glorious temple, and purity and justice in the worship and moral life of Israel. This was the disciples' hope as well, but their hopes were dashed with Jesus's crucifixion (Luke 24:21). Now with Jesus raised from the dead, their hope is revived. In Acts 1:6 the apostles are thinking of the kingdom in terms of the promises made to Israel and the restoration of national sovereignty, but Jesus has in mind a larger vision of the kingdom. Before it comes, the church must proclaim the gospel of Jesus Christ to all people everywhere in the power of the Spirit (1:8). Then the ascended Jesus will return and fully establish his kingdom (1:9–11).

Before embarking on this mission, however, the church must select a replacement for Judas to be the twelfth apostle (1:15–26). Peter sets the selection criteria, and then the assembled disciples choose by casting lots, a well-known and ancient form of discovering the divine will and appointing people to positions.

The apostles and the rest of the disciples met and preached in Solomon's Colonnade in the temple (Acts 3:11; 5:12). In this model at the Israel Museum (Jerusalem), Solomon's Colonnade runs along the far (east) side of the temple mount.
Todd Bolen/BiblePlaces.com

However, Philo calls casting lots "that uncertain and fortuitous divider, the lot" (*Quis Rerum Divinarum Heres* 179). On the other hand, the Roman orator Cicero offers his brother Quintus's opinion that discerning the divine will by lot "is not in itself to be despised" and that "I am inclined to think that they may, under the power of God, be so drawn as to give an appropriate response" (*De Divinatione* 1.18.34). Once the Spirit was given on Pentecost (2:1–4), the disciples no longer relied on lots since the Spirit directed their labors. Dreams, however, continued to be regarded as a form of divine direction (16:6–10).

THE MISSION IN JERUSALEM (2:1–8:3)

The coming of the Spirit occurs on Pentecost (2:1–4), a feast that, during the first century, celebrated the renovation of the old covenant (see *Jubilees* 6:17, "The feast of weeks [Pentecost] . . . [is] to renew the covenant in all (respects), year by year"). On this feast day God's people receive his Spirit as the blessing of the new covenant according to his promise (Jer. 31:33; Ezek. 11:19; 36:26–27). In his sermon (Acts 2:14–36), Peter understands the event as fulfilling Joel 2:28–32 and as a sign of the advent of the "last days" (Acts 2:17). But the central focus of his message is Christ and proclamation. Peter includes four basic points (2:22–39): the fulfillment of prophecy; a summary of Jesus's ministry, death, and triumph (resurrection and ascension); quotations of the Old Testament that testify about the Messiah; and a call to repentance. In response to Peter's preaching, about three thousand express their faith and repentance through baptism (2:37–41).

Luke also presents a number of cameos on communal life in the early church (2:42–47; 4:32–5:16; 6:1–6). "All the believers were one in heart and mind" (4:32), and private property was used to benefit those in need. They gave to the neediest among them (2:45b) and "no one claimed that any of their possessions was their own, but they shared everything they had" (4:32). In so doing, the church embodies the classical ideal of friendship, a result of this *koinōnia* ("sharing"), there are no needy members of the congregation (4:34). Barnabas is a prime example of the ideal of true friendship (4:36–37), while Ananias and Sapphira violate it by embezzling what they previously dedicated to the Lord for those in need (5:1–11). Their act echoes the sin of Achan (Josh. 7). At some point, longstanding prejudices between Aramaic-speaking and Greek-speaking Jewish Christians from the Diaspora hinder the church from responding in true friendship to widows (6:1–6).

As the church vigorously carries out the commission to preach the gospel, opposition to the community arises. The Jewish leadership is "greatly disturbed" because of how the apostles are "teaching the people [and] proclaiming in Jesus the resurrection of the dead" (4:2).

Koinonia and Friendship

The statement "friends are one soul" (cf. Acts 4:32) was proverbial in antiquity. When Aristotle was asked, "What is a friend?" he replied, "A single soul dwelling in two bodies" (Diogenes Laertes, *Lives of Eminent Philosophers* 5.20). Aristotle quotes a proverb of his day, "Friends' goods are common property," and then affirms, "This is correct, since community [*koinōnia*, 'sharing'] is the essence of friendship" (*Nichomachean Ethics* 8.9.1 [1159B]).

In the church, the ideal community of friends, no rule demands each to hand over their resources for distribution to all (see 5:4). Rather, the early Christians responded to the necessity of others (4:35). This perspective accords with Aristotle's comment on sharing property: "For individuals while owning their property privately put their own possession at the service of their friends and make use of their friends' possessions as common property" (*Politics* 2.2.5 [1263A]).

Multiple *mikvehot*, baths for ritual washing, have been found south of the Temple Mount in Jerusalem. This was one place in Jerusalem where three thousand people could have easily been baptized in a day.
Todd Bolen/BiblePlaces.com

Although Peter and John are arrested and warned not to preach or teach in Jesus's name (4:18), they declare their obligation to God (4:19) and continue to give bold witness to the gospel (4:23–31), empowered by the Spirit (4:31; 5:12–16). They proclaim Jesus as the Messiah (5:17–42), with significant results (6:7). The persecution reaches a peak after Stephen's martyrdom (6:8–8:3).

Stephen's account of Israel's history highlights two fundamental points. First, the Israelites have a history of rejecting God's servants sent to them, such as Joseph (7:9), Moses (7:23–29, 39–40), and the prophets (7:52a); even now they reject Jesus, "the Righteous One" (7:52b). However, God was with those whom his people rejected (7:9, 30–35, 38). Second, God's presence with his people does not depend on any sacred site. God appeared to Abraham in Mesopotamia (7:2), was with Joseph in Egypt (7:9), and revealed himself to Moses at Mount Sinai (7:30–34, 38). Their ancestors had the tabernacle, which went everywhere with them (7:44–46). God does not dwell in houses made by human hands (7:48–50; cf. 1 Kings 8:27; Isa. 66:1–2).

Stephen's sermon, therefore, is pivotal in Luke's narrative. The disciples again present Jesus to the Jewish nation, and once again, the nation as a whole rejects the call to repent and believe that Jesus is the promised Messiah. The door is now open to take the gospel out to the wider world, and there is no abiding link between the worship of God and the temple in Jerusalem. The next step is the mission to the gentiles.

THE MISSION IN JUDEA, SAMARIA, AND THE SURROUNDING REGIONS (8:4–12:25)

The persecution that now breaks out is severe (8:1–3). Many leave Jerusalem and become scattered throughout the surrounding regions, preaching the gospel as they go (8:4). Luke also shows that the expansion of Christianity is ethnic as well.

God-Fearers

Cornelius, the Roman centurion, was a "God-fearer"—a person who "feared God" (10:2). God-fearers (cf. also 13:16, 26, 43; 16:14; 17:4, 17; 18:6–7) were gentiles who sympathized with Judaism and adopted some but not all Jewish theology and practice. They did not become full proselytes, which required circumcision for men and baptism for men and women. Epictetus, a Stoic philosopher, notes the difference between a God-fearer and a proselyte: "Why do you act the part of a Jew, when you are a Greek? Do you not see in what sense men are severally called Jew, Syrian, or Egyptian? For example, whenever we see a man halting between two faiths, we are in the habit of saying, "He is not a Jew, he is only acting the part." But when he adopts the attitude of mind of the man who has been baptized and has made his choice, then he both is a Jew in fact and also is called one" (Cited in Arrianus, *Dissertationes* 2.9.19–20).

The city of Caesarea, where the Roman soldier and God-fearer Cornelius was converted, was a gentile city.
Bill Schlegel/BiblePlaces.com

Josephus on the Death of Herod Agrippa I

Luke's account of the death of Herod Agrippa I (12:20–23) is strikingly similar to that of Josephus (*Ant.* 19.8.2 [344–350]): "On the second day of these shows, [Herod] put on a garment made wholly of silver, and of a contexture truly wonderful, and came into the theatre early in the morning; at which time the silver of his garment being illuminated by the fresh reflection of the sun's rays upon it, shone out after a surprising manner, and was so resplendent as to spread amazement over those that looked intently upon him; and presently his flatterers cried out, one from one place, and another from another . . . that he was a god."

Josephus then recounts his dreadful death.

Philip goes to Samaria (8:5–25). The Samaritans were descendants of the non-Jewish settlers in the northern kingdom after the Assyrian conquest (2 Kings 17:24–41), though the Samaritans considered themselves true descendants of Israel.

Luke emphasizes that the inclusion of gentiles in the church is fully legitimate in two ways. First, their inclusion comes through divine intervention. Both Peter and Cornelius have similar visions (10:1–23), and these visions are retold in the following narratives (10:30–32; 11:5–10). And through the Holy Spirit, the Lord tells Peter what to do (10:19–20; 11:11–12). Divine confirmation comes while Peter is speaking—the Lord pours out his Spirit on the gentiles gathered at the house of Cornelius (10:44–47; 11:15–17). The conclusion is inevitable. Second, none other than Peter himself, the principal leader of the church, leads this admission of the gentiles, a move the church in Jerusalem subsequently confirms.

An aerial view of Joppa and its harbor from the north. Cornelius sent men to Joppa, and they would have entered the city from the north (Acts 10:7–8).
Bill Schlegel/BiblePlaces.com

The city of Antioch in Syria was the third largest urban center in the Roman empire. Although located twenty-four miles inland, the city enjoyed access to the Mediterranean via the Orontes River. This is an artist's re-creation of how it may have looked in the first century.
Balage Balogh/www.archaeology illustrated.com

Peter says, "Surely no one can stand in the way of their being baptized with water. They have received the Holy Spirit just as we have" (10:47). The church in Jerusalem agrees: "So then, even to Gentiles God has granted repentance that leads to life" (11:18).

The mission of the church continues with the spread of the gospel north to Antioch and west to the island of Cyprus (11:19–30). Antioch, the third largest urban center in the empire, known as the "Pearl of the East," becomes the hub of the church's mission out to the wider world (see ch. 13 and beyond). This comes as no surprise since the city is a political and military center.

Nothing appears able to detain the spread of the gospel, including rulers such as Herod Agrippa I, grandson of Herod the Great (Acts 12). Luke records his opposition to the gospel and his untimely end, an account paralleled in Josephus.

THE MISSION TO THE ENDS OF THE EARTH (13:1–28:31)

Paul's First Missionary Journey and the Jerusalem Council (13:1–15:35)

With Paul's first missionary journey, the church adopts a new policy regarding evangelism. The church begins a direct mission to the gentiles instead of simply evangelizing them as a result of the dispersion generated by the persecution in Jerusalem (11:19–20).

The church launches this mission from Antioch, not Jerusalem, under divine direction and with the affirmation of the whole church in that city (13:1–3). Paul and Barnabas set sail

An inscription from Pisidian Antioch bears the name of Sergius Paulus, the proconsul of Cyprus (Acts 13:4–12). Paul and his associates may have gone to Pisidian Antioch at the suggestion of Sergius Paulus, whose family owned an estate in the area.
www.HolyLandPhotos.org

The Gospel of Christ Versus Magic

Luke demonstrates the triumph of the Lord over magic and satanic powers (cf. 8:9–24; 13:9–12; 19:11–20). Court magicians who functioned as astrologers were common in the ancient world; even Felix in Judea had a Cyprian Jewish magician (*Ant.* 20.7.2 [141–144]). Through magic formulas people attempted to obligate and manipulate the powers and make them do something for them (see Simon's desire in 8:19–20). Ancient sources sometimes identified Jews who possessed special magical ability; some even portrayed Moses or Solomon as magicians (see *Testament of Solomon* 1:3–2:9).

The names of powerful deities, including the names of God, Jesus, and angels, appear in magic as part of the quest to gain power over demons: "The God of Abraham, the God of Isaac, the God of Jacob, the God of us, rescue Aurelia from every evil spirit and from every epileptic fit and seizure, I implore you Lord Iao, Sabaoth, Eloaion, Ouriel, Misichael, Raphael, Gabriel, Sariel, Rasochel, Ablanathanalba, Abrasax, xxxxxx nnnnnna oaaiiiiiiiiiiixouuuuu uuaaoooooooooono. . . ."[2]

The gospel spreads beyond Judea to Samaria, Ethiopia, and Syria.

for Cyprus, Barnabas's home (4:36; 15:39). The gospel reaches the highest corridors of power in the evangelization of the proconsul Sergius Paulus, a name known also from ancient inscriptions (13:4–12; see photo p. 297). But the Jewish false prophet Elymas, a court magician (13:6–7), opposes the gospel and is struck blind by God. In this way, Luke demonstrates the superiority of the gospel over ancient magic (see also 8:9–24; 19:18–20).

Paul and Barnabas make their way into Galatia, where Paul preaches in the synagogue in Pisidian Antioch (13:13–52). He preaches a sermon that parallels Peter's Pentecost address in Acts 2. For the first time we hear Paul's declaration of justification by faith (13:38–39), a theology he discusses at length in Romans and Galatians (see, e.g., Rom. 1:16–17; 3:21–24). After Jewish rejection of the gospel in the city, Paul announces his mission to the gentiles, citing Isaiah 49:6 (Acts 13:47–48; see 1:8).

After Paul and Barnabas evangelize Iconium, Lystra, and Derbe, they return through the cities to strengthen the churches and establish leadership. Then they return to Antioch in Syria (Acts 14). The evangelization of the gentiles, though ordained by God, generates a dispute, as some Jewish believers insist that the male gentile converts be circumcised like male proselytes to Judaism (Acts 15:1). Since Jesus was the Jewish Messiah, this insistence on circumcision is understandable (see Gen. 17:10–14, 23–27; Ex. 12:44, 48).

Becoming a Jewish Proselyte

The conversion of gentiles to Judaism entailed submission to the rite of circumcision for males and a commitment to observe all the laws of Scripture, not only the moral code. W. D. Davies explains the procedure: "The process by which a man was made a proselyte was threefold: it consisted of circumcision, immersion in water (i.e., baptism), and the presentation of an offering in the temple. Of these rites baptism assumed a growing importance."[3] There was, however, some debate whether circumcision was essential. Josephus writes regarding the gentile King Izates that Ananias, a Jewish counselor, argued Izates could "worship God without being circumcised, even though he did resolve to follow the Jewish law entirely" (*Ant.* 20.2.4 [38–48]). But the prevailing view was that it was necessary for male converts to be circumcised.

Herod completely rebuilt Samaria, naming it after Augustus, whose Greek name was Sebaste. Temples, a basilica, even a stadium have all been excavated.
Todd Bolen/BiblePlaces.com

From the gentile perspective, this "salvation without circumcision" was welcome news since the thought of such surgery was abhorrent for the Greek. This seeming mutilation of the body was a barrier to gentile conversion to Judaism—but now this barrier has been abolished. This is the first issue dealt with in the Jerusalem council, although the larger question is whether discipleship of Christ first entails conversion to Judaism, and the relationship of Christianity to Judaism. A person does not have to abandon their own ethnicity to become a disciple of Christ. The second issue taken up in the council is how those Jewish Christians who remain faithful to the Jewish law can sit at table and have fellowship with gentiles who are ritually unclean and whose food is ceremonially unclean because they have not adhered to the ceremonial laws. Fellowship around the Lord's table would be difficult in such situations, but the council's decision addresses the issue (15:20; cf. Gal. 2:11–14).

Hope for the Gentiles

According to the Old Testament and intertestamental Jewish literature, Israel held out hope that the gentile nations would convert from their idolatry and worship God (Isa. 2:1–4; Tobit 14:6–7: "Then the nations in the whole world will all be converted and worship God in truth. They will all abandon their idols ... and in righteousness they will praise the eternal God"; see also Ps. 22:27–28; Isa. 42:6; 49:6). The conversion of the gentiles in Acts is understood as the realization of this hope.

Separation from Gentiles

How could devout Jews associate closely with gentiles in light of their purity laws (Lev. 11)? One distinguishing mark of Israel was their refusal to eat gentile food, which the Jews considered ceremonially unclean. These dietary laws were part of the long history of resistance to Hellenistic influence, as the Maccabean conflict demonstrates (see 1 Macc. 1:62–63).

The vision of Peter in Acts 10 opens the way for this leading Christian to go to the house of Cornelius in Caesarea. The visit troubles him (10:9–17), as do the dietary compromises (10:28), for which he is criticized (11:3). The Lord, however, reminds Peter that all foods are clean.

Paul's first missionary journey

Paul's Second Missionary Journey (15:36–18:22)

Paul's second missionary journey (15:36–18:22) brings him back through the churches founded on the first missionary journey and on to the Aegean port city of Troas, where he receives the well-known "Macedonian call" (15:36–16:10). In a vision Paul sees a Macedonian man who implores him, "Come over to Macedonia and help us" (16:9).

Because of a conflict with Barnabas over taking John Mark along, Paul takes Silas (15:36–40) and adds Timothy to his company (16:1–4). Luke, the author of Acts, joins them at Troas since the narrative in Acts switches to the first-person plural (16:10–13). Luke apparently remains in Philippi since the narrative continues in the third person (see the other "we" sections in 20:5–15; 21:1–18; 27:1–28:16). Paul and his companions evangelize the Roman province of Macedonia, preaching in the Roman colony of Philippi (16:11–40), the free city of Thessalonica (17:1–9), and Berea, the seat of the confederation of Macedonian cities, called the *koinon* (17:10–13).

Paul and his companions must flee Berea; they sail by ship (likely embarking from Dion) and travel the coastal waters down to the nearby Roman colony of Corinth, which stands on the isthmus between mainland Greece and the Peloponnese (18:1–17).

The "Macedonian Man"

In his vision (16:9) Paul sees a Macedonian man who is likely dressed in traditional Macedonian garb. Antipater of Thessalonica refers to L. Calpurnius Piso, the Roman proconsul in Macedonia, who himself took up the region's traditional costume (note how the hat does the talking): "A broad-brimmed hat, from olden times the Macedonian's comfortable gear, shelter in snowstorm and helmet in war, thirsting to drink your sweat, valiant Piso, I come, an Emathian [an ancient name for Macedonia] to Italian brows."[4]

Paul's second missionary journey

Through his account of these journeys, Luke emphasizes the mounting and severe hostility that Paul and the early Christians endure. But the important story for the first readers of Acts is that Paul and his companions are innocent of all charges; those who profess faith in Christ pose no threat to the empire. Any opposition is due to financial loss (16:19), jealousy (17:5), false charges and social prejudice (16:20–21), incitement (17:13), philosophical arrogance (17:18, 21), and hostility from the unbelieving Jewish community (17:5, 13; 18:6, 12). Luke shows Theophilus how Paul is vindicated before the authorities in Philippi, Athens, and Corinth (16:35–40; 17:19–20, 32–33; 18:12–17). Though severe opposition arises, God is with Paul and his companions (16:25–34; 18:9–10).

Luke repeatedly emphasizes that the gospel is sent "first to the Jew," as Paul himself notes (Rom. 1:16). Paul first preaches the gospel to the Jewish community in a city; if they reject Jesus as the Messiah, Paul turns to the gentiles (Acts 16:13–15; 17:1–4, 10–12, 17; 18:5–6). The early church faced a dilemma: Why were so many gentiles becoming followers of Jesus the Messiah while God's own people were not? Had God forsaken his people (see Rom. 9–11)? Luke records the repeated offer of the gospel to the Jews and, in his final summary, observes, "Some were convinced by what [Paul] said, but others would not believe" (Acts 28:24). So Paul states, "Therefore I want you to know that God's salvation has been sent to the Gentiles, and they will listen!" (28:28).

The forum in Philippi, where Paul was accused and flogged before the authorities of this Roman colony (Acts 16:19–24). *Reproduced by permission from Carole Raddato*

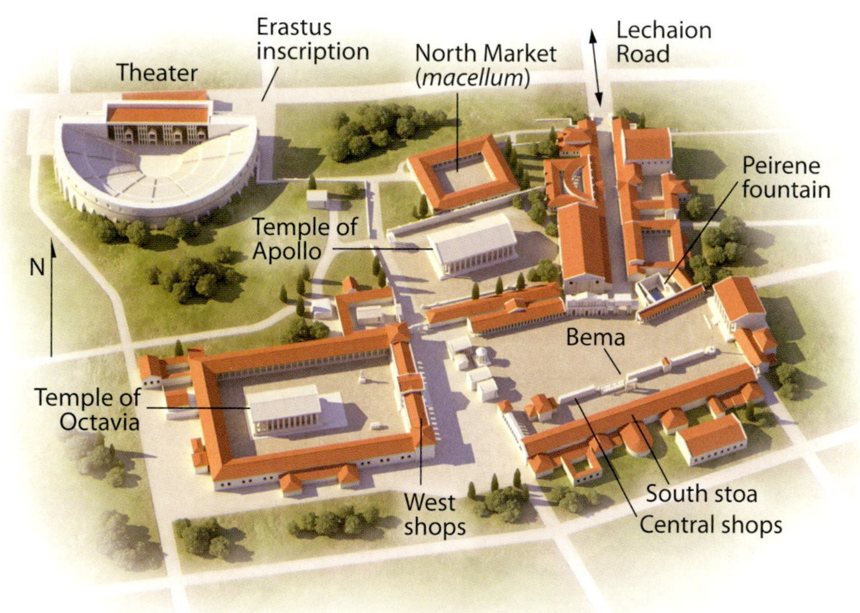

Paul was accused before Gallio, the Roman proconsul of Achaia, at the *bēma* (Latin: *rostrum*) in Corinth (Acts 18:12–17). *© 2011 by Zondervan*

A third emphasis in this section is the relationship between faith in Christ and other systems of belief. The gospel is the fulfillment of Jewish hopes contained in Scripture, and Luke repeatedly highlights how Paul returns to the sacred text to expound the message of Christ in the synagogue. In Thessalonica, for example, Paul goes to the synagogue "and on three Sabbath days he reasoned with them from the Scriptures, explaining and proving that the Messiah had to suffer and rise from the dead. 'This Jesus I am proclaiming to you is the Messiah,' he said" (17:2–3). Likewise, in Berea he goes to the synagogue and lays out the message; the Jews of that city receive the message and eagerly examine the Scriptures to see whether Paul is right (17:11). In Athens and Corinth he proclaims Jesus as the Messiah in the synagogues (17:17; 18:5).

The Thessalonians had constructed an imperial temple in the city to honor Julius Caesar and his adopted son, Augustus, pictured here.
Todd Bolen/BiblePlaces.com

The Roman agora in Athens was filled with altars, images of the gods, and temples.
Todd Bolen/BiblePlaces.com

A reconstruction of the stoa in Athens, where Paul likely stood before the city council, the Areopagus, whose duties included the admission of new deities to the Athenian pantheon.
© 2015 by Zondervan

On Admitting Foreign Deities in Athens

The charge against Paul in Athens that he was "advocating foreign gods" (17:18–20) echoed the charge leveled against Socrates centuries before: "Socrates is guilty of rejecting the gods acknowledged by the state and of bringing in strange deities: his is also guilty of corrupting the youth" (Xenophon, *Memorabilia* 1.1.1). Paul's presentation before the Areopagus may have been an initial hearing of the type needed before new and foreign deities could be added to the Athenian pantheon.

Jewish Exorcists and "Ephesian Letters"

Magic was such a dominant feature of life in Ephesus that many magical incantations were known as "Ephesian Letters" (Plutarch, *Table Talk* 7.5). The potency of magic spells was bound up with their secrecy. To reveal the secret was to render the spell powerless. The scene in Acts 19:18–19 is not only one of repentance but of destroying the power of magic. The book burning is a clear sign that these believers have renounced their former life. Burning books to control ideas was known in antiquity (1 Macc. 1:56), but this action in Acts is voluntary.

But Luke also shows how the gospel is superior to popular religion (16:16–18) and the philosophical constructs popular during the era (17:16–34). In Athens, Paul confronts Epicurean and Stoic philosophers (17:18). His address to the council of the city, the Areopagus, is an artful refutation of the tenets of these philosophies. At the same time, Paul affirms God's presence and providential care for all before the gospel arrived (17:24–28). While he severely criticized idolatry (17:16, 29–31), the apostle was able to affirm some truths found in philosophers such as Epimenides (though some question this identification) and Aratus, both quoted in 17:28.

While Paul does not specifically quote Scripture in his message in Athens, he repeatedly refers to biblical truth: God is the creator of all (17:24; cf. Ps. 146:6), all humans have been formed from one ancestor (17:26; cf. Gen. 1:27–28; 2:7), and God has determined the boundaries for people (17:26b; cf. Deut. 32:8). Luke's presentation of the gospel repeatedly demonstrates that, despite the church's persecution and subjection to legal proceedings, the gospel is the true way of salvation.

Paul's Third Missionary Journey (18:23–20:38)

Paul's third missionary journey begins after he returns to Jerusalem and then travels to Antioch in Syria (18:22–23). Paul first visits the churches founded on his previous travels, then arrives in Ephesus (18:24–19:21), the "mother city" of the province of Asia, located at the terminus of the Cilician Road.

Most of Luke's account of this journey records the gospel's penetration into Ephesus (19:1–41) and his address to the Ephesian elders (20:17–38). Between these events, Paul travels back through Macedonia and Achaia (20:1–6; see his plans in 19:21), spends a brief time in Troas (20:7–12), then bypasses Ephesus and stops at Miletus (20:13–16). Paul's ministry in Ephesus lasts for three years (20:31). Ephesus was a "free" city, not a Roman colony (like Philippi and Corinth). It was the capital of the Roman province of Asia and its most populous city (between 200,000 and 250,000).

Luke's account of the Ephesian ministry highlights the evangelism of those who had only heard the message of John the Baptist (19:1–7), evangelism in the synagogue and rejection of the gospel by the Jewish community (19:8–10), and the extraordinary miracles God works through Paul (19:11–20). The superiority of Christ over Jewish exorcists and the compelling claims of Christ over against magic make for a powerful story for those facing the frightful power of demons and seeking protection from magic spells.

Ephesus was also the center of the Artemis cult; the temple dedicated to her was one of the wonders of the ancient world. Pilgrims from everywhere visited this religious center as Artemis was becoming a universal deity. So effective is the evangelization of Ephesus through the powerful proclamation of the gospel, however, that the trade in silver shrines commemorating Artemis is severely diminished, and a near riot ensues because of the way the goddess appears to be brought into dishonor (19:23–41). Paul's proclamation of the gospel does include a direct attack against idolatry (19:26; cf. 14:8–18; 17:16–31).

Paul's final address to the Ephesian elders given in Miletus upon return from Macedonia and Achaia (20:17–38) summarizes the apostle's ministry and serves as his last testament. With this sermon Paul's Aegean ministry comes to a close.

Paul's third missionary journey

The Temple of Artemis in Ephesus

In his second century AD travelogue, Pausanias comments on the glory of the temple of Artemis: "The land of the Ionians has the finest possible climate, and sanctuaries such as are to be found nowhere else. First because of its size and wealth is that of the Ephesian goddess" (Description of Greece 7.5.4). Antipater of Thessalonica found it to be one of the grandest sights in the ancient world: "I have set eyes on the wall of lofty Babylon ... and the statue of Zeus by Alpheus, and the hanging gardens, and the colossus of the sun, and the huge labor of the high pyramids, and the vast tomb of Mausolus; but when I saw the house of Artemis that mounted to the clouds, those other marvels lost their brilliancy."[5]

Tunnel entrance into the Ephesus theater
Gary M. Burge

The theater in Ephesus (Acts 19:23–41, see v. 38)
Erik Cleves Kristensen/Flickr, CC BY 2.0

Paul's Return to Jerusalem and Subsequent Imprisonments (21:1–28:31)

As chapter 20 ends, an even more dangerous chapter opens, as the prophecies given to Paul predicted (21:4, 10–14). The last part of Acts is taken up with Paul's return to Jerusalem (21:1–22:21) and his imprisonment in Jerusalem, Caesarea, and Rome (22:22–28:31). Familiar themes resurface: the persecution of the apostle and his innocence before all charges (26:30–32), the presentation of the gospel to Jews in Jerusalem and Rome and their rejection of it (21:37–22:29; 28:17–27), and the offer of the gospel to the gentiles (21:17–19; 22:21; 28:28). Paul goes to the imperial city as an "ambassador in chains" (23:11; 26:32–27:1; 28:16; see Eph. 6:20).

Decorative sculpted column base from the Artemis temple in Ephesus.

Josephus on the Rebellion of the Egyptian

Josephus records that the Roman governor Felix sent out his cavalry and infantry against a rebel called "the Egyptian" and killed four hundred (cf. Acts 21:38). The Egyptian, who styled himself as a God-sent liberator, escaped. Josephus writes: "Now these impostors and deceivers persuaded the multitude to follow them into the wilderness, and pretended that they would exhibit manifest wonders and signs. . . . Moreover, there came out of Egypt about this time to Jerusalem one that said he was a prophet, and advised the multitude of the common people to go along with him to the Mount of Olives. He would show them from there how, at his command, the walls of Jerusalem would fall down" (*Ant.* 20.8.5 [167–170]).

In 9:15 God told Ananias that the apostle Paul was God's "chosen instrument to proclaim my name to the Gentiles and their kings and to the people of Israel." In chapters 24–26 Paul testifies before King Agrippa II and the Roman governors of Judea, Felix, and then Festus. In the end, he travels to Rome, where he presents his gospel before Emperor Nero. Luke ends the story telling only of Paul's two-year imprisonment in Rome, where he continues to preach the gospel (28:30–31). Nothing can quench his burning passion to proclaim Christ.

The Artemis temple in Ephesus. Note the image of the deity, eight frontal columns, and the sculpted column drums in the coin minted in Ephesus for Emperor Hadrian (AD 117-38).
Classical Numismatic Group, Inc./www.cngcoins.com

COMPOSING THE STORY

Luke uses various sources in writing this two-volume work, including eyewitness accounts and written documents (Luke 1:1–2). The sources for this second volume include testimony that came from the early Palestinian church as well as the apostle Paul. Luke's "we" sections (16:10–13; 20:5–15; 21:1–18; 27:1–28:16) suggest that the author himself was Paul's traveling companion and an eyewitness to part of the history described in the scroll. Ancient historiography considered that the presence of a historian at some of the events described added credibility to the account.

There has been considerable debate about the literary genre of Luke and Acts (see ch. 10). Is it a novel, a scientific treatise, a biography, or a history? The question of genre is important because a genre raises certain expectations and suggests a particular strategy for reading the document. Luke-Acts presents itself as both a biography and a history (see sidebar).

History or Biography?

The debate about whether Luke-Acts should be regarded as a history or a biography is based on ancient discussion of these two genres. Plutarch, for example, said, "For it is not Histories that I am writing, but Lives" (*Alexander* 1.2). For him, writing history meant chronicling the flow of events, while in biography the concern was with character portraits (see sidebar on "Luke and Plutarch" in ch. 10 for the quotation).

The first-century BC Latin biographer Cornelius Nepos similarly distinguished these genres in *Pelopidas* 1.1: "I am in doubt how to give an account of his merits; for I fear that if I undertake to tell his deeds, I shall seem to be writing a history rather than a biography."

Ancient Historians on Writing History

Polybius (*Histories* 2.56.10–12) distinguishes historical writing from poetry, saying:

> A historical author should not try to thrill his readers by such exaggerated pictures, nor should he, like a tragic poet, try to imagine the probable utterances of his characters or reckon up all the consequences probably incidental to the occurrences with which he deals, but simply record what really happened and what really was said, however commonplace. For the object of tragedy is not the same as that of history but quite the opposite. The tragic poet should thrill and charm his audience for the moment by the truth of the words he puts into his characters' mouths, but it is the task of the historian to instruct and convince for all time serious students by the truth of the facts and the speeches he narrates.

History was concerned with "a faithful narration of facts" (Tacitus, *Agricola* 10). Lucian, in his essay *How to Write History*, repeatedly advocates for such faithfulness. Luke presents his two-volume work as an historical narrative (Luke 1:1) based on the best historical testimony available to him, including that of eyewitnesses (1:2). He is diligent in his investigation and makes significant attempts to arrange his narrative in an orderly way (1:3).

Ancient historians remark on their concern for faithfulness in their writing. The father of ancient historiography, Thucydides, noted that while he found it difficult to record the exact words spoken by some figure, he attempted to remain faithful to the actual sense of what was said: "With reference to the speeches in this history, some were delivered before the war began, others while it was going on; it was hard to record the exact words spoken, both in cases where I was myself present, and where I used the reports of others. But I have used language in accordance with what I thought the speakers in each case would have used, adhering as closely as possible to the general sense of what was *actually spoken*" (*History of the Peloponnesian War* 1.22, italics added).

Insofar as we can verify his history, Luke's presentation is strikingly accurate. Colin Hemer noted in his comparative study of Acts and ancient historical sources:

"Here we discovered a wealth of material suggesting an author or sources familiar with the particular locations and at the times in question. Many of these connections have only recently come to light with the publication of new collections of papyri and inscriptions. . . . By and large, these perspectives all converged to support the general reliability of the narrative, through the details so intricately yet often unintentionally woven into the narrative."[6]

The prevailing skepticism regarding Luke's faithfulness to the events recorded in Acts is not warranted.

AUTHOR AND DATE

The arguments regarding the authorship and date of Luke (see ch. 10) hold true for Acts since the same person composed this two-volume work for the same recipient. As noted in the discussion on Luke, the testimony of the early church is unanimous that Luke was the author of these books.

Our assessment of the date of composition will depend, in part, on our understanding of the purposes of the book in light of the statement in 28:30: "For two whole years Paul stayed there in his own rented house." Was Luke-Acts composed at the end of that two-year period, giving us a date of composition of about AD 62, well before the martyrdom of Peter and Paul under Nero? Or, since Luke's concern is to tell the story of the movement of Christianity from the Jewish confines to the "ends of the earth," could the volumes have been written even after Paul's death (which is hinted at in 20:25, 38; 21:13; 25:11)? In other words, would the first reader have come to these verses and said, "Paul's death happened as predicted"?

Questions for Discussion

1. Compare the message of the apostles' sermons in Acts 2, 13, and 17 with our contemporary telling of the gospel. How is our message the same as theirs? How is it different?
2. Miracles, including speaking in tongues and prophecy, were a common element of the apostolic proclamation and the life of the early church. Are such phenomena for the church today? Frame your response with reference to Luke's presentation of the Spirit's coming and theology of the Spirit in Acts.
3. Discuss the key elements of Christian mission according to Acts, including the message, method, and recipients of the gospel.
4. How can we proclaim the gospel in a world of religious pluralism? What lessons can we learn from Acts as we reflect on this present-day issue?
5. Who are the excluded people in our society? Does the church reach them with the gospel of Christ? Do our current practices reflect Luke's emphasis on the gospel to the excluded?

BIBLIOGRAPHY

Introductory

Bruce, F. F. *The Book of Acts*. NICNT. Rev. ed. Grand Rapids: Eerdmans, 1988.
Fernando, A. *Acts*. NIVAC. Grand Rapids: Zondervan, 1998.
Larkin, W. J. *Acts*. IVPNTC. Downers Grove, IL: InterVarsity Press, 1995.
Marshall, I. H. *The Acts of the Apostles*. TNTC. Grand Rapids: Eerdmans, 1980.
Stott, J. R. W. *The Message of Acts*. BST. Downers Grove, IL: InterVarsity Press, 1990.

Advanced

Bock, D. L. *Acts*. BECNT. Grand Rapids: Baker, 2007.
Barrett, C. K. *The Acts of the Apostles*. ICC. 2 vols. Edinburgh: T. & T. Clark, 1994, 1998.
Fitzmyer, J. A. *The Acts of the Apostles*. AB. New York: Doubleday, 1998.
Keener, C. S. *Acts: An Exegetical Commentary*. 4 vols. Grand Rapids: Baker, 2012–15.
Peterson, D. G. *The Acts of the Apostles*. PNTC. Grand Rapids: Eerdmans, 2009.
Schnabel, E. J. *Acts*. ZECNT. Grand Rapids: Zondervan, 2012.

NOTES

1. M. Hengel, *Acts and the History of Early Christianity* (Philadelphia: Fortress, 1980), 67.
2. G. H. R. Horsley, *New Documents Illustrating Early Christianity* (North Ryde, N.S.W.: Macquarie University Press, 1986), 6:192–93.
3. W. D. Davies, *Paul and Rabbinic Judaism* (Philadelphia: Fortress, 1980), 121.
4. A. S. F. Gow and D. L. Page, *The Greek Anthology* (Cambridge: Cambridge University Press, 1965), 1:37.
5. Ibid., 1:69.
6. C. J. Hemer, *The Book of Acts in the Setting of Hellenistic History* (Tübingen: Mohr, 1989), 412.

Chapter 13

PAUL OF TARSUS: LIFE AND TEACHINGS

The Cilician road passed through Tarsus, Paul's home.
www.HolyLandPhotos.org

Besides Peter, the most prominent leader in the early church was Paul, a man from the Greek city of Tarsus. His conversion is a cornerstone in Acts, where Luke describes the event three times (Acts 9:1–9; 22:3–21; 26:1–23). Through his vision on the Damascus road, Paul becomes a witness of Christ's resurrection (1 Cor. 15:3–11) and an apostle with a special commission to proclaim the gospel among the gentiles (Gal. 2:7–8). From both Acts and Paul's letters, we can develop his life and teachings.

Peter describes Paul as a "dear brother" who wrote many letters but whose message was distorted by some within the churches (2 Pet. 3:15–16). Echoes of his teaching can be heard in other New Testament letters, such as 1 Peter and Hebrews, and the leaders of the postapostolic church recount many of the traditions surrounding his life, including his martyrdom in Rome under Nero.

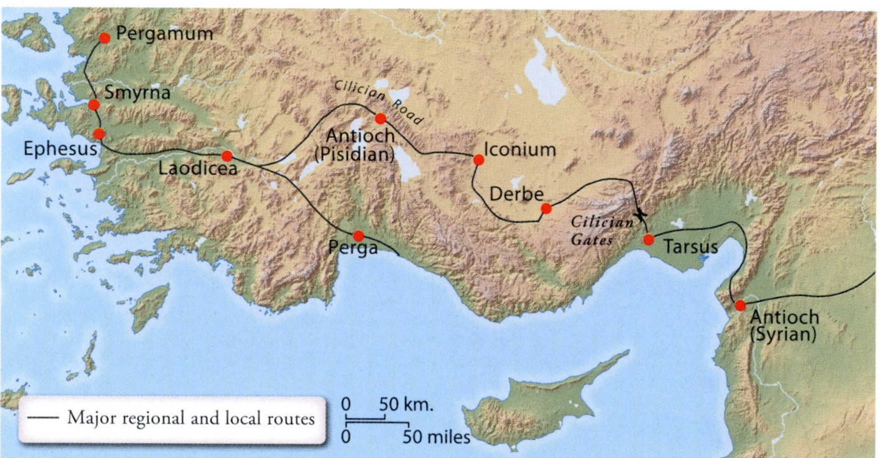

The city of Tarsus was located on the Cilician Road, the major east-west road in southern Asia Minor.

The principal route that connected the eastern section of the empire with Rome went through the narrow pass of the Taurus mountain range known as the Cilician Gates, located about thirty miles from Tarsus. A modern road traverses the same route.
Public Domain

Paul's influence on theology has been enormous. He offers the clearest and most detailed exposition of the Christian faith. Although he worked hard and suffered severely for the gospel, he refused to seek honor for himself since he knew that his efforts were divinely empowered: "To this end I strenuously contend with all the energy Christ so powerfully works in me" (Col. 1:29). To understand the shape and history of early Christianity, we must explore the life and teachings of Paul.

SAUL OF TARSUS

Paul was a Jew and also a Roman citizen (Acts 16:37–38; 22:25–29; 23:27), born in the free city of Tarsus, the capital of the province of Cilicia. As a Roman, Paul would have had three names: *praenomen*, *nomen*, and *cognomen*. A Roman's *cognomen* acted as a surname and, in the apostle's case, this was the Latin *Paullus* (Gk. *Paulos*), which identified him as a member of the *Paulli* family. He was known also as Saul (Gk. *Saulos*, a transliteration of the Semitic *Shaul* (7:58; 8:1; 13:9). The name was likely his *supernomen*, a kind of nickname used chiefly with Jews.

Tarsus was "no ordinary city" (21:39), lying thirty miles south of the pass through the Taurus Mountains called the Cilician Gates along the great Cilician Road, which crossed the southern section of Asia Minor.

The inhabitants of Tarsus were so well-known for learning that Strabo, the Roman geographer, remarked, "The people at Tarsus have devoted themselves so eagerly, not only to philosophy, but also to the whole round of education in general, that they have surpassed Athens, Alexandria, or any other place" (*Geography* 14.5.13). Strabo continues that the inhabitants who study there "complete their education abroad." Saul followed this pattern by studying in Jerusalem under the rabbi Gamaliel, grandson of the famous rabbi Hillel (22:3; cf. 5:34). Strabo makes special note of the schools of rhetoric in Tarsus, and Paul's letters evidence his familiarity with ancient rhetorical discourse. Although he received rigorous training in the Torah, Saul could also have read Homer, Euripides, and other Greek literature without the fear of incurring "uncleanness" or ritual defilement (Mishnah *Yadayim* 4:6; and Acts 17:28; 1 Cor. 15:33).

Paul presents a detailed summary of his Jewish heritage in Philippians 3:5: "circumcised on the eighth day, of the people of Israel, of the tribe of Benjamin, a Hebrew of Hebrews; in regard to the law, a Pharisee." That he was an Israelite by birth is clear from his reference to circumcision according to Jewish law. Since Saul was zealous for the traditions of his people (Gal. 1:14), he likely married, as most Jewish men did, in his early twenties. But in Acts, Paul is a single man (1 Cor. 7:8), and we can only speculate what may have happened to his spouse.

PERSECUTOR AND CONVERT

We first meet Saul at Stephen's martyrdom (Acts 7:54–58; 8:1; 22:20), after which he launches an aggressive wave of persecuting any Jews who acknowledge Jesus as the promised Messiah (Acts 8:3). Paul is enraged by this new sect and sets out to destroy it (Gal. 1:13, 23; 1 Cor. 15:9; Phil. 3:6). He deems belief in Jesus as Messiah to be blasphemy, and in his zeal (Gal. 1:13–14) he sets out to persecute Jesus's disciples, sowing terror and deep fear (Acts 9:26).

But God has other plans for Saul. We cannot understand Paul's theology apart from his encounter with the risen Christ on the road to Damascus, where, by his own account, Jesus Christ "took hold" of him (Phil. 3:12).

At his conversion Paul sees a light and hears Christ's voice, but he also sees the Lord (Acts 9:17; 22:14). Paul recalls this event in his letters: "Have I not seen Jesus our Lord?" (1 Cor. 9:1); "and last of all he appeared to me also" (1 Cor. 15:8; cf. Gal. 1:15–16). Paul is struck blind and led by the hand into Damascus (Acts 22:11). The powerful Saul is now helpless. His whole life has become radically reoriented.

The Zeal for God

The zeal Paul demonstrated in persecuting the church is not simply religious fanaticism. Paul saw his devotion for God and his law as part of a noble history in Israel, which lauded those who showed outstanding courage to defend and avenge what was holy.

For example, Scripture remembered Phinehas's zeal, which led him to violence against an Israelite man and a Midianite woman indulging in sexual sin and the worship of Baal (Num. 25:1–15). Later, 1 Maccabees 2:54 recalls the event, "Phinehas our ancestor, because he was deeply zealous, received the covenant of everlasting priesthood" (see also 2:58). According to Sirach 45:23, "Phinehas son of Eleazar ranks third in glory for being zealous in the fear of the Lord."

Paul understood his persecution of the church as part of this tradition. His righteous zeal was the source of his greatest sin (1 Tim. 1:13–14). Yet precisely at this point, Paul realizes he became the recipient of God's gift of grace: "I was shown mercy because I acted in ignorance and unbelief. The grace of our Lord was poured out on me abundantly, along with the faith and love that are in Christ Jesus."

Saul or Paul?

Paul lived in a bilingual world. And many in this world carried two names. Among his Jewish friends and family, where Aramaic and Hebrew were common, his name was Saul. But as he moved into Greek-speaking areas, he adopted the Roman name Paul (Gk. *Paulos*). Acts 13:9 tells us that Paul used both names. We see the same occurring in Peter's life. His Hebrew name was Simon (*Shimon*), but Jesus renamed him Cephas (*Kephas*, John 1:42). Because Cephas means rock or stone in Aramaic, his Greek name became Peter (Gk. *Petros*), which also means rock.

This Roman road, which runs between Syria and Petra, is similar to the road to Damascus on which Paul encountered the risen Christ. "Damascus Road" has become a metaphor for conversion because of the story of Paul's vision along this highway.
Alistair Duncan, © Dorling Kindersley/DK Images

In a world that held faithfulness to tradition as a high value, Saul's conversion must have appeared confusing. In fact, that type of change was hardly commendable according to the ancient worldview. Cicero, for example, quotes the Stoic opinion that "the wise man never 'supposes' anything, never regrets anything, is never wrong, never changes his mind" (*Pro Murena* 61). Paul explains his unusual change by appealing to divine intervention, which he views as the outworking of God's plan for him before he was born (Gal. 1:15–16). He becomes convinced that the crucified Jesus of Nazareth is indeed alive. In fact, contrary to all Jewish teaching, Paul comes to understand that it was necessary for the Messiah to suffer death and rise from the dead and that Jesus is the Messiah (Acts 17:3). In reality, his conversion was not an abandonment of his ancestral heritage but the fulfillment of it.

HERALD OF THE GOSPEL

Paul's conversion includes Jesus's instruction that he will be a witness to what he had seen and heard. Soon he feels compelled to proclaim this experience both to his own people and to gentiles (Acts 9:15; 22:14–15; 26:15–18). In fact, Paul begins immediately to proclaim in Damascus that Jesus indeed was the long-anticipated Messiah, the promised king (9:19b–22). Sometime during this period, Paul goes away to "Arabia" (see sidebar) and then returns to Damascus, where he stays for three years (Gal. 1:15–18a). Reaction to his preaching becomes so severe that he has to escape the city by night (Acts 9:23–25; 2 Cor. 11:33), and he goes back to Jerusalem (Gal. 1:18b).

During Paul's brief visit to Jerusalem with Peter he also meets with James (Gal. 1:18–19) and Barnabas presents him to the church in the city (Acts 9:26–29). The accounts in Galatians and Acts are difficult to reconcile here since in Galatians he notes that he saw no apostle save Peter and then James, the Lord's brother. In Acts, however, Barnabas presents him to the apostles. Most likely the apostles whom Luke mentions in Acts are only Peter and James (who was considered an apostle). While Paul seeks to demonstrate to the Galatians his independence of Jerusalem, Luke emphasizes Paul's acceptance by the Jerusalem church.

Paul in Arabia

Paul mentions his sojourn in Arabia in Galatians 1:17: "I went into Arabia. Later I returned to Damascus." Acts does not mention this journey. Arabia was the Nabatean kingdom south of Damascus. During this period it was a vassal state of Rome but in AD 106 became a Roman province.

Petra was the ancient capital of the Nabateans. Although their language was a form of Arabic, some Nabatean inscriptions were written in Aramaic, and presumably Paul was able to communicate successfully among these people using Aramaic or Greek. Paul may have gone to Nabatea for a season of contemplation or, more likely, to proclaim the gospel to Arab gentiles, per the Lord's command (Acts 9:15; Gal. 1:15–17).

Paul must have angered the Nabateans with his activity in their area, since after returning to Damascus, the ethnarch of the Nabatean king, Aretas IV, tried to seize Paul (2 Cor. 11:32; Damascus was under Nabatean jurisdiction). Arabs had heard the gospel on the day of Pentecost (Acts 2:11). Now they were Paul's first audience.

Petra was the capital of the Arabian kingdom of the Nabateans.
David Wünschel/123RF.com

Paul speaks openly in Jerusalem about Jesus as the Messiah and becomes a lightning rod for conflict (Acts 9:29). He quickly leaves and travels to northern Syria (Antioch?) and finally arrives in Cilicia, where his home of Tarsus was located (Gal. 1:21). Following his departure from Judea, Luke says with a touch of irony, "Then the church . . . enjoyed a time of peace" (Acts 9:31).

The following years Paul's ministry is taken up with his mission to the gentiles (Gal. 2:6–9). We are acquainted with his journeys through his letters addressed to his churches, but much of our knowledge about this missionary enterprise comes from Acts, which recounts three missionary journeys (see ch. 12) when Paul traveled extensively on the roads and sea lanes of the empire.

Paul's journey to Rome

Paul the Apostle

Paul repeatedly identifies himself as an "apostle of Christ Jesus," who attributes his apostleship to an act of God (2 Cor. 1:1; Eph. 1:1; Col. 1:1). God called him directly to this service (1 Cor. 1:1; cf. Gal. 1:1) to be the apostle to the gentiles (Rom. 1:5; 11:13 Gal. 2:8).

What was an apostle? In secular Greek *apostolos* ("apostle") describes a messenger sent on a mission. But the New Testament concept of "apostle" appears indebted to the Hebrew concept of the *Shaliach*. Leaders utilized authorized messengers to sign contracts and make business arrangements that were binding on the sender. The Mishnah teaches, "A man's *Shaliach* is like [the man] himself" (*Berak*. 5:5). Since he was an appointed apostle, Paul's words come with the authority of Christ himself.

Romans could obtain passage to the ports of the Mediterranean on cargo vessels (Acts 28:11). Safe sea lanes and the roads gave Romans a high degree of mobility.
Marco Prins/www.livius.org

After his third missionary journey, Paul is arrested in Jerusalem and sent to Caesarea, where he is imprisoned until his journey to Rome as a captive (Acts 21:27–28:31). Acts ends rather abruptly without saying what became of Paul there. We know Paul wrote a number of letters during his imprisonment (his so-called "Prison Epistles": Ephesians, Philippians, Colossians, and Philemon). Despite his captivity, Paul continues to proclaim the gospel of Jesus Christ to all who come into contact with him. In fact, he describes himself as an "ambassador in chains" (Eph. 6:20; see Phil. 1:7, 13). He considers himself a "prisoner of Christ Jesus" (Eph. 3:1; 4:1; Philem. 1, 9, 23). He even proclaims the gospel to Caesar's elite Praetorian Guard (Phil. 1:13).

Although Nero provoked a wholesale persecution against the Christians, accusing them of setting the city of Rome on fire (which Nero himself is rumored to have set), Paul does not appear to have been martyred as was Peter during this assault. Shortly before the great fire, he was released from imprisonment and presumably set out to visit his churches. Eusebius, the early church historian, said, "Tradition has it that after defending himself the Apostle was again sent on the ministry of preaching, and coming a second time to the same city suffered martyrdom under Nero" (*Eccl. Hist.* 2.22.2).

On the Road and on the Sea

The system of roads that stretched throughout the empire and linked Italy and the provinces with Rome illustrated Roman dominance over the landscape. Along these all-weather highways traveled Roman officials and soldiers, colonists, those engaged in trade, and heralds of various religions, philosophers, and pilgrims. Roman mile markers dotted the highways, and itineraries offered travelers information about where towns were located and the distances between them. Both Pompey and Augustus pacified the Mediterranean, clearing out most of the pirates. Thus, travel became relatively quick and easy. While exiled in Thessalonica, Cicero once complained about how crowded the Via Egnatia and other roads had become.

Yet there were dangers. Robbers could fall on an ill-armed company, and the sea was known for its treachery (see Acts 27). Antipater of Thessalonica once said, "Approve not the grievous labor of the treacherous ocean or the heavy toil of perilous seafaring. As a mother is more delightful than a step-mother, by so much is the earth more desirable than the gray sea."[1]

Paul agreed: "Three times I was shipwrecked, I spent a night and a day in the open sea. . . . I have been in danger from rivers, in danger from bandits, in danger from my fellow Jews, in danger from Gentiles; in danger in the city, in danger in the country, in danger at sea" (2 Cor. 11:25–26). Yet he kept on the move, bringing the gospel to city after city.

But the apostolic calling to proclaim the gospel to the gentiles always lies in tension with Paul's concern for the newly founded congregations: "Besides everything else, I face daily the pressure of my concern for all the churches" (2 Cor. 11:28). Out of this tension he wrote his letters to the previously established churches.

From his last letters and the testimony of the early church, we can reconstruct some of Paul's activities between his two Roman imprisonments. The Pastoral Epistles (1–2 Timothy, Titus) contain casual references to places Paul visited, journeys not recorded in Acts. Apparently, he evangelized Crete (Titus 1:5) and traveled to Nicopolis, Troas, and Miletus (Titus 3:12; 2 Tim. 4:13, 20).

Some question remains whether Paul ever reached Spain (the Roman province *Hispania*) during this period (cf. Rom. 15:24, 28). Corduba (the modern Córdoba)

Paul sailed from the ancient harbor in Caesarea, bound as a prisoner on his way to Rome.
Bill Schlegel/BiblePlaces.com

Nero's Persecution of Christians

Tacitus recounts the terror of the blaze that consumed ten of Rome's fourteen districts. "Nero was seeking the glory of founding a new capital and endowing it with his own name" (*Annals* 15.40). But Nero needed a scapegoat in order to deflect the suspicion that the blaze was set by imperial order: Therefore, "Nero substituted as culprits, and punished with the utmost refinements of cruelty, a class of men, loathed for their vices, whom the crowd styled Christians" (15.44). Tacitus describes Nero's cruelty: "First, then, the confessed members of the sect were arrested; next, on their disclosures, vast numbers were convicted, not so much on the count of arson as for hatred of the human race.... They were covered with wild beasts' skins and torn to death by dogs; or they were fastened on crosses, and, when daylight failed were burned to serve as lamps by night.... Hence there arose a sentiment of pity, due to the impression that they were being sacrificed not for the welfare of the state but to the ferocity of a single man" (15.44).

Christians

The New Testament uses various terms to describe the followers of Jesus: "believers" (1 Thess. 1:7), "saints" or "holy people" (Phil. 1:1), "Nazarene sect" (Acts 24:5), "disciples" (Acts 11:26), and followers of "the Way" (Acts 9:2; 19:9, 23; 22:4, 14, 22). "Christian," however, was not a self-designation of the believers. The name identified them as partisans of Christ, similar to the "Herodians" (Mark 3:6; 12:13), and early on the name had a pejorative sense.

The Roman historian Tacitus, commenting on the persecution under Nero's reign, derided the believers as people "whom the crowd styled Christians" (*Annals* 15.44). We are not surprised, therefore, that Peter urges the believers, "If you suffer as a Christian, do not be ashamed, but praise God that you bear that name" (1 Pet. 4:16). From earliest times, that term for believers was not honored; instead, it was a source of shame. At times Roman authors misconstrued the name, calling the believers "*Chrestianoi*," as if the founder of the group were named "Chrestus." Suetonius appears to commit such a gaff when he comments that Claudius expelled the Jews from Rome "on account of disturbances at the instigation of Chrestus" (*Life of Claudius* 25; cf. Acts 18:5).

After Paul's first imprisonment in Rome, he traveled to various places such as Crete, Nicopolis, Troas, Miletus, and possibly Spain.

was the home of the philosopher Seneca and his brother Gallio, who became the proconsul of Achaia (Acts 18:12), while the orator Quintilian and later three emperors came from the province. The New Testament is silent on whether Paul was able to reach this goal. Ancient literature identified Gades in Spain (modern Cádiz) as "the ends of the earth," and Paul may have been driven to evangelize it because of the Lord's commission in Acts 1:8 (see sidebar on "The Ends of the Earth" in ch. 12). Large numbers of non-Greeks lived in Hispania. These were the "barbarians," those "others" considered to be "uncivilized," but Paul wanted to honor them by bringing them the gospel (Rom. 1:14).

Clement of Rome, who wrote at the end of the first century, comments that Paul did reach "the limits of the West" (*1 Clement* 5:7—perhaps meaning Spain).

The forum in ancient Rome. Paul had planned to pass through Rome on his way to Spain.
Bjsamelsonjones/Wikimedia Commons, Public Domain

The Muratorian fragment, a list of books considered canonical by the Roman church, written near the close of the second century, comments that Acts does not include "Paul's journey when he set out from Rome for Spain."

Paul later returned to Rome. He may have been at Corinth when the persecution in Rome broke out (2 Tim. 4:20), and news of the violence likely spread to the church in that Roman colony. Did Paul return to aid the suffering believers in the imperial city? We can only speculate, but we know that he was captured again. During this second Roman imprisonment, Paul wrote 2 Timothy, where he clearly anticipates his imminent demise (4:6). This second Roman imprisonment ended in martyrdom according to Eusebius: "It is related that in his [Nero's] time Paul was beheaded in Rome itself and that Peter likewise was crucified" (*Eccl. Hist.* 2.25.5). Paul's last recorded words demonstrate the confidence in his work and the level of his hope even in that dark hour: "For I am already being poured out like a drink offering, and the time for my departure is near. I have fought the good fight, I have finished the race, I have kept the faith. Now there is in store for me the crown of righteousness, which the Lord, the righteous Judge, will award to me on that day—and not only to me, but also to all who have longed for his appearing" (2 Tim. 4:6–8).

Paul's apostolic legacy has survived his death, and he still speaks to the church today through his letters.

A BRIEF CHRONOLOGY OF PAUL'S LIFE

Assembling a chronology of Paul's life is no easy task since we do not have a full account of his early years, nor do the New Testament documents include much information about his travels between the first and second imprisonment in Rome. Events mentioned in his letters are sometimes not even recounted in Acts (e.g., see his list of sufferings in 2 Cor. 11:23–27). Nevertheless, we can reconstruct many of the details of his life.

A Chronology of Paul's Life

(Note that all dates are AD and approximate)

	Paul's Life		Paul's Letters
5–10	Paul's Birth		
[30 (or 33)	Crucifixion of Jesus]		
32/33 (or 34)	Paul's Conversion		
35 (or 36)	First Visit to Jerusalem		
46 (or 47)	Second Visit to Jerusalem		
47–48	First Missionary Journey	48	Galatians (South Galatia theory date)
49	Jerusalem Council		
49–52	Second Missionary Journey	50–51	1 and 2 Thessalonians
		51	Galatians (North Galatia theory date)
52–57	Third Missionary Journey	54	1 Corinthians
		56	2 Corinthians and Romans
57–59	Caesarean Imprisonment		
59	Trial before Festus and Agrippa II		
59–60	Voyage to Rome		
60–62	First Roman Imprisonment		
		60–62	Ephesians, Philippians, Colossians, Philemon
62–64	Release and Travels		
		65–66	1 Timothy and Titus
67–68	Reimprisonment	67–68	2 Timothy
68	Martyrdom in Rome		

PAUL'S TEACHINGS

Some Critical Issues

We know the contours of Paul's teaching through his letters, though not all Paul's writings survived. We do not have a letter sent to the Laodicean church (Col. 4:16) or the first letter he wrote to the Corinthians, penned before our 1 Corinthians (1 Cor. 5:9). Some scholars have questioned whether all the Pauline letters in the New Testament were truly written by him. While no one doubts the authenticity of Romans or 1 Corinthians, books such as the Pastoral Epistles have come under severe attack (see ch. 21). In outlining Paul's theology, should we include the letters whose authenticity is questioned? Nevertheless, scholars of all persuasions have summarized Paul's theology and confidently attested to his accessibility to us. No other New Testament author, apart from Luke, gives us so much material to work with.

Paul, who spoke publicly as this Greek orator, denounced polytheism and idolatry as he proclaimed the one true God (1 Thess. 1:9). Some viewed Paul as just another itinerant philosopher, but Paul refused to let them cast him in this role (1 Cor. 2:1–5). *corneliagraco/Flickr, CC BY 2.0*

Yet even with his rich collection of writings, questions remain regarding whether Paul's theology is entirely consistent. Since he wrote in response to situations as they arose, some insist we should not expect any internal coherence in his teaching. Others argue that Paul's theology should be divided into stages, since there is development in his thought. Among those who search for some center of Paul's theology, there is no consensus on which doctrine should be viewed as the focal point. Instead of a "center," should we describe his thought in a manner that is less static and more dynamic? Does the very notion of a "center" minimize important aspects of his thought?

Discussion of Paul's theology has taken a dramatic turn in recent years as the traditional reading of Paul, inherited from the Reformers, has come under attack by the so-called "new perspective" on Paul. The serious student of Paul's thought is faced with a dizzying array of questions as she or he seeks to tease out the fundamental structures of the apostle's teaching.

But although Paul's letters take up a broad spectrum of problems, he addresses these issues within a coherent theological framework that recalls God's act of creation, his salvation through the cross and resurrection of Christ, and the final consummation when Christ returns. Thus, when dealing with the error of idolatry or the issue of asceticism, Paul orients his response around God's creative act (Rom. 1:22–25; 1 Tim. 4:3–4). When facing human sin, the agony of death, or the division between Jews and gentiles, he responds with reference to the cross and resurrection of Christ (1 Cor. 15:3–4; Eph. 2:11–16; 1 Thess. 4:13–16). When commenting on the rejection of Christ in his day or the disorder in the universe, his gaze is on Christ's return (Eph. 1:9–10; Phil. 2:9–11).

Foundational Ideas for Paul

Paul's starting point is a belief in the unity of God. The *Shema*, the Jewish confession that Israelites repeated every morning and evening, is Paul's foundation: "Hear [Heb. *Shema*], O Israel: The Lord our God, the Lord is one" (Deut. 6:4–9). Paul echoes the *Shema* in his letters, such as in his statement that God wants all people to be saved and to come to know the truth, "for there is one God" (1 Tim. 2:5). The claim that God is one means for Paul that there is one Savior for all humanity (2:6). In a world awash in religious pluralism, Paul boldly declares, "For even if there are so-called gods, whether in heaven or on earth (as indeed there are many 'gods' and many 'lords'), yet for us there is but one God, the Father, from whom all things came and for whom we live" (1 Cor. 8:5–6).

Paul understands the worship of idols, the creation of human hands, as the central source of sin since humans reject the revelation of the one God and worship and serve that which is created rather than the Creator (Rom. 1:18–25). His proclamation of the gospel among the gentiles begins with a call to abandon idols in favor of the one God of all (Acts 14:11–18; 17:22–31; see 1 Thess. 1:9). Paul recognizes God's agency in the world and acknowledges that God indeed reveals himself broadly to humanity (Rom. 1:20; Acts 17:26–28). While respectful and no blasphemer of other religions (Acts 19:37), he resoundingly condemns idolatry (Rom. 1:21–23; Acts 17:24–25, 29–31).

Through the Damascus road event, God showed Paul that there is also only "one mediator between God and mankind, the man Christ Jesus" (1 Tim. 2:5). Paul undoubtedly knew the stories about Jesus even before his encounter with the risen Christ. When speaking to Agrippa II, he declared, "The king is familiar with these things, and I can speak freely to him. I am convinced that none of this has escaped his notice" (Acts 26:26). None of this escaped Paul's notice either. But when Paul encountered the risen Jesus and heard his voice (Acts 9:17; 22:14–15; 1 Cor. 15:8), he understood Jesus to be the royal "Son of God." He was descended from David, according to the promise of 2 Samuel 7:11–16, but he was also the one "who through the Spirit of holiness was appointed the Son of God in power by his resurrection from the dead: Jesus Christ our Lord" (Rom. 1:4).

Many "Lords"

The title *kyrios* ("lord") was a mark of respect (similar to "sir") or a term meaning slave master (Eph. 6:9; Col. 4:1). For the Greek-speaking Jews, *kyrios* was also the divine title for YHWH used in the Greek Old Testament (the Septuagint).

But gentiles also used *kyrios* to refer to deities. For example, if you were inviting someone to dine with you at the temple of the Egyptian deity Serapis, you might write, "Nikephoros asks you to dine at a banquet of the Lord [*kyrios*] Sarapis in the Birth-House on the 23rd, from the 9th hour."[2] The gods Isis, Apollo, Artemis, Athena, Hermes, Asclepius, and Dionysus were all called *kyrios*. And in the imperial cult that honored the emperor as a deity, *kyrios* is often found. Even Nero is called "the lord of all the world."

Jesus as Lord and Savior

Among the gentiles Paul's announcement that Jesus is the Christ (or Messiah) would not have been readily understood. Paul's central proclamation among them was that "Jesus Christ is Lord" (Phil. 2:11). "Lord" was commonly recognized as a title of both deities and rulers, as part of the imperial cult. This Christian proclamation directly challenged these other claims to lordship. Paul writes to the Corinthians that while there were many called "lords," in fact "there is but one Lord, Jesus Christ, through whom all things came and through whom we live" (1 Cor. 8:6).

In a similar way, Paul proclaimed that Jesus is the "Savior" (Phil. 3:20; 2 Tim. 1:10; Titus 1:4), and this title likewise linked Jesus with God (Isa. 43:11). This title was also ascribed to a variety of deities and appears in the imperial cult. Augustus was styled as "the god and savior, emperor" and various deities, such as the god of healing Asclepius, were called "savior."

People longed for salvation from disaster, disease, and death. Temples dedicated to "Zeus the savior" could be found at harbors (Strabo, *Geography* 9.1.15). The Egyptian goddess Isis was thought to offer healing and immortality. The common concern for salvation found its hope and fulfillment in Jesus Christ (Acts 16:29–32). Through Jesus Christ, those who believe are saved (1 Cor. 1:21; 15:2; Eph. 2:8). While salvation is a process that begins in the present (1 Cor. 1:18) and includes the Spirit's work of washing and renewing a person (Titus 3:5), Paul frequently speaks of Christ's salvation as a future event—we will be saved from God's wrath through him (Rom. 5:9).

The temple at Epidaurus in Greece was the center of the healing cult of Asclepius, although temples to the god were erected in other cities as well, such as Corinth. The votive offerings pictured above come from the Asclepion at Corinth. *www.HolyLandPhotos.org*

Given Paul's liberal use of the titles "Lord" and "Savior" for Jesus Christ, we are not surprised to hear him call Jesus "God." In Titus 2:13 Paul speaks of the "blessed hope" that is "the appearing of the glory of our great God and Savior, Jesus Christ." Similarly, Romans 9:5 speaks of "the Messiah, who is God over all, forever praised!" The exalted status of Christ is so high that Paul describes him as the one who brought the world into existence and the one for whom creation exists (Col. 1:15–16; "firstborn" implies his preeminence as in Ps. 89:27). He exercises authority over all as Lord (1 Cor. 15:25–26; cf. Ps. 110:1). Paul's high Christology contrasts sharply with modern attempts to reduce Jesus to nothing more than a moral teacher, a traveling sage, or a cultural ideal.

But Paul also rigorously affirms the humanity of Christ. He "made himself nothing by taking the very nature of a servant, being made in human likeness. And being found in appearance as a man, he humbled himself by becoming obedient to death" (Phil. 2:7–8). God's saving purposes are accomplished through him since God, "sending his own Son in the likeness of sinful flesh, and to deal with sin, he condemned sin in the flesh" (Rom. 8:3 NRSV).

The Death and Resurrection of Christ

For Paul, the crucifixion of Jesus was a sacrifice for the sins of humanity (Rom. 4:25; 1 Cor. 15:3; Gal. 1:4). This death for sin fulfilled the promise of the ancient Scriptures: "Christ died for our sins according to the Scriptures" (1 Cor. 15:3; see Isa. 53:12). During Paul's time, Jewish theology did not understand Isaiah 53 as a messianic prophecy; to preach "Christ crucified" (1 Cor. 1:23) was a patent contradiction. How could the promised Messiah be subject to such shameful treatment?

Asclepius, the god of healing, was one of the many deities called "savior." *Marie-Lan Nguyen/Wikimedia Commons, CC BY 2.5*

A View of the Cross

Platus pejoratively called someone destined for crucifixion a "wretched gallows-bird" (*Pot of Gold* 522). This form of execution was called the *summum supplicium* ("the ultimate torture") and was reserved for the lowest social status, especially slaves and noncitizens. The execution began with beating; then the condemned was stripped, nailed or tied to the crossbeam, and hoisted high enough so his feet did not touch the ground. Crucifixion normally took place in full view of the public, which added shame (see also sidebar on "Foolishness of the Gentiles" in ch. 16).

Paul boldly proclaimed the message of "Christ crucified" (1 Cor. 1:23). This late second- to early third-century AD jasper gemstone is one of our earliest portrayals of Jesus's crucifixion.
© The Trustees of the British Museum

Paul's challenge in the synagogue was to show from Scripture that "the Messiah had to suffer" (Acts 17:3).

The message of the cross was likewise difficult for the gentiles to accept, as Paul acknowledges: "We preach Christ crucified: a stumbling block to Jews and foolishness to Gentiles" (1 Cor. 1:23). To preach that a crucified Jew was Savior and Lord would have been difficult to accept. And crucifixion was the ultimate torture (see sidebar on "A View of the Cross"). But Paul states: "To those whom God has called, both Jews and Greeks, Christ [is] the power of God and the wisdom of God" (1 Cor. 1:24). Crucifixion was a dishonorable death, and early Christians suffered dishonor due to their allegiance to Christ. Yet Paul knew that the cross of Christ was the way of salvation and therefore affirmed, "I am not ashamed of the gospel, because it is the power of God that brings salvation to everyone who believes: first to the Jew, then to the Gentile" (Rom. 1:16).

Paul saw Christ's death through the sacrificial system of the temple in Jerusalem. He declares to the Corinthians that "Christ, our Passover lamb, has been sacrificed" (1 Cor. 5:7); his death is "a sacrifice of atonement" that turned away God's wrath (Rom. 3:25). The repeated references to Christ's blood return us to the sacrificial nature of Christ's death since that blood was poured out in death for sin (1 Cor. 11:25; Eph. 1:7; Col. 1:20). The significance of Christ's death does not end, however, at the cross; its twin theme is the resurrection, when God vindicated Jesus's life. On his journey to Damascus, Paul saw the risen Christ and later proclaimed that Jesus was truly alive (Acts 25:19). His understanding of the resurrection was also rooted in the prophetic testimony that Christ would be raised, as he says: "He was raised on the third day according to the Scriptures" (1 Cor. 15:4; cf. Acts 2:24–32).

Paul elaborates on the resurrection in 1 Corinthians 15 in response to some within the church who denied that deceased believers would be raised (v. 12). While Paul affirms an intermediate conscious state between the death and resurrection of the believer (2 Cor. 5:6–8; Phil. 1:20–23), his hope is fixed on the resurrection of the dead, since indeed Christ was raised from the dead (1 Thess. 4:13–18). So united is the resurrection of the believers with the resurrection of Christ that Paul viewed the Corinthian denial of the believers' resurrection as entailing the denial of Christ's resurrection (1 Cor. 15:12–19).

As a result of Christ's work on the cross and his resurrection, God has inaugurated the *new covenant*, as represented in the Lord's Supper (1 Cor. 11:23–26). The blessings of the new covenant were that God would write his law on his people's heart, they would all have the knowledge of God, and God would forgive their sins

(Jer. 31:31–34). Paul emphasizes the benefits of forgiveness (Eph. 1:7; Col. 1:14), knowing God through Christ (Gal. 4:8–9; Eph. 1:17; Phil. 3:8, 10), and fulfilling the law by the power of the Spirit (Rom. 8:4; cf. 2:15). The death and resurrection of Christ have also *justified* believers (4:25; 5:1, 9), meaning they are declared righteous in Christ through faith (3:21–26). Through Christ's death God is both the righteous Judge who deals with sin and the One who acquits those who have faith in Christ. Furthermore, those who were enemies of God because of their sin are now *reconciled* to him and are at peace with him (5:1, 10–11; Eph. 2:13). Through Christ's redemptive act we are saved from the wrath of God (Rom. 5:9–10).

THE NEW PERSPECTIVE ON PAUL

In the 1970s a debate erupted among New Testament scholars trying to understand Paul's theology in light of his Jewish context.[3] This debate has resulted in a "new perspective" on Paul that today challenges many conventional interpretations of the apostle.

Traditionally, many have thought that Paul saw Judaism as a religion that required a person to earn their salvation through meritorious works of religious law. Because of our inability to obey God's law, our relationship with him is broken—and only Christ's work on the cross has solved our need for righteousness. Our justification, then, is a gift that compensates for our sin—that offers us grace. In this view, Paul inherited a severe legalism from Judaism that taught that by obeying the law, God's wrath could be appeased. God's grace in Christ is truly good news because it offers us a way of escape. Paul was converted *to Christ*, but more importantly, converted *from Jewish legalism*.

But today many question whether Judaism embraced such a view of the law. In this new view, the legalism Christians have projected onto first-century Judaism originated with Luther's struggle with the legalism of medieval Catholicism. Keeping the Jewish law, according to the new perspective, was a response to God's grace and commitment, not a means of achieving it. A Jew does not obey the law in order to earn salvation; Jews obey the law because of their status as members of God's covenant community. But then why did Paul emphasize grace as if it were contrasted to the law? The answer: the gentile mission of the church. Gentiles who did not have the Jewish law would view it as an obstacle to conversion. Thus, Paul underscored the power of grace without law among non-Jews.

If then Paul had no complaint with his Jewish heritage (cf. Phil. 3:4–6), in what sense can we say he was "converted"? According to the new perspective, Paul's conversion began in the discovery of Jesus of Nazareth, the resurrected Messiah. He was critical of things such as circumcision and dietary rules because they impeded the gentile mission and kept Jewish Christians and gentile Christians apart. But does this mean that in Paul's mind Judaism outside Christ is a sufficient and saving faith? Scholars are divided. Some believe that to find some inadequacy in Judaism anchors an anti-Jewish attitude in the heart of Paul's theology. These scholars develop a "two covenant" theology for Paul, meaning that salvation could be found for Jews in their covenants and gentiles could find salvation in Jesus's covenant. But most believe Paul presented Christ as a necessary continuation of God's saving work in history, which Jews also must join. There is one covenant, one means of salvation in Christ.

While this debate about first-century Judaism and the law will continue, it has offered an important corrective to our understanding of the New Testament and its world. The characterization of the Jewish faith as nothing more than legalism ignores not only the rich teaching of the Old Testament about the grace and mercy of God but also the many writings of Jews in antiquity who knew that obedience to God could only spring from experiencing his grace.

Paul argues in Romans that both gentile and Jew are under sin and subject to God's wrath and that Christ's justification is effective for both peoples (Rom. 3:21–31). While Paul's conversion was truly not in the same category as that of the gentiles, who turned to God from idols, he did undergo a radical transformation in his perspective regarding God's Messiah. In this conversion he affirmed the promises made to his ancestors that are now fulfilled in Christ. Paul also found that the righteousness by which he stood before God was the righteousness of God through Christ (2 Cor. 5:21; Phil. 3:8–9).

THE IMPLICATIONS OF THE GOSPEL

For Paul, justification has social dimensions regarding Jewish and gentile fellowship (Gal. 2:11–21), and the reconciliation Christ brings about extends to the whole cosmos (Eph. 2:16; Col. 1:20). The salvation of Christ also has dramatic effects in the lives of the believers. They are formed together into a new community, the church, which has both local manifestations (1 Cor. 1:2; 1 Thess. 1:1) and a universal dimension (Eph. 1:22–23). God has taken both Jew and gentile and made them into one new humanity (2:14–15), and together they are reconciled to God (2:16–17).

The social distinctions that separated humanity—gender, ethnicity, socioeconomic status—are of no importance as this new and diverse community comes together as one (Gal. 3:28; Col. 3:11). The Roman Empire was hardly egalitarian in its perspective on social class. Society expected that a person would remain within their place in the social order, though some social mobility was possible (e.g., a slave becoming a freedman or freedwoman). People were classified as either slave or free, citizens or noncitizens, patricians or plebs, Romans, Greeks, Macedonians, Jews, or "barbarians."

Gender distinctions were also important. The amazing social mix within

Christianity, however, caught the attention of Pliny the Younger, governor of the Roman province of Bithynia around AD 112. In writing to Emperor Trajan about the "Christian problem," he stated:

> This made me decide it was all the more necessary to extract the truth by torture from two slave-women, whom they call deaconesses. . . . I have postponed any further examination and hastened to consult you. The question seems to me to be worthy of your consideration, especially in view of the number of persons endangered; for a great many individuals of *every age and class, both men and women*, are being brought to trial, and this is likely to continue. It is not only the towns, but villages and rural districts too which are infected through contact with this wretched cult (*Epistles* 10.96).

Paul's view of Christ's cross embraces his understanding of the Christians' participation in the victory over sin. Since the blessing of the new covenant included the writing of God's law on the heart as well as forgiveness, Paul regarded union with Christ in his death as a death to sin. This is symbolized in baptism and framed as a liberation from slavery to sin (Rom. 6:1–23). Paul knows full well that humanity is incapable of doing what God requires because of our fallen human nature, the "flesh" (*sarx*, 7:13–25). Yet Christ has not only justified believers (8:1) but also empowered his people with the Spirit so that they can do what pleases God (8:1–13). The high moral standards Paul describes in his letters (see, e.g., Rom. 12–15; Eph. 4–6; Col. 3–4) form a roadmap for those liberated by Christ from sin's slavery and enabled by God's Spirit.

Paul's theology is also oriented to the future. In a world marked by violence, disease, death, and despair, Paul was filled with hope. When he faced his darkest moment during his second Roman imprisonment, he knew that a crown of righteousness awaited him (2 Tim. 4:6–8). Because of Christ's resurrection, those who died in Christ would be raised at the time of his return (1 Thess. 4:13–18), an event he calls the *parousia* (1 Cor. 15:23; 1 Thess. 2:19; 4:15; 5:23; 2 Thess. 2:1).

This return of Christ is the consummation of human history, a time when all will confess that Jesus is Lord (Phil. 2:9–11). He will have then "destroyed all dominion, authority and power"—all forces natural and supernatural that are against God. He reigns now and will continue to do so "until he has put all his enemies under his feet," including death itself (1 Cor. 15:24–25). Then God will be all in all.

Slaves were common in Rome, and Christians were among them. Here two women slaves fight as gladiators in the arena. This plaque recognizes their release from slavery and gives their names, Amazon and Achillia.
Reproduced by permission from Carole Raddato

Questions for Discussion

1. In what ways does Paul's theology help us understand the place of Christianity in the midst of a society marked by religious pluralism?
2. Compare Paul's proclamation about Christ with the understanding of salvation preached in the contemporary church. How is the contemporary message similar and how does it differ from what Paul proclaimed?
3. What are the implications of the "new perspective" on Paul? Compare the fundamental observations of this perspective with the preaching you have heard.
4. What are the social effects of salvation? Does Paul reflect on the role of Christians in the wider society?
5. What place does eschatology (the teaching about the "last things") have in the theology of the church today? What place does eschatology have in your understanding of the Christian faith and your present life? Compare Paul's emphasis, including the link between eschatology and ethics.

BIBLIOGRAPHY

Introductory

Barclay, J. M. G. *Paul and the Gift*. Grand Rapids: Eerdmans, 2015.

Bruce, F. F. *Paul: Apostle of the Heart Set Free*. Grand Rapids: Eerdmans, 1977.

Capes, D. B., R. Reeves, and E. R. Richards. *Rediscovering Paul*. Downers Grove, IL: InterVarsity Press, 2007.

Gorman, M. *Apostle of the Crucified Lord: A Theological Introduction to Paul and His Letters*. Grand Rapids: Eerdmans, 2004.

Marshall, I. H. *New Testament Theology*. Downers Grove, IL: InterVarsity Press, 2004.

Polhill, J. *Paul and His Letters*. Nashville: Broadman & Holman, 1999.

Schreiner, T. R. *Paul: Apostle of God's Glory in Christ*. Downers Grove, IL: InterVarsity Press, 2001.

Advanced

Dunn, J. D. G. *The Theology of the Apostle Paul*. Grand Rapids: Eerdmans, 1998.

Murphy-O'Connor, J. *Paul: A Critical Life*. Oxford: Clarendon, 1996.

Neyrey, J. H. *Paul: In Other Words*. Louisville: Westminster John Knox, 1990.

Ridderbos, H. *Paul: An Outline of His Theology*. Grand Rapids: Eerdmans, 1975.

Schnabel, E. J. *Early Christian Mission*. Vol. 2. *Paul and the Early Church*. Downers Grove, IL: InterVarsity Press, 2004.

Wright, N. T. *Paul and the Faithfulness of God*. 2 vols. Minneapolis: Fortress, 2013.

NOTES

1. A. S. F. Gow and D. L. Page, *The Greek Anthology* (Cambridge: Cambridge University Press, 1965), 2:57.

2. G. H. R. Horsley, *New Documents Illustrating Early Christianity* (North Ryde, N.S.W.: Macquarie University Press, 1986), 1:5.

3. See E. P. Sanders, *Paul and Palestinian Judaism* (Philadelphia: Fortress, 1977).

Chapter 14

THE LETTER TO THE GALATIANS

The ancient theater of Psidian Antioch, a major city in the Roman province of Galatia. Psidian Antioch was a trading center on a highland plateau in Asia Minor. Paul knew its importance and crossed through the city on each of his missionary tours.
Todd Bolen/BiblePlaces.com

The letter to the Galatians gives us a glimpse into the earliest days of Paul's theological career. Unlike the calm, reasoned style of many of his other letters, here Paul uses forceful polemic, as if something vital to the message of the gospel is in jeopardy. He is no doubt at the beginning of his ministry—precisely *where and when* needs to be determined—and already he has learned about opponents who have denied what he teaches. He is astonished that the Christians of this region have succumbed to false teaching, and he is eager to straighten them out.

In each of Paul's letters, we will see how important it is to understand context and setting. Each letter springs from particular circumstances in Paul's life, and arguments found in, say, Galatians are going to be entirely different from concerns expressed in Thessalonians. Galatians is a dramatic case study of this. Knowing what is happening before and after this letter was penned will determine a great deal about how we interpret it.

A number of important questions have shadowed this letter (each championed by lists of scholars). We will begin by clarifying where this letter stands in Paul's life and thinking. Where has Paul been? What has happened to cause the conflicts in the letter? Who are his opponents? What did they teach? Why is their teaching viewed so critically by Paul? And when was this letter penned in relation to other major events in the history of the early church?

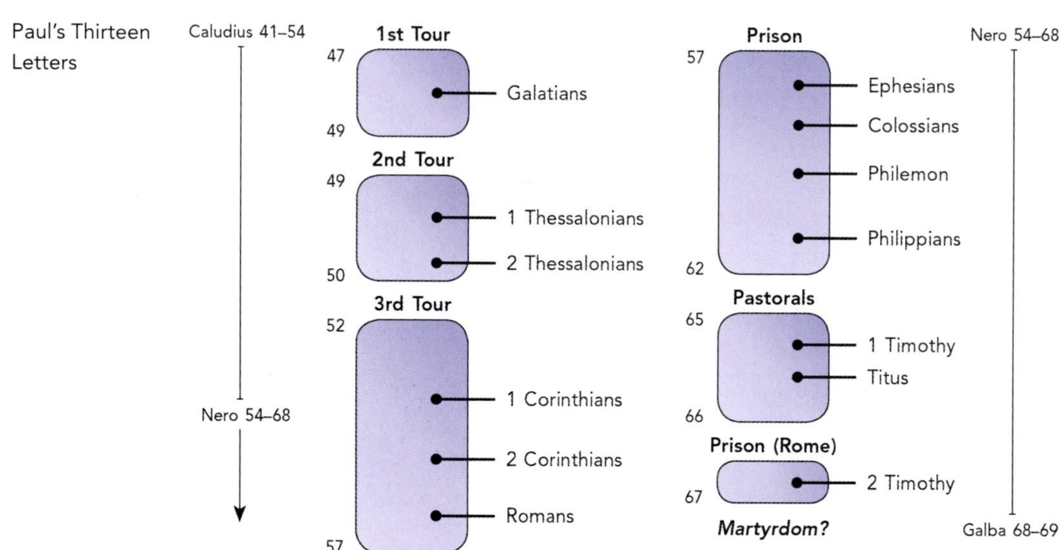

Paul's Thirteen Letters

WHERE WAS GALATIA AND WHY DOES IT MATTER?

It's clear from the intimacy and argument of the letter that Paul had previously visited Galatia. The book of Acts refers to Paul visiting Galatia on his second

(16:6) and third (18:23) journey. The problem is that much of what Paul argues here regarding the Jewish law and gentile compliance had been resolved at a theological council in Jerusalem (Acts 15). And this gathering had taken place before Paul's second journey. So the problem is simple: Why does Paul have to argue a theological point following the very council that had clarified that point? If Paul's visit to Galatia was after the Jerusalem Council and that council had decided in favor of gentile freedom, was the council a failure? Did some reject it? The problem to be solved: What is the relation between the Jerusalem Council of Acts 15 and the letter of Galatians? We need to begin by locating Galatia.

Paul's First Tour	Jerusalem Council	Paul's Second Tour
Acts 13–14	Acts 15	Acts 16–18

Galatia was located in the region geographers call Anatolia (or Asia Minor)—modern-day Turkey. The small historic ethnic region of Galatia was in north-central Anatolia, where Celts and Gauls had migrated some three hundred years before Christ (Strabo, *Geography* 12.5.1; 567). The Romans recognized it as its own kingdom for many years before Paul began his ministry. A quick look at a map[1] indicates that the cities of Pisidian Antioch, Lystra, and Derbe—the cities of Paul's first tour—were not in this region and instead belonged to the southern area populated by people called Phrygians. Most early Christian (Patristic) commentators assumed this northern location for Galatia because this is how they understood the geography of their own time. And for them, Paul never entered this region till his second tour.

The Jerusalem Council: Ethnic Reconciliation

The Jerusalem Council of Acts 15 was the first theological council of the church. Because a delegation of Jewish Christians had traveled north and announced the requirement that gentiles obey the Jewish law (circumcision in particular), representatives from the church at Syrian Antioch (including Paul) traveled to Jerusalem in protest. Following a variety of speeches that are only minimally represented in Acts, James, the leader of the Jerusalem community, proclaimed: "It is my judgment, therefore, that we should not make it difficult for the Gentiles who are turning to God" (Acts 15:19) and with these words declared the freedom of gentiles from ceremonial law. In a word, Paul's theology had won the day. However, James did say if Jew-gentile relationships were to go forward, gentile Christians needed to make cultural concessions, completely avoiding practices that were offensive to Jews (such as idolatry). It is quite possible that some Jewish Christians disagreed with the council's decision and continued to promote circumcision at least for Jewish believers.

A map of Imperial Galatia, including the cities of Pisidian Antioch, Lystra, Derbe, and Iconium. Note that the Roman province included the ethnic region of Galatia.

A Roman road entering Pisidian Antioch. Paul traveled roads such as this throughout his career.
www.HolyLandPhotos.org

This position was challenged in the nineteenth century by a Scottish New Testament scholar (and archaeologist) named William Ramsay (1851–1939). As an intrepid Victorian traveler using wagons and horses (and who enjoyed tea set out on elegant china by his wife every afternoon), Ramsay journeyed throughout Asia Minor, studying what remained of the cities and locations mentioned in the New Testament. He happened upon a remarkable theory that has since been largely substantiated. Ramsay hypothesized that when Paul referred to the geographic regions of his travels, he did not mean "ethnic" regions but was using "imperial," or governmental, regional designations (1 Cor. 16:5, 15, 19). It so happened that in 25 BC, Rome had reorganized central Asia Minor and created an imperial region called The Province of Galatia that swept south to the Taurus Mountains and included cities like Pisidian Antioch. When Paul visited this city on his first missionary journey, he was visiting the Roman imperial province of Galatia. About two hundred years later (second century AD) Rome again reorganized central Asia Minor, shrinking Galatia back to its ethnic parameters.

For most scholars this question is settled. In the New Testament, Galatia refers to an imperial Roman province that reached south beyond Pisidian Antioch. Paul preferred going to those areas that were developed with large population centers, where his efforts at evangelism would be rewarded. The southern regions not only had these cities but had roads that facilitated Paul's travel. Ethnic Galatia

Paul's First Journey	**Jerusalem Council**	**Paul's Second Journey**
Imperial Galatia	The Gentile Decree	Imperial Galatia
Acts 13–14	Acts 15	Acts 16–18

(the north) was sparsely populated and its road system was undeveloped. The crux, however, is here: *Paul visited Galatia on his first missionary tour (Acts 13–14) as well as on his second missionary tour (Acts 16).* The remaining question is when he wrote his letter.

The Intrepid William Ramsay of Scotland

Professor William Ramsay of Aberdeen University (Scotland) traveled to Asia Minor regularly to pursue his passion for reconstructing the background and setting of New Testament history. He had studied in Germany at Tübingen University and heard many critical theories deconstructing the reliability of New Testament history. His career goal—at Oxford and then Aberdeen—was to see if these theories were true. His splendid books *St. Paul the Traveler and Roman Citizen* (1895) and *The Letters to the Seven Churches of Asia* (1905) are superb introductions to his efforts.

Sir William Mitchell Ramsay
Public Domain

Another well-traveled Victorian, Gertrude Bell (known as Gertie Bell), shared many of these trips with Ramsay and his wife. Bell spoke fluent Arabic, was known to countless tribes in the region, and was a well-known advisor to the British Foreign Service. She was even responsible for drafting the map of the Middle East as we know it today. Notes such as these from Bell's journals give insight into their adventures together.[2]

Gertrude Bell in Iraq, sorting archaeological finds.
Historia/Shutterstock

> Madan Shehar
> Saturday, May 25, 1907
>
> The Ramsays arrived yesterday. I was in the middle of digging up a church when suddenly two carts hove into sight and there they were. It was about 3 in the afternoon. They instantly got out, refused to think of going to the tents, Lady Ramsay made tea (for they were starving) in the open and Ramsay oblivious of all other considerations was at once lost in the problems the church presented. It was too delightful to have someone as much excited about it as I was.[3]

The Timing of Paul's Letter

The timing of Paul's letter is a matter of some debate because we need to decide where it falls in relation to the Jerusalem Council of Acts 15. If the letter was before the council, it can be dated to AD 49, and its arguments anticipate the council. If it is after the council, it belongs to the early 50s and shows that the council did not convince every member. Three positions are common.

(1) The so-called North Galatian Theory has been the majority view of the church for centuries. Some contemporary scholars who still defend this position argue that Paul is addressing the churches of this northern ethnic region and that he only visited here on the second tour, hence, after the Jerusalem Council. By this reasoning, Paul's letter refers to the Jerusalem Council of Acts 15 in Galatians 2:1–10. In these verses Paul says he visited Jerusalem with an entourage of colleagues (including Barnabas; Acts 15:2) and met with the apostolic leadership. He describes his theological opponents and names James, Peter, and John as "pillars" of the church who affirmed his work (Gal. 2:9–10). To sum: this view believes that the visit to Galatia *followed* the Jerusalem Council. (Some severe critics in this position believe Paul does not refer to any decree in Galatians because the events of Acts 15 never occurred.)

(2) Other scholars are drawn to the South Galatian Theory, arguing that Paul's formative visit to Galatia occurred *before* the council, on the first tour, and that this letter anticipated the arguments of the council. Most scholars concede today that Paul was in Galatia on the first tour, but it remains to be seen if Paul *wrote* the letter before the council. By this view, Paul's description of the visit to Jerusalem in Galatians 2:1–10 refers to the so-called "famine visit" of Acts 11:27–30. And indeed, there are many parallels. These scholars also claim if the decree of Acts 15 had occurred, then Paul should have mentioned it in his letter. But in Galatians he does not. Plus they wonder why after the council James (who publicly gave way at the council) is still sending out emissaries who contradict Paul (Gal. 2:12).

Paul's First Tour	***Paul writes Galatians?***	**Jerusalem Council**	**Paul's Second Tour**	***Paul writes Galatians?***
Acts 13–14		Acts 15	Acts 16–18	

(3) Today a widely-held mediating position affirms that Paul is referring to (southern) imperial Galatia in all his travels and that Paul likely never entered northern, ethnic Galatia. Thus, Paul went to Galatia on both tours (his first and his second). However, Paul's description in Galatians 2:1–10 does refer to the Jerusalem Council of Acts 15. We cannot know why Paul fails to mention the previous decree from Acts 15, but we have a parallel in 1 Corinthians which was written after the Jerusalem Council as well. In 1 Corinthians Paul discusses food sacrificed to idols and sexual morality—two issues the decree also settled. If Paul had the decree, why doesn't he mention it in 1 Corinthians?

This letter followed the Jerusalem Council as well, and here Paul discusses food sacrificed to idols and sexual morality—two issues the decree also settled. If Paul had the decree, why doesn't he mention it in 1 Corinthians? In this view,

Paul had already delivered the gentile decree to Galatia during his second tour, and his opponents had rejected it. But above all, a close comparison between Galatians 2:1–10 and Acts 15 demonstrates a surprising number of parallels: the issues (circumcision and gentiles), the outcome (gentile freedom), and the agreement of James and Peter.

The key here is to see that Galatians is shaped by ideas being debated in the earliest days of the church. And the Jerusalem Council in Acts 15 presents us with the critical issues—the first theological issues—that the early church had to contend with. Some believe it is vital to see the letter as preceding the council. Still others argue that it followed the council and that Paul is forced to revisit the issues of that gathering because the decree of gentile freedom had been rejected.

For the present, we will assume that Galatians was penned sometime near AD 48, preceded the work of the Jerusalem Council (Acts 15), and was Paul's first letter. We will also assume that it gives us our earliest glimpse into Paul's theological thinking and opens a window into the first theological quarrel in early Christian history.

THE CONTROVERSY: A JERUSALEM DELEGATION IN GALATIA

We need to think of the cities of Asia Minor as filled with people who had a wide array of religious interests. A city like Pisidian Antioch was a highland trading crossroads, where travelers from the "far east" (Syria, Mesopotamia, Persia) might have mingled with Greeks, Romans, and the local Phrygians, who were known for their ecstatic worship of the goddess Cybele. Temples from older Greek gods still existed alongside Roman shrines, whose gods in some cases simply occupied the older temples. In this mix we would find communities of Jews who struggled with the age-old problem of faithfulness to their religion while mingling with the "modern" Hellenistic cultures around them. Some Jews certainly were won over to this gentile world and compromised much; others held firm to their faith and as a defensive posture may have exhibited a rigidity that isolated them.

Cybele was worshiped throughout the Roman Empire, especially in Asia Minor, where she was often known as Agdistis. *www.HolyLandPhotos.org*

It is evident that Paul is writing to gentiles in Galatians (Gal. 4:8–9). In fact, when Paul and Barnabas passed through the Galatian city of Lystra (Acts 13–14), the crowd was so impressed with them that they gave the two men the ultimate speaker's compliment, "The gods have come down to us in human form!" (14:11). They called Paul Hermes (because he spoke so much), and Barnabas they called Zeus (the chief god of the Greek pantheon). Even the priest at Zeus's temple in Lystra tried to sacrifice to them (14:13). Still others referred to Paul as "an angel of God" (Gal. 4:14). To say the least, Paul and Barnabas were distressed. But these

Hellenistic religious instincts also showed up in other ways. Many there were interested in superstitious beliefs that left them in bondage and fear, and they no doubt paid homage to "spirits" and imagined spiritual forces (Gal. 4:8–11).

After Paul and Barnabas completed their work during their first tour in southern imperial Galatia (Pisidian Antioch, Lystra, Iconium, Derbe), they departed for Judea and left behind fledgling Christian communities that were fragile but who understood the fundamentals of the gospel. These were some of the world's earliest Christian churches. They had no written Christian Scriptures but only knew what Paul taught—which likely left them vulnerable. And while Paul was away, something happened. It appears that a delegation of teachers from Judea arrived in Galatia in Paul's absence and met with these young churches. This is when the trouble began. They contradicted Paul's teaching and taught the Galatians that in some manner Christians had to take on the markers of Judaism if they were to be fully attached to Christ. Suddenly, topics like circumcision and Sabbath observance were a part of the Galatian vocabulary.

How do we know this? Paul must have learned about this crisis while he was in Syrian Antioch before his second tour. He penned Galatians as a furious complaint against these teachers, and using the words from this letter, we can reconstruct what is going on. He is unafraid to call them out personally ("some people are throwing you into confusion" Gal. 1:7) and says that they should be condemned for what they have done (1:9; 5:10). He even names the culprits as "certain men came from James" (2:12), which tells us that this delegation had originated in Jerusalem, more importantly, from the Christian church there led by James, the brother of Jesus (1:19). In a bit of grim irony, he even says that these promoters of circumcision should emasculate themselves (5:12). These are harsh words. Paul feels so strongly about this that he postpones his second tour. The Galatian crisis likely ignites the debates leading up to the Jerusalem Council (Acts 15). It is no surprise that at the council, Paul was intent on having a "clarifying conversation" with James.

The problem is that these teachers from James have made firm inroads in Galatia. Paul writes, "I am astonished that you are so quickly deserting the one who called you to live in the grace of Christ and are turning to a different gospel" (1:6). He also says, "You foolish Galatians! Who has bewitched you? Before your very eyes Jesus Christ was clearly portrayed as crucified" (3:1). He is almost in despair as he thinks how these new Christians have suddenly begun to carry the burden of the law and have lost the joy and freedom he had preached to them. "I have wasted my efforts on you" (4:11). They had returned to slavery (4:9) but now of a type they had never known before: it was slavery to Jewish laws and obligations that had no business in their lives. The letter of Galatians is Paul's attempt to oppose what these teachers have said and to remedy the situation.

Jews in Syrian Antioch

Jewish life in Roman cities could at times be tenuous. At other times Jews flourished in some of the most important cities of the empire. Syrian Antioch (not to be confused with Pisidian Antioch) was a major Hellenistic city in the east with a long history before the New Testament era. The Jewish historian Josephus wrote that Jews in Antioch lived there "by reason of the size of the city, wherein the kings ... granted them the enjoyment of equal privileges of citizens with the Greeks themselves. They also made proselytes of a great many of the Greeks perpetually and thereby after a sort brought them to be a portion of their own body" (*Jewish War*, 7.3.3 [43–45]).

But conflicts could arise. The Emperor Caligula wanted to put his statue in the Jerusalem Temple, thereby forcing Jews to pay homage to imperial leadership. In many cities, including Antioch, rioting broke out. Twenty-five years later, during the First Revolt (AD 66–70), Jewish leaders were frequently massacred (*Jewish War* 7.3.3 [47–48]). Such tensions between Jewish identity and the majority gentile culture flared up regularly and no doubt appeared in the early churches. This is valuable because such circumstances in Syrian Antioch may be illustrative of what happened in the Roman cities of Galatia. Jewish communities lived alongside gentile communities, and a struggle for Jewish cultural preservation was a daily affair.

PAUL WRITES GALATIANS

The Roman world was no different from our own when it came to composing professional letters. There were rules, and well-educated people followed them. Formal letters followed a model we can easily see in the tiny third letter of John. Gracious opening lines identify the writer and his recipient (3 John 1). This is followed by a prayer of blessings for the reader (2–4), the body of the letter (5–10), a delicately written ethical exhortation (11–12), and a polite close, often with a blessing of "peace" (13–15).

Now look at Galatians and note how many elements are missing. Galatians is a "rebuke letter" penned to someone you might know quite well but who has disappointed you profoundly. In a papyrus remnant from the third century (P.Oxy. 1.123.5–9), we can hear this tone easily in the words of a father rebuking an errant son, "I am very much surprised, my son, that till today I have not received any letter from you, telling me about your welfare."[4] This is Paul's tone as well. He launches forcefully, abruptly, into his concerns, almost as if he can't help himself. This letter is a rebuke, and because of this, scholars commonly study the letter to see persuasive (or rhetorical) speech patterns known in antiquity.

The opening lines of Galatians demonstrate Paul's rhetorical style well. Note that there is no word of thanks for the Galatians, not even kind wishes for their welfare. Paul can give praise to God for his rescue from "the present evil age," but there is no praise to God for the Galatian church (compare Col. 1:3 or 1 Thess. 1:2).

Why is this? Because they have "so quickly" (1:6) abandoned the gospel itself. It was not long ago that Paul had been there, and now, before the gospel has barely taken root, they have let the core of its message disintegrate.

THE MESSAGE OF GALATIANS

The fundamental concern on Paul's mind is the ongoing role of the Jewish law in the purposes of God. Paul contends that gentiles are not obligated to fulfill the law as represented in the requirement of circumcision. But entailments certainly follow. Circumcision was only the beginning, and we can expect that other strictures such as dietary law and Sabbath observance were sure to follow. But this leads Paul to think more globally about the law and its ongoing place even in Judaism. For Paul, Christ was the great disrupter of all things in heaven and on earth—in the gentile world and within Judaism. But to endorse a Christ-formed view of the law, to promote a rearrangement of the duties of the law, this certainly would bring controversy. Paul is not necessarily arguing with those who believe circumcision (or the law) is a prerequisite for salvation. He is arguing against those who make circumcision a necessary entailment that marks true believers from those who fail to understand God's will. For Paul's opponents then, uncircumcised gentiles live on the margin of God's grace until they choose to be obedient to the law.

Paul's opening words (1:1–5) show that these teachers have begun by challenging Paul's own authority. They probably pointed to their own authority as being commissioned perhaps by James and some of the leading apostles in Jerusalem. Paul, on the other hand, had "lesser" credentials. This attack does not surprise Paul. What he is contending for will bring enormous offense to his opponents; but this does not trouble him, because he is an apostle ("one sent") commissioned by Jesus Christ himself. This is the force of Paul's contention: God is the architect of what has happened in Christ. And in Christ the gospel has come to the world, and in its defense, Paul will confront any opposition.

Paul then launches into the gravity of the present situation (1:6–11). The Galatians have deserted the gospel. Even if an angel were to bring another message, that angel (Paul says) should be cursed by God! And if this is true, the same can be said for these Jerusalem messengers (1:9). They are bearing a "different" gospel. In other words, Paul is willing to be controversial, willing to make a stir, because he is not working to please a human audience. His efforts are entirely directed to honoring God.

Paul's Personal Story (1:12–2:21)

Paul begins by laying down facts that demonstrate his credibility. He outlines carefully the origin of his gospel as a direct revelation of Jesus Christ. He knows that his story is well-known. He was a persecutor of the church who treated Jesus's followers violently because he viewed them as deeply compromised and mistaken. Plus he was a proficient theologian exceeding many of his peers. Both facts make his conversion story that much more remarkable and compelling. He was not an ambivalent Jew. He understood his faith and promoted it aggressively. He could not be easily persuaded. And this truth strengthens the power of his conversion story (see Acts 9). Jesus's revelation to him (recorded elsewhere only in Acts) is the basis of his argument: *this gospel has come to him directly from God*. After his conversion Paul did not confer with those whom he knew were Christians. He immediately departed to the deserts east of Judea ("Arabia"), was discipled by Christians such as Annas in Damascus, and there for three years was forced to rearrange the meaning of his life and purpose. Jesus had disrupted everything. The man who had promoted the law, separated himself from gentiles, and persecuted the church—this man would now become an evangelist bringing the grace of God to the wider gentile world.

Paul in the Desert of Arabia

Paul's entry into the wilderness of Judea represents an ancient tradition in Judaism. The wilderness deserts are just east of every major city in the central mountains of Judea. And then there are the expansive, huge deserts reaching south toward Egypt (where the Israelites wandered for decades), northeast toward Syria, and directly east and southeast into Arabia. Because these deserts were a place where Israel's faith was forged (see Deut. 6–10), great leaders of the Bible *inevitably* spent time there. From Moses to John the Baptist, God called and formed many people in the desert. John the Baptist even insisted that if anyone wanted to encounter God and be renewed through his baptism, they had to leave Jerusalem and enter the deserts where John worked. Even Jesus entered the desert for forty days after his baptism. Paul did the same.

Syrian desert
yeowatzup/Wikimedia Commons, CC BY 2.0

Mapping Paul's Early Years

In Galatians 2:1 Paul says that fourteen years elapsed before he came to Jerusalem on the famine visit. This small reference is vital when we reconstruct the early years of Paul by bringing together our sources both in Acts and Galatians. If we assume that Paul's chronological marker in Galatians is his conversion, we know that he spent three years in the desert south of Damascus. Then we know that following a fifteen-day visit to Jerusalem, he left for Tarsus. Acts 11 tells us that Barnabas came to Tarsus, located Paul, and brought him to Syrian Antioch as copastor for one year. Now we learn that after fourteen years, he comes to Jerusalem. Can we pull these threads together?

One convenient synthesis offers this outline: (1) Paul spent three years in Arabia, (2) ten years near Tarsus, (3) and one year pastoring with Barnabas in Syrian Antioch. This gives us the fourteen years needed to explain his reference in Gal 2:1. If this reconstruction is correct, it means that Paul had been a Christian for thirteen years before he was invited into Christian leadership.

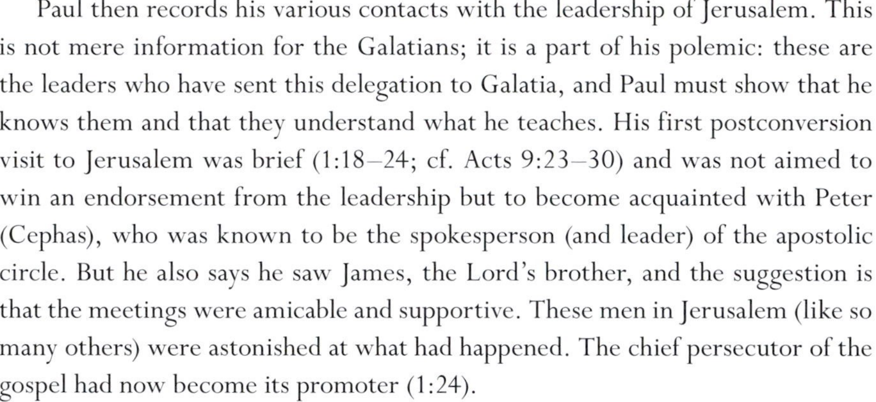

Paul then records his various contacts with the leadership of Jerusalem. This is not mere information for the Galatians; it is a part of his polemic: these are the leaders who have sent this delegation to Galatia, and Paul must show that he knows them and that they understand what he teaches. His first postconversion visit to Jerusalem was brief (1:18–24; cf. Acts 9:23–30) and was not aimed to win an endorsement from the leadership but to become acquainted with Peter (Cephas), who was known to be the spokesperson (and leader) of the apostolic circle. But he also says he saw James, the Lord's brother, and the suggestion is that the meetings were amicable and supportive. These men in Jerusalem (like so many others) were astonished at what had happened. The chief persecutor of the gospel had now become its promoter (1:24).

Paul's second visit to Jerusalem (2:1–11) took place during what we have termed the "famine visit" (Acts 11), and, of course, this presumes the South Galatian Theory (see above). Paul tells how he came to Jerusalem with Barnabas and Titus, but then as they brought aid to the church, a controversy erupted. Unlike Barnabas, a Jewish Christian, Titus was a gentile convert. Soon the leaders in Jerusalem asked if Titus ought to obey the Jewish law by being circumcised. This implies that Jewish Christians at least in these years understood that they were required to keep the law as a natural supplement to their faith in Christ. The problem now was that they were imposing these expectations on a gentile.

Paul resisted. And not surprisingly, Titus did as well (Gal. 2:3). For Paul, what was at stake was a fundamental aspect of the gospel itself (2:5). This was not a peripheral matter but a point he was willing to argue vehemently. Then we read something remarkable. Paul names the Jerusalem leaders (James, Peter/Cephas, and John) and says that they endorsed his work among the gentiles. As Peter worked among Jews, so Paul was to go to the gentiles. There is explicit support for Paul's view about gentiles, but we can assume safely that at least in the minds of some Jewish-Christians, the Jewish law continued to be a valid way of life for Jewish converts to Christ.

It wasn't until Peter came to Syrian Antioch (2:11–14) that things broke apart. The fragile agreement Paul thought he had with the Jerusalem leaders was shattered. Syrian Antioch had grown into the first multicultural church where gentile and Jewish believers could live side by side. Peter "used to eat with the gentiles" (2:12), but then a delegation from James arrived who said that Christians who obeyed the law (circumcision) should remain set apart. Did they view themselves as superior?

Relief from the second century of a teacher with disciples
Wikipedia/Shakko

Circumcision

Circumcision is the surgical removal of a sheath of skin (the foreskin) found at the end of the penis. This was done on the boy's eighth day after birth (and is still done today among Jews, Muslims, and many Christians—sometimes as religious ceremony, sometimes as tradition). Circumcision was used widely in antiquity but was adopted by the Jews and considered the "tribal mark" of God, sealing Israel's relationship to the covenant. After Abraham was called into a covenant relationship with God (Gen. 12–15), he was circumcised (Gen. 17). Genesis 17:10–14 (ESV) makes the rule explicit:

> This is my covenant, which you shall keep, between me and you and your offspring after you: Every male among you shall be circumcised. You shall be circumcised in the flesh of your foreskins, and it shall be a sign of the covenant between me and you. He who is eight days old among you shall be circumcised. Every male throughout your generations, whether born in your house or bought with your money from any foreigner who is not of your offspring, both he who is born in your house and he who is bought with your money, shall surely be circumcised. So shall my covenant be in your flesh an everlasting covenant. Any uncircumcised male who is not circumcised in the flesh of his foreskin shall be cut off from his people; he has broken my covenant.

The Romans thought that circumcision was astonishing. They abhorred it and thought that the practice was extreme in the least. This makes it even more remarkable that in Galatia gentile Christians were having circumcision imposed on them.

This fourth-century AD inscription from Aphrodisias, Asia Minor, provides clear evidence that gentile god-fearers were part of Diaspora synagogues. The inscription begins with the phrase "and to these god-fearers" and is followed by a list of gentile names. *Stephen H. Sanchez/BiblePlaces.com*

Did they view these gentile Christians as unclean? When Peter heard this message, out of fear he drew back from the gentile Christians and separated himself from them. The controversy must have been so intense that even Barnabas joined ranks with the so-called "procircumcision group." Paul was furious, and he had one term for this: hypocrisy. He confronted Peter and the rest of the mistaken Jerusalem Christians publicly (2:14).

In Galatians 2:15–21 we may have Paul's earliest theological reflection *in writing* about the essence of the gospel. He can point to Judaism's own theological heritage ("we who are Jews . . . know . . ." 2:15–16) to buttress an argument he will flesh out in Romans 1–8, and this no doubt is what he argued that day in Syrian Antioch. *Our fundamental relationship with God is based not on satisfying the law but rather on the grace of God that we receive by faith.* Christ died so that those who were experiencing death under the law might find life and renewal. "Christ lives in me" means that the gift of God was not simply the cross but a transforming union with the Son of God that changes how I live "in this body." All this—all of it—is a gift of God's grace. Our success with God is not anchored to our enduring efforts; it is anchored to the enduring character of God's goodness.

To sum up, Paul has undermined his opponents' arguments. He has validated the authority of his revelation, unmasked the hypocrisy of the Jerusalem leadership, and now launches his theological thesis, which is as old as Judaism itself: salvation is found in grace alone and no place else. Supplemental markers of spiritual identity (such as circumcision) are of little use.

Outline of Galatians

- I. Greetings (1:1–5)
- II. Rebuke (1:6–5:1)
  1. Paul's Rebuke to the Galatians (1:6–11)
  2. Paul's Autobiographical Narrative (1:12–2:21)
     - a. Paul's Call (1:12–17)
     - b. Paul Meets Apostles in Jerusalem (1:18–2:10)
     - c. Paul Confronts Peter in Antioch (2:11–21)
  3. Paul's Theological Argument (3:1–5:1)
     - a. Abraham's Example (3:1–14)
     - b. The Law and the Promise (3:15–29)
     - c. Heirs of God (4:1–11)
     - d. A personal appeal (4:12–20)
     - e. Abraham and Sarah (4:21–5:1)

III. Paul's Moral Concerns (5:2–6:10)
   1. Circumcision (5:2–15)
   2. Life in the Spirit (5:16–6:10)
IV. Closing Summary and Greetings (6:11–18)

Paul's Theological Argument (3:1–5:1)

Paul simply cannot comprehend how the Galatians could have abandoned the purity of the gospel of grace. And he begins with an experiential argument. The genesis of anyone's faith is found in the initiative of God's love. It was the gift of God—God moving toward us, God providing his Spirit—that gave birth to our spiritual walk. If this is true, then salvation is based on a gift and not on efforts under the law. We meet this gracious overture from God in our faith, and this meeting is the spark that ignites our new life in Christ.

For Paul, Abraham is the premier example of this truth (3:6–9; cf. Rom. 4). Before he had faith, before he was circumcised, even before he could present to God a merit-worthy life, God spoke promises to him (see Gen. 12). Abraham heard these overtures and "believed God, and it was counted to him as righteousness" (Gal. 3:6; Gen. 15:6). Abraham was circumcised (Gen. 17), but this was never a prerequisite or a disqualifying entailment of his righteousness. Paul could not say it more clearly: Abraham was righteous *without circumcision*.

The law indeed had its function: to unmask our truest condition—sin—and show us its consequences—death (Gal. 3:10–11, 19, 22; Rom. 7:7). In our immaturity, the law served as a "guardian," guiding us away from things that might harm us (3:23–25). The Hebrew Scriptures point out the only way to life: "The righteous will live by faith." Paul uses this short verse from Habakkuk 2:4 in Galatians 3:11 as well as Romans 1:17 to score two points: faith alone is fundamental to our salvation, and this view is anchored in the Old Testament. In other words, Paul is not departing from his Jewish heritage. He is reclaiming it.

Then Paul makes a perfectly stunning return to Abraham (Gal. 3:15–18). The promise of God was to Abraham and his "offspring" (or seed, singular). And since this means one person (singular), we now know that the one "offspring" of Abraham is Christ. The principle of grace established in Abraham's covenant cannot be annulled by any subsequent covenant (even that of Moses). Therefore, the gospel *of Jesus* is in fact the gospel *of Abraham*, and those who belong to this Abrahamic-Jesus community are those who belong to Christ—not those who obey Judaism's laws. For Paul, Abraham and Christ are the two nodal points from which all theological reflection must begin and end.

Again, Paul is making a foundational argument about grace. Beyond that, however, he is raising questions about the identity of God's people. Attachment to Abraham through attachment to Christ is now the basis of belonging to God.

Gentiles who have embraced Christ by faith, therefore, belong to Abraham! "If you belong to Christ, then you are Abraham's seed, and heirs according to the promise" (3:29). No longer can emissaries from Jerusalem claim a spiritual exceptionalism thanks to ethnicity or circumcision. Christ has again been the great disrupter, but now he has done so socially. Ethnicity, gender, and social class are each upended in Christ (3:28). This "disruptive argument" is the heart of Paul's gospel to the gentiles. They too can become children of Abraham. As Paul will later write, Abraham is "the father of us all" (Rom. 4:16).

Ruins of a Roman aqueduct near Pisidian Antioch, modern day Yalvac, Turkey
Valery Shanin/123rf.com

Mount Sinai
Marcelo Alexandre Rabelo/123rf.com

> ### Imitate Me
> In Galatians 4:12 Paul points to himself as a model for the Galatians to follow and says they ought to imitate him. This request was common among teachers and students in antiquity. Seneca advocates this in his letter to his friend Lucilius: "We can get rid of most sins, if we have a witness who stands near us when we are likely to go wrong. . . . Happy is the man who can make others better. . . . Choose a master whose life, conversation, and soul-expressing face have satisfied you; picture him always to yourself as your protector and your pattern" (*Epistles* 11:8–10).

Paul knows that exceptionalism is what is driving this argument in Galatia. And he knows it from his own history. There are those who believe blessings descend from Abraham and Sarah to the covenant of Moses and that those who live within that legacy are privileged. In perhaps his most shocking analogy (which sounds extremely strange to us today) Paul inverts this line of blessing, comparing heirs to slaves (4:1–31). Slavery describes both Jews and gentiles. Some are slaves to the elemental spirits of the universe; others resemble children who, like slaves, live under laws. But now in Christ the fullest inheritance of Abraham has been given. Slavery should be finished. The promises offered to Abraham in the Old Testament have now been realized in Jesus Christ. And if this is true, why would anyone want to return to slavery (or the law, 4:21)? Paul then exploits the idea of slavery by returning to the story of Abraham, Sarah, and Hagar: two women, two sons. And yet unbelievably Paul says that the son of the slave Hagar (Ishmael) represents Mount Sinai and its covenant! "She is in slavery with her children" (4:25). Christ's people, on the other hand, are the true children of Isaac, because their lives are anchored to the grace Abraham witnessed in his life. Hagar is Jerusalem and Isaac is the church? This is theological disruption beyond imagining.

Paul's Moral Concerns (5:1–6:10)

Central to any theological discussion must be its ethical value. Paul and his opponents know this. Which theological position will lead to virtuous, godly change? Which view—Paul's or his opponents'—will inspire godly righteousness? In Galatia, the emissaries from Jerusalem no doubt argued that circumcision was not merely a matter of obedience to God's law but that obedience to the law was beneficial for living a moral life. In other words, there was moral risk in Paul's teaching: to withdraw the requirements of the law might lead to lawlessness.

Paul wants to be clear. In this discussion, circumcision is of no value (5:1–6). Instead, the pursuit of circumcision (and its entailments) will become a detriment to our relationship with Christ. Paul says, "You . . . have been alienated from Christ; you have fallen away from grace" (5:4), because sustainable change cannot come from law or fear. Genuine change springs from grace. Thus, for Paul, neither circumcision nor uncircumcision matter. What matters is singular: Have we encountered the grace of God? Are we united by Christ and filled with his Spirit?

But if the law (and circumcision) is no longer an assignment for these Galatians, is it possible that they will exploit this grace and, assuming the generosity of God, live immorally? Here Paul anticipates not only a pastoral problem but a Jewish objection. Will the absence of the law lead to immorality?

This question causes Paul to pen what has become some of his most famous verses (5:16–25). The follower of Christ who walks by the Spirit, who bears the fruit of the Spirit, will exhibit a more enduring claim to righteousness than anyone under the law. For Paul and his ethics, moral transformation is mystical inasmuch as it begins with inner transformation rather than external discipline. These lists of virtues are not checklists for human effort, but outcomes of a life wed to growth in Christ and the Spirit.

If this growth is taking place, Paul wants to see concrete outcomes within the Galatian churches of Asia Minor (6:1–10). How we treat each other matters, or as Paul will say at the end, "Neither circumcision nor uncircumcision means anything; what counts is the *new creation*" (6:15, emphasis added). When Paul visits his churches, this is what he hopes to see: Christ-followers as new creations who through their lives demonstrate the power of the gospel. In Paul's words, he wants his own life—and that of the Galatians—to reflect two values: to glory in Christ alone (not the law) and to not only celebrate the work of Christ on the cross but to live a cruciform life, a life shaped by the cross. This life, lived in union with Christ, shows the "marks of Jesus" on its owner.

PAUL'S THEOLOGICAL INTERESTS

From beginning to end, Paul is not simply defending a minor theological point of view. He believes that an epic shift has occurred in history. Paul has deftly asserted the secure place of gentile Christians in the family of God and defined for the first time the relationship of the law to the gospel. Christ has brought to reality what Abraham's children were meant to be. It is fair to say Paul did not deny his Judaism, but rather, he was drawn deeper, through his faith in Christ, into what it means to belong to Israel. God is now making children out of "many nations" (Rom. 4:17; Gal. 4:7). Paul's first benediction for his churches is this, and its theological weight is enormous: "Peace and mercy to all who follow this rule—to the Israel of God" (6:16). What rule? The Abrahamic-Messianic rule of grace and faith. What community of people is enjoying this Abrahamic-Messianic blessing? The church, now boldly given the Old Testament's most honorific title.

Paul's reframing of the "children of Abraham" was a disconcerting idea to many within the Jewish-Christian world. And non-Messianic Jews no doubt wondered about their identity. Did they still have a place in Paul's theology? Paul doesn't answer this last question here, but he will feel the weight of it later, and we will find his answer at the end of his letter to the Romans (Rom. 9–11).

AUTHOR AND DATE

Scholars question the authorship of many of Paul's letters. But four of Paul's thirteen letters are rarely questioned: Galatians, 1 and 2 Corinthians, and Romans. Scholars are virtually unanimous that Paul is the author of Galatians. The date of Galatians depends entirely on where we locate it in connection with Paul's three missionary journeys. We have argued (see above) for the South Galatian Theory and date the letter about AD 48. On the other hand, if the letter were written after the second missionary tour, it might be AD 51. The date of the letter is important not simply to establish a chronology for Paul but to establish the arguments surrounding the controversy at the Jerusalem Council of Acts 15.

Questions for Discussion

1. Explain the differences between the North and South Galatian theories.
2. What was the central issue dealt with at Paul's meeting with James, Peter, and John in Jerusalem at the "famine visit"?
3. What are the chief concerns of Paul's opponents in Galatia?
4. How does Paul theologically link Abraham and Christ? How does that impact gentile and Jewish self-understanding?
5. Explain Paul's understanding of moral transformation and the Spirit. Why is this ethic "mystical"?

BIBLIOGRAPHY

Introductory

Aune, D. E. *The New Testament in Its Literary Environment*. LEC. Ed. Wayne A. Meeks. Philadelphia: Westminster, 1987.

Esler, P. F. *Galatians*. New Testament Readings Series. New York: Routledge, 1998.

Stowers, S. K. *Letter Writing in Greco-Roman Antiquity*. LEC. Ed. Wayne A. Meeks. Philadelphia: Westminster, 1986.

Wilson, T. *Galatians: Gospel Rooted Living*. Preaching the Word. Wheaton: Crossway, 2013.

Advanced

Bruce, F. F. *Commentary on Galatians*. NIGTC. Grand Rapids: Eerdmans, 1982.

Dunn, J. D. G. *Commentary on Galatians*. BNTC. Grand Rapids: Baker, 1993.

Keener, C. *Galatians: A Commentary*. Grand Rapids: Baker, 2019.

Longenecker, R. N. *Galatians*. WBC. Grand Rapids: Zondervan, 1990, 2015.

Martyn, J. L. *Galatians*. AB. New York: Doubleday, 1997.

Moo, D. J. *Galatians*. BECNT. Grand Rapids: Baker Academic, 2013.

Schreiner, T. *Galatians*. ZECNT. Grand Rapids: Zondervan, 2010.

NOTES

1. I always encourage students to purchase one of two atlases: (1) A. Curtis, *The Oxford Bible Atlas*, 4th ed. (New York: Oxford University Press, 2007) or (2) P. Lawrence, *The IVP Atlas of Bible History* (Downers Grove, IL: InterVarsity Press, 2006). IVP published a concise edition of the Lawrence atlas in 2012.

2. *Desert Queen* by Janet Wallach (2005) tells the fascinating story of her life.

3. From *The Letters of Gertrude Bell* (1927), 1:239, cited in S. Neill, *The Interpretation of the New Testament, 1861–1961* (Oxford: Oxford University Press, 1964), 141.

4. N. A. Dahl, "Paul's Letter to the Galatians: Epistolary Genre, Content, and Structure," in ed. D. A. Nanos, *The Galatians Debate* (Peabody, MA: Hendrickson, 2002), 119. This papyrus document is dated to the third or fourth centuries of the common era.

Chapter 15

1 AND 2 THESSALONIANS

A decorative grave stele depicting two Roman residents from the Macedonian city of Thessalonica
Todd Bolen/BiblePlaces.com

The two letters to the Thessalonians are among Paul's earliest letters. Soon after establishing this church during his second missionary journey (AD 50), Paul, Silas, and Timothy were forced to leave town because civil disturbances broke out in the wake of their proclamation of the gospel. Despite repeated attempts, Paul states that he was unable to return to this fledgling church. The persecution that resulted spilled over to these new believers. Would the Thessalonians stand firm in the faith?

Paul traveled on to Berea and then south by sea to Athens, where he decided it was better to be left alone and to send Timothy back to Thessalonica. While anxiously awaiting a report about the church, Paul traveled to Corinth. Timothy finally arrived with news—and it was good. Despite severe opposition, the Thessalonians continued in their new faith. Paul penned 1 Thessalonians right after receiving Timothy's report. The letter is, above all, a thanksgiving to God for the faith, love, and enduring hope that marked this church.

We do not know how much time elapsed between 1 and 2 Thessalonians, though it was not long. Paul was probably still in Corinth when further news about the Thessalonians arrived. Persecution intensified, and in response Paul assured the Thessalonians that God would intervene, punishing their persecutors and relieving the believers' suffering. Some in the church were proclaiming that the day of the Lord had already come. Finally, some believers were not working, contrary to Paul's teaching and example.

THE SETTING OF 1 AND 2 THESSALONIANS

The City of Thessalonica

Antipater of Thessalonica (first century AD) wrote an epigram in which he referred to his hometown as "the mother of Macedonia." The city was a mixture of native Macedonians and Roman immigrants. It exhibited great loyalty to the emperor and the Roman people and enjoyed the benefits of that relationship.

Cassander, king of Macedonia, founded the city in 316 BC and named it after his wife Thessaloniki, half-sister of Alexander the Great. When the Romans attempted to rule the Mediterranean world, the Macedonians fought three wars against them. In 168 BC Rome gained the final victory and dismantled the Macedonian monarchy, dividing the former kingdom into four districts and making Thessalonica the capital of the second administrative area.

In 149 BC Andriscus, a man who claimed to be the son of the former king Perseus, organized a revolt against Roman domination. Thessalonica sided with the Romans and hailed Metellus, the Roman

Tetradrachm of Alexander minted by Lysimachus, and gold stater minted by Brutus. Note the similarities, including the Horn of Ammon.
Harlan J. Berk, Ltd.

commander, as their "savior and benefactor." Rome remembered the loyalty of the city and named Thessalonica as the capital of the reorganized province of Macedonia.

A century later, after the assassination of Julius Caesar, assassins Brutus and Cassius fought a decisive battle against Octavian (Augustus) and Mark Antony for control of the empire just outside the Macedonian city of Philippi. Thessalonica sided with Octavian and Mark Antony, who won. As a reward for her loyalty, Antony granted Thessalonica the high honor of becoming a "free city." As such, the Romans did not garrison troops there, and they allowed the citizens of Thessalonica to govern themselves according to their traditional laws and customs.

Cassander founded the city of Thessalonica in 316 BC. The city would become the principal port of the Macedonian kingdom.
Harlan J. Berk, Ltd.

Coin of Andriscus, who claimed to be the son of the last Macedonian king Perseus.
Harlan J. Berk, Ltd.

Thessalonica was granted free city status due to its loyalty to Mark Antony and Octavian, as commemorated on this coin.
Harlan J. Berk, Ltd.

Religion in Thessalonica

Thessalonica, as other cities of the empire, was full of idols. The epigramist Philip of Thessalonica recorded the names of twenty deities. He preserved for us a prayer to Artemis for the emperor: "Artemis ... dispatch this very day that hateful sickness away from the best of Emperors.... For Philip will offer the smoke of frankincense above your altars, and will make splendid sacrifice of a mountain-roaming boar" and to Apollo from a sailor: "Be gracious in return, and send upon the sails a favorable breeze running with us to the harbors of Actium."[1]

Antipater, another epigramist, preserved the prayer of a woman to Aphrodite: "Bithynian Cythera dedicated me, the marble image of your form, Cyprian goddess [Aphrodite], according to her vow. Do you make a large gift in return for a small one, as your custom is; a husband's loving heart is all she asks."[2] Another woman, blind and childless, offered hers to Artemis: "Both prayers were heard by Artemis, midwife in child-bearing and light-bringer of white-gleaming rays."[3]

When Octavian and Mark Antony later fought against each other, Thessalonica sided with Octavian, a wise and strategic move, since Octavian defeated Antony at the Battle of Actium in 31 BC. As in the past, Rome remembered Thessalonica and favored the city because of its loyalty.

Thessalonica prospered under Roman rule. Many Romans immigrated to the city, bringing their wealth with them. The city honored these Romans with public inscriptions that praised them for their benefactions. The city established a cult to honor the goddess Rome and the Roman benefactors and also constructed a temple of Caesar to honor Julius Caesar and his adopted son, Augustus. Thessalonica enjoyed great privileges and benefited immensely from the Roman presence and rule.

THE GOSPEL COMES TO THESSALONICA

During Paul's second missionary journey, he, Silas (Acts 17:4), and Timothy (see 16:1–3; 17:14–15; 1 Thess. 1:1; 2:7, 13) arrived in Thessalonica to preach the gospel. They had traveled down the Via Egnatia from Philippi, where Paul and Silas had been beaten and jailed without trial (Acts 16:16–40; 1 Thess. 2:2). Despite this suffering, these Christian messengers gathered courage to proclaim the gospel in Thessalonica, even in the face of great opposition.

Acts 17:1–9 records Paul's ministry in Thessalonica. He went into the Jewish synagogue where, during three Sabbath days, he used the Scriptures to persuade those gathered that the anticipated king of Israel, the Messiah, had to suffer and that Jesus was this Messiah (17:3; cf. 9:22; 18:5, 28). While some Jews believed, the larger response came from the "God-fearing Greeks" (17:4; see sidebar on "God-Fearers" in ch. 12). The apostles apparently undertook a wider evangelistic effort among the gentiles since most in the church had "turned to God from idols to serve the living and true God" (1 Thess. 1:9).

Poseidon, Aphrodite, Sarapis, Isis—Thessalonica, as most ancient cities, embraced religious pluralism. *Gene L. Green*

The Decrees of Caesar

Cassius Dio talks about "Caesar's decrees," which the Thessalonians invoke in Acts 17:7. Augustus decreed that "the seers were forbidden to prophesy to any person alone or to prophesy regarding death even if others should be present. Yet so far was Augustus from caring about such matters in his own case that he set forth to all in an edict the aspect of the stars at the time of his own birth. Nevertheless, he forbade this practice."[4]

The emperor Tiberius issued another decree: "But as for all the other astrologers and magicians and such as practiced divination in anyway whatsoever, he put to death those who were foreigners and banished all the citizens that were accused of still employing the art at this time after the previous decree [*dogma*] by which it had been forbidden to engage in any such business in the city."[5]

These remains of the central agora in Thessalonica are from the second century AD and later. Archaeologists have recently uncovered first-century structures.
Marco Verch/Flickr, CC BY 2.0

Since Paul's explanations and proofs persuaded so many God-fearers, including many prominent women (Acts 17:4), those of the synagogue who were not persuaded became jealous and managed to stir up a mob against Paul and Silas. The riot that ensued soon inflamed the whole populace.

The charges leveled against Paul and his companions before the city officials (Gk. *politarchas*; see 17:6, 8) were well calculated: "These men who have caused trouble all over the world have now come here" (v. 6). News about how the gospel had caused civic unrest in places like Philippi had reached Thessalonica (cf. 16:19–24). Rome did not tolerate civil disturbances, and even a free city like Thessalonica would be expected to deal severely and quickly with anyone accused of inciting them.

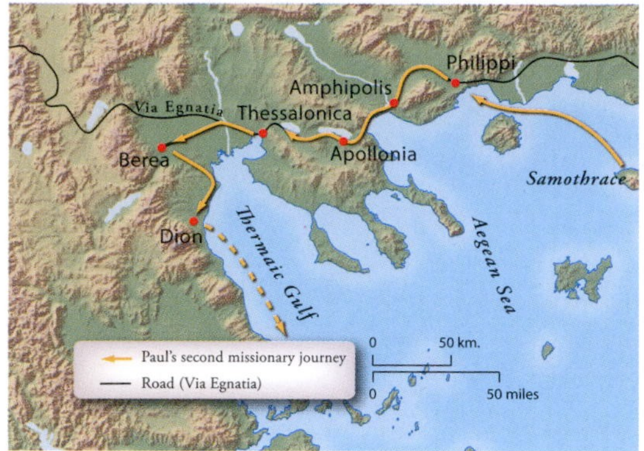

Note how Paul traveled off the Via Egnatia to arrive at Berea. He perhaps sailed for Athens from Dion.

The second part of the accusation was that Paul and Silas, along with those like Jason (their patron) were "defying Caesar's decrees, saying that there is another king, one called Jesus" (17:7). These imperial decrees, emitted during the reigns of Augustus and Tiberius, made it illegal to predict the death of any person, especially the emperor. The apostolic prediction of a coming king implied the passing of the current ruler.

Paul's proclamation of "another [coming] king" (see 1 Thess. 1:10; 4:16; 5:2–3; 2 Thess. 2:3–8) may have sounded like the promise of a renewed monarchy for the Macedonians. Upon hearing such accusations, the city officials knew they had to act because the city's privileged status with the Romans was at stake. Consequently, Paul and his companions fled the town under the cover of night (Acts 17:10).

Paul, Silas, and Timothy traveled to Berea, where they proclaimed the gospel. But after disturbances broke out there, the Berean believers sent Paul to the coast, and he sailed to Athens (Acts 17:10–15). Soon afterward Silas and Timothy joined Paul in Athens (cf. Acts 17:15; 1 Thess. 3:1) but then returned to Macedonia, leaving Paul on his own.

Paul repeatedly tried to return to Thessalonica but was hindered by circumstances that he attributes to satanic opposition (1 Thess. 2:17–18). He was deeply concerned about this church since they were recent converts, now on their own, who were suffering persecution because of their faith (1:6; 2:14; 3:3–4). They were also experiencing moral problems (4:1–8) and theological confusion (4:13–5:11). Paul's anxiety moved him to send Timothy back to Thessalonica to encourage the believers and to find out whether "in some way the tempter had tempted you and that our efforts might have been in vain" (3:5).

This inscription from the Vardar Gate in Thessalonica has the names of the city's politarchs. The politarchs are mentioned in Acts 17:6 and 8. The inscription reads: "The politarchs are Sosipatros, son of Kleopatra and Lukios Pontius Secundus; Aulos Auios Sabeinos; Demetrios, son of Phaustos; Demetrios son of Neikopolis; Zoilos, son of Parmenion and of Meniskos; Gaios Agilleos Poteitos; the treasurer is Tauros, son of Ammia and of Reglos (i.e. Regulus); the gymnasiarch is Tauros, son of Tauros and Reglos."
Todd Bolen/BiblePlaces.com

From Athens, Paul traveled to Corinth (Acts 18:1). The wait for Timothy's return from Thessalonica must have been agonizing. Paul saw himself as the Thessalonians' father in the faith (1 Thess. 2:11), and his care for them was as tender as a nursing mother's (2:7). Would they stand firm in the faith despite the suffering they were facing?

Outline of 1 Thessalonians

- I. The Epistolary Greeting (1:1)
- II. Opening Thanksgiving—The Coming of the Gospel and Its Reception (1:2–10)
- III. The Body of the Letter (2:1–5:22)
    1. The Gospel's Arrival in Thessalonica (2:1–3:13)
        - a. The Apostles' Entry to the City (2:1–12)
        - b. The Thessalonians' Reception of the Gospel (2:13–16)
        - c. The Apostles' Exit and Attempts to Return (2:17–20)
        - d. Timothy's Mission (3:1–5)
        - e. The Second Thanksgiving to God for the Thessalonians (3:6–10)
        - f. The Prayers to Return to Thessalonica (3:11–13)
    2. The Life That Pleases God (4:1–5:22)
        - a. Introduction: A Life Pleasing to God (4:1–2)
        - b. Sexual Sanctification (4:3–8)
        - c. Responses to the Thessalonians' Questions (4:9–5:11)
            - i. About Fraternal Love (4:9–12)
            - ii. About Those Who Died (4:13–18)
            - iii. About the Time of the Day of the Lord (5:1–11)
        - d. Leadership and Community (5:12–13)
        - e. Life in Community (5:14–15)
        - f. Communion with God (5:16–18)
        - g. Prophecy in the Community (5:19–22)
- IV. The Final Prayer, Greetings, and Blessing (5:23–28)

THE MESSAGE OF 1 THESSALONIANS

Paul wrote 1 Thessalonians promptly after Timothy's arrival in Corinth (1 Thess. 3:6; cf. Acts 18:5). Timothy brought "good news" of the church's faith, love, and steadfastness in hope, even amid their persecutions (1 Thess. 1:3; 3:6, 8). These believers were steadfast in faith despite the overwhelming conflict they endured. Hearing Timothy's report, Paul overflowed with thanks to God and joy over the Thessalonians (3:9; see also 1:3; 2:13) and offered earnest and constant prayers to God that he and his companions might return to the church to "supply what is lacking in your faith" (3:10).

Following ancient convention, Paul begins the letter with the names of the authors, followed by that of the recipients and then a salutation (1:1–2). He goes on to offer an extended thanksgiving for the Thessalonian believers (1:3–10). Paul commonly uses these thanksgivings to introduce the main topics of the correspondence, and 1 Thessalonians is no exception. He reminds the readers of how the gospel came to them (vv. 3–5) and of their reception (vv. 6–10; topics repeated in 2:1–2 and 2:13–16, respectively). Woven in here are notes about the character of the gospel messengers (1:5b), the sufferings endured (1:6), the mission of the church (1:8), and their eschatological hope (1:10).

Although Timothy delivered a good report about the steadfastness and Christian character of the Thessalonian believers, the news was not all good. Paul and his companions felt compelled to defend their personal character (2:1–12), most likely because of some accusation concerning why Paul had not returned. Paul responds that they were genuinely concerned for the well-being of the Thessalonians and did not preach with questionable motives. He reminds the church that he and his companions had entered the city to preach in spite of great opposition (vv. 1–2) and that their message, methods, and motives were pure (vv. 3–5). They did not come looking for honor or financial gain but genuinely cared for them as a nursing mother (vv. 6–9). Their character was blameless, and like a father, they encouraged the moral progress of the church (vv. 10–12).

Other scholars, however, contend that Paul's purposes in chapter 2 are didactic, not apologetic. Paul presents himself and his companions as moral examples for this congregation to follow. But 2:1–12 begins a large section (2:13–3:13) that records Paul's attempts to provide continuing pastoral care for this fledgling congregation. He did not neglect them or fail to show interest in them, for he made every effort to return and, when he was hindered from accomplishing this, sent Timothy in his stead (2:17–3:5). When Timothy finally returned from Thessalonica, Paul rejoiced over the Thessalonians' faith, love, and steadfastness and declared his longing and prayers to see the church again (3:6–13). While 2:1–12 appeals to what they know about the sincere motives of Paul and his companions, 2:13–3:13 tells the story of their continued care for the well-being of the church.

But there were other problems in the church. Paul delivers a stern warning to those Thessalonians who dismissed his commands about sexual morality (4:1–8). He advises them that "anyone who rejects this instruction does not reject a human being but God, the very God who gives you his Holy Spirit" (4:8).

The Thessalonian congregation apparently also has some questions for Paul, which they conveyed via Timothy (cf. 4:9). Their first concern was about *philadelphia* ("love among the members of this family" of believers, see 4:9–10).

Looking for Fame

Paul told the Thessalonians that he did not preach the gospel "looking for praise" (1 Thess. 2:6). He shunned the prestige or fame that so many rhetoricians and sophists sought in those days. Orators in ancient society were akin to today's rock music legends or Hollywood stars. Numerous ancient authors said their desire for money, honor, and fame were primary motivations.

Dio Chrysostom denounced those orators "who are lifted aloft as on wings by their fame and disciples," and singled out a certain sophist who was "being destroyed by popular opinion; for his liver swelled and grew whenever he was praised and shriveled again when he was censured."[6] Epictetus spoke out against such orators who persuaded young men to follow in their tracks: "And so it's for this, is it, that young men are to travel from home, and leave their parents, their friends, their relatives, and their bit of property, merely to cry 'Bravo!' as you recite your clever little mottoes?"[7] He painted a caricature of such men, who in effect say: "'But praise me.' What do you mean by 'praise'? 'Cry out to me, "Bravo!" or "Marvelous!"'"[8]

This was not Paul's style. He did not arrive in Thessalonica seeking glory or money.

In the very heart of the city at the agora (market), archaeologists have found the remains of a first-century circular bath next door to a brothel.
Todd Bolen/BiblePlaces.com

Perhaps the striking mix of people from different ethnic groups, social strata, and gender created tension in the social fabric of this new community. The second question concerned the destiny of the dead in Christ (4:13–18). Some in the church had died since Paul's departure, and the Thessalonians were grief-stricken since they did not fully understand the doctrine of the resurrection of believers. Paul responded that as Christ died and rose again, so the believers who died would be raised (4:13–16). This resurrection would occur at Christ's advent, or *parousia* (4:15).

The *Parousia* of Christ

Paul's description of Christ's *parousia* ("coming," 4:15) echoes accounts of the *parousia* of an emperor to a city, an occurrence that marked the beginning of new eras and was celebrated by the minting of coins and the erection of ceremonial structures. Usually a delegation of officials out of the city went out to meet the coming dignitary and then would accompany the person back to town. Josephus records the coming of Vespasian to Rome:

> And as this goodwill to Vespasian was universal, those that enjoyed any remarkable dignities could not have patience enough to stay in Rome, but hurried to meet him at a very great distance from it; nay, indeed, none of the rest could endure the delay of seeing him, but did all pour out of the city in such crowds, and were so universally possessed with the opinion that it was easier and better for them to go out than to stay there, that this was the very first time that the city joyfully perceived itself almost empty of its citizens; for those that stayed within were fewer than those that went out. But as soon as the news was come that he was close by, and those that had met him at first related with what good humor he received everyone that came to him, then it was that the whole multitude that had remained in the city, with their wives and children, came into the road, and waited for him there; and for those whom he passed by, they made all sorts of acclamations, on account of the joy they had to see him, and the pleasantness of his countenance, and styled him their benefactor and savior, and the only person who was worthy to be ruler of the city of Rome. And now the city was like a temple, full of garlands and sweet odors (Josephus, *War* 7.4.1 [68–72]).

Paul writes that both the resurrected and living believers will file out to meet the coming Ruler (1 Thess. 4:16–17), implying that they will return with him.

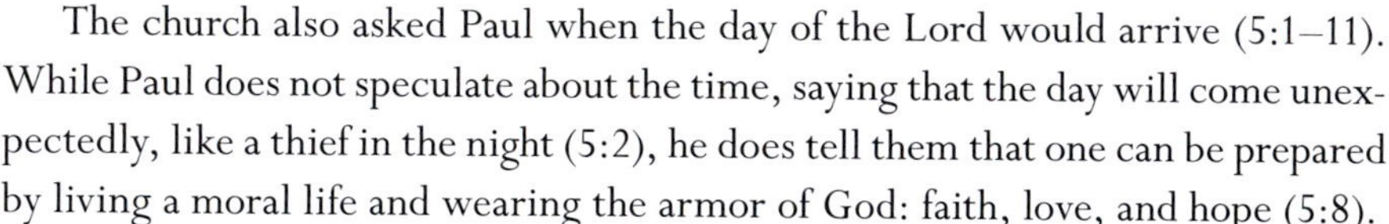

The church also asked Paul when the day of the Lord would arrive (5:1–11). While Paul does not speculate about the time, saying that the day will come unexpectedly, like a thief in the night (5:2), he does tell them that one can be prepared by living a moral life and wearing the armor of God: faith, love, and hope (5:8).

Timothy also informed Paul that the Thessalonian believers did not recognize and honor their new leaders (5:12–13). And some members of the church were not working (5:14; cf. 4:11–12). Paul classifies them as the "disruptive," since they refused to live by the community rule on this matter (see also 2 Thess. 3:6–15). After teaching the Thessalonians about good relationships with others, both inside and outside the church (5:14–15), and with God himself (5:16–18), Paul instructs them about receiving and evaluating prophetic messages (5:19–22). The letter closes with a final prayer for their sanctification (5:23–24), greetings, and a blessing (5:25–28).

Outline of 2 Thessalonians

I. The Epistolary Greeting (1:1–2)
II. The Thanksgiving and Prayers for the Thessalonians (1:3–12)

1. The First Thanksgiving for the Thessalonians (1:3–4)
2. The End of the Persecutors (1:5–10)
3. Prayers for the Thessalonians (1:11–12)

III. The Body of the Letter (2:1–3:15)

1. The Advent of the Day of the Lord (2:1–17)
   a. Do Not "Become Easily Unsettled": False Doctrine about the Day of the Lord (2:1–12)
   b. The Second Thanksgiving for the Thessalonians (2:13–14)
   c. The Exhortation to Stand Firm (2:15)
   d. The Second Prayer for the Church (2:16–17)
2. The Final Instructions (3:1–15)
   a. The Mutual Prayers (3:1–5)
   b. The Problem of Those Who Refuse to Work (3:6–15)

IV. The Final Prayer and Greetings (3:16–18)

THE MESSAGE OF 2 THESSALONIANS

Three topics taken up in 1 Thessalonians return in this letter: persecution, the day of the Lord, and work. Paul, however, does not address other issues, such as the character of the apostolic messengers or sexual immorality in the church. Probably the messenger who carried 1 Thessalonians to the church returned to Paul in Corinth with further news about the believers and their situation. After the epistolary greeting (2 Thess. 1:1–2), Paul offers his thanks to God for the church, as he did in the first letter (1:3–4). He underscores the Thessalonians' faith, love, and perseverance through persecution, which is the fruit of hope (cf. 1 Thess. 1:3; 3:6–8; 5:8). These characteristics mark the Thessalonians to such a degree that Paul can lift them up as an example to other churches.

Then Paul discusses the topic of persecution (2 Thess. 1:5–9). The Thessalonians' persecution (cf. 1 Thess. 1:6; 2:14; 3:2–4) has continued and intensified. Paul reminds them that they are suffering for the kingdom and that their persecutors will be judged by God. Second Thessalonians 1:5–10 graphically describes the cataclysmic nature of this divine retribution: The Lord Jesus will be "revealed from heaven in blazing fire with his powerful angels," and the Thessalonians' persecutors "will be punished with everlasting destruction." By contrast, relief is promised to these believers (1:7), and Paul reminds them that they will glorify the Lord at his return (1:10). Chapter 1 ends with a reminder of Paul's constant prayers that the name of the Lord be glorified among them and that they be glorified "in him" (1:11–12).

Second Thessalonians 2:1–12 is an interpretive jungle. The Thessalonians faced not only external persecution but also internal doctrinal confusion that threatened to destabilize them. A teaching was circulating among the believers that the final consummation, which included the return of Christ and the resurrection/rapture of the church (2:1–2), had "already come" (or, possibly, was "right at hand"). Paul does not know the source of this unsettling perspective—perhaps a "prophecy" (lit., "spirit"; cf. 1 John 4:1–3), a message or teaching, or a letter with Paul's name falsely inscribed on it.

In response, Paul assures the Thessalonians that two events will precede the day of the Lord (2:3). (1) "Rebellion" (*apostasia*) commonly referred to apostasy from the faith. A "rebellion" could be any movement against an established authority, either religious or political. Such an event is characteristic of the last times (1 Tim. 4:1)—a perspective also found in Jewish apocalyptic writings. (2) The "man of lawlessness" will be revealed. Paul no sooner mentions this figure than he highlights his final doom (2:3). In the ancient Mediterranean world, people attributed divine status to some rulers and honored them with both temple and cult. The imperial cult flourished in the eastern provinces of the Roman Empire. Even Thessalonica had a temple that honored the emperor as divine.[9]

Paul does not identify this "man of lawlessness" with any current or past emperor, but he does note that some (unidentified) power is "holding him back" (2:6–7). Is it the empire, the emperor, government, the law, the preaching of the gospel, Paul himself, God the Father, or the Holy Spirit (interpreters have suggested all of these)? We simply do not know, though Paul assumes the Thessalonians do know because of his initial instruction (2:5). In any case, 2:7 does not imply that the Holy Spirit will be taken out of the world, and with him the church, as some who propose a "pretribulation" rapture of the church argue. Some authors suggest that this power who "holds it back" should be understood as an agent who prefigures and anticipates the coming of the "man of lawlessness." Paul's main aim is to remind the church of these events and to assure them of Christ's final victory over all hostile powers (2:8–12), including this "man of lawlessness" and those he deceived.

After thanking God for the church (2:13–14), calling the Thessalonians to adhere to the teaching they have already received (2:15), and pronouncing a blessing on them (2:16–17), the apostle asks for prayers for his mission (3:1–2). He then underscores his settled assurance in the Lord's ability to take care of his own (3:3–5; cf. 1 Thess. 5:23).

The third major issue Paul addresses has to do with work (3:6–15), another matter he has previously instructed them about (3:10; cf. 1 Thess. 4:11–12), and offers himself as an example (2 Thess. 3:7–9). Despite his teachings and warnings, some have remained "disruptive," not heeding the apostolic instruction and refusing to work (3:11). Many argue that some Thessalonians are not working because of their expectations concerning the day of the Lord. If that day has come or is soon to come (2:2), why continue to work? Though Paul must correct the Thessalonians' understanding about eschatology, he does not make any connection between that issue and the problem of work.

Another reading of the situation is that some Thessalonians continue to act as dependent clients, relying on rich patrons in the city or the church for benefits such as money, food, and even public representation. Such personal patronage was a significant feature of economic life in the Roman Empire. Clients often arose early to appear at the house of their patron to give him or her a morning greeting. They would support their patrons in public assembly and at times would follow the patron through town. While Paul encourages benefaction toward those with genuine need (1 Thess. 4:9–10; 2 Thess. 3:13), he calls the believers to abandon their status as dependent clients and to work for their living. In 3:6–15 he calls the church to undertake disciplinary action toward those who are disorderly. Those who refuse to work should be noted, admonished, and shunned, though they should not be treated with hostility as if they were enemies. Note also that no patron in the church has any obligation to support them (3:11–15).

The Temple of Caesar in Thessalonica

A fragmentary inscription found in the city of Thessalonica commemorates the building of the imperial temple in Thessalonica. Note that the inscription mentions the chief city officials, the *politarchs* (cf. Acts 17:6, 8):

> . . . proconsul . . . of Latomia buil[t the] **tem[ple] of Caesar**. In the time of priest and agon[othete of **Im]perator Caesar Augustus son [of god]**. . .-oms son of Neikopol[eomms, priest] of the gods, Dom[. . . son of . . .]-pos, and (priest) of Roma a[nd Roman] benefactors, Neik[. . . son of] Paramonos. In the term of the **Politarchs** Diogenems son [of. . .] Kleomn son of P. . ., Zompas son of Kal. . ., Eulandros son of . . ., Promtogenems son of . . ., and the superinp[tendent] of the work, trea[surer of the city] Somsomnos s[on of . . .] [In the term of the] architec[t] Dionysiu[s son of . . .].[10]

Juvenal on How Clients Are Entertained

The Thessalonian believers who are not working are acting like any client of a socially superior patron. Juvenal, the Latin satirist who wrote near the end of the first century AD, penned his fifth satire about the meager rations and dishonorable treatment that clients sometimes received when invited to a banquet by their patron. See sidebar on "Juvenal and Persius on Patrons" in chapter 4 for a quote.

AUTHOR AND DATE

Paul wrote 1 Thessalonians from Corinth on his second missionary journey. The book opens with the names of Silas and Timothy, the cofounders of the church along with Paul (1 Thess. 1:1). The letter has many verbs in the first person plural ("we"), which may indicate that Silas and Timothy had a significant role in the letter's composition. Paul only occasionally steps out of the group to express his particular concerns (2:18; 3:5; 5:27). Joint composition of letters was a known practice in the ancient world. For example, in Cicero's letter *Ad Atticum* he says, "For my part I have gathered from your letters—both that which you wrote in conjunction with others and the one you wrote in your own name" (11.5.1). Paul, however, had the major hand in writing this letter (cf. 5:27).

Early external evidence that supports the authenticity of 1 Thessalonians is firm, though not extensive. Eusebius regarded 1 Thessalonians as a genuine Pauline letter. References to the book appear early in such writings as the second-century *Didache*, the *Letters of Ignatius* (d. 135), and the *Shepherd of Hermas*. Tertullian comments that even the heretic Marcion considered the book to be genuine, and Tertullian concurs. In the second half of the second century, the Muratorian Canon and Irenaeus regarded it as an authentic work by Paul. Currently, scholars universally regard this epistle as authentic.

Second Thessalonians is another matter. This letter enjoyed the same solid support in the early church. In the second century, Ignatius and Justin Martyr make use of it, while Polycarp and Irenaeus attribute it to Paul, as do Clement of Alexandria and Tertullian in the third century. The Muratorian Canon also classifies this letter as authentic.

But in the nineteenth century, some scholars raised questions. One argument was that the style is so strikingly similar to that of 1 Thessalonians that it must have been written by someone imitating Paul (though this phenomenon can also be used to argue in favor of Pauline authorship). A second argument against Paul's authorship is that 2 Thessalonians addresses a more general situation. However, the specific situation of the church is clearly defined in all three chapters (the persecutions, the questions about the day of the Lord, and the problem of work).

Finally, some say this letter reflects "post-Pauline" theology. For example, the eschatology of the letter is not linked with joy. Also, there appears to be a tension between 1 Thessalonians 5:1–11, which speaks of an unexpected end, and 2 Thessalonians 2:1–12, which outlines the events that will precede the day of the Lord. And the author speaks about the "teachings" handed down to the Thessalonians (2:15), a marker that appears to class this book with the post-Paulines. But the severity of the suffering the church is facing generates the serious tone of the eschatological teaching in chapter 1. The tensions between an imminent end and signs that precede the end appear in Jewish eschatology and even in Jesus's teachings (Mark 13). And the mention of the "teachings" is commonplace in Paul's writings (e.g., 1 Thess. 2:13; 4:1–2; cf. 1 Cor. 15:1–8). Most scholars today affirm its Pauline authorship.

The recipients of the book are believers in Thessalonica, organized into a "church" (*ekklēsia*; 1 Thess. 1:1). The majority are gentiles who have "turned . . . from idols" (1:9), with some Jewish believers (Acts 17:4). Most are of the artisan class, who worked with their hands to make a living (1 Thess. 4:11).

Since the occasion of the letter is Timothy's return from the Thessalonian church (1 Thess. 3:6), the date of composition can be set during Paul's visit to Corinth when Timothy, along with Silas, arrived from Macedonia (Acts 18:5). Paul spent a year and half in that city, during which time Gallio was named as

The Gallio inscription from Delphi dates the term when L. Iunius Gallio served as proconsul of the province of Achaia. During this time, Paul was in Corinth, where he penned the Thessalonian correspondence. The inscription helps us date Paul's sojourn in Corinth and the date of his letters to the Thessalonians. The inscription reads: "Tiberius Claudius Caesar Augustus Germanicus, 12th year of tribunician power, acclaimed emperor for the 26th time, father of the country, sends greetings to [________]. For long I have been well-disposed to the city of Delphi and solicitous for its prosperity, and I have always observed the cult of the Pythian Apollo. Now since it is said to be destitute of citizens, as my friend and proconsul L. Iunius Gallio recently reported to me..."[11]
www.HolyLandPhotos.org

the proconsul of the Roman province of Achaia (18:11–12). An inscription from Delphi indicates that Gallio was named to this post in AD 51, which gives us the approximate date for 1 Thessalonians.

First Thessalonians is one of the earliest epistles of the apostle Paul, second only perhaps to Galatians, which Paul wrote at the end of the first missionary journey (see ch. 14). The apostle wrote 2 Thessalonians not long after the first letter, during his eighteen-month stay in Corinth. Some of the same themes appear in both letters, such as the persecutions, questions about the end, and the problem of the "disruptive" who refused to work.

Some scholars, however, argue that the canonical order of the books derives from the fact that 1 Thessalonians is longer and has nothing to do with which one was written first. A few modern authors have argued that some evidence points to 2 Thessalonians as being the first letter. But note how 2 Thessalonians 2:15 looks back to a previous letter written to the church: "Stand firm and hold fast to the teachings *we passed on to you*, whether by word of mouth or *by letter*" (emphasis added)—most likely 1 Thessalonians.

Questions for Discussion

1. Isolate Paul's teaching on suffering in 1 and 2 Thessalonians. How does the apostle construct a "theology of suffering" for these persecuted believers? Why are these believers able to stand firm in their faith in the face of severe opposition?
2. How does Paul use the teaching about the last things to help the Thessalonian believers? Are his concerns speculative or pastoral and moral?
3. Describe the character of good Christian leadership according to these letters. How does Paul's leadership ethic compare with that of contemporary Christian leaders?
4. What importance does Paul place on sexual ethics? How does he underscore the importance of sexual purity?

BIBLIOGRAPHY

Introductory

Fee, G. D. *The First and Second Letters to the Thessalonians*. NICNT. Grand Rapids: Eerdmans, 2009.
Green, G. L. *1 and 2 Thessalonians*. PNTC. Grand Rapids: Eerdmans, 2002.
Gupta, N. *1–2 Thessalonians*. NCCS. Eugene, OR: Cascade, 2016.
Holmes, M. W. *1 and 2 Thessalonians*. NIVAC. Grand Rapids: Zondervan, 1998.
Marshall, I. H. *1 and 2 Thessalonians*. NCB. Grand Rapids: Eerdmans, 1983.

Advanced

Bruce, F. F. *1 and 2 Thessalonians*. WBC. Waco, TX: Word, 1982.
Malherbe, A. *1 Thessalonians*. AB. Garden City, NY: Doubleday, 2001.
Shogren, G. S. *1 & 2 Thessalonians*. ZECNT. Grand Rapids: Zondervan, 2012.
Weima, J. A. D. *1–2 Thessalonians*. BECNT. Grand Rapids: Baker, 2014.

NOTES

1. A. S. F. Gow and D. L. Page, *The Greek Anthology* (Cambridge: Cambridge University Press, 1965), 1:303.
2. Ibid., 1:19.
3. Ibid., 1:79.
4. Cassius Dio, *Hist*. 56.25.5–6, as quoted in E. A. Judge, "The Decrees of Caesar at Thessalonica," *RTR* 30 (1971): 3. See also a similar decree from Tiberius, p. 4.
5. Cassius Dio, *Hist*. 57.15.8, as quoted in ibid., 4.
6. Dio Chrysostom 12.5; 8.33; cf. 12.5; 32.11; 77/78.27; Plutarch, *Moralia* 78A; 131A.
7. Epictetus 3.23.32.
8. Epictetus 3.23.23–24. On this theme, see especially B. W. Winter, "Entries and Ethics of the Orators and Paul (1 Thessalonians 2:11–12)," *TynBul* 44 (1993): 61–63; A. J. Malherbe, "'Gentle as a Nurse': The Cynic Background to 1 Thess ii," *NovT* 12 (1970): 214.
9. See H. L. Hendrix, "Thessalonicans Honor Romans" (ThD diss., Harvard University, 1984), 107–8.
10. Cited in ibid., 107–8.
11. J. Murphy-O'Connor, *St. Paul's Corinth* (Collegeville, MN: Liturgical, 1990), 161.

Chapter 16

1 CORINTHIANS

The *diolkos* served as a dry canal to pull ships over land between the Saronic Gulf and the Gulf of Corinth.
www.HolyLandPhotos.org

The Corinthian congregation was embroiled in a variety of problems since the demands of their newly acquired faith and the cultural values surrounding them often pulled the members in opposite directions. Divisions were a hallmark of this church. It was broken into disputing factions that hailed one minister of the gospel over another, as if each preacher were nothing more than a leader of a philosophical school. Members took each other to court, and some used their Christian liberty in ways harmful to others in the congregation. Socioeconomic differences separated members at the Lord's Table. The church polarized over the gifts of the Spirit, with some members acting as if they were superior. Furthermore, many in the church engaged in immoral sexual practices, including visiting prostitutes. The Corinthian church also had doctrinal issues. Certain believers denied a future resurrection of the dead, a perspective Paul viewed as a tacit denial of the resurrection of Christ.

This letter is an impassioned attempt to correct these problems as well as to respond to inquiries about aspects of Christian faith and practice. Although written to a group of Christians whose social world was distinctly different from ours, its message is a powerful one for the church today. Our problems are, in many ways, not so distant from theirs. We too must find our way between apostolic teaching and values of contemporary culture that sometimes oppose the Christian faith.

THE SETTING OF 1 CORINTHIANS

The City of Corinth

Corinth was the capital of Achaia and was strategically located. It stood on an isthmus between mainland Greece and the Peloponnese; thus, it controlled all north-south travel and trade. But more important, Corinth was a strategic hub for one of the east-west routes in the empire. Ships sailing from Italy docked at Lechaeum, Corinth's port on the Gulf of Corinth. Those sailing from Asia arrived at Cenchreae, on the Saronic Gulf (see Acts 18:18–19; Rom. 16:1). Seafarers preferred to avoid sailing around the Peloponnese on these east-west journeys because this route added six days to the trip and the waters around the Maleae peninsula on the southern part of the Peloponnese were treacherous. Strabo recalls the ancient dictum, "But when you double Maleae forget your home" (*Geography* 8.6.20–23).

To facilitate east-west trade, a dry canal, called the *diolkos*, was constructed in the sixth century BC and continued in use up through the ninth century AD. Sometimes goods were carried across the isthmus on a stone track. At other times ships were hoisted on wheeled wagons and rolled to the other side. Corinth controlled all this trade and grew rich as a result. The city played host to travelers from across the Mediterranean world. This rich cosmopolitan center built its economy on the many people who came through her gates. Into this bustling city, Paul came to preach the gospel.

The Roman provinces of Macedonia, Achaia, and Illyricum

Corinth and the surrounding *territorium*

The temple of Apollo in Corinth is one of the structures from classical Corinth that survived until Roman times.
© 2012 by Zondervan

The Babbius monument reads, "Gnaeus Babbius Philinus, aedile and pontifex, had this monument erected at his own expense, and he approved it in his official capacity as duovir."[1] This former slave not only served as city manager (*aedile*) and priest (*pontifex*) but became one of the two principal governing officials of Corinth (*duovir*).
www.HolyLandPhotos.org

The Coming of the Romans

During the third century BC, Corinth was a Greek city-state in alliance with other cities of Achaia to form the Achaean League. Rome's eastward expansion ended in a military showdown with Corinth in 146 BC. Mummius descended on Corinth with 32,000 Roman infantry and 3,500 cavalry. He captured the city, ordered the men to be killed, and handed the women and children over to slavery. He sent Corinth's wealth to Rome and destroyed its walls and buildings. The Romans left Corinth practically deserted for a hundred years.

The Roman Destruction of Corinth (146 BC)

Ancient authors who describe the defeat of Corinth tell a tale of brutality and pain. Pausanius graphically paints this picture:

> As soon as night fell, the Acheans who had escaped to Corinth after the battle fled from the city, and there fled with them most of the Corinthians themselves. At first Mummius hesitated to enter Corinth, although the gates were open, as he suspected that an ambush had been laid within the walls. But on the third day after the battle he proceeded to storm Corinth and set it on fire. The majority of those found in it were put to the sword by the Romans, but the women and children Mummius sold into slavery (*Description of Greece* 7.16.7–8).

Antipater of Thessalonica composed an epigram which pulses with the terror and pathos of that moment:

> I, Rhodope, and my mother Boisca, neither died of sickness,
> nor fell by the enemy's sword.
> But we ourselves, when fierce Ares burnt the city of Corinth,
> our fatherland, chose a brave death.
> My mother slew me with the slaughtering knife,
> nor did she, sorrowful woman, spare her own life,
> But tied the noose around her own neck, for to die in
> freedom was better than slavery.[2]

Roman Corinth

Shortly before his assassination in 44 BC, Julius Caesar ordered the recolonization of Corinth, naming it *Colonia Laus Iulia Corinthiensis*. The colonists were mostly freedmen, plebeians (common Roman citizens), and Roman legionary veterans. Rome secured the deep loyalty of these colonists by granting them land allotments (six to seven acres per colonist) and placing them in an environment that had lost none of its strategic advantage, which meant prosperity for many of them. But such success was the exception rather than the rule.

Rebuilt Corinth was a strategic boon for Rome since it gave her a point from which to expand her influence east and to facilitate trade. It became the largest city of Roman Greece, with a population at around eighty thousand in the city and another twenty thousand in the surrounding countryside. Although located on Greek soil, the new colony was a thoroughly Latin city, with mostly Latin inscriptions. The main exceptions were those related to the Isthmian games, since those who participated in this biannual event came from the Greek-speaking world. The city's architecture was Italian, and the images of the emperor portrayed him in Roman dress.

Although Corinth was located on Greek soil, first-century Corinth was a Roman colony, as evidenced by the predominance of Latin inscriptions in the city.
© 2012 by Zondervan

The Isthmian Games were supervised by Corinth. Shown here are the remains of an ancient starting line used in the Isthmian Stadium. Paul refers to the games in 1 Corinthians 9:24–27.
Heritage Image Partnership Ltd/ Alamy Stock Photo

This relief found at Isthmia commemorates the prizes won by an athlete at various games, including the Isthmian games.
The Metropolitan Museum of Art, Public Domain

But why were Paul's Corinthian letters (and Romans, for that matter) written in Greek and not Latin? Corinth began to experience a gradual increase in the presence of Greeks in the city. These were not citizens but *incolae* (foreign residents without full civic rights) and not, therefore, part of the social elite. By the second century, Favorinus wrote that Corinth, "though Roman, has become thoroughly Hellenized" (Philostratus, *Lives* 37.25–37). The fact that the letter was written in Greek may reflect the Christian reality—the gospel made the greatest inroads among those of the lower classes who spoke Greek (see 1 Cor. 1:26).

Corinth was the seat of the Roman proconsul. L. Iunius Gallio, brother of the great philosopher Seneca, was the proconsul during part of Paul's eighteen-month stay in the city (Acts 18:12). Gallio assumed the post on July 1, AD 51, but left early. Seneca commented on his untimely departure: "When, in Achaia, he began to feel feverish, he immediately took ship, claiming that it was a malady of the place" (*Letters* 104.2). Acts 18:12–17 underscores Gallio's judicial power as Paul stood before him at the *bēma* (Gk.), or *rostra* (Latin), a speaker's platform erected during the Augustan period.

The city itself had two chief magistrates (*duoviri*) elected each year by the assembly of citizens. It also had a senate. The business managers of the city (*aediles*) were also elected annually. They took care of public works (buildings, streets, market supervision) and managed the city's income. An inscription found near the theater names one of these officials: "Erastus in return for his aedileship laid (the pavement)

Paul appeared before the proconsul Gallio at the *bēma* (Latin *rostra*) located in the Corinthian agora. This elevated platform served as a place to give public speeches and hold legal tribunals.
Todd Bolen/BiblePlaces.com

Crinagoras on Corinth

Not long after Julis Caesar refounded the city in 44 BC, the poet Crinagoras lamented the low level of society that characterized the city from the start: "What inhabitants, O luckless city, have you received, and in place of whom? Alas for the great calamity to Greece! Would, Corinth, that you be lower than the ground and more desert than the Libyan sands, rather than wholly abandoned to such a crowd of scoundrelly slaves, you should vex the bones of the ancient Bacchiadae."[4] The Bacchiadae were the ancient aristocratic rulers of classical Corinth. The social composition of the Roman city was quite different from its glorious past.

at his own expense" (in Latin: *ERASTVS PRO AEDILIT[at]E S(ua) P(ecunia) STRAVIT*). Since the inscription dates from around AD 50, Erastus may be the "city treasurer" (*oikonomos*) mentioned in Romans 16:23 (Romans was written from Corinth).

Strabo once noted that "Corinth is called 'wealthy' because of its commerce, since it is situated on the Isthmus and is master of two harbors, of which the one leads straight to Asia, and the other to Italy" (*Geography* 8.6.20a). A number of the rich, such as Erastus, embraced the gospel (Rom. 16:23; 2 Tim. 4:20), and those with households large enough to accommodate the believers opened their homes for the church's common meal (1 Cor. 11:17–18). A significant group of believers in the church enjoyed high socioeconomic status.[3]

But not everyone had access to such wealth. Paul comments that this church was filled with those who had neither economic power nor social status (1 Cor. 1:26). When the whole church gathered to eat the Lord's Supper, some went hungry (11:21). And the believers' different responses to the eating of idol meat may have been due to the economic disparity between the rich, accustomed to eating meat regularly, and the poor, who consumed meat only on special occasions. The second century AD orator Alcifrón commented on the stark economic disparity he witnessed in the city: "No more did I enter Corinth than I realized that shamelessness of the rich there and the disgrace of its poor" (*Letters of Parasites* 24 [3.60]).

As the *aedile* of Corinth, Erastus would have been responsible for the care of the city, including paving streets. The inscription honors him as one who personally paid for the street by the theater. The person honored in the inscription may be the same Erastus named in Romans 16:23.
www.HolyLandPhotos.org

THE GOSPEL COMES TO CORINTH

Paul evangelized Corinth during his second missionary journey (Acts 18:1–18). He arrived there distressed (18:9–10; 1 Cor. 2:3), especially after the ill-treatment he suffered in Macedonia and the dishonoring ridicule he endured in Athens. Silas and Timothy joined him after their return from Macedonia, arriving with an offering from the Macedonian churches for his support (Acts 18:5; 2 Cor. 11:7–9). Aquila and Priscilla also joined him (Acts 18:2–3; see 1 Cor. 16:19). Paul spent eighteen months in Corinth (Acts 18:11) and wrote the Thessalonian letters during this period.

After Paul left Corinth, Apollos came to the city and the Corinthian church received him warmly (Acts 18:27–19:1). Apollos was an eloquent Alexandrian Jew trained in rhetoric (18:24–25), whose oratorical skills were notably stronger than Paul's (1 Cor. 2:4; 2 Cor. 10:10). His presence in Corinth accounts for his prominence in the minds of some Corinthians (1 Cor. 3:4–6).

After leaving the city, Paul wrote his first letter to the Corinthian church, a document that has not survived but which Paul references in Acts 5:9–11. Around AD 55, while Paul was in Ephesus on his third missionary journey (Acts 19; 1 Cor. 16:8, 19), "some from Chloe's household" in Corinth arrived with news about the congregation (1 Cor. 1:11–12). These were likely Chloe's slaves or business associates who had become believers. A more official delegation visited Paul (16:15–18), who presumably brought a letter from the church asking him various questions (7:1; cf. 7:25; 8:1; 12:1; 16:1, 12). Paul wrote what we now call 1 Corinthians in response to the report from Chloe's people and to answer these questions.

Around the same time, Paul sent Timothy to Corinth (4:17; 16:10–11). Paul had previously dispatched Timothy to Thessalonica to aid the church there (1 Thess. 3:1–5; Timothy's later missions are noted in Phil. 2:19–22; 1 Tim. 1:3). Paul seems to expect that his letter will arrive before Timothy.

THE MESSAGE OF 1 CORINTHIANS

Scholars have evaluated the Corinthians' problems in Corinth in various ways. Some have attempted to find "a common source"[5] to all the issues, variously identified as Gnosticism, Hellenistic-Jewish wisdom speculation, factionalism, a conflict with Paul, or dualistic thought coupled with an over-realized eschatology. Others adopt a more eclectic reading of the evidence, looking at the Corinthian situation as a patchwork of issues. Witherington, for example, identifies five basic problems in this church: partisan attachments to Christian leaders, continued adherence to cultural values, pride and insult in using spiritual gifts, sexual issues, and disagreement over eschatology, including the resurrection and the believer's present reign.[6] He and others argue that we should identify the variety of cultural, philosophical, and religious influences that impinged on this church located at one of the major crossroads of the Roman empire.

Outline of 1 Corinthians

- I. Opening Greeting and Thanksgiving (1:1–9)
- II. Paul's Response to Reports about the Corinthian Church (1:10–6:20)
  - 1. Division Over Leadership and Wisdom (1:10–4:21)
  - 2. Immorality in the Community (5:1–6:20)
    - a. Incest and Church Discipline (5:1–13)
    - b. Lawsuits among Believers (6:1–11)
    - c. Prostitution (6:12–20)
- III. Paul's Response to the Corinthians' Letter (7:1–16:12)
  - 1. Concerning Marriage (7:1–40)
    - a. About Marriage and Divorce (7:1–16)
    - b. General Principle: Remain as You Were When Called (7:17–24)
    - c. About Betrothal (7:25–40)
  - 2. Concerning Food Sacrificed to Idols (8:1–11:1)
    - a. Conduct Governed by Knowledge or Love (8:1–13)
    - b. Having but Not Using Freedom (9:1–27)
    - c. Eating in Temples and Homes (10:1–11:1)
  - 3. Concerning Worship (11:2–14:40)
    - a. Gender Roles and Head Coverings (11:2–16)
    - b. The Lord's Supper (11:17–34)
    - c. Spiritual Gifts (12:1–14:40)
      - i. Unity and Diversity of the Gifts (12:1–30)
      - ii. The Way of Love (12:31–13:13)
      - iii. The Use of Tongues, Prophecy, and Other Gifts (14:1–40)
  - 4. The Resurrection of the Dead (15:1–58)
  - 5. Concerning the Collection, Travel Plans, and Apollos's Visit (16:1–12)
- IV. Final Exhortation, Blessing, and Greetings (16:13–24)

Division in the Church

After opening greetings (1:1–3) and thanksgiving (1:4–9), Paul addresses the problem of divisions in the church (1:10–4:21). Paul has been informed of factionalism that has arisen among the members of the church as they align themselves behind various Christian leaders: "One of you says, 'I follow Paul'; another, 'I follow Apollos'; another, 'I follow Cephas'; still another, 'I follow Christ'" (1:12; see 3:4). Paul was the founder of the church, Apollos was an eloquent Alexandrian

Jew who ministered there (Acts 18:24–28), and Cephas is the Aramaic name of Peter (John 1:42), who apparently traveled through Corinth (1 Cor. 9:5). There was either a final "Christ group" or Paul himself interjects his correction to their factionalism—he simply belongs to Christ.

Paul is not quoting the Corinthians' exact words, as though they are making such childish claims, but rather employs the rhetorical technique called "impersonation," displaying an adversary's thoughts as if they were expressing them. Borrowing language that was often employed to encourage political concord and peace, Paul exhorts the Corinthians authoritatively in the name of the Lord Jesus Christ "that all of you agree with one another in what you say and that there be no divisions among you, but that you be perfectly united in mind and thought" (1:10).

Popular Orators in the Streets of Corinth

Dio Chrysostom describes the acclaim he received when he entered a city: "I am escorted with much enthusiasm and respect, the recipients of my visits being grateful for my presence and begging me to address them and advise them and flocking around my door from early dawn ... all without my having incurred any expense" (*Discourses* 47.22).

Commenting on the days of Diogenes of Corinth, Dio (8.9) notes how well-known this city was for such displays in support of this or that orator: "That was the time, too, when one could hear crowds of wretched Sophists around Poseidon's temple shouting and reviling one another, their disciples, as they were called, fighting with one another, many writers reading aloud their stupid works, many poets reciting their poems while others applauded them ... and peddlers not a few peddling whatever they happened to have."

Philostratus notes how the students of one sophist became so angry with another orator that they had their slaves beat the other orator to death (*Lives of the Sophists* 588).

Foolishness to the Gentiles

Why is the message of the cross foolishness to the gentiles (1:23)? Crucifixion was principally reserved for slaves and dangerous criminals (see sidebar on "A View of the Cross" in ch. 13). Cicero underscores the shame of crucifixion:

> How grievous a thing it is to be disgraced by a public court ... to suffer a fine ... to suffer banishment; and yet in the midst of any such disaster we retain some degree of liberty.... But the executioner, the veiling of the head and the very word "cross" should be far removed not only from the person of a Roman citizen but his thoughts, his eyes and his ears. For it is not only the actual occurrence of these things but the very mention of them that is unworthy of a Roman citizen (*Pro Rabirio Perduellionis Reo* 5.16).

The message that the crucified Jew, Jesus, was the Savior of humanity sounded foolish indeed.

From there he launches a discussion about wisdom and the message of the cross (1:18ff.). Traveling experts in rhetoric, known as sophists, were well-known in Corinth. Orators drew crowds and attracted students by their rhetorical expertise. Philo of Alexandria notes that sophists were "winning the admiration of city after city, and . . . drawing well-nigh the whole world to honor them" (*On Agriculture* 143). Some Corinthian believers view the Christian messengers as nothing more than sophists who came to town and, accordingly, divided into rival schools around each one. Paul, for his part, distances himself from the rhetorical finery of the sophists (2:1–5). The Corinthians, however, are concerned about form over content.

Paul knows that the heart of the problem is a fundamental misunderstanding of the gospel. The message of the cross is not simply another brand of philosophical "wisdom" (1:18–25; 2:4–5), but a demonstration of God's power and wisdom (1:22–25). And to emphasize rhetorical form and eloquence empties the cross of its power (1:17). In Paul's view, the power to persuade rests in God (2:4–12). So while the world views God's means of salvation, the cross, as foolishness and weakness (1:18, 23), those who believe this "foolishness" of the cross are saved (1:21). This "foolishness" of God is wiser than human wisdom, and his supposed "weakness" is stronger than any human accomplishments (1:25). By contrast, human wisdom cannot lead a person to know God (1:21).

Paul also counters the Corinthians' factionalism by underscoring the true position of Christian ministers. They are not sophists who need honor and praise, but rather "servants" (3:5) and "co-workers" under God (3:9). One plants, another waters, but God causes the growth (3:6–7). Thus, the church does not belong to any minister but to God (3:9). For this reason, the Corinthians should not exalt one minister over another (3:5; 4:6).

Immorality in the Community

Chapter 5 deals with incest in the church. A man has entered an illicit sexual relationship with his stepmother, possibly marrying her after his father died (5:1). Perhaps this is a wealthy family who could lose the inheritance of the deceased husband were she to marry into another family. Both the Old Testament (Lev. 18:7–8; 20:11; Deut. 22.30; 27:20; Ezek. 22:10–11) and Roman custom prohibited this kind of relationship. *The Institutes of Gaius* 1.63 says, "Neither can I marry her who has aforetime been my mother-in-law or step-mother." Cicero commented: "The mother-in-law marries the son-in-law, no one looking favorably on the deed, no one approving it, all foreboding a dismal end to it. Oh, the incredible wickedness of the woman . . . unheard of since the world began! Oh, the unbridled and unrestrained lust! Oh, the extraordinary audacity of her conduct!" (*Pro Cluentio* 5.14–6.15. Surprisingly, Cicero does not mention the man's role in this union.)

Yet the Corinthians are boasting about this union and take no disciplinary action (5:2), perhaps since this individual is a member of the social elite.

Paul addresses the man's sin (his stepmother does not appear to be a church member) and exhorts the church to excommunicate him (5:3–5; cf. Matt. 18:15–20), although he holds out hope for the person's redemption. While the Corinthians tolerate such sin in their midst, they paradoxically disassociate themselves from unbelievers, having misinterpreted Paul's earlier teaching about church discipline (5:9–13). The church must be pure and should take action to maintain its purity, but this does not mean they should distance themselves from people in the surrounding culture.

Moreover, some Corinthian believers are taking each other to court (6:1–11). Paul discourages believers from trying their legal cases before "the unrighteous" (6:1 NRSV). Roman courts were often corrupt, and the way legal proceedings were conducted would hardly promote *concordia* ("harmonious agreement") among the Corinthians. Paul encourages arbitration in the church to settle disputes (6:5) and, in the end, states that suffering wrong is better than doing wrong (6:7–8; cf. Matt. 5:38–42; Rom. 12:17, 19; 1 Pet. 2:23; 3:9).

In 6:12–20 he returns to the problem of sexual immorality, addressing the practice of consorting with prostitutes. Jews normally did not visit prostitutes, but the Greeks and Romans considered prostitution acceptable, and it became a "Main Street" affair. Prostitutes registered with a city magistrate (the *aedile*), and moralists like Cicero and Cato condoned it as a safeguard against adultery (see sidebar).

The Corinthians argued that sex was a natural function of the body. As the body needed food, so the body needed sex (6:13). But Paul insists that such behavior cannot be allowed in the church. How can someone take the members of Christ and join them to a prostitute? As in 1 Thessalonians 4:3–8, he calls believers to a life of sexual purity. Their bodies are not their own but have been redeemed at the price of Christ's death and become the temple of God's Spirit. The body has a role in God's plan since he

Going to Court in the Roman World

Only those with superior social status could prosecute, so "justice for all" was not a cornerstone of the Roman legal system. Cases would only be brought against social equals or inferiors, so we may assume that the believers instigating legal proceedings are part of the social elite. Judges and juries were easily influenced by bribes. Verdicts would go to the highest bidder. By the second century AD, Apuleius critiqued the courts, saying, "Nowadays all juries sell their judgements for money" (*The Golden Ass* 10.33). Not long after Paul was in Corinth, Dio Chrysostom commented on the "lawyers innumerable perverting justice" (*Discourses* 37.16–17). People used the courts to avenge themselves against their enemies.

Prostitution in the Ancient World

The Roman Cato praised a young man who came out of a brothel since going to such a place would keep him away from other men's wives. But when he saw the young man repeatedly going to the brothel, he said, "I praised you, since I assumed you came here now and again, not that you lived here!" (Horace, *Satires* 1.2.32).

While Strabo notes that the temple of Aphrodite in Corinth owned more than a thousand temple prostitutes (*Geography* 8.6.20), this remark refers to classical Corinth. There is no evidence that this practice continued into the Roman period. But there was prostitution in Corinth, as in most cities of the empire.

will raise it up as Christ was raised from the dead. So our bodies are for the Lord, and we must honor God with them (1 Cor. 6:13–20).

Corinthian Questions—Marriage

In chapter 7 Paul begins to answer the questions the Corinthians have written to him (7:1). He begins with sexuality, marriage, divorce, the single life, widows, and "virgins." In light of Paul's Jewish heritage, that he prescribes the single life is shocking (7:7); Jews viewed marriage positively (cf. Gen. 2:18–25). Sometime after Paul, the Talmud records the words of Rabbi Johanan: "He who is twenty years old and not married spends all of his days in sin" (*b. Kidd.* 29b).

Paul's concerns are not simply about marriage but on sexual relationships within marriage (7:1–7). Some of the Corinthians, although married, were arguing for celibacy. Paul states that while there may be cause for abstention, this should be by mutual consent, only for a season, and for only one reason: prayer. Marital relationships should resume so that Satan does not take advantage of a lack of self-control.

The Stoics and Cynics on Marriage

During the first century, a debate raged between the philosophical schools of the Stoics and the Cynics about marriage. Marriage brings great responsibilities, so should one enter into such a union? Stoics stated that the divine principle governed the universe and one must live in harmony with it; this included marriage. Cynics understood marriage simply as a social convention. They longed for freedom to pursue philosophy, unencumbered by the concerns of this life, including marriage.

Jewish Reflections on Marital Relations

Paul is not the only Jewish author to comment on the frequency of sexual relations in marriage and offer reasons for abstention (1 Cor. 7:5). The Mishnah reflects early debates on this issue:

> He who takes a vow not to have sexual relations with his wife—the House of Shammai say: [He may allow this situation to continue] two weeks. And the House of Hillel say: For one week. Disciples go forth for Torah study without [the wife's] consent for thirty days. Workers go out for one week. The sexual duty of which the Torah speaks [Ex. 21:10]: (1) those without work [of independent means]—every day; (2) workers—twice a week; (3) ass-drivers—once a week; (4) camel drivers—once in thirty days; (5) sailors—once in six months. The words of R. Eliezer (*m. Ketub.* 5:6).

The *Testament of Naphtali* 8.8 likewise affirmed, "There is a time for having intercourse with one's wife, and a time to abstain for the purpose of prayer." Paul's advice in 1 Corinthians 7:5 seems to have been commonplace.

Paul echoes Jesus's teaching about divorce in 7:10–16 (see Matt. 5:31–32; 19:3–12) but adds that a believer should not separate from an unbelieving spouse simply because they do not share the faith (cf. 1 Pet. 3:1–6). Nor should a believer's new existence be used as an excuse to change one's social status (7:17–24). Paul concludes his teaching on marriage with a curious section on "virgins"—likely women betrothed but not yet married (7:25–40). Paul in no way prohibits marriage, but he does offer the advantages of unmarried life (7:32–35).

Corinthian Questions—Meats Offered to Idols

Next Paul discusses the pressing question of whether Christians may eat food offered to idols (1 Cor. 8–10). The first issue is whether a Christian may eat meat sacrificed in gentile temples and subsequently sold in the marketplace.

Next is whether one may eat at the tables located in the idol temples. While Paul allows Christians to eat idol meat, he does insist that if such actions provoke a weak brother or sister to eat in violation of their conscience, the strong believer should not eat such meat (8:7–13). But the Christian's freedom does not extend to eating meat in the idol temple since such action necessarily involves one in the idol cult (10:14–22).

An inscription found at Corinth notes that Quintus Cornelius Secundus, along with his wife, sons, and daughter built "the meat market [. . .] along with [. . .] and the fish market."
www.HolyLandPhotos.org

A third question concerns an invitation to eat at an unbeliever's house. Should a Christian do so, especially if the meat served has been sacrificed to idols (10:27–30)? While Paul deals specifically with eating idol meat and the question of community, the issue of how to act toward one's patron runs through this section. Should believers risk dishonoring patrons by refusing? This presented a dilemma to some.

The *macellum*, or meat market (today often called "The North Market"), was located next to the temple of Apollo.
Joshua Clutterham/BiblePlaces.com

An Invitation to Dine at a Temple

Banquets were sometimes held within an ancient temple that had dining rooms (*triclinia*) attached to it. In Corinth, the temple of Asclepius has numerous dining rooms, while that of Demeter and Kore had at least forty.

Hosts often sent invitations for such meals on the day of or the day before the feast. If your patron or social superior invited you, refusal was difficult. One such invitation reads, "Herais asks you to dine in the (dining-)room of the Sarapeion at a banquet of the Lord Sarapis tomorrow, namely the 11th, from the 9th hour." Another invitation is said to come from the deity himself: "The god calls you to a banquet being held in the Thoereion tomorrow from the 9th hour."[7]

One of the couches in a dining room, or *triclinia*, of the temple of Asclepius in Corinth, where worshippers could share a meal in the presence of the deity.
Gene L. Green

How does chapter 9 fit into Paul's discussion? Here Paul addresses the topic of Christian freedom (9:1) but also the attendant social responsibility placed on Christians (9:19). Certain social circumstances should limit the believer's use of Christian freedom, and Paul places himself as an example of such limitation (9:3–7, 12b, 15, 19). Not using freedom for the sake of another in the community does not mean a person has lost freedom.

The deceased is reclining at this funerary banquet.
Walters Art Museum

Corinthian Questions—Worship

In chapters 11–14, Paul discusses worship issues. He begins the section with the oft discussed head coverings for men and women (11:2–16). Some Corinthian men appear to have participated in the Corinthian worship services with their heads covered (11:4), while some women were praying and prophesying with their heads unveiled (11:5). In this context Paul discusses gender roles, which, from his cultural perspective, were expressed through head coverings (11:3, 7–12).

Why would some Corinthian men in the church cover their heads in worship?

The Jewish custom of head-covering in prayer postdates the New Testament and so does not help us understand the problem. But Roman men and women who officiated in gentile cults covered their heads with part of their flowing toga as they offered sacrifices. Those who participated as priests were of the social elite, and the Corinthian men Paul refers to were likely of this class. In *Roman Questions*, Plutarch asks, "Why is it that when they worship the gods, they cover their heads, but when they meet any of their fellow-men worthy of honor, if they happen to have the toga over the head, they uncover?" (*Moralia* 266C).

Second, Paul insists that the women should be veiled in worship and not leave their heads uncovered (11:5–6). Roman portraits and sculptures frequently depict women, at least those of the upper class, with their heads uncovered. But the evidence is not unanimous. Veiling seems to have something to do with a woman's relationship to her husband; according to Plutarch, this was the common practice of Roman women. So why were some Corinthian women throwing off the veil? The Villa of the Mysteries in Pompeii depicts women devotees of the Dionysus cult with their heads (and more) uncovered and hair down. In such cults, women could take part in ways normally inaccessible to them in their male-dominated societies. Perhaps women in the Corinthian church, as in the Dionysus cult, were throwing off their head-covering (which would have indicated their proper relationship to their spouse) and using the Christian cult as a form of "social liberation."

Paul discusses gender roles and the Christian church. He talks about "headship" (11:3) but also emphasizes both men and women's dependency on each other (11:11–12). Interpreters have understood the "head" as either "source" (11:8, 11–12) or "authority," but not "superiority of nature." The authors of this book understand that Paul's emphasis is on the mutual dependence of men and women and do not interpret "headship" as granting authority to the man. However, Christians will probably continue to debate this issue (hopefully, charitably) for years to come.

Next Paul discusses the Lord's Supper, the symbolic sharing of the bread and wine that Jesus instituted among the disciples. The early church celebrated it during common banquets (11:17–34; cf. Matt. 26:26–29; Mark 14:22–25; Luke 22:14–20). Banqueting as a religious ceremony was common in the ancient world, often done to remember the dead.

Food and wine were served at these annual events to commemorate the life of the deceased or of some hero. These were private feasts, and only a select group participated. The Corinthian believers were following contemporary custom by celebrating a Christian banquet in honor of Christ's death, but at these events, some were excluded and went hungry (11:20–21). Others became drunk (even though the wine commonly served was a mixture of wine and water). These groups had their "own private suppers" (11:21); from Paul's perspective, this was not the Lord's Supper, which symbolizes the common life of the church (10:16–17).

Paul returns the Corinthians to the fundamentals of the Lord's Supper, which recalls and proclaims the sacrificial death of Christ, the new covenant, and the promise of Christ's coming kingdom (11:23–26). He warns the Corinthians against partaking in this meal "in an unworthy manner" (11:27)—meaning when it was divisive and exclusive. Taking the Lord's Supper together as a celebration of our common salvation implies that believers act and live together as Christ's body.

Paul's next worship issue is his discussion of the gifts of the Spirit (chs. 12–14). While he pays particular attention to tongues and prophecy in chapter 14, he mentions many other gifts in the Corinthian church (12:7–11, 28–30; cf. 1:7; Rom. 12:6–8; 1 Thess. 5:19–22). From Paul's perspective, the gifts of the Spirit are not given to a special elite group but to believers for the benefit of others (1 Cor. 12:7). In chapter 14 he repeatedly reminds the Corinthians that the gifts must be used for building up other members of the community (14:3–5, 12, 26; cf. 1 Pet. 4:10–11).

The development of Paul's argument emphasizes this very point. He first presents the gifts (12:1–11), then discusses the body of Christ (12:12–27), and then returns to the issue of the gifts (12:28–31). Next is a lengthy discourse on love (13:1–13). Each member must use his or her gifts for the benefit of others, in love, and for the church's upbuilding (see Rom. 12:4–10, where Paul runs the same argument). This is Paul's antidote to the factionalism of this church.

On the Resurrection

In the last major section, we learn that some Corinthians deny the (future) resurrection of believers (15:12), perhaps because of the Greek notion that "when you're dead, you're dead." Aeschylus said, "When the earth has drunk up a man's blood, once he is dead, there is no resurrection" (*Eumenides* 647–648). But since the resurrection of the believers is linked inextricably with Christ's resurrection, Paul argues that to deny believers' resurrection is, in fact, to deny Christ's (15:13, 16; cf. Phil. 3:21). For Paul, the Christian hope is not life eternal in heaven (though cf. 2 Cor. 5:6–10; Phil. 1:20–24), but the resurrection of the dead. If Christ has not been raised, our faith is in vain and we have no salvation (15:14–19). Christianity is more than ethics but the promise of immortality and the triumph over death and hell (15:54–57).

Paul ends his letter with an exhortation about the collection for the poor believers in Jerusalem (16:1–4; cf. 2 Cor. 8–9), his forthcoming visit (16:5–9), and the visit of Apollos (16:12). He closes with the final greetings (16:13–24), which include the Aramaic prayer "Maranatha!" ("Come, Lord!").

Bust of Aeschylus, the ancient Greek tragedian who said there is no resurrection.
Reproduced by permission from Carole Raddato

COMPOSING 1 CORINTHIANS

The array of issues the apostle takes up in 1 Corinthians is almost dizzying. Divisions, questions about marriage and sexuality, litigation and idol meats, head coverings, banqueting and the Lord's Supper, spiritual gifts, and the resurrection give the letter an eclectic feel. Some students of the letter have concluded that its fragmented nature demonstrates that the letter is a compilation of various letters Paul wrote to the Corinthian church. But this eclectic nature stems rather from the multifaceted nature of the Corinthians' problems as they worked out the meaning of their new faith in Christ. We should also remember that Paul "wrote" his letters using an amanuensis, who would have taken dictation on wax tablets before transcribing the work onto papyrus (see 16:21, where Paul adds his final greeting). Thus, the document's cohesion surprises us more than its multicolored contents.

The Amanuensis

Ancient authors often used a secretary or amanuensis when composing documents. These people took dictation, sometimes using a form of shorthand, but they could edit what the author dictated, or the author could even instruct them to compose a letter around certain themes. Nevertheless, the author assumed full responsibility for the document's final form. The presence of a scribe is sometimes indicated in the letter itself (see Rom. 16:22; Gal. 6:11; 1 Pet. 5:12), but often we become aware of a secretary's presence because of a change in handwriting at the end, where the author adds the final greeting.

Marble stele of Timocrates, a scribe from Atheus, second century AD.
Lanmas/Alamy Stock Photo

AUTHOR AND DATE

Contemporary scholars have not seriously questioned the authenticity of 1 Corinthians. Paul wrote it in Ephesus on his third missionary journey (1 Cor. 16:8, 19; cf. Acts 19:1–41). He was closely associated with Aquila and Priscilla (and their house church in Ephesus), who, along with others, conveyed greetings to the Corinthians (16:19–20). Paul's Ephesian ministry lasted around three years (see 20:31), although the exact duration of his stay appears to have been closer to twenty-seven months (19:8, 10). Scholars suggest various dates for this period, with late AD 52 until early AD 55 being the most likely dates. Most believe 1 Corinthians was written partway through Paul's Ephesian ministry, sometime around the spring of AD 54 (1 Cor. 16:8).

Questions for Discussion

1. The misuse of the gifts of the Spirit (chs. 12–14) is one factor that contributed to the divisions in the church. Identify the problems and note how Paul corrects them. Does he restrict or prohibit the use of the gifts in the church?
2. Is Paul's teaching on eating meat offered to idols (chs. 8–10) relevant for us who live in societies where such practices are nonexistent? What principles have significance for us?
3. Discuss Paul's teaching on sexuality in contrast with contemporary sexual norms.
4. Should Christians ever go to court against each other? Compare the Corinthians' situation and context with modern litigation. How does Paul's teaching apply today?
5. How do members of your church understand the Christian hope in the face of death? Compare and contrast 1 Corinthians 15 with our current views about the fate of the deceased.

BIBLIOGRAPHY

Introductory

Blomberg, C. *1 Corinthians*. NIVAC. Grand Rapids: Zondervan, 1995.
Hays, R. B. *First Corinthians*. Interpretation. Louisville: John Knox, 1997.
Keener, Craig S. *1–2 Corinthians*. NCBC. Cambridge: Cambridge University Press, 2005.
Oropeza, B. J. *1 Corinthians*. NCCS. Eugene, OR: Cascade, 2017.
Vang, P. *1 Corinthians*. TTC. Grand Rapids: Baker, 2014.

Advanced

Ciampa, R. E, and B. S. Rosner, *The First Letter to the Corinthians*. PNTC. Grand Rapids: Eerdmans, 2010.
Fee, G. D. *The First Epistle to the Corinthians*. NICNT, rev. Grand Rapids: Eerdmans, 2014.
Fitzmyer, J. A. *First Corinthians*. AB, rev. New Haven: Yale University Press, 2008.
Garland, D. *1 Corinthians*. BECNT. Grand Rapids: Baker, 2003.
Thiselton, A. C. *The First Epistle to the Corinthians*. NIGTC. Grand Rapids: Eerdmans, 2000.
Witherington, B. *Conflict and Community in Corinth: A Socio-Rhetorical Commentary on 1 and 2 Corinthians*. Grand Rapids: Eerdmans, 1995.

NOTES

1. J. Murphy-O'Connor, *St. Paul's Corinth* (Wilmington, DE: Glazier, 1983), 27.
2. A. S. F. Gow and D. L. Page, *The Greek Anthology* (Cambridge: Cambridge University Press, 1965), 7:493.
3. B. Witherington, *Conflict and Community in Corinth* (Grand Rapids: Eerdmans, 1995), 22–23.
4. Gow and Page, *Greek Anthology*, 9.284.
5. This phrase comes from C. Blomberg, *1 Corinthians*, NIVAC (Grand Rapids: Zondervan, 1995), 23.
6. Witherington, *Conflict and Community in Corinth*, 74.
7. G. H. R. Horsley, *New Documents Illustrating Early Christianity* (North Ryde, N.S.W.: Macquarie University Press, 1986), 1:5.

Chapter 17

2 CORINTHIANS

Acrocorinth was a monolithic rock mountain standing over the Hellenistic city of Corinth. In the classical period before Paul, the famed temple of Aphrodite stood here.

Paul as an Orator

Paul's supposed "timid" character (10:1), poor bodily presence (10:10b), and lack of eloquence (10:10c) all marked him as an orator who was not honorable according to ancient standards. Some Corinthians said he was *tapainos*, which could mean "timid" (NIV) or "humble" (NRSV), but here more likely means "base" or "servile." Honorable people were not "servile" like slaves. Marcus Aurelius said, "Is it not better to use what is in your power like a free person than to concern yourself with what is not in your power like a slave or servile person?" (9.40; Epictetus, *Diatr.* 1.9.33). Personal presence or appearance was a great concern among students of rhetoric (Epictetus, *Diatr.* 3.1). Orators should be able to say, "Look . . . both I and my body are witnesses to the truth of my contention" (3.22.88). Epictetus notes that the great orator Diogenes "used to go about with a radiant complexion, and would attract the attention of the common people by the very appearance of his body." Above all, people expected public orators to have refined rhetorical skills. Cicero praised the orator Sulpicius, saying, "His voice was strong and at the same time pleasing and of brilliant timbre; his gesture and bodily movement extraordinarily graceful . . . his language was swift and of easy flow without being either redundant or verbose" (*Brutus* 55.203). The "super-apostles" weighed Paul by these standards and found him wanting. Apparently they were persuading the Corinthians. Paul's retort was that the Corinthians, under the influence of the "super-apostles," were "judging by appearances" and did not recognize the authority that the Lord had given him (2 Cor. 10:7–11).

Second Corinthians is filled with heart. The letter is almost embarrassingly personal, exuding the pathos of the deep relationship between the apostle Paul and this church. Paul had been severely criticized, the Corinthians had been grieved, the church had failed to complete the collection for the believers in Judea, and new trouble was brewing as self-styled "super-apostles" had gained a foothold in the congregation. Paul was invested in this church and, as a father who loved them (cf. 1 Cor. 4:14–15), he persisted in helping them and restoring their relationship with him through letters, personal visits, and emissaries. The letter overflows with tears, joy, tales of arduous journeys, suffering, stern words about boasting, and other pointed warnings—all for the sake of the gospel. The full story of Paul's relationship with this congregation is not easy to reconstruct with precision, but the depth of his love and concern for them cannot be missed (2 Cor. 12:15). Paul's goal is full reconciliation for the church—first with God and also with himself (5:11–6:13).

THE SETTING OF 2 CORINTHIANS

Chapter 16 of this text outlines the early relationship between the apostle Paul and the Corinthian church (see ch. 16, The Gospel Comes to Corinth). Paul founded the church on his so-called second missionary journey. Subsequently he wrote them a letter that is lost to us (1 Cor. 5:9–11). While Paul was in Ephesus (16:8) during his third missionary journey, some news arrived about the church, and he received a letter from them asking him a variety of questions (1:11–12; 16:15–18; and 7:1). In response, Paul penned and dispatched 1 Corinthians. He also sent Timothy, his younger associate, to assist the church (4:17; 16:10–11). But Timothy was not the letter carrier. Paul utilized other messengers, most likely Stephanus, Fortunatus, and Archaicus, who had to come to Paul from Corinth (16:15–18). Regular sea traffic along the shipping lane between Ephesus and Corinth facilitated communication between the apostle and this church.

It would take four days for a messenger who went from Ephesus to Corinth to cover 290 miles (466 kms) by sea, including stops at islands along the way. When Paul sent Timothy to Corinth, however, he traveled another route—through Alexandria Troas, west across the Aegean to Macedonia, then south to Corinth (Acts 19:21–22; 1 Cor. 4:17; 16:10–11). This trip of about 934 miles (1,500 kms) would have taken him more than two weeks.

Timothy finally arrived in Corinth and found that all was not well with the church. Some "super-apostles," whom Paul also calls "false apostles," had made their way into the church (2 Cor. 11:5–15). Paul heard about this (we are not sure how) and responded by traveling straight from Ephesus over to Corinth himself, making what he calls a "painful visit" (2:1). This was the second of Paul's visits to the church. Paul speaks about this journey to Corinth and his hopes for a subsequent third visit in 12:14 and 13:1–2. The second encounter did not turn out well, since he met with opposition from the congregation (2:5–11; 7:12). Indeed, someone had "grieved" Paul and, indeed, others in the congregation.

Paul left Corinth and then wrote what has come to be known as his "sorrowful letter" to them. He determined that it was best not to come back and have another hard round with them (2:1) but instead penned a letter: "I wrote you out of great distress and anguish of heart and with many tears, not to grieve you but to let you know the depth of my love for you" (2:4). The letter caused them sorrow and hurt them, "but only for a little while" (7:8). Unfortunately, as the first letter Paul wrote to the church, this correspondence is lost to us.

Titus, another of Paul's coworkers who appears prominently in 2 Corinthians, was the letter carrier (7:5–16). Titus was well received and, indeed, he was able to help encourage the Corinthians regarding the collection for the churches in Judea (8:6). Titus caught up with Paul in Macedonia, though we do not know if they met up in Philippi, Thessalonica, or Berea (7:5–6). The letter Paul sent the Corinthians had brought them sorrow, and they turned around and wanted to clear themselves with Paul (7:7b-13). Paul exclaimed, "By all this we are encouraged" (7:13).

But another problem had arisen. Some "super-apostles" had entered the church and exalted themselves while denigrating Paul. Paul also calls them "false apostles" (11:5, 13). These people critiqued the apostle as being servile, having an unimpressive personal presence, and not being an eloquent speaker (10:1, 7–11). They contrasted his presence with his letters: "For some say, 'His letters are weighty and forceful" (10:10). They dishonored him greatly, and the Corinthians were being taken in by them.

In response to all this news, Paul wrote 2 Corinthians. Timothy was with him at the time, but Paul charged Titus with carrying the letter to Corinth (1:1; 8:16–24). Paul mentions Titus's other travel companions, each of whom Paul simply calls "our brother." Paul himself planned another visit to Corinth (12:14; 13:1–4), perhaps to address the problems the false apostles caused.

𝔓[46], a second-century papyrus manuscript, contains 2 Corinthians. *Image digitally reproduced from the Papyrology Collection, Graduate Library, University of Michigan, P.Mich.inv. 6238.*

AUTHOR AND DATE

All regard 2 Corinthians as a genuine composition of the apostle Paul. The early church fathers received it as authentic, and as such, it was included in the canonical lists of the early church. We have allusions to the book as early as the end of the first century AD, when Clement of Rome wrote to the Corinthian church.[1] Ignatius (c. AD 110), the Letter to Diognetus (AD 130 to the second century), and Polycarp echo it (AD 69–155). It was among the books listed in the Muratorian Canon (AD 170) and even that of Marcion, the heretic (AD 140). It also appears in the second-century papyrus manuscript known as P[46]. Not until the late second century and into the third century do we hear the letter quoted by Irenaeus, Clement of Alexandria (d. ca. AD 215), Origen (d. AD 254), and Tertullian (d. c. AD 240).[2] Similarly, contemporary scholars have overwhelmingly received 2 Corinthians as an authentic Pauline correspondence.

SINGLE LETTER OR COMPOSITE DOCUMENT?

Students of 2 Corinthians often discuss whether Paul composed 2 Corinthians as a unified document or if the document is comprised of two or more letters that were subsequently joined together. Many regard 2 Corinthians as a compilation of various Pauline letters. Although all surviving ancient copies of 2 Corinthians include the letter as a single composition, the document's internal evidence suggests that it was composed in stages or existed originally as separate letters that were then compiled together into one.[3] Paul most likely composed this and other letters over a period of time. This may account for some of the seams and disjunctures in the document that scholars have identified. On the other hand, we have no non-Christian parallels to the phenomenon of joining various letters together into one.[4] While ancient authors often included material from various sources, making composite letters from pieces of correspondence does not appear to have been common practice.

Scholars, however, present various pieces of evidence that suggest 2 Corinthians was a composite document. Some identify 2 Corinthians 2:14–7:4 as a separate document since there appears to be a seam between 2:13 and 2:14 and then another between 7:4 and 7:5. Paul talks about his trip to Macedonia in 2:13, then picks up the topic again in 7:5, suggesting that the intervening section from 2:14 through 7:4 was originally a separate treatise. Did Paul simply digress for a time before returning to the topic of his trip to Macedonia?

Another separate section may be 6:14 through 7:1. In these verses Paul speaks about relations with unbelievers, and some have suggested that this section is the "lost letter" Paul references in 1 Corinthians 5:9–11, in which he discussed the issue of the Corinthians' associations with various kinds of people. Note how Paul appeals to the Corinthians, saying "Open wide your hearts also" in 2 Corinthians 6:13 and then picks up this very idea in 7:2, where he says, "Make room for us in your hearts." Some even regard 2 Corinthians 6:14–7:1 as a non-Pauline fragment.

Conversations through Letters

Demetrius compared letters with conversations. Echoing Artemon, the editor of Aristotle's letters, he stated, "A letter should be written in the same manner as a dialogue" (*Eloc.* 233). Cicero drew a similar line between letters and casual conversation: "Although I have nothing to write to you, I write all the same because I feel that I am talking to you" (*Att.* 12.53 [295]); and 8.14.1 [164]). Seneca likewise responds to comments about his letter-writing, saying, "You have been complaining that my letters to you are rather carelessly written. . . . I prefer that my letters should be just what my conversation would be if you and I were sitting in one another's company or taking walks together—spontaneous and easy" (*Ep.* 75.1).

How Many Letters?

We know that Paul wrote at least four letters to the Corinthians, two of which are part of the New Testament canon:

- The "lost letter" mentioned in 1 Corinthians 5:9–11
- 1 Corinthians
- The "sorrowful letter" mentioned in 2 Corinthians 2:3–4 and 7:8–12
- 2 Corinthians

Second Corinthians could have been written as one single document. But various scholars suggest that it is a compilation of multiple letters, all written by Paul:

- Letter A = 2 Corinthians 1:1–2:13 and 7:5–8:24
- Letter B = 2 Corinthians 2:14–7:4
- Letter C = 2 Corinthians 9:1–15
- Letter D = 2 Corinthians 10:1–13:14 (possibly the "sorrowful letter" mentioned in 2 Cor. 2:3–4; 7:8–12)

In addition, some recognize a letter fragment inserted into Letter B:

- Letter E = 2 Corinthians 6:14–7:1 (possibly the "lost letter" mentioned in 1 Cor. 5:9–11)

Alternately, others identify only three letters:

- Letter A = 2 Corinthians 1:1–8:24
- Letter B = 2 Corinthians 9:1–15
- Letter C = 2 Corinthians 10:1–13:14

Still others say two Pauline letters were combined to form 2 Corinthians:

- Letter A = 2 Corinthians 1:1–9:15
- Letter B = 2 Corinthians 10:1–13:14

However 2 Corinthians was composed, scholars heartily agree that Paul was the author of the content of this letter. In its final form, 2 Corinthians comes to us as an apostolic communication.

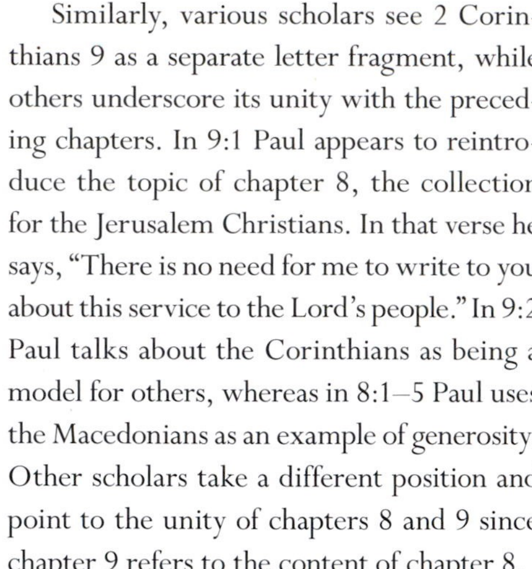

Similarly, various scholars see 2 Corinthians 9 as a separate letter fragment, while others underscore its unity with the preceding chapters. In 9:1 Paul appears to reintroduce the topic of chapter 8, the collection for the Jerusalem Christians. In that verse he says, "There is no need for me to write to you about this service to the Lord's people." In 9:2 Paul talks about the Corinthians as being a model for others, whereas in 8:1–5 Paul uses the Macedonians as an example of generosity. Other scholars take a different position and point to the unity of chapters 8 and 9 since chapter 9 refers to the content of chapter 8.

The most striking disjuncture, however, comes at 2 Corinthians 10:1, leaving some to argue that at least two letters were joined together, the first being chapters 1–9 and the second 10–13. Paul begins to defend himself vigorously in 10:1–6, a topic unrelated to the previous discourse about the collection for Jerusalem (1–9) and in tension with the good news Titus had delivered (7:13b-16). Paul could have received additional news about some "false apostles" that he then took up in the latter chapters (11:5, 13). On the other hand, some say these last chapters are the lost "sorrowful letter" Paul mentions in 2 Corinthians 2:3–4, which was composed before 2 Corinthians 1–9. Then chapters 10–13 were combined with 1–9 but placed after them. The commendatory language of chapters 1–9 changes markedly as Paul deals with the vexing problem of those who set themselves up as "super-apostles" and denigrated Paul's ministry. But the change in tone could be accounted for by additional negative news coming to the apostle after he composed the first nine chapters. For example, a letter from Cicero speaks about changes in a letter's tone due to changes in circumstances. Cicero said, "A propos of what I wrote above about Curio being frozen up, he's warm enough now. . . . He had not done this when I wrote the earlier part of this letter" (*Fam.* 8.6.5 [88.5]).[5]

Scholars will continue to debate whether 2 Corinthians is a composite document. The majority hold that the book is a compilation, but various scholars regard it as having literary unity.[6] In support of their position, letter writers did not always compose their documents with the type of logical structures we might expect. Ancient authors compared letters with conversations, which, unlike well-crafted essays and speeches, often drop topics and later take them up again. The shifts and disjunctures in 2 Corinthians may be evidence that Paul wrote as if the Corinthians were present with him. Indeed, when reading this highly personal letter, we have a sense that we are listening to one side of a highly emotional conversation.

However 2 Corinthians was composed, we read within these pages the deep struggles the apostle had with the Corinthian congregation and also witness his determination to help them overcome a multitude of issues.

THE MESSAGE OF 2 CORINTHIANS

In 2 Corinthians Paul spends considerable time talking about his relationship with the Corinthian church, including his visits, letters, and the emissaries sent to them. Woven through this narrative are extended sections in which he talks about the character of his apostolic ministry and the many sufferings he endured carrying it out. He is also concerned about the welfare of the church in Jerusalem and invests considerable energy encouraging the Corinthians to finalize the offering for that church. The letter ends with a confrontational section wherein he deals with a group of false apostles, also called "super-apostles," who had infiltrated the congregation and challenged Paul's apostolic authority. This lively letter brings the reader into the heart and heat of Paul's service for Christ and his concern for the church.

Outline of 2 Corinthians

I. Epistolary Greeting (1:1–2)
II. Thanksgiving to God amid Sufferings (1:3–11)
III. The Character of Paul's Apostolic Ministry (1:12–7:16)
    1. Paul's Change in Plans (1:12–2:13)
    2. Apostolic Ministry in the New Covenant (2:14–7:4)
    3. Paul's Plans and Titus's Report (7:5–16)
IV. The Offering for the Poor in the Jerusalem Church (8:1–9:15)
    1. Call to Complete the Offering (8:1–15)
    2. Titus's Forthcoming Visit to Corinth (8:16–9:5)
    3. Generosity in Giving (9:6–15)

Comfort in Suffering

Paul repeatedly refers to God's comfort or consolation in 1:3–7. The terms Paul uses here (*paraklēsis/parakaleō*) appear throughout the letter (2:7–8; 5:20; 6:1; 8:4, 6, 17; 7:4, 6–7, 13; 9:5; 10:1; 12:8, 18; 13:11). In some contexts they refer to an exhortation, in others a request, and yet others as the comfort that comes to someone enduring affliction or oppression. In the first verses of 2 Corinthians, the latter sense is in mind. But the "comfort" the apostle experiences likely embraces something beyond emotional encouragement. Isaiah repeatedly describes God's promised salvation as bringing "comfort" or "deliverance" to God's people through the Servant of the Lord (Isa. 40:1; 51:3, 12; 61:1–2; 66:13). Paul, therefore, is able to say that as he shares in Christ's sufferings, so too, he knows the saving comfort that comes through him (2 Cor. 1:5).

Jars of Clay

Perishable earthenware vessels were common in Paul's day. When broken, they would be tossed in the trash. Though fragile and unattractive, they were eminently useful. The clay pot became a metaphor for the frailty of human life (Ps. 32:12; Jer. 19:10–11). Paul talks about the "treasure" of God's glory revealed in Christ being carried in the fragile vessel of his body (4:6–7). In the Roman world, coin hoards and other valuables were sometimes placed in such pots for safe keeping. Paul has this practice in mind.

A hoard of Roman coins hidden in a locally made cooking pot discovered at Llanvaches, Monmouthshire, in 2006. These are at the Caerleon Museum. From the date of the latest coin, the hoard was probably buried around AD 160.
Reproduced by permission from Helen Hall

V. The Defense of Paul's Apostolic Ministry (10:1–13:10)
   1. Paul's Apostolic Authority (10:1–18)
   2. The False Apostles (11:1–15)
   3. Paul's Boasting About His Sufferings and Vision (11:16–12:10)
   4. Paul and the Super Apostles (12:11–13)
   5. Paul's Third Visit (12:14–13:10)

VI. Epistolary Closing: Final Exhortations, Greetings, and Prayer (13:11–14)

Thanksgiving to God amid Sufferings (1:3–11)

Paul opens 2 Corinthians by blessing God for his comfort amid the sufferings he has endured (1:3–11). So deep were the troubles he faced while in the province of Asia that he feared death (1:9–10). Despite the peril, Paul placed his hope in God and found that the compassionate Father comforted him (1:3–7, where he mentions the Father's "comfort" ten times). Paul recognizes, first, that he is entirely dependent on God's care and, second, that the comfort he and Timothy, his coauthor (1:1), received is to be used to comfort others (1:3–4; cf. 7:6–7, 13).

The Character of Paul's Apostolic Ministry (1:12–7:16)

Paul begins this section on his apostolic ministry (1:12–7:16) with an apologetic explaining why he did not

Triumphal Processions

"Thanks be to God, who always leads us as captives in Christ's triumphal procession" (2 Cor. 2:14).

Triumphal processions were glorious events that celebrated the victories of military generals or emperors. In such celebrations the deities received honor, and captives from the conflict were led in the procession. Paul shows that Christ is the victor, and the smell of the incense meant life for those participating in the victory but death for the vanquished, since often they were executed at the end. Surprisingly, Paul depicts himself as a captive in the procession. This may mean that he views himself as a prisoner who would then be spared at the end or, more likely, as one who had been vanquished by God and had died in Christ.

Bas-relief from the Arch of Marcus Aurelius, dated AD 176–180, Rome
Peter Horree/Alamy Stock Photo

Relief of the imperial triumph, Arch of Titus
Jebulon/Wikimedia Commons, Public Domain

return to Corinth as planned (1:12–2:13). The Corinthians knew he was planning to come through Corinth on his way to Macedonia (crossing straight from Ephesus to Cenchreae, the city's port on the Aegean Sea) and then come back through Corinth upon returning from Macedonia (1:15–16). From Corinth he would then head to Judea. But Paul changed plans, not wanting to make yet another "painful visit" to the church (1:23–2:4). Recall that Paul had made a painful visit that caused them, and someone in particular, considerable grief (2:2, 5–11), and he had also sent them the "sorrowful letter" (2:3–4; 7:8–9). So instead of returning to Corinth, Paul went on to Troas to preach the gospel (2:12–13).

Adversity and Virtue

In the ancient Mediterranean world, the wise person was someone who was able to face the adversities of life and yet maintain their virtue and composure. Seneca says, for example, "A good man will do what he thinks it will be honourable for him to do, even if it involves toil; he will do it even if it involves harm to him; he will do it even if it involves peril; again, he will not do that which will be base, even if it brings him money, or pleasure, or power. Nothing will deter him from that which is honourable, and nothing will tempt him into baseness" (*Ep.* 76.18).

Epictetus stresses that hardships may come from the divinity to train a person and make that person an example: "These are the terms upon which now He brings me here, and again He sends me there; to mankind exhibits me in poverty, without office, in sickness; sends me away to Gyara, brings me into prison. Not because He hates me—perish the thought! And who hates the best of his servants? Nor because He neglects me, for He does not neglect any of even the least of His creatures; but because He is training me, and making use of me as a witness to the rest of men" (*Diatr.* 3.24.113–114). Paul's catalog of hardships are calculated to show his virtue over against his opponents in Corinth (cf. Phil. 3:2–11).[7]

Was Paul someone who did not keep his word? Was he unreliable? Paul vigorously denies it (1:18–22). As today, people in antiquity severely criticized unreliable leaders. Suetonius records a letter of Emperor Tiberius, who said, "I shall always be consistent and never change my ways so long as I am in my sense" (*Tib.* 67.4). In contrast, Suetonius notes that Claudius was given to inconsistency: "But in hearing and deciding cases he showed strange inconsistency of temper" (*Claud.* 15:1). The same held true for his rule as emperor: "In this office too he was variable, and both his theory and his practice were inconsistent" (16:1; see also *Dom.* 3:2). To show that he was not inconsistent, Paul sought to clarify why he changed plans. He patterned his life after God, who is faithfully consistent (1:18).

A Roman soldier stands over a Jewish female slave representing Judea, captured during the First Revolt (66–70 AD). Paul experienced the might of Rome in his imprisonments under Roman guard.
Photo courtesy of Freeman & Sear, Los Angeles, CA

Paul goes on to explain in detail the nature of his apostolic ministry (2:14–7:4). He affirms that he is a competent minister of God's new covenant (3:6). He contrasts his ministry with some who are only in it for the money (2:17) and who need letters of recommendation to verify their legitimacy (3:1). Paul likely has in mind the "super-apostles," whom he critiques later in the book (11:1–15). In Paul's day, itinerant philosophers strolled into towns with profit on their mind. Lucian slammed such "philosophers [who] sell their lessons as wine-merchants their wines—most of them adulterating and cheating and giving false measure" (*Hermot.* 59). Paul distances himself from such well-known types both here and elsewhere (1 Thess. 2:1–12, esp. vv. 5, 9).

Paul is a competent minister of the new covenant with God (3:4–4:6; cf. Jer. 31:31; Luke 22:20; 1 Cor. 11:25; Heb. 8:8–13). The contrast between this covenant and the old covenant could not be more striking. Paul talks about "letters

Yoked Together with Unbelievers

In 6:14 through 7:1, Paul talks about relationships with those who were not followers of Christ. He states, "Do not be yoked together with unbelievers" (6:14). Some have suggested that this segment is an interpolation into 2 Corinthians and it originally existed as the lost letter Paul attempts to clarify in 1 Corinthians 5:9–13. Paul uses the agrarian image of two different kinds animals, like an ox and a donkey, being yoked together (Deut. 22:10). Paul's point was not to say Christians should have no relationships whatsoever with those who do not share their faith. He clarifies this in 1 Corinthians 5:10: "In that case you would have to leave this world." Rather, 2 Corinthians 6:14–7:1 emphasizes separateness in the context of idolatry: "What agreement is there between the temple of God and idols?" (6:16). Paul previously reproved the Corinthians for participating in the banquets held in the temples dedicated to the idols (1 Cor. 10:14–22). Paul's concern also has a moral element, since here in 2 Corinthians he speaks about righteousness and wickedness, light and darkness, uncleanness and purity, as well as holiness. The exhortation closes the door on Christian participation in any way with idolatry (see 1 John 5:21), but it also serves as a call not to be tethered in relationships that serve to compromise moral integrity. Paul is not calling Christians to be antisocial but reminds them of God's moral imperative.

on stone" (3:7), referring to the law in the old covenant. The law did not empower people to fulfill its requirements and therefore brought condemnation (see Rom. 7:4–25). But the ministry of the new covenant is "not of the letter but of the Spirit; for the letter kills, but the Spirit gives life" (2 Cor. 3:6; see Rom. 8:1–13). The "letter" that "kills" is not the study of Scripture, as some say. Paul's thought here is similar to Romans 7–8, where he states that "through Christ Jesus the law of the Spirit who gives life has set you free from the law of sin and death" (Rom. 8:2). Paul regards the glory of the new covenant as greater than that which marked Moses's ministry under the old covenant (2 Cor. 3:12–18; cf. Ex. 34:27–35).

Despite the glory of the new covenant and its ministry, Paul says that it is marked by suffering (4:7–5:10). The agonies and the hope that mark Paul's service for Christ are graphically laid out in a series of contrasts: "We have this treasure in jars of clay to show that this all-surpassing power is from God and not from us. We are hard pressed on every side, but not crushed; perplexed, but not in despair; persecuted, but not abandoned; struck down, but not destroyed. We always carry around in our body the death of Jesus, so that the life of Jesus may also be revealed in our body" (4:7–10).

Just a few verses later, Paul again picks up the theme of the hardships he has endured as a servant of God (6:4–7): "As servants of God we commend ourselves in every way: in great endurance; in troubles, hardships and distresses; in beatings, imprisonments and riots; in hard work, sleepless nights and hunger; in purity, understanding, patience and kindness; in the Holy Spirit and in sincere love;

in truthful speech and in the power of God." Paul includes two other catalogs of his hardships in this letter (11:21b–33; 12:7–10). Over and again Paul wants his readers to see God and his work. The only thing Paul can boast about is his weakness, for God's power is seen there (11:30; 12:9–10).

In the midst of his sufferings and the prospect of death, Paul maintains hope in God. Paul recognizes that death means passing into Christ's presence (5:6–10; cf. Phil. 1:22–23), but he also anticipates the resurrection of the body (2 Cor. 5:1–5; cf. 1 Thess. 4:13–18; 1 Cor. 15). The intermediate state of being "at home with the Lord" (2 Cor. 5:8) is a consolation but not the final destiny for Christians, in Paul's view.

Paul encouraged the Corinthians to support their fellow believers in Judea with money for famine relief. This coin depicts Nero (AD 54–68).
Z. Radovan/www.BibleLand Pictures.com

At the heart of Paul's apostolic service was the ministry of reconciliation, another name for God's salvation (5:11–6:2). Paul understands that Christ's coming had inaugurated a "new creation." That new thing God is doing through Christ is reconciliation: "All this is from God, who reconciled us to himself through Christ and gave us the ministry of reconciliation: that God was reconciling the world to himself in Christ, not counting people's sins against them. And he has committed to us the message of reconciliation" (5:18–19; cf. Rom. 5:10–11; 11:15; Eph. 2:14–18; Col. 1:19–23). Paul sees his own place within this cosmic plan of God to reconcile people to himself through Christ. As Harris says, at the heart of reconciliation is the idea of "exchange or substitution of peace for war, of love for anger, or of friendship for enmity . . . a transformation of relations . . . in the sense that friendly relations now replace former hostility. Reconciliation restores humans to a proper relationship with God . . . and with fellow human beings."[8] Reconciliation, the restoration of peace and harmony, is the core of the Christian understanding of salvation.

Equality

When Paul speaks about the offering for the poor in Jerusalem, he touches on the topic of equality: "The goal is equality" (8:14). He appeals to Exodus 16:18, when during the distribution of the manna in the wilderness everyone had what they needed. A similar sentiment marked the church in Jerusalem, which carefully cared for the needy (Acts 2:42–47; 4:32–5:10; 6:1–7). Philo also discussed how equality is part of the divine plan (*Her.* 141–206; and *Let. Aris.* 263). Such equanimity was a common topic in ancient discussions on friendship. Aristotle said, "It is thought that what is just is something Forms of partnerships. that is equal, and also that friendship is based on equality, if there is truth in the saying 'Amity is equality'" (*Eth. eud.* 7.9.1, 1241b). Euripides likewise stated, "Far finer, my son, to honor Equality, which binds friends to friends, cities to cities, and allies to allies. For Equality, men find, conduces to lawfulness, whereas the lesser is always hostile to the greater and making war against it" (*Phoen.* 535–540). Paul reframes this ancient discussion within the gospel. Care should be extended to the neediest in the church.

The section (1:12–7:16) ends with Paul's restatement of his plans and notes Titus's report about the Corinthian church (7:5–16). As mentioned above, some believe this section was part of an original correspondence that ends in 2:12–13 and then resumes in 7:5. Whatever the case, in 7:5–16 Paul continues to explain why he did not come to Corinth but went to Macedonia instead. He says he was relieved when he heard the effect of Titus's visit and their response to the sorrowful letter (7:8). They had turned around and lamented the breach in the relationship with Paul. Paul affirms the church heartily, that is until chapters 10 through 13, where he takes up the problem of the "false apostles" who had entered the church.

The Offering for the Poor in the Jerusalem Church (8:1–9:15)

At the beginning of chapter 8, Paul turns abruptly to take up the question of the collection for the poor believers in Jerusalem (8:1–9:15). This is not the only place the New Testament documents discuss this offering. When Paul went to Jerusalem to present the gospel, he preached to the pillars of the church—James, Peter, and John. He and Barnabas received their approval, "the right hand of fellowship" (Gal. 2:9), and were commissioned to preach to the gentiles. "All they asked was that we should continue to remember the poor," Paul says, "the very thing I had been eager to do all along" (Gal. 2:10). The offering for the poor in Jerusalem was also a topic in Paul's letter to the Romans. When he composed that epistle, he was on his way to Jerusalem with this very offering. Paul remarks that "Macedonia and Achaia were pleased to make a contribution for the poor among the Lord's people in Jerusalem" (Rom. 15:26). Paul regarded this offering not only as a means to relieve suffering in the Jerusalem church but also as reciprocity: "If the gentiles have shared in the Jews' spiritual blessings, they owe it to the Jews to share with them their material blessings" (Rom. 15:27). The way one gave thanks in the ancient world was through reciprocity (see ch. 20).

First-century iron hoe used in a vineyard. The poor, often freedmen, would engage in subsistence farming. City History Museum, Barcelona. *Laumas/Alamy Stock Photo*

Paul prompts the Corinthians to give generously by showing them the example of the Macedonian church, which, though poor and afflicted, had given beyond their ability (2 Cor. 8:1–7). Moreover, the Lord himself served as an example for them to follow (8:8–9). The Corinthians had begun to collect for the Jerusalem poor but had not finished (8:10–9:5). Paul does not want them to be unprepared and ashamed before the Macedonian believers who might come with him to collect the offering (9:4). Paul not only offers the Corinthians examples of generosity and appeals to their honor but also reminds them to sow generously that they may reap an abundant harvest (9:6–11). The result of this offering will be thanks and praise to God (9:12–15). Paul regards such material help for the neediest as an integral part of the gospel. He frames it as a dimension of their service to

God (8:19–20; 9:1, 12–13) just as much as proclaiming the message of the gospel (3:7–9; 4:1; 5:18; 6:3; 11:8). He even designates the gift as "grace" (*charis*, 8:1, 4, 6–7; 9:14), which is modeled after God's gift of grace through Jesus Christ (8:9; 9:8, 14). Generosity is at the heart of the gospel, and Paul calls the Corinthians to participate.

The Defense of Paul's Apostolic Ministry (10:1–13:10)

In the final section of 2 Corinthians, Paul engages in an all-out defense of his apostolic ministry (10:1–13:10). Paul addresses the problem of the "super-apostles" (11:5; 12:11), whom he calls "false apostles, deceitful workers, masquerading as apostles of Christ" (11:13). He is unsparing in his critique: "And no wonder, for Satan himself masquerades as an angel of light" (11:14). The problem is not simply that these people had come to Corinth but that the Corinthians were taken in by them. The Corinthians were deceived by them and had put up with their alternative version of the gospel: "If someone comes to you and preaches a Jesus other than the Jesus we preached, or if you receive a different spirit from the Spirit you received, or a different gospel from the one you accepted, you put up with it easily enough" (11:4). Not only that, but these "super-apostles" had denigrated Paul. Their charges were that he was not versed in rhetoric and his personal presence was not what one would expect of a great orator. His letters, they said, were "weighty and forceful, but in person he is unimpressive and his speaking amounts to nothing" (10:10). They also argued that Paul was somehow inferior since he did not receive offerings from the church (11:7–11). They were intent on shaming Paul before the Corinthians while boasting about themselves (11:12).

Some in Corinth denigrated Paul because he was not an eloquent orator such as the ones who were well known in the city (2 Cor. 10:10). This bust is of Cicero, the most well-known orator. *Anthony Majanlahti/Flickr, CC BY 2.0*

Paul offers a partial profile of these "super-apostles" but does not elaborate on the character of their teaching. They were Jewish (11:22) and versed in rhetoric to a degree that they could make a persuasive appeal to the Corinthians and even out-did Paul in this (11:5–6). They had come into Paul's sphere of ministry (10:13–14) and denigrated Paul as someone who lived according to the flesh (*kata sarka*), that is, "by the standards of this world" (10:2). He shows no patience with their tactics since he regards them as seductive (11:3; "led astray" refers to seduction) and deceitful people who masquerade as "apostles of Christ" and "servants of righteousness" (11:13–15). Unlike Paul, they needed letters of commendation (3:1) and lauded themselves before the Corinthians (10:12). These "false apostles" claimed to be followers and ministers of Christ (10:7; 11:13–14). But Paul regards them as folk who are peddling the gospel for profit (2:17), although he seems to concede that they are Christians (11:23).

We can only speculate on the nature of the false apostles' teaching or who they were. Paul charges them with preaching a different Jesus, a different Spirit, and a different gospel (11:4). Their emphasis on rhetoric may indicate that they

Boasting

Speaking about the type of boasting orators engaged in, Dio Chrysostom asked, "Will you not discard that disgraceful and immoderate craving for notoriety? Will you not be cautious about poking fun at everybody else, and, what is more, before persons who, if I may say so, have nothing great or wonderful to boast of?" (32:60). Self-adulation was a character flaw that could annoy people and generate criticism from others. Quintilian mounts a devastating critique of orators and others who praised themselves:

> First of all, then, any boasting about oneself is wrong, but an orator's boasting of his own eloquence is especially wrong. It not only bores the hearers but generally also disgusts them. The human mind has a certain natural loftiness and pride that does not find it easy to bear a superior; consequently, we gladly help the humble and submissive to their feet, because we feel this shows our superiority, and whenever rivalry has vanished, humanity steps in. On the other hand, anyone who rates himself too highly is thought to be oppressive and contemptuous, and to be diminishing others rather than increasing his own stature (11.1.15).

Such people exalted their own status and looked down on others. Plutarch critiqued Cicero for his boasting, saying, "So at this time Cicero had the greatest power in the state, but he made himself generally odious, not by any base action, but by continually praising and magnifying himself, which made him hateful to many" (*Cic.* 24.1). Paul was determined to boast in the Lord alone (cf. 1 Cor. 1:31).

were heavily influenced by Sophists, who placed value on rhetorical skills above all else. These were splendid orators who could draw large crowds and who gained considerable prestige through their public speaking. Indeed, these were the "rock stars" of the Mediterranean world. For them, it was all about the show and applause. They were quite prominent in and around Corinth in Paul's day. Talking about Isthmia, just down the road from Corinth, Dio Chrysostom said, "That was the time, too, when one could hear crowds of wretched sophists around Poseidon's temple shouting and reviling one another, and their disciples, as they were called, fighting with one another" (*Or.* 8.9). In his *Lives of the Sophists*, Philostratus talks about Favorinus, who "was proclaimed a sophist by the charm and beauty of his eloquence." Accordingly, "When he delivered discourses in Rome, the interest in them was universal, so much so that even those in his audience who did not understand the Greek language shared in the pleasure that he gave; for he fascinated even them by the tones of his voice, by his expressive glance and the rhythm of his speech" (489, 491–92). The Corinthians were likely taken in by the "super-apostles," who had honed their own rhetorical skills.

Paul's response to these false apostles is sustained and devastating. They were all show; he had substance. Surprisingly, Paul mentions "boasting" twenty-three times in these chapters.[9] Paul lays out how the "super-apostles" boasted about gospel work that Paul himself had undertaken (10:15–16). They had boasted about their accomplishments "in the way the world does" (11:18) and were shameless in the way they paraded their accomplishments (11:21b).

The Corinthian church had a problem with boasting, though Paul reminded them that they were hardly high-status people (1 Cor. 1:26–31; 4:6–7). He called them to boast only in the Lord (1:31, citing Jer. 9:23–24). But now the Corinthians are being taken in by the boasting of the "super-apostles."

Paul responds vigorously. He affirms that he is empowered by God to bring down arguments that are against the knowledge of God (2 Cor. 10:1–6). He talks about his own authority to build the Corinthians up and not tear them down (10:6–11). Paul refuses to engage in boasting about other's work as if he had done it himself. Indeed, if he is going to boast, it is only going to be about the Lord's work (10:12–17). He is genuinely concerned for the well-being of the Corinthians, not about his own fame (11:1–4). Paul undercuts the critiques that the "super-apostles" leveled against him about his support. He did not receive money from the Corinthians since others supported him while he was there (11:5–11). After leveling charges against these false apostles and their teachings (11:12–15), Paul does begin to boast. But he does not boast about status or great accomplishments but rather his sufferings for the gospel (11:16–33). He could boast about his vision (12:1–10) only because he was driven to it. But he would rather boast of his weakness, since in it God's power is seen (12:9). Paul reminds the Corinthians of the miraculous signs that accredited his apostolic ministry (12:11–13), but he defends his ministry only because he cares for the church and loves them deeply (11:11; 12:15).

Paul closes the letter with an appeal to the Corinthians to examine themselves. He reaffirms that his goal is to build them up, despite the severity of his words (13:5–10). Paul calls the church to mutual harmony before ending with the public call for them to "greet one another with a holy kiss" (13:11–12). This call reminds us that the letter was to be read aloud to the whole assembled congregation. We can only imagine the emotion that filled the Corinthian church at that moment. Paul closes with what we can regard as a Trinitarian wish-prayer: "May the grace of the Lord Jesus Christ, and the love of God, and the fellowship of the Holy Spirit be with you all" (13:14).

Questions for Discussion

1. Given Paul's arguments in 2 Corinthians, how would Paul respond to contemporary television preachers and highly popular megachurch leaders?
2. What responsibility do affluent and not-so-affluent churches have toward poor believers, both within and outside their congregations?
3. Discuss how the "ministry of reconciliation" Paul outlines in 2 Corinthians 5:11–6:2 should be understood and practiced in the contemporary church's mission.
4. What might it mean for Christians today to "not be yoked together with unbelievers" (2 Cor. 6:14)?
5. Discuss Paul's theology of suffering in 2 Corinthians. What are its contours, and how does Paul develop this theology elsewhere? Be sure to indicate how he relates this theology to Jesus Christ.

BIBLIOGRAPHY

Introductory

Baker, W. R. *2 Corinthians*. The College Press NIV Commentary. Joplin, MO: College Press, 1999.
Belleville, L. *2 Corinthians*. NTC. Downers Grove, IL: InterVarsity Press, 1996.
Collins, R. F. *Second Corinthians*. Paideia. Grand Rapids: Baker, 2013.
Hafemann, S. J. *2 Corinthians*. NIVAC. Grand Rapids: Zondervan, 2000.
Keener, C. S. *1–2 Corinthians*. NCBC. Cambridge: Cambridge University Press, 2005.

Advanced

Barnett, P. *The Second Epistle to the Corinthians*. NICNT. Grand Rapids: Eerdmans, 1997.
Guthrie, G. H. *2 Corinthians*. BECNT. Grand Rapids: Baker, 2015.
Harris, M. J. *The Second Epistle to the Corinthians*. NIGTC. Grand Rapids: Eerdmans, 2005.
Martin, R. P. *2 Corinthians*. WBC. Grand Rapids: Zondervan, 2014.
Seifrid, M. A. *The Second Letter to the Corinthians*. PNTC. Grand Rapids, Cambridge, UK, and Nottingham: Eerdmans and Apollos, 2014.
Thrall, M. E. *A Critical & Exegetical Commentary on the Second Epistle to the Corinthians,* 2 vols. ICC. Edinburgh: T & T Clark, 1994–2000.

NOTES

1. Compare 1 Cl. 5:6, "Seven times he bore chains; he was sent into exile and stoned," with 2 Cor. 11:23, 25, 32–33 which speak of his bonds, stoning, and escape from Damascus; 1 Cl. 36:2, "through this one we see the reflection of his perfect," with 2 Cor. 3:18 since both speak about a reflected image.

2. For summaries of the evidence, see M. J. Harris, *The Second Epistle to the Corinthians: A Commentary on the Greek Text*, NIGTC (Grand Rapids and Milton Keynes: Eerdmans and Paternoster, 2005), 2–3; M. E. Thrall, *A Critical and Exegetical Commentary on The Second Epistle to the Corinthians*, 2 vols. (ICC; T&T Clark, Edinburgh, 1994, 2000), 1.2–3.

3. The arguments surrounding composition are detailed and complex. See, for example, Harris, *The Second Epistle to the Corinthians*, 8–51; G. H. Guthrie, *2 Corinthians*, BECNT (Grand Rapids: Baker Academic, 2015), 23–32; Thrall, *The Second Epistle to the Corinthians*, 1.3–49.

4. Thrall, *The Second Epistle to the Corinthians*, 1.45, n. 300.

5. Guthrie, *2 Corinthians*, 29.

6. Thrall compiled a list of the positions held by a wide variety of scholars (*The Second Epistle to the Corinthians*, 1.47–49). Guthrie includes a helpful summary of arguments forwarded by those who hold to the letter's unity (*2 Corinthians*, 29–32).

7. See J. T. Fitzgerald, *Cracks in an Earthen Vessel: An Examination of the Catalogues of Hardships in the Corinthian Correspondence* (Atlanta: Scholars Press, 1988).

8. Harris, *The Second Epistle to the Corinthians*, 435–436.

9. 2 Cor. 10:8, 13–17; 11:10, 12, 16–18, 21, 30; 12:1, 5–6, 9.

TO THE ROMANS

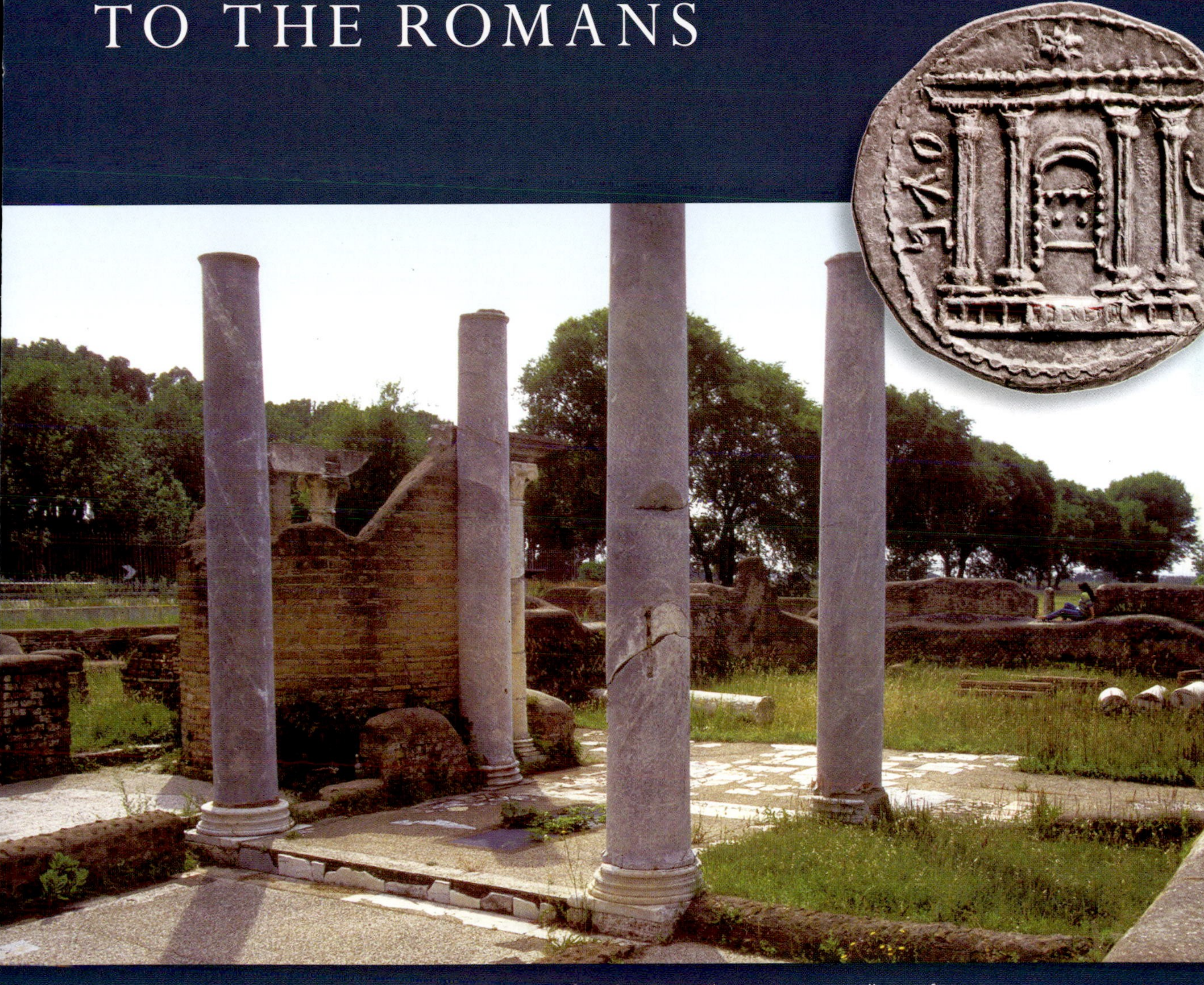

Evidence of a Jewish community near Rome was found in Ostia. These ruins may well stem from a synagogue.

Gladiators

Gladiators (from *gladius*, "sword") were fighters who dueled to death for the public in Rome. In AD 107 Emperor Trajan sent ten thousand gladiators into the arena over a period of four months.

Gladiators fought with a variety of weapons. The *Samnites* entered hand-to-hand battle with a large shield, a visor, a helmet, and a short sword; the *retiarius* ("net man") attempted to entangle his fully armed opponent and finish him off with a trident; the *essedarii* ("chariot men") fought from chariots; the *lauearii* ("lasso men") aimed to lasso their opponents; the *andabatae* fought on horseback with closed visors (i.e., blindfolded!).

Exhibitions usually began with sham fights with wooden swords and javelins. During the real fighting, a losing gladiator could appeal for mercy to the crowds, who signaled either to spare his life (thumbs up) or to continue with his death (thumbs down).

One of the most famous Roman gladiators was Spartacus, who escaped from gladiator school in 73 BC and organized such a volatile slave revolt that it threatened the Roman republic. His throng of runaway slaves and rebel gladiators defeated three Roman armies on the slopes of Mount Vesuvius.
Gary M. Burge

At the end of his third missionary tour, Paul remained in Corinth for three months and reflected on his future ministry. Once again, he looked west, wanting to go as far as Spain. But first he hoped to go to the imperial capital of Rome, where a Christian community was already growing.

Paul's letter to the Romans is his longest (which explains why it is first in the New Testament canon of Paul's letters). While some view it as his best systematic treatment of the Christian faith, Paul nevertheless writes with an awareness of critical issues that need to be addressed. Although he has never visited this church, Christian couriers commonly brought news of developments throughout the Mediterranean. The Roman Christians were thus well-known in Greece (Rom. 1:8; 16:3ff.), so Paul can write to them addressing specific issues.

THE CITY OF ROME

Rome was an astonishing city. By the first century an extensive system of aqueducts provided most of the city with clean water. Sewer systems, public latrines, and public baths increased levels of sanitation. Multistoried buildings with internal plumbing were common. Augustus (27 BC–AD 14) installed a police force and fire prevention units. Monuments, government buildings, libraries, racecourses, and theaters displayed impressive feats of engineering and architecture. In every respect, Rome offered the refinements and efficiencies that were unparalleled elsewhere in the empire.

Rome had served as the capital of the entire Mediterranean world for nearly two centuries and was a famous cultural and intellectual center.

The lure of this city, with its hundreds of miles of paved roads, brought scores of people from all corners of the empire—civilized and uncivilized (cf. 1:14). Medical colleges and gladiator spectacles were equally popular. By the end of the second century AD, Rome reached the pinnacle of its power, prosperity, and population—estimated at nearly one million.

Religion was central to Roman political and social life. Priests frequently counseled the senate on issues like making war and interpreting the law. Religious oracles were consulted to predict the future. Extravagant religious festivals were part of the fabric of everyday life. It was not, however, one religion, but a blend of many. The Romans usually assimilated the gods of conquered people, merging them with the Roman pantheon, and required those conquered to adopt Roman divinities. To desecrate any temple in the empire was a capital crime.

A temple dedicated to all Rome's gods, the Pantheon, was built in open fields outside the ancient city (the *Campus Martius*). It stood prominently in Paul's day.
djedj/Pixabay

The Romans occupied southern Spain (or Iberia) from the second century BC, but Augustus completed its conquest from 26–19 BC. This Roman bridge is found in Salamanca, Spain.
Tono Balaguer/Shutterstock

Access to Rome was via the Tiber River, which flowed into the Adriatic Sea at the city of Ostia. A great maritime city since the fourth century BC, Christians in Rome would know the port well. This coin from Nero (AD 54–68) shows the Ostia harbor lighthouse (with statue), Tiber reclining below, and four successive uses of the harbor: two ships entering at full sail, two being rowed out, a large ship at anchor (whose sails are being gathered in), and a ship alongside a quay being unloaded.

This is why the Romans struggled with Jewish (and later, Christian) claims to theological exclusivity. Refusal to embrace the imperial religious spirit deemed Jews and Christians haughty, exclusive, and intolerant. Eventually this led to persecution.

Paul is fully aware of the religious and social climate of this city. He knows that the Roman church is gentile but is also anchored in a Jewish community. This multicultural environment brings its own challenges. Jews might seek privileges in their ethnic heritage; gentiles might discriminate against Jewish fellow believers.

THE SETTING OF ROMANS

Paul is facing a major transition in his ministry (15:19–23). Having preached the gospel "from Jerusalem all the way around to Illyricum" (15:19, present-day Bosnia and Serbia), he concludes, "There is no more place for me to work in these regions" (15:23). Thus, Paul hopes to visit Rome on his way to Spain.

Paul mentions two people whose names help us locate this writing in the city of Corinth: Gaius, Paul's host while visiting the church in Corinth (cf. 16:23; 1 Cor. 1:14) and Phoebe (Rom. 16:1), a deacon in the church at Cenchreae (a port six miles east of Corinth). Paul's commendation of Phoebe (16:1–2) indicates that she will be delivering this letter. Most scholars agree that Paul writes this letter at the end of his third missionary journey (cf. Acts 20:2–3). Therefore, we must think of him as a veteran of many years, experienced in theological debate and having well-formed ideas about the church and its beliefs.

Paul has just completed a collection of money from his gentile churches and is planning to give it to the poorer churches in Judea (Rom. 15:25–27; cf. 1 Cor. 16:1–4; 2 Cor. 8–9). As he writes Romans, the delicacy of this gesture is on his mind. Will the ethnic tensions, racial pride, and theological differences between gentile and Jewish Christians surface again? Will Jewish believers in Jerusalem reject this gift and jeopardize the fragile unity of the church? This delicate balance of Jewish and gentile interests can be seen particularly in Romans 14, where Paul diplomatically addresses concerns from festival recognition to religious restrictions on diet.

Then there are his opponents in Judea, whom he has known since he was a young Pharisee. Will they continue to pursue him (15:31)? Paul thus asks that the Christians in Rome pray for his protection and that the contribution he takes to Jerusalem "may be favorably received by the Lord's people" (15:31).

One plausible view is that Paul writes this extensive letter because he has ominous feelings about what will happen in Judea (15:30–33). If he is arrested or even killed, this letter will be a theology legacy, guiding the Roman church (and perhaps others) in his absence. But Paul is also looking to the Roman Christians for practical financial support. His journey to Spain will be expensive, and so the Roman church can offer him help (15:26–29).

THE CHURCH IN ROME

Claudius ruled from AD 41–54 and was famous for his decree to expel Jews from Rome who were caught up in a debate about "Chrestus" (a confusion with the Greek *Christos*), referring to Christ.
Public Domain

The origins of Christianity in Rome are uncertain. By the first century BC, Rome possessed a large Jewish population, perhaps as many as fifty thousand. Many Jews arrived as slaves after 63 BC, when Pompey conquered Jerusalem. The strong commercial ties between Rome and Judea attracted even more Jews. Archaeologists know of nearly a dozen synagogues in Rome. It is plausible to assume that the Roman congregation began in these synagogues during the early decades of the first century (cf. Acts 2:10).

But gentiles likely joined as well, raising a variety of disputes well-known to Paul. Evidence of widening tensions *within* the Jewish community comes in the late 40s, when Emperor Claudius expelled Jews and Jewish-Christians from the city (AD 49; cf. Acts 18:1–2). As a result, the leadership of Roman Christianity rapidly became gentile.

Claudius's expulsion affected the Christian couple Aquila and Priscilla, who fled to Corinth and hosted Paul there (Acts 18:1–3). But they returned to Rome, and Paul anticipates seeing them again (Rom. 16:3). The motif "first to the Jew, then to the Gentile" (1:16), which runs throughout Paul's letter, evidences the ethnic diversity of the Roman congregation. But little more can be known.

Paul is aware, of course, that he is addressing Christians with Jewish heritage. He speaks of circumcision, the law of Moses, Abraham's significance, and the fate of unbelieving Israel, as if his readers enjoy a deep Jewish heritage. He even identifies with them by referring to Abraham as "the forefather of us Jews" (4:1) and greets his fellow Jews in chapter 16 (Priscilla, Aquila, and others, vv. 3–4, 7, 11).

At the same time, Paul clearly has gentile Christians in mind in this letter. The sins of idolatry cataloged in chapter 1 are characteristic of the gentile world. Paul assures these gentiles that they are among those called to "belong to Jesus Christ" (1:6) and are central to God's plan of salvation (11:13–25). They are the focus of Paul's commission (see 15:15–17, cf. 1:13).

The Edict of Claudius

The Roman historian Suetonius writes that Claudius "expelled the Jews from Rome because they were constantly rioting at the instigation of Chrestus" (*Life of Claudius* 25.4). Who is Chrestus, and why would Claudius banish the entire Jewish population and not only this "troublemaker"?

The spelling and pronunciation of this common Greek name is close to the Greek word *Christos*, meaning "Messiah." Suetonius has most likely confused the two words. Tensions probably flared up when Jews returning from Jerusalem claimed that Jesus of Nazareth was indeed the long-awaited *Christos*. Claudius's edict likely affected both Jews and Jewish Christians, since the Romans considered both part of the same group.

THE PURPOSE OF ROMANS

We have already summarized a few of the reasons Paul may have written Romans, particularly as he moves farther west to expand his mission into new frontiers. He is in Corinth and wants to work in the far west; Rome and Spain are now his new destinations. The church of Syrian Antioch supported his journeys in the eastern half of the Mediterranean (Acts 13:1–4). Now as he moves farther west, he wants to locate a different "anchor church," one with the vision and resources to assist him in expanding his mission.

Paul knows that the Christians in Rome understand the gospel, but perhaps there are errors in their belief or maybe teachers have criticized Paul's teachings. Romans 1:16; 3:8; and 9:1–2 imply that Paul feels under attack and needs to defend himself and his understanding of the faith. This explains his frequent use of rhetorical questions his opponents (apparently) raised, whether real or hypothetical (i.e., 2:17–24; 3:1, 5–8). If Paul is going to rely on this church as a strategic ally in his mission, he must establish himself as a decisive teacher, dispel any doubts about his positions, and lay out "my gospel" (2:16).

But Paul's interest in the Roman church is not simply pragmatic. He also cares for their pastoral needs and no doubt has a good idea of what they are. The diversity of this community leads naturally to the subject of conflict. Thus, his argument in 9:1–11:36 shows how gentiles and Jews have both participated—and will participate—in the plan of God's salvation. He wants them to experience a genuine unity as "one body . . . liv[ing] in harmony with one another" (12:5, 16) and to pursue a life of righteousness (12:1–15:13) with no discrimination between the "weak" and the "strong" regarding the law (14:1; 15:1, 7).

Scholars have always struggled to find a unifying theme for the entire letter. Chapters 1–8 seem to summarize salvation; 9–11 describe the fate of unbelieving Israel; and 12–16 provide social and personal ethical guidance. This traditional view is widely supported but may need to be revised. The New Testament professor Robert Jewett, for instance, thinks that the climax of the letter is in chapter 16. For him, the aim of the letter is social: Paul wants to move on to Spain, where today we know there were no significant Jewish settlements. This would be a mission to "barbarians" (in a Roman view), and Paul wants to enlist support from the Roman church. But he knows that problems of hierarchy so prevalent in Roman society are rampant in the Roman congregations. Well-educated, socially powerful people are discriminating against poorer Jewish believers who could claim little Roman honor (see 14:10). Paul then is writing a gospel that turns the Roman honor system on its head: the gospel is about the "shame" of the cross and the empowerment of those who embrace it in faith. Righteousness then is not about reconciliation with God, per se, but about a community in which public honor is distributed to all, including those in the lower classes.

The "righteousness of God" is thus: *righteousness that comes from God rather than righteousness that springs from Roman practice*. It is righteousness that restores a person not simply to God but to the public life they have never enjoyed. And if these Roman Christians see that at the heart of the gospel is God's love and elevation of those who are "less," those who have been shamed in Roman life, then they will see Paul's mission to the barbarians in Spain to be consistent with what he preaches.

Certainly there is much in this view that is admirable. The gospel has genuine implications for how the less honorable are elevated as Christ's shame at the cross was amended in the resurrection. But it is a significant step to redefine Paul's sense of "righteousness" as something social and communal and not redemptive and salvific.

The temple of Romulus in Rome. According to a legend known since the third century BC, Rome was founded by the twins Romulus (Lat. The Roman) and Remus, who were rescued from the Tiber River and raised by a wolf.
Public Domain

AUTHORSHIP AND LITERARY UNITY

Paul's authorship of Romans is rarely disputed. It claims to be from Paul (1:1) and was upheld through the earliest centuries. Its language echoes that of other so-called undisputed letters (Galatians, 1–2 Corinthians, and Philippians).

A more complex question is the literary unity of the letter. Some scholars

Tertius Wrote Romans?

In Romans 16:22 Paul's scribe identifies himself: "I, Tertius, who wrote down this letter, greet you in the Lord." This raises an interesting question: How much editorial influence did Tertius exercise on the content of this letter?

Writers in antiquity usually enlisted an amanuensis, or scribe, to help compose letters. Authors gave scribes varying degrees of freedom in the actual wording of the text, ranging from much freedom in composition to dictation word-for-word. Most likely Paul dictated Romans to Tertius, though some wonder whether Paul wrote out a first draft and Tertius put it in final form.

Paul's Use of Diatribe

Paul uses several rhetorical devices to carry his argument. One of these is the diatribe, a series of questions to which the answer is an emphatic no (Gk. *mē genoito*, "may it never be"). Some examples:

3:5: Is God unjust to inflict wrath upon lawbreakers? *No!*

3:9: Are Jews better off than gentiles in God's eyes? *No!*

6:1: Shall Christians keep sinning so that grace may increase? *No!*

7:7: Is the law sin? *No!*

doubt that chapter 16 was a part of Paul's original letter. Some early manuscripts end the letter at 16:24. The final "benediction" (16:25–27) even appears elsewhere (e.g., after 14:23 or 15:33). Some speculate that Paul originally wrote chapters 1–14 (or 1–15) with the doxology as his original ending. Some argue that the list of greetings in 16:1–24 stems from another copy of the letter sent to Ephesus, which would explain how Paul knows so many people.

But no Greek manuscript omits chapter 16, and Paul's extensive travels and contacts throughout the Mediterranean may explain its extensive list of names. Priscilla and Aquila (16:3) are a good example. Paul met them in Corinth, yet they were originally from Rome.

THE LITERARY FORM OF ROMANS

Many interpreters agree on the major divisions of the letter. This is because Paul incorporates several literary devices and grammatical features that signal the beginning and end of sections. Paul opens and closes his letter in typical ancient fashion: greeting, thanksgiving, reason for writing, and his theme. His conclusion includes upcoming plans, commendations, and a doxology.

Within this framework, Paul develops a series of sections: doctrinal instruction that underscores the main argument of the gospel, an application of this gospel to Jew-gentile relations, and ethical exhortations. He often advances his argument by offering a number of questions and answers to show how someone can draw incorrect conclusions when they learn about the gospel. In the final section he describes the impact of the gospel on the life of the church and then on the community at large.

Outline of Romans

I. Salutation and Introduction (1:1–17)

II. Theological Explanation of the Gospel (1:18–11:36)

   1. The Human Dilemma: Universal Sin and Guilt (1:18–3:20)
   2. The Divine Solution: Justification (3:21–5:21)
   3. The Christian Prospect: Sanctification (6:1–8:39)

4. God's Plan for Israel: Rejection and Restoration (9:1–11:36)

III. Ethical Exhortation: Practical Implications of the Gospel (12:1–15:13)
1. Practicing Righteousness in the Body (12:1–21)
2. Practicing Righteousness in the World (13:1–14)
3. Christian Liberty and Christian Charity (14:1–15:13)

IV. Conclusion (15:14–16:27)
1. Paul's Upcoming Ministry, Travel Plans, and Prayer Requests (15:14–33)
2. Recommendation of Phoebe and Greetings (16:1–16)
3. Final Remarks and Doxology (16:17–27)

The first century witnessed an explosion of literary production. Books circulated on papyrus scrolls, and letters were sent on smaller sheets of papyrus (seen here on a wall fresco at Pompeii in the hands of the child). In the late first century or early second century, Christians began using the sewn papyrus codex, or book.
Public Domain

THE THEOLOGICAL ARGUMENT OF ROMANS

Salutation and Introduction (1:1–17)

The introduction immediately sets the tone and direction and echoes many other letter openings of Paul. For instance, he identifies himself as an apostle (1:1), greets the saints with "grace and peace" (1:7), and gives thanks for their faith (1:8). Aware of his need to build rapport with a church he has never visited, Paul expands his greeting (1:1–7) to reveal the credibility of his apostolic calling and gentile ministry. He explicitly mentions his frustrated attempts to visit, despite his longing to see them (1:8–15).

The Roman Christians were ordinary citizens of the empire, such as this Roman couple whose sculpture was completed during the late Republican period (first century BC).
Kathryn Andrus

Above all, Paul's introductory paragraphs offer the thesis that will be defended throughout the letter (1:16–17): the gospel offers the power of God for salvation to everyone who believes, both Jews and Greeks. Note that Paul refers to shame—as if there were something in this message that was unexpected, even shame-producing to some. "I am not ashamed of the gospel" (1:16) unmasks what some Romans might think. Paul says that the gospel is about power, that the power of God will resolve humanity's most profound questions. Roman scholars might expect him to refer to wisdom or learning or discipline as the solution to humanity's corruption. But Paul does not. Paul says that in the gospel the righteousness of God has been revealed—in a manner that fully conforms with Old Testament principles of righteousness (1:17; Hab. 2:4). Paul is now ready to discuss the theological and ethical implications of this thesis.

A Theological Explanation of the Gospel (1:18–11:36)

The human dilemma: universal sin and guilt (1:18–3:20). In 1:18 Paul launches his first doctrinal section on the nature of the human condition. He describes the sinfulness and guilt of gentiles (1:18–32), Jews (2:1–3:8), and all humanity (3:9–20). God's wrath is revealed against sinful humanity for repudiating his truth (1:18). Paul reaches back to the beginning to highlight the universality of sin (1:19–23): human rebellion is a willful attempt to reject God and usurp his role as Creator. This results in inappropriate sexual relations (1:24), misdirected worship (1:25), and corrupted ethics (1:26–32) that destroy the very fabric of human society. Note carefully that Paul's first argument is that the human mind and human moral capacity are broken (1:28) and therefore there is no hope for restoration from below, from the realm of creaturely life. In fact, creation has been divinized and worshiped because a true consciousness of the Creator has been lost.

Even the Jews, God's people privileged with the custodianship of his Word (3:2), have rejected his truth. They too will be judged, for "God does not show favoritism" (2:11). Jews should not place confidence merely in having the law, for breaking it puts them in a worse position than gentiles (2:17–27). True Jewishness, Paul clarifies, focuses on the importance of the inward work of the Spirit over against ethnic identity markers, like circumcision (2:28–29).

Paul concludes this section with numerous quotes from Psalms: "Jews and Gentiles alike are all under the power of sin. . . . There is no one righteous, not even one" (3:9–10; cf. Ps. 14:1–3). Indeed, all human beings are sinful and without excuse, rightfully condemned for not living according to conscience (gentiles) or the law (Jews).

The divine solution: justification (3:21–5:21). Paul then develops his solution. The sacrificial death of Christ is the basis for justification, and we appropriate the benefits of his death by faith (3:21–26). Since Jew and gentile alike are justified by faith alone, there is no room for personal boasting (3:27–31). To illustrate the principle of righteousness by faith, Paul highlights the story of Abraham (4:1–25), using as his key text Genesis 15:6: "Abraham believed God, and it was credited to him as righteousness" (Rom. 4:3ff.). Abraham's righteous status was declared *before* his circumcision (Gen. 17:10–14), which set in place an important pattern. Works of the law cannot be a precondition for salvation. Therefore, righteousness by faith is freely available to Jews and gentiles alike—thus making Abraham the spiritual father of all believers.

Acquiring a new position with God brings remarkable results: peace with God, grace that transforms character, and hope in the midst of suffering (5:1–11). This new status of righteousness is given to us by Christ, the new head of a new humanity (5:12–21). As Adam imputed to humanity a propensity to sin from which there is no escape, Christ as head can now do the same in reverse, repairing what was broken in Eden.

Temples in Rome

Religion thrived in Roman culture. The Romans developed complex mythologies. Jupiter (god of lightning, thunder, and rain; Greek Zeus) headed the Roman pantheon. Devotion to these gods took concrete form in impressive structures of worship, like the temple of Jupiter.

Likely Paul has this background in mind when he writes: "Although they claimed to be wise, they became fools and exchanged the glory of the immortal God for images made to look like a mortal human being and birds and animals and reptiles" (1:22–23).

The Temple of Jupiter in the Roman city of Pompeii
Reproduced by permission from Pegasi Numismatics

Paul's Use of *Hilastērion* in 3:25

God presented Christ as a *hilastērion* (3:25). Interpreters have long debated the meaning of this term, particularly because it is central to Paul's entire argument about Christ. For some, the word refers to a work that appeases another's wrath. If this is Paul's meaning, then Christ is our "propitiation" (KJV, NASB, ESV), meaning he has appeased God's anger. Others believe it refers only to the wiping away of sins. If the latter is correct, then Christ is our "expiation" (RSV) for sin.

Others suggest that *hilastērion* may refer to the cover on the ark of the covenant, called the "atonement cover" (the main meaning of this term in the LXX). On the Day of Atonement, a priest sprinkled blood on the *hilastērion* to turn away God's wrath. Over time, the atonement cover represented for Jews the place where God dealt with their sins. For Paul, then, Christ's sacrificial death on the cross is where God dealt with human sin. He has turned away God's wrath and wiped away our sins. The phrase "sacrifice of atonement" (NIV, NRSV) attempts to encompass this wider meaning.

The Christian prospect: sanctification (6:1–8:39). The gospel offers not only freedom from condemnation but also a way of escape from the dilemma of our moral paralysis. It offers *restoration*, a return to human goodness and holiness that can only be regained by a renewed relationship with God. Therefore, Paul discusses the tyranny of sin (Rom. 6), the condemnation brought about through the law (ch. 7), and the hopeful restoration given through the work of the Spirit (ch. 8).

Some might exploit God's offer of free grace, saying that Paul's teaching inspires *antinomianism*—sinning so that God's grace may forgive that much more. This view betrays a misunderstanding of baptism (6:1–14) and conversion (6:15–23). Union with Christ in baptism frees us from the *compulsion* to sin: "Sin shall no longer be your master" (6:14). Thus, we can yield our lives to God rather than to sin. The benefits are remarkable: freedom (not to do anything we want, but to live as we were designed), holiness (to be like God), and eternal life (6:23).

Paul sustains this discussion by moving through a variety of metaphors. Slavery (6:20–23) and marriage (7:1–3) model how a new relationship with the law has come about. Through redemption we have acquired a new Master in God, who now owns us (6:22). Likewise, the death of a spouse changes the binding obligations of a marriage, and so our death to the law (our former spouse) enables us to conduct our lives for God. The struggle to fulfill the law (7:14–20) is the hallmark of a life lived in the flesh, a life in bondage to sin. God's work in the gospel offers a new prospect: that sin no longer reigns (6:12; 8:2), that our captivity is over (7:23), and that we now live safe from condemnation (8:1).

Grafting is a process in which new branches are joined to an older olive tree, in order that both tree and new branches might grow together. Romans 11:17–24 uses this metaphor to describe the inclusion of the gentiles into God's chosen people.
Manuel Trinidad Mesa/ Shutterstock

The hopeful prospect of the gospel is not only found in the work of Christ. Paul now turns to the transforming work of the Holy Spirit (8:1–30). He sees two opposite choices before us: the flesh (or sinful nature) and the Spirit (8:5). The former refers to a life lived in captivity to sin that results in death; this life cannot obey the law or please God (8:5, 7). The alternative is life in the Spirit of God (mentioned nineteen times in Rom. 8). Just as justification is a gift of God's goodness, so sanctification is another expression of his grace. The Spirit indwells and transforms (8:9), implants holy desires (8:5), controls the mind (8:6), gives life (8:11), puts to death evil deeds (8:13), leads to self-control (8:14), confirms our spiritual adoption (8:15), and intercedes on our behalf with the Father (8:26).

Above all, the Spirit confirms within us that God continues to be on our side, giving us a new status as his adopted sons and daughters (8:14–17). Despite our suffering and feelings of futility, God remains on our side, promising a future that holds a glorious promise of both our own redemption and that of the entire earth

Who is the "I" in Romans 7?

Is Christian perfection possible? Proponents who say either yes or no must come to terms with Romans 7:14–25. In this text the person speaking is obviously struggling with sin. But who is this "wretched man" who cries out for deliverance (7:24)? Does this "I" refer to Paul before or after his conversion, or perhaps to something else?

Three interpretations are common: (1) Paul describes his struggle before conversion, as a Jew representing Israel's experience with the law ("I" = unregenerate Paul/Israel). (2) Paul describes his own experience after conversion ("I" = regenerate Paul). (3) Paul is not writing autobiographically but rather symbolically for all humanity ("I" = Adam/humanity).

Why is this important? The question is this: *Once one becomes a follower of Christ, is baptized, and receives the Holy Spirit, will sin be fully defeated?* Is perfection possible? Those who believe the converted Paul is writing about his own Christian life will point to the nature of Christian life: there is ongoing struggle with sin despite the work of God through his Spirit to sanctify us.

(8:18–25). *This is the fundamental source of our peace* (5:1). God is in control, and for those who love him, every good plan is in place (8:28–30). No object—celestial or creational—can separate us from God's love (8:37–39).

God's plan for Israel: rejection and restoration (9:1–11:36). These chapters are often separated from 1–8 as if they are an unnecessary feature of the apostle's argument. But this is a mistake. Paul has been describing the jeopardy and hope that belongs to every human community: both Jew and Greek. God is sovereign in working out a plan for the restoration of his creation. But one obstacle remains: if God has been at work in Judaism, bringing a Messiah who will restore the world and repair the lost righteousness of humanity, why did Jesus's own people (the Jews) fail to embrace this good news? Again, Paul returns to his main themes: God's faithfulness and grace, God's plan to save and renew, and the importance of embracing what he has done.

At the center of Paul's consciousness is a deep and troubling anguish about the Jewish people, his own people (9:2). He believes that Jesus is the Messiah, that his resurrection vindicates every claim about him, and that Paul's own conversion is personal proof that God is at work in Christ. But Judaism has not completely embraced its Messiah. Everywhere he goes, Paul finds strong resistance to his preaching. His discussion in this section no doubt represents countless hours of argument in synagogues during his three missionary tours.

One debater's voice looms large: If Jesus Christ is central to God's program for righteousness—and since his Jewish people have not universally acclaimed this program—has God's effort failed (9:6)? Paul feels so deeply here that he would sacrifice himself for his own people if it were possible (9:3–4).

Israel and the Church in Romans 9–11

The interpretation of Romans 9–11 is one of the most contentious subjects in the theology of Paul. This was true throughout Christian history and is particularly true today with the birth of modern Israel in 1948 and the growth of Christian Zionism in the twentieth century.

Is Paul challenging Jewish ethnic privilege? Is Paul denying Jewish exceptionalism? That is, if God made a covenant with Abraham (and his descendants), is Paul now making faith in Christ a prerequisite for enjoying the benefits of that covenant? For some theologians, this is precisely what Paul is doing: Jews and gentiles now have equal access to the grace of God in Christ because faith is within reach of both. Thus, Paul can argue in Romans 9 that it is the remnant of Israel, those who share the faith of Abraham—a faith now found in Paul himself—a faith that finds Jesus as its object, that saves.

The difficulty is that in Romans 11 Paul implies that God's interest and love for Israel is exceptional for the sake of their ancestors (11:28). He also holds out hope that "all Israel will be saved" (11:26). Does this mean that Israel can be saved without Jesus? Paul would never write this. Does this mean that Paul expects *in hope* that all Jews will be saved through the gospel? This is possible. Or does Paul mean that Israel will still have a future place in God's plan for history and at some future time (Christ's second coming?) Israel will join the saved community of Christ when they embrace him in faith?

The disputes surrounding this one theme are enormous. And they turn on the idea of privilege: Can one ethnicity have privileges from God not shared by any other? Paul imagines the people of God as an ancient olive tree (11:17), and at its root is Abraham, "the father of us all" (4:16). Paul reminds his Jewish community that they may be broken off from that olive tree (11:17, 20). This is sobering. He reminds gentiles that they are branches grafted in. But they can be broken off too (11:21), so there must be no anti-Judaism among gentile Christians. There must be no arrogance among any who are part of the tree. What Paul eagerly anticipates is the *regrafting* of his own unbelieving people back into the tree (11:24). In that day, gentiles and Jews will together share the family of Abraham, the ancestor of all who have faith.

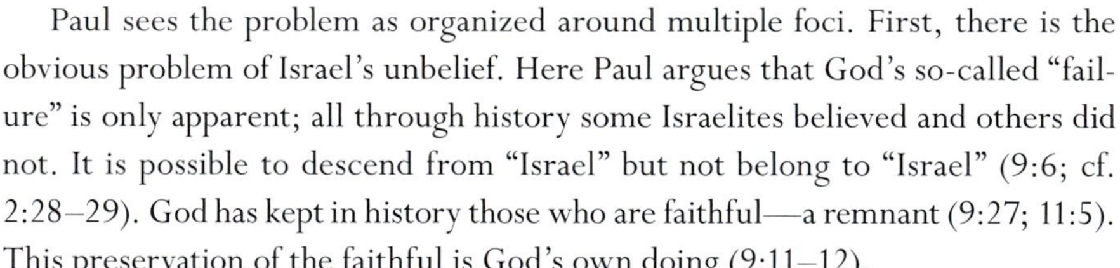

Paul sees the problem as organized around multiple foci. First, there is the obvious problem of Israel's unbelief. Here Paul argues that God's so-called "failure" is only apparent; all through history some Israelites believed and others did not. It is possible to descend from "Israel" but not belong to "Israel" (9:6; cf. 2:28–29). God has kept in history those who are faithful—a remnant (9:27; 11:5). This preservation of the faithful is God's own doing (9:11–12).

But if God is responsible for this believing remnant, then is his mercy capricious? How can he still find fault (9:19)? Paul says that this divine freedom is the freedom a potter has over clay. The clay only becomes what it is, thanks to the potter's hand. Every gesture is an act of mercy since the clay is useless in its natural state. God acts to save, and he has saved many Jews who now proclaim Jesus's messiahship.

If ethnicity is no guarantee to becoming God's people (9:25–26), the way is then open for gentiles to become God's children. This means that Israel's zeal for religion based on works is misdirected (9:32). Their effort promoted a righteousness born not from God but from within Judaism.

In every case, it is not the person's pedigree that matters but his or her faith. It is one's desire to yield to God's purposes in history that matters. Paul demonstrates this principle by citing Jeremiah, Isaiah, Leviticus, Deuteronomy, Joel, and the Psalms. Paul also notes that Isaiah and Moses ushered in a warning for those who continue in their disobedience (10:21).

Therefore, God has not failed or rejected his people, because Paul himself and the many whom God has preserved now represent the true faith of his people. But a remnant implies another larger body that has failed to attain the goal. What of them? Paul sees this as another opportunity for grace, since as a result of Israel's unbelief, the gentiles have now entered God's family, or been grafted into God's olive tree (11:17–24). This unexpected development will provoke Jewish envy (11:11–12), so that they may eventually be grafted back into the tree.

Paul's heartfelt desire is for the salvation of *all fellow Jews* (11:28–36). He acknowledges that even though unbelieving Jews are "enemies" (11:28) of the gospel, God loves them for the sake of their ancestry because God does not revoke his covenant love on a whim. God loves Israel—which reminds gentiles that any anti-Jewish sentiments are sin. And yet by refusing Christ, these Jews have entered the deepest tragedy yet: separation from the very ancestral olive tree that has sustained them.

Ethical Exhortation: Practical Implications of the Gospel (12:1–15:13)

In Paul's mind, right thinking and believing produce right living. Paul now outlines four areas that require sincere Christian reflection: community ethics (12:1–21), political ethics (13:1–7), personal ethics (13:8–14), and the relationship of the "strong" and the "weak" (14:1–15:13). This final section is so long it suggests that Paul may be addressing a common problem either troubling the Roman church or his churches in general (it also appears in 1 Corinthians 8–10).

No system of ethics is successful without the moral and spiritual transformation of the practitioner (12:1–2). When this happens, genuine, reasoned worship takes place. Yet the opposite is often the case. Christians become proud of their status and damage the community in which they live. Paul reminds the Romans that all gifts are tokens of God's mercy and are given to strengthen and serve others. The community of faith thus becomes a place where service trumps competition and humility outweighs pride. Generosity, love, liberality, and patience are hallmarks of a redeemed life.

But no Christian community can live in isolation from the social and political realities of the world. The church must live within the empire. So Paul charges the church to submit to the authorities and live as good citizens (13:1–7). However, what sets the church apart is not its good citizenship but its belief that the state is not the final authority in matters of truth. The state must answer to God. Hence, Christians are not called to blind political obedience but to be subject when the state conforms to its calling under God.

The Voice of Jesus in Romans

In chapters 12–16 Paul unveils the ethical implications of the gospel. These commands often parallel the teachings of Jesus. As a result, scholars suggest that Paul has access to some of the same sources the gospel writers used.[1] Compare, for example, the following texts:

Romans	Gospel Parallel	Paul's Instruction
12:14	Luke 6:27–28	Bless those who persecute you; bless and do not curse.
12:17	Matt. 5:39	Do not repay anyone evil for evil.
13:7	Mark 12:17	If you owe taxes, pay taxes; if revenue, then revenue.
13:8–9	Mark 12:31	Love your neighbor as yourself [sum of commandments].
14:10	Matt. 7:1–2	You, then, why do you judge your brother or sister?
14:14	Luke 11:41; Mark 7:19	I am convinced . . . that nothing is unclean in itself.
16:19	Matt. 10:16	Be wise about what is good, and innocent about what is evil.

When Paul tells the Roman Christians to support those in public authority (13:1–7), he is walking a delicate line between politics and gentile religion since religious structures were a part of Roman society. In Pompeii, the public forum housed public courts (basilica), the market (macellum), as well as temples such as the great Capitolium (or the Temple of Jupiter), dedicated to the gods Jupiter, Juno, and Minerva.
Public Domain

Life in the empire is also life in the marketplace, with legal transactions, property rights, and friendships. Here too Paul calls on Christians to be exemplary in their conduct (13:8–14). The church should be the one place where people act differently toward one another, where Christians do not simply look after one another but where goodness is extended to others regardless of their faith. This is what it means to be a light to the world.

Finally, Paul reflects on the problem of religious and ethnic diversity that was characteristic of the first-century church (14:1–15:13). What happens when someone with strict and conservative scruples (like the Jew) decides to live in a community that celebrates its freedom in Christ? Tensions develop. The unity of the church and the preservation of the weaker believer should rank higher than our own freedom. Paul knows that food laws have disappeared in Christ (14:14), yet he refuses to injure a brother or sister for the sake of his own freedom.

Nine Women in Romans 16

Paul's greetings in all his letters include fifty-four men and thirteen women, most of whom are coworkers. All told, 20 percent of the names he lists are women. This should dispel any doubt about Paul having female coworkers.

Romans 16 follows this pattern. Paul mentions nine women. Phoebe is called a "deacon" in 16:1, but he also mentions Mary, Tryphena, Tryphosa, and Persis as "work[ing] very hard" for the Lord (a phrase Paul uses for his own work in 1 Cor. 4:12; 15:10). Priscilla and Aquila are a husband-and-wife team. Junia (not Junias, a male name) is well-known even among the apostles. Paul also greets Julia and the sister of Nereus.

Conclusion (15:14–16:27)

Paul closes his letter by returning to several themes of the introduction (cf. 1:8–15). He describes more fully his ministry to the gentiles, his reasons for writing, and his future travel plans (15:14–33). A recommendation of Phoebe (16:1–2) and numerous greetings to believers (16:3–16) give a warm relational tone. Paul concludes with a warning about false teachers (16:17–20), final greetings from his coworkers (16:21–24), and a doxology (16:25–27).

THE CENTRAL THEME OF ROMANS

From the time of the Reformation, most Protestants studying Romans have emphasized the personal justification of the believer before God. Individual salvation, justification by faith, and freedom from God's wrath were located at the center of Paul's letter. This debate turned a sharp corner in 1963 when Krister Stendahl wrote an article in the *Harvard Theological Review* entitled "The Apostle Paul and the Introspective Conscience of the West."[2] Stendahl argued that Paul is not preoccupied with matters of personal salvation and that we can find this emphasis only if we read Romans through the lens of Augustine's or Luther's anxieties about sin and justification.

For Stendahl and many subsequent interpreters of Paul, Paul's interests lie in a deeper question of how gentiles who do not possess the law gain full access to God's promises for salvation. In this view, the climax of Paul's thought is found in Romans 9–11, where Paul redefines the meaning of "Israel" theologically as God's people, both Jews and gentiles living together as one people in Christ. This "new perspective" on Romans thus sees Jew-gentile relations as the epicenter of Romans. Both Jews and gentiles share equal jeopardy before God's wrath—and both share equally in his grace. (See the New Perspective on Paul, chapter 13.)

This view does acknowledge numerous secondary themes in Romans. Individual salvation is one of them, but it is subsidiary to a wider concern about the law, gentile hope, and Jewish advantages. As some scholars today prefer, Romans should be viewed as a "dialogue with Judaism."[3] Or, as James Dunn puts it, Paul is dialoguing with himself—Paul the Jewish rabbi talking with Paul the Christian apostle.[4] For instance, when Paul argues against "works of the law," is he arguing against religious efforts by Jews trying to secure their place with God, or is he thinking about Jewish identity markers, such as circumcision and food laws that isolated Israel from other nations? If the latter, then Paul is arguing against an assumed sense of privilege that hinders the gospel among gentiles. This shift from a "vertical" to a "horizontal" understanding of Romans determines how scholars organize and interpret the letter.

In response, it seems difficult to doubt that Paul is addressing an individual crisis in Romans. He writes not simply about a Jewish and gentile problem but about a human problem. The individualism of Romans can certainly be defended, though it cannot be brought into the center of the apostle's thought. For Paul it is the *individual* Jew or gentile who is fallen, who benefits from Christ's work on the cross, who exhibits faith, and who then is rescued from Adam's curse. But this individual never lives a privatized spiritual life outside a redeemed *community*. The redeemed community has moved from a status "in Adam" to a place "in Christ" and now must seek its relation to the historic people of God known as "Israel."

Keeping this debate in mind, interpreters have often seen Paul's interest as centered on the law (mentioned seventy-two times in Romans)[5] or on the righteousness of God attained through faith (1:17). Others see this complex of ideas as one idea subsumed in "the gospel," which Paul mentions at the beginning (1:1, 2, 9, 15) and end of his letter (15:16, 19). The gospel is even the main theme of Paul's thesis statement in 1:16, "I am not ashamed of the gospel."[6]

But what is the content of this gospel? Here key themes merge: Paul is making clear that both Jews and gentiles live under a parallel jeopardy—the threat of the law, which discloses our failure to satisfy God's righteousness. But that righteousness has now been met by God himself. In Christ, God satisfied the law and made his righteousness alive within the community of faith. *This is the good news of the gospel.* Since it is appropriated by faith and not the law, it is accessible to both Jews and gentiles. Through grace, God offers genuine human renewal. If we do not recognize this new work of God in Christ, if we continue to pursue the law (9:30–31), a renewed community made up of Jews and gentiles—a new Israel—is impossible.

Questions for Discussion

1. How do the details from Paul's situation (i.e., his missionary context) and the Roman church (i.e., Jewish and gentile diversity) help us understand Romans?
2. Why does Paul send a letter of such theological complexity to a congregation he has neither established nor visited?
3. How does Paul explain the despair of human sinfulness yet maintain the dignity of the human race?
4. What distinctive themes does "the new perspective on Paul" sound in the interpretation of Romans?
5. In Romans 11 Paul recognizes the special status of Jews in God's plan of salvation. How, if at all, should this theological understanding affect international politics with modern-day Israel?

BIBLIOGRAPHY

Introductory

Bruce, F. F. *Romans*. TNTC. Grand Rapids: Eerdmans, 1985.
Jewett. R. *Romans. A Short Commentary*. Minneapolis: Fortress, 2013.
Moo, D. J. *Romans*. NIVAC. Grand Rapids: Zondervan, 2000.
Osborne, G. R. *Romans*. IVPNTC. Downers Grove, IL: InterVarsity Press, 2004.
Stott, J. *Romans: God's Good News for the World*. Downers Grove, IL: InterVarsity Press, 1994.

Advanced

Dunn, J. D. G. *Romans*. 2 vols. WBC. Waco, TX: Word, 1988.
Fitzmyer, J. *Romans*. AB. New York: Doubleday, 1993.
Jewett, R. *Romans: A Commentary* [Hermeneia Series]. Minneapolis: Fortress, 2007.
Keener, C. S. *The Mind of the Spirit. Paul's Approach to Transformed Thinking*. Grand Rapids: Baker, 2016.
Moo, D. J. *The Epistle to the Romans*. NICNT. Grand Rapids: Eerdmans, 1996.
Schreiner, T. R. *Romans*. BECNT. Grand Rapids: Baker, 1998.

NOTES

1. C. Blomberg, *The Historical Reliability of the Gospels* (Leicester, England: Inter-Varsity Press, 1987), 223.
2. The original article can be found in *HTR* 56 (1963): 199–215, and later was reprinted in K. Stendahl, *Paul among Jews and Gentiles* (Philadelphia: Fortress, 1976). See also E. P. Sanders, *Paul and Palestinian Judaism* (Philadelphia: Fortress, 1977).
3. D. Moo, *The Epistle to the Romans*, NICNT (Grand Rapids: Eerdmans, 1996), 28.
4. J. D. G. Dunn, *Romans*, WBC (Waco, TX: Word, 1988), 1:lxiii.
5. See F. Thielman, *Paul and the Law: A Contextual Approach* (Downers Grove, IL: InterVarsity Press, 1994).
6. D. Moo, *Romans*, NIVAC (Grand Rapids: Zondervan, 2000), 26.

AND EPHESIANS

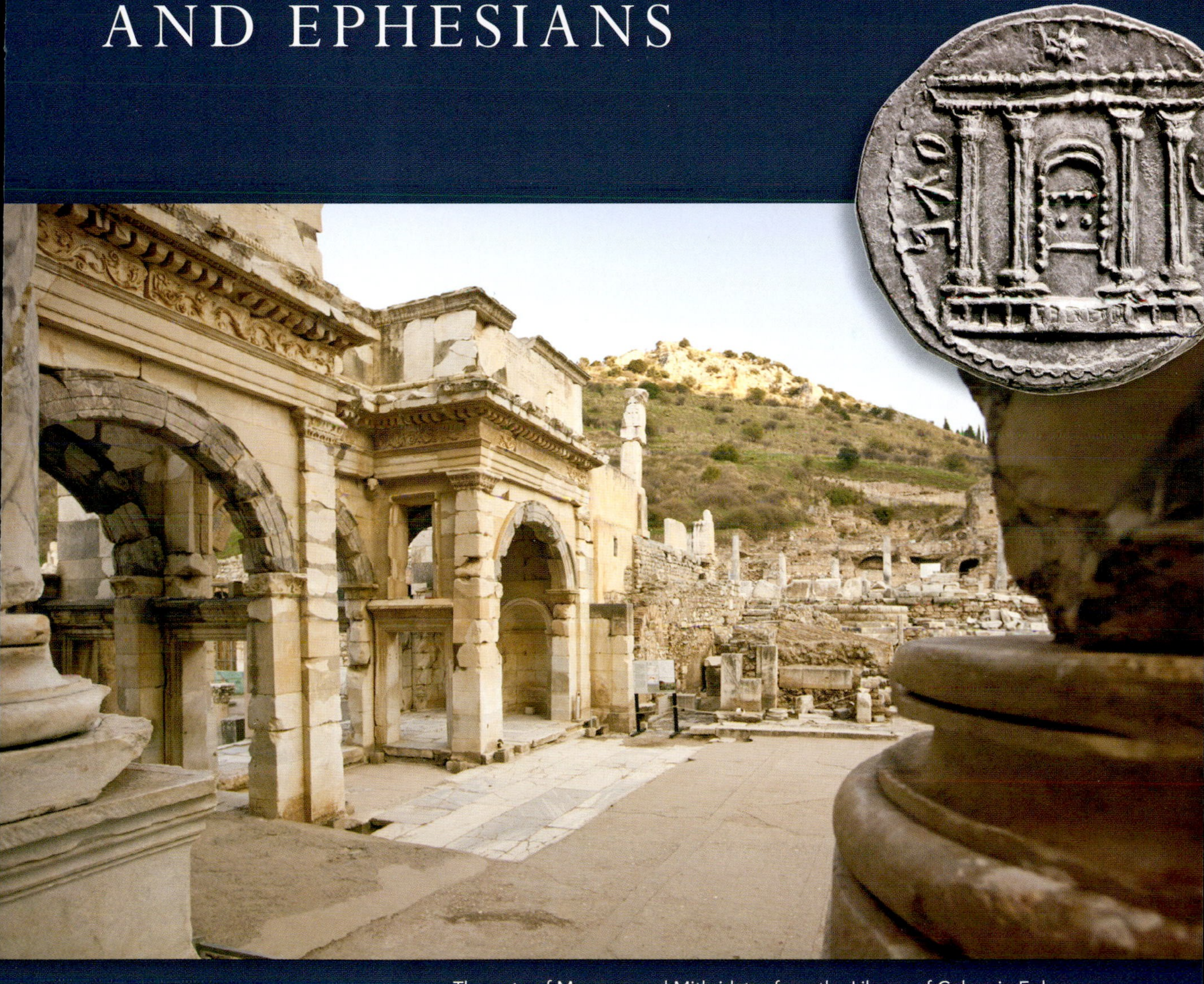

The gate of Mazaeus and Mithridates from the Library of Celsus in Ephesus

Paul's letters to the Colossians and the Ephesians are two of the so-called Prison Epistles, the others being Philippians and Philemon. Paul wrote these four letters while imprisoned, most likely in Rome (Eph. 3:1; 4:1; 6:20; Phil. 1:7, 12–18; Col. 4:3, 10, 18; Philem. 1, 9, 23). Paul had been brought for trial before the Roman procurator M. Antonius Felix in Caesarea Maritima (Acts 23:23–27). When Felix's successor, Porcius Festus, wanted to send Paul to be tried in Jerusalem, the apostle appealed to have the emperor hear his case. This was a right that Roman citizens could use if they believed they might not receive a fair trial (25:1–12; 22:25–29). Paul was sent to Rome and remained in custody there for a few years (Acts 26:32–28:31). This was the first of his two known Roman imprisonments. He composed the Prison Epistles during this period and dispatched Ephesians and Colossians with Tychicus, his messenger (Eph. 6:21–22; Col. 4:7–8; and Acts 20:4; 2 Tim. 4:12; Titus 3:12). Paul also sent Onesimus with him, since he was returning him to Philemon in Colossae (Col. 4:9; Philem. 1, 8–21). Although the two letters went out at the same time, Colossians was likely the first one written.

Colossae tell
Steven H. Sanchez/BiblePlaces.com

Letter Messengers

Paul used the services of Tychicus to make sure Colossians and Ephesians arrived safely at their destinations (Eph. 6:21–22; Col. 4:7–8). The Roman imperial postal service, the *cursus publicus*, was not available to private citizens. Private individuals used messengers whose duty was not only to carry the correspondence but also to offer additional comments. Hence authors sometimes included the messenger's name in the letter as a guarantee that the sender authorized the messenger's commentary. Messengers were so valuable that the Roman senator Cicero once remarked to Atticus that he did not have any news to send but wrote anyway: "I cannot refrain from entrusting letters to folk who are bound for Rome" (*Att.* 8.14.1). One ancient letter writer lamented that he did not have a messenger at hand: "I wrote you this letter at night, having found an opportunity, but I was not able to send it" (*p. Mich.* 476.20–21). The government of the vast Roman empire depended on the *cursus publicus* to function, and so too Christian apostles required their own commissioned couriers to maintain contact with the churches throughout the Mediterranean world. Tychicus was one of them, as was Phoebe (Rom. 16:1–2), Stephanus (1 Cor. 16:15–16), Epaphroditus (Phil. 2:25–30), and Onesimus (Philem. 10–12).

THE SETTING OF COLOSSIANS

Colossae was located on the Lycus River in a region known as Phrygia, a southern section of the Roman province of Asia. Colossae was well-known for its wool industry (Strabo 12.18.16) and was once considered a famous city. Its importance was eclipsed during the Roman period, however, by its larger neighbor Laodicea. Laodicea lay about nine miles (fifteen km) to the northwest (Col. 4:16) and was connected to Colossae via a principle east-west trade route through the region. Many deities had shrines in Colossae, including Artemis of Ephesus, Artemis the Huntress, Zeus, Demeter, Tyche, Nike, Dionysus, Athena, Leto, Isis, Sarapis, Hygieia, and Helios, among others. This gentile city also held a sizeable Jewish population, as did other cities in Asia Minor. Josephus recounts that two thousand Jewish families were once sent to Phrygia to help calm social unrest in the region (*Ant.* 12.3.4 [147–153]). Around AD 60 or 64, Colossae was shaken by a sizeable earthquake. Tacitus said that Laodicea was laid in ruins by this event (*Ann.* 14.27). Possibly Colossae met a similar fate, but we cannot be sure of the extent of the destruction since the site has not been excavated by archaeologists. Most likely Paul wrote to the church before that epic event.

We find no record in Acts, Colossians, or the other Pauline epistles that the apostle preached the gospel in Colossae. Paul mentions that the Colossians had not met him (Col. 2:1) and that he had only heard about them and their faith in Christ

The unexcavated theater in Colossae
Gary M. Burge

The city of Colossae has not been extensively excavated, so our understanding of city life in the first century AD comes principally from literature and coins. This coin with bust of Demos was minted in Phrygia, Colossae AD 180–92.

Photograph © Museum of Fine Arts, Boston

(1:4–5a, 9). Epaphras had preached the gospel to them, and he had also conveyed news about the church to Paul (1:5b–8). At the end of the letter, we learn that Colossae was Epaphras's home and that he earnestly prayed for the Colossian believers so that they might "stand firm in all the will of God, mature and fully assured" (4:12). Epaphras also showed great concern for the churches in Laodicea and Hierapolis (4:13), both near Colossae, and was possibly their founder as well. Among the other members of the Colossian church were free men such as Philemon and Archippus (Philem. 1–2; Col. 4:17), the slave Onesimus (Philem. 10–11), and the women Apphia and Nympha. Nympha was a wealthy woman who hosted a church in her home, a church she possibly led (Philem. 2; Col. 4:15). Paul's statement in Colossians 1:27 about God's mystery being "known among the Gentiles" may suggest that the Colossian church was comprised largely of non-Jews.

Epaphras had come to Paul in Rome and ended up being Paul's "fellow prisoner," but we do not know the reason for his incarceration (Philem. 23; cf. Col. 4:10; Rom. 16:7). In his letter Paul heartily commends Epaphras as a "servant of Christ Jesus" and his "dear fellow servant, who is a faithful minister of Christ on our behalf" (4:12; 1:7). The apostle remarks that the Colossians had received "the true message of the gospel" from Epaphras (1:5), the very same gospel that was spreading across the world and bearing fruit, as it was doing among the Colossians (1:6). Paul, then, wrote this letter to call them to "continue to live your lives in him, rooted and built up in him, strengthened in the faith as you were taught" (2:6–7). Apparently Paul was concerned about teachings circulating that were antithetical to the gospel that the Colossians had been taught (2:8, 16). Likely Epaphras had reported the situation to Paul. In Colossians the apostle urges the church not to yield to such beliefs but exhorts them, saying, "Continue in your faith, established and firm, and do not move from the hope held out in the gospel" (1:23).

The Colossian Problem

The nature of the aberrant teaching in Colossae has been the subject of considerable debate. We only possess Paul's response to the problem, so reconstructions of the situation remain tentative at best. Indeed, some have argued that Paul is simply warning about potentials for error rather than fighting a coherent system of belief. The Colossians seemed to be holding to the gospel (1:3–8). On the other hand, Paul's question in 2:20 suggests that they had already been influenced to some extent by this teaching: "Why, as though you still belonged to the world, do you submit to its rules?" Whether these influences had infiltrated the church or not, they were genuine threats to the faith that the Colossians had embraced through Epaphras's ministry.

The first reference to the teaching is 2:8: "See to it that no one takes you captive through hollow and deceptive philosophy, which depends on human tradition and the elemental spiritual forces of this world rather than on Christ." While we may not be able to outline all the details of this "philosophy" from the letter itself, the apostle's warnings present a rough outline of its character. "Philosophy" was a term that could be used of religious systems. Josephus and Philo both called Jewish teachings "philosophy," and later Justin Martyr tagged Christianity as "the true philosophy." The philosophy Paul was concerned with was, however, "hollow," or empty, as opposed to the richness of God's mystery (1:27) and "deceptive" in contrast with the truth of the gospel (1:5). The philosophy was merely a "human tradition" and was not of divine origin (2:8b, 22), although those who promoted the philosophy claimed to have received divine revelation in visions and consequently regarded themselves as superior to others (2:18). Paul was concerned about the persuasive rhetoric of those who held the philosophy.

Belief in the controlling power of the zodiac was common in the ancient world and can be found in both the gentile and Jewish worlds. Ephesian Artemis (Acts 19:23–41) has the signs of the zodiac around her neck (below), and the mosaic floor of the Jewish synagogue in Beth Alpha near Beit Shean, Israel, has a zodiac design. Although this synagogue dates from the third century AD, Jewish belief in the zodiac can be found much earlier.[1]

Z. Radovan/www.BibleLand Pictures.com

Gary M. Burge

In 2:8 and 2:20 Paul expresses concern over belief in the power of "the elemental spiritual forces of this world" (Gk. *stoicheia tou kosmou*). The term *stoicheia* could mean some kind of basic principles or *ABCs*, as in Hebrews 5:12. In other contexts the word refers to the "elements" that, according to ancient thought, made up everything: earth, fire, water, and air, or more simply the "elements" out of which the universe was made. In other texts the *stoicheia* are spiritual powers or even stars and the signs of the zodiac. Most likely Paul has this latter sense in mind, these "spiritual forces" being equivalent to the spiritual "rulers/powers" and "authorities" mentioned elsewhere in the letter (Colossians 1:16; 2:10, 15). These hostile forces were sometimes identified with the stars, which controlled people's destinies and the universe. The pseudepigraphic *Testament of Solomon* describes certain spirits who come and proclaim, "We are thirty-six elements, the world rulers of darkness of this age" (18:1–5; 8:2). These were associated with the zodiac. Diogenes Laertius similarly calls the signs of the zodiac "the twelve elements"

(6.102). These malignant spiritual powers could control destiny but also brought sickness and community disharmony. Paul believed that there were hostile forces in the world that were not visible (1:16) yet assailed human beings (Eph. 6:10–17).

Another aspect of the teaching Paul was concerned about was asceticism. The philosophy imposed strict rules about what one could eat, drink, or touch (2:16, 20) and prescribed "harsh treatment of the body" to subdue the desires of the flesh (2:23). In addition to these ascetic practices, it required ritual observance of certain religious days, that is, "a religious festival, a New Moon celebration or a Sabbath day" (2:16), and it is possible circumcision was obligatory (2:11). All this suggests that Jewish elements were mixed in with the philosophy. The philosophy also obligated them to display "false humility," a form of self-abasement before the powers (2:18, 23). Some in the ancient world believed that a person could come close to the deity through ascetic practices, including carefully observing sacred times. Paul regards all these regulations as ultimately ineffectual, though they appeared to embody true wisdom (2:22–23).

Especially concerning was the philosophy's insistence on "self-abasement and worship of angels" (2:18 NRSV), which explains the following note about "self-imposed worship" (2:23). Paul sees deep danger here, saying that this practice could "disqualify you" (2:18 NRSV) or deprive them of the prize. The veneration of angels was found within ancient magic as well as Judaism during this period. Angels were invoked in place of the deity, as people called on them to protect and provide for them. Angels served as intermediaries between humans and the deity, who was transcendent. Jewish magical texts also witness to the way some called on the angels for assistance.[2] Origen, for example, quotes Celsus's critique of the Jewish practice: "The first point relating to the Jews which is fitted to excite wonder, is that they should worship the heaven and the angels who dwell therein" (*Contra Celsus* 5.6).

Some have suggested that the problem Paul and Epaphras faced was a form of Judaism, while others identified it as Gnosticism, the dualistic philosophy that held that matter is evil and spirit is good. But the problem was more likely a syncretistic blend of various beliefs stemming from gentile sources and a strain of Judaism. The question was how someone could control the supernatural powers that held sway over people's lives. People in the region of Colossae held the belief that the deity was high and inaccessible, and therefore one needed intermediaries who could be invoked for protection and help. Magic in the form of angel veneration, ascetic practices, and the observance of certain days were all deemed necessary to gain some form of control over the powers.[3] Paul calls this for what it is—a vacant and deceitful philosophy (2:8). He wants the believers in Colossae and Laodicea to recognize the exalted place of Christ, who nullifies their need for these rituals. Christ is above all as both the Creator and Redeemer. None other is needed.

Paul's Response

Above all else Paul wants the Colossians and the Laodiceans to know the exalted place of Christ. On the one hand, he disparages the errant ideas that are a threat to their faith. When addressing the insistence on keeping Jewish ritual laws regarding eating, drinking, and keeping certain holy days, Paul responds, "These are a shadow of the things that were to come; the reality, however, is found in Christ" (2:17). Speaking of the ascetic restrictions that the philosophy imposed, he says, "These rules, which have to do with things that are all destined to perish with use, are based on merely human commands and teachings" (2:22). Such regulations appear wise "but they lack any value in restraining sensual indulgence" (2:23). More seriously, he is concerned that the proposed "false humility and the worship of angels" will, in the end, "disqualify you" (2:18). Indeed, those who promote the false philosophy "have lost connection with the head," by which he means Christ (2:19a; and 1:18; 2:10). There can be no growth in the community without this connection to Christ (2:19b; cf. 1 Cor. 12:14–26). The false philosophy that appeared so wise had the net effect of separating believers from Christ. Indeed, Paul reminds them that through the gospel they "died with Christ to the elemental spiritual forces of this world" (2:20).

Over against the loss that comes through the philosophy, Paul opens the readers up to the greatness of Christ's person and work. To begin with, Paul includes theological themes expressed elsewhere in his letters. For example, Christ's death on the cross brings reconciliation with God (Col. 1:21, 22; Rom. 5:10; 2 Cor. 5:18, 20), and believers are "buried with him in baptism, in which you were also raised with him through your faith in the working of God, who raised him from the dead" (Col. 2:12; Rom. 6:1–10). Believers put off the old self and put on the new (Col. 3:5–10; Rom. 13:11–14) and have now become members of Christ's body, the church (Col. 1:18; 3:15; Rom. 12:4–5; 1 Cor. 12:12–31). Here, as elsewhere, Paul affirms that Christ has broken down the barriers between ethnic and social groups (Col. 3:11; Gal. 3:28), and Paul calls for love within the community (Col. 3:14; 1 Cor. 13:1–13).

Elsewhere in the letter, Paul declares, "God was pleased to have all his fullness dwell in him" and "in Christ all the fullness of the Deity lives in bodily form" (1:19; 2:9). This is one of the most robust statements of the incarnation in all Paul's letters (cf. John 1:14). Paul links the incarnation

The Firstborn over All Creation

In 1:15 Paul claims that Christ is the "firstborn." This appears to state that he was the first being to be created. But Paul negates this understanding of the term in 1:16: "For in him all things were created." "Firstborn" was a Jewish term for preeminence and authority (see Prov. 8:22; Heb. 1:6). David, for example, was called the firstborn in Psalm 89:27: "I will appoint him to be my firstborn, the most exalted of the kings of the earth." He was not, however, the first of father Jesse's children but rather the youngest (1 Sam. 16:1–13). In the Greco-Roman world, "firstborn" was also a word for one's legal heir. Christ is also "the beginning and the firstborn from among the dead" (Col. 1:18). Although Christ was the first to be raised from the dead (see 1 Thess. 4:13–18; 1 Cor. 15), he also holds the place of highest authority as the last part of 1:18 clarifies: "so that in everything he might have the supremacy."

with Christ's work of redemption (1:20) and states that he is superior over "every power and authority" (2:10).

Paul affirms that Christ stands supreme over all creation (1:15–17) and his death has the effect of reconciling all things on earth and in heaven (1:18–20). In the first creation, everything was created through Christ and all creation is for him. He existed before it, and he sustains creation as well (1:15–17). Paul boldly states that "the Son is the image of the invisible God" (1:15), that is, he is the one through whom God is revealed and known.

But Christ is also head over God's new creation. He is over the church and was the first to rise from the dead. Through his death and resurrection, God reconciles all things to himself, both in earth and heaven (1:18–20). Christ is sovereign over the first creation and over God's new creation.

Given Christ's exalted status as Creator and Redeemer, Paul talks about the "mystery of God, namely, Christ, in whom are hidden all the treasures of wisdom and knowledge" (2:2–3). Paul's mission is to make known the mystery of Christ among the gentiles, which includes this stunning truth: "Christ in you, the hope of glory" (1:27). Paul declares that "Christ is all" and with regards to the believers he "is in all" (3:11). The portrait of Christ is the most exalted of all Paul's letters, apart from Ephesians. But Paul elevates Christ to such a high level that some have wondered whether this is truly a letter penned by the apostle (see Author and Date).

Given who Christ is and what he has done in creation and redemption, the philosophy based on "human tradition" that pays heed to the "elemental spiritual forces of this world" brings no benefit but only loss.

Paul's Ethics

The soaring Christology of Colossians is tightly linked with Paul's ethical admonitions in the second part of this letter (3:1–4:6). What Christ has accomplished in redemption has moral implications for the ones whom he has redeemed. As elsewhere in his letters, Paul affirms that believers have died with Christ and have been raised with him as well. He holds the hope that as Christ was glorified, so they will be (3:1–4; see Rom. 6:1–14). The reality that they have "died" and "been raised with Christ" carries within it the call to "put to death, therefore, whatever belongs to your earthly nature" (3:5). Similarly, Paul taught the Roman believers that they had died with Christ but that now they are to "count yourselves dead to sin but alive to God in Christ Jesus" (Rom. 6:11). The moral imperative is buried within the indicative of Christ's act, and their identification with him. In Colossians this means that they should put off the sins that characterized their former life (3:5–10), including the prejudices that divided them (3:11). But he also calls them to put on the virtues that are markers of the true Christian life (3:12–17).

Virtue and Vice Lists

Virtue and vice lists were a common form of moral instruction in the Mediterranean world. Vice lists outlined the types of behaviors of people who had not achieved full potential, and virtue lists depicted the good life of a wise person. While vice lists outlined morally dishonorable behavior, the virtue lists showed what conduct was honorable. Virtues brought freedom, while vices resulted in moral bondage. Diogenes Laertius, for example, says, "Amongst the virtues some are primary, some are subordinate to these. The following are the primary: wisdom, courage, justice, temperance. Particular virtues are magnanimity, continence, endurance, presence of mind, good counsel." He also lists dishonorable behavior: "Similarly, of vices some are primary, others subordinate: *e.g.* folly, cowardice, injustice, profligacy are accounted primary; but incontinence, stupidity, ill-advisedness subordinate" (7.92–93, 110–112). The most well-known of Paul's vice and virtue lists are the works of the flesh and the fruits of the Spirit in Galatians 5:19–26. In Colossians 3:12–14 he inserts a virtue list after a vice list in 3:5–8. Christian virtue and vice lists were infused with the values of the gospel and thereby redefined what constituted honorable and dishonorable behavior. Christians regarded love as the highest virtue (1 Cor. 13:13).

Both here and in Ephesians, Paul includes an extensive section of what has been called a "household code" (*Haustafel* in German) in 3:18–4:1. Similarly, in Ephesians 5:21–6:9 Paul presents another household code, a form of teaching found also in 1 Peter 2:18–3:7. Household codes outlined the reciprocal duties and obligations of the various members of ancient households: wives and husbands, children and parents, slaves and masters. The focus of the codes was household management, but they also extended to people's duties to civil authorities, since the state was conceived as a household. Given this, the household code in 1 Peter includes teaching on responsibilities to the emperor and civic magistrates (1 Pet. 2:13–17).

Relief of an ancient Roman family, the National Museum, Istanbul, Turkey
Gary M. Burge

The household codes presupposed a hierarchical social order that included both superordinate and subordinate members of society. Parents and the emperor were superordinate, for example, while children and citizens were subordinate. Paul and Peter adopted this form of teaching but, as in the case of the virtue and vice lists, infused them with Christian values. Husbands are told to "love your wives and do not be harsh with them" (Col. 3:19), and masters are called to do "what is right and fair, because you know that you also have a Master in heaven" (4:1). At the same time, the household codes had an apologetic function, since they demonstrated that the Christian communities did not pose a threat to social order.

Paul's household codes, as that in 1 Peter, showed believers how to live according to Christian values within the social structures of that day. They did not,

The Household Codes

Before and during Paul's time, many ancient moral philosophers wrote about household management. In his *Politics*, Aristotle said, "Every state is composed of households . . . and the household in its perfect form consists of slaves and freemen. The investigation of everything should begin with its smallest parts, and the primary and smallest parts of the household are master and slave, husband and wife, father and children; we ought therefore to examine the proper constitution and character of each of these three relationships, I mean that of mastership, that of marriage . . . , and thirdly the progenitive relationship" (1.2.1–2 [1253b]). The apostles developed their own ideas about household management.

however, prescribe the preservation of those social structures as understood in the ancient Mediterranean world. While we affirm civil authority, we do not believe we must live under the rule of an emperor or king (1 Pet. 2:13). The church was instrumental in the abolition of slavery, regarding the institution as antithetical to the values of the gospel.[4] The household codes in the New Testament point to how Christians were to live within the structures of Roman society but do not codify ancient Roman social structures for all time.

Outline of Colossians

I. Epistolary Greeting (1:1–2)
II. Thanksgiving and Prayer for the Colossian Church (1:3–14)
III. The Supremacy of Christ in Creation and Redemption (1:15–23)
IV. Paul's Ministry and God's Mystery (1:24–2:5)
V. The Hollow and Deceptive Philosophy (2:6–23)
VI. New Moral Life in Christ (3:1–4:6)
   1. Death and Resurrection with Christ (3:1–4)
   2. Put to Death Vice and Put on Virtue (3:5–17)
   3. The Christian Household Code (3:18–4:1)
   4. Final Exhortations (4:2–6)
VII. Final Greetings (4:7–18)

THE SETTING OF EPHESIANS

Paul wrote Ephesians during his first Roman imprisonment and dispatched this letter, along with Colossians, in the hands of his messenger Tychicus, who was also charged with telling the recipients about Paul's situation (Eph. 6:21–22; Col. 4:7–8). Paul called himself "a prisoner for the Lord" (Eph. 4:1) and "an ambassador in chains" (6:20), recognizing that his bonds were for the cause of Christ and that his incarceration was an opportunity for ministry (cf. Phil. 1:12–14). Paul continued to exhibit deep concern for the welfare of the churches despite having had his liberty taken away. His letters made his voice heard and emphasized his apostolic authority to the churches even though he was physically absent.

Some of the oldest manuscripts of Ephesians do not include the words "in Ephesus" in 1:1. This textual problem (see ch. 27 on The Text of the New Testament) leads many scholars to conclude that this book may not have been written to the Ephesian church. Paul ministered there for two to three years (Acts 19:1,

Polycarp of Smyrna on Circulating Letters

At the beginning of the second century AD, Polycarp, the bishop of Smyrna, in the province of Asia, commented to the Philippians about circulating letters:

> Both you and Ignatius have written to me that if anyone is going to Syria he should take along your letter. I will do so if I have the opportunity—either I or someone I send as a representative on your behalf and mine. We have forwarded to you the letters of Ignatius that he sent to us, along with all the others we had with us, just as you directed us to do. These accompany this letter; you will be able to profit greatly from them, for they deal with faith and endurance and all edification that is suitable in our Lord (*Phil.* 13.1–2).

A letter could bring benefit even though the correspondence was not written to that person. Such is the situation of contemporary readers of the New Testament letters.

10; 20:17–18, 31), yet this letter says that he had only "heard" about their faith (Eph. 1:15) and that they had "heard" about his ministry (3:2). The epistle is devoid of personal greetings at the end, a strange phenomenon if he were writing to a well-known congregation. One suggestion is that this was a circular letter, like Galatians (Gal. 1:2), sent to the churches in the province of Asia, with Ephesus being one of the cities the letter passed through. On the other hand, some scholars note that many later Greek manuscripts include "in Ephesus," as do ancient versions (translations). The earliest textual witnesses, however, favor the exclusion of "in Ephesus," as does the lack of personal references. Common practice in the early church was to circulate apostolic letters, even those destined for a particular congregation (Col. 4:16).

While we may not be able to identify precisely who the original recipients of this letter were, the correspondence itself offers us evidence of the contours of the community or communities to which it was written. These believers, as noted, had not met Paul, but his apostolic authority was recognized among them (Eph. 1:1). They also knew about his ministry and his imprisonment

Apostolic Presence and the Epistles

Paul lived in the tension between his call to spread the gospel throughout the empire (Gal. 1:15–16; 2:9) and the need to care for the churches. In his absence he sent associates like Timothy and Titus to care for the congregations (1 Cor. 16:10–11; 2 Cor. 12:17–18; Phil. 2:19; 1 Thess. 3:2; Titus 1:4–5), but he also sent letters to address their needs. In the ancient world, letters were read aloud. For Paul's letters, this would have been done when the Christians assembled (1 Thess. 5:27). It was as if the apostle stood before them; letters were regarded as a substitute for an absent person. In a letter to Lucilius, Seneca the philosopher said:

> I thank you for writing to me so often; for you are revealing your real self to me in the only way you can. I never receive a letter from you without being in your company forthwith. If the pictures of our absent friends are pleasing to us, though they only refresh the memory and lighten our longing by a solace that is unreal and unsubstantial, how much more pleasant is a letter, which brings us real traces, real evidences, of an absent friend! For that which is sweetest when we meet face to face is afforded by the impress of a friends' hand upon his letter—recognition (*Ep.* 40.1).

(3:2, 13). When addressing them directly, Paul calls them "Gentiles by birth" (2:11) and says that he is "the prisoner of Christ Jesus for the sake of you Gentiles" (3:1; and 3:6, 8; 4:7). These gentiles have "faith in the Lord Jesus and your love for all God's people" (1:15), but we do not know how the gospel came to them. They had heard the good news of Christ and had received essential Christian teaching, including ethical instruction (1:13; 4:20–24). But they needed instruction about their relationship with Jewish believers and the promises God had given to that nation (2:11–3:13). Paul's appeal in 4:14 about no longer being "infants, tossed back and forth by the waves, and blown here and there by every wind of teaching" may imply that they were relatively recent converts to Christ and could be swayed by errant teaching. These gentile believers also apparently needed the most basic instruction regarding proper Christian conduct (4:25–5:2). The household code indicates that the congregations were inclusive, comprised of men and women, parents and children, and masters and slaves (5:21–6:9). Some were on the lower rung of the socioeconomic ladder (4:28b).

THE MESSAGE OF EPHESIANS

We are not entirely sure why Paul composed this letter. When Paul wrote Romans, for example, he announced his forthcoming visit to the city and his desire that the church assist him as he journeyed onward to Spain (Rom. 1:11–13; 15:23–29). He composed 1 Corinthians as a response to the news he received about the church and to answer questions the church had put to him (1 Cor. 1:10–12; 7:1). But many scholars hold the view that Ephesians had no distinct purpose. Why did Paul write it?

Some have suggested that Ephesians was originally a sermon preached at a baptism, since it exhorts the young believers to live out their Christian calling. There is "one baptism" (Eph. 4:5), Paul reminds them, and now they "must no longer live as the Gentiles do" (4:17) but should "live as children of light" (5:8). Others have picked up on Paul's warning about being tossed to and fro by false teaching (4:14) and then endeavor to identify the false teaching. Some argue that it was Gnosticism, a dualistic philosophy that regarded matter as evil and spirit as good. Gnosticism promised salvation through esoteric knowledge (*gnosis*). Yet others claim the letter is a polemic against the way gentile Christians dishonored Jewish Christian believers (2:11–3:13). Others see the letter as Paul's attempt to address the issue of Christian conflict with cosmic spiritual powers (6:10–17). As Clinton Arnold says, "Ephesians appears to have been written to a group of churches in western Asia Minor needing help in developing a Christian perspective on the 'powers' and encouragement in their ongoing struggles with these pernicious spirit-forces."[5]

The Powers

In Ephesians 6:10–20 Paul reminds the believers of the spiritual battle they are in: "For our struggle is not against flesh and blood, but against the rulers, against the authorities, against the powers of this dark world and against the spiritual forces of evil in the heavenly realms" (v. 12). Acts 19:19 reminds us that Ephesus was known for magic, but this was not the only place it was practiced (Acts 8:9, 11; 13:6, 8). Artemis of Ephesus was known for her power. One ancient invocation to her said, "O Great Artemis of the Ephesians, help! Display your power upon this young man who has died. For all the Ephesians know, both men and women, that all things are governed by you, and that great powers come to us through you."[6] Power was one of the greatest concerns in ancient religion. In this context of conflict with "the powers," Paul affirms the victory of Christ and that Christians clothed with the "full armor of God" can stand against them. Paul exhorts these believers, saying, "Finally, be strong in the Lord and in his mighty power" (Eph. 6:10).

Against the backdrop of Ephesus's marketplace, Paul proclaimed the gospel of Jesus.
iStock.com/smartin69

On the other hand, while the "powers" are indeed Paul's concern, the whole of the letter cannot be explained with reference to that spiritual conflict. The letter also evidences no trace of negative gentile attitudes toward Jewish Christians, nor are there echoes of the distinctives of the later Gnostic heresy, such as salvation via knowledge or dualism. The letter is what it appears to be on the surface—an epistle—and does not have marks of being originally a Christian homily, whatever the occasion.

The occasion of Ephesians is best discerned by returning to the content of the letter and its audience. In the first place, these new gentile converts to Christ needed to know the basics of Christian morality. This is the concern of the second half of the book (4:1–5:9). How they were now to live in contrast to their former life is repeatedly emphasized (4:1, 14, 17, 20, 25, 29; 5:1, 3, 8, 15). They also needed to know how to live as believers within the social structures in which they were embedded. The household code in 5:21–6:9 discusses the issue at length. Also, they needed deep understanding about how to live over against the spiritual powers that were so well-known within the surrounding culture. There is a spiritual battle, but Christ is the victor, and believers stand with him against these forces (6:10–17).

But Paul also invests considerable energy in telling these gentile believers what place they hold in God's plan in relation to his promises to Israel (2:11–3:13). We do not know for certain the reason for this lengthy section on the relationship between the gentiles and the Jewish people. Most likely these gentile converts held questions about their place and status with respect to the great promises made to Israel, statements they had heard when Scripture was read. Were they included in God's plan and what was their relationship with the promises made to the ancestors of the Jewish people?

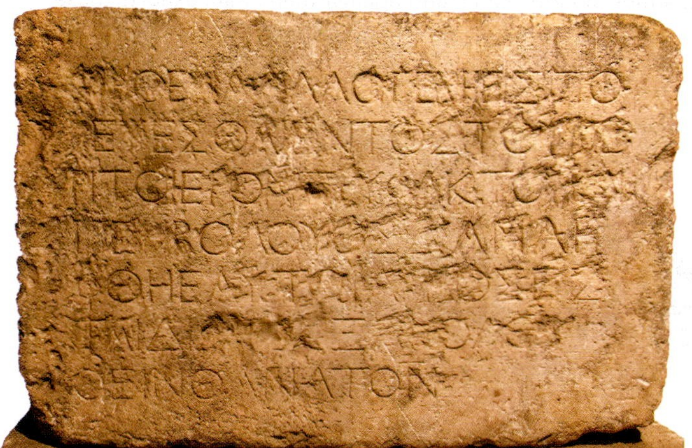

Paul seeks to show the gentiles that although they had been "separate from Christ, excluded from citizenship in Israel and foreigners to the covenants of promise, without hope and without God in the world," they have now "been brought near by the blood of Christ" (2:12–13).

The *soreg* was a wall that divided the Court of the Gentiles from the temple. The inscription warned gentiles not to pass beyond the wall. It reads: "No gentile may enter beyond the dividing wall into the court around the Holy Place; whoever is caught will be to blame for his subsequent death." Paul appears to reference this wall as a symbol of gentile exclusion, Istanbul Archaeological Museum. *Todd Bolen/BiblePlaces.com*

Notice the *soreg* on both sides of this model of the temple. *© 2018 by Zondervan*

Ethnicity and the Church

In Ephesians 2:11–3:13 Paul writes extensively about the respective place of Jews and gentiles in God's plan, as he does throughout Romans (Rom. 1:16–17; 9:1–11:36). The gentiles "once were far away" but have now "been brought near by the blood of Christ" (Eph. 2:13). He has made "the two groups one" (2:14), and his purpose was to "create in himself one new humanity out of the two, thus making peace" (2:15) between themselves and then with God. Paul astonishingly claims that God's purpose was "to reconcile both of them to God through the cross," not as separate entities but "in one body" (2:16). He links reconciliation with God with reconciliation of people from these, and other, ethnic groups. But both the Jerusalem Council (Acts 15) and Galatians clarified that conversion to Christ did not mean that someone must abandon their ethnicity to follow Christ. Gentile believers did not have to become Jewish proselytes through the ritual of circumcision and adoption of dietary laws. Unity between the varied social groups did not mean the suppression of one's ethnic identity.

In the Roman world, a person's identity was marked in a variety of ways, the first being the place where they were from (Matt. 21:11; 26:69; 27:57; Acts 9:11; 16:14; 18:2), which regarded as a contributing factor to their ethnic characteristics. As Ptolemy said, "For if the seed is generically the same, human for example, and the condition of the ambient the same, those who are born differ much, both in body and soul, with the difference of countries" (*Tetrabiblos* 1.8; and Pliny the Elder, *Nat.* 2.80.189). Place was also a marker for social status. Paul, for example, said, "I am a Jew, from Tarsus in Cilicia, a citizen of no ordinary city" (Acts 21:39). In contrast, Nathanael remarked on Jesus's town, saying, "Nazareth! Can anything good come from there?" (John 1:46).

While identity was linked with place, it could also result in ethnocentrism. Indeed, ethnocentric attitudes were prevalent in the Roman world. The "other" for the Greeks were the Barbarians, as the Samaritans were for the Jews (John 4:9). "Barbarians" did not speak Greek and were considered uncivilized. The Greeks, therefore, regarded the Jews as barbarians and uncivilized (Josephus, *C. Ap.* 2.14 [148]; Juvenal 6.155). Aristotle quotes the saying: "'Tis meet that Greeks should rule barbarians,'" then remarks, "implying that barbarian and slave are the same in nature" (*Pol.* 1.1, 1252b). Paul makes the astounding statement in Romans 1:14, "I am a debtor both to Greeks and to barbarians" (NRSV). Ethnic stereotyping was common. Josephus remarks that the Scythians "delight in murdering people and are little better than wild beasts" but that at least they "think it their duty to uphold their national customs" (*C. Ap.* 2.37 [269]). Paul, in contrast, includes Scythians among those included in Christ (Col. 3:11).

The miracle of the gospel is the inclusion of people of all ages, both genders, every social class, multiple cities, and all ethnicities. Paul said to the gentiles, "You are no longer foreigners and strangers, but fellow citizens with God's people and also members of his household, built on the foundation of the apostles and prophets, with Christ Jesus himself as the chief cornerstone" (Eph. 2:19–20). The mystery of the gospel is that "the Gentiles are heirs together with Israel, members together of one body, and sharers together in the promise in Christ Jesus" (3:6). Those who were divided by origin, ethnicity, custom, and prejudice shared a common baptism, sat at one table, and shared life together in Christ, while at the same time not abandoning their identity. Both diversity and unity were found in their common bond with Christ and each other.

Deep within this section is the question of ethnic identity and the gospel of Christ (2:14–18). Paul and the early church invested considerable energy working through the relationship in Christ between Jews, gentiles, and all ethnicities, as well as the varied social classes and both genders (Gal. 3:28; Col. 3:11; Rom. 9–11). They also developed practical guidelines regarding how those of varied social groupings could worship and eat together and help one another (Acts 15:19–29; Rom. 14:1–15:13; Gal. 2:10; 1 Cor. 11:17–34; 16:1–4; 2 Cor. 8–9). Unity in Christ was expressed in concrete ways.

Finally, Ephesians addresses some of the larger questions found also in Colossians. Paul tells of the overarching purposes of God in reconciling humanity (2:15–16) but also "to bring unity to all things in heaven and on earth" (1:9–10). This is the cosmic dimension of the reconciling "mystery" of God (1:9; 3:2–6; cf. Col. 1:19–20). Christ is sovereign over everything in heaven and earth (1:20–23). The apostle demonstrates that believers have died and risen with Christ and shows how "God raised us up with Christ and seated us with him in the heavenly realms in Christ Jesus" (2:6). Paul affirms Christ's absolute transcendence, authority, and saving power and that his followers are participants in his victory by grace. As he discusses Christ's authority, he affirms the identity of the gentile believers, who find their place in God's plan in relation to Israel and the whole cosmos. Their inclusion is part of the overarching eternal plan of God. They have been chosen, predestined, and redeemed through Christ's cross and have come to know their place in God's plan through the proclamation of the gospel (1:3–14).

Outline of Ephesians

I. Epistolary Greeting (1:1–2)
II. God's Plan for All Creation and Humanity (1:3–3:21)
   1. Praise to God for Spiritual Blessings in Christ (1:3–14)
   2. Thanksgiving and Prayer for the Believers (1:15–22)
   3. God's Salvation by Grace through Faith (2:1–10)
   4. The Inclusion of the Gentiles in God's People (2:11–3:13)
   5. Prayers for the Believers (3:14–21)
III. Living a Life Worthy of God's Calling (4:1–6:20)
   1. Life Together in One Body (4:1–16)
   2. No Longer Living Like Other Gentiles (4:17–5:7)
   3. Living as Children of Light (5:8–20)
   4. The Christian Household Code (5:21–6:9)
   5. Taking on the Armor of God (6:10–20)
IV. Epistolary Closing and Prayer (6:21–24)

THE RELATIONSHIP BETWEEN COLOSSIANS AND EPHESIANS

Scholars have long recognized the intimate relationship between the contents of Colossians and Ephesians. At least a third of the vocabulary found in Colossians is also in Ephesians, and certain sections of the letters read almost the same. For example, the letters' final greetings are nearly identical at one point (Eph. 6:21–22; Col. 4:7–8), and throughout, expressions in the one seem to be duplicated in the other (compare, e.g., Eph. 1:4 and Col. 1:22; Eph. 1:7 and Col. 1:14; Eph. 2:5 and Col. 2:13; Eph. 4:2 and Col. 3:12, 14). Both letters include a household code, unlike any of the other Pauline letters, and both emphasize the transcendent supremacy of Christ in creation and redemption. How do we account for the similarities and differences between these letters?

One proposed solution is that the author of Ephesians had Colossians at hand. Literary borrowing was done in the ancient world (see ch. 5 on the synoptic problem and ch. 24 on the relationship between 2 Peter and Jude). Those who hold that the author of Ephesians used Colossians argue that Ephesians was a pseudepigraphic letter written by someone other than Paul. Others, however, hold that the similarities and differences between the letters may be accounted for by assuming that Paul wrote both around the same time. Their differences are due to the unique situations of their respective readers. This explanation assumes Pauline authorship for both letters and holds that the apostle composed both from Rome and dispatched them both with Tychicus, his messenger (Eph. 6:21; Col. 4:7). This explanation fits the existing evidence but depends on the assessment of the authenticity of the letters. Did Paul write both Colossians and Ephesians?

𝔓46, one of the earliest manuscripts of Ephesians dates to the second century AD and does not include the words "in Ephesus."
Papyrology Collection, Graduate Library, University of Michigan, P.Mich.inv. 6238, 146 recto

AUTHOR AND DATE

Both Colossians and Ephesians purport to be by Paul (Col. 1:1; Eph. 1:1), who identifies himself as an apostle and states that he is a prisoner bound in chains (Eph. 3:1; 4:1; 6:20; Col. 4:10, 18). The early church received these letters as genuine communications from the apostle Paul. Eusebius, the fourth-century early church historian, noted that they were among the "recognized" books in the New Testament, in contrast with other "spurious" documents, such as the

Acts of Paul (*Hist. eccl.* 3.15.2, 4). Every early canonical list named these letters as authentic letters of the apostle Paul (see ch. 27). And recognized Christian authors in the second and third centuries AD used both books. Justin Martyr, Irenaeus, Tertullian, Clement of Alexandria, and even the heretic Marcion acknowledged Colossians as authentic. Clement of Rome, Ignatius, Hermas, Polycarp, and Irenaeus all referenced Ephesians in their writings, demonstrating belief in its authenticity. The early church cast no shadow of doubt over the authenticity of either Colossians or Ephesians.

In contrast, questions about Colossians's authenticity arose early in the nineteenth century and have continued to this day. The style of the letter is different from other undisputed Pauline epistles, such as Romans and 1 Corinthians. Eduard Lohse counts thirty-four words in this work that appear nowhere else in the New Testament and another twenty-eight not found in Paul's other writings. Moreover, the grammatical style shows marked stylistic differences compared with the other known Pauline letters. He concludes, "It is generally conceded that the liturgical-hymnic style points to considerable differences from the speech and manner of expression used in the chief Pauline letters."[7]

While acknowledging the differences, we need not conclude that these are decisive markers of inauthenticity. First, Colossians takes up the peculiar issues of the philosophy that was at the door of the church, and this situation evoked at least some of the unique language in the letter. Second, Paul's prolonged imprisonment may account for changes in style, at least to some extent. Third, the role of the secretary or amanuensis must be considered. Secretaries were commonly employed when authors wrote, and Paul used their services (see Rom. 16:22). Paul added a final greeting in his own hand (Col. 4:18), a common practice when ancient authors utilized an amanuensis (Gal. 6:11; 2 Thess. 3:17). These final greetings authenticated the content of the letter. We know that secretaries sometimes took dictation, but they could also edit or even compose the letter under the guidance of the author.[8] Cicero, the great Roman orator, used the services of his secretary Tiro: "Your services to me are past all reckoning—at home, in the forum, in the city, in my province, in private as in public affairs, in my literary pursuits and performances" (*Fam.* 16.4.3; 16.3.2). Given the assistance a secretary could and did offer authors, the stylistic differences are not sufficient to bring the letter's authenticity into doubt.

But contemporary authors have also noted theological differences in this letter. The high Christology in Colossians 1:15–20 is unique among the Pauline writings, apart from Ephesians. The letter also speaks of the church not only as a local congregation but as a universal entity (1:18), as opposed to Paul's use of the term elsewhere as local congregations (compare, e.g., Gal. 1:2). The character of "hope" in this letter is not developed as a Christian virtue (1 Cor. 13:13) but rather as part of the author's discussion about the meaning of the gospel, which he summarizes as "hope" in 1:3–8 (see also 1:27). The ethical instruction in the household code in Colossians also finds no parallel in Paul's letters, apart from Ephesians (3:18–4:1).

But Colossians is theologically similar to other Pauline letters. The letter is replete with Pauline themes such as the death and resurrection of Christ, faith, and the lordship of Christ. Theological differences in the letter can be traced to the unique situations the apostle addresses but also reflect developments in his own understanding of the scope of Christ's work. The Christology of the letter is more developed than in 1 Corinthians, for example, but from the beginning Paul recognized Christ as the exalted heavenly Lord (see 1 Thess. 4:13–18, one of the earliest of Paul's letters). Developments in the apostle's Christology or ecclesiology need not surprise us. The concept of "hope" here is not alien to Paul either (cf. Rom. 8:22–25). The inclusion of the household code is not a marker that another author wrote the book, since such teaching appears to have been common in the early church (see 1 Pet. 2:18–3:7).

The personal greetings that fill the end of this book point to the authenticity of the letter, since the recipients would have readily recognized a forgery. The letter to the Colossians bears the marks of authenticity and was received as such by the early church. We should acknowledge it as an authentic apostolic correspondence as well.

The epistle to the Ephesians is similar to Colossians in a number of ways, as has already been discussed. The similarity of Ephesians and Colossians has been used as evidence that an unknown author composed Ephesians using Colossians as a template. But if we postulate that Paul wrote these two letters at about the same time yet addressed different situations, the problem of similarity dissolves. We must allow the apostle some "reruns," as with any public speaker or writer. In any case, most authors acknowledge that Colossians was likely the first of the two epistles written and that Ephesians echoes Colossians.

As with Colossians, the authenticity of Ephesians is sometimes denied based on stylistic differences with the other universally acknowledged Paulines. There are around ninety words in Ephesians not found in the other Pauline letters, and the author uses extremely long sentences in a style unlike Paul's.[9] The letter is replete with unique phrases, grammar, and ambiguities that make his meaning sometimes difficult to ascertain.[10] Yet here again, we must take into account the strong role an amanuensis could have in composition. The presence of a secretary in composition or editing would not diminish the named author's role, since authors normally checked the work of the secretary before adding a greeting and dispatching the correspondence.

The absence of personal greetings at the end of the letter is not an argument against the authenticity of Ephesians. It may have been a circular letter, since the words "in Ephesus" in 1:1 were likely not part of the original text. Galatians was a circular letter, and it is devoid of personal greetings as Ephesians. We cannot argue against authenticity based on this lack.

Both Colossians and Ephesians come to us as authentic works of Paul, but we also recognize the presence of an authorial community, that is, people who joined with Paul in the composition, distribution, and explanation of these letters. Paul was not an independent agent but was dependent on a wider circle of associates who played significant roles as he carried out his apostolic mission.

Questions for Discussion

1. What implications does Paul's teaching about Christ's supremacy as Creator and Redeemer as discussed in Colossians and Ephesians have for the Christian life in society today?
2. How should the church interpret and use the household codes today, given that they called believers to live out their faith in social orders different from those in contemporary society?
3. Are Christians still engaged in spiritual warfare today and, if so, in what ways?
4. What contemporary theological trends may be identified as a "philosophy" that poses a threat to the gospel (Col. 2:8)?
5. How are Paul's teachings on ethnicity in Ephesians relevant for the life of the church in a multicultural society?

BIBLIOGRAPHY

Colossians: Introductory

Bird, M. F. *Colossians and Philemon.* NCCS. Eugene, OR: Cascade, 2009.
Garland, D. E. *Colossians and Philemon.* NIVAC. Grand Rapids: Zondervan, 1998.
Gupta, N. K. *Colossians.* SHBC. Macon: Smyth & Helwys, 2013.

Colossians: Advanced

Barth, M., and H. Blanke. *Colossians.* AB. New York: Doubleday, 1994.
Dunn, J. D. G. *The Epistles to the Colossians and to Philemon.* NIGTC. Grand Rapids: Eerdmans, 1996.
Moo, D. J. *The Letters to the Colossians and to Philemon.* PNTC. Grand Rapids: Eerdmans, 2008.
Pao, D. W. *Colossians and Philemon.* ZECNT. Grand Rapids: Zondervan, 2012.
Wilson, R. M. *A Critical and Exegetical Commentary on Colossians.* ICC. London: T&T Clark, 2005.

Ephesians: Introductory

Bruce, F. F. *The Epistles to the Colossians, to Philemon, and to the Ephesians.* NICNT. Grand Rapids: Eerdmans, 1984.
Cohick, L. H. *Ephesians.* NCCS. Eugene, OR: Cascade, 2010.
Snodgrass, K. *Ephesians.* NIVAC. Grand Rapids: Zondervan, 1996.

Ephesians: Advanced

Arnold, C. E. *Ephesians.* ZECNT. Grand Rapids: Zondervan, 2010.
Barth, M. *Ephesians.* AB. Garden City: Doubleday, 1974.
Best, E. *A Critical and Exegetical Commentary on Ephesians.* ICC. Edinburgh: T&T Clark, 1998.
Hoehner, H. W. *Ephesians. An Exegetical Commentary.* Grand Rapids: Baker Academic, 2002.
Lincoln, A. T. *Ephesians.* WBC. Dallas: Word, 1990.
Thielman, F. *Ephesians.* BECNT. Grand Rapids: Zondervan, 2010.

NOTES

1. J. H. Charlesworth, "Jewish Astrology in the Talmud, Pseudepigrapha, the Dead Sea Scrolls, and Early Palestinian Synagogues," *HTR* 70 (1977): 183–200.

2. For the texts, see C. E. Arnold, *The Colossian Syncretism: The Interface between Christianity and Folk Belief at Colossae* (Grand Rapids: Baker, 1996), 8–89.

3. Ibid., 234–238, 310–312.

4. See M. A. Noll, *The Civil War as a Theological Crisis* (Chapel Hill: University of North Carolina Press, 2006).

5. C. E. Arnold, *Ephesians: Power and Magic: The Concept of Power in Ephesians in Light of Its Historical Setting* (Grand Rapids: Baker, 1992), 167.

6. Cited in Ibid., 22.

7. E. Lohse, *Colossians and Philemon*, Hermeneia (Philadelphia: Fortress, 1971), 84–91.

8. E. R. Richards, *Paul and First-Century Letter Writing: Secretaries, Composition and Collection* (Downers Grove, IL: InterVaristy Press, 2004), 59–93.

9. C. L. Mitton, *Ephesians*, NCB (Grand Rapids: Eerdmans, 1982), 4–5.

10. F. Thielman, *Ephesians*, BECNT (Grand Rapids: Baker Academic, 2010), 5–7.

AND PHILEMON

The basilica and forum at Philippi

Todd Bolen/BiblePlaces.com

After landing at the harbor in Neapolis, Paul took the Via Egnatia to Philippi.

On his second missionary journey, Paul founded the church in Philippi. His mission in the city landed both him and Silas in jail after being beaten and publicly dishonored (Acts 16:22–32; 1 Thess. 2:2). When Paul writes to the Philippian church, he is again a prisoner, this time in Rome. The persecution he endured in Philippi is now also the experience of the Philippian believers.

Despite the pain he and the first readers suffer, the Philippian letter overflows with tremendous joy (mentioned twelve times). Paul pens the best-known words from the letter, "rejoice in the Lord always" (4:4), while bound with chains and wondering whether he will live or die. He calls the Philippian church not to be afraid of their adversaries but to understand that "it has been granted to you on behalf of Christ not only to believe in him, but also to suffer for him" (1:29).

Paul is also troubled about the Judaizers (see below). In addition, the church is experiencing internal strife involving two female leaders. Nevertheless, Paul calls the congregation to humble service, presenting them Christ's example, and assures them that in the final day every being in God's universe will recognize Christ as Lord.

THE CITY OF PHILIPPI

Paul arrived at Philippi after crossing the Aegean Sea during his second missionary journey. He and his companions (Silas, Timothy, and Luke) had set sail from Troas to Philippi's port city, Neapolis (16:11).

From Neapolis, Paul and his companions traveled to Philippi, located some ten miles (sixteen km) inland. Midway through the journey they would have stopped for water at an ancient inn (*mansio*) before finally passing through the Neapolis Gate to enter Philippi.

When the Romans defeated the Macedonian empire in the mid-second century BC, Philippi (named after Philip II, the father of Alexander the Great) came under Roman control. The Romans divided the former Macedonian kingdom into four districts. Philippi was in the first district, although the principal city there was Amphipolis (some late Latin manuscripts of Acts 16:12 say Philippi was "a city of the first district of Macedonia, a colony" instead of being "the leading city of that district").

Philippi became a Roman colony and received the name *Colonia Iulia Philippensis* in honor of Julius Caesar. Shortly thereafter it became *Colonia Augusta Iulia Philippensis*, honoring Augustus. This city prospered since it presided over an extensive territory (*territorium*) and had legal status as an Italian city. This was *Italian soil* in Macedonia. Thus, the colonists paid no land or poll taxes and enjoyed full Roman citizenship. The law and judicial system were Roman. The main language in the streets was Latin, not Greek. However, four of the people we know from the Philippian story have Greek names (Lydia, Epaphroditus, Euodia, Syntyche; see Acts 16:14; Phil. 2:25; 4:2); only one was Latin (Clement in 4:3). This may say something about the social classes that were most open to the gospel, since in this city the Latin-speaking Romans held the wealth and power.

The harbor of Neapolis, today called Kavala, is the port city of Philippi.
Ververidis Vasillis/Shutterstock

Paul, Silas, Timothy, and Luke traveled the Via Egnatia, which passed through Philippi.
William D. Mounce

The city of Philippi
© 2011 by Zondervan

A tetradrachm minted at Amphipolis, the capital of the "first district" of Macedonia. The inscription reads *Makedonōn prōtēs* ("First of the Macedonians").
Harlan J. Berk, Ltd.

This coin commemorates the victory of Mark Antony and Octavian over Brutus and Cassius at the Battle of Philippi.
MUSA Numismatic Art/www.vcoins.com

THE SETTING OF PHILIPPIANS

Luke tells the story of the founding of the Philippian church in Acts 16. On his second missionary journey, Paul headed west down the Cilician Road to the Roman province of Asia (Ephesus was likely his goal), but was "kept by the Holy Spirit from preaching the word in the province of Asia" (16:6). Silas accompanied Paul, and since he was a prophet, the prohibition was likely communicated through him (15:32). Likewise, "the Spirit of Jesus" did not allow Paul to head north to the province of Bithynia and Pontus (16:7). He, Silas, and Timothy (15:40; 16:1–3) traveled to the western port of Troas.

This city was a Roman colony and known as one of the great seaports of antiquity, having a population between thirty thousand and one hundred thousand. In a vision (Acts 16:9), Paul saw a Macedonian man (perhaps dressed in their well-known broad brimmed hat), urging him to travel to Macedonia to help them. Plutarch noted at the end of the first century AD that "in popular belief . . . it is only in sleep that men receive inspiration from on high" (*Moralia* 589D). Paul and his companions responded to the vision as a divine summons (cf. Num. 12:6) and embarked by sea, sailing west to Macedonia.

The winds favored the trip from Troas to Neapolis, making this a mere two-day journey. Traveling the other direction took longer (cf. 20:6). Paul and his company departed from Neapolis and headed to Philippi on the Via Egnatia, the great Roman military and commercial artery that traversed the whole province of Macedonia. Paul arrived in the city around AD 49 or 50.

Philippi did not have a large enough Jewish population to form a synagogue (ten men were required to establish a synagogue; cf. *m. Sanh.* 1:6; *Pirque Aboth* 3:6). Instead, a group of women gathered by a river outside the city gate in "a place of prayer" (Gk. *proseuchē*), a word that can denote a building but here refers simply to a place where prayers are offered.

Since Philippi was a Roman colony, most of the inscriptions from the city are in Latin. This one honors a Roman named Cornelius. *Gene L. Green*

Paul's first convert is, surprisingly, neither a Macedonian nor a man. Lydia (Acts 16:14) is from Thyatira (see Rev. 2:18–29), a city of the region of Lydia (hence her name) in Asia Minor. Thyatira is the center of a purple-dye industry, and Lydia has come to Philippi to ply her trade. She embraces the gospel, and both she and the members of her household (including slaves) believe and are baptized (16:14–15). She is wealthy enough to own a home and becomes the patroness of the gospel messengers while they are in the city. Her house is the meeting place of this first church in Roman Macedonia (16:15, 40).

The second woman mentioned in Acts 16 is on the opposite end of the social spectrum. She is a slave girl possessed by a spirit and engaged in divination for pay, with all the profits going to her owners (16:16; in *De Divinatione* 1.5.9 Cicero defines "divination" as "the foreseeing and foretelling of events considered as happening by chance").

A high-order oracular spirit possesses the slave girl. Her owners would have paid a great price for this woman with such supernatural talent. When Paul casts the spirit out of her, her owners find their profits drastically cut. Both the spirit and their hopes of gain have gone out (lit.) (16:18–19)! According to Lucian, a Greek author who wrote *Alexander the False Prophet*, Alexander engaged in divination and was able to charge one drachma and two obols per question, which totaled something like seventy thousand to eighty thousand drachmas a year (a Greek drachma being equal to a Roman denarius, the wage for a day's labor). This was great profit, indeed.

When Paul entered Philippi, he joined a group of Jews who worshiped at the river adjacent to the city (Acts 16:13). One possible site is the Krenides River. *Todd Bolen/BiblePlaces.com*

A Python Spirit

The spirit that inspired the slave girl in Philippi, a "Python spirit," was well-known in antiquity because of its association with the famous oracle in Delphi. Plutarch, the priest of Delphi at the end of the first century AD, commented, "The god himself after the manner of ventriloquists ... called now Pythoness, enters the bodies of his prophets and prompts their utterances" (*Obsolescence of Oracles* 414E). The Python was the serpent that Apollo killed (Ovid, *Metamorphoses* 1.438–447), and the prophetesses at Delphi took their name from this creature.

The "Python spirit," which possessed the slave girl in Philippi, was associated with the ancient oracular site of Delphi in Greece.
Elgreko/Shutterstock

The girl's owners extract revenge. They seize Paul and Silas and drag them "into the marketplace to face the authorities" (16:19). The accusation against them does not mention the financial loss but plays on prejudice and Roman pride. The first accusation is: "These men are Jews" (16:20). Anti-Jewish sentiments were rife in the Roman world. Men like Philostratus voiced the common prejudice that "the Jews have long been in revolt not only against the Romans but against humanity" (*Apollonius* 5.33).

Second, Paul and Silas "are throwing our city into an uproar" (16:20). The Romans loved order above everything else and were determined to maintain it.

The final accusation leveled against the two is: "advocating customs unlawful for us Romans to accept or practice" (16:21). In ancient society all people were expected to follow their ancestral traditions. The Roman Livy remarked, "How often . . . has the task been assigned to the magistrates of forbidding the introduction of foreign cults . . . and of annulling every system of sacrifice except that performed in the Roman way" (*Hist*. 39.8–19).

The scene that follows is frightening and a great affront to Paul and Silas's honor. The crowd attacks, strips, and beats them with rods, under direction of the civil authorities. The civic magistrates have them thrown into jail and confine them to the innermost cell with feet secured in stocks (16:22–24; cf. 1 Thess. 2:2; Phil. 1:30). Not many months afterward, Paul recounts the incident to the Thessalonians: "We had previously suffered and been treated outrageously in Philippi, as you know" (1 Thess. 2:2), and later he reminds the Philippians of the suffering he experienced in the city (Phil. 1:30). The magistrates' actions, however, violate Roman law, for Paul and Silas "are Roman citizens" (Acts 16:37). Beating a Roman citizen without due process was a great crime. "To bind a Roman citizen is a crime, to flog him is an abomination, to slay him is almost an act of murder" (Cicero, *Against Verres* 2.5.66.170). Anyone who treated a Roman citizen in such an illegal manner faced the prospect of heavy penalties (16:37–40).

Despite such hostility, humiliation, and suffering, Luke emphasizes God's intervention. As Paul and Silas sing hymns to God at midnight, an earthquake shakes the prison, opens the doors, and unfetters the chains (16:25–26). Most Romans would view this as a divine omen. Any guard who allowed a prisoner to escape was liable to the punishment of the prisoner (*Code of Justinian* 9.4.4); thus, the Philippian jailer seeks to take his own life (16:27). But Paul assures him that nobody has escaped. He therefore asks Paul and Silas, "Sirs, what must I do to be saved?" (16:30).

The theater in Philippi dates from the pre-Roman period. The Plain of Philippi, where Mark Antony and Octavian defeated Julius Caesar's assassins Brutus and Cassius, is in the background.
iStock.com/MikePax

The response has echoed through the church for centuries: "Believe in the Lord Jesus, and you will be saved—you and your household" (16:31; cf. 11:14; 16:15). His household would have included slaves as well as family members. In Roman culture the father (*pater familias*) had a decisive role regarding the religious practices of the household. But Luke also adds that each member of the household hears the Word of God, believes, and is baptized (16:32–34). Before leaving town and heading to Thessalonica, Paul meets with the Philippian believers in Lydia's house (16:40).

PAUL WRITES TO THE PHILIPPIANS

The Philippian church stayed in contact with Paul after his first visit by sending him offerings early on when he was in Thessalonica (Phil. 1:5; 4:15–16) and again while he was imprisoned in Rome (4:10–19). The church had recently dispatched Epaphroditus with this gift for Paul (2:25; 4:18). This church, along with other Macedonian congregations, also displayed extraordinary generosity in sending relief aid to the Jerusalem church (2 Cor. 8:1–5).

Paul writes this letter according to the ancient customs of letter writing, beginning with the name of the author, followed by the name of the recipient and an opening greeting (Phil. 1:1–2). He begins the body proper with a thanksgiving for the church, woven with a prayer (1:3–11). The body of the letter comprises the bulk of the composition (1:12–4:20), after which Paul closes with final greetings (4:21–23). While ancient letters ended with good wishes for health, Paul prefers to end with a benediction (v. 23).

In his letter, Paul acknowledges the Philippians' generosity and offers commendation for Epaphroditus as he returns to Philippi (he is the one who likely carries this letter, though the explanation about his illness may indicate the need for some account about whether he accomplished his mission to Paul). Paul also hopes to soon send Timothy to the church and offers another letter of commendation for him, who will gather news for Paul about the church (2:19–24).

While Paul acknowledges the gift he has received from the Philippians, he never specifically says thank you (see 4:13–20). Note what Seneca writes: "Not to return gratitude for benefits is a disgrace, and the whole world counts it as such" (3.1.1). A person was socially obligated to return thanks. In acknowledging the Philippians' gift, however, Paul makes it clear that

Letters of Commendation

Embedded in Philippians are two letters of commendation, one for Timothy (2:19–24) and another for Epaphroditus, the Philippians' messenger to Paul. Pseudo-Demetrius, who wrote on epistolary theory, described this type of letter:

> The commendatory type, which we write on behalf of one person to another, mixing in praise ... in the following manner:
>
> So-and-so, who is conveying this letter to you, has been tested by us and is loved on account of his trustworthiness. You will do well if you deem him worthy of hospitality both for my sake and his, and indeed for your own. For you will not be sorry if you entrust to him, in any matter you wish, either words or deeds of a confidential nature. Indeed, you, too, will praise him to others when you see how useful he can be in everything.[1]

he is not seeking more benefits from them (4:17). He frames their generosity as a sacrifice to God and as participation in the cause of the gospel (4:18, 14–15). In the end, God is the One who will repay them for the benefit they have conferred on Paul (4:19). This is truly hearty thanks, as the reciprocity comes from God himself.

Outline of Philippians

I. Epistolary Greetings (1:1–2)
II. Thanksgiving and Prayers for the Philippians (1:3–11)
III. Body of the Letter (1:12–4:20)
    1. Paul's Imprisonment, Anticipated Release, Either through Life or Death (1:12–26)
    2. Exhortation to Unity (1:27–2:18)
        a. The Call for Unity (1:27–2:4)
        b. The Example of Christ (2:5–11)
        c. Corporate Conduct (2:12–18)
    3. Letters of Commendation for Timothy and Epaphroditus (2:19–30)
    4. Warning against Incursion of the Judaizers (3:1–21)
        a. Watch Out for the "Mutilators of the Flesh" (3:1–4a)
        b. Paul's Past and Present Values and Credentials (3:4b–14)
        c. Following Paul's and Other's Example (3:15–21)
    5. Final Exhortations: Stand Firm, Be United, Follow Paul's Teaching and Example (4:1–9)
    6. Thanks for the Philippians' Generosity (4:10–20)
IV. Final Greetings and Blessing (4:21–23)

In addition, Philippians contains the marks of a letter of friendship. In the ancient world, such letters stressed reciprocity in giving and receiving benefits and included notes about how physical absence did not imply absence in heart (1:27; 2:12). Pseudo-Demetrius presents a model of this kind of letter: "Even though I have been separated from you for a long time, I suffer this in body only. For I can never forget you or the impeccable way we were raised together from the childhood up."[2] Philippians abounds with expressions of affection (1:7–8; 4:1), emphasizes Paul's prayers for them and their prayers for him (1:4, 19), and stresses the church's partnership with him in suffering for the gospel (1:29–30; 2:17–18).

As Paul writes to the Philippians, they face hostility in the city (1:27–30). The same antagonism Paul and Silas experienced in Philippi has spilled over into the church. Paul calls the church to hold firmly to their faith and to shine as lights in a dark world (2:14–16). Adherence to the gospel means participating in practices that appear anti-Roman (Acts 16:20–21). Perhaps this is why Paul emphasizes that "our citizenship is in heaven" (Phil. 3:20) and that "above all, you must live as citizens

Humility

Paul underscores Christ's self-humiliation and offers Christ's self-sacrifice as an example for the Philippian believers (2:1–8). But in the Roman world, the type of reversal of status that Christ willfully endured was considered degrading. The "humble" person was someone of inferior social status (James 1:9). Such a person had little social power compared with mighty rulers (Luke 1:52). They were unable to influence society by means of their wealth, social standing, or political position.

To humble others was to weaken them (Diodorus Siculus 19.67.3) and to humble oneself was to degrade oneself (Plutarch, *Moralia* 116E). Yet Christ came as someone who submitted himself to humiliation, to the point of taking the status of a slave and submitting to death. His honor came from the Father, who "exalted him to the highest place" (2:9).

of heaven, conducting yourselves in a manner worthy of the Good News about Christ" (1:27 NLT). Paul reminds the church that the sufferings they endure for the gospel are the same as those he is presently facing in Rome (1:12–26, 30).

The persecutors are not the Philippians' only opponents. Paul warns them about the Judaizers (see ch. 14), using rather strong language: "Watch out for those dogs, those evildoers, those mutilators of the flesh. For it is we who are the circumcision, we who serve God by his Spirit, who boast in Christ Jesus, and who put no confidence in the flesh" (3:2–3). These Judaizers are attempting to turn gentile believers into Jewish proselytes in order to be saved, demanding especially the gentiles' submission to circumcision and dietary laws (Acts 15:1). This letter simply warns the believers about them without suggesting that they have already put down roots in Philippi.

There is, however, another group of opponents mentioned in this letter, whom Paul characterizes as "enemies of the cross of Christ" (3:18). Are these the Philippians' persecutors (1:27–28) or are they the Judaizers (3:1–6)? Whatever their identification, Paul calls the Philippian church to follow his example and that of others (3:17) and to conduct themselves as citizens of heaven, who live in expectation of the coming of the Savior, the Lord Jesus Christ (3:20–21).

The church is also experiencing some internal tensions. In 4:2–3 Paul calls on two leading women in the church, Euodia and Syntyche, "to be of the same mind in the Lord" (4:2; cf. 2:2). These women were Paul's coworkers (4:3). Earlier, Paul appeals for concord within the congregation (1:27; 2:1–4), so perhaps the dispute has spilled over into the church itself. Paul's exhortation does not imply that their relationship has degenerated into enmity; in fact, he commends these women highly: "They have contended at my side in the cause of the gospel, along with Clement and the rest of my co-workers, whose names are in the book of life" (4:3).

AUTHOR AND DATE

Philippians very early received wide acceptance as an authentic letter of Paul. Irenaeus, Clement of Alexandria, and Tertullian ascribed it to Paul. Around AD 135 Polycarp wrote a letter to the church in which he mentions Paul's previous correspondence to them (*Philippians* 3:2). Most today consider this letter a genuine Pauline letter.

An ordinary traveler could traverse from Rome to Philippi in thirty-seven days if traveling the main roads (775 miles), twenty-one days if traveling by sea (1,580 miles). The Rome-to-Colossae trip would take eighteen days.

Although Paul authored the book, he may have inserted a hymn into the letter. Some have identified Philippians 2:6–11 as an early hymn to Christ. Most modern translations block out the section in poetic form (see also Col. 1:15–18; 1 Tim. 3:16). But the section diverges somewhat from ancient Greek hymns and should perhaps be viewed as prose that approaches poetic style. In any case, this section teaches about the self-humiliation and exaltation of Christ and is integral to the letter.

One of the most vexing questions of Philippians has to do with its date. While we know that Paul was imprisoned when he wrote Philippians (1:7, 12–14, 17, 30), scholars cannot agree about where he was. While most consider he was in Rome (Acts 28:16, 30, between AD 60 and 62), some argue for an earlier date, either during Paul's captivity in Caesarea (Acts 23:33–26:32) or even in a presumed Ephesian imprisonment that took place during his three-year stay there (19:8, 10; 20:31; cf. 2 Cor. 1:3–11).

Both external evidence and Philippians itself support the Roman imprisonment. In the second century, the Latin prologue to this book (Anti-Marcionite Prologue) identified Rome as the place of composition, as do the postscripts added to a number of New Testament manuscripts. In Philippians, Paul refers to the *praetōrion* (1:13), a company of Caesar's elite personal guard, which numbered as many as a thousand men. This is another marker of the Roman origin of the letter.

Paul was a prisoner in Rome when he wrote Philippians. He refers to the elite praetorian guard (here pictured in this second-century AD relief) in 1:13. These soldiers were charged with the protection of the emperor and the suppression of social elements that could cause unrest.

Reproduced by permission from Jérémy-Günther-Heinz Jähnick

This letter envisions various communications between Paul and the Philippians (see 2:25–30 for a number of messages that went back and forth). We should not suppose that they dispatched special messengers for each exchange of news. People heading in a certain direction were commonly encouraged to serve as messengers to carry news and letters. Cicero, for example, once quipped that though he had no fresh news to share with Atticus, "I cannot refrain from entrusting letters to folk who are bound for Rome" (*Ad Atticum* 8.14.1 [164]).

Slave Tags

Some slaves had to wear ID tags with instructions about how to return the slave. One tag said, "I have run away. Capture me. When you have returned me to my master, Zoninus, you will receive a reward." Another read, "I am Asellus, slave of Praeiectus, who is an administrative officer in the Department of the Grain Supply. I have escaped my post. Capture me, for I have run away. Return me to the barbers' shop near the temple of Flora."[3]

This Roman slave tag says, "I have fled, hold me; when you bring me back to my master Zoninus you receive a solidus [gold coin]."
Sebastià Giralt/Flickr, CC BY-SA 2.0

THE SETTING OF PHILEMON

Philemon is Paul's shortest existing letter. Yet one of the more recent commentaries on this book is 561 pages! Philemon is the length of typical personal correspondence in the Roman world. Its content is intensely personal, and we wonder why the early church ever preserved a letter like this. Obviously, many in both the ancient and modern church have recognized the importance of this brief letter. Why is this? Philemon tells the story of the runaway slave Onesimus, who encountered Paul in Rome and became a convert to Christ. Paul sends him back to his master, Philemon, making intercession on Onesimus's behalf. The story is replete with issues surrounding the intersection of grace and slavery.

In reading the letter, we discover a list of familiar names. Paul and Timothy appear in the opening greeting (v. 1; cf. Col. 1:1). The letter itself is filled with references to people we encounter in Colossians, such as Archippus (v. 2; Col. 4:17), Onesimus (v. 10; Col. 4:9), Aristarchus (v. 24; Col. 4:10), Demas, Luke (v. 24; Col. 4:14), and Mark (v. 24; Col. 4:10). Epaphras, the founder of the Colossian church, is also mentioned in both letters (v. 23; Col. 1:7; 4:12). Presumably Paul wrote this letter at the same time as he penned Colossians.

Most important, however, is the social location of Philemon, Onesimus, and Paul. Onesimus is a slave (v. 16) who has become a believer, and Paul appeals to his master, Philemon, to receive him back as if he were the apostle himself (v. 17).

Masters managed their slaves and at times the control they exercised turned cruel. Beatings were frequent and could be severe, including flogging and mutilation. If a slave was required to give testimony in court, torture

Roman Slaves

At the beginning of the imperial period, there were about two million slaves in Italy alone, with one slave for every three free persons.[4] People became slaves by being taken captive in war and by being kidnapped (1 Tim. 1:10). Convicted criminals and those unable to pay their debts could become slaves. Parents left unwanted children exposed, where they either died or were found and raised as slaves. Children born to slave parents also became slaves.

Slaves were personal property and could be bought and sold. In fact, the more slaves a person had, the greater his or her social status. Slavery was not racial, however, as it was in the New World, nor were they necessarily uneducated. Some slaves were tutors and *paedagogues* (cf. Gal. 3:24). They cooked, cleaned, built buildings and roads, cut and styled hair, did laundry, made clothes, and even managed financial affairs.

preceded testimony so that, supposedly, the slave would speak the truth. Sexual abuse of slaves was common. If a slave was killed, the penalty was burning at the stake or crucifixion. But it was not in the master's best interest to kill a slave, since slaves were a costly investment. Some masters were kind and could show genuine compassion to their slaves, yet others were capricious and cruel (1 Pet. 2:18–20).

Occasionally, slaves ran away, especially if they were treated severely or unjustly (see 1 Pet. 2:18). An escaped slave could be crucified or given over to death in a gladiatorial show. To identify their slaves, masters sometimes branded them or required them to wear a metal ID tag (see sidebar). Rewards were offered for the capture of runaway slaves. Onesimus was clearly in a precarious position.

One of the wonders of early Christianity was its ability to absorb people of all genders, races, and socioeconomic classes. Note Galatians 3:28: "There is neither Jew nor Gentile, neither slave nor free, nor is there male and female, for you are all one in Christ Jesus." Common faith in Christ leveled the usual stratified social distinctions that separated humanity in general and Roman society in particular. This understanding eventually resulted in the abolition of slavery.

THE LETTER TO PHILEMON

Paul is imprisoned when he writes this letter (vv. 1, 9–10, 13, 23), likely in Rome (see Colossians). During his captivity, he encounters Onesimus, who becomes a convert to Christ under Paul's ministry (v. 10). We have no idea how these two met. Perhaps Onesimus is a runaway slave who is imprisoned before being returned to his master. Another possibility is that Onesimus seeks Paul out since he is in trouble and surmises that Paul may have some influence with his Christian master. In any case, Onesimus responds to the gospel, and now Paul is able to call him a "dear brother," whom he even commends to the Colossian church (v. 16; cf. Col. 4:9).

Outline of Philemon

I. Epistolary Greeting (vv. 1–3)
II. Opening Thanksgiving (vv. 4–7)
III. The Body of the Letter (vv. 8–22)
  1. The Initial Appeal (vv. 8–11)
  2. Onesimus's Return (vv. 12–16)
  3. The Final Appeal (vv. 17–21)
  4. A Room Request (v. 22)
IV. Final Greetings and Blessing (vv. 23–25)

Since he was a runaway slave, Onesimus would face an uncertain fate upon returning to Colossae. But Paul appeals to his master, Philemon, to receive him not as a slave but as a brother (v. 16) and to treat him with leniency. He sends Onesimus back with clear signs of his deep affection for this new believer (v. 12), noting to Philemon that he would like to keep Onesimus as an assistant (vv. 12–14). Paul has a keen sense of God's sovereignty here. Although he makes no excuse for Onesimus's wrongdoing, Paul points out God's hand in the unfolding events. Onesimus became separated from Philemon for a short time in order that Philemon might have him back forever as a brother (vv. 15–16). This slave, whose name means "useful," has become truly that (v. 11).

Paul implies that Onesimus may have done some wrong to Philemon (vv. 17–19). Paul himself vows to pay any debt he owes, but also reminds Philemon of the spiritual debt he owes Paul (v. 20). In a rather astounding move, Paul takes then the pen from his secretary and writes the final highly personal appeal in his own hand (v. 19). He is convinced of Philemon's generous character (v. 21). Paul announces a forthcoming visit, since he expects his release from captivity (v. 22; cf. Phil. 1:19).

AUTHOR AND DATE

While scholars have engaged in considerable debate concerning the Pauline authorship of Colossians (see comments on that letter), few have raised doubts concerning the authenticity of Philemon. Although 1:1 mentions Timothy along with Paul, the first-person verbs are in the singular. And Paul even writes in his own hand at one point (v. 19). Timothy does not seem to have had a significant role in the composition of this letter. But perhaps the amanuensis was Timothy himself.

Since Paul penned the letter at the same time as Colossians, the date can be fixed in the early 60s, during Paul's first Roman imprisonment (compare Col. 4:9 with Philem. 10, and see the discussion of Colossians).

Questions for Discussion

1. How does Paul understand the relationship between his imprisonment and his mission in his letter to the Philippians?
2. Look at Philippians 2:12–13. Is Paul's call to "work out your salvation with fear and trembling" a corporate or an individual task?
3. Why does Paul commend Epaphroditus and Timothy so highly to the believers in Philippi? What character traits mark them as exemplary servants of the gospel?
4. Do Paul's statements about loss and serving Christ in Philippians 3:1–14 mean we should give up all our plans and ambitions in order to be servants of the gospel?
5. What methods of persuasion does Paul use to encourage Philemon to receive Onesimus back as a brother? How does he use, and refrain from using, his authority as an apostle?
6. Slavery is still a reality in different parts of the world (see www.globalslaveryindex.org; www.antislavery.org; and other websites on modern slavery). What should our Christian response be to this institution? For a discussion of the problem during the Civil War in the United States, see Mark A. Noll, *The Civil War as a Theological Crisis* (Chapel Hill: University of North Carolina Press, 2006).

BIBLIOGRAPHY

Philippians: Introductory

Martin, R. P. *Philippians*. NCB. Grand Rapids: Eerdmans, 1976.
Osiek, C. *Philippians, Philemon*. ANTC. Nashville: Abingdon, 2000.
Still, T. D. *Philippians and Philemon*. SHBC. Macon: Smyth & Helwys, 2011.
Thielman, F. *Philippians*. NIVAC. Grand Rapids: Zondervan, 1995.

Philippians: Advanced

Bockmuehl, M. *The Epistle to the Philippians*. BNTC. Peabody, MA: Hendrickson, 1998.
Fee, G. D. *Paul's Letter to the Philippians*. NICNT. Grand Rapids: Eerdmans, 1995.
Hansen, G. W. *The Letter to the Philippians*. PNTC. Grand Rapids: Eerdmans, 2009.
Hawthorne, G. F. *Philippians*, rev. R. P. Martin. WBC. 2nd ed. Nashville: Nelson, 2004.
Reumann, J. *Philippians*. AB. New Haven: Yale University Press, 2008.
Silva, M. *Philippians*. BECNT. Rev. ed. Grand Rapids: Baker, 2005.
Witherington, B., III. *Paul's Letter to the Philippians: A Socio-Rhetorical Commentary*. Grand Rapids: Eerdmans, 2011.

Philemon

Barth, M., and H. Blanke. *The Letter to Philemon*. Grand Rapids: Eerdmans, 2000.
Fitzmyer, J. A. *The Letter to Philemon*. AB. New York: Doubleday, 2000.
McKnight, S. *The Letter to Philemon*. Grand Rapids: Eerdmans, 2017.
See also most commentaries on Colossians (which often include Philemon).

NOTES

1. A. Malherbe, *Ancient Epistolary Theorists* (Macon, GA: Scholars, 1988), 33.
2. Ibid.
3. J. Shelton, *As the Romans Did* (Oxford: Oxford University Press, 1997), 177.
4. Ferguson, *Backgrounds of Early Christianity* (Grand Rapids: Eerdmans, 2003).

Chapter 21

THE PASTORAL LETTERS: 1 TIMOTHY, 2 TIMOTHY, TITUS

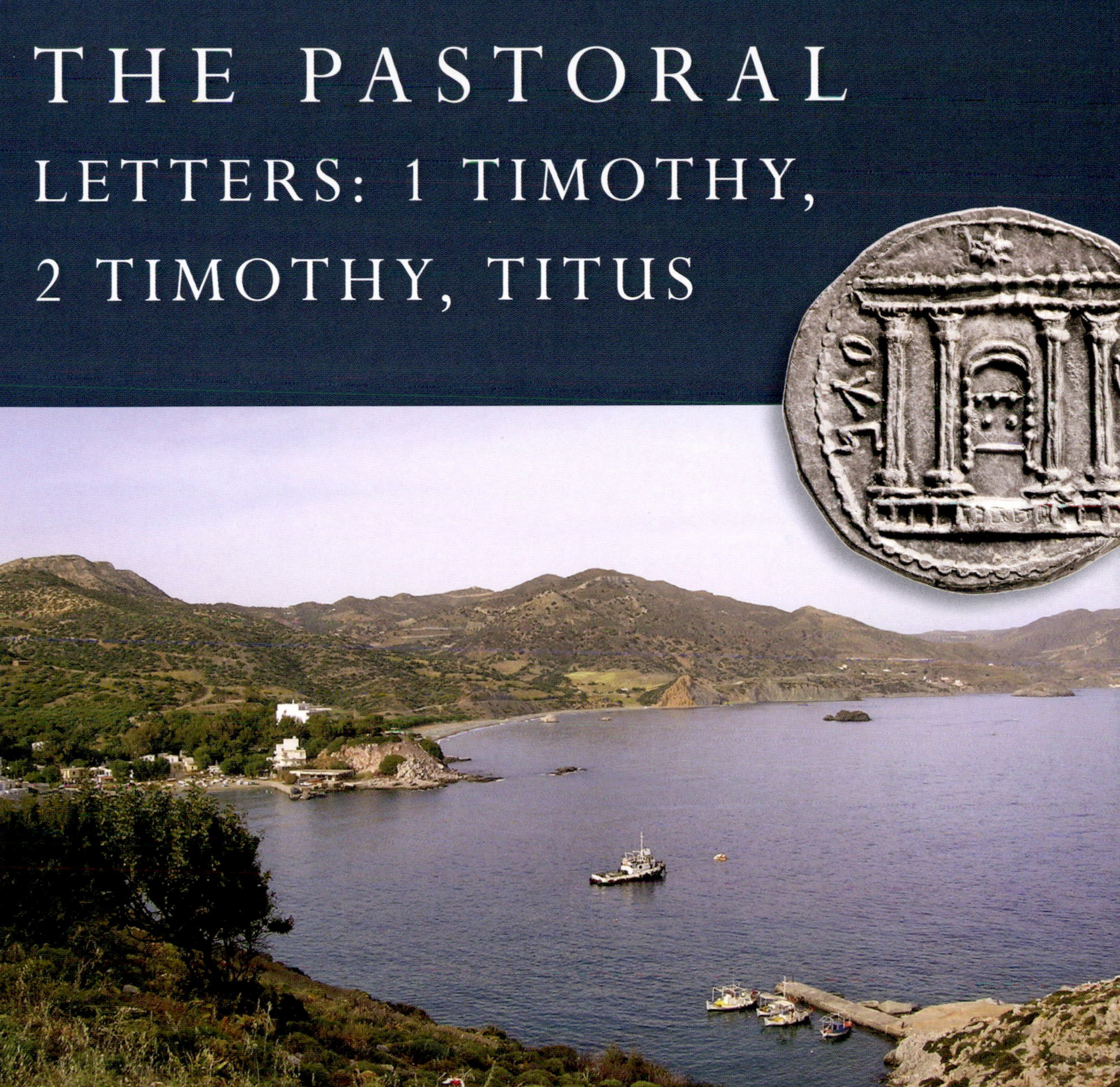

Paul wrote to Titus when he was leading a church in Crete. Fair Havens harbor in south Crete also hosted Paul on his imprisonment trip to Rome (Acts 27:8–12).
Todd Bolen/BiblePlaces.com

When we open the Pastoral Letters (1 Timothy, 2 Timothy, Titus), we find ourselves in a very different historical and theological context than we have seen before. These are personal letters addressed to leaders of churches in Crete (Titus) and Ephesus (Timothy). The title "Pastorals" comes from the Latin word for shepherd (*pastor*) and became the principle word to describe those who tend the church (or flock) of God, which Titus and Timothy are doing. These three letters have been grouped together under this name since the eighteenth century in order to recognize their common purpose and their similarities. Today it is common to refer to "the Pastorals" when indicating these three letters.

The letters also present us with a number of historical questions. For example, we do not know the order of their writing. But it seems that 2 Timothy must have been last because Paul has been imprisoned and views the genuine possibility of his own imminent death (see 2 Tim. 4:6). But there are more pressing questions than this. For instance, we have been able to anchor most of Paul's letters in some historical framework in a reconstruction of his life. The first six letters of Paul (Romans, 1 Corinthians, etc.) can fit into the outline of Paul's life in Acts. The so-called "prison letters" (Ephesians, Colossians, Philemon, Philippians) likely stem from Paul's imprisonment described in Acts 28. But here in these three letters we have geographical references that seem foreign to Paul's life. In 1 Timothy 1:3 Paul has been in Ephesus and then went to Macedonia. In Titus 1:5 and 3:12, Paul has just left Crete and is headed to Nicopolis (Greece). In 2 Timothy 1:17 Paul is in Rome but has just come from Troas, where he was with someone named Carpus (4:13).

Curetes Street, one of the three main streets in Ephesus, had statues and shops on both sides of the street.
Tatiana Popova/Shutterstock

Pseudonymity, or False Writing

A common theory today is that the Pastorals were penned by some unknown person who was using Paul's name to advance their own ideas. This is called pseudonymity.

Because the ancient world did not have publication controls, such as a "copyright," that we have today, there were many instances of authors writing in the name of another: hence, the terms pseudonymity ("false name") or pseudepigraphy (false writing). In some cases, writers imitating a famous author might employ his or her name to advance the prestige of their writing (the names Homer and Virgil were used frequently this way). Sometimes students would honor their masters by writing what they had learned *in the name of the teacher* (some works attributed to Plato came from this source). Occasionally there were deliberate forgeries intended to increase sales—and these were met with harsh criticism. The physician/author Galen knew of these and tells that the competition between the libraries of Alexandria and Pergamum was such that they spawned an active forgery market so that each could boast holdings of Plato, Aristotle, and others. He was outraged that his medical works and those of fellow physician Hippocrates had been rewritten and corrupted (see Galen, *Hippocratis de natura hominis commentarium,* Books 1–2). Even early Christians indulged in this as well. The late first-century bishop of Rome, Clement, had many spurious works credited to him.

The question is whether such *false attribution* was known to NT writers. Some scholars will point to Ephesians and the Pastorals, as well as 2 Peter, as examples of NT pseudepigraphy. But we must be clear: this practice was controversial and generally rejected. Complaints about the practice abound in antiquity. From Herodotus (fifth century BC) to Strabo (first century AD), we read protests about false attribution.

In the NT period, Jews practiced it too. Writings were attributed to biblical figures from the past that had nothing to do with them (Enoch and Ezra), and some recorded the "testaments" or last words of biblical characters falsely (*The Testament of the Twelve Patriarchs*, *The Testament of Job*, etc.). But Christians after the New Testament era did the same. *The Apocalypse of Peter* and *The Gospel of Thomas* are two of many examples of pseudepigraphy.

In the New Testament itself, there is an acute awareness of this issue. The end of 2 Thessalonians refers to forgeries written in Paul's name, and the apostle is out to stop it (see 2:2 and 3:17). This echoes the concerns of Jews, Romans, and Greeks that the authenticity of a writing was tied to the certainty of its origin. This was especially true of letters (our concern in the Pastorals). When the New Testament collection (or canon) was being formed, early Christian leaders rejected pseudonymity as unacceptable. When Serapion (d. AD 211), bishop of Antioch, read *The Gospel of Peter* and his research led him to believe it was not from Peter, he rejected it. Tertullian (AD 160–225) did the same with *The Acts of Paul and Thecla.* Cyril of Alexandria (d. AD 444) promoted four gospels and rejected the rest as "falsely written."

To maintain that the Pastorals are pseudepigraphical, we have to imagine that someone not only imitated Paul but inserted historical and personal notes in order to make the forgery persuasive, and this at face was deceptive. Many prefer a mediating position, at least arguing that these letters came indirectly from Paul and represent materials that the apostle actually wrote but were reshaped by someone else.

Some scholars believe we can locate these events in Paul's three well-known journeys and thus sync the Pastorals with Paul's other writings. By this view, 1 Timothy would fit between 1 Corinthians and 2 Corinthians, Titus between Romans and Philippians, and 2 Timothy would be the last (or thirteenth) letter of Paul penned during his Roman imprisonment that we read about in Acts.

But most scholars reject this view. It is common to think that Paul was released from his Roman imprisonment in Acts 28 and continued on more journeys that Luke did not record. It was in this new setting that these three letters were penned. Second Timothy then describes a second more severe imprisonment that likely took Paul's life. Still other critical scholars believe the letters were written some decades after Paul's life. By this view, they were written by a disciple of Paul or written by an imitator who was (falsely) using Paul's name. We need to look at this closely.

Above all, the Pastorals provide us with a glimpse into the life of the church well beyond the raucous years of its beginning. Time has passed. New questions have arisen for mature leaders and congregations to answer. The passionate arguments, say, of Galatians, are past and the need is for firm structures of leadership, guidance in moral living, and warnings about unfortunate false teaching. These themes had genuine importance for the ancient church and have an inestimable value for us today.

1 TIMOTHY

We know about Timothy from the Book of Acts. During Paul's second missionary journey, he entered the cities of Derbe and Lystra and there met a young man named Timothy. Luke notes that his mother was a Jewish-Christian believer and that his father was Greek—and by this we can infer that Timothy's father was neither Jewish nor Christian but likely participated in the imperial religious traditions of Rome. In 2 Timothy 1:5 we learn that Timothy's mother's name was Eunice and his grandmother was Lois. Paul came to know the family and writes warmly about the richness of their faith in God. This *maternal Jewish identity* made Timothy a Jew (m. *Qiddushin* 3:12), and because Paul was ministering in Jewish synagogues, he decided to take Timothy with him. But one thing was lacking: Timothy was not circumcised (a situation his father no doubt enforced), and this would have discredited Paul's ministry since some might have called Timothy an apostate. Paul had Timothy circumcised (Acts 16:3) since the public knew his family and knew that Timothy did not carry the full markers of Jewish identity.

With this little story, we gain a glimpse into the complexity of ethnic, religious, and national identity in the first century. Timothy was from a mixed marriage—and while his mother and grandmother no doubt raised him to have a profound personal faith, still, his father likely suppressed public signs of Jewish individuality. Timothy's home was filled with stories of Jewish history. And he grew up learning about Jesus. Judaism, Jesus, and Roman gods swirled around the family's life. It makes us wonder how Timothy's parents built a truce around all this. Did Timothy frequent gentile temples as a child? Did Timothy follow Jesus? Did he know the Hebrew scriptures? We may need to say yes to each of these.

When we open this letter, many years have passed since Timothy's first days with Paul. The apostle has recently been at the Aegean port of Ephesus, and he apparently left there to travel north to Macedonia (Northern Greece). Timothy had been left behind in Ephesus as a teacher and pastor. By now Timothy is well-known among Paul's colleagues around the Mediterranean. Priscilla, Aquila, Onesiphorus, Eubulus, Pudens, Linus, and Claudia each know him (2 Tim. 4:19–21). Nevertheless, he is young ("don't let anyone look down on you because you are young," 1 Tim. 4:12) and needs to be reminded of his family legacy of faith (1 Tim. 1:3–7; 6:12) and of the worship gathering when Timothy was commissioned by a prophetic word from God (1 Tim. 1:18; 4:11–16).

He needed this reminder because Paul has learned—and this is the setting of the letter—that the church in Ephesus is struggling with a variety of problems. Some are blending gentile religious ideas with faith in Jesus. Others are living immoral lives that discredited that faith. Paul writes that Timothy must hold to a good faith and good conscience (1:19) and promote these ideals in the church. "Train yourself to be godly," Paul writes, because this training holds promise not only for this life but for the life to come (4:7–10). Paul memorably tells him to "pursue righteousness, godliness, faith, love, endurance and gentleness" (6:11).

Outline of 1 Timothy

I. Opening (1:1–2)
   Note the absence of Paul's customary blessing and prayer
II. The Twin Anchors of Faith: Right Belief and Right Conduct (1:3–20)
III. Guidelines on Public Worship (2:1–15)
IV. Guidelines for Church Leadership (3:1–16)
   1. Bishops (3:1–7)
   2. Deacons (3:8–13)
   3. A Public Creed (3:14–16)
V. Protection Against False Teachings (4:1–16)
VI. Social Instructions for the Church (5:1–6:19)
   1. Men, Women, and Widows (5:1–16)
   2. Elders (5:17–25)
   3. Slaves (6:1–2)
   4. The Good Fight of the Gospel (6:3–19)
VII. Closing Exhortation (6:20–21)

Relief of Nike, the goddess of victory, holding the wreath of glory. This relief was located near the remains of the Domitian temple, signifying that Ephesus was loyal to imperial mythology. *Reproduced by permission from Carole Raddato*

Essential Concerns in 1 Timothy

It is evident in this letter that Timothy is confronting challenges to his leadership that neither he nor Paul expected. Throughout this letter—and throughout so many other writings of Paul—the same twin emphases return. Jesus's followers must know what they believe (orthodoxy, or right belief), and they must know how they are to live (orthopraxy, or right activity). But the problem lies deeper. The pressure on Timothy must have been acute, and so Paul worries that even Timothy himself might be swayed by some charismatic teachers and their speculative doctrines. "Timothy, guard what has been entrusted to your care. Turn away from godless chatter and the opposing ideas of what is falsely called knowledge" (6:20). This is an exhortation alerting Timothy not only to the state of his church but to the state of his own heart.

Two distinguished women from the Roman imperial era, the National Museum, Istanbul
Gary M. Burge

The temptation at the Ephesian church was to blend belief systems from the non-Christian world with those found in the church. When Paul warns against obsessions with genealogies, myths, and religious speculation (1:4; 4:7), he is talking about teachers (1:7) who want a platform in the church and yet have no real understanding of the essential claims of the gospel. We can be sympathetic to these tendencies. At this time, the Ephesian church did not have a New Testament to assess these teachings. They only had the instruction of Paul and his disciples, like Timothy. The forces of religious culture were certainly strong. Roman religious life and Roman political life merged (as they do today), and these themes suddenly were attached to the church's message. We can easily imagine a power struggle: Timothy representing Paul's teaching, and others offering contributions from their own religious speculations and the dominant Roman imperial cult.

Paul reminds Timothy that the essence of discipleship also centers on "love, which comes from a pure heart and a good conscience" (1:5; 5:24–25). This is the second aspect that has been neglected in Ephesus. The gospel does not merely announce a set of theological convictions, but it calls for a new way of living that is shaped by God's Spirit. This does not mean that Christians are sinless—Paul himself admits that he is foremost among sinners (1:12–15)—but that Christians do not promote immorality as acceptable. The mercy of God found in the gospel should change us. For Paul, the conscience (a keen sensitivity to what is right) is a vital guide to our conduct. And those who ignore it place their entire faith at risk (see 1:20 and the case study of Alexander and Hymenaeus).

These two concerns (right thinking, right living) thread themselves through every chapter of the letter. Paul hopes that gatherings for worship will reflect these two values (1 Tim. 2), and he explains criteria for leadership in the church (bishops, elders, deacons) centered on these (1 Tim. 3 and 5). Leaders must be moral exemplars *and* know the essence of the gospel. These leaders, as well as Timothy himself, must be truly unwavering in this, because Paul knows that there are many who have ruined their faith because they have dabbled in doctrines that do not belong in the church.

Women in 1 Timothy 2

Eight verses in 1 Timothy 2 have become a storm center of debate. The crux comes in 2:11–12, where Paul says that he wants women to learn in silence, be submissive, and never teach or have authority over men. This is perplexing because we know that women appear regularly in Paul's churches as leaders. There were female prophets (Acts 21:9; 1 Cor. 11:5) and female deacons (Rom. 16:2; 1 Tim. 3:11). Paul even uses the term "co-worker" (Gk. *sunergos*) for women (Euodia and Syntyche), just as he does men (Phil. 4:3). Priscilla was well-known in Paul's churches (Acts 18:2, 26), was a Christian before Paul, and had been imprisoned for her faith—showing her public profile as a Christian leader. Some believe she even discipled Apollos in Acts. Lydia hosted a church in her own home (Acts 16:14–15, 40), and, as Cynthia Westfall has shown (*Paul and Gender*, 2016), this meant far more than domestic service. As host, she led this church. Widows seem to be organized into an order for public service (1 Tim. 5:9–16), but we are unclear what this is. A woman named Junia was even called an apostle and was famous among the other apostles (Rom. 16:7). In all his writing, Paul recognizes fifty-four men and thirteen women, which means that 20 percent of the names he commends are female. The problem is that many people often fail to identify these as female names. In Romans 16 Paul mentions nine women, and he commends Mary, Tryphena, Tryphosa, and Persis using the same language he employs for himself and his ministry colleagues. Paul never sees gender as a criterion for the distribution of gifts in the Spirit. In Galatians 3:28 he even dismisses the privileges of gender, along with the supposed privileges of race and social class.

How do we make sense of these eight verses in 1 Timothy 2? The key may be in Paul's use of "have authority" in 2:12 ("I do not permit a woman to teach or have authority over men" RSV). This term (Gk. *authenteo*) occurs only here in the NT. But in over three hundred later occurrences in other Greek literature, there is no instance of it expressing benevolent pastoral care of another. When it describes a relationship, it implies harm or force, such as "to take over" or "to take charge without permission" or "hijack." Sometimes it refers to violence. Therefore, when Paul is describing women in these verses, he is not making a universal pronouncement about all women (or women today); this would contradict his other teachings. Paul is talking about *specific women*, divisive or sectarian women, who are trying to take over Timothy's church in Ephesus. They are immodest (2:9), disorderly, and lacking public decorum (2:11). They might deny child-bearing or pregnancy (2:15). And they have forgotten that Eve (as well as Adam) was guilty of the original sin of humanity (2:14).

The problem is that we have universalized a teaching of Paul from these verses when it needs to be kept within its historical context. Paul is concerned with what happens when Christians gather in worship (2:8). We do not universalize Paul's word that men lift their hands when they pray (2:8). Nor do we universalize Paul's prohibition of women wearing gold or pearls or braided hair (2:9). These are descriptors of modest spirituality that are bound to Timothy's contextual location two thousand years ago. Timothy's opponents in Ephesus we now know included a group of women who brandished threatening authority against Timothy and his leaders. Paul says that they—these challengers—need to be silenced. They may not teach (2:12).

Bishops and Elders

In the Pastorals we find a new emphasis on established offices for church leadership: the deacon (Gk. *deaconos*), the elder (*presyteros*), and the bishop (*episcopos*). While deacons likely took up the practical needs of the church, elders and bishops were responsible for oversight and teaching. In later centuries, elders worked within a single congregation, while bishops gave oversight to many. (This is the order found in the Catholic, Anglican, Eastern Orthodox, and Methodist traditions.)

Some scholars wonder whether elders and bishops are one and the same. Criteria for elders (1 Tim. 5:17–22; Titus 5:1–6) and bishops (1 Tim. 3:2–7; Titus 1:7–9) show considerable overlap. And Titus 1:7 (Gk. *dei*, for) implies that they are not separated. In this view, leaders were elders (senior members) who gave oversight to the church (the essential meaning of *episcopos*). The elders must be selected carefully ("Do not be hasty in the laying on of hands," 1 Tim. 5:22), and then they would join a council of elders (1 Tim. 4:14), which is precisely the model of Jewish councils in synagogues (Acts 22:5).

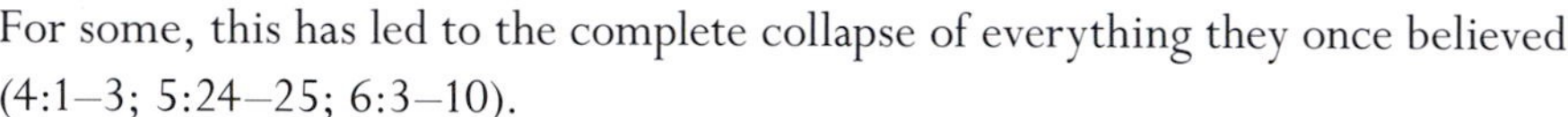

For some, this has led to the complete collapse of everything they once believed (4:1–3; 5:24–25; 6:3–10).

Nevertheless, Timothy's context has intimidated him (4:11–16), so it makes sense that Paul recognizes that Timothy must surround himself with leaders—both men and women—who have understood and embraced Paul's gospel and are willing to lend support against those who would challenge it. This is, in Paul's language, "the good fight of the faith" (6:12). But above all, Timothy himself is at risk (6:20). If Jesus could hold a courageous and uncompromised faith before Pontius Pilate (6:13), Timothy now must do the same before his opponents. This gives us some insight into what is at stake. Timothy's opponents are powerful, and he must acknowledge the test he is under.

TITUS

This very short personal letter is private correspondence between Paul and one of his most trusted converts. Although Titus is not mentioned in Acts, he appears in a number of Paul's letters. Here in this letter we gain a glimpse of Paul's commitment to this man, simply in his greeting, "To Titus, my true son in our common faith: Grace and peace from God the Father and Christ Jesus our Savior" (1:4). After his conversion, Titus was brought by Paul to Jerusalem during what we called Paul's "famine visit" (see ch. 14). It was a controversial visit, since few Jewish Christians believed at the time that gentiles could embrace the gospel fully without taking on Jewish religious markers such as circumcision. Titus was Paul's model of the uncircumcised Roman whose faith was unimpeachable (Gal. 2:1–3). When some wanted Titus to be circumcised to complete his discipleship,

The harbor of Fair Havens, modern Kali Limones. Located south of Greece, Crete hosted many Christian communities and was frequented by Titus and Paul.
www.HolyLandPhotos.org

Paul adamantly refused. For Paul, Titus's experience in Jerusalem was a test case for freedom from the law offered in the gospel.

Crete is the fourth-largest island in the Mediterranean Sea.

We also learn about Titus during Paul's tumultuous relationship with the Corinthians while Paul was in Ephesus. After Paul's "painful visit" to Corinth, Titus delivered Paul's "severe letter" to Corinth (possibly 2 Cor. 10–13) and met Paul later to report the grief and regret of the congregation (2 Cor. 2:13; 7:6, 13–14). Paul described Titus as his "partner and co-worker" (2 Cor. 8:23), and we can easily imagine him as one of Paul's most trusted allies. On his third trip, Paul was taking up a collection for Judea, and Titus returned to Corinth to gather their money (2 Cor. 8:6). On this visit, he brokered a reconciliation that would finally come between Paul and Corinth.

At some later time (we cannot know when), Paul continued to send Titus as a courier representing him. In a distressing verse during Paul's final imprisonment (2 Tim. 4:10), he describes his despair at being abandoned by a man named Demas, who had departed to Thessalonica. And he describes his longing to see Crescens, who had left for Galatia, and Titus, who had gone to Dalmatia. Recall that Titus had been with Paul at Nicopolis, in northwest Greece (Titus 3:12; Rom. 15:19), a city that belonged to Dalmatia, a district in the south part of Illyricum. Titus knew the area well, and it makes sense that Titus would work there. However, this is the last reference we have to Titus.

Essential Concerns in Titus

There are many similarities between 1 Timothy and Titus. We can assume that Paul has been in Crete and that he has left Titus there to amend what he sees as difficulties in the many churches that have been planted. The advice he gave Timothy in 1 Timothy, he now wants to give to Titus.

Outline of Titus

- I. Opening (1:1–4)
    1. Note the absence of Paul's customary blessing and prayer
- II. Appointing Elders and Bishops in Crete (1:5–9)
- III. False Teaching in Crete (1:10–16)
- IV. Guidelines for Community Behavior and Belief (2:1–3:11)
    1. Moral Guidelines (2:1–10)
    2. Theological Guidelines (2:11–3:11)
- V. Personal Closing, Greeting, and Blessing (3:12–16)

The opening of the letter shows that Paul's twin emphases are still on his mind. He is writing "to further the faith of God's elect and their knowledge of the truth that leads to godliness" (1:1). The knowledge of the truth refers to right belief (orthodoxy), and godliness refers to right living (orthopraxy). These two features must be hallmarks of every Christian's identity. When Paul refers to false teachers, he can say it is possible to profess to know God—but then deny him by our very deeds (1:16). Even for Titus, his teaching must show integrity, gravity, and soundness while his life is a model of good deeds (2:7). Right teaching and right living are central to Paul's thoughts.

This double test is to be applied to leaders Titus must appoint. Therefore, the profiles of elders and bishops (1:5–9) must be held to these standards. They must be able to "encourage others by sound doctrine" (1:9) while also exhibiting the virtues we expect from those who are named "God's stewards" (1:7 RSV). What the leaders model should also be reflected in the lives of all believers, and here Paul gives notes for older men and women, younger men, and slaves (2:1–10). On the other hand, Titus (like Timothy) must have the courage to discredit and remove those whose lives or beliefs are unacceptable, and Paul is unsparing in his language for them (1:10–16). Titus must declare aloud what is required and exhort his church "with all authority" (2:15).

Paul's words about public conduct both here and in 1 Timothy suggest that Paul is aware that followers of Christ must be morally excellent not only in the church but *within the city* where they reside. "Be subject to rulers and authorities," "be obedient," "be gentle toward everyone," (3:1–2). The ethical call we read here is often compared to virtue lists in use elsewhere in the Roman world. It means that when a Roman citizen examined the lives of Christians, they would at once recognize lives that were virtuous even by gentile standards.

2 TIMOTHY

Second Timothy is widely accepted as Paul's final letter. He is in prison (2:9), feeling the despair of isolation (1:15), eager to be visited by old friends (1:16–18; 4:9, 21), and aware of the seriousness of the charges against him (4:16) and how fortunate he is to be alive (4:17). He has dogged opponents, such as people named Alexander (4:14), Phygelus, and Hermogenes (1:15), and for the first time we hear him reflecting on the very possibility of his own martyrdom (4:6–8). Paul has already been making appearances in court, and he feels the weight of jeopardy.

Outline of 2 Timothy

I. Opening and Prayer of Thanksgiving (1:1–5)
II. Encouragement to Timothy (1:6–14)
III. The Struggle to Remain Faithful (1:15–2:13)
  1. Threats and Opposition (1:15–18)
  2. Singular Determination (2:1–7)
  3. A Reminder of the Message (2:8–13)
IV. Examples of Truth and Falsehood (2:14–3:9)
V. The Cost of Faithfulness (3:10–4:8)
VI. Personal Requests and Greetings (4:9–22)

Preserved from first-century Egypt is a personal letter from Sarapion to Diodoros. Second Timothy reflects the openness and warmth of personal letters.
Sarpiōn. Private letter, [1st cent. AD]. p.duk.inv 98, David M. Rubenstein Rare Book & Manuscript Library, Duke University

This is Paul's most personal letter, and unlike 1 Timothy and Titus, it does not supply directions for church leaders and provides minimal theological instruction. There are numerous personal references—names, crises, unmet desires, disappointments—which give the letter an immediacy and urgency.

Essential Concerns in 2 Timothy

This letter reflects the aspirations and hopes of a man looking back at his legacy. Paul reminisces about his own achievements (3:10–17), but not to highlight the grace of God or in recklessness of self-promotion as he did in Philippians 3. Here Paul is honestly looking back at the notebook of his life, reflecting on what his choices have cost him. He mentions various persecutions and reflects broadly now: "Everyone who wants to live a godly life in Christ Jesus will be persecuted" (3:12). This verse is not only Paul summing up what it cost to be courageously faithful but has been a sobering reminder for Christians throughout the centuries who likewise experience severe opposition.

But we need to remember that this is not simply Paul reminiscing. He is writing to Timothy, and his aim is to instruct Timothy in courage and model for him what a courageous life looks like. His (final?) exhortations are explicit:

Nero: Infamous Persecutor of Christians

Born in AD 37, Nero Claudius Caesar ruled as Rome's fifth emperor, from AD 54–68. His first five years of rule were comparatively peaceful, since his able teacher Seneca ran the government. But Nero chafed under the supervision of wiser minds. He murdered his mother and his wife. Thereupon Seneca retired (Nero forced him to commit suicide in AD 65), and Nero, now free, ruined the Roman economy and thinned out the ranks of the senate by accusing many of treason.

Nero's unique evil was evident in condemning Christians as scapegoats for a fire that burned much of Rome in AD 64 (see sidebar "Nero's Persecution of Christians" in ch. 13).

Nero was the adopted son of Emperor Claudius. His rule from AD 54–68 places him at the center of Paul's later life. According to Christian tradition, Paul was martyred under Nero in Rome, and this may be the setting of 2 Timothy.
Phoenix Data Systems

"You then, my son, be strong in the grace that is in Christ Jesus" (2:1). This is why he reminds Timothy of his courageous family (1:3–7) and his commissioning when Paul personally laid hands on him (1:6). He openly talks about the temptation for Timothy (or anyone) to be ashamed of their faith (1:8) or to wither at the first sight of danger (2:1–7). Timothy must know that a courageous faith can be compromised a hundred ways: unnecessary public entanglements (2:4), speculative theological quarrels (2:16, 23), youthful impulsivity (2:22), bending to what the crowd demands to hear (4:3–5), terrible influences (3:2–6), and aggressiveness (rather than gentleness) when we represent the truth (2:25). A courageous follower of Jesus must know his or her goal: like an athlete aiming for the trophy or the farmer aiming for the harvest (2:5–6). Timothy must be single-minded.

Two final concerns preoccupy Paul. If he does not survive this final imprisonment, he knows that his legacy is found in two places. He has manuscripts (parchments, 4:13) and he has people, and both speak to the gospel for which he has given his life. What is this trove of manuscripts he wants? Every scholar would love the answer. But Paul also knows and lists the other repositories of his message: the faithful who have made the same investment he has made. He names Luke, Mark, Tychicus, Prisca, Aquila, Onesiphorus, Erastus, Trophimus, Eubulus, Prudens, Linus, and Claudia—these are some of the men and women Paul is thinking about in his last days. And Timothy and Titus are among them. They have maintained a long obedience in the same direction. They are truly and fully disciples who will carry on the gospel. And in his final year, it is this knowledge that buoys the apostle Paul.

AUTHOR AND DATE

Since the birth of critical biblical scholarship in the early 1800s, the Pauline authorship of these three letters has been challenged. And today this is the prevailing view among scholars. We learned about these questions when we studied 2 Thessalonians and the "prison letters," but what we found there can be doubled for the Pastorals. For instance, there is the problem of language. Scholars have meticulously cataloged every word written by Paul and, using computers, have tried to build a profile of his usual style. Each of us has a writing style complete with grammar preferences and word choices. When the Pastorals are compared with Paul's other letters—especially those that are undisputed (Galatians, Romans, 1–2 Corinthians), we find striking differences. The Pastorals have 848 words, and 36 percent of these do not occur in any of Paul's other writing. In fact, 175 of these are completely unique to the Pastorals and are found no place else in the NT. For instance, here in these letters we find the Greek word *eusebeia* ("godliness"), but it is never used by Paul elsewhere. There is a long list of these. God is called "sovereign" and "king of kings" here but not elsewhere by Paul. And the flip side is true. Words that Paul seemed to prefer are absent. But in addition to word choice, we all have habits of grammar that we do not think about: how we connect sentences and clauses, if we prefer rhetorical argument or cascading modifiers, or how we use prepositions. In a word, the style of these letters is completely unlike Paul's other letters. This is one of the chief arguments that Paul did not pen the letters.[1]

But this sort of argument is not unassailable. Some have tried to argue that this is an older, more mature Paul, and with age his writing style has changed. This solution has been deemed unpersuasive to almost all scholars. Others have said that we have new subjects here, such as guidelines for church offices, and these require different word choices. Also Paul here is not engaged in dense argumentation as he is in, say, Galatians. This too would require a shift in writing form. Still, the differences are troubling and for some insurmountable. This has led many conservative scholars to question *direct* Pauline authorship. For them there is a cumulative case made of the historical context, language, and even theology so that a conservative scholar such as I. Howard Marshall can write that these data cast "doubts on the traditional defense of direct Pauline authorship."[2] Marshall believes that Paul's writing is here, but that it originated in a way we might not expect.

Scholars like Marshall have tried to find another way forward. We know that Paul used trusted scribes (called amanuenses) in his writing (see Rom. 16:22), and they had freedom to contribute broadly to published compositions. Others suggest that a close disciple of Paul brought together many of the apostle's notes not long after his death. This does not mean that they engaged in deception; it was a respectful reuse of materials they could not take credit for themselves (see sidebar "Pseudonymity, or False Writing"). This means we have an *indirect,* though substantial, link between Paul and the letters, and the style has been affected either by a scribe or a disciple.

Nevertheless, we must be clear. It is not implausible that we have direct Pauline authorship here, and arguments for it still hold. There are many senior New Testament scholars who defend it. But at this point we simply need to be aware that this controversy exists and will be with us permanently.

Questions for Discussion

1. When Paul writes these letters, where is he located in his career and travels?
2. Evaluate the controversy surrounding Paul's authorship of these letters. What is at stake and why is this important?
3. What controversies surrounded Timothy at Ephesus? What message does Paul want Timothy to hear?
4. Why would Paul call for the silence of women in 1 Tim. 2:8–15?

BIBLIOGRAPHY

Introductory

Carson, D. A. "Pseudonymity and Pseudepigraphy" in *Dictionary of New Testament Background*. Ed. Craig A. Evans and Stanley E. Porter. Downers Grove, IL: InterVarsity Press, 2000.

Dunn, J. D. G. "Pseudepigraphy" in *Dictionary of the Later New Testament and Its Developments*. Eds. Ralph P. Martin and Peter H. Davids. Downers Grove, IL: InterVarsity Press, 1997.

Liefeld, W. L. *1 and 2 Timothy and Titus*. NIVAC. Grand Rapids: Zondervan, 1999.

Stott, J. *Guard the Truth: The Message of 1 Timothy and Titus*. Downers Grove, IL: InterVarsity Press, 1996.

Towner, P. H. *1–2 Timothy, Titus*. IVP NTC. Downers Grove, IL: InterVarsity Press, 1994.

Advanced

Johnson, T. L. *The First and Second Letters to Timothy*. AB. New York: Doubleday, 2001.

Knight, G. W., III. *The Pastoral Epistles: A Commentary on the Greek Text*. NIGTC. Grand Rapids: Eerdmans, 1992.

Marshall, I. H. *A Critical and Exegetical Commentary on the Pastoral Epistles*. ICC. Edinburgh: T&T Clark, 1999.

Meade, D. G. *Pseudonymity and Canon*. WUNT 39. Tübingen: Mohr, 1986.

Mounce, W. D. *1 and 2 Timothy, Titus*. WBC. Waco, TX: Word, 2000.

Towner, P. H. *The Letters to Timothy and Titus*. NICNT. Grand Rapids: Eerdmans, 2006.

Westfall, C. *Paul and Gender: Reclaiming the Apostle's Vision for Men and Women in Christ*. Grand Rapids: Baker Academic, 2016.

Yarbrough, R. W. *The Letters to Timothy and Titus*. PNTC. Grand Rapids: Eerdmans, 2018.

NOTES

1. For a full chart of these differences, see P. N. Harrison, *The Problem of the Pastoral Epistles* (London: Oxford University Press, 1921) summarized by D. Hagner, *The New Testament: An Historical and Theological Introduction* (Grand Rapids: Baker Academic, 2012), 614–22 and I. H. Marshall, *The Pastoral Epistles: The International Critical Commentary* (London: T&T Clark, 1999), 60–79.

2. Marshall, *The Pastoral Epistles*, 79.

THE HEBREWS

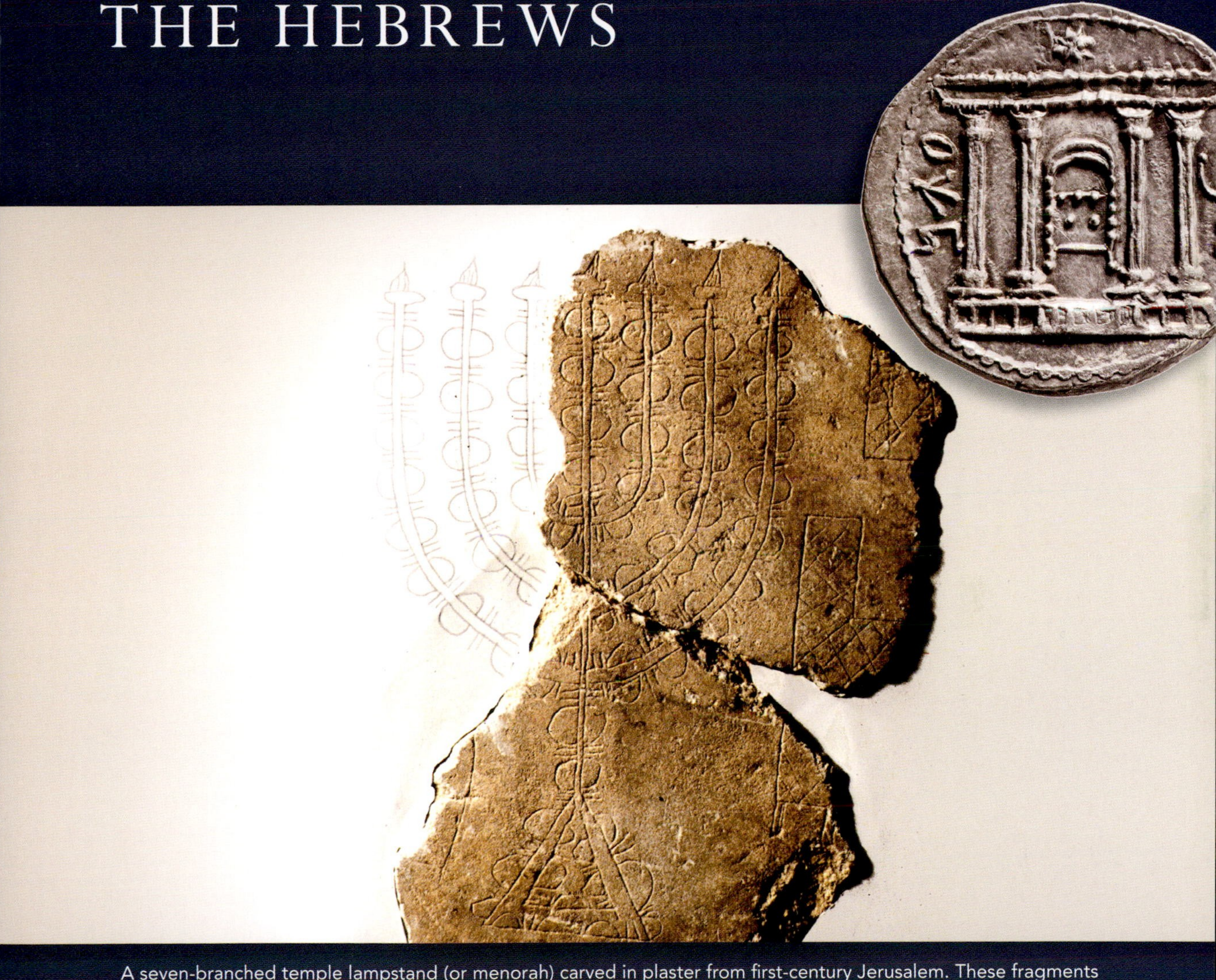

A seven-branched temple lampstand (or menorah) carved in plaster from first-century Jerusalem. These fragments were found in the Jewish Quarter Excavations amid the debris of the ruins from Jerusalem's destruction in AD 70.

The letter to the Hebrews is replete with texts that reverberate in the hearts and minds of Christians. We readily recognize the exaltation of Christ in the opening words of the letter: "In the past God spoke to our ancestors through the prophets at many times and in various ways, but in these last days he has spoken to us by his Son, whom he appointed heir of all things, and through whom also he made the universe" (1:1–2). Over and again we have heard Hebrews's declaration that "the word of God is alive and active. Sharper than any double-edged sword, it penetrates even to dividing soul and spirit, joints and marrow" (4:12). The eleventh chapter on faith opens with words many have memorized: "Now faith is the substance of things hoped for, the evidence of things not seen" (11:1 KJV). Church leaders intone the doxology in 13:20–21 at the end of Sunday services. Yet much of this book is alien to non-Jewish Western Christians. Its pages are filled with talk about angels, Sabbath rest, Jesus's high priesthood, Melchizedek, the covenants, the tabernacle, and blood sacrifice. On the other hand, some Christians, like the late Kwame Bediako from Ghana in Africa, joyfully affirm that "The epistle to the Hebrews is OUR epistle!"[1] He and others resonate with Hebrews's familiar themes of mediation, sacrifice, and ancestors. Melchizedek holds special significance for African Christians, since this figure is a non-Jew who received God's blessing. Whether we read Hebrews as Western or non-Western Christians, we all ask what this canonical text meant to its first readers and what it means for us now.

THE GENRE OF HEBREWS

The book of Hebrews does not look like a letter. Unlike our New Testament letters and those from the Mediterranean world, it lacks the name of the author, the recipients, and an opening prayer or thanksgiving at the beginning. On the other hand, the book closes with a letter ending that includes a final blessing (Heb. 13:20–21; cf. Phil. 4:23), along with personal information and greetings (Heb. 13:23–24; cf. Phil. 4:21–22). The author even remarks to his readers that he has "written to you quite briefly" (Heb. 13:22; cf. 1 Pet. 5:12) and concludes with the familiar words "Grace be with you all" (Heb. 13:25; cf. 2 Cor. 13:14). But the absence of the usual epistolary opening has led some to suggest that Hebrews was originally a sermon. Indeed, the author identifies his message as a "word of exhortation" (Heb. 13:22; cf. Acts 13:15). If Hebrews was first presented as a sermon, why was the letter-ending added? If it was originally a letter, was the opening somehow lost? We may never be able to solve this "riddle of Hebrews," as many have called it.

We should recall, however, that the line between letter writing and public discourse was not entirely clear. Letters were read aloud to their recipients, who gathered together to listen (1 Thess. 5:27; Col. 4:16). Ancient authors who discussed public rhetoric sometimes spoke about letter writing as well. They classified letters as "epideictic" rhetoric. In contrast with "judicial" rhetoric of the courtroom and "deliberative" rhetoric of public assembly, people used "epideictic" rhetoric to inform hearers about what kind of conduct was honorable or shameful. "Epideictic" rhetoric, therefore, concerned itself with praise for honorable behavior and blame for dishonorable. This rhetorical concern is evident throughout Hebrews.

Aristotle on Three Types of Rhetoric

"Therefore there are necessarily three kinds of rhetorical speeches, deliberative, forensic, and epideictic. The deliberative kind is either hortatory or dissuasive; for both those who give advice in private and those who speak in the assembly invariably either exhort or dissuade. The forensic kind is either accusatory or defensive; for litigants must necessarily either accuse or defend. The epideictic kind has for its subject praise or blame" (*Rhet.* 1358b [1.3]). Aristotle added that "the epideictic style is especially suited to written compositions" (1414a [3.6]). Hebrews is a fine example of epideictic rhetoric due to its concern with honor and shame, praise and blame (e.g., Heb. 2:7, 9; 3:3, 5:4; and 3:17; 12:2, 16–17).

THE FIRST READERS

We cannot definitively identify the genre of Hebrews, nor do we know who wrote the book, a topic discussed below. The recipients are not named either, although we can glean considerable information about them and their situation from the letter itself. The title *Pros Hebraious* ("To the Hebrews") appears in most early Greek manuscripts, but as with other New Testament book titles, this one was not an original part of the composition. However, it serves as evidence that from the earliest centuries Christians held that the book was directed to Jewish people who confessed Christ (Heb. 3:6, 14).

On the other hand, some contemporary scholars have argued that the recipients were gentile believers or a mixed congregation of Jews and gentiles. The author calls them not to have "a sinful, unbelieving heart that turns away from the living God" (3:12). This could mean they were tempted to abandon the one true God. Although Hebrews is replete with references to Israel's history and Jewish practices, some would argue that many other New Testament texts directed to gentile believers draw from the well of the Old Testament. First Peter was written to gentile Christians, yet it uses the language drawn from Exodus 19:6 and Isaiah 43:20–21 to describe them: "You are a chosen people, a royal priesthood, a holy nation, God's special possession" (1 Pet. 2:9). In Galatians Paul draws extensively on the story of Israel to explain the new existence of these gentile believers. They are blessed with Abraham (Gal. 3:6–9; Gen. 15:6) and are children of the promise through Isaac (Gal. 4:21–31; Gen. 16:15–16; 17:16; 21:2–3, 10). Early on, gentile Christians came to view themselves as included in Israel's story. Might this be the case with the recipients of Hebrews?

The theory that the first audience of this book were gentiles or included numerous gentiles is, however, difficult to sustain. The problem the author confronts is

In addition to numbers of Jewish people in the city of Rome during the first century AD, the port of Rome, called Ostia, had a Jewish synagogue built during the reign of Emperor Claudius. This menorah is one of two capitals below which the Torah scrolls were kept.
www.HolyLandPhotos.org

the readers' return to Judaism and not their reversion to gentile religious practices. The book does not warn against idolatry, and nowhere is the audience clearly or implicitly marked as gentile (cf. Eph. 3:1). Hebrews repeatedly shows the superiority of the new covenant God has established through Christ over the old covenant (Heb. 1:4; 6:9; 7:7, 19, 22; 8:6; 9:11, 23; 10:34; 11:16, 35, 40; 12:24)—not over gentile religious practices. He does not contrast gentile religion with Christian faith but occupies himself with how the Jewish sacrificial system contrasts with the sacrifice of Christ (Heb. 9–10). The author presupposes that his readers knew the Old Testament well, suggesting that these were Jewish Christians. To be sure, such familiarity could be testimony to gentile converts' mastery of the Jewish Scriptures in Greek (the Septuagint, or LXX). But it is less likely that they would have known the Jewish history of the Maccabees, which the author also references (cf. Heb. 11:35b and 2 Macc. 6:18–7:42; 4 Macc. 5–18). Hebrews opens by stating that "In the past God spoke to our ancestors through the prophets" (1:1). With these words the author marks himself and his readers as Jewish and descendants of Abraham (2:16). The most likely conclusion is that the recipients were all or almost entirely Jewish converts to Jesus, the Messiah.

Hebrews offers a bit of evidence about the location of the book's first recipients. In 13:22–25 the author gives his final exhortation and blessing, along with information about Timothy and a visit to the assembled believers. He also greets the leaders and all the people and then says, "Those from Italy send you their greetings" (13:24). These words may suggest that the author writes from Italy and sends out greetings with those who are from there. They could have been in Rome. Under this reading, 13:24 would not offer any information about the location of the recipients but only the author. On the other hand, it may be that the author is with those who have come from Italy and now he sends this communication to believers back home. In this case, the letter may have been written to Jewish believers in the Italian city of Rome. The imperial city was home to about forty to sixty thousand Jewish residents.[2]

The author states that he is with those "from Italy," an expression similar to John 11:1, which says that Lazarus was "from Bethany," and Matthew 21:11, which states that Jesus was "the prophet from Nazareth" (see also Acts 18:2 and 2:5; 6:9; 10:23b). The author did not write in the company of believers in Italy (cf. 1 Cor. 16:19; 1 Pet. 5:13) but rather stands with a group that has come from there. Interestingly, the first time we hear Hebrews quoted is in 1 Clement, written by Clement of Rome at the end of the first century or beginning of the second century AD.

This evidence notwithstanding, some ancient and contemporary commentators have suggested that the recipients resided in Jerusalem or even some other locale. A few have argued that the readers had been members of the Qumran community where the Dead Sea scrolls were found, a position that has not found wide acceptance.[3] In any case, the interpretation of the book does not depend on knowing the readers' residence.

The recipients of Hebrews were not new believers, but their situation was precarious, so much so that the author exhorts them: "Do not throw away your confidence; it will be richly rewarded" (10:35).

Hebrews and 1 Clement

Clement of Rome wrote to the church in Corinth sometime around the turn of the first century. Clement cites and alludes to the Old Testament, mainly from the Greek translation called the Septuagint, along with a number of books that later became part of the New Testament canon: 1 Corinthians, Romans, Galatians, Paul's Prison and Pastoral Epistles, 1 Peter, James, Acts, and John's gospel. He also references Hebrews in a number of places.[4] Compare, for example, 1 Clement 36:2 and Hebrews 1:3–4, noting how Clement weaves Hebrews into his thought:

> *Hebrews 1:3–4:* The Son is the radiance of God's glory and the exact representation of his being, sustaining all things by his powerful word. After he had provided purification for sins, he sat down at the right hand of the Majesty in heaven. So he became as much superior to the angels as the name he has inherited is superior to theirs.
>
> *1 Clement 32:1:* Through this one we gaze into the heights of the heavens; through this one we see the reflection of his perfect and superior countenance; through this one the eyes of our hearts have been opened; through this one our foolish and darkened understanding springs up into the light; through this one the Master has wished us to taste the knowledge of immortality. He is the radiance of his magnificence, as superior to the angels as he has inherited a more excellent name.

THE RECIPIENTS' SITUATION

The first readers of Hebrews were second-generation Christians who had not personally heard Jesus but learned the faith from first-generation believers (2:3–4). They received testimony about Jesus, accompanied by miraculous signs that bore testimony to the gospel. When Hebrews was written, the recipients were not new converts but had been Christians for some time (5:11–14). In 6:4–5 we learn that their conversion was genuine, since they had been "enlightened" by the gospel (cf. Heb. 10:32; Eph. 1:18); "tasted," or experienced, God's gift saving grace (cf. Heb. 2:3; Rom. 5:15; and 1 Pet. 2:3); and received the Holy Spirit (cf. Heb. 6:4; Rom. 8:9). They also had heard God's word (cf. Heb. 1:3; 2:1–3; 4:12) and experienced the "powers of the coming age" (6:5; cf. 2:4). They had confessed their faith (3:1; 4:14; 10:23).[5] Their conversion had included both inward moral cleansing and water baptism (10:22). Their newfound faith had resulted in service for those in need (6:9–12). Their adherence to Christ had cost them dearly, however. At one time they had endured severe persecution, which included social ostracism, verbal abuse, and the loss of property, though not life (10:32–35). At that time they stood with the persecuted and had suffered themselves. Although they previously lost goods, they knew that they "had better and lasting possessions" (10:34).

Apostasy from the Faith

The author of Hebrews addresses the problem of apostasy in various warnings. He exhorts the readers not to abandon the gatherings of believers as some have done already (10:25). He appeals to the recipients not to "drift away" (2:1), "fall short" (4:1; 12:15), or "shrink back" (10:39). In 6:6 he speaks about those "who have fallen away," and in 10:26–27 he warns: "If we deliberately keep on sinning after we have received the knowledge of the truth, no sacrifice for sins is left, but only a fearful expectation of judgment and of raging fire that will consume the enemies of God." He even states that it is impossible for those who have experienced the full blessing of God and have fallen away "to be brought back to repentance" since "they are crucifying the Son of God all over again and subjecting him to public disgrace" (6:4–6). Over and again Hebrews recalls the dark destiny of those in Israel's history who turned away from God (Heb. 3:7–4:11 and Ps. 95:7–11 and Num. 14; Heb. 10:26–39 and Deut. 32:35–36, Ps. 135:14 and Hab. 2:4). Hebrews's warnings against apostasy could not be more dire.

The early church struggled deeply with apostasy. Peter warned, "It would have been better for them not to have known the way of righteousness, than to have known it and then to turn their backs on the sacred command that was passed on to them" (2 Pet. 2:21). In his first letter, Peter alerted his readers to the devil, who "prowls around like a roaring lion looking for someone to devour" (1 Pet. 5:8). Paul feared that the young Thessalonian believers had been tempted by "the tempter" and that the apostolic labors among them would have been in vain (1 Thess. 3:5). Demas, once Paul's companion, forsook him, since he "loved this world" (2 Tim. 4:10).

The problem of apostasy continued after the apostolic era. In the early second century AD, Pliny the Younger wrote to Emperor Trajan about the "Christian problem" in the province of Bithynia and the measures he took to arrest the movement. In one correspondence he described the way some Christians had turned from the faith: "Others, whose names were given to me by an informer, first admitted the charge and then denied it; they said that they had ceased to be Christians two or more years previously, and some of them even twenty years ago. They all did reverence to your statue and the images of the gods in the same way as the others, and reviled the name of Christ" (*Letters* 10:96). Not all continued in the faith in the face of persecution.

These texts stand over against those that speak of God's ability to keep his own. Jesus spoke about his sheep, saying, "No one will snatch them out of my hand" and "no one can snatch them out of my Father's hand" (John 10:28–29). Peter assured the persecuted believers that they "are shielded by God's power until the coming of the salvation that is ready to be revealed in the last time" (1 Pet. 1:5). God can keep his own.

The church will continue to debate the question whether apostasy is indeed possible. Some would say Hebrews warns those who are not truly in the faith[6] or who were taking steps toward the faith. Others contend that Hebrews only presents apostasy as a theoretical possibility. Still others say the book warns believers not to abandon Christ. But note that the author addresses the situation of those who are willful and deliberate in their abandonment, not those who fail due to weakness. Whatever the conclusion on this matter, Hebrews warns its readers to continue to follow Christ faithfully and to not turn their backs on him. He is God's final word.

They had not, however, come to the point of shedding blood for their faith (12:4), a possible reference to the fact that nobody had been martyred. However, they had suffered severe social dishonor.

But these believers' firm faith was now starting to erode. The author expresses deep concern over their lack of maturation in the faith, given how long they had been followers of Christ (5:11–6:3). Fissures in the community had appeared, since some abandoned the gatherings of believers (10:24–25). Socially, the community continued to be "outside" and marginalized, suffering dishonor. They were beginning to slip away. Over and again the author warns them of the perils of abandoning Christ and reverting to Judaism. He urges them not to drift away and exhorts them to remain faithful to Christ (2:1–4; 3:6–19; 4:1–2, 11; 6:1–12; 10:26–31, 35–39; 12:1–17, 25–29; 13:9–15), knowing that Christ himself had suffered shame yet received honor from God (12:1–3). Indeed, among the catalog of the faithful in chapter 11 were those who suffered for their faith to the point of death and had shown themselves to be truly honorable (11:37–38). They held to faith and were commended (11:39–40) and, as such, were an example for the first recipients of this book. But the author also repeatedly underscores the dire consequences of abandoning their faith in Christ. Apostasy was a frightful possibility. Hebrews calls them to follow Christ faithfully, even embracing his shame (13:13).

Outline of Hebrews

I. God's Revelation through His Son (1:1–4)
II. The Son and the Angels (1:5–2:18)
    1. The Son's Superiority over Angels (1:5–14)
    2. The First Warning against Apostasy (2:1–4)
    3. The Humanity and Exaltation of the Son (2:5–18)
III. The Son, Moses, and Joshua (3:1–4:13)
    1. The Son is Superior to Moses (3:1–6)
    2. The Second Warning against Apostasy (3:7–19)
    3. Joshua's Rest and the Call to Enter God's Sabbath Rest (4:1–13)
IV. The Son as the Great High Priest (4:14–10:18)
    1. Jesus the Merciful High Priest (4:14–5:10)
    2. The Third Warning against Apostasy (5:11–6:8)
    3. God's Sure Promise (6:9–20)
    4. Jesus's Superior Priesthood in the Order of Melchizedek (7:1–28)
    5. Jesus the High Priest of a Superior Covenant (8:1–13)
    6. The Superior Tabernacle (9:1–10)
    7. Jesus's Superior Sacrifice (9:11–10:18)
V. The Call to Perseverance in the Faith (10:19–12:29)
    1. The Exhortation to Draw Near to God (10:19–25)

The symbol of an anchor is used to secure believers in their faith (Heb. 6:19). This stone anchor used by Greek and Roman ships was discovered near Palmachim, Israel. Beit-Miriam Museum, Israel.
Todd Bolen/BiblePlaces.com

2. The Fourth Warning against Apostasy (10:26–31)
3. Perseverance amid Suffering (10:32–39)
4. The Examples of Faith (11:1–40)
5. Following Jesus in the Race (12:1–3)
6. God's Discipline (12:4–13)
7. The Fifth Warning against Apostasy (12:14–17)
8. Coming to the Heavenly Mount Zion (12:18–29)

VI. Final Exhortations (13:1–19)
VII. The Benediction and Greetings (13:20–25)

THE MESSAGE OF HEBREWS

The message of Hebrews goes beyond warning the recipients not to turn away from Christ and calling them to remain faithful to him. The book repeatedly shows the first readers and hearers that the way of salvation God laid out in Christ is superior to the blessings they had received under the old covenant. Indeed, the author uses the word *better* (or greater) thirteen times in the book (1:4; 6:9; 7:7, 19, 22; 8:6 [2X]; 9:23; 10:34; 11:16, 35, 40; 12:24). He tells them of Christ's superiority over the prophets, angels, Moses, Joshua, Aaron, and the Levitical priesthood. He demonstrates that Jesus Christ has inaugurated a superior covenant, serves in a better heavenly tabernacle, and offered himself as a superior sacrifice, thus providing a new and living way to draw near to God. At the same time, the author reminds the readers that the "old" is passing away. Speaking of the new covenant, he says, "By calling this covenant 'new,' he has made the first one obsolete; and what is obsolete and outdated will soon disappear" (8:13). Given these realities, he repeatedly calls them not to turn away from Christ (2:1–4; 3:7–19; 5:11–6:8; 10:26–31; 12:14–17) and exhorts them to stand firm in the faith, to persevere, and to enter into what God has promised (3:1; 4:14–16; 6:1–3; 10:19–25, 36–39; 12:1–3, 28–29).

Angels fly above a scene of the sacrifice of Isaac, from the Basilica of San Vitale, sixth century AD.
Spatuletail/Shutterstock

Jesus and the Prophets

Hebrews opens with the dramatic claim that God had spoken in previous generations through the prophets but "in these last days he has spoken to us by his Son" (1:2). The "last days" are the time when God's promises through the prophets are fulfilled (Acts 2:17). Through the Son, God now makes his final revelation. In these first words, the author declares the superiority of Christ's revelation over that of the Old Testament prophets. He goes on to demonstrate how exalted the Son is, thereby securing his place of authority. He is the Creator, heir, sustainer, Redeemer, and is sovereign over all things. And he is "the radiance of God's glory and the exact representation of his being" (Heb. 1:3). He shares the nature of God and therefore fully represents his person and will. The opening verses of Hebrews present some of the highest Christology of the New Testament books (cf. John 1:1–5, 14). Confidence in him starts here.

Jesus and the Angels

Given who the Son of God is, the author can claim he is "much superior to the angels" (1:4 and 1:5–2:18). Why did he deem it necessary to make this claim? While angels appear in various roles in the Old Testament (i.e., Gen. 19:1; Pss. 19:11; 103:20), Jewish theology during the intertestamental period ascribes increasingly important roles to them. They are regarded as the ones through whom God gave the law and knowledge (Gal. 3:19; Heb. 2:2; Jub. 1:28; 10:10–14). They served as mediators between humanity and God, since they stand in his presence (Matt. 18:10; Tob. 12:11–15; 1 En. 9:1–11). Some held that angels govern the world (Deut. 32:8 LXX; Dan. 10:13, 20; 1 En. 60:15–21). Hebrews, however, declares that angels are only ministers (Heb. 1:14) who worship the Son (1:6). The Son is superior to them, since everything is under his authority (1:8–14; 2:5–9).

Hebrews and the Old Testament

Starting with the second section of the book (1:5–2:18), the author of Hebrews supports his argument with constant reference to the Old Testament. In his discussion of Christ's superiority over angels, he cites Psalm 2:7 (1:5a), 2 Samuel 7:14 with 1 Chronicles 17:13 (1:5b), Deuteronomy 32:43 (1:6), Psalm 104:4 (1:7), Psalm 45:6–7 (1:8b-9), Psalm 102:25–27 (1:10–12), Psalm 110:1 (1:13), Psalm 8:4–6 (2:6b–8a), Psalm 22:22 (2:12), and Isaiah 8:17–18 (2:13). Throughout the following argument, he supports his position by appealing to Scripture, citing the Septuagint (LXX), the Greek translation of the Old Testament. Most of his citations come from the Psalms, although he also draws heavily upon the Pentateuch and somewhat less from the Prophets. The author utilizes a variety of interpretive techniques, such as typology (9:1–11) and midrash (3:7–4:11), to show how the ancient Scriptures point to Christ and guide the Christian community. Although he regards Christ as God's fullest revelation, he repeatedly recognizes that God spoke in these texts through the agency of the Holy Spirit (Heb. 1:1). The author introduces quotations by saying "the Holy Spirit says" (3:7; cf. 9:8; 10:15) or by indicating that God is the author (1:13; 4:3; 5:5; 7:12; 10:5, 7, 8, 30; 13:5) instead of naming the human author of the text.

Hebrews declares that the Old Testament texts point to Christ and are fulfilled in him.

At the same time, Hebrews argues that the new revelation in Christ surpasses the old, and supersedes it (4:8; 7:11; 8:7, 11; 10:9). This claim runs counter to the common notion in the Mediterranean world that older things were better than newer things. Socrates was condemned, for example, for bringing to Athens "new deities" (Xenophon, *Mem.* 1.1.1; cf. Acts 17:19). Christ's revelation, though new, transcends the old.

Angels

Hebrews discusses the role of angels in relation to Christ and believers. The author reminds the readers that angels are nothing less than "ministering spirits sent to serve those who will inherit salvation" (1:14). During the Second Temple Period, Jewish authors ascribed increasingly significant roles to angels as agents of God (Jub. 38:10), protectors of God's people (1 Enoch 100:5), executors of God's judgments (1 Enoch 56), and mediators of God's revelation (Jub. 1:27–29; 10:10–14). They were deemed to be spiritual beings created by God who praised his work of creation (Jub. 2:2–3). Hebrews recognizes their significant role yet affirms Christ's superiority over them.

Indeed, he is sovereign even over the world to come (Heb. 2:5–8). Given his position of superiority over the angels and the message they mediated—the law (2:2)—the author calls the readers not to drift away and ignore the great salvation Christ brings (2:1–3). The ethical demand emerges from Christ's gift of salvation.

In discussing Christ's exaltation over the angels, the author also goes to lengths to show how fully Christ identified with humanity. At the same time, he explains that Christ's humanity and suffering do not negate his exalted position. He suffered death for everyone (2:9), was made perfect through his sufferings (2:10), and was honored to be of the human family (2:11), whom he came to liberate from the power and fear of death (2:14–15). He renders aid for "Abraham's descendants" (2:16), having been made "fully human in every way" as their high priest (2:17), even being tempted as humans and yet was without sin (2:18; 4:15). He atoned for human sin through his death (2:17). Powerful as they are, no angel could accomplish that.

Jesus, Moses, and Joshua

The role of Moses in the history of Israel cannot be overestimated. Moses was from the tribe of Levi (Ex. 2:1) and, as such, was regarded as a priest in Jewish literature (Philo, *Vit. Mos.* 2.66–186). Moses was the only one God spoke to "face to face, as one speaks to a friend" (Ex. 33:11; Num. 12:7–8). Moses led Israel out of Egypt in the exodus (Heb. 3:16), and through him God gave the law to his people. Although Moses faithfully discharged his duties as a servant in God's house (3:2, 5), Jesus is superior as the builder of the house and the "Son over God's house" (3:3, 6). The "house," in the author's understanding, is both the whole universe (3:4; cf. 1:2, 10) and God's people (3:6; 10:21). As a means to warn the readers not to rebel against Christ (3:7–19), Hebrews recalls the disobedience of Israel and the consequences of their rebellion.

In 4:1–13 the author develops the theme of "rest," which he first presented in the warning against rebellion (3:7–11 and 4:3, citing Ps. 95:7–11). The rest promised to Israel was the land of Canaan, into which Joshua was going to lead them (4:2, 8). Hebrews, however, recalls the disobedience of the nation and God's judgment, which did not allow many to enter the rest promised in that new land (4:6; see Num. 14:21–23). The rest in that promised land was only a type of the greater Sabbath rest that God enjoys and to which he calls believers (4:6–11). Rest becomes a rich metaphor for the totality of God's promised salvation, elsewhere in the book called a heavenly country and city (11:16) and a kingdom that cannot be shaken (12:28). The example of Israel's disobedience and subsequent exclusion from the Promised Land serves as yet another warning to the readers not to abandon Christ.

Wall painting from the Dura-Europos synagogue of Moses parting the Red Sea
Wikimedia Commons, PD-US

Jesus, the Great High Priest

Central to Hebrews's theology and exhortation to hold on to the faith is the high priesthood of Jesus: "Therefore, since we have a great high priest who has ascended into heaven, Jesus the Son of God, let us hold firmly to the faith we profess" (4:14). His high priesthood occupies the central section of the author's argument (4:14–10:25) and appears throughout the book (2:17; 3:1; 4:14–14; 5:1, 5, 10; 6:20; 7:26; 8:1, 3; 9:7, 11, 25; 13:25). Although the author focuses on the heavenly ministry of Jesus as the high priest, he affirms that, as every priest, Jesus is like those he serves. High priests were selected from among the people and were beset with the same weaknesses. Given this, the high priests were "able to deal gently with those who are . . . going astray" (5:2). Indeed, Jesus learned obedience to the Father through severe suffering (5:7–8). Being human and tempted as all humans are, he is able "to empathize with our weaknesses" (4:15). The author is careful to add, however, that though he was temped, "he did not sin."

Fragment of Q11 Melchizedek
Courtesy of The Leon Levy Dead Sea Scrolls Digital Library; Israel Antiquities Authority, photo: Shai Halevi

Melchizedek in the Dead Sea Scrolls and Hebrews

In the Dead Sea Scrolls from Qumran, one short book discusses the place of Melchizedek. The book 11QMelchizedek draws upon Leviticus and Deuteronomy regarding the year of Jubilee (Lev. 25:13; Deut. 15:2), Isaiah about God's rule (52:7) and his liberation of the captives (Isa. 61:1–3), and various texts from Psalms that speak of God's judgment (Pss. 7:8–9; 82:1–3). The book regards Melchizedek as the one who brings in God's liberating jubilee: "He will proclaim liberty for them, to free them from [the debt] of all their iniquities. And this will [happen] in the first week of the jubilee which follows the ni[ne] jubilees" (11QMelch 2.5–7). Melchizedek will also carry out God's judgment according to this text: "But, Melchizedek will carry out the vengeance of God's judges." He will also free them from the devil, that is, "from the hand of Belial" (2.13, 25). In this text Melchizedek is understood as an angelic being that opposes the devil and brings in God's liberation and judgment. In contrast, Hebrews interprets Melchizedek as a type of Christ, since that ancient figure is both king and high priest, as is Jesus.

After the reminder of the Son of God's constancy, Hebrews exhorts the readers yet again not to turn away from Christ (5:11–6:8). They had not matured as they ought (5:11–6:3). After this the author inserts the third warning against apostasy (6:4–8). His warning could not be more severe. What hope is there for those who deliberately turn their back on Christ, since "to their loss they are crucifying the Son of God all over again and subjecting him to public disgrace" (6:6)? The author, however, sounds a note of hope that they will not turn from the Son of God (6:9–12). He remains convinced that they will choose the right path despite their present precarious position.

Throughout this section, the author argues that the high priesthood of the Son of God is an eternal priesthood "in the order of Melchizedek" (5:6, 10; 6:20; 7:1–28). The problem with regarding Jesus as high priest is that he was not a descendant of Levi, the Jewish tribe designated by God to serve as priests (Lev. 8–10). Jesus, however, was of the tribe of Judah and should not, therefore, qualify as a priest (7:11–19). Hebrews, however, recognizes Jesus's high priesthood as in the line of Melchizedek, quoting Psalm 110:4 (Heb. 5:5, 10; 6:20; 7:17). Scripture first introduces Melchizedek in Genesis 14:18–20, where he appears as "king of Salem" and "priest of God Most High." Melchizedek represented another kind of priesthood that was not connected with the descendants of Abraham. Hebrews argues that Melchizedek's priesthood is superior to that of Aaron and the Levites,

Matt Ragen/Shutterstock

This colorization of the spoils panel on the Arch of Titus in Rome, commemorating the defeat of Jerusalem and the destruction of the temple, combined scholarly research from ancient literary sources, identifying pigments from Roman sculptures, matching color evidence from Roman wall paintings, and implementing modern 3D modeling software to re-create the scene as vividly and accurately as possible. Hebrews 9:2 mentions the lampstand and the table as items in the Holy Place of the tabernacle.

© 2018 by Learning Sites, Inc., the Institute for the Visualization of History, Inc., and the Yeshiva University for Israel Studies

since Abraham, Levi's forefather, paid tithes to Melchizedek and Melchizedek in turn blessed him (Heb. 7:1–10). As Hebrews says, "the lesser is blessed by the greater" (7:7). Jesus's priesthood "in the order of Melchizedek" is therefore superior to that of the tribe of Levi. Moreover, it is a priesthood that lasts forever (5:6; 6:20; 7:14, 20–25) and will not be abrogated. So once again the author of Hebrews shows the superiority of the Son of God over a central institution of Judaism, the Levitical priesthood.

Hebrews not only tells the first readers about the Son of God's superior high priesthood but also elaborates about the superiority of the new covenant established through a better sacrifice, Christ himself (8:1–10:18). The new covenant (8:7–13; 9:11–22; Jer. 31:31–34) is superior since it brings people to a true knowledge of God, writes God's laws on peoples' minds and hearts, and offers forgiveness of sins. This covenant was established through the blood and sacrifice of Christ, which was once and for all (10:10)—it did not have to be repeated like the sacrifices of the old covenant (9:11–14, 27–28; 10:1–18). The superiority of Christ's sacrifice is such that his blood was offered in the heavenly sanctuary, not an earthly sanctuary or tabernacle (8:3–6; 9:1–10, 23–28; see Ex. 25–27). The earthly tabernacle was simply an image of the superior heavenly one (9:11).

Reconstructed four-horned altar from Beersheba at the Israel Museum, Jerusalem. Sacrifices prescribed by the Mosaic law had to be repeated on altars such as these. Christ's sacrifice for sin meant the end of sacrifices.
© 2018 by Zondervan

Christ's sacrifice and offering, as well as the sanctuary where he offered them, are far superior to the old covenant, and their efficacy is superior. Christ "has appeared once for all at the culmination of the ages to do away with sin by the sacrifice of himself" (9:26). Therefore, any other "sacrifice for sin is no longer necessary" (10:18).

The Call to Perseverance

At the end of the extended discussion regarding the new covenant, the sacrifice of Christ, and the heavenly tabernacle, the author inserts yet another call to persevere in the faith (10:19–25) and warns the readers of the consequences of rejecting the Son of God (10:26–31). He wraps up the warning with yet another hope-filled call to persevere in the faith as they had done in the past when they endured severe persecution (10:32–39).

Chapter 11 is one of the most well-known passages from Hebrews. Here the author presents the people of faith throughout the history of Israel to serve as examples for his readers to emulate. After citing Habakkuk 2:3–4 (Heb. 10:37–38), he reminds them that they and he "do not belong to those who shrink back and are destroyed, but to those who have faith and are saved" (10:39). He then makes a statement on the nature of faith that countless Christians have memorized: "Now faith is confidence in what we hope for and assurance about what we do not see" (11:1). Attridge suggests the translation, "Faith is the reality of things hoped for, the proof of things unseen" and comments that "faith . . . is obedient fidelity and trusting belief and both components are essential. The perception of reality that faith provides give the basic motivation to endure trials and tribulations."[7] The kind of trust and obedience to which the author calls his readers is exemplified in the characters presented in the following examples of virtue. This type of list of exemplar people who demonstrated virtue appears in other Jewish literature as well (4 Macc. 16:16–23; Wis. 10:1–21). Hebrews reminds the readers that some of God's people accomplished honorable and noteworthy deeds through faith (11:4–35a) but that others "were tortured . . . faced jeers and flogging, and even chains and imprisonment" and "were put to death by stoning . . . sawed in two . . . killed by the sword . . . went about . . . destitute, persecuted and mistreated" (11:35–38). Whether these worthies in the past saw deliverance or destitution, they "were all commended for their faith" (11:39). The author takes this moment to call his readers to faith yet again, saying, "Yet none of them received what had been promised, since God had planned something better for us so that only together with us would they be made perfect" (11:39–40). The call to emulate such faith could not be stronger.

The author of Hebrews gives them one more example of faith amid adversity—Jesus himself (12:1–3). He calls them to view hardship as God's discipline (12:4–13) and warns them again not to reject God's blessing (12:14–17). He summarizes the privilege they have as they come "to Mount Zion, to the city of the living God" (12:22) and urges them to "be thankful, and so worship God acceptably with reverence and awe, for our 'God is a consuming fire'" (12:28–29, citing Deut. 4:24).

Hebrews concludes with a series of final exhortations (13:1–19) at whose heart is the final reminder and appeal: "Jesus also suffered outside the city gate to make the people holy through his own blood. Let us, then, go to him outside the camp, bearing the disgrace he bore. For here we do not have an enduring city, but we are looking for the city that is to come" (13:12–14). In calling his readers to endure in faith, he points them directly to Jesus, through whom they offer their sacrificial worship of praise and doing good for others (13:15–16).

AUTHOR AND DATE

The church father Origen commented on the authorship of Hebrews, saying, "But who wrote the epistle, in truth God knows" (cited by Eusebius, *Hist. eccl.* 6.25.14). Hebrews is an anonymous document whose authorship can be guessed but not affirmed with certainty. In the early church, many believed that the apostle Paul penned the book. Origen expresses his views regarding the possibility of Pauline authorship, saying, "But as for myself, if I were to state my own opinion, I should say that the thoughts are the apostle's, but that the style and composition belong to one who called to mind the apostle's teachings and, as it were, made short notes of what his master said. If any church, therefore, holds this epistle as Paul's, let it be commended for this also. For not without reason have the men of old time handed it down as Paul's" (6.25.13–14). Eusebius also recalls the view of Clement of Alexandria, saying, "As for the Epistle to the Hebrews, he says indeed that it is Paul's, but that it was written for the Hebrews in the Hebrew tongue, and that Luke, having carefully translated it, published it for the Greeks" (6.14.2–3). But Origen notes that the style of the Greek is not Paul's. Despite this, the Western church accepted the book as Paul's, up through the fourth century.

The arguments against Pauline authorship are strong, however. Paul always includes his name in his compositions, but the author of this book does not identify himself. The style of the book is different from that of Paul. The author notes that he is dependent on the testimony of first-generation followers of Christ (Heb. 2:3–4), something that Paul denies (Gal. 1:11–17; 1 Cor. 15:3–10). The central theme of Jesus's high priesthood never appears in Paul's known writings. On the other hand, Paul commonly refers to the Lord as "Christ Jesus," and he repeatedly talks about Jesus's resurrection. Hebrews, however, never utilizes this title and only once refers to Jesus's resurrection (13:20). The most certain thing we can say about authorship is that Paul did not write the book.

Many others have been suggested as possible authors. Luke was named as a candidate, given Clement of Alexandria's comment and the excellent Greek style of the book. The author knows Timothy, as did Luke (2 Tim. 4:11; Heb. 13:23). Clement of Rome has also been suggested as the author since he is the first to show traces of Hebrews in his letters to the Corinthian church at the end of the first century AD. Barnabas, Paul's travel companion on his first missionary journey, is another possible author. Two likely candidates are Apollos and Silas (also known as Silvanus; 1 Pet. 5:12; Acts 15:40), both Hellenistic Jews who would likely be able to produce the fine Greek style of Hebrews. Apollos is an especially attractive suggestion, given his noted rhetorical skill and his knowledge of Scripture (Acts 18:24). He was from Alexandria, which may account for the similarities between the argumentation of Hebrews and that of Philo of Alexandria.[8] Priscilla is another person named as a possible author, as is Mary, the mother of Jesus, but the masculine participle used when the author refers to himself precludes these possibilities (11:23). In the end, all these and other suggestions are only conjectures.

We know, however, that the author was a second-generation Christian who had heard eye-witness testimony about the Lord Jesus (Heb. 2:3). He was part of the Pauline circle, which included Timothy (13:23). The person had a deep knowledge of the Old Testament but was entirely dependent on the Septuagint. He was well versed in rhetoric and likely in Greek philosophical thought. The book is a marvel of persuasive power. Given this and the fact that he is deeply versed in Jewish literature and practice, the author is most likely a Hellenistic Jewish Christian. We do not know where the author was located, save that he lived somewhere outside Italy (see section The First Readers, earlier in the chapter). He could have been in Jerusalem or, less likely, in Alexandria in Egypt.

Even though the book's author cannot be identified with certainty, the early church readily received Hebrews into the canon. The book was used very early in the church, with *1 Clement*, citing it often as did Polycarp and *2 Clement*. Tertullian and Clement of Alexandria cited it, and Origen liberally quoted it. On the other hand, the Muratorian Canon does not mention it, and Eusebius does not include it in his list of recognized books. Eusebius does not include it in his lists of disputed and spurious books either (*Hist. eccl.* 3.25.1–7). But he seems to have regarded it as a work by the apostle Paul and included it among the Paulines in his general statement about the acceptance of the epistles of Paul. But he expressed some doubt about Pauline authorship, saying, "And the fourteen letters of Paul are obvious and plain, yet it is not right to ignore that some dispute the Epistle to the Hebrews" (3.3.4).

Over against this question about authorship, Hebrews was used early and widely in the churches. They warranted its inclusion into the list of books Christians regard as canonical and therefore authoritative. Jerome expressed the sum of the matter best: "The Epistle which is inscribed to the Hebrews is received not only by the Churches of the East, but also by all Church writers of the Greek language before our days, as of Paul the apostle, though many think that it is from Barnabas or Clement. And it makes no difference who it is, since it is from a churchman, and is celebrated in the daily readings of the Churches" (*Epistle* 129).

The date the author wrote the book is elusive as well, though Hebrews offers a bit more evidence in this matter. We know the author lived within the time of first-generation Christians (2:3). Some time had passed since his readers had come to faith in Christ, and they had passed through a period of persecution for their faith (5:12; 10:32–35). The persecution had waned and so too their faith. Since Clement of Rome cited the book at the end of the first century AD, Hebrews could not have been penned later than the 90s. Timothy was still alive and known (13:23). The sacrifices in the Jerusalem temple were still being offered, it appears (9:6–10; 10:1–2). If indeed they were still being offered, we could safely date the book to a time before the destruction of the temple by the Romans in AD 70. In this case, a date of composition in the 60s is highly likely. On the other hand, Hebrews is interested in the tabernacle and not the temple, so the note about sacrifices may not be a strong marker of the date as some suggest. Indeed, the repeated emphasis on the replacement of the Jewish sacrificial system may point to a date later than AD 70. The best we can say is that the book may have been written in the 60s or possibly in the 70s through the 80s.

Questions for Discussion

1. Hebrews is an impassioned plea not to turn away from Christ. Is it possible to lose one's salvation?
2. What relevance does the ancient sacrificial system have for Christians today, locally and globally?
3. Explore the nature of the new covenant in Hebrews and other Old Testament and New Testament texts. What does the new covenant offer Christians?
4. Discuss the issue of suffering in Hebrews, both in relation to Christ and believers. What does faith in the midst of suffering look like?
5. The author of Hebrews calls the readers to go to Jesus "outside the camp" (13:11). What did this mean for the first readers of Hebrews and what is its significance for Christians today?

BIBLIOGRAPHY

Introductory

Guthrie, G. H. *Hebrews.* NIVAC. Grand Rapids: Zondervan, 1998.

Laansma, J. C. *The Letter to the Hebrews: A Commentary for Preaching, Teaching, and Bible Study.* Eugene, OR: Cascade, 2017.

Schreiner, T. R. *Commentary on Hebrews.* Nashville: Broadman & Holman, 2015.

Thompson, J. W. *Hebrews.* Paideia. Grand Rapids: Baker, 2008.

Advanced

Attridge, H. W. *The Epistle to the Hebrews.* Hermeneia. Philadelphia: Fortress, 1989.

Bruce, F. F. *The Epistle to the Hebrews.* NICNT. Grand Rapids: Eerdmans, 1990.

Cockerill, G. L. *The Epistle to the Hebrews.* NICNT. Grand Rapids: Eerdmans, 2012.

deSilva, D. A. *Perseverance in Gratitude: A Socio-Rhetorical Commentary on the Epistle to the Hebrews.* Grand Rapids: Eerdmans, 2000.

Koester, C. R. *Hebrews.* AB. New York: Doubleday, 2001.

Lane, W. L. *Hebrews.* 2 vols. WBC. Dallas: Word, 1991.

NOTES

1. K. Bediako, *Jesus and the Gospel in Africa: History and Experience* (Maryknoll, NY: Orbis, 2004), 20–33.

2. J. D. G. Dunn, *Romans 1–8*, WBC (Dallas: Word, 1988), xlv-xlvi.

3. While similarities with the theology of the Dead Sea Scrolls community exist, they fall short of proving that converts from Qumran were the recipients. See E. F. Mason, "Hebrews and the Dead Sea Scrolls. Some Points of Comparison," *PRSt* 37 (2010): 457–79.

4. See D. A. Hagner, *The Use of the Old and New Testaments in Clement of Rome* (NovTSup 34; Leiden: Brill, 1973).

5. All these verses use the Greek term *homologia*, which refers to their "confession" of faith.

6. Commenting on Hebrews 6:4–6, F. F. Bruce says, "In these verses he is not questioning the perseverance of the saints; we might say that rather he is insisting that those who persevere are the true saints." *The Epistle to the Hebrews*, NICNT (Grand Rapids: Eerdmans, 1990), 144.

7. H. W. Attridge, *The Epistle to the Hebrews* (Hermeneia; Philadelphia: Fortress, 1989), 305, 308.

8. Ibid., 29.

Chapter 23

THE LETTER OF JAMES

This fifth-century mosaic from the Beth Shan synagogue uses all the well-known symbols of Jewish religious life in the first century: the temple candelabra, incense shovel, and ram's horn.

Z. Radovan/www.BibleLandPictures.com

Tension among rich and poor is one of the main motifs in James. These are examples of distinguished Roman citizens. The National Museum, Istanbul. *Gary M. Burge*

Martin Luther famously remarked that the epistle of James is "an epistle of straw" (alluding to 1 Cor. 3:12) compared with the gospel of John, 1 John, Paul's epistles, and 1 Peter. These books, he said, "show you Christ and teach you all that is necessary and salvatory for you to know." Luther, however, expressed more charitable thoughts about the book elsewhere: "I praise it and consider it a good book, because it sets up no doctrines of men but vigorously promulgates the law of God." Yet, in the end, he voiced profound concerns about the epistle, since in his opinion, "it is flatly against St. Paul and all the rest of Scripture in ascribing justification to works [2:24]." And "it does not once mention the Passion, resurrection, or the Spirit of Christ."[1] In contrast, Bede the Venerable (d. AD 735), the great English church historian, lauded the book highly, saying that James "encourages the righteous not to fall away from the faith in temptations, he reproves sinners and advises them to refrain from sinning and to make progress in virtues lest what they had received as sacraments of the faith might turn out to be for them not only fruitless but also a cause of damnation."[2] Throughout church history Christians have evaluated James quite differently.

Contemporary judgments about the epistle of James vary widely as well. Some detach the book from the historical James, the half-brother of Jesus, who led the Jerusalem church, regarding it as yet another example of early Christian pseudepigraphy. Others laud it as a powerful book that stands within the prophetic tradition and the teaching of Jesus, since it defends the cause of the poor and stands against their oppressors. Is James simply "straw" or does it faithfully translate the teaching of Jesus into the life of the church and society?

THE SETTING OF JAMES

Readers of James sometimes come away with the impression that the book is merely a cobbled-together collection of wise and memorable sayings. Martin Luther held this opinion, exclaiming that James "throws things together so chaotically" since it appears that he "took a few sayings from the disciples of the apostles and tossed them off on paper."[3] In a similar vein, Martin Dibelius called the letter *paraenesis*, that is, "a text which strings together admonitions of general ethical content" and lacks continuity.[4] But are there central concerns the epistle addresses, and does James have a cohesive message?

James indeed contains some of the most memorable verses in the New Testament, seemingly randomly arranged. He exhorts his readers to "consider it pure joy, my brothers and sisters, whenever you face trials of many kinds, because you know that the testing of your faith produces perseverance" (1:2–3). He follows that familiar line with the call and promise that "if any of you lacks wisdom, you should ask God, who gives generously to all without finding fault, and it will be given to you" (1:5). In the second chapter, James declares that believers are "justified by works and not by faith alone" (2:24 ESV), appearing to contradict Paul (compare Rom. 3:28; Gal. 2:16). James checks the language of his readers with the scorching remark, "The tongue also is a fire, a world of evil among the parts of the body" (3:6). Many contemporary readers regard these and other texts as James's guide for personal piety. Concerns about trials and testing (1:2–18), doing God's word (1:22–25; 2:1–26), living harmoniously in community (4:1–12), the tongue (1:26–27; 3:1–12), patience in suffering (5:7–11), and faith (5:13–18) all resonate with many believers.

Clothing of the wealthy is depicted by this statue of a woman's torso from the first century AD.
Public Domain

But Christians in Latin America and other places in the world, where a large gap between the fortunes of the rich and the poor is part of the social landscape, see another set of issues that tie the letter together and evoke James's teaching. They hear James speaking into his world as well as their own as he traces the primary problem of socioeconomic disparity and its devastating effects, even within the Christian community. Mexican scholar Elsa Tamez says, "If the Letter of James were sent to the Christian communities of certain countries that suffer from violence and exploitation, it would very possibly be intercepted by government security agencies. The document would be branded as subversive because of the paragraphs that vehemently denounce the exploitation by landowners (5:1–6) and the carefree life of the merchants (4:13–17)."[5]

The Rich and the Poor

Latin American theologian Gustavo Gutiérrez called poverty "institutionalized violence," a structural social issue and not a condition produced by fate or a person's unwillingness to work.[6] James does not blame the poor for their state but rather focuses on the way rich people exploit them for profit and take them to court (5:1–6; 2:6). For their part, the believers discriminate against them (2:2–4) and do not respond to their need (2:14–17).

In James's day wealth and poverty were linked to the land. Those holding land prospered (Luke 12:16–21), while those without land suffered economic insecurity, with its attendant ills of malnutrition and low life expectancy. James rails against rich landowners in the assembly who refused to pay their workers, in violation of God's command (Lev. 19:13; Deut. 24:15; Jer. 22:13). The author of Sirach similarly said that "the bread of the needy is the life of the poor; whoever deprives them of it is a murderer. To take away a neighbor's living is to commit murder; to deprive an employee of wages is to shed blood" (34:25–27; Tobit 4:14). Likewise, Pseudo-Phocylides urged, "Give the laborer his pay, do not afflict the poor" (19). The poor could not find justice in the courts since the courts were weighted to favor those of higher social status. Indeed, one could not take a social superior to court, so the poor could not hope for legal remediation. The rich, in turn, could drag the poor into court for not paying debts and rents. James calls out the rich as those who oppress the poor (James 2:6), just as Malachi denounced "those who oppress the hired workers in their wages" (Mal. 3:5 NRSV).

The Diaspora

James addresses his letter "to the twelve tribes in the Dispersion" (1:1 NRSV). The "dispersion" may designate Jews who lived outside their homeland (John 7:35; Ps. Sol. 8:28; 9:2) or the place where they lived beyond Palestine (Jdt. 5:19). They were separated from their homeland, aliens in their communities, and subject to suspicion and discrimination at the hands of the majority culture. As one Jewish text said, "In the dispersion you shall be regarded as worthless" (T. Ash. 7:2–3). In 2 Maccabees 1:27 we hear the prayer, "Gather together our scattered people, set free those who are slaves among the gentiles, look on those who are rejected and despised." But assimilation to the values and the lifestyle of the surrounding culture was also a reality among Diaspora peoples. This appears to be the case with some within the community James addresses (James 4:4–6). They had adopted wealth and pride as their core values (5:1–6) and gave greatest honor to those who entered the community with "a gold ring and fine clothes" (2:2). They failed to recognize that God has "chosen those who are poor in the eyes of the world to be rich in faith" (2:5).

First-century Jewish diaspora

James 1:27 defines pure religion as reaching out to the most vulnerable in society—the orphan and the widow in James's day. The extensive section on justification and the nature of faith centers on the way the community marginalizes and neglects the poor while honoring the rich (2:1–26). The society of James was highly stratified, with men and women on the lower rungs experiencing acute depravation (1:27; 2:15–16; 5:4, 6). The rich, on the other hand, dressed elegantly and were given great honor in the assembly of believers (2:2–3). Yet these very people oppressed the poor by exploiting them, dragging them into court, and withholding wages from them as they hoarded their own wealth (2:6; 5:1–6). The rich coveted and fed their desires, fought and quarreled, and showed themselves to be primarily friends of the world who pursued their own interests (4:1–12). Then they arrogantly boasted about their economic prowess (4:13–17) and heaped up wealth (5:2–3). They talked good religion, but their actions told another story (1:22–24; 2:1–26). The community was tested, given their social situation (1:2–18). When we read James considering the economic realities within the Mediterranean world and our own, the letter's principle concern with wealth and poverty in relation to God and community snaps into focus.

The first readers of James were members of the Diaspora, Jews who lived outside Palestine, aliens in the societies where they lived and displaced from their homeland (1:1): "to the twelve tribes in the Dispersion" (NRSV), or "scattered among the nations" (NIV).

Similar to James, Peter's first epistle is addressed to those who are "the exiles of the Dispersion" (1 Pet. 1:1 NRSV). Peter appears to use "Dispersion" figuratively, referring to both Jewish and gentile members of the congregations he addresses. Some would insist that the "twelve tribes" in James 1:1 is also used figuratively to designate all Christians, both Jewish and gentile. But James's letter has a decidedly Jewish orientation and setting. The readers are people who twice daily confessed the *Shema* (Deut. 6:4–9), which begins: "Hear, O Israel, the LORD our God, the LORD is one" (see James 2:19). The place of their gathering is called a "synagogue" (Gk. *sunagōgē*, translated "assembly"), a term that refers to the religious gathering place of the Jewish people (Matt. 4:23; Mark 1:21; Luke 4:16; John 6:59; Acts 6:9) and never the Jesus-followers of the New Testament. Yet the Jewish members of this "synagogue" had faith in the Lord Jesus Christ (James 2:1; and 1:1), so their synagogue was distinguished from others that had not responded to the message that Jesus was the Messiah.

The location of these Jewish Christians cannot be ascertained with certainty. They may have been part of the Jewish Diaspora somewhere in the Mediterranean world. On the other hand, Jews were also scattered in lands toward the Euphrates River. Therefore, the letter might be addressed to Jewish Christians both to the east and west of Palestine. James was an encyclical document, carried to the scattered Jewish people (1:1) by a messenger, similar to the way Paul's letter to the Galatians (Gal. 1:2) and Peter's first epistle (1 Pet. 1:1) were distributed. In such cases, it would have been common for the letter to be read aloud to the community (1 Tim. 4:13), copied, then sent onward to recipients in other localities.

Outline of James

I. Opening Epistolary Greeting (1:1)
II. Introduction to Principle Themes: Testing, Wisdom, Poverty and Riches, Doing the Word, and the Tongue (1:1–27)
III. Faith without Works Is Dead (2:1–26)

IV. Controlling the Tongue and the Whole Body (3:1–12)
V. True Wisdom from Heaven (3:13–18)
VI. Verbal Conflict in the Community (4:1–12)
VII. Gaining Riches and Oppressing the Poor (4:13–5:6)
VIII. Patience in Suffering (5:7–12)
IX. Closing Prayer and Help for the Sick in Body and Sin (5:13–20)

THE MESSAGE OF JAMES

James and Jesus

In developing his message to these Jewish believers, James draws heavily on the teaching of Jesus, principally from his Sermon on the Mount. James talks about asking and receiving, as does Jesus (James 1:5; Matt. 7:7–8), and they both emphasize doing God's word, not simply hearing it (James 1:22–25; Matt. 7:24). Jesus's teaching on God's attention to the poor is prominent in James's letter (James 2:5; Matt. 5:3; Luke 6:20). James's epistle highlights Jesus's love command (James 2:8; Matt. 22:39–40) and shares the Lord's concern for mercy (James 2:13; Matt. 5:7). Jesus talked about the reversal of status when the Lord would exalt the humble (James 4:10; Matt. 23:12) and how the rich would suffer great loss (James 5:1; Luke 6:24–25). Jesus takes a stand against swearing, as does James (James 5:12; Matt. 5:34–37). In his commentary on the letter, Peter Davids lists thirty-six parallels between the teachings of Jesus and James.[7] Although James does not attribute his teaching to Jesus, he draws deeply on Jesus's wisdom for his own time and weaves in the Lord's instruction throughout his epistle. Although James does not refer to Jesus frequently, he recontextualizes the Lord's teaching for these assemblies. James's readers had faith in Christ (2:1), had his name invoked over them (2:7), and anticipated his coming (James 5:6–8). Now they learn how to follow Jesus's way amid the complexities of their world.

James and the Old Testament

James not only appeals to the teaching of Jesus but also depends on the Old Testament for some of his teaching. He especially focuses on Leviticus 19, which helps guide his exhortation regarding the care of the poor (Lev. 19:10 and James 2:1–6, 15–16, 25), not swearing falsely (Lev. 19:12; James 5:12), not holding back wages from workers (Lev. 19:13; James 5:1–6), not showing partiality (Lev. 19:15; James 2:1–11), not slandering another (Lev. 19:16; James 4:11), and loving your neighbor (Lev. 19:17–18; James 2:8). James also quotes the book of Proverbs in 4:6 (Prov. 3:34) and 5:20 (Prov. 10:12) in his teaching on humility and forgiveness. James reflects deeply on the Old Testament Scripture as well as the teaching of Jesus in developing relevant moral guidance for his readers.[8]

James and Paul

In both Romans and Galatians, Paul makes the case that God justifies a person through faith in Christ and not because of a person's observance of the law (Rom. 3:28; Gal. 2:16; 3:11). Appealing to Genesis 15:6, he argues that Abraham was not justified by works but rather though faith in God (Rom. 4:2–3; Gal. 3:8–9). James, on the other hand, boldly declares that a person is justified before God through works and not by faith alone (James 2:24). He, too, quotes Genesis 15:6 yet declares, "Was not our ancestor Abraham justified by works when he offered his son Isaac on the altar?" (James 2:21 NRSV; cf. Gen. 22). James stands in the tradition of Jesus's teaching, but does he set out to contradict Paul? Some scholars say James and Paul represent two distinct streams in early Christianity. Paul, on the one hand, espouses a law-free gospel directed at the gentiles, while James forwards a law-affirming gospel for the Jews.[9]

Every commentary on the epistle of James discusses this issue at some length. At the start we should recall that James, along with Peter and John, affirmed the gospel Paul preached when he laid it out to these three "pillars" in the Jerusalem church (Gal. 2:1–10). Given James's assent to Paul's teaching, we should not hastily adopt the view that James set out to challenge Paul's understanding of the gospel as Luther concluded. First of all, James was not engaged in the same fight as Paul, who disputed with the Judaizers' theology in Galatia. Those people sought to establish observance of the law, including circumcision, as the foundation of salvation (Gal. 5:2–6; see chapter 14). For his part, James addresses people whose confession of faith in God (2:19) produced nothing more than empty piety in the face of human need (2:15–16). Such faith, according to James, is "dead" (2:17, 20, 26). He argues that true faith shows itself through its deeds (2:18). James appeals to Abraham precisely because his faith in God led to action (2:21–24) and likewise recognizes Rahab's active faith (2:25). These affirmations are in complete harmony with Paul, who states in Galatians 5:6 that "the only thing that counts is faith working through love" (NRSV). Likewise, Paul commends the Thessalonians for their "work produced by faith" (1 Thess. 1:3).

Not only are Paul and James fighting on different fronts in Galatians and the epistle of James, but they attach slightly different concepts to their vocabulary. Whereas Paul talks about "the works of the law" in Romans 3:28, James talks about those works or deeds that benefit others or show obedience to God (James 2:15–16, 21–25). Some have suggested that the term "justify" is conceptually different in the two authors' writings, with James using it to refer to a demonstration of righteousness (as in Matt. 11:19), and Paul understanding it in the sense of a declaration of righteousness. Douglas Moo does not feel that this is a satisfactory explanation of the differences between James and Paul and offers an alternative avenue of interpretation based on the different prepositions the authors use (those little words count!). "Paul uses the preposition *ek* in the relevant texts to indicate the *instrument* of justification: we are justified before God through our faith and not through our works. James, we suggest, is using the preposition in a looser sense, to say works are necessarily involved in, or related to, God's justifying verdict."[10] In the end, both James and Paul wish to speak about the character of true faith, and this is James's central concern throughout his letter (cf. Eph. 2:8–10).

Literary Borrowing

James engages in the ancient practice of *imitatio* (Gk. *mimēsis*), that is, using authoritative sources for his own purposes. Horace, for example, commented on how to adopt sources while adapting them to make the material one's own: "It is hard to treat in your own way what is common: . . . In ground open to all [*publica materiaes*, material part of the public domain] you will win private rights [*privati iuris*] if you do not linger along the easy and open pathway, if you do not seek to render word for word as a slavish translator, and if in your copying [*desilies imitator*] you do not leap into the narrow well" (*Ars Poetica* 131–4). Horace here talks about how an author creatively adapts sources for an author's own ends. Dionysius of Halicarnassus said that authors should change the source by "subtraction, addition or alteration" and not simply copy it (*On Literary Composition* 6). Those sources worthy of *imitation* were known as "the books," literature produced by recognized and honored authors. As other ancient authors, James engaged in this ancient practice of literary borrowing, using honored source materials but modifying them to his own ends. This practice was distinguished from *furtum* (Gk. *klopē*), or theft, what we would today call "plagiarism."

James and 1 Peter

There are a number of verses in James that are strikingly similar to 1 Peter. Both James and 1 Peter group together a quotation from Proverbs 3:34 about God resisting the proud and giving grace to the humble (James 4:6; 1 Pet. 5:5b), submitting to God and resisting the devil (James 4:7; 1 Pet. 5:8–9), and humbling yourself before God, who will exalt you (James 4:8, 10; 1 Pet. 5:6). James and Peter speak in similar ways about suffering, testing, and joy (James 1:2–4; 1 Pet. 1:6–7), and they both cite Isaiah 40:4–8 (James 1:10–11; 1 Pet. 1:24–25). God's word, they say, gives them birth (James 1:18; 1 Pet. 1:23). Did James have 1 Peter at hand when he wrote, or did Peter borrow from James?

We know that early Christian authors used each other's writings. Second Peter 2 makes extensive use of Jude, and both Matthew and Luke used Mark when composing their gospels. Such literary borrowing was common in ancient literature. Authors would use authoritative sources but then modify them for their own ends. James has done this with the Old Testament and Jesus's teaching.

It may be that in this case, both Peter and James drew from common Christian teaching that circulated in the churches before the epistles were penned. This is most likely the case, since the contents of James and 1 Peter are strikingly different. A similar phenomenon appears in Ephesians 5:21–6:9, Colossians 3:18–4:1, and 1 Peter 2:18–3:7, all texts that share common teaching on slavery and marital relationships. Similarly, 1 Peter 2:13–17 and Romans 13:1–7 address the question of submission to the state in remarkably similar ways. Peter and Paul most likely drew from a common stock of early Christian teaching, sometimes known as the "domestic code" (or in German, *haustafeln*).

The common material in James and 1 Peter—as that in 1 Peter, Colossians, Ephesians, and Romans—informs us that the early church engaged in extensive teaching before the composition of these canonical letters. Early Christian authors drew from that teaching, along with texts at hand, like the Old Testament and the teachings of Jesus that had been handed down, as they worked out their theological formulations and ethical instruction.

James's Teaching

Whereas Paul and Peter were deeply concerned with challenges to the character of early Christian theology, James's focus is on correct conduct, or *orthopraxis*. Proper conduct was as important as right theology. Indeed, James affirms that the theology of these Jewish-Christian synagogues was correct: "You believe that there is one God. Good!" But he then reminds them that "even the demons believe that—and shudder" (2:19). What James wants to see is a faith in God that issues in good deeds that show one's faith. Indeed, "faith without deeds is dead" (2:26). So while epistles like Galatians, Colossians, and 2 Peter challenge views that did not jibe with apostolic doctrinal instruction, James is primarily concerned with genuine conduct and diversions from it.

"The rich who oppress you"—Poverty and Riches

For those who enjoy affluence, James's primary teaching is difficult to hear. In this letter his principle, though not exclusive, focus is on poverty and wealth. The world where James and his readers lived was not inherently fair, and there was no "middle class." A great gap divided the rich and the poor, with the rich holding the vast majority of the land and wealth. The rich were also rapacious, and the poor suffered at their hands. As Sirach 13:3–5 said:

> A rich person does wrong, and even adds insults;
> a poor person suffers wrong, and must add apologies.
> A rich person will exploit you if you can be of use to him,
> but if you are in need he will abandon you.
> If you own something, he will live with you;
> he will drain your resources without a qualm.

A gold and carnelian ring with an engraved figure of a winged Nemesis. Found on Cyprus, this ring is representative of Roman decorative jewelry ca. first to third century AD. *The Metropolitan Museum of Art*

James pulls no punches when he asks "Is it not the rich who are exploiting you? Are they not the ones who are dragging you into court?" (2:6; see Amos 8:4). The rich wore a gold ring, a marker that they may have been of a high social class like the equestrian, and could have been wealthy merchants (2:2). They wore fine, or shiny, clothing (see Luke 7:25; 16:19), which also publicly displayed their social status and wealth. Such people came into the assembly or synagogue and were given the place of honor: "Here's a good seat for you" (2:3). James reminds the rich that they will fade like a wildflower under a blazing sun. They "will fade away even while they go about their business," so they should now "take pride in their humiliation" (1:10–11). We do not know if James has in mind those who accepted Jesus as the Messiah or whether they were simply visiting the messianic synagogue (cf. 1 Cor. 14:23). Since in some places James speaks directly to them (5:1–6), we may assume that they had found a comfortable home with these gatherings of believers, whatever the character of their own commitment to the Messiah Jesus.

In addition to the way the rich publicly show their wealth (2:2), exploit others, and use the courts to their own ends (2:6), they "are blaspheming the noble name of him to whom you belong" (2:7). Economic and legal exploitation stand alongside their irreligious contempt for the one whom the believers hold most sacred. To blaspheme the name of Christ entails degrading those who believe in him (2:1) and belong to him (2:7b). The rich could particularly be in mind when James talks about the tongue, since these people boast (cf. 3:5 and 4:16) and curse (cf. 3:9 and 2:7). James 4:1–10 may likewise address the rich, given this section's warnings about unbridled desire that is willing to kill in order to get (cf. 4:2 and 5:5), covetousness (cf. 4:2 and 4:13; 5:3), pleasure (cf. 4:3 and 5:5), friendship with the world, and pride with the attendant call to humility (cf. 4:6–10 and 1:10). In 4:13–17 James speaks out against the rich, whose principle value is "profit," without any reference to God.

Roman fresco from Pompeii of people playing with dice. Much like today, dice were used in the ancient world for fun as well as for gambling. *Public Domain*

Seneca on the Folly of Seeking Wealth

Seneca, the Roman philosopher, spoke about the equestrian Cornelius Senecio. His critique of this rich man parallels those of James, as he comments on this man's passing: "He who was venturing investments by land and sea, who had also entered public life and left no type of business untried, during the very realization of financial success and during the very onrush of the money that flowed into his coffers, was snatched from the world!" Seneca goes on to comment: "But how foolish it is to set out one's life, when one is not even owner of the morrow! . . . To say: 'I will buy and build, loan and call in money, win titles of honour, and then, old and full of years, I will surrender myself to a life of ease.' Believe me when I say that everything is doubtful, even for those who are prosperous." James would differ with Seneca, however, in his affirmation that the future is in God's hands. He will judge the greedy rich (5:3–5) and show favor to the humble poor (4:6; 1:9).

They boast about their economic schemes, which even include the injustice of not paying the wages of poor laborers (5:1–6). The rich hoard the wealth, while the poor cry out to God for relief (5:3–4). They are willing to drag the poor into court and even murder those who have no recourse (5:6; cf. 2:6). James lets them know that their riches will rot and that they will face judgement (5:1–3, 5).

In this fresco from Pompeii, the couple is shown as learned. The woman has a stylus to her lips and holds a wax tablet. Her husband holds a scroll. This couple wanted to be seen as scholarly and well-read. James's letter may have attracted such couples, who were being urged to act on the faith they learned. *Wikimedia Commons, PD-US*

James addresses the poor as well, telling them of God's special care for them. Though their situation is marginal, James infuses them with hope. James taps into the idea of a great reversal: those of humble circumstances will find themselves in a high position (1:9), the dominant theme in Mary's Magnificat (Luke 1:46–55). James does not idealize poverty. In the first chapter, he frames the discussion of the poor and rich (1:9–11) with teaching about trials and perseverance (1:2–8, 12), including notes of joy (1:2) and deep hope in God's reward (1:12). Threaded through James's discussion is the question of honor, one of the highest values in the ancient world. Poverty not only meant a lack of sufficient resources but also carried the social stigma of dishonor. The poor walk into the assembly with dirty clothes and are told before onlookers, "'You stand there' or 'Sit on the floor by my feet'" (2:3b). Philo of Alexandria spoke of "disrepute following in the wake of poverty" (*Gig.* 29). Jesus had already turned the table on the dishonor of poverty, saying, "Blessed are you who are poor" (Luke 6:20). Indeed, this blessedness was linked to their inheritance of the kingdom of God. James focuses in on the way God honors the dishonored poor by asking, "Has not God chosen those who are poor in the eyes of the world to be rich in faith and to inherit the kingdom he promised to those who love him?" (2:5).

Looking in the Mirror

James 1:23–24 is remarkably similar to Plutarch's exhortation in his book *On Listening to Lectures*. He talks about someone who "rises to leave the barber's shop" and "stands by the mirror and feels his head, examining the cut of his hair and the difference made by its trimming" (42B). He compares this act to one who goes home after hearing a lecture, saying, "It would be a shame not to direct his gaze forthwith upon himself and to note carefully his own spirit." Self-examination must follow hearing. He then goes on to quote Ariston, who said that "neither a bath nor a discourse is of any use unless it removes impurity" (*Moralia* 32B). Doing must follow self-examination. James calls for focused and intent looking "into the perfect law that gives freedom" (1:25) as the first step.

In Pliny's *Natural History* (36.66 [193]), he notes that glass mirrors were invented in the first century AD in Sidon, located in what is now modern Lebanon. The earliest extant examples of glass mirrors date from the second century. This first-century mirror resembles those found in the Vesuvius area.
Public Domain

James's lengthy section on faith, works, and justification wraps around the question of how the assembly should respond to the poor who come through the door (2:2). The poor have "physical needs" (2:16b). So it will not do for the assembly of believers to simply hand them pious words that imply God will take care of them: "Go in peace; keep warm and well fed" (2:16a). True faith will show itself in deeds (2:17–26). If the assembly "does nothing about their physical needs, what good is it?" (2:16). James will not countenance any dichotomy between faith and deeds (2:18), since "as the body without the spirit is dead, so faith without deeds is dead" (2:26). In other words, neglect of the poor is a sign of dead faith. "Religion that God our Father accepts as pure and faultless is this" says James, "to look after orphans and widows in their distress and to keep oneself from being polluted by the world" (1:27).

James places considerable emphasis on doing what God's Word says (1:22–25). James compares the person who listens to the Word (reading was done aloud in the synagogues; Luke 4:16–19) but does not put it into action to someone who sees their face in a mirror, then turns and forgets what they look like (James 1:23–24).

James picks up the theme of "doing" as a sign of true wisdom (3:13–18). James only knows one kind of faith: that which shows itself through "deeds done in the humility that comes from wisdom" (3:13).

Trials, Testing, and Perseverance

Closely related to his teaching on riches and poverty is James's instruction regarding trials, testing, and perseverance. Indeed, James brackets his teaching on the poor and the rich (1:9–11) between his instruction regarding trials and testing (1:2–8 and 13–15). The letter suggests that the trials he has in mind are those that marginalized people endure. He lets them know that the trials they are enduring will test their faith but that the outcome of the process will be perseverance (1:2–4). They should not view such trials as temptations from God (1:13–15). James picks up this theme of patience in the midst of suffering once again in the last chapter of the letter (5:7–11). They can persevere because they know that the Lord is coming and his coming is near. James orients them to the final day so that they may endure in the present time, but he also turns their attention to the prophets in the past who suffered and persevered (5:10–11). Perseverance thrives between memory and hope. James does not teach them simply to be passive but to be determined in faith with tenacity, joy, and true grit.

The Tongue

James also focuses on issues related to the tongue. He values hearing and doing more than speaking (1:19–21). He lets his readers know that empty claims about faith have no value if they are not linked to deeds (2:14). In fact, pious words cannot substitute for concrete acts of charity (2:15–16). Therefore, those who consider themselves religious need to reign in their religious speech and show their religion through looking after the needy and vulnerable (1:26–27). The epistle offers a special warning to those who teach, since they will be strictly judged by God. James believes that the tongue is extremely unruly and is the most difficult part of the body to control (3:3–12). The one who can control their tongue is "able to keep their whole body in check" (3:2). James's teaching on the tongue is in harmony with Proverbs (Prov. 12:18; 13:3; 18:21) and the teaching of Jesus (Matt. 5:21–22; Mark 7:20–23). Controlling the tongue as a key component of virtue appears to be linked with his discussion regarding the rich. The tongue "makes great boasts" (James 3:5), something that is characteristic of the rich merchants whom James derides (4:13–17). James's emphasis on the need to control the tongue does not hold much currency in the contemporary world, where electronic speech can set society ablaze: "Consider what a great forest is set on fire by a small spark. The tongue also is a fire, a word of evil among the parts of the body" (3:5–6). James knows that the character of a person is linked with what comes out of their mouth (3:9–12), or as Jesus said, "For the mouth speaks what the heart is full of" (Luke 6:45).

Controlling one's speech is comparable to controlling a horse with a bit, according to James. This statue of a horse with a bit is from the Mausoleum at Halikarnassos, ca. 350 BC, British Museum, London. *Public Domain*

The Community

Running throughout the letter and intersecting with the previous teaching is James's deep insistence on harmonious community relations. His concerns about poverty and riches, perseverance amid trials, and good speech are meant to promote concord and mutual care while hacking and disrupting divisions. The call to concord begins early in the letter, where James addresses those who are family and beloved (1:16, 19). As direct as this letter is, James draws everyone in as siblings who are truly loved. Given the tensions in the communities, he exhorts them early, saying, "Everyone should be quick to listen, slow to speak and slow to become angry" (1:19). He then calls them to care for the weakest and the poor rather than showing the greatest honor to the rich (1:26–2:26). His sharp teaching about the tongue is meant to put out the fires of discord that words can set ablaze (3:1–12, especially vv. 5, 9–10). They should avoid slandering each other (4:11–12) and grumbling against one another (5:9). When he prescribes wisdom, James links it with the social virtue of humility, which is the opposite of "bitter envy and selfish ambition," which yield "disorder and every evil practice" (3:14, 16). True wisdom from God begets purity but is also "peace-loving, considerate, submissive, full of mercy and good fruit, impartial and sincere" (3:17).

Vice and Virtue Lists

James 3:17 contains one of the many virtue lists in the New Testament. Such lists are sometimes placed in contrast with a list of vices. The most famous of these vice and virtue lists in the New Testament is Galatians 5:19–23, Paul's teaching on the works of the flesh and the fruit of the Spirit. Other such lists are scattered throughout the New Testament (2 Cor. 6:6–8; Eph. 4:31–32; 5:9; Phil. 4:8; Col. 3:12; 1 Tim. 4:12; 6:11; 2 Tim. 2:22; 3:10; 1 Pet. 3:8; 2 Pet. 1:5–7). Such lists were common in Greco-Roman moral philosophy as well as Jewish literature. Diogenes Laertius, for example, enumerates virtues this way:

> Amongst the virtues some are primary, some are subordinate to these. The following are the primary: wisdom, courage, justice, temperance. Particular virtues are magnanimity, continence, endurance, presence of mind, good counsel.

He then adds some comments about them:

> And wisdom they define as the knowledge of things good and evil and of what is neither good nor evil; courage as knowledge of what we ought to choose, what we ought to beware of, and what is indifferent; justice; . . . magnanimity as the knowledge or habit of mind which makes one superior to anything that happens, whether good or evil equally; continence as a disposition never overcome in that which concerns right reason, or a habit which no pleasures can get the better of; endurance as a knowledge or habit which suggests what we are to hold fast to, what not, and what is indifferent; presence of mind as a habit prompt to find out what is meet to be done at any moment; good counsel as knowledge by which we see what to do and how to do it if we would consult our own interests (7.92–93).

These lists were comprehensive but outlined what kinds of behavior mark the life of a truly wise or good person by showing which behaviors were honorable or shameful. They detail for their readers what a truly moral person does and avoids and are therefore pieces of a larger and comprehensive understanding of virtue. Oftentimes we skip over such lists without careful consideration of each element. Biblical authors, as well as their philosophical counterparts, expected their readers to understand the dimensions of each virtue or vice without spelling out all the implications, although sometimes they marked out a particular virtue or vice's character. James's list in 3:17–18 marks out the social virtues that promote harmony within the community: "Peacemakers who sow in peace reap a harvest of righteousness" (v. 18).

In his quest for unity in the assemblies of believers, he warns them against "fights and quarrels" (4:1) that have their roots in desires (*hēdonōn*; cf. 1 Pet. 1:14; 2:11; 4:2) and covetousness. Prayer is to mark their life together, especially prayer for the sick among them (5:13–18). Part of community harmony is the confession of sin and turning back those who have engaged in sin (5:19), offering forgiveness to the one who has transgressed (5:20).

James is deeply concerned for harmony within the community and recognizes that sin, which breaks harmony, is also the responsibility of the community. Confession and forgiveness with mutual prayer will keep the assembly together and well, both morally and physically. James would heartily endorse the view that members of the community are their brothers' and sisters' keepers.

Sin and Sickness

In calling for the assembly to pray for those who are sick and assuring them of God's ability to make them well, James adds, "If they have sinned, they will be forgiven." He goes on to say, "Therefore confess your sins to each other and pray for each other so that you may be healed" (5:15–16). The link between sin and sickness also appears in Jesus's teaching when he healed a lame man (Mark 2:1–12). This connection had Jewish roots (Deut. 28:20–22, 27–29; Ps. 38:3; Sir. 18:21; 38:15; and *b. Ned.* 41a, "a sick man does not recover from his sickness until all his sins are forgiven him"). But Jesus also warned against concluding that all disease was the result of sin (John 9:1–5). Throughout the gospels Jesus heals people without any call for confession of sin or offer of forgiveness. There are other causes of sickness, as we know today. We cannot conclude that every ailment is the result of sin, something James acknowledges. But sinful behavior can result in bodily ailment, a sober reminder from James.

The Martyrdom of James

Josephus, the Jewish historian, wrote about the martyrdom of James. His commenting on this event shows how prominent a figure the half-brother of Jesus was in Jerusalem during the middle of the first century AD. Josephus talks about the high priesthood of Ananus, saying,

> The younger Ananus, who, as we have said, had been appointed to the high priesthood, was rash in temper and unusually daring. He followed the school of the Sadducees, who are indeed more heartless than any of the other Jews . . . when they sit in judgement. Possessed of such a character, Ananus thought that he had a favourable opportunity because Festus was dead and Albinus was still on the way. And so he convened the judges of the Sanhedrin and brought before them a man called James, the brother of Jesus who was called the Christ, and certain others. He accused them of having transgressed the law and delivered them up to be stoned (*Ant.* 20.9.1 [199–200]).

THE CONTENT OF JAMES

James begins with an opening greeting, as was common in letters from the era (1:1). Although it lacks the common epistolary closing, it ends with a prayer for health similar to the wish-prayers for health that were part of Greco-Roman letter closings (5:13–20). The body of James is not the easiest to outline. Some even argue that the letter does not have a logical structure. But the first chapter of James introduces many of the topics later taken up in the letter, similar to the way the opening thanksgiving in Paul's letters offer an introduction to the letters' contents.

AUTHOR AND DATE

The author of this epistle identifies himself simply as "James, a servant of God and of the Lord Jesus Christ" (1:1a). Nowhere else in the letter does he provide any further details about who he is. We can glean from the introduction and his writing that he was a believer in Jesus Christ (1:1a; 2:1) and that he was well versed both in Jesus's teaching and the Old Testament. Most likely he was Jewish. He was apparently well-known among a wide variety of synagogues throughout the Jewish diaspora beyond Israel (1:1b; 2:2) and held a considerable amount of authority among them. Unfortunately, the internal evidence from the letter leaves us few clues regarding his identity.

James was a common name in Israel during the early first century AD, so we are not surprised to find a number of people called James within the pages of the New Testament. James, the son of Zebedee and brother of John, was among the twelve apostles (Mark 1:19; 3:17; Acts 1:13; 12:2), as was James, the son of Alphaeus (Mark 3:18; Acts 1:13). James, the father of Judas, is referenced twice (Luke 6:16; Acts 1:13), and we also read about James the Younger, who was the son of Mary, the wife of Cleopas (Mark 15:40; 16:1; Matt. 27:56; Luke 24:10; and John 19:25). James, the half-brother of Jesus, appears multiple times in the New Testament narrative (Mark 6:3; Acts 12:17; 15:13; 21:18; Gal. 1:19; 2:9; 1 Cor. 15:7; Jude 1). Most likely the author of the letter can be found among this list.

In the earliest preserved depiction of Jesus's family (ca. AD 100), Mary is holding the infant Jesus and the man to the left is identified by many as a prophet. The group is under a fruit tree. Jesus's siblings (including James) are rarely found in ancient Christian art. *Public Domain*

Given that we know nothing about James the father of Judas or James the Younger, they appear to be the least likely candidates. James, the apostle who was the son of Alphaeus, is likewise obscure. One of two most prominent people who carried the name was James, the brother of John. He was one of the inner circle of three apostles who were closest to Jesus, along with Peter and John (Mark 1:29; 5:37; 9:2; 13:3; 14:33). But James was martyred early under Herod Agrippa I (Acts 12:1–2), making his identification as the author less likely than the final James, the brother of Jesus. As the leader of the early church after Peter and as a person who was well-known beyond Israel (Gal. 2:12), he is the most likely author of the book.

The early church fathers, however, were mixed in their assessment of the book's authorship. Irenaeus (ca. AD 130–202) appears to use the book but does not name the author of his source. Origen (AD 185–253) quoted the book and attributed it to James, the brother of Jesus. In the fourth century AD, Augustine, Cyril, Gregory of Nazianzus, and Athanasius all regarded it as canonical. On the other hand, the Muratorian canon does not include the book, and Eusebius (fourth century) said, "The first of the epistles named catholic is said to be by James the brother of the Lord, but some see it as forged" (*Hist. eccl.* 2.23.25) and said it was one of the disputed books (3.25.3). Jerome also noted a view circulating about James that "it is asserted, was published under his name by another" (*Vir. ill.* 2).[11] In the end, however, the church received James as canonical and recognized James, the brother of Jesus, as its author. Doubts about the book's authenticity may have arisen due to its decidedly Jewish character and the absence of any reference to Christ's death and resurrection.

Some contemporary scholars have raised doubts about the letter's authenticity due to the quality of the Greek style. But the Greek of the letter, though quite good, would have been within the range of a Jewish leader who had come from Galilee. Also, we cannot discount the role of an unnamed scribe or amanuensis in providing stylistic help to the author.

If indeed James, the half-brother of Jesus, is the author of the book, we have a good amount of information about him. He was one of many of Jesus's siblings (Matt. 13:55–56), another being Jude, the author of the epistle which goes under his name (Jude 1). James was not a believer during Jesus's earthly ministry (John 7:2–5) but became a witness of the resurrected Jesus (1 Cor. 15:7) and was present with the apostles and Mary, his mother, on Pentecost (Acts 1:14; 2:1). Peter became the leader of the church in Jerusalem but soon left James in charge (Acts 12:17). James was clearly regarded early on as one of the "pillars" of the Jerusalem church, along with Peter and John (Gal. 2:9). He exercised the decisive leadership role in the Jerusalem Council (Acts 15:12–21), where he was conciliatory regarding gentile and Jewish Christian relations (so also Acts 21:17–25). He clearly stood against those who said that gentiles had to become proselytes of Judaism and be circumcised to be saved. Paul mentions that the Judaizers claimed authority from him when they arrived in Antioch (Gal. 2:12), but James's position regarding gentile circumcision was clearly other than what they proposed. Eusebius confirms James's leadership role, saying that "the episcopal seat at Jerusalem was committed by the apostles" to him (*Hist. eccl.*2.23.1). Eusebius also comments that James was called "the Just" and that he met his end when he was "thrown from a wing of the temple and beaten to death with a fuller's club" (*Hist. eccl.* 2.1.5). James and the other relatives of Jesus (see Jude 1) held considerable authority in the early church (Eusebius, *Hist. eccl.* 3.20.8; 1.7.14).[12]

Our assessment of the date of James's letter depends largely on whether we regard James as an authentic letter of James, the brother of Jesus, or whether it is a pseudepigraphic epistle. If the letter was not written by James, it could have been written as late as the middle of the second century AD.[13] If it is an authentic letter by James, as we contend, it could not have been written later than AD 62. According to Josephus, James became a martyr at the hands of the high priest Ananus after the procurator Festus died and before Albinus assumed the position (*Ant.* 20.9.1 [200]). This would give us a date of around AD 62 for his death. Likely it was written after James became the leader in the church at Jerusalem in the early 40s (Acts 12:17). The book was therefore written somewhere during this period. The issues taken up in the Jerusalem Council (Acts 15, AD 48–49), such as gentile inclusion and circumcision, are absent from the book, and it appears to come from a time when Paul's teaching on justification by faith was known but misinterpreted (James 2). We suggest a date before the Council. Most likely James was written somewhere between AD 42 and 48, making it one of the earliest of our New Testament documents.

Questions for Discussion

1. Discuss the issue of whether James contradicts Paul's teaching on faith, works, and justification.
2. How might James's teaching on the rich and the poor help us understand how to respond to these issues in the church and in society?
3. How might James's teaching on the tongue be applied to contemporary community relations and the use of social media?
4. What does James teach us about the causes of suffering and the response to it?
5. Trace the various threads of James's teaching about community relationships. How might they be applied in your Christian community?

BIBLIOGRAPHY

Introductory

Brosend, W. F. II. *James and Jude* NCBC. Cambridge: Cambridge University Press, 2004.
Moo, D. J. *James.* TNTC. Rev ed. Downers Grove, IL: InterVarsity Press, 2015.
Nystrom, D. P. *James.* NIVAC. Grand Rapids: Zondervan, 1997.
Tamez, E. *The Scandalous Message of James. Faith Without Works is Dead.* New York: Crossroad, 2002.

Advanced

Allison, D. C., Jr. *James: A Critical and Exegetical Commentary.* ICC. London: Bloomsbury T&T Clark, 2013.
Blomberg, C. L., and M. J. Kamell. *James.* ZECNT. Grand Rapids: Zondervan, 2008.
Davids, P. H. *The Epistle of James.* NIGTC. Grand Rapids: Eerdmans, 1982.
Johnson, L. T. *The Letter of James.* AB. New York: Doubleday, 1995.
Martin, R. P. *James.* WBC. Waco: Word, 1988.
McCartney, D. G. *James.* BECNT. Grand Rapids: Baker, 2009.
McKnight, S. *The Letter of James.* NICNT. Grand Rapids: Eerdmans, 2011.
Moo, D. J. *The Letter of James.* PNTC. Grand Rapids: Eerdmans, 2000.

NOTES

1. M. Luther, *Word and Sacrament*, ed. E. Theodore Bachmann; vol. 35 of *Luther's Works*; ed. Helmut T. Lehmann (Philadelphia: Muhlenberg Press, 1960), 362, 395–96.

2. Bede the Venerable, *The Commentary on the Seven Catholic Epistles*, trans. D. Hurst (Kalamazoo, MI: Cistercian Publications, 1985), 8.

3. Luther, *Word and Sacrament*, 397.

4. M. Dibelius, *James*, rev. Heinrich Greeven, Hermeneia (Philadelphia: Fortress Press, 1975), 3, 5.

5. E. Tamez, *The Scandalous Message of James: Faith without Words Is Dead* (New York: Crossroad, 1990), 1.

6. Gustavo Gutiérrz, *A Theology of Liberation: History, Politics and Salvation* (Maryknoll, NY: Orbis, 1988), citing the Episcopal Conference at Medellin (1968).

7. P. H. Davids, *The Epistle of James: A Commentary on the Greek Text*, NIGTC (Grand Rapids: Eerdmans, 1982), 47–50.

8. D. G. McCartney, *James,* BECNT (Grand Rapids: Baker Academic, 2009), 44–45.

9. J. D. G. Dunn, *Unity and Diversity in the New Testament: An Inquiry into the Character of Earliest Christianity* (Philadelphia: Fortress Press, 1977), 251–52.

10. D. J. Moo, *James*, TNTC (Downers Grove, IL: InterVarsity Press, 2015), 63.

11. The external evidence regarding the authenticity of the book is assembled in J. B. Mayor, *The Epistle of James* (Minneapolis: Klock & Klock, 1977), lxvi-lxxxiv; D. C. Allison, Jr., *A Critical and Exegetical Commentary on The Epistle of James,* ICC (New York: Bloomsbury, 2013), 13–18.

12. See R. Bauckham, *Jude and the Relatives of Jesus* (Edinburgh: T&T Clark, 1990).

13. This is the position of D. R. Nienhuis, *Not by Paul Alone: The Formation of the Catholic Epistle Collection and the Christian Canon* (Waco, TX: Baylor University Press, 2007), 238.

Chapter 24

1 AND 2 PETER AND JUDE

The Temple of Augustus in Pisidian Antioch, located in the Roman province of Galatia.
Todd Bolen/BiblePlaces.com

Peter sent his letters to churches in the Roman provinces of northern Asia Minor.

The early church faced two main crises: persecution and false teaching. These three small letters bring us into the swirl of these dangers. First Peter addresses believers in Asia Minor who are enduring hostilities and exhorts them to maintain the holy way of life and to do good even to those who revile them for their faith. Both Jude and 2 Peter battle against heresies that diverge from the apostolic tradition and are leading believers into immorality.

These are not the only battles surrounding these books. Contemporary scholarship has debated the authorship of each letter. Did Peter write both 1 and 2 Peter? If so, why are their styles so different? Is Jude a pseudepigraphical document or is it truly a composition of Jude, brother of James and half-brother of Jesus? Doubts about these books today parallel those in the ancient church, which, for example, questioned the authenticity of 2 Peter. Moreover, both Jude and 2 Peter present an apocalyptic vision of coming judgment. That vivid portrayal of final doom stands in sharp contrast to contemporary notions of Christianity as "sweetness and light." How do we listen to their message today?

THE SETTING OF 1 PETER

Peter addresses his first letter "to God's elect, exiles scattered throughout the provinces of Pontus, Galatia, Cappadocia, Asia and Bithynia" (all Roman provinces in Asia Minor). He composes this letter while in "Babylon" (5:13), a common code name for Rome (e.g., Rev. 14:8; 16:19; 17:5, 9, 18).

The many rural allusions may suggest that these are not urban Christians (1 Pet. 1:22–24; 2:25; 5:2–4, 8). But at the beginning of the second century, Pliny the Younger, governor of Bithynia, commented on the gospel spreading from urban centers to surrounding areas: "It is not only the towns, but villages and rural districts too which are infected through contact with this wretched cult" (*Letters* 10.96). Peter addresses both men and women (3:1–7), and the churches Peter addresses have believers from divergent socioeconomic strata. Some are slaves (2:18), while others are free and even have sufficient economic power to be benefactors (2:13–17). Some women can afford costly apparel and jewelry (3:3). The recipients of the letter have only recently become Christians (1:3, 12, 23; 2:2; 4:3, 15).

Several passages suggest that these are Jewish believers (e.g., the Diaspora in 1:1; also the citation of numerous Old Testament texts, such as 2:9–10). But 4:3 implies that they are gentiles, for they formerly participated in local banquets and engaged in idolatry. Furthermore, their contemporaries are surprised that they no longer participate in such activities (4:4). They have broken from a traditional ancestral way of life, along with its religious observances and civic cults (1:18). In a society that lauded duty and adherence to tradition, their conversion was a serious social breech indeed. They no longer attend banquets held under the auspices of the deities (4:3–4). Wives do not participate in the cult of their husbands (3:1–2), bringing them into a fearful position because of the threat of abuse (3:6). The power of fathers over their children (the *patria potestas*) extends into the area of religion.

Slaves too would encounter grave problems if they participated in religious activities not sanctioned by their masters. Columella (first century AD) gave this advice about slaves who served as overseers: "He shall offer no sacrifice except by direction of the master" (*On Agriculture*, 1.8.5). Cato said, "He must perform no religious rites," with only a few exceptions (*On Agriculture* 5.3). We can only imagine the fate of Christian slaves who refused to accompany their masters when offering sacrifice to the gods.

Community reaction against the Christian converts mainly takes the form of social ostracism and verbal abuse. Christians are reviled and reproached (3:9; 4:14, 4), and accused of doing evil (2:12; 3:16a). "Evildoers" are either criminals (4:15) or those engaged in practices like magic. People who do not fulfill their social obligations toward the gods could also be called "evildoers." These charges echo the slander heard in Rome, where, according to Tacitus, the Christians were "loathed for their vices" (*Annals* 15.44). Such verbal attacks were a source of grave social humiliation or dishonor. Peter insists that such public ridicule is the ignorance of foolish people (2:15).

The Christians' contemporaries are not adverse to call them to account for their new religious allegiance (3:15–16) since ancient religion is a public affair. The gods, after all, serve as patrons and protectors of the communities. Noncompliance by Christians is a social threat. But 1 Peter does not seem to envision any state-sponsored persecution, though physical attacks are not out of the picture (4:1), especially where authoritative relationships govern religious practice. Slaves are subject to beatings (2:19–20), and women face similar abuse (implied in 3:6).

Plutarch on Women's Religion

Plutarch praises the woman who subjects herself to her husband, even in questions of religious devotion: "A wife ought not to make friends of her own, but to enjoy her husband's friends in common with her. The gods are the first and most important friends. Wherefore it is becoming for a wife to worship and to know only the gods that her husband believes in" (*Advice to Bride and Groom* 140D).

Ridicule and Social Shame

Social shame is illustrated in an inscription from Epidaurus that speaks of "being ashamed as being ridiculed by others."[1] First-century philosopher Musonius Rufus speaks of the shame people experience "if someone gives them a malignant glance or laughs or strikes them or reviles them."

Notice the lions on the left and right of this third-century marble sarcophagus. The detail depicts the story of Endymion. Peter identifies the force behind persecution as the Devil, who is described as a roaring lion (1 Pet. 5:8).
Public Domain

Two slaves hold a bull that has been prepared for the sacrifice about to take place.
Public Domain

The crux of the matter is the reaction of the Christians to their situation. Some have begun to be ashamed of their faith (4:16; cf. Rom. 1:16; 2 Tim. 1:8).

Some believers are tempted to retaliate (3:9; cf. 2:23). In the Roman world, revenge was a social obligation to maintain your honor in society; offering the other cheek was not an option. One Roman mother said, "You will say that it is wonderful to avenge yourself upon your enemies. I consider vengeance as important as anyone."[2] Fear and terror are setting in among these new Christians (3:6, 14), and they are tempted to conform to a more socially acceptable lifestyle (1:14; 4:2–3) and so commit apostasy. Peter identifies the force behind their persecutions as the devil, who "prowls around like a roaring lion looking for someone to devour" (5:8). The lion was used in funeral reliefs as a symbol of death (see 2 Tim. 4:17; cf. Ps. 22:13).

THE MESSAGE OF 1 PETER

Peter responds to this situation by making the Christians fully aware of the overarching grace of God toward them and calling them to stand firm in this grace instead of returning to their former way of life (5:12). "Grace" summarizes the message of the book. It embraces God's activity on their behalf, as well as the call to a holy way of life. Grace is rooted in God's election (1:1–2), predicted through the prophets, and brought into history through the sufferings, death, and glorification of Christ (1:10–12). God will bring them his grace at the final unveiling of Christ (1:13). Christian messengers proclaim God's grace in the gospel (1:12), and through God's grace believers can stand strong and firm in the face of hostility (5:10).

First Peter is an impassioned plea to maintain a holy way of life (1:14–16) in the midst of the moral and social problems of the believers. Peter calls them to live "good lives among the pagans" (literally "gentiles," here meaning those who do not believe in Christ, 2:11–12). The believers should respond to evil with good and not retaliate (3:9), and resist the devil by standing firm in the faith (5:8–9). But his message also shows how to change their status in the community. They must do "good deeds" to silence the opposition (2:12, 15) and live in such a way that their detractors will be ashamed of their ill-treatment (3:16). Good conduct will serve as a witness to the gospel and win over the opposition—whether a woman's unbelieving husband (3:1–2) or anyone opposed to the Christians (2:12). The "day [God] visits us" (2:12) is the time when God will come to humanity, either to save or judge (Gen. 50:24–25; Ex. 3:16; Isa. 10:3; Luke 19:44). They hope their persecutors will "glorify God," which may imply that Peter hopes that Christian testimony through word (2:9) and deed (2:12) will bring them to conversion.

This call to good works is closely tied with civic benefaction in the ancient

Reproduced by permission from Carole Raddato

momo/Flickr, CC BY 2.0

In 1 Peter, the apostle emphasizes the importance of virtue over privilege. Those who are free people should not use their freedom as a pretext for doing evil (2:16), and wealthy women should invest in character rather than adornment. The elaborate hairstyles depicted was possible through the assistance of a slave hairdresser.

world (2:13–15). Peter reminds his readers that the governor will "commend those who do right" (2:14). In the ancient world, public inscriptions honored civic benefactors, praising their good deeds for the community.

Peter therefore calls the believers to participate in the life of their communities, seeking to "do good" for all, not only for those of faith (cf. Acts 10:38; Gal. 6:10). Such social engagement might oblige the persecutors to change their opinion of Christians.

Outline of 1 Peter

I. Epistolary Salutation (1:1–2)
II. The Christian Existence (1:3–2:10)
   1. The New Life (1:3–12)
   2. The Call to Sanctification (1:13–2:3)
   3. The New Existence as the Elect and Holy People of God (2:4–10)
III. The Christian Obligations (2:11–5:11)
   1. In the Structures of Society: General Exhortations (2:11–3:12)
   2. In the Structures of Society: Under Persecution (3:13–4:6)
   3. In the Christian Community (4:7–11)
   4. In the Structures of Society: Under Persecution (4:12–19)
   5. In the Christian Community (5:1–7)
   6. In the Structures of Society: Under Persecution (5:8–11)
IV. Final Exhortation and Salutation (5:12–14)

Honoring Civic Benefactors

The city of Athens resolved to praise the benefactor Menelaus "because he is a good man and does whatever good he can for the people of Athens." Another inscription honors a benefactor who did "whatever good he is able to perform for the citizens." An inscription from the island of Kos illustrates the social obligation to honor benefactors: "so that we ourselves may be seen by those who propose to bestow benefactions on us to give appropriate rewards."[3]

A public inscription of thanksgiving from Bythinia, thanking Lucius Julius Frugi for his benefactions (ca. AD 150).
1991 Thomas Corsten

Civic Benefactors

Greek inscriptions honoring civic benefactors featured prominently throughout the cities of the empire. The inscriptions heaped praise on the benefactors. A typical inscription reads: "Let it be recorded to offer praise ... that he does good because he does indeed do good ... and to render him a benefactor because he is able to be a good man and because he does good ... to praise him and to establish him ... as a benefactor of the Athenians" (*Inscriptiones graecae* [Berlin: de Gruyter, 1924], 82, 93, 118). Those who were recipients of benefaction were under a social obligation to display proper gratitude toward the benefactor.

COMPOSING 1 PETER

Wax tablets known as diptychs were used to make first drafts of compositions, which were then transferred to papyrus. Peter's scribe or amanuensis (5:12) would have written down the apostle's message on such tablets before making the papyrus copy to be sent. This reproduction was made of wood with a bronze stylus and held together by a leather strap (9.5 x 17 x 9.5 x 2 cm).
Courtesy of the Princeton University Library

According to 5:12, Peter composed this letter "with the help of Silas, whom I regard as a faithful brother." The Greek text uses "Silvanus," the Latin form of the Greek name "Silas." This person is probably the same Hellenistic Jewish believer who traveled with Paul (Acts 15:40; 1 Thess. 1:1; 2 Thess. 1:1). Some scholars hold that Silvanus is the messenger who delivered this letter to the various Christian communities, while others argue that he served as Peter's amanuensis. If Silvanus had a secretarial role, he would have had some liberty in the composition, which likely includes adjustments to the grammatical style, a common scribal practice. Early testimony about Peter indicates that he needed help with the Greek language. Papias, for example, indicates that Mark was his interpreter. Whether or not it was Silvanus, someone likely served as Peter's amanuensis.

Peter, however, indicates that he is responsible for the letter's content ("I have written to you briefly" [5:12]). He uses a variety of sources, such as the Old Testament (e.g., 1:16 [Lev. 19:2]; 2:6 [Isa 28:16]) and the teaching of Jesus, especially the Sermon on the Mount (cf. 4:14 with Matt. 5:10–11). The striking similarities between Peter and Paul's teaching on a Christian's obligation to the state (cf. 2:13–17 and Rom. 13:1–4) and the domestic code (cf. 2:18–3:7 with Eph. 5:21–6:9; Col. 3:18–4:1) suggest that both authors draw on early Christian instruction for new believers. Affinities between 1 Peter and James on watchfulness and resisting the devil (cf. 5:6–9 with James 4:6–10) likewise indicate common source material.

AUTHOR AND DATE OF 1 PETER

In 1:1 the author identifies himself as "Peter, an apostle of Jesus Christ," while 5:1 indicates that he is an "elder" and "a witness of Christ's sufferings." The early church was unanimous in recognizing this book as an authentic letter of Peter. The earliest testimony comes from 2 Peter 3:1, which states: "This is now my second letter to you." Eusebius grouped books the church used into three categories: genuine, disputed, and false. He lists 1 Peter with the first group (*Eccl. Hist.* 3.3.1). Various second-century church fathers know of this letter, such as Papias (*Eccl. Hist.* 3.3.2), Irenaeus (who cites it), Tertullian (*Against Heresies* 5.7.2), and Clement of Alexandria (*Paedagogus* 1.6.43).

But a number of contemporary scholars question the book's authenticity, partly because of its fine Greek style. Could a Galilean fisherman have composed such a letter? We can attribute its grammatical style to Silvanus (5:12) or some other amanuensis.

Another argument is that the persecutions reflected in the book are state-motivated, which did not occur until the time of Domitian (AD 95) or Pliny the Younger (AD 112). But these believers are not facing state-organized persecution. In 3:15 the word "answer" or "defense" (*apologia*) need not imply legal proceedings (Acts 22:1; 1 Cor. 9:3); moreover, this defense is to be given "to everyone," not only civil authorities. To "suffer as a Christian" (1 Pet. 4:16) does not necessarily reflect the situation under the governor Pliny, who discussed with Emperor Trajan "whether it is the mere name of Christian which is punishable, even if innocent of crime, or rather the crimes associated with the name" (*Letters* 10.96). From very early, Christians understood their sufferings as being "for the Name" (Acts 5:41). The situation reflected in this letter is that of first-century Christians, regardless of where they lived.

If indeed 1 Peter is an authentic work of the apostle, we may date it sometime before his death, which occurred during Nero's persecution of Christians, whom he blamed for the fire in Rome (AD 64). Some have even understood the "fiery ordeal" of 4:12 as a reference to that persecution, since Nero used Christians as human torches to illuminate his garden at night (Tacitus, *Annals* 15.44). But although Peter writes *from* Rome during Nero's reign (5:13), its recipients are scattered throughout Asia Minor, and the Neronian persecution did not extend outside the imperial city. Early church testimony confirms that Peter met martyrdom in Rome (sometime between AD 64 when the fire broke out and AD 68 when Nero died). A likely date for the letter is the early 60s.

THE SETTING OF 2 PETER

In 2 Peter 3:1 the author states: "This is now my second letter to you." His first letter took up the pressing problem of persecution; here the crisis is internal, as heresy has crept in and threatens these congregations. This letter warns those who "are firmly established in the truth" (1:12) not to abandon the faith. Peter's appeal here is urgent since he knows his death is imminent (1:12–15).

The situation is also urgent since false teachers are exerting their influence on the church (1:5, 10, 15), as the false prophets had in Israel. Peter reveals their error: "They will secretly introduce destructive heresies, even denying the sovereign Lord who bought them" (2:1). The heretics deny the coming of the Lord and future judgment, and this theological diversion is coupled with libertine morality (2:14, 18–19; 3:3–9). To bolster their case, they repudiate apostolic teaching, which they classify as *mythos* ("myth") (1:16), and question the divine inspiration of the prophets (1:20–21). Peter warns of the dire outcome of this heresy: "swift destruction" (2:1, 3; 3:7, 16).

The skepticism about the Lord's coming (3:3–10) is based on the apparent delay of his advent (3:4, 9; cf. 2:3). Their sexual immorality (2:2, 10, 14, 18), drunkenness, and gluttony (2:13) result from a distortion of Paul's teachings (3:15–16), turning "freedom" into moral license (2:19a). In reality, corruption has enslaved such people (2:19b).

Greed motivated the heretics (2:3, 14) as they exploit members of the church. Peter highlights their arrogance as they "despise authority" (2:10) and mock the teaching about the second coming (3:3–4). Their "denial" of "the sovereign Lord" is not only verbal, since in their conduct they do not acknowledge him as the Master of their life (2:1; cf. 1 Tim. 5:8; Titus 1:16). This is shocking since the Master is the very one "who bought them" (2 Pet. 2:1).

At one time the heretics were participants in the faith but "left the straight road and have gone astray, following the road of Balaam son of Bosor" (or Beor, 2:15 NRSV). These people have forgotten that they were cleansed from past sins (1:9). They entice others to their way, and as a result, unstable souls succumb to their error (2:14, 18–22). They are apostates who had "escaped the corruption of the world by knowing our Lord and Savior Jesus Christ" and yet were "again entangled in it and are overcome" (2:20). Peter appeals to his readers not to be carried away with this error (3:18), as some already have. Two proverbs of the day described their condition: "'A dog returns to its vomit,' and, 'A sow that is washed returns to her wallowing in the mud'" (2:22).

Denying the Master Who Bought Them

The language in 2:1 evokes images drawn from ancient slavery, especially the act of freeing a slave, known as manumission (see 1 Cor. 7:22–23). One manumission inscription reads: "Apollo the Pythian bought from Sosibius of Amphissa, for freedom, a female slave, whose name is Nicaea, by race a Roman, with a price of three minae of silver and a half-mina."[4] This slave became free by being sold, in effect, to the deity (Apollo). Though freed from slavery to sin (Rom. 6:17–18), the Christian now belongs to another Master, Christ.

A very small marble manumission fragment inscribed in Greek with eight lines of writing on both sides. Only two to seven letters from each line are legible.
Courtesy of The Spurlock Museum, University of Illinois at Urbana-Champaign

What is this error? Those who view 2 Peter as pseudepigraphic say the letter is an attempt to curb Gnosticism, which believed in salvation via esoteric knowledge (1:2, 3, 5–6, 8; 2:20; 3:18). This movement did not arise until the second century AD (although certain elements were present in the first century). But there are no traces in the letter of the later Gnostic dualism, which viewed the material world as evil and the spiritual as good. The author links their immorality with skepticism about final judgment and a distortion of Pauline teaching about Christian liberty, not with Gnostic dualism. Although Peter does mention "knowledge" in

The Epicureans on Prophecy

Diogenes Laertius quotes Epicurus as saying: "No means of predicting the future really exists, and if it did, we must regard what happens according to it as nothing to us" (10.135). Plutarch derides the Epicureans, "who ... have an arrogant contempt, as they themselves aver, for all such things as oracles," which were believed to predict the future (*Obsolescence of Oracles* 434D).

Epicurus
Public Domain

The Epicureans on the Delay of Divine Judgment

In a fictitious dialogue, Plutarch discusses Epicurus's argument that delay in divine judgment is strong evidence against divine providence. Plutarch's son-in-law Patrocleas comments, "The delay and procrastination of the Deity in punishing the wicked appears to me the most telling argument by far." Olympichus adds that "his slowness destroys belief in providence" (*On the Delays of the Divine Vengeance* 548C-D, 549B).

the letter, he has in view personal knowledge of God and Christ (1:2–3, 8; 2:20; 3:18).

Another possible explanation of the heretics' teaching is the influence of Epicureanism (see ch. 4). Epicureans rejected the notion of a future divine judgment and based their belief on the apparent delay in divine vengeance on evil. Peter appears to respond to their perspective in 3:9: "The Lord is not slow in keeping his promise, as some understand slowness. Instead he is patient with you, not wanting anyone to perish, but everyone to come to repentance."

The Epicureans also denied divine providence and believed that everything happened by chance. A corollary to their rejection of providence was their skepticism regarding predictive prophecy. How could even the gods predict that which happened by chance?

But Peter rejects these notions (3:3–4) and affirms that God was active in the world in the past, having brought it into being, and so he will act in the future (3:5–7). In fact, God has judged the world (2:4–10a), and he has not been absent from its history. Even if the Epicureans had not influenced the heretics, a climate of skepticism in the first century brought into question the possibility of predictive prophecy, a trend that Cicero traces back to the Greek author Carneades (Cicero, *On Divination* 2.3.9–12).

THE MESSAGE OF 2 PETER

In light of the danger of apostasy, Peter urges his readers to be diligent in their moral progress (1:5–8) and so confirm their "calling and election" (1:10). His call to growth becomes his summary message: "Grow in the grace and knowledge of our Lord and Savior Jesus Christ" (3:18). He links this growth with the moral life of the believer (1:8). Second Peter is an impassioned plea to reject the heretics' notions about judgment and moral responsibility and to affirm that delay in divine judgment is due to nothing less than God's mercy as he calls people to repentance (3:8–10). But judgment will come, which should shape the present conduct of the believer (3:11–13). This was also Paul's message (3:14–16).

Outline of 2 Peter

I. Epistolary Greeting (1:1–2)

II. Letter Body: A Warning against False Teachers (1:3–3:17)

   1. Body Opening: God's Call to Glory and Virtue (1:3–11)
   2. Body Middle: The Apostolic Testimony and the False Teachers (1:12–2:22)
      a. A Call to Remember (1:12–21)
      b. The Coming and the Judgment of the False Teachers (2:1–22)
   3. Body Closing: A Call to Holiness (3:1–17)
      a. A Call to Remember Prophetic and Apostolic Teaching (3:1–2)
      b. Understand This: The Scoffers of the Last Day (3:3–7)
      c. Do Not Ignore This: One Day Is as a Thousand Years (3:8–10)
      d. Since All These Things Will Pass Away: Living in Light of the End (3:11–13)
      e. While Waiting for These Things: Diligence to Be Found Blameless (3:14–17)

III. Letter Closing: A Doxology (3:18)

COMPOSING 2 PETER

Peter is aware of a corpus of Paul's writings whose message the heretics have distorted (3:15–16). Our author admits that Paul's letters contain teachings that are difficult to understand, although he appears confident that the heretics' interpretation of those teachings is wide of the mark. Apart from this reference (2:19), 2 Peter is not otherwise dependent on Paul's writings.

But Peter does make extensive use of Jude, which he apparently has at hand. A good portion of Jude is reproduced in 2 Peter 2, and both letters present their material in roughly the same order. For example, Jude reminds his readers of God's past judgment of the angels, who are "bound with everlasting chains for judgment" (Jude 6), which Peter adapts: "God did not spare angels when they sinned, but sent them to hell, putting them in chains of darkness to be held for judgment" (2:4). Compare the verses found in the chart to the right:

2 Peter and Jude—a Comparison

Jude	2 Peter
v. 4	2:1–3
v. 6	2:4
v. 7	2:6
v. 8	2:10
v. 9	2:11
v. 10	2:12
v. 11	2:15
v. 12a	2:13
vv. 12b–13	2:17
v. 16	2:18
vv. 17–18	3:2–3

It is unlikely that Jude used Peter. Were that the case, we would expect teaching from 2 Peter 1 and 3 to appear in Jude's letter. It is also unlikely that both authors used a common source. A careful comparison of these verses shows that Peter modifies material from Jude, shaping it in his refutation of the heretics.

Neither should we assume that since Jude is Peter's source, the heretics denounced in both letters are the same people. The issues raised, while similar, are distinct.

Some have identified 2 Peter as a testament or a farewell speech (notes 1:12–15). Various examples of such literature from antiquity have been preserved (e.g., *Testaments of the Twelve Patriarchs*, *Testament of Abraham*), and testamentary material appears in other ancient writings (e.g., *1 Enoch*, *Jubilees*). This genre usually involves gathering family and friends around one's deathbed, reflecting on the dying person's character, calling them to avoid certain sins, and exhorting them to live a righteous life. It also contains blessings and curses, and visions of the future.[5] Richard Bauckham observes that since testaments are always pseudepigraphical, 2 Peter cannot be an authentic work of Peter.[6] But although 2 Peter includes a testamentary section (1:12–15), it does not share other common features of this genre, and we should not classify this entire letter as a testament.

AUTHOR AND DATE OF 2 PETER

The authorship of 2 Peter has been debated since ancient times. The *Apocalypse of Peter* knew of the book, as did many of the church fathers. In the second century Justin Martyr referred to it, Clement of Alexandria wrote a commentary on it, and Irenaeus echoed it. A translation appeared in Egypt in the third century, and people such as Origen accepted it as genuine. But even Origen noted that some doubted its authenticity. In the fourth century Jerome commented that considerable doubt existed about its authenticity, citing stylistic differences with 1 Peter (Jerome accounts for the differences through different secretaries). Eusebius said most churches accepted it as authentic, although he entertained doubts. The church, however, finally recognized 2 Peter as part of the Christian canon.

In contemporary biblical scholarship, the debate over authorship revolves around different grammatical style in 1 and 2 Peter; sometimes the same concepts are expressed by different terminology (cf. 1 Pet. 1:13 and 2 Pet. 2:16 on Christ's coming). But since antiquity, stylistic differences have been attributed to Peter's amanuensis, possibly Silvanus (1 Pet. 5:12). The distinct situations of each letter evoked unique vocabulary, and these may account for the lexical differences between them. Second Peter 3:16 seems to point to a second-century date of composition since Paul's writings have been collected and classified as "Scripture." But Paul's letters were circulated and collected early (Col. 4:16), and the elevation of Paul's letters to "Scripture" is not out of line with Paul's own understanding of the inspired nature of his writings (1 Cor. 2:16; 7:40; 14:37; 2 Cor. 13:3). Some argue that concern over the delay in Christ's coming (3:4) reflects a second-century situation, but teaching about the delay had been woven into the earliest strata of Christian literature (see Matt. 25:1–13; Luke 12:35–48; James 5:7–8).

The arguments against the authenticity of 2 Peter are not entirely compelling, and doubts that have arisen have reasonable explanations. We should consider this an authentic work of Peter. The date of the letter is just before Peter's death (sometime between AD 64 and 68).

THE SETTING AND MESSAGE OF JUDE

Jude does not write the letter he originally intended. Apparently he was eager to compose a letter to a church or churches in Palestine to reflect on the "salvation we share" (v. 3). But Jude finds himself constrained to change his tone because some teachers have come from the outside whose conduct is ungodly. They pervert the teaching on grace (v. 4), transforming it into an excuse for licentious conduct that denies the only Master and Lord, Jesus Christ. Their theological novelty does not agree with the faith handed down as a sacred tradition (v. 3b).

Jude's letter pleads for the believers "to contend for the faith that was once for all entrusted to God's holy people" (v. 3). It calls them to build themselves up and stand firm in the faith (vv. 20–21). But the troublers of the church are persuasive and have swayed some members. Jude calls the church to show mercy on those who are wavering (v. 22) but also to rescue those who have succumbed to the temptation (v. 23). Yet Jude is concerned that the rescuers themselves do not become ensnared by the heresy.

These heretics are promoting a theology that grace frees a person from moral constraint, but they deny the Lord by their immorality (v. 4). They reject any form of authority over their conduct (v. 8a) and are especially bombastic in their rejection of "glorious ones" (v. 8b NRSV), a reference to angels, whom Jewish theology understood as mediators of divine law (Acts 7:53; Gal. 3:19). They claim their teaching is inspired since it came to them in dreams (v. 8), a universally recognized form of divine communication. New, inspired revelation is set over against apostolic tradition (vv. 4, 17).

Roman fresco of a banquet at the Palazzo Massimo alle Terme, Rome. Jude 12 refers to "love feasts," which may have included the Lord's Supper (cf. 2 Pet. 2:13). *Reproduced by permission from Carole Raddato*

Some have broadly characterized the error as "antinomianism." Jude portrays the heretics as not only being in error (vv. 11b, 13) but also as corrupt people. He draws special attention to their unbridled sexuality (vv. 4–8, 12, 16, 18), avarice (v. 11), and pride-filled verbal excess (vv. 8–9, 10, 16, 18). What moves them are animal instincts (v. 10), not the Spirit (v. 19), the source of Christian virtue.

These heretics are also intent on persuading others to join with them. They stealthily make their way in among the members of the church (v. 4) and act like friends (though they are nothing more than flatterers, v. 12). People recognized them as leaders but, like Cain, Balaam, and Korah, they are actively influencing others for ill (v. 11). They are effective in persuading members of the church to follow their ways, though not all who are tempted fully embrace their error (vv. 22–23).

Jude informs his readers/hearers that destruction awaits such people, as was predicted long ago (v. 4). Their presence, in effect, is a sign of the last times (v. 18). Yet Jude is confident that God is able to keep the disciples from falling into their trap (v. 24). They must avail themselves of faith and love (vv. 20–21) and mercifully come to the aid of any who are becoming ensnared (vv. 22–23). Jude is confident that this situation rests in God (vv. 24–25).

Outline of Jude

- I. Epistolary Greeting (1–2)
- II. Letter Body: An Exhortation to Fight for the Traditional Faith (3–23)
    1. Disclosure of Jude's Purpose for Writing: An Exhortation to the Beloved (3–4)
    2. A Call to Remember: Predictions about the Heretics and Fulfillment (5–19)
        - a. Text and Comment: Exodus, Angels, Sodom and Gomorrah, and Those Who Defile the Flesh, Reject Authority, and Slander Glorious Ones (5–8)
        - b. Text and Comment: Michael Did Not Blaspheme the Devil but These Blaspheme What They Do Not Understand (9–10)
        - c. Text and Comment: Cain, Balaam, Korah, and Those Who Are Blemishes in the Community Meals (11–13)
        - d. Text and Comment: The Prophecy of Enoch and Those Who Are Grumblers, Complainers, Flatterers (14–16)
        - e. Text and Comment: The Apostolic Prophecy and Those Who Are Worldly, Lacking the Spirit (17–19)
    3. Exhortations to the Beloved (20–23)
- III. Closing Doxology (24–25)

COMPOSING JUDE

A striking feature of Jude's letter is his use of pseudepigraphical literature. In verse 6 he refers to an angelic fall, which is an interpretive tradition based on Genesis 6:1–4 and elaborated extensively in *1 Enoch* 6–12 and other Jewish texts. In verse 9 Jude refers to the dispute over the body of Moses between the archangel Michael and the devil—a story drawn from the *Assumption of Moses*. The most striking use of extrabiblical literature is in verses 14–15, where Jude quotes *1 Enoch* 1:9. New Testament authors sometimes make use of extrabiblical texts as they elaborate their arguments. Paul, for example, quotes Epimenides (Acts 17:28; Titus 1:12), Aratus (Acts 17:28), and Menander (1 Cor. 15:33). Some in the early church rejected Jude's letter because the author quoted these pseudepigraphical books. Others said that since Jude quoted 1 Enoch, the church should accept that book. Augustine argued the position that has held until today: Although Jude quotes 1 Enoch, we will not accept that book nor reject Jude. We may say that Jude, as Paul, affirmed what they deemed was true regardless of its source but, at the same time, did not embrace everything from such extrabiblical sources.

Fragment of 1 Enoch
Courtesy of The Leon Levy Dead Sea Scrolls Digital Library; Israel Antiquities Authority, photo: Shai Halevi

AUTHOR AND DATE OF JUDE

The author identifies himself as Jude, "a brother of James" (v. 1). Jude's reference to James is likely the well-known James, the Lord's brother, one of the "pillars" of the Jerusalem church (Gal. 2:9). The author is most likely the same person who is named, along with James, as one of Jesus's siblings (Matt. 13:55; Mark 6:3). Since honor in the Mediterranean world is shared among family members, the honor ascribed to James as the leader of the Jerusalem church would enhance the status of Jude. In other words, in identifying himself as the "brother of James," Jude claims authority that parallels Paul's affirmations of his apostleship (Gal. 1:1).

Some confusion existed in the early church regarding Jude. But in his *Comments on the Epistle of Jude* (1–4), Clement of Alexandria not only states that Jude is the Lord's brother but comments on the author's reluctance to identify himself as such: "Jude, who wrote the Catholic Epistle, the brother of the sons of Joseph, and very religious, whilst knowing the near relationship of the Lord, yet did not say that he himself was His brother. But what said he? 'Jude, a servant of Jesus Christ,'—of Him as Lord; but 'the brother of James.' For this is true; he was His brother, (the son) of Joseph."

Jude was read early in the church and was accepted in the second-century Muratorian Canon and that of Athanasius in the mid-fourth century. Clement of Alexandria esteemed Jude highly enough to write a commentary on it. The letter was likely written around the middle of the first century.

Questions for Discussion

1. First Peter presents a robust theology of suffering. Discuss this theology in relation to Peter's theology about God, Christ, and the end times. Is the theology of suffering a topic of reflection in the contemporary church?
2. Should Christians be engaged in social action in society? Integrate the teaching of 1 Peter into your response.
3. Is "heresy" a category that we can maintain in a pluralistic culture? Discuss the tension between theological novelty and apostolic tradition in light of 2 Peter and Jude.
4. What role does eschatology play in the field of Christian ethics? What insight can be gained from Jude and 2 Peter?
5. Examine Jude's use of pseudepigraphical literature. Does Jude consider such writings to be authoritative?

BIBLIOGRAPHY

Introductory

Davids, P. H. *The First Epistle of Peter*. NICNT. Grand Rapids: Eerdmans, 1990.
———. *The Letters of 2 Peter and Jude*. PNTC. Grand Rapids: Eerdmans, 2006.
Green, M. *The Second Epistle of Peter and the Epistle of Jude*. TNTC. Grand Rapids: Eerdmans, 1987.
Grudem, W. *The First Epistle of Peter*. TNTC. Grand Rapids: Eerdmans, 1988.
Marshall, I. H. *1 Peter*. IVPNTC. Downers Grove, IL: InterVarsity Press, 1991.
Mbuvi, A. N. *Jude and 2 Peter*. NCCS. Eugene, OR: Wipf & Stock, 2015.
McKnight, S. *1 Peter*. NIVAC. Grand Rapids: Zondervan, 1996.
Moo, D. J. *2 Peter and Jude*. NIVAC. Grand Rapids: Zondervan, 1996.
Schreiner, T. R. *1, 2 Peter, Jude*. NAC. Nashville: Broadman & Holman, 2003.

Advanced

Achtemeier, P. J. *1 Peter*. Hermeneia. Minneapolis: Fortress, 1996.
Bauckham, R. J. *Jude, 2 Peter*. WBC. Waco, TX: Word, 1983.
Elliott, J. H. *1 Peter*. AB. New York: Doubleday, 2000.
Feldmeier, R. *The First Letter of Peter*. Waco: Baylor University Press, 2008.
Green, G. L. *Jude and 2 Peter*. BECNT. Grand Rapids: Baker, 2008.
Jobes, K. *1 Peter*. BECNT. Grand Rapids: Baker, 2005.
Michaels, J. R. *1 Peter*. WBC. Waco, TX: Word, 1988.
Neyrey, J. H. *2 Peter, Jude*. AB. New York: Doubleday, 1993.

NOTES

1. J. H. Moulton and G. Milligan, *The Vocabulary of the Greek Testament* (Grand Rapids, Baker Academic, 1995), 15.
2. Cited in D. F. Epstein, *Personal Enmity in Roman Politics 218–34 BC* (London: Croom Helm, 1987), 20.
3. B. Winter, *Seek the Welfare of the City* (Grand Rapids: Eerdmans, 1994), 28, 34–35.
4. A. Deissmann, *Light from the Ancient East*, trans. L. Strachan (New York: Kessinger, 2003), 323.
5. J. Charlesworth, ed., *The Old Testament Pseudepigrapha*, 2 vols. (New York: Doubleday, 1983, 1985), 1:773.
6. R. Bauckham, *Jude, 2 Peter*, WBC (Waco, TX: Word, 1983), 134.

Chapter 25

THE LETTERS OF JOHN

Early Christians such as John were competing with colossal religious temples throughout the empire. To speak of a God who appeared in a Jewish man named Jesus hardly compared with the glorious temple of Bacchus in Baalbek, Lebanon.

Jonny Blaze/Flickr CC BY 2.0

Three short letters in the New Testament have been attributed to John. Unmistakable thematic connections with the fourth gospel suggest that the letters originated with the author of that gospel. The letters are an enigma, however. While 2 John and 3 John have the usual features of ancient letters, 1 John bears no such marks: it is more like a tract or an essay aimed at a problem.

To understand the three letters, we must attempt to reconstruct the social and theological history of John's community of Christians by using clues in these letters. Threatening heresies are sweeping John's churches. His letters address these issues forcefully in order to protect the unity of the church and identify those undermining his authority. Rather than arming the community for combat against *external* pressures, these letters indicate that the conflicts are now *internal*. John's letters address these issues forcefully in a manner that both protects the unity of the church and identifies those who are undermining his authority.

Roman families generally had "family altars" for venerating their ancestors. Here incense could be burned and prayers said regularly. The letters of John describe life among Roman Christians who are forging a new identity *as Christians*, and undoubtedly they had to decide what to do with such traditional practices. This altar is about twenty-four inches tall and may have had a statue on its upper platform. The national Museum, Istanbul.
Gary M. Burge

THE CONTEXT OF JOHN'S LETTERS

According to Irenaeus (ca. AD 130–202), bishop of Lyons, John was a leading figure in Asia Minor (Eusebius, *Eccl. Hist.* 3.23). Clergy traveled to Ephesus simply to learn from him and hear his stories about Jesus. Irenaeus says he obtained this information from Polycarp, bishop of Smyrna, who himself received instruction from John (*Against Heresies* 2.22.5). Eusebius also notes that John, who reclined near the Lord at the Last Supper (John 13:25), was buried in Ephesus (*Eccl. Hist.* 3:31).

John's community of believers lives on the frontiers of Judaism. His church is heterogeneous: Jewish Christians with little knowledge of Greek live alongside Greeks, who know little of the Old Testament. Their common bond is a firm allegiance to Jesus, their Messiah, and John is their leader. Yet since John himself and his "Christian message" are rooted in Judaism, this community naturally lives near the synagogues of Ephesus.

These were the formative years when prized stories about Jesus were being preserved, including a collection of John's personal accounts. John's gospel offered generous amounts of teaching from Jesus, who predicted the sort of persecution the church was having. Among Jesus's teachings were those that promised an intimacy with him through the Holy Spirit; John includes phrases like "rebirth," "drinking living water," and "eating the bread of life." This was a gospel that encouraged those believers prone to mystical experiences of the faith.

Indeed, John's gospel is an *empowering gospel* that shaped this Christian community. Jesus and the Father lived inside these spiritually reborn believers (John 14:23). The Holy Spirit promised to provide them with incredible powers: to recall Jesus's words (14:26), to work miracles greater than those of Jesus (John 14:12), to have prayer answered (John 14:13–14), and to confront a hostile world (John 16:8). They even had the power to forgive sin (John 20:23). Above all, the Spirit gave them the power of *prophecy*, to continue speaking with Jesus's voice, revealing *new things* not recorded in Scripture (16:13).

In other words, John's community was a *pneumatic* community—a community that made the Spirit (Gk. *pneuma*) a vital feature of its life. Believers were ready to experience the Spirit in its fullness. In short, John's theology established the context for a pneumatic/charismatic Christianity.

But something serious has happened to this church's life. The once-unified congregation is beginning to tear apart, and this crisis seems fueled by a misuse of the gospel's teachings about the Spirit. There are threats within the fellowship itself. John says that it is "the last hour" for the community (1 John 2:18).

Lengthy scholarly debate has tried to identify these dissenters. They are likely a group of John's former followers who know his gospel well, claim to be inspired by the Spirit, and challenge John's understanding of Jesus Christ's person and work. They are succeeding, because the community is splitting, harsh words are being exchanged, and the vocabulary once reserved for those in "the world" is now aimed at fellow Christians.

John's Tomb in Ephesus

Eusebius cites a remarkable quote from Papias, bishop of Hierapolis in Asia Minor (c. AD 60–130), that he (Papias) was mentored by John. But Eusebius also refers to a second John in Ephesus—"John the elder." Thus, Ephesus had two tombs attached to the name "John" (*Eccl. Hist.* 3.39.6).

Today visitors to Ephesus can see the ruins of a large Byzantine church built by Emperor Justinian (483–565). This marks the traditional burial place of John.

Tradition says that John was buried in Ephesus. In the sixth century, Justinian built a church in Ephesus to commemorate it.
Gary M. Burge

Valentinus and Heracleon

Valentinus was a second-century Egyptian Gnostic teacher who moved to Rome (136–165) to gain greater authority. He may have authored *The Gospel of Truth*, a document that shows remarkable parallels to John's writings.

Heracleon was a student of Valentinus. His chief contribution was a full Gnostic commentary on the gospel of John, though only fragments survive in the writings of his severe critics and in quotations in Origen's commentary on John.

Both Valentinus and Heracleon show the welcome reception John's writings had in Gnostic circles. Presumably the raw forms of Gnosticism embraced this gospel not long after it was written.

The letter of 1 John supplies our primary evidence for this division, where we read of the painful departure of this group (2:19–26) and warnings about "deceivers" and "liars" who twist the truth of Christ (2:22; 2 John 7). We read of theological debates (1 John 5:5–8) being fought among teachers claiming to be filled with the Holy Spirit (2:20–21; 4:1–6). The letter's repeated emphasis on love hints at the severity of the situation.

John's letters are a response to those misinterpreting the fourth gospel. For some scholars these letters served as a commentary on the gospel. Others describe them as an "epilogue," designed to circulate with his gospel to root out erroneous interpretations.

John's "communities" were likely small gatherings of Christians in house churches. This artist's rendering shows the earliest Christian church building known, from Dura-Europos, Syria, early third century.
© 2010 by Zondervan

Hippolytus, a third-century theologian, describes how his Gnostic opponents admired Johannine language, which explains why the earliest commentaries on John were written by Gnostic theologians (e.g., Heracleon; see sidebar). This is probably why the orthodox church only cautiously embraced this gospel. There is a surprising lack of interest in John's writings among the second-century writers. As many scholars believe, it was the letters of John—1 John in particular—that redeemed the fourth gospel for the New Testament.

LITERARY FORM

The letters of 2 and 3 John have all the usual features of first-century letters: the author and recipient identified at the beginning, a blessing or prayer ("Grace, mercy, and peace"), and a "greeting" at the end. The letters also contain personal references and allusions that suggest they are intended for a specific situation. Some suggest that 3 John is the best New Testament example of first-century epistolary format.

But the same cannot be said for 1 John, which is least like a first-century letter. It lacks an address or name. No conclusion ends the document—5:21 sounds abrupt, as if the writer's thoughts are cut off. There are no personal comments. This is unusual when we consider the crisis in the church that the author is trying to correct. Compare this with how Paul writes in Galatians. When Paul faces a similarly distressing crisis, he shows lots of personal emotion, exacting exhortations, and a personal awareness of his opponents.

This absence of the usual conventions of letter writing in 1 John has led many to suggest that this document is not a personal letter but a general treatise or a sermon for wide distribution (John uses the plural "you" twenty-two times). Perhaps it is a pamphlet engaged in some sort of polemic. When we think of it this way, suddenly its use and value shifts. Imagine 1 John as an instructional outline, helping struggling churches and their pastors make headway among those who are eager to dilute the gospel.

Discovering a recognizable structure of thought in 1 John has proven impossible. Scholars find either spirals of cyclical thought or unconnected units. Some see two main divisions, each with a declaration: "God is light" (1:5) and "God is love" (4:8). The gospel of John, which also enjoys a bipartite form, may be the *structural model* for 1 John. Similarities between the fourth gospel and 1 John are numerous. And while we cannot be sure of many of their historical details, one thing is certain: *there is a relationship.* The same author likely penned both, and themes raised in the gospel are finding new attention in this subsequent letter (see below, "Author and Date").

Outline of 1 John

- I. Prologue (1:1–4)
- II. God Is Light (and We Should Walk Accordingly) (1:5—3:10)
    1. Thesis: The Light and the Darkness (1:5–7)
    2. Resist Sinfulness (1:8–2:2)
    3. Obey God's Commands (2:3–11)
    4. Defy the World and Its Allure (2:12–17)
    5. Renounce Those Who Distort the Truth (2:18–27)
    6. Live like God's Children (2:28–3:10)
- III. God Is Love (and We Should Walk Accordingly) (3:11–5:12)
    1. Love One Another in Practical Ways (3:11–24)
    2. Beware of False Prophets (4:1–6)
    3. Love One Another as Christ Loves Us (4:7–21)
    4. Obey God and Thereby Conquer the World (5:1–5)
    5. Never Compromise Your Testimony (5:6–12)
- IV. Conclusion (5:13–21)

It seems clear that 2 John and 3 John do not have a careful theological structure. As personal letters, they simply begin with a greeting and then develop one theme after another. Both letters are concerned about living the truth, which means loving those who abide with the family of God and chastising those who dismantle that family. In each case John warns against those who would fragment the community of believers. But the surprising thing here is that he identifies the opponents of the church as coming from *within* its ranks, not from some outside setting.

AUTHOR AND DATE

While Christian tradition has attributed these letters to John the apostle, the letters are anonymous (except that 2 and 3 John call their author "the elder"). This title may simply refer to a man of high esteem in the church, though elsewhere the apostles call themselves "elders" (1 Pet. 5:1). This situation is complicated by Eusebius's reference to two Johns (see sidebar on "John's Tomb in Ephesus," above).

While 2 and 3 John appear to come from the same pen, does 1 John originate with this same author described as "the elder"? There are striking similarities of style and content among all three writings that suggest common authorship.[1] A more compelling question is whether the same pen wrote the gospel of John. As early as the third century, church fathers made this claim on the basis of similarities in content and style, especially between 1 John and the gospel. These parallels are similar to those found between Luke and Acts or Colossians and Ephesians. Thus, most scholars today affirm common authorship for 1 John and the gospel. Therefore, if John the apostle wrote the gospel, he most likely wrote all three letters.[2]

If this is indeed true, those who place the gospel in the late first century locate the letters anywhere from AD 90 to 110. However, arguments for such a late date are being seriously criticized, and increasingly the gospel has been given an earlier time frame (closer to AD 70 or 80). Allowing time for the development of the heresy described in the letters, a date between 70 and 90 is likely.

THEOLOGICAL THEMES IN JOHN'S LETTERS

The theological emphases of the letters are intimately tied to the controversy that has placed the community under siege. The reason John repeatedly talks about love, sin, and the truth is rooted in the views of certain heretics.

The Views of the Heretics

It is clear that John is addressing an oppositional movement in his letters, but it is impossible to identify it with any specificity. We can only outline their beliefs using clues within these letters. But this is difficult. Writers rarely describe their opponents' views completely (or fairly), and we have no first-hand documents from John's adversaries. And some things John opposes in his letters may not derive from his opponents. For instance, in 1 John 4:18 he says there is no fear in love because perfect love casts out fear; John may be chastising his followers here, not the heretics.

John returns repeatedly to two intimately connected themes: the doctrine of Christ (Christology) and ethical behavior. The opponents have embraced an incorrect view of Christ that has led them to make wrong judgments about Christian living.

Christology. John's opponents hold the following beliefs: They deny the Son (1 John 2:23), deny that Jesus Christ came in the flesh (1 John 4:2; 2 John 7), and deny that Jesus is the Christ (1 John 2:22). Affirmations in the letters that buttress John's own Christology are: Jesus is the Christ (1 John 5:1), Jesus Christ has come in the flesh (4:2), Jesus is the Son (2:23; 3:23; 5:11) or the Son of God (1:3, 7; 3:8, 23; 4: 9, 10, 15), and Jesus Christ came "by water and blood" (5:6).

From these statements we can deduce that John's opponents are Christians who have begun to deviate from the traditional understanding of Jesus Christ. It is clear that they are followers of Jesus, but they are in sharp disagreement about the nature of what occurred within Jesus's own life. This was a pivotal issue the church needed to resolve: Was Jesus a human phenomenon, that is, a man in whom God had spoken? Or was Jesus a divine phenomenon, a visitor "from above," one who brought God himself into human history? This is not a question of hearing God's voice in Jesus. An Old Testament prophet could make that claim, and surely some were making this claim of Jesus. At stake here is the notion that in the person of Jesus something of God himself was present. As we will see, the gospel of John had already weighed in firmly on this topic.

Jesus Is Not the Christ

In a polemical verse, John writes: "Who is the liar? It is whoever denies that Jesus is the Messiah" (1 John 2:22). At first glance it would seem that John's opponents deny the messiahship of Jesus. But this is not what they are saying. They deny that *Jesus* is the Messiah. That is, they believe in a redemptive revealer named Christ, but he was not made truly human in the man Jesus. Simply put: they want Christ; they don't want Jesus.

In 4:2 John reinforces his claim: "Every spirit that acknowledges that Jesus Christ has come in the flesh is from God." Note also 2 John 7: "Many deceivers, who do not acknowledge Jesus Christ as coming in the flesh, have gone out into the world. Any such person is the deceiver and the antichrist." This is John's strong theological rejection of those who would reframe Jesus's identity using Docetism.

Claims for prophetic inspiration were common in antiquity and contributed to the confidence of John's opponents. Called "oracles," none were more famous than those at Delphi, Greece, which gave their utterances in the inner halls of the temple of Apollo.
Todd Bolen/BiblePlaces.com

Cerinthus and the Bathhouse

Irenaeus (*Against Heresies*, 3.3.4) relates an interesting story he heard from Polycarp about John meeting the heretic Cerinthus in the public baths at Ephesus. John cried out, "Let us save ourselves; the bath house may fall down, for inside is Cerinthus, the enemy of the truth."

Cerinthus distinguished *Jesus* and *Christ*. Jesus was the earthly man of Nazareth, while Christ was a heavenly deity who descended on Jesus at his baptism and departed before the crucifixion. Thus, *the man Jesus* died on the cross, not the Son of God. John's statement in 1 John 2:22 probably reflects this distinction (see also 5:1, 11).

A typical bath in Ephesus. A floor was laid over the pillars, and hot air from a fire circulated underneath, warming the bath. Polycarp wrote that John met the heretic Cerinthus at such a bath.
Todd Bolen/BiblePlaces.com

These opponents in 1 John are convinced that Jesus Christ is indeed a divine phenomenon, that God himself was present in him. But once this idea is settled, another problem arises. If this is truly a divine event, if Jesus Christ is truly the Son of God—can we imagine that God himself, in his fullest perfection, could assume human flesh? The key term here is "incarnation," which refers to the event of God entering *fully* into our humanity. John's opponents want to affirm the divinity of Jesus Christ but are unconvinced that he truly appropriated our humanity. This discussion of Jesus's "identity" in all its dimensions is called Christology. And this had become the dividing issue in the community.

Most scholars believe John's opponents embraced a Christology that elevated Christ's divinity at the expense of his humanity. It is easy to see how this happened. The Hellenistic world affirmed a universe populated by numerous deities, and elevating Christ into their company was easy. But this same world rejected the idea that such divinities entered our material world, since it is morally imperfect and subject to decay. This stark separation between the "above" and the "below," the divine and the human, spirit and flesh, is called dualism, and it was one of the first theological hurdles the church faced. The mere idea of Jesus's incarnation was problematic in a world that was fully dualistic. In a word, John's opponents promoted a Christology that was not incarnational.

In this dualistic outlook, Christ is separated from our world and belongs with the deities of heaven. But then what do we make of the visibility of Jesus during his ministry? Surely if he was divine, he was not a phantom. His first followers saw him, heard him, and touched him. One solution many supported was that Jesus only "appeared" to be human. This term (appeared) is important and represents the Greek term *dokeō*. Such Christians were "Docetists," meaning they said Christ "appeared" in the flesh but did not assume our full humanity. Where did this view come from? Some scholars point to the gospel of John itself. The fourth gospel presents a highly divine Jesus linked utterly with God ("In the beginning was the Word and the Word was with God; and the Word was God;" "I and the Father are one."). But this new interpretation of Jesus may have also been justified by the gospel's understanding of the Spirit. Jesus had promised that the Spirit would lead his followers into matters they could barely understand (John 16:12–14). This is why John later tells his church to "test the spirits" (1 John 4:1), because not every anointing necessarily comes from God. The very gospel that gave birth to their faith is being jettisoned (cf. 2 John 9).

We have cautiously rebuilt the christological context from which John's opponents are working. The *incarnate* Jesus Christ no longer occupies the central place in Christian faith. While the opponents may have a nominal interest in the Jesus of history, they look for inspired spiritual experiences that lift them above the views of John.

Ethics. John's letters give a sustained critique of the moral disposition of the heretics, whose theology apparently makes ethical behavior of no consequence for the Christian life. John mentions that his opponents boast that they:

- are "without sin" (1:8, 10)
- "have fellowship" with God but walk in the darkness (1:6)
- "know" God but are disobedient (2:4)
- are "in the light" but hate their fellow Christians (2:9)
- "love God" but hate their brothers and sisters (4:20)

John also repeats affirmations that shed light on the nature of the opponents' ethical position:

- to abide in God is to obey him (2:6)
- to sin willfully shows you have not known God (3:3–6; 5:18)
- whoever acts sinfully belongs to the devil (3:7–10)
- we should love one another (3:11–12, 17–18)
- refusing to love your brother or sister means you have not inherited eternal life (3:14–15)
- God is love—and to know him is to love (4:8–10)

To be sure, the doctrine of Jesus Christ was central to the debates in John's church. And evidently these debates had turned harsh and divisive. Poor theology had led to unethical conduct. And the result had been genuine harm to the community. Language that may have once been used for non-Christians hostile to the church now has found a new use within the church itself.

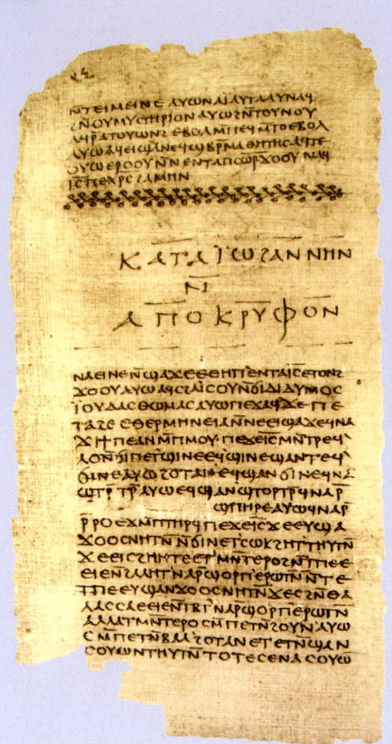

The *Gospel of Thomas*, Saying 29

The discovery of the *Gospel of Thomas* in Egypt (1945) has given us a poignant view into what happened to early Christians who jettisoned an orthodox framework for thinking theologically. Here we have 114 "secret sayings" claiming to be from Jesus. But in them are Gnostic categories that denigrate the material world. Saying 29 illustrates this well: "Jesus said, 'If the flesh came into being because of spirit, it is a wonder. But if spirit came into being because of the body, it is a wonder of wonders. Indeed I am amazed at how this great wealth has made its home in this poverty.'"

First John contradicts this sort of thinking. The author embraces the material world: "That which was from the beginning ... which we have *seen with our eyes*, which we have looked at and our *hands have touched*—this we proclaim concerning the Word of life" (1:1, emphasis added).

The end of the *Apocryphon of John* and the beginning of the *Gospel of Thomas*. Nag Hammadi codex II, folio 32.
Wikimedia Commons, PD-US

The origin of this misconduct, or worse, the ability to say they have no sin, comes from the same dualism that fueled the christological problem. If this material world is of no account, if "the flesh" does not matter to God, then what matters is spiritual experience, engagements with God that are "beyond the flesh" where God lives. Dualism devalues the world and therefore must deny not only the incarnation but the importance of conduct in the world. So if they deny their own sinfulness ("things in the flesh do not matter!"), they will feel no need for Christ's atoning death on the cross. Theirs is a "deeper" religion, fueled by nontraditional insights gleaned from the Spirit (1 John 2:20–23; 4:1). They refuse to submit to the leadership that promotes these teachings and are intolerant of those who disagree with them.

The opponents are not simply indifferent to those who disagree with them; they are intolerant. This explains the repeated times that John refers to "hating" fellow Christians. Conflict has resulted from the opponents' superior spirituality. These people have become elitist in their view of themselves, and those who seek to exhort them, if they cannot catalog similar experiences for themselves, have no credibility.

John's Secondary Concerns

Various secondary themes are evident throughout the letters. These appear by accident because they are a part of the refutation the author is making against his opponents.

The Holy Spirit. If John's gospel is central to this community's spiritual formation, the Spirit obviously plays a pivotal role in discipleship. In 4:13 John reassures his followers that possessing the Spirit is characteristic of those who "live in [God]." Such abiding is not simply a matter of orthodox confession (4:15) or loving conduct (4:16). Abiding in God is experiential—a personal experience with the Holy Spirit. Therefore, the false teachers must buttress their authority with some pneumatic experience. This explains why in 4:1–3 John calls the church to "test the spirits." Believers must be able to spot "false prophets" (4:1).

This is a pneumatic (or "spirit-filled") context. Note that John does not use his apostolic authority as Paul often does. He cannot say, "Look. I'm an apostle and my judgments are binding." Instead, he urges the church to test the spirits to see if they are affirming traditional beliefs about Jesus—thereby undercutting the authority of these prophets. His tactic, therefore, is characteristic of those struggling against rival leadership claims in a "charismatic" setting. One cannot deny the Spirit. Thus, one must teach discernment and urge Christians to weigh claims made in the Spirit.

But John goes further. If these opponents are claiming a superior spirituality, he reminds the church that each member has been equally anointed with the Spirit (2:20, 27). In other words, spiritual discernment is the task of *every* person. No one may claim exclusive spiritual insight.

Discernment and tradition. These letters remind us that the church is the custodian of the truth. The believing community must discern false belief and practice and distinguish between truth and error. While this theme is explicit only in 4:1ff, it is presumed throughout 1 John (cf. also 2 John 8).

But how can we discern truth from falsehood? If a prophet urges something new under the authority of the Spirit, how can it be weighed? John believes that the church is accountable to the historic revelation given in Jesus Christ and passed down through the apostles. Individual inspiration must be weighed against truth revealed in Scripture and tradition.

Throughout 1 John the author affirms that what was "from the beginning" should be the anchor (1:1; 2:13–14; 3:11). John continually urges his readers to recall what they first learned and to measure everything else by it. "Let what you heard *from the beginning* abide in you. If what you heard *from the beginning* abides in you, then you will abide in the Son and in the Father" (2:24 NRSV, emphasis added).

"The beginning" refers to the historic coming of Jesus Christ and the preservation of that revelation. What is revealed in the incarnation must be the litmus test for all new theological insights. Thus in 1:1–3 John points to what he saw with eyes and touched with hands—the incarnate Christ, fully linked to our full humanity. *Historic Christology must be the touchstone for all Christian belief.* His exhortation in 2:12–14 twice reminds the fathers—those who are older—to rekindle their acquaintance with the ancient teachings.

This theological anchor in historic Christology is reminiscent of the gospel of John. In his farewell discourse, Jesus talks about the Spirit and the limits of what he will do. As Jesus's words cannot deviate from the Father's words (John 5:19), so too the Spirit will reiterate what Jesus himself has said (14:26; cf. 16:13). Father, Son, and Spirit provide a revelation that is self-consistent.

Since John did not possess the New Testament as we do today, he had to elevate "tradition" or historic teaching passed down with apostolic authority. No doubt his own record of Christ—the gospel of John—serves as a reservoir of such traditional teachings. Were John with us today, he would undoubtedly point to Scripture as an apostolic archive of teachings against which to weigh modern teachings. Yet other, more ancient Christian communities (such as the Catholic and Orthodox churches) would object to such a narrow explanation of "tradition." To them tradition means more—the archive of normative religious truth passed down through the church from generation to generation. John affirms that Christian wisdom and truth—anchored in right Christology—are cumulative and binding.

Love, unity, and fellowship. The gospel and letters of John place a high premium on the quality of Christian community. Jesus's command in John 13:34 and 15:12, 17 make clear that love should be the hallmark of his followers. In John 17 Jesus prays for harmony and unity among his followers so "that all of them may be one," based on the model of the oneness of the Father and the Son (vv. 20–23).

No doubt the division in John's church has placed unity and love first on the church's agenda. He even makes love a command: Christians who love God *must* love their brothers and sisters in the church (1 John 4:21). This teaching John anchors "from the beginning" as well (3:11; 2 John 5). In 1 John 3:23 he almost sums up the Christian life with two exhortations: believing in Jesus Christ and loving one another.

But John accompanies this exhortation with a theological basis. Initially, he says, God first loved us (4:19). Love cannot be fueled by human energy. It originates from God when we apprehend the depth of his love for us (4:7a) and when we are born anew by *his* Spirit (4:7b). Intimate knowledge of God is the same as enjoying the intimate reciprocity of God's love: he loves us, we love him, and this love spills over to those near us. Conversely, not to love is evidence that someone does not truly know God (4:8).

Christ Jesus is the material expression of God's tangible love. Once again, historic Christology addresses the issues of ethics. Because Christ laid down his life for us, we ought to do the same for one another (3:16; see especially 4:10).

John describes living in God's love, knowing him, and obeying his commands as "walk[ing] in the light." When people live in the light together, they *corporately* experience God's love and unity, and fellowship results (1:5–7). But the reverse is also true. When people exhibit hostility and division, when they "hate" (to use John's term), they prove they live "in the darkness" (2:9–11). Such so-called Christians are "liars" and hypocrites (4:20).

John uses the language of family (1 John 2:12–14, 28; 5:2) to describe Christian believers' relationships with each other. This was unconventional in antiquity and underscored the unique community early Christianity aspired toward.
Gary M. Burge

The ongoing history of John's church is visible in 2 John and 3 John. Various theories have been offered for the chronological order of these three letters. Some suggest 2 John is John's original letter and 1 John is his expansion—a fulfillment of his wish to write much more (2 John 12). But how does 2 John make sense if the recipients have not read 1 John? Second John is an exhortation—a reminder—of things said in 1 John. The shorter letters should be interpreted in light of 1 John.

These letters show us a community that takes its faith seriously. Some have wondered whether it fosters a sectarian outlook in which inner love and cohesion are as absolute as the boundary the community has erected between itself and the world. Christians are taught to reject the world (1 John 2:15–17; 4:4–5) and to practice a love within the community that has no natural counterpart (4:19–21; 2 John 5; 3 John 5–6). They must view themselves as the elect of God (1 John 5:19–20; 2 John 7–9).

Does such a community finally collapse under its own internal pressures? The intensity of its vision arms its critics with an intolerance that finally tears the church apart. When we read 1 John 2:18–19, this group has departed, though John still views them from the doorway of the church as former members. But by the time we read 2 John 7, the rupture seems complete. Now they are in the world and allied with the antichrist, and John forbids further contact (2 John 10–11).

These letters bear eloquent testimony to the vulnerability of the church when it lives on the frontiers of the world and is subject to its influences. They warn us of anyone "who runs ahead and does not continue in the teaching of Christ" (2 John 9)—particularly when such teachers are from within the ranks.

Roman Rest Stop Discovered

The Roman road system, famous for its excellent construction and safety, recognized the need for rest stops. One road stretching across Europe gave up its secrets in December 2004, when an archaeological team discovered a Roman rest stop in Neuss, Germany. It offered a chariot service station, a gourmet restaurant, and a hotel with central heating.

Christians relied on the hospitality of other believers when they traveled. Thus, John commends Gaius in 3 John 5 for welcoming his emissaries. To welcome someone meant hospitality, acceptance, friendship, and loyalty.

The short letters of John remind us that the early Christians did not live in isolation but enjoyed a communications network of couriers that used the Roman road system. Pictured here is a Roman road located in Side, Turkey, identical to Roman roads built throughout the eastern empire.
Arthur Lomarainen/Shutterstock

THE CONTEXT OF 3 JOHN

In 3 John, the church is in the grips of the theological struggle described in 1 John and confronted in 2 John. John himself once wrote to the church, but an influential man named Diotrephes rejected his letter (3 John 9). John then sent emissaries to the church, but Diotrephes refused to acknowledge them (v. 10). He even rejected John publicly (v. 9) and spread rumors about him. Diotrephes even forcefully stopped anyone who showed sympathy to the visitors or tried to speak with them.

The missionaries found a courageous host, however, in a man named Gaius. We cannot tell if Gaius belonged to Diotrephes's house church or lived nearby. Gaius knew Diotrephes but did not feel threatened by his power. He offered hospitality to traveling Christians and helped finance their journey (3 John 5–6). He sent them "on their way" (v. 6)—which means giving them money—and they returned to John with their report about the church's rebellion and Gaius's faithfulness (v. 3).

John wants to visit this church personally but cannot at the present (v. 14). He knows he must shore up the true believers there and encourage their faithfulness—those like Gaius who still walk in the truth, whom he calls "friends" (v. 14; cf. v. 1). So John plans a strategy: commend Gaius for his hospitality and encourage him to continue. Thus, when John comes for a visit, he has allies who will stand for Christ and against Diotrephes.

Verse 12 introduces the courier of the letter—Demetrius. The hospitality and financial support shown to other Christian travelers will undoubtedly be extended to Demetrius, a personal friend of John. John says, even "the truth" (v. 12) speaks well of him.

This strong affirmation of Demetrius anticipates what Diotrephes might say about him. Since Diotrephes rejects John, he will reject Demetrius. John's testimony should strengthen Gaius's confidence in Demetrius, but the problem will only be solved when John confronts Diotrephes personally.

Questions for Discussion

1. How did emphases in the gospel of John influence the false teachings that John must address later?
2. Why was the early church reluctant to embrace the gospel of John fully?
3. How does John confront opponents who claim that their teaching stems from Jesus himself speaking through the Spirit?
4. How can a faulty understanding of the incarnation lead to a willingness to live immorally?
5. How do we balance a commitment to love with a commitment to separate ourselves from those who contradict the truth?

BIBLIOGRAPHY

Introductory

Bruce, F. F. *The Epistles of John*. Grand Rapids: Eerdmans, 1970.

Burge, G. M. *Letters of John*. NIVAC. Grand Rapids: Zondervan, 1996.

Jobes, K. *1, 2, and 3 John*. ZECNT. Grand Rapids: Zondervan, 2014.

Thompson, M. M. *1–3 John*. IVPNTC. Downers Grove, IL: InterVarsity Press, 1992.

Advanced

Brown, R. E. *The Epistles of John*. AB. New York: Doubleday, 1982.

Kruse, C. G. *The Letters of John*. PNTC. Grand Rapids: Eerdmans, 2000.

Marshall, I. H. *The Epistles of John*. NICNT. Grand Rapids: Eerdmans, 1978.

Smalley, S. *1, 2, 3 John*. WBC. Waco, TX: Word, 1984.

NOTES

1. R. E. Brown, *The Epistles of John*, AB (New York: Doubleday, 1982), 14–35, 755–59 (charts).

2. For the credibility of this tradition, see G. M. Burge, *Interpreting the Gospel of John* (Grand Rapids: Baker, 1992), 37–54.

THE REVELATION OF JOHN

A street in ancient Pergamum called "The Sacred Way" leads to the city's Asclepion. This well-known city had a Christian community whom John addresses in Revelation 2:2–17.

Todd Bolen/BiblePlaces.com

The seven churches that received John's revelation and letters (Rev. 1:11; 2:1–3:22) and the island of Patmos (1:9)

The Revelation of John is perhaps the best-known New Testament writing while being the least understood. Revelation begins with familiar epistolary elements, such as the introduction of the author, an address to the readers, an opening blessing, and praise to Jesus Christ (1:4–6). The second and third chapters hold a series of small letters addressed to churches located in the Roman province of Asia: Ephesus, Smyrna, Pergamum, Thyatira, Sardis, Philadelphia, and Laodicea (1:11; 2:1–3:22). As many other New Testament documents, the book ends with a benediction: "The grace of the Lord Jesus be with God's people. Amen." (22:21; cf. 1 Cor. 16:23–24; 2 Cor. 13:14; Phil. 4:23; 1 Thess. 5:28; 2 Thess. 3:18). Yet such familiar features dissolve into a vision of the exalted Christ (1:7–20). As chapter four opens, John is summoned to bear witness of things transpiring in heaven: "Come up here, and I will show you what must take place after this" (4:1). What follows are fabulous and terrifying scenes of the heavenly throne of God and cataclysmic judgments upon the world (4:1–19:8). The series of visions culminates with the appearing of Christ, identified as the "KING OF KINGS AND LORD OF LORDS," the coming of the millennium, the judgment of Satan and the deceased, and visions of the new heaven, new earth, new Jerusalem, and restored Eden (19:11–22:5). The exalted Christ instructs John to compose letters to the seven churches in Asia (2:1, 8, 12, 18: 3:1, 7, 14) and to write down the visions revealed to him (1:11, 19; 10:4; 14:13; 19:9; 21:5). The whole book is circulated to the seven churches, who are to read it aloud to the gathered assembly of believers: "Blessed is the one who reads aloud the words of this prophecy" (1:3a). But the blessing comes with a call to "hear it and take to heart what is written in it," not adding or taking away anything from these words (1:3b; 22:17–18). Though Revelation is filled with both familiar and unfamiliar cadences, it was a book that spoke powerfully to the church in John's day. And it speaks to ours.

THE GENRES OF REVELATION

A Letter

The book of Revelation contains seven short epistles addressed to churches in Asia (chapters 2–3). But the whole book is also laid out as a large letter from John to the seven churches, sharing key epistolary features, such as opening with the name of the author and the recipients followed by a prayer and praise to Christ (1:4–6). The letter ends with a well-known epistolary blessing (22:21). In the ancient world, reading was commonly done aloud, and Christian leaders expected that their letters would be recited to the gathered company of believers (Acts 8:30; 1 Thess. 5:27). Revelation was no exception. The first "readers" actually heard this book. John exhorts them not to change any of the contents of what he had written since Jesus himself gave this testimony to John through his angel (22:16, 18–22).

An Apocalypse

While Revelation is framed as a letter, the body of the composition from chapter 4 onward is an example of apocalyptic literature. The opening verse of the book identifies it as such: "The revelation (Gk. *apokalypsis*) from Jesus Christ" (1:1). The term means "to uncover" or "reveal" something previously hidden. Apocalyptic literature flourished between about 200 BC until around AD 100. It was literature born in crisis that exhorted God's people and offered them hope amid the myriad of social troubles they were enduring. Apocalyptic has been defined as "a genre of revelatory literature with a narrative framework, in which a revelation is mediated by an otherworldly being to a human recipient, disclosing a transcendent reality which is both temporal, insofar as it envisages eschatological salvation, and spatial insofar as it involves another, supernatural world."[1] These features appear throughout this book as it starts with the revelation of the exalted Jesus to John (1:1, 9–20; 22:16), explains events that are present and future (1:19; 22:12), and shows John these visions in an other-worldly heavenly realm (4:1). The book offers its readers a divine perspective on their current realities using highly symbolic imagery. Apocalyptic literature anticipates the end of the empire and the renewal of the world. As apocalyptic literature, Revelation supports the people of God against the unbridled hostility of Roman imperial power. The first readers faced persecution during Emperor Domitian's reign, and this letter-apocalypse was calculated to lift their eyes to God's ultimate control of history. The empire does not wield ultimate power, whatever its claims.

A Prophecy

Revelation also displays elements of the prophetic genre. Indeed, Revelation self-identifies as "prophecy" (1:3; 22:7, 10, 18, 19; also 10:11). As Old Testament prophetic literature, Revelation recounts the prophet's call and commissioning to become God's spokesperson (1:9–11). The prophet receives revelations from God, both orally and in visions (1:12–20). The received oracles can be both threatening and benevolent (i.e., 2:2–7, 9–11, 13–17; 8:13; 12:10–12; 14:13; 16:15; 19:9).[2] While judgment upon injustice marks Revelation's oracles against the empire, it also exhorts and offers hope to the people of God. The message is not about escape from their present troubles but an affirmation that the readers should now heed Christ's call and thus receive his blessing.

Each of these genres contribute to our interpretation of Revelation. The book is concerned with ethics and God's intervention in the present and future. It joins events on earth with divine activity in heaven. Many of our contemporary readings of Revelation turn it into a source of speculation about the future and dates rather than recognizing its powerful message about God's sovereignty over all life, the hope he offers his people in the middle of severe trials, and the call to align our lives with his purposes. Christ is with his people, whom he calls to patient endurance (1:9; 2:3; 3:10; 13:10; 14:12). Revelation also warns against all powers, political and religious, that exalt themselves over God. John's writing demonstrates that Christ has all authority in heaven and on earth (Matt. 28:18; Rev. 19:16). The prayer Jesus taught the church—"Your kingdom come, your will be done, on earth as it is in heaven" (Matt. 6:10)—finds its answer here. As Revelation 11:15 proclaims, "The kingdom of the world has become the kingdom of our Lord and of his Messiah, and he will reign for ever and ever."

THE SETTING OF REVELATION

John received his visions while on Patmos, an island located in the Aegean Sea, west of the Roman province of Asia (1:9). This small island of just over thirteen square miles is located about seventy-seven miles from Ephesus. The journey by sea from the island to Ephesus would have taken almost two days. John was exiled on Patmos "because of the word of God and the testimony of Jesus" (1:9), that is, because of his witness to the gospel of Christ. While others suffered the death penalty for their witness (2:13; 6:9; 20:4), John possibly endured the loss of *caput*, citizenship or liberty.[3] John was subjected to the *relegatio in* (or *ad*) *insulam*, banishment to an island. Patmos was not a penal colony, as some have suggested, but exile to an island was a well-known civil punishment.

The island of Patmos
Todd Bolen/BiblePlaces.com

Banishment to an Island

Relegatio ad insulam was a form of judicial punishment in John's day (Rev. 1:9). Suetonius speaks about this form of banishment, decreed by Emperor Titus: "After these had been soundly beaten in the Forum with scourges and cudgels, and finally led in procession across the arena of the amphitheatre, he had some of them put up and sold, and other deported to the wildest of the islands" (*Titus* 8.5). The satirist Juvenal twice remarked about people being exiled on the island of Gyara: "If you want to be Somebody, do a daring deed deserving of cramped Gyara and the dungeon" (1.73) and "In discontent he seethes at the narrow limits of the universe as if confined on the rocks of Gyara or tiny Seriphus" (10:168–69). Exile to an island could be permanent or temporary.

The persecution that landed John on Patmos most likely took place during the reign of Emperor Domitian at the end of the first century AD. Some have suggested that John was exiled earlier, during the persecution of believers under Nero that began in AD 64. Speaking of the rumor that Nero had caused the great fire in Rome, the historian Tacitus said, "Therefore, to scotch the rumour, Nero substituted as culprits, and punished with the utmost refinements of cruelty, a class of men, loathed for their vices, whom the crowd styled Christians" (*Annals* 10.44). But the attack against Christians under Nero did not extend beyond Rome. Widespread persecution also occurred during Domitian's time. Eusebius stated, "The only emperors who were ever persuaded by malicious men to slander our teaching were Nero and Domitian, and from them arose the lie, and the unreasonable custom of falsely accusing Christians" (*Hist. eccl.* 4.26.9). We do not have clear evidence, however, that Domitian promoted an empire-wide persecution. Much of the hostility against the churches of Asia could have been due to their noncompliance with local civic expectations regarding participation in the imperial cult. Still, numerous scholars argue that John has in mind the sufferings many believers endured during Domitian's reign.

Suetonius notes that Domitian promoted the imperial cult and began to demand that he be addressed as both "lord" and "god": "With no less arrogance he began as follows in issuing a circular letter in the name of his procurators, 'Our Master and our God bids that this be done.' And so the custom arose henceforth of addressing him in no other way even in writing or in conversation" (*Domitian* 13). *© Museums Victoria/Heath Warwick https://collections.museumvictoria.com.au/items/64107*

Support for a late-first century dating of Revelation comes from the ancient church historian Eusebius, who cites Irenaeus as his source: "At this time, the story goes, the Apostle and Evangelist John was still alive, and was condemned to live in the island of Patmos for his witness to the divine word. At any rate Irenaeus, writing about the number of the name ascribed to the anti-Christ in the so-called Apocalypse of John, states this about John in so many words in the fifth book against Heresies. 'But if it had been necessary to announce his name plainly at the present time, it would have been spoken by him who saw the apocalypse. For it was not seen long ago but almost in our own time, at the end of the reign of Domitian'" (*Hist. eccl.* 3.18). Eusebius also notes that John did not remain exiled after the death of Domitian: "After Domitian had reigned

The reverse of this second-century coin minted in Ephesus depicts four temples in Ephesus: The Temples of Hadrian, Caracalla, Artemis (upper left), and the Sebastoi (lower right). The latter temple was erected under Domitian as part of the imperial cult. © The Trustees of the British Museum

fifteen years, Nerva succeeded. The sentences of Domitian were annulled, and the Roman Senate decreed the return of those who had been unjustly banished and the restoration of their property. . . . At that time, too, the story of the ancient Christians relates that the Apostle John, after his banishment to the island, took up his abode at Ephesus" (3.20.8–9).

Revelation itself offers some support that the book was written during Domitian's time. The emperor Nero had committed suicide in AD 68, yet around the end of the first century, many believed that he had come back to life or never actually died. That popular belief may be echoed in Revelation 13:12 and 14. The first beast's "fatal wound had been healed" and the second beast "ordered them to set up an image in honor of the beast who was wounded by the sword and yet lived." Worship of the supposedly divinized ruler was at the heart of the imperial cult. Domitian had promoted the imperial cult in the province of Asia at the end of the first century, including the erection of an imperial temple in Ephesus in AD 89/90. Previously, imperial temples had been built in Pergamum (29 BC; see Rev. 2:13), Smyrna (AD 21), and elsewhere in the province. Indeed, we have evidence of the presence of the imperial cult in the very cities John addresses in Revelation.[4]

The Imperial Cult

The imperial, or ruler, cult was a prominent feature in the cities addressed in John's Revelation. People honored the emperor as a god. Cities erected temples to him and established priesthoods dedicated to the imperial cult. Cities honored their imperial patron through such homage. One inscription from Ephesus dated to 49 BC said: "The cities of Asia and the [communities] and the county districts (honour) Galius Julius, son of Gaius, Caesar, Pontifex Maximus, Imperator and counsel for the second time, descendant of Ares and Aphrodite, the god who has appeared visibly and universal savior of the life of human beings."[6] In 29 BC Augustus allowed for the construction of a temple in Ephesus dedicated to "Dea Roma," the goddess Rome, and "Divus Julius," the divine Julius Caesar. At the same time, Augustus allowed a temple to be erected in Pergamum to honor him and "Dea Roma." Religious devotion mixed with the prospect of economic advantage through the emperor's benefaction. A letter from the proconsul of Asia, Paullus Fabius Maximus, underscores the importance of imperial honors in the cult: "[It is difficult to say] whether the birthday of the divine emperor has caused more joy, or more benefit. We may rightly set it at the beginning of all things; not indeed in terms of the order of nature, but because of the advantage (accruing to us). He has re-established all that had decayed and turned to disaster. Thanks to him, the whole world presents a different aspect. Had not the emperor, who is the common happiness of all the human race, been born, then the world would have fallen victim to corruption." The proconsul proposed that "the cities should have one and the same New Year's Day: the birthday of the divine emperor."[7]

The Book of Revelation bears witness to the persecution Christians endured for not conforming to the social expectation of honoring the emperor as a god. Revelation is a vivid polemic against the imperial cult.

Imperial temple in Ankara, Turkey, built ca. 25–20 BC. An inscription on its walls reads *Res Gestae Divi Augusti* (Deeds of the Divine Augustus).
Reproduced by permission from Carole Raddato

Domitian's promotion of the ruler cult "provided a climate in which enormous pressure was placed on Christians to be loyal citizens and participate in the imperial cult."[5] Civic officials during the era were eager to support the ruler cult, since it formed part of the system of benefaction. Benefits would accrue to those cities that showed due loyalty. Rejection of the imperial cult became an antisocial act. This is the situation envisaged in Revelation 13:15, where noncompliance with the imperial decree to worship the beast could result in death. The imperial cult is one of the principle concerns in Revelation (see also 13:4; 14:9; 15:2; 16:2; 19:20). Faithfulness to Christ meant noncompliance with the cult (20:4).

INTERPRETING REVELATION

Some interpreters of Revelation regard the bulk of the book from chapter 4 onward as a symbolic survey of what will occur at the end of time. Others understand it as a description of events during John's own day. Yet others tell us that the book describes the whole sweep of history from John's day until the coming of Christ. On the other hand, some argue that the book is not concerned with historical events at all, whether past, present, or future, but simply portrays the enduring struggle between good and evil in the world. No reader should approach Revelation without understanding the differences between these varied approaches to the book.

Preterist Interpretation

The preterist (which means "past") or contemporary-historical approach to Revelation's message holds that the events described therein are those transpiring during the first century AD. In symbolic form the book recounts the persecution of Christians under the Roman Empire. The beast of Revelation 13 is either the empire or the emperor, and Babylon (17:1–18) is the city of Rome. Under this reading, the book shows believers during John's day that though they are being persecuted, their oppressors will be overthrown at the time of Christ's advent. All the events of the book have to do with the church's conflict with the Roman Empire during the days of Domitian. This view is the most common among contemporary commentators.

An alternative preterist view is that the book speaks primarily about Israel and the destruction of Jerusalem under the military leadership of Titus in AD 70. The problem with this approach is that it necessitates an early date for the writing of Revelation, before AD 70. It also limits its scope of the book to Israel, whereas Revelation speaks of a more universal judgment (Rev. 6:15; 16:12–16; 17:1–5). A third form of the preterist view regards Revelation as a description of conditions under the Roman Empire during John's day and up to the fall of Rome in AD 476 (Rev. 18:1–24). The virtue of the preterist approaches to Revelation is that the book provides a message clearly directed to its first readers in the cities of Asia. On the other hand, the preterist view diminishes the book's significance for successive generations.

Historicist Interpretation

The historicist approach to Revelation was popular among the Reformers and others. Under this reading, the book prophetically describes the whole sweep of history from John's day all the way up to the present. Luther and Calvin identified the pope as the Beast of Revelation. Subsequent interpreters who used this approach identified the Beast as Napoleon, Mussolini, Hitler, or others. In 1887 William Milligan wrote about this approach to Revelation, saying, "To this day no belief is more commonly entertained than that in the visions of St. John we may read of the establishment of Christianity under Constantine, of Mohammed, of the Papacy, of the Reformation of the sixteenth century, of the French Revolution, of not a few in short of the greatest movements by which, since the beginning of the Christian era, the Church and the world have been stirred."[8] The historicist approach, however, is not widely held today, since there is absolutely no agreement regarding which people and events of history should be identified with the book's symbolism. The historicist view also suffers from cultural myopia since its interpretation is limited to the history of Western civilization. The perspectives of Revelation stretch well beyond the West (1:5, 7; 3:10; 11:15).

Idealist Interpretation

Those supporting the idealist approach to interpreting Revelation argue that the book does not describe historical events either in John's day, through history, or even in the future. Rather, Revelation depicts the enduring struggle between good and evil in symbolic form. The book speaks about God's judgment on sin wherever and whenever it occurs. The beast cannot be identified with any particular person in history but rather stands for all rulers and empires who oppose God. Milligan remarked that Revelation lays out "great principles and not special incidents." He charges that "we are not to look in the Apocalypse for special events, but for an exhibition of the principles which govern the history both of the world and the church." The book therefore becomes "a spring of elevating encouragement and holy joy to Christians in every age."[9] The virtue of this view is that we can understand how Revelation's message is for all churches in all times. The problem, however, is that it disconnects Revelation from historical events in John's day or any concrete future events. Revelation's message is indeed about real events, places, and people that are here portrayed symbolically.

Futurist Interpretation

One of the most popular approaches to Revelation regards everything that occurs from 4:1 onward as events that will take place immediately preceding the advent of Christ and beyond to the final events of history. Some who embrace the futurist interpretation of Revelation propose that the catching away of the church to meet the Lord (1 Thess. 4:13–18) will happen before a seven-year tribulation period preceding Christ's coming. This secret "rapture" to the heavens occurs in 4:1: "After this I looked, and there before me was a door standing open in heaven. And the voice I had first heard speaking to me like a trumpet said, 'Come up here, and I will show you what must take place after this.'" Others who hold to a futurist interpretation argue that Revelation 4:1 is only experienced by John, to whom it was addressed, and is not about the rapture of the church. Rather, the church will pass through the period of tribulation before the advent of Christ. The problem with the futurist interpretation is the way it disconnects the bulk of the message of Revelation from the church in John's day. The futurist view has generated considerable unwarranted speculation about times and dates regarding the Lord's return, especially among those who hold that 4:1 refers to the "rapture" of the church. We should note that the belief in a secret catching away of the church before the "great tribulation" did not originate until early in the 1830s.[10]

Combined Views of Interpretation

Many interpreters of Revelation hold that various approaches to interpreting Revelation should be combined. While we may set aside the *historicist* interpretation on the grounds already mentioned, the book indeed portrays the enduring struggle between good and evil. This is the significant contribution of the *idealist* approach. Revelation also graphically portrays the conflicts the church faced or would face during the first century, as Christians refused to participate in the imperial cult and were persecuted for their noncompliance. The book offered them hope that their sufferings were not the final word. History belongs to God, who takes care of his people whatever adversity confronts them (3:10; 7:1–17). This *preterist* view clearly shows how Revelation spoke to the first Christians who heard its message. But the *futurist* approach reminds us of the final events of history and the promise of God's ultimate intervention to right all wrong (Rev. 4–22). Not all Revelation's prophecy has been realized. The book speaks both about the present (preterist) and future (futurist) in a way similar to ancient prophecy. George Ladd reminds us that "the prophets had two foci in their prophetic perspective: the events of the present and the immediate future, and the ultimate eschatological event. These two are held in dynamic tension often without chronological distinction, for the main purpose of the prophecy is not to give a program or chart of the future, but to let the light of the eschatological consummation fall on the present (2 Pet. 1:19)."[11] Under this combined view, the historical events of John's day prefigure the final events of history. Present realities are tied to the eschatological future.

THE MESSAGE OF REVELATION

Revelation begins as a letter that, after the opening prayer, turns to recount John's vision of the exalted Christ (Rev. 1). After the stage is set, John pens a series of letters to seven churches in Asia (Rev. 2–3). Following the letters, John is taken up to heaven to see visions of God's heavenly court (Rev. 5–6) and becomes a witness to three series of seven judgments symbolized by seals that are opened (6:1–8:1), trumpets that sound (8:2–11:19), and bowls that are poured out (15:1–16:21). But before the seven bowls are poured out, Revelation reveals the Dragon, the Beasts, and the Lamb (12:1–14:20). The book ends with the final judgment of Babylon (17:1–19:10) and the coming of Christ in victory (19:11–15). The millennium period that follows (20:1–10) gives way to the final judgment (20:11–15) and the establishment of the new heaven, new earth, new Jerusalem, and new Eden (21:1–22:5).

Outline of Revelation

I. Prologue (1:1–3)
II. Epistolary Greeting (1:4–8)
III. Inaugural Vision of the Exalted Christ (1:9–20)
IV. The Letters to the Seven Churches of Asia (2:1–3:22)

V. John's Visions in Heaven (4:1–22:5)
   1. The Throne of God, the Scroll, and the Lamb (4:1–5:14)
   2. The Seven Seals (6:1–8:5)
   3. The Seven Trumpets (8:6–11:19)
   4. The Dragon, the First and Second Beasts, and the Lamb (12:1–14:20)
   5. The Seven Bowls (15:1–16:21)
   6. The Fall of Babylon (17:1–19:5)
   7. The Coming of the Word of God with the Armies of Heaven (19:6–21)
   8. The Millennial Reign of Christ (20:1–6)
   9. The Final Judgment of Satan and the Dead (20:7–15)
   10. The New Heaven, New Earth, New Jerusalem, and New Eden (21:1–22:5)

VI. Epilogue (22:6–21)

The Prologue and Epistolary Greeting (1:1–8)

Although John penned this book, the readers learn from the beginning that this is "the revelation from Jesus Christ" (1:1). His authority stands behind the book as the one who shows "his servants what must soon take place" (1:1). The contents of this book are, in the first place, a message from Christ to the churches in John's day (1:11). The opening greeting of this extended letter focuses on Jesus Christ, who gave witness, died, rose from the dead, and is now "the ruler of the kings of the earth" (1:5). Although many have speculated about the meaning of the symbols in Revelation, every reader needs to keep in view that the book is principally about Jesus Christ, his salvation, and his rule. Revelation is the culmination of the New Testament story.

The obverse of this coin bears the image of Domitian and the reverse bears the image of his son who had died yet is portrayed as young Jupiter, who sits on a sphere and is surrounded by seven stars. The imagery denotes his sovereignty over the whole world. The inscription reads, "divine Caesar, son of the emperor Domitian." Christ stands as the counterpoint to such claims (Rev. 1:16). *Classical Numismatic Group, Inc./www.cngcoins.com*

Inaugural Vision of the Exalted Christ (1:9–20)

In the opening vision, John sees "someone like a son of man" (1:13), as in the vision in Daniel (Dan. 7:13; Rev. 1:7, 13). This vision of Jesus identifies him with the Ancient of Days (cf. Dan. 7:9–10; Rev. 1:12–16). He is the one who was dead but is now alive and holds all authority over death and Hades, the abode of the dead (Rev. 1:18). But he is also seen with seven stars in his right hand (1:16). The image depicts his sovereignty and is likely a counterpoint to Domitian's imperial claims to world dominion and power.

The stars, along with the seven lampstands (1:12), also demonstrate Christ's sovereignty over the churches and their "angels" (1:20). The angels (messengers) may be their human leaders or, more likely, angelic beings in charge of the churches. The seven churches of Asia are offered assurance that, in the midst of their sufferings, Christ, and no other, is the true sovereign.

The Letters to the Seven Churches of Asia (2:1–3:22)

These short seven letters are filled with references to the situations of the churches and allusions to the surrounding environment of every city. For example, near Laodicea lay Colossae with its cold-water supply and Hierapolis, which was known for its hot springs. Both water supplies were beneficial. But the Laodicean church's faith was like lukewarm, unpalatable water (3:15–16).

Laodicea had a medical school whose leadership was well known in the field of ophthalmology during the first century. Many salves were used for treatment of the eyes in antiquity, but we find frequent reference to "Phrygian powder," Phrygia being the region where Laodicea was located. The church had become metaphorically blind. Christ now counsels them to obtain from him "salve to put on your eyes, so you can see" (3:18).[12]

The hot thermal mineral waters that flowed through pipes from Hierapolis were lukewarm and unpalatable by the time they reached Laodicea.
© 2012 by Zondervan

Hierapolis baths
Todd Bolen/BiblePlaces.com

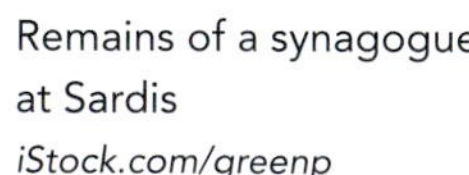

Remains of a synagogue at Sardis
iStock.com/greenp

Each of the seven letters follows the same outline. First, they begin with a reference back to the initial vision of the exalted Christ in chapter 1 (cf., e.g., 2:1 and 1:12–13, 16, 20). Second, they offer a comforting statement that the sovereign and exalted Lord is with his churches and that he knows their condition (e.g., 2:2, 9, 13). Third, as in epideictic rhetoric, the letters praise the churches for their honorable deeds and blame them for their shameful conduct (e.g., 2:2–6, 9, 13–15). Raymond Brown notes that "three sorts of problems confront the seven churches: false teaching (Ephesus, Pergamum, Thyatira); persecution (Smyrna, Philadelphia); and complacency (Sardis, Laodicea)."[13] The fourth element is a call to hear what the Spirit says to the churches and the exhortation to turn from evil and hold fast to what they have (e.g., 2:7, 10, 16–17a). Finally, the letters end with a promise to those who overcome the adversity and temptations they face (e.g., 2:7, 11, 17b).

The letters to the seven churches show Christ's knowledge of and concern for his people. Though exalted, he remains their vigilant leader. These churches do not represent seven church ages, as some popular expositors suggest, but rather show how Christ is engaged with his people in the midst of the theological, social, and spiritual issues they face. The letters offer assurance and hope as they call believers to stand firm in the faith and to not give way to evil.

John's Visions in Heaven (4:1–22:5)

From 4:1 onward, John presents the visions given him when taken up into the heavens: "After this I looked, and there before me was a door standing open in heaven. And the voice I had first heard speaking to me like a trumpet said, 'Come up here, and I will show you what must take place after this'" (4:1). The voice calls John up to the heavenly places to see the unfolding of the final events of history. Apparently this is not a physical journey, since he clarifies that he was "in the spirit" (4:2; cf. Paul's account of his vision in 2 Cor. 12:1–4). The voice is a summons to John, not to the whole church at the time of the rapture as some have suggested. John does not describe the church's escape hatch from the troubles of this age.

The Throne of God, the Scroll, and the Lamb (4:1–5:14)

In chapter 4 John shows his readers the throne of God in heaven. The scene around the throne echoes Ezekiel 1, where "the heavens were opened and I saw visions of God" (Ezek. 1:1). Around the throne of God, he sees "twenty-four elders" (Rev. 4:4), who appear to be celestial beings with ruling authority since they sit on thrones. These worship God (4:11; 5:14), offer John the meaning of the visions (5:5; 7:13–17), and have a special relation with the people of God (5:8b; 11:16–18; 14:1–3). Four living creatures gather around the throne as well

The scroll with seven seals (Rev. 5:1) had seals along the outer edge that were attached to strings wrapped around the scroll. The signet of the owner of the scroll was pressed into clay when the scroll was sealed. Any tampering with the scroll would have been evident to all. The seals pictured here are called *bullae* and on display at the Israel Museum.
© 2018 by Zondervan

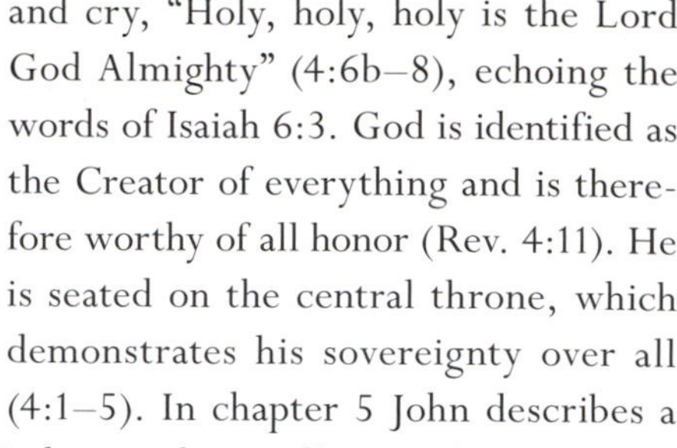

and cry, "Holy, holy, holy is the Lord God Almighty" (4:6b–8), echoing the words of Isaiah 6:3. God is identified as the Creator of everything and is therefore worthy of all honor (Rev. 4:11). He is seated on the central throne, which demonstrates his sovereignty over all (4:1–5). In chapter 5 John describes a sealed scroll and the Lamb to whom God gives the scroll, since he is deemed worthy to open it when none other can (5:2–3, 7, 9–10). Once again, Revelation identifies Christ as the one who has redeemed all humanity through his death and who exercises his sovereign rule.

Reproduction of a papyrus scroll found in Egypt and sealed with a clay *bullea* and seal impression.
Historic Connections, www.historicconnections.com

Numerous suggestions have been made regarding the meaning of the scroll. Is it the eternal decrees of God, a contract-deed of the world, an account of the destiny of humanity and the world, the Lamb's Book of Life (3:5; 13:8; 17:8; 20:12, 15), the Old Testament, or the prophecy itself? Given that the scroll is handed to the Lamb by the One who sits on the throne (5:7), it is likely a royal decree. A document from the Dead Sea Scrolls speaks of the books of King Darius of Persia, saying, "Among the books was found a scroll sealed with seven seals of the ring of Darius, his father" (4Q550). The Lamb breaks the seals, and the final decrees of God are enacted.

The Seven Seals (6:1–8:5)

As the seven seals are broken, the four horsemen of the Apocalypse appear (6:1–8). This is the beginning of divine judgment as they come to conquer, take peace from the earth, and bring famine and death. The fifth seal is opened, and the scene shifts to those who had been martyred (6:9–11), indicating that the church is indeed passing through this time of tribulation and has not been "raptured" in 4:1. The opening of the sixth seal brings on cataclysmic events in the heavens and on earth. None will escape the wrath of the Lamb, no matter how high their social status (6:12–17). On the other hand, God seals and cares for his own (7:1–17), despite the sufferings they endure.

As the seventh seal is broken, there is a dramatic pause—silence in heaven (8:1–5)—before the seven trumpets sound (8:6–11:19). Interpreters of Revelation take different positions on whether the seven seals, trumpets, and bowls are progressive events that follow one after another or whether the trumpets and the bowls recapitulate or recount the judgments of the seven trumpets in greater detail. The former view is the simplest reading of Revelation, whereas the recapitulation view recognizes how the seventh seal, trumpet, and bowl all point to the same final climax of God's judgments (8:1–5; 11:15; 16:17). A third

The Number 7 in Revelation

Chapters 6–16 present visions of seven seals broken, seven trumpets sounding, and seven bowls poured out. These may be viewed as successive events. Intervening visions are found between the sixth and seventh seals and trumpets, and between the seventh trumpet and the bowls:

Seals	*Trumpets*	*Bowls*	
123456(intervening vision)7	*123456(intervening vision)7*	*(intervening vision)*	*1234567*

Alternately, seals, bowls, and trumpets may not depict successive events but may recapitulate the judgments depicted in the previous series:

Seals	*1*	*2*	*3*	*4*	*5*	*6*	*(intervening visions)*	*7*
Trumpets	*1*	*2*	*3*	*4*	*5*	*6*	*(intervening visions)*	*7*
Bowls	*1*	*2*	*3*	*4*	*5*	*6*		*7*

option is that opening the seventh seal carries within it the seven trumpets and likewise the seventh trumpet carries within it the seven bowls. Under any of these readings, the seven seals, trumpets, and bowls are all parts of God's judgment.

The Seven Trumpets (8:6–11:19)

Angels sound the seven trumpets, the first four of which burn a third of the land, contaminate a third of the sea with blood, poison a third of the rivers and springs, and darken a third of the celestial bodies (8:6–12). The fifth trumpet brings figurative locusts on the earth (cf. Ex. 10:1–20), while the sixth results in the death of a third of humanity (9:1–21). God's wrath has come (11:18). Two witnesses of God appear but are then martyred before the seventh trumpet sounds (11:1–14). These may represent the whole church or possibly two historic witnesses, such as Enoch and Elijah or Moses and Elijah (cf. Mark 9:4). Another angel sounds the seventh trumpet and proclaims the victory of God, recalled in the Hallelujah Chorus of Handel's *Messiah*: "The kingdom of the world has become the kingdom of our Lord and of his Messiah, and he will reign for ever and ever" (11:15).

A painted vase with a Greek soldier blowing a salpinx, a straight bronze trumpet used by soldiers to signal and get a crowd's attention
The Print Collector/Alamy Stock Photo

The Dragon, the First and Second Beasts, and the Lamb (12:1–14:20)

Before the seven bowls are poured out, Revelation inserts visions of the woman and the dragon (12:1–17), the beast out of the sea (13:1–10), the second beast out of the earth (13:11–18), and finally the Lamb of God (14:1–6). John describes the woman as "clothed with the sun, with the moon under her feet and a crown of twelve stars on her head" (12:1). Although the woman has been variously identified as the church or even female deities such as Artemis and Isis, she is most

Nero Redivivus

The belief that Nero was still alive was widespread in the late first century AD. Dio Chrysostom said, "For so far as the rest of his subjects were concerned, there was nothing to prevent his continuing to be Emperor for all time, seeing that even now everybody wishes he were still alive. And the great majority do believe that he is, although in a certain sense he has died not once but often along with those who had been firmly convinced that he was still alive" (*Or.* 21).

likely Israel, given the imagery taken from Joseph's dream: "I had another dream, and this time the sun and moon and eleven stars were bowing down to me" (Gen. 37:9). She then gives birth to the Messiah (Rev. 12:4–5). John identifies the dragon as the devil, Satan himself, who deceives and was set to destroy the Messiah (12:3–9). Through the mayhem the focal point of Revelation remains the gospel story.

The first beast in John's vision is slain and returns to life, likely an allusion to the belief that Nero had come back to life or had never died (13:1–10).

The second beast promoted the ruler cult and may be identified as Domitian. This beast ordered the inhabitants of the earth "to set up an image in honor of the beast who was wounded by the sword and yet lived" (13:14). The counterpoint to the dragon and the beasts is the Lamb and the 144,000 "who had been redeemed from the earth" (14:3). The number is symbolic of all those who "were purchased from among mankind" (14:4). The juxtaposition of the beast with the Lamb calls for a decision announced by the angels: either fear God, giving him glory and worshiping him as the one who made all things (14:6–7), or worship the beast and experience the wrath of God (14:9–20). Revelation calls its readers to align with God and his purposes.

The Seven Bowls (15:1–16:21)

Before the seven bowls of God's wrath are poured out, John sees a vision of seven angels with seven plagues of God's wrath (15:1–8). As God's wrath is coming to completion, John also describes his vision of those who emerged victorious over the beast. Together they intone the hymn of Moses, which extolls God's mighty deeds (15:3–4; cf. Ex. 15:1–18). The redeemed are like the people of Israel who were liberated from Egypt in the exodus. The gospel story is again viewed as God's new exodus. As in the first exodus, plagues are poured out as the bowls of God's wrath are emptied (16:1–21). The final declaration comes as the seventh angel pours out his bowl: "It is done!" (16:17).

The Fall of Babylon (17:1–19:5)

The fall of Babylon is a symbolic portrayal of the overthrow of Rome. Babylon was a common code name for Rome (see 1 Pet. 5:13), which here is identified as the "seven hills on which the woman sits" (Rev. 17:9). The woman is one who sits "on a scarlet beast" (17:3) and is identified as "BABYLON THE GREAT" (17:5). The fall of Babylon-Rome is an overthrow of all her immorality and material excess (18:1–3), and the merchants who grew rich by her lamented her downfall (18:9–20).

Her wealth and excess are shattered (18:21–24). The doom of Babylon, or Rome, stands as a dreadful warning for all times that God will judge the world's excesses of wealth and moral corruption (cf. James 5:1–6). The lament over Babylon's judgment is matched by the praise of God in heaven for her downfall (19:1–10).

The Coming of the Word of God with the Armies of Heaven (19:6–21)

The climax of Revelation comes with the advent of Christ, the Word of God (19:13), who is also called the "KING OF KINGS AND LORD OF LORDS" (19:16). Just as he was deemed worthy to open the scroll handed him by God, so now he is hailed as the one who "treads the winepress of the fury of the wrath of God Almighty" (19:15). His coming marks the overthrow of the beast and those who serve him (19:19–21). For the suffering Christians in Asia and for Christians through the ages, the promise of Christ's advent and participation in the marriage feast of the Lamb are the greatest of hopes amid conflicts, adversities, and opposition (19:6–9). God reigns supreme throughout the ages and down to the end.

The Millennial Reign of Christ (20:1–6)

Interpreters of Revelation have understood the millennial reign of Christ in various ways (20:2–5). Those who hold to a *premillennial interpretation* state that Christ will return before a literal one thousand years, or a millennium. Before this time the situation in the world will become worse and worse. A variation on that view is that the one thousand years is a real period of peace under the rule of Christ, but the time span is not a literal one thousand years. Christ comes *before* this millennial rule is established. Others, however, align with a *postmillennial interpretation.* Under this view the millennium is a figurative period. Christ will not return before the millennium but rather *after* it is established by the church, which has taken up the task of redeeming the world and spreading the gospel of Christ in both word and deed. At the end of this period, Christ will return. Many interpreters, however, opt for an interpretation that is less optimistic. They hold to an *amillennial interpretation*, which states that there will not be a millennium established by the church prior to the return of Christ or inaugurated by Christ after his return. Rather, the millennium is only a symbolic way of speaking of the triumph of Christ and the present age of the church in the world where both good and evil coexist.

The Final Judgment of Satan and the Dead (20:7–15)

Surprisingly, Revelation contemplates a period after the millennium when Satan will be released and judged (20:7–10) and the dead will be judged according to their deeds (20:11–15). These are the ones who do not take part in Christ's millennial reign (20:4–6). These events will set the stage for the final renewal of all God's creation.

The New Heaven, New Earth, New Jerusalem, and New Eden (21:1–22:5)

Before the final epilogue (22:6–21), John records the vision of the renewal of all God's creation, including a new heaven, new earth, new Jerusalem, and restored Eden. The key to this section is God's proclamation, "I am making everything new!" (21:5). This section is filled with promise and serves as the great hope for the church in John's age and through time: "Those who are victorious will inherit all this, and I will be their God and they will be my children" (21:7). The promise here echoes that given to the victorious in the seven churches in chapters 2 and 3. As Christ said to the Ephesian church, "To the one who is victorious, I will give the right to eat from the tree of life, which is in the paradise of God" (2:7; and see 2:11, 17, 26–28; 3:5, 12, 21). The promise of God in the end serves to motivate faithful service to him in the present.

The message Revelation teaches is that the people of God will endure suffering, which, for many, will mean martyrdom (12:11; 13:7; 14:13). The Apocalypse also describes how the judgments of God will be measured out (14:10, 19; 15:1). Evil does not have the final word. Revelation also shows that God's faithful servants are not destined for wrath (1 Thess. 5:9; Rom. 5:9) but are protected from it (Rev. 7:3–4; 9:4; cf. Israel in Egypt in Ex. 8:22–23; 9:2–4, 26; 10:23). God is selective in his wrath (Rev. 14:9–10; 16:2), but this does not mean that his people will not suffer. The churches are called to remain faithful during this period of great adversity (2:7, 11, 17, 26–28; 3:5, 12), knowing that God can keep his own and offers them a future resplendent with hope. They should not give way to the idolatrous worship of the empire and the allure of its immoral practices. Revelation calls its readers to honor and worship God. At its heart, Revelation is about Jesus Christ—his death, resurrection, and sovereignty—and the victory God's suffering people have through him (1:5; 7:14; 12:11). In the most vivid ways possible, Revelation affirms that God rules, Christ triumphs, their enemies are defeated, God's people flourish, and Christ's universal rule is established.

AUTHOR AND DATE

John penned this book either while on the island of Patmos or from Ephesus after his exile (1:1, 4, 9; 22:8), but he attributes the book's message to Jesus Christ (1:1, 12–20). The Revelation of Jesus Christ comes with the authority of the Lord himself, who communicates to John through the Holy Spirit (2:11, 17, 29; 3:6, 13, 22; 14:13; 19:10; 22:17). By pointing to the Holy Spirit's agency, John stands as a prophet who communicates God's message (1 Sam. 10:6; 2 Sam. 23:2; Zech. 7:12), while the visions he received locate him within the apocalyptic tradition. He was, as Richard Bauckham says, a "prophetic visionary."[14]

John was a common name in the first-century Jewish community. The author says nothing about himself, so identifying which John wrote this book presents a challenge. We can say he was known to the seven churches of Asia (Rev. 1:9–11). He was also most likely a native speaker of Aramaic. The Greek of Revelation is replete with mother-tongue interference, that is, the author's Greek style shows a considerable level of Semitic influence. Some, however, attribute the unique features of his Greek style to the influence of the Septuagint or a combination of these two factors. In either case, we can safely identify the author as Jewish, not only because of his linguistic ability but also his extensive use of the Old Testament. Revelation alludes to the Old Testament more than any other book of the New Testament, although John does not name his sources (e.g., Rev. 1:7, which draws from Dan. 7:13 and Zech. 12:10).

We have met a few people named John in the pages of the New Testament. John the Baptist is not likely the author, although he and his disciples have been suggested. John Mark, the author of the gospel of Mark, is another unlikely candidate, as Eusebius rightly saw (*Eccl. hist.* 7.25.15). Many of the early church fathers attribute the book to John the apostle. Justin Martyr said, "And further, there was a certain man with us, whose name was John, one of the apostles of Christ, who prophesied, by a revelation that was made to him, that those who believed in our Christ would dwell a thousand years in Jerusalem" (*Dial.* 81.4). Irenaeus concurs, saying, "John also, the Lord's disciple, when beholding the sacerdotal and glorious advent of His kingdom, says in the Apocalypse: 'I turned to see the voice that spoke with me. And, being turned, I saw seven golden candlesticks'" (*Adv. Haer.* 4.20.11). Other church fathers agree with this ascription (Clement of Alexandria, *Strom.* 6.106–7; Tertullian, *Adv. Marc.* 3.14.3; Hippolytus, *De antichristo* 36–42).

The problem with the identification of the apostle John as the author is that the style of Revelation is distinctly different from the gospel or epistles of John. Also, the apocalyptic visions in Revelation find no parallel in other writings attributed to John. There are also marked theological differences between Revelation and the Johannine writings. While the gospel and epistle of John emphasize love, Revelation focuses on God's wrath. At the same time, both the gospel of John and Revelation refer to Jesus as the Word of God (John 1:1, 14; Rev. 19:13) and the Lamb (John 1:29, 36 and Rev. 5:6, 8). Both include "I am" statements from Jesus (John 10:11; 14:6; Rev. 1:8, 17–18) and identify him as the source of "living water" (John 7:37–39; Rev. 22:1). Moreover, the unique style of Revelation may be attributable to the nature of the visions John received. Also, John may not have had the help of an amanuensis or community, as was the case when he penned the gospel (John 21:24b). Despite the difficulties of identifying the apostle John as the author, we cannot dismiss this ascription outright.

An alternative theory of authorship is that a person known as John the Elder wrote Revelation. Eusebius discusses the question of authorship of Revelation and notes that there were two tombs in the city of Ephesus with the name of John on them and that there was another John referred to as John the Elder (*Hist. eccl.* 7.25–9–16; 3.39.2–4). Could this John be the author of Revelation? While this theory would solve the problem of the differences in style and perspective between the Johannine literature and Revelation, it remains no more than an interesting possibility that lacks solid evidence. The most likely author of the book of Revelation remains the apostle John.

Remains of a gate for the Hellenistic acropolis at Patmos, third century BC, a location that may have been active at the time of the writing of the book of Revelation.
Todd Bolen/BiblePlaces.com

Questions for Discussion

1. The letters to the seven churches in Revelation 2–3 addressed the situations of the Christian communities in the Roman province of Asia in the first century AD. What is their enduring message for churches today?
2. Compare the teaching on the state in Romans 13:1–7 and 1 Peter 2:13–17 and that found in Revelation. How and why do they differ? How does each of these texts inform our understanding of Christians' relationship to government today?
3. The various hymns of praise throughout Revelation, such as 5:9–10 and 11:15–18, outline the character of God and Christ. Locate these hymns and discuss their theology, comparing their emphases with those of contemporary Christian music.
4. Throughout the New Testament, teaching about eschatology, or the "last things," is intimately linked with Christian ethics rather than speculation about times and dates. As a prophetic book, how does Revelation connect eschatology with Christian conduct and hope?
5. Examine the ways your church understands the millennium in Revelation 20. How does that affect its views regarding Christian presence and work in contemporary society?

BIBLIOGRAPHY

Introductory

Fee, G. D. *Revelation.* NCCS. Eugene, OR: Cascade, 2011.

Gorman, M. J. *Reading Revelation Responsibly: Uncivil Worship and Witness—Following the Lamb into the New Creation.* Eugene, OR: Cascade, 2011.

Keener, C. S. *Revelation.* NIVAC. Grand Rapids: Zondervan, 2000.

Witherington, B., III. *Revelation.* NCBC. Cambridge: Cambridge University Press, 2003.

Advanced

Aune, D. E. *Revelation.* 3 vols. WBC. Nashville: Nelson, 1997–98.

Beale, G. K. *The Book of Revelation.* NIGTC. Grand Rapids: Eerdmans, 1999.

Koester, C. R. *Revelation.* AB. New Haven: Yale University Press, 2014.

Mounce, R. H. *The Book of Revelation.* NICNT. Grand Rapids: Eerdmans, 1997.

Osborne, G. R. *Revelation.* BECNT. Grand Rapids: Baker, 2002.

Smalley, S. S. *The Revelation to John.* Downers Grove, IL: InterVarsity Press, 2005.

NOTES

1. J. J. Collins, "Introduction: Towards the Morphology of a Genre," *Semeia* 14 (1979): 2. For an updated discussion of the genre, see J. J. Collins, ed., *The Oxford Handbook of Apocalyptic Literature* (Oxford: Oxford University Press, 2014).

2. F. D. Mazzaferri, *The Genre of the Book of Revelation from a Source-Critical Perspective* (Berlin: Walter de Gruyter, 1989), 379–83.

3. D. E. Aune, *Revelation 1–5* (Dallas: Word, 1997), 82.

4. W. Howard-Brook and A. Gwyther, *Unveiling Empire: Reading Revelation Then and Now* (Maryknoll, NY: Orbis, 1999), 103; S. R. F. Price, *Rituals and Power: The Roman Imperial Cult in Asia Minor* (Cambridge: Cambridge University Press, 1984), 249–74.

5. D. E. Aune, *Revelation 6–16* (Nashville: Thomas Nelson, 1998), 780.

6. Cited in Hans-Josef Klauck, *The Religious Context of Early Christianity: A Guide to Graeco-Roman Religions* (Minneapolis: Fortress, 2003), 290.

7. Klauck, *The Religious Context of Early Christianity*, 290–98.

8. W. Milligan, *The Revelation of John* (New York: Macmillan, 1887), 127.

9. Ibid., 153, 155.

10. On the origins of the pretribulation rapture theology, see G. E. Ladd, *The Blessed Hope* (Grand Rapids: Eerdmans, 1956) and R. H. Gundry, *The Church and the Tribulation* (Grand Rapids: Zondervan, 1973). Also see G. L. Archer and D. J. Moo, *Three Views on the Rapture: pre-, mid-, or post-Tribulation?* (Grand Rapids: Zondervan, 1996).

11. G. E. Ladd, *A Commentary on the Revelation of John* (Grand Rapids: Eerdmans, 1972), 13. See, for example, the way Nathan's prophecy to David embraced both his son Solomon and his descendant Jesus (2 Sam. 7:11b–16).

12. C. J. Hemer, *The Letters to the Seven Churches of Asia in their Local Setting* (Grand Rapids: Eerdmans; Livonia, Mich.: Dove, 1989), 186–91, 196–99. We do not have clear evidence that Laodicea's water was tepid, however.

13. R. E. Brown, *An Introduction to the New Testament* (New York: Doubleday, 1997), 782.

14. R. Bauckham, *The Climax of Prophecy: Studies on the Book of Revelation* (Edinburgh: T&T Clark, 1993), 150.

Chapter 27

THE PRESERVATION AND COMMUNICATION OF THE NEW TESTAMENT

Codex Sinaiticus, showing the final page of John's gospel, fourth century AD.

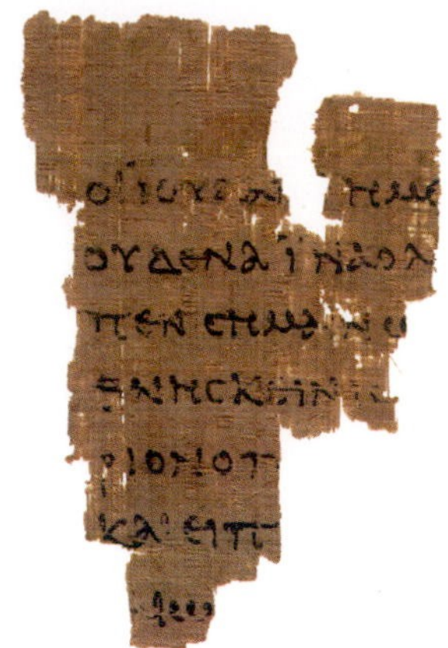

Scholars believe this is the earliest New Testament manuscript fragment in our possession (cataloged as $\mathfrak{P}^{52}$). It is a very small papyrus piece (2.5 x 3.5 inches) dated from AD 125–150.
Reproduced by courtesy of the University Librarian and Director, The John Rylands University Library, The University of Manchester

The New Testament we read today is the result of many centuries of effort. Manuscripts originally written on papyrus were copied and preserved from generation to generation. Leading authorities and church councils determined which writings should enter the church's final collection of twenty-seven books. And as the New Testament moved out of the Greek-speaking world, scholars had to translate its words into new languages.

Each of these three areas—text criticism, the canon, and translation theory—are important disciplines. A modern English translation has inherited a long history of debate and decision-making, and we now turn to these issues.

THE TEXT OF THE NEW TESTAMENT

We do not possess any of the original autographs of New Testament texts. But these originals were carefully copied and preserved, and today we possess an abundance of manuscripts—over 5,700 (from the second to the fourteenth centuries)—that give us some portion of the New Testament.[1]

The earliest copies of important New Testament writings were circulating by the late first century. The first formal printing of the Greek New Testament did not take place until 1516. For 1,400 years, therefore, the New Testament was subject to the hazards of hand-copying. In the earliest centuries, the Christians who produced these manuscripts were well-intentioned, pious believers who wanted to pass on to others copies of valuable Christian works. The evidence shows they were incredibly successful, but they did make inevitable minor mistakes, which textual criticism seeks to reverse.

The Writing of Ancient Books

In antiquity a variety of materials was used for writing surfaces: wood, bone, broken pottery, papyrus, and parchment (treated animal skin). For the earliest New Testament period, papyrus is the most important for our study. Fifteen-foot stalks of papyrus were harvested from the Nile Delta, cleaned, flattened, and cut into twenty-inch strips. These were laid side by side, overlapping each strip so that its natural glue would bond the pieces together. Then a second layer running at right angles was laid down and glued. This final sheet was then trimmed, making a page about 20 x 9 inches. This page was polished into a smooth writing surface.

The making of papyrus
Veronika Kovalenko/Shutterstock

Next, workers glued numerous sheets side by side to make a commercial roll for consumers, such as professional scribes, who cut off only the length needed.

The scribe used ink made of charcoal and water (along with a variety of acids). He marked a section with pin pricks to square and frame a writing area, and then began writing in columns about three inches wide.

Papyrus was grown in Egypt from the third millennium BC. By the New Testament era, it had become the chief source of writing material.
toeytoey/Shutterstock

The scroll, made of either papyrus or parchment, was the earliest and most important form of writing for official documents in the Hellenistic world ("volume" comes from the Latin *volumen*, "roll"). Late in the first century, however, another invention surfaces. For some time, secretaries had taken temporary notations on wood tablets with a waxed surface. These could be tied together at the margin, making a "book." Some scribes left the papyrus as sheets, folded them in the middle, and stitched sheets together at the center. This was called a "codex," which became a favorite form for the early Christians.

Text Variants

Many copies of New Testament books circulated in the earliest centuries, with varying levels of quality. Some copyists introduced errors by accident, and these were copied diligently by later scribes. In other cases, copyists intentionally made changes in order to improve the text. By comparing texts together, we can uncover errors and reconstruct what was in the original text. In this effort, New Testament scholarship has been extremely successful. Such "variant readings" are cataloged, organized, evaluated, and presented in any critical edition of the Greek New Testament.

Scribal methods were well-known in Judea as well. This ink well (along with four others) was discovered at Qumran near the Dead Sea. Since all were in one room, the area has been popularly called Qumran's "scriptorium."
Z. Radovan/www.BibleLandPictures.com

Where do these variants come from? Inadvertent errors were common. Some came from simply seeing the text incorrectly. A scribe might misread an abbreviation. In 1 Timothy 3:16 some manuscripts tell us that "God was manifest in the flesh." Others read: "who was manifested in the flesh" (RSV). In Greek, God was often abbreviated as QMSM; "who" is OS. These two words were easily confused.

Sometimes a line might end the same way a previous line ends, and the copyist's eye would skip a line. A variant reading of John 17:15 thus has Jesus praying the wrong prayer: "I do not pray that you should keep them from the evil one." Jesus actually prays, "My prayer is not that *you take them out of the world but that* you protect them from the evil one" (emphasis added).

The Greek letters PMA often abbreviate the word *pneuma* ("spirit"). But POMA is the Greek word for drink. So at 1 Corinthians 12:13, some texts read: "All were made to drink of one drink" instead of "all [were] given the one Spirit to drink." The error makes little sense.

Occasionally the scribe knows another New Testament text so well that his mind inserts words from elsewhere. Luke 11:1–2 offers a shorter version of the

A Scribe's Complaint

Codex Vaticanus is one of the most important biblical texts we own. It is a vellum (animal skin) codex from the fourth century and is located in the Vatican. It has 759 sheets (617 Old Testament, 142 New Testament). Each sheet has three columns with forty-two lines to a column. It contains the entire Septuagint (except Maccabees and Manasseh). The New Testament lacks the Pastoral Epistles, Philemon, and Revelation. Because the ink was faded, at some point a later scribe decided to write over each letter. When something seemed unclear, he felt free to "correct" it.

There is an odd comment in the margin at Hebrews 11:3. A later scribe, frustrated that someone had changed something unnecessarily, scribbled the following in the margin: "Fool and knave! Can't you leave the old reading alone and not alter it?"[2]

Lord's Prayer, which can be found in full form in Matthew 6:9–13. Here is the original abbreviated prayer, but placed in brackets are inserted scribal "harmonizations." The final addition in the last line is a remarkable expansion coming no doubt from the scribe's own piety.

[our] Father [who is in heaven]
Let your name be holy
Let your kingdom come
[let your Holy Spirit come upon us and cleanse us]

Sometimes the scribe cannot make sense of what he sees, or he doesn't entirely like it, and he tries to improve it. These are *intentional* changes. John 5:4 does not exist in most modern New Testaments because a later scribe decided to explain why the lame man was trying to get into the pool: "An angel of the Lord would stir the water." Scribes were also unclear about where this miracle occurred. Various manuscripts offer: Bethzatha, Bezatha, Belzetha, Bethsaida, Bethesda. Most text critics prefer Bethzatha.

Intentional changes like this in John 5 are benign. Sometimes scribes tried to clarify what seemed unclear or wrong. Mark 1:2 gives a composite quote from Isaiah and Malachi but credits it to Isaiah. Some scribes sought to improve this

The Soldier's Remark

Sometimes scholars suggest textual emendations to the New Testament when there is *no* evidence for them in any manuscript. For example, in Mark 15:34–35 Jesus calls out to God (*"Eloi! Eloi!"*). Some of those standing nearby (likely including the Roman soldiers) misunderstand this Aramaic phrase and say, "Listen, he is calling *Elijah*. . . . Let's see if Elijah comes to take him down." However, there is limited Jewish evidence for seeing Elijah as a rescuer, nor (if the Roman soldiers are involved) would they likely even know about Elijah.

Some scholars therefore suggest that the Greek text misrepresents what actually took place. The word for Elijah in Greek is *Helias*. But if we change one letter it becomes *Helios*, the "sun"—which represented a god in antiquity. When Jesus is on the cross, darkness covers Jerusalem (15:33). Therefore, these scholars insist, it would be natural for the soldiers and others around the cross to think that Jesus is calling on the sun to restore him. But earlier copyists of the gospel of Mark confused *Helios* for *Helias*, and soon the change was permanent.[3] This may be a creative suggestion, but it is purely speculative. There is no textual evidence to support it, and it is doubtful that it improves the text.

by changing Mark: "as it says in *the prophets*." Other scribes were motivated by doctrine. In Mark 13:32 Jesus says, "But about that day or hour no one knows, not even the angels in heaven, nor the Son, but only the Father." Scribes could not reconcile this statement of Jesus's ignorance with his divinity and their solution was simple. They removed the phrase "nor the Son."

Text Types

The earliest manuscripts of the New Testament are papyrus fragments; we possess about 115 of these. These generally come from the period up to the fourth century and give us excellent insight into the earliest informal development of our texts. They are classified with a P and are numbered [P^{52}, P^{66}]. For instance, P^{66} dates to AD 200 and holds 104 6 x 5-inch pages containing numerous chapters from John's gospel. The earliest copies of Peter's two letters are P^{72}, a third-century codex.

From the fourth to the ninth century we have 310 majuscule manuscripts written on parchment. When Christianity became an official faith in the empire, the copying of manuscripts was done by professional scribes who carefully produced beautifully embellished and formatted documents for study and worship. Some of these codices are classified with symbols (Sinaiticus is indicated by א [Hebrew letter *aleph*]), but each of these also receive a number preceded by a zero: 01 Codex Sinaiticus, 02 Codex Alexandrinus, 03 Codex Vaticanus, 032 Codex Washingtoniensis, and so on.

In the ninth century a smaller cursive handwriting style developed for more rapid copying. We have 2,877 of these, generally called "minuscules." These manuscripts are classified with simple Arabic numbers: Codex 1 is a twelfth-century codex now in Basel, and Erasmus used it to print the first Greek New Testament. Codex 565 is the Codex Purpureus Petropolitanus ("the purple codex of St. Petersburg") and comes from the tenth century.

Portions of the New Testament also appeared in the worship literature of the early church, called "lectionaries." Here texts were arranged according to the sequence of desired readings for the church year. We now have 2,432 manuscripts of this order. These are classified by *l* (e.g., *l*45) or Lect. (Lect.55).

Another source of information about the early New Testament is the "versions"—translations as early as the second century, such as Syriac, Latin, Coptic, and Armenian. An early version may reflect a text reading just like a Greek manuscript but do so indirectly. A second indirect source is the "patristic citation." The church fathers wrote letters and sermons and cited the New Testament texts in their library. Thus, if a bishop in Alexandria quoted a text in the early fourth century, that citation is one more witness to texts circulating in this period.

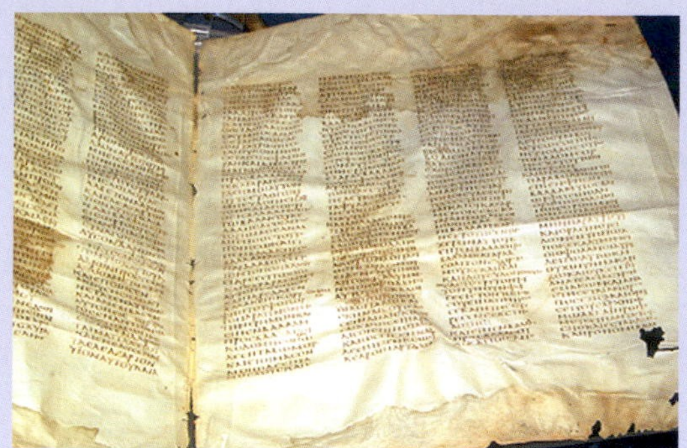

Codex Sinaiticus is an important uncial manuscript copied in the fourth century. It was discovered at St. Catherine's monastery on Mount Sinai in the nineteenth century. Shown here is the ending of 1 John and beginning of 2 John.
Public Domain

Codex Sinaiticus Discovered

The German scholar Constantin von Tischendorf pursued ancient manuscripts in the nineteenth century. In 1844 he visited St. Catherine's monastery on Mount Sinai, and according to his report (disputed by the monks at St. Catherine's), in their library he saw parchment sheets piled and ready for the fire. He saved forty-three pages from the Greek Old Testament, urged the monks to stop, borrowed these texts, and returned to Leipzig, where he published them in 1846.

In 1853 and 1859 Tischendorf returned to Mount Sinai with a copy of the published sheets he took in 1844. One monk said he had something better. From his closet he unwrapped a complete codex containing much of the Old Testament and the entire New Testament in pristine condition. Tischendorf studied it all night, and after lengthy negotiations the monastery presented it to their protector, the Russian czar, as a gift. This text, Codex Sinaiticus, was published in 1862. Scholars now believe the codex originates from the fourth century. Later, St. Catherine's offered up many more manuscripts, including twelve more sheets from Codex Sinaiticus.

St. Catherine's monastery is perhaps the oldest continually occupied Christian monastery in the world.
Marc Ryckaert/Wikimedia Commons, CC BY 3.0

Text Families

Comparative analysis of text variants remained in its infancy until the seventeenth century (though Jerome refers to an edited Greek New Testament from Lucian of Antioch in the early fourth century). Desiderius Erasmus (1469–1536) was one of the earliest critical students of the Greek New Testament. His scholarship led to a publication of a variety of ancient texts (Jerome, Seneca, Plutarch), including the Greek New Testament in 1516. He based his text on Byzantine manuscripts resembling those coming from Lucian. By the late sixteenth century, scholars felt this was the best text possible—called the Received Text or the *Textus Receptus*; it became the basis for the 1611 King James Version.

But soon scholars began to find other manuscripts outside the *Textus Receptus* tradition. For instance, in 1627 the patriarch of Constantinople presented King Charles I of England with Codex Alexandrinus, an exquisite fifth-century vellum codex containing 773 10 x 12-inch pages of text; most of the Old and New Testaments were there except for lost leaves from Matthew, John, and 2 Corinthians. Such discoveries convinced scholars that more had to be done. Theoretical principles had to be developed to bring order out of chaos.

The solution came in the eighteenth century when scholars agreed that a text variant could not be decided by the sheer number of manuscripts that supported it. They spoke of text "genealogies" or "families," where one early text a scribe reproduced in turn became the source for multiple others. If twenty manuscripts were copied from a poor original, these twenty only represented the one manuscript and did not bring twenty different readings. They belong to a family. Families were determined by tracking the errors and classifying the manuscripts that held them. Thus, manuscripts could be sorted and their relative value assessed.

By the early nineteenth century, scholars began publishing Greek texts that rivaled the venerated *Textus Receptus*. Scholars were hunting for new manuscripts, and even the

This page from the United Bible Society's Greek New Testament shows the Greek text and the textual apparatus for Luke 11. Note how footnotes point to textual data where variant readings are listed. Each entry in the apparatus is then given a letter grade.

The Greek-English New Testament: UBS Fifth Revised Edition and New International Version, © 2015 by Zondervan

11.3-11 ΚΑΤΑ ΛΟΥΚΑΝ 486

3 τὸν ἄρτον ἡμῶν τὸν ἐπιούσιον δίδου ἡμῖν τὸ καθ᾽ ἡμέραν·
4 καὶ ἄφες ἡμῖν τὰς ἁμαρτίας ἡμῶν,
καὶ γὰρ αὐτοὶ ἀφίομεν παντὶ ὀφείλοντι ἡμῖν·
καὶ μὴ εἰσενέγκῃς ἡμᾶς εἰς πειρασμόν[4].
5 Καὶ εἶπεν πρὸς αὐτούς, Τίς ἐξ ὑμῶν ἕξει φίλον καὶ
πορεύσεται πρὸς αὐτὸν μεσονυκτίου καὶ εἴπῃ αὐτῷ, Φίλε,
χρῆσόν μοι τρεῖς ἄρτους, **6** ἐπειδὴ φίλος μου παρεγένετο ἐξ
ὁδοῦ πρός με καὶ οὐκ ἔχω ὃ παραθήσω αὐτῷ· **7** κἀκεῖνος
ἔσωθεν ἀποκριθεὶς εἴπῃ, Μή μοι κόπους πάρεχε· ἤδη ἡ
θύρα κέκλεισται καὶ τὰ παιδία μου μετ᾽ ἐμοῦ εἰς τὴν κοίτην
εἰσίν· οὐ δύναμαι ἀναστὰς δοῦναί σοι. **8** λέγω ὑμῖν, εἰ καὶ οὐ
δώσει αὐτῷ ἀναστὰς διὰ τὸ εἶναι φίλον αὐτοῦ, διά γε τὴν
ἀναίδειαν αὐτοῦ ἐγερθεὶς δώσει αὐτῷ ὅσων χρῄζει. **9** κἀγὼ
ὑμῖν λέγω, αἰτεῖτε καὶ δοθήσεται ὑμῖν, ζητεῖτε καὶ εὑρήσετε,
κρούετε καὶ ἀνοιγήσεται ὑμῖν· **10** πᾶς γὰρ ὁ αἰτῶν λαμβά-
νει καὶ ὁ ζητῶν εὑρίσκει καὶ τῷ κρούοντι ἀνοιγ[ήσ]εται[5].
11 τίνα δὲ ἐξ ὑμῶν τὸν πατέρα αἰτήσει ὁ υἱὸς ἰχθύν[6], καὶ ἀντὶ

καὶ ἐπὶ τῆς γῆς (*see* Mt 6.10) ℵ[1] (ℵ* οὕτω καί) (ℵ[2] A C D P W Δ Θ 892 *omit* τῆς) Ψ *f*[13] 28 33 157 180 205 (565[supp] *omit* σου) 579 597 700 1006 1010 1071 1241 1243 1292 1424 1505 *Byz* [E F G H] *Lect* it[aur, b, c, d, e, f, ff2, i, (l), q, r1] vg[mss] syr[p, h] cop[bo] eth slav (Titus-Bostra) Cyril

[4] **4** {A} πειρασμόν 𝔓[75] ℵ[*,2] B L 1 700 1342 vg syr[s] cop[sa, boPt] arm geo Marcion[acc. to Tertullian] Origen Cyril; Tertullian[vid] Augustine[vid] // πειρασμὸν ἀλλὰ ῥῦσαι ἡμᾶς ἀπὸ τοῦ πονηροῦ (*see* Mt 6.13) A C D W Δ Θ Ψ *f*[13] 28 33 157 180 205 565 579 597 892 1006 1010 1070 1241 1243 1292 1424 1505 *Byz* [E F G H] *Lect* it[aur, b, c, d, f, ff2, i, l, q, r1] vg[mss] syr[c, p, h] cop[boPt] eth slav Diatessaron[syr] (Titus-Bostra) // *transposes* ἀλλὰ ῥῦσαι … πονηροῦ *after* γῆς (*footnote 3*) ℵ[1]

[5] **10** {C} ἀνοιγήσεται (*see* 11.9; Mt 7.8) 𝔓[45] ℵ C L Θ Ψ *f*[1] *f*[13] 28 33 157 180 579 597* 700 892 1241 1292 1342 1505 *Byz*[pt] *Lect*[pt, AD] arm geo Macarius/Symeon // ἀνοιχθήσεται A W Δ 205 565 597[c] 1006 1010 1071 1243 1424 *Byz*[pt] [E F G H] *Lect*[pt] (ἀνοιγήσεται *or* ἀνοιχθήσεται it[aur, b, c, d, f, ff2, i, l, q, r1] vg cop[sa] Speculum) // ἀνοίγεται 𝔓[75] B D cop[bo]? DHH

[6] **11** {B} ἰχθύν 𝔓[45] (𝔓[75] ἰσχύν) B 1241 it[ff2, i, l] syr[s] cop[sa] arm Marcion[acc. to Epiphanius] Origen Epiphanius // ἄρτον μὴ λίθον ἐπιδώσει αὐτῷ; ἢ καὶ ἰχθύν (*see* Mt 7.9) A (C ἢ καὶ ἰχθύν … ἐπιδώσει *after verse 12*) (D αὐτῷ ἐπιδώσει) W Δ Θ Ψ *f*[1] *f*[13] 180 205 597 1010 1071 1243 1292 1342 1424 *Byz* [E (F

7 Μή … πάρεχε Mt 26.10; Lk 18.5; Ga 6.17 **8** διὰ … χρῄζει Lk 18.5

Vatican permitted the world to study its famous Codex Vaticanus. As the complexity of the problem increased, the science of textual criticism forced it to yield to principles of order and reason.

Today every New Testament student should be familiar with a critical edition of the Greek New Testament. Its heritage begins with the critical work of the great Cambridge scholars B. F. Westcott and F. J. A. Hort. They carefully explained their methodology and produced a Greek New Testament based on sound principles that are still used today. One rule controlled all they did: "The first step towards obtaining a sure foundation is the constant application of the principle that knowledge of documents should precede final judgment upon readings."[4] No other rule is more important. A text variant belongs to a document, and that document belongs to a family whose heritage can be reconstructed and evaluated.

A critical edition of the Greek New Testament provides a recommended Greek text, but each page indicates where other manuscripts differ. This information is called a *critical apparatus*. In the widely used United Bible Society text, an editorial team has graded each variant reading (*A* for a certain reading to *D* for an uncertain reading). Even though many textual issues are still debated, the church has never had more reason for confidence in its New Testament Scriptures.

THE CANON OF THE NEW TESTAMENT

The early Christians preserved their Scriptures through a process of copying and distribution, but at some point the church's leadership had to give guidance concerning which writings were deemed beneficial. They had to develop criteria by which Christian leaders could adopt texts as "Scripture." This authoritative collection of New Testament books is called "the canon."

Josephus and the Canon

In the late first century, Josephus describes Judaism's authoritative texts: "Our books, those which are justly accredited, are but two and twenty, and contain the record of all time . . . no one has ventured either to add, or to remove, or to alter a syllable; and it is an instinct with every Jew, from the day of his birth, to regard them as the decrees of God, to abide by them, and if need be, cheerfully to die for them" (*Against Apion* 1.8 [37–43]).

Definitions

The term *kanōn* ("canon") had two basic definitions in the ancient world. It could refer to a measuring ruler, something that guides or regulates belief or practice. But since a ruler has units of measurement etched on it, that series of marks is also called a canon or a list. Today, we use both senses: "The 'canon' of scripture is understood to be the *list* of books which are acknowledged to be, in a unique sense, the *rule* of belief and practice."[5]

Most Jews in Jesus's day agreed on a common core of authoritative texts, including the Pentateuch, the Former Prophets (Joshua, Judges, Samuels, and Kings), the Latter Prophets (Isaiah, Jeremiah, Ezekiel, and the Minor Prophets), and writings such as the Psalms. But was there an official Jewish canon in the first century? Those who understand "canon" to mean a list from which nothing can be removed or added believe the Jewish canon is later than Jesus's day. But those who see "canon" as recognition of a particular book's authority hold that Judaism in Jesus's day did operate with a canon.

Historical Evidence from Patristic Authors

Within the New Testament itself, we have hints of collections of writings and claims of authority about those writings. In 2 Peter 3:15–16, Peter declares that Paul's letters are collected and known among many churches. Paul himself encourages the Colossians to share his letter with the church in nearby Laodicea (Col. 4:16). Of course, Jesus's words were given the utmost authority, not only in the gospels but also in Paul (see 1 Cor. 7:10, 17).

Already in the second century, we see a pattern of both revering New Testament Scripture and collecting it into an authoritative body of texts. Clement of Rome (ca. AD 95) asks his readers to "especially remember the words of the Lord Jesus which he spoke when he was teaching gentleness and long suffering" (*1 Clement* 13.1–4; see also 46.7–8). The *Epistle of Barnabas* announces, "As it is written, 'many are called, but few are chosen'" (4:14; see Matt. 22:14). Did this author have access to a copy of Matthew's gospel?

The author of *2 Clement* (mid-second century) writes: "Another scripture also says, 'I came not to call righteous, but sinners'" (2:4–6, citing Matt. 9:13 or Mark 2:17). Ignatius, bishop of Antioch (ca. AD 50–110), directly claims a superiority of Jesus's words over the Old Testament: "For I heard some men saying, 'If I find it not in the charters [Old Testament], I do not believe in the Gospel.'[6] . . . But to me the charters are Jesus Christ, the inviolable charter is his cross, and death,

Ignatius was one of the first martyrs of the second century, killed during Emperor Trajan's rule (AD 98–117). He declared to the Roman Christians as he faced his martyrdom, "Let me be given to the wild beasts, for through them I can attain unto God. I am God's wheat, and I am ground by the teeth of wild beasts that I may be found pure bread [of Christ]" (Letter to the Romans 4.1, translation J. B. Lightfoot). This art piece was done by Francesca Francanzama (1612–1656). *Public Domain*

and resurrection, and the faith which is through him" (*Phld.* 8.2). Each of these writers either knew of a gospel or at least of some collection of Jesus's sayings.

Justin Martyr (ca. AD 150) speaks of the gospels as the "memoirs of the Apostles," useful to establish doctrine (*First Apology* 66.3; 67.3). These "memoirs" truthfully tell the story of Jesus (*Dialogue with Trypho* 103.8). For Irenaeus, the church has "the gospel in fourfold form, [but] held together by one Spirit," and he denounces those who "reject the form of the gospel and introduce either more or fewer faces of the gospels" (*Against Heresies* 3.11.8). He was referring to the four canonical gospels (Matthew, Mark, Luke, and John), denouncing those who would "reject the form of the gospel and introduce either more or fewer faces of the gospels" (ibid.). This "fourfold" gospel is presumably the accepted norm throughout the church.

In the second century Marcion not only edited Paul's letters but removed anything that validated the Old Testament and Jewish faith. He was declared a heretic, and his "canon list" survives only in the pages of his antagonist, Tertullian (*Against Marcion*).

Canon Boundaries

Throughout the second century, Christian writers also refer to texts not included ultimately in the canon, such as the *Shepherd of Hermas*, the *Didache*, the *Wisdom of Solomon*, and the *Epistle of Barnabas*. For example, Irenaeus cites the *Shepherd of Hermas* in his *Against Heresies* 4.20.2. Gradually, texts such as these were determined as outside canonical authority. An early canon list, the Muratorian Canon (ca. AD 200), is missing both its beginning and ending. What remains includes the following: the gospels of Luke and John, Acts, the letters of Paul (1 and 2 Corinthians, Ephesians, Philippians, Colossians, Galatians, 1 and 2 Thessalonians, Romans, Philemon, Titus, and 1 and 2 Timothy), Apocalypse of John, Jude, 1 and 2 John, Wisdom of Solomon, Apocalypse of Peter (though the list notes that some think this last work should not be read in church). By the fourth century, Athanasius spoke of the *Didache* and the *Shepherd* as important for teaching purposes, but not as part of the canon (*Festal Letter* 39).

In the early fourth century, Eusebius (ca. AD 263–339) referred to three categories of texts: "recognized, disputed, and spurious" (*Eccl. Hist.* 3.25.1–7). "Recognized books" included the four gospels as well as Acts and the letters of Paul (14, including Hebrews, see 3.3.4), 1 John, and 1 Peter. He adds, "if it seems right, the Apocalypse of John." James, Jude, 2 Peter, and 2–3 John were "disputed." He also claims that the *Acts of Paul*, *Shepherd of Hermas*, *Apocalypse of Peter*, *Epistle of Barnabas*, and the *Didache* are spurious (*Church History* 3.25.1–7).

Eusebius offers three criteria for identifying a "recognized" book. (1) The book must be true. Did its contents match the *regula fidei* ("rule of faith"), a summary of essential tenets of Christianity as determined by the apostles who knew Jesus? This rule established that the historical figure Jesus of Nazareth was crucified for the sins of humanity, was raised by God's power, and is now seated at God's right hand. He is both fully God and fully human. In the second and third centuries, heresies challenged the *regula fidei*, so several church fathers pointed to the traditions handed down from the apostles (see 1 Cor. 15:3–11; Ignatius, *Trall.* 7; Irenaeus, *Against Heresies* 3.2).

(2) A book must be genuine, that is, written by an apostle or their associate. For example, Mark wrote a gospel for Peter, and Luke was connected with Paul. The early church would not have knowingly accepted a pseudepigraphic or anonymous writing (see chs. 8, 9, and 21). Those writings claiming to be written by an apostle (e.g., *Gospel of Thomas*) but holding views that differed sharply with teachings of Matthew, John, and Paul, were rejected.

(3) The book must be widely used among all the churches. Augustine wrote: "Prefer those [writings] that are received by all Catholic Churches to those which some of them do not receive" (Augustine, *On Christian Doctrine*, 2:12).[7]

By ca. AD 325, the New Testament canon was essentially in place. In 367 Athanasius wrote the earliest complete New Testament list in his 39th *Festal Letter* 2, 7–10.

> I also resolved to set forth in order the writings that are in the list and handed down and believed to be divine. . . . Those of the New Testament . . . are . . . four gospels [Matthew, Mark, Luke, John]. Then after these are Acts of the Apostles and the seven letters of the Apostles called the 'Catholic' letters [James, 1 and 2 Peter, 1, 2, 3 John, Jude]. In addition, there are fourteen letters of Paul the apostle [Romans, 1, 2 Corinthians, Galatians, Ephesians, Philippians, Colossians, 1, 2 Thessalonians, Hebrews, 1, 2 Timothy, Titus, Philemon]. Last, from John again comes the Revelation. These are springs of salvation . . . let no one add to them or take away aught of them.[8]

In 397 the Council of Carthage confirmed the twenty-seven books of the New Testament canon.

Tatian's *Diatessaron*

A disciple of Justin Martyr, Tatian (early second century), produced a single gospel by blending and editing Matthew, Mark, Luke, and John into one narrative. This *Diatessaron* ("harmony of four") was popular in Syria until the early fifth century. Tatian was a member of an ascetic group known as the Encratites. They were vegetarian, which may be why Tatian edited John the Baptist's diet description from Mark's "locusts and wild honey" to "milk and honey." Eusebius criticized the *Diatessaron* because Tatian combined the four gospels (*Eccl. Hist.* 4.29.6), which he felt should not be changed.

The *Diatessaron* was used extensively within the Syriac-speaking churches until the early fifth century. This is a Greek fragment of the Diatessaron found in 1933. It comes from the first half of the third century.
Beinecke Rare Book and Manuscript Library, Yale University

TRANSLATING THE NEW TESTAMENT

Translation in Antiquity

Greek and Latin were the principal languages of the Empire, as is contained in this bilingual inscription in Latin and Greek from Larnaca, Cyprus. Latin above: "Julia Donata, the freedwoman of Olympus, lies here" and in Greek below: "Good Ioulia Donata the freedwoman of Olympos, farewell."
The Metropolitan Museum of Art

The Mediterranean world had a mix of languages, with the two main tongues being Greek and Latin. The Romans were generally more willing to learn other languages than the Greeks, and any educated Roman was expected to know these two. Archaeologists have discovered many bilingual inscriptions. In such a world, translation became a common practice. As noted in chapter 3, the Greek-speaking Jews of the Diaspora used the Septuagint (LXX), a Greek translation of the Hebrew Scriptures.

The early Christians were the beneficiaries of ancient translations. The LXX became their Bible, even though other Greek translations took place later (e.g., those by Aquila, Theodotion, and Symmachus). In fact, most of the quotations of the Old Testament in the New Testament writings are based on the LXX. The multiple translators of the LXX did not hold a unified translation theory, and as a result, some sections were translated literally (e.g., Judges and Ruth), while others were more of a paraphrase (e.g., Daniel and Job). We can sometimes recognize the influence of the LXX on the New Testament authors when we examine New Testament quotations of Old Testament texts (compare Mark 7:6–7, quoting Isa. 29:13 from the LXX, and Isa. 29:13 as translated from the Hebrew in a modern translation).

But even for those Jews living in Palestine, translation was necessary since the language of the street was Aramaic rather than Hebrew. These translations from Hebrew to Aramaic were first done orally. The Mishnah's *Megillah* 4.1 instructs: "He that reads from the Law . . . may not read to the interpreter more than one verse, or, in [a reading from] the Prophets, three verses." In other words, the reader must not run too far ahead of the translator. Eventually these translations were written down and became known as the *targumim* (ch. 3). The interpretive traditions incorporated into the *targumim* may have influenced the translators of the LXX.

This is a beautiful page from a Bible translated into Ethiopic, seventeenth century.
Wikimedia Commons, PD-US

Ancient authors discussed how translation should be done. Cicero, commenting on the translation of the Greek orators Demosthenes and Aeschines, said, "And I have not translated them as a literal interpreter, but as an orator giving the same ideas in the same form and mould, as it were, in words conformable to our manners; in doing which I did not consider it necessary to give word for word, but I have preserved the character and energy of the language throughout" (*De optimo genere oratorum* 14).

Jerome (AD c. 345–c. 419) echoes Cicero's concern to translate the ideas of the original and not give a word-for-word translation. He even noted that a literal translation may obscure the sense, since the goal is to "look for the meaning" (*Letter* 57.6). Jerome quotes extensively from Cicero as his authority, affirming his statement, "If all that I have written is not to be found in the Greek, I have at any rate striven to make it correspond with it" (*Letter* 57.5).

Early Christian Versions

Early Christians needed a Latin translation of the Scriptures since not everyone knew Greek. Pope Damascus specifically asked Jerome to revise the existing Latin translations of the gospels (known as Old Latin), using the Greek text. He did the Old Testament as well, translating first from the LXX but then from the Hebrew text. Jerome's work became the Latin translation known as the Vulgate.

But not everyone spoke Latin or Greek, so other translations of the Scriptures, known as "versions," came into being. Christians in Egypt spoke Coptic, and so a Coptic version appeared (start of the third century). In Africa an Ethiopic version of the Bible was done (cf. Acts 8:26–39).

The gospel took hold in Syria early on (cf. Syrian Antioch in Acts 11:19–30), so that some of the oldest versions are Syriac (Old Syriac in the second century, the Peshitta in the second and third centuries). Armenian, Georgian, and Arabic versions of the Bible survive from the early centuries as well. This robust enterprise of translation shows that the church understood that the message of Christ had to come to people in languages they could understand.

The beginning of the Gospel of Matthew from this bilingual translation. Coptic text is on the left, and Arabic is on the right, dated to 1663.
The British Library, Public Domain

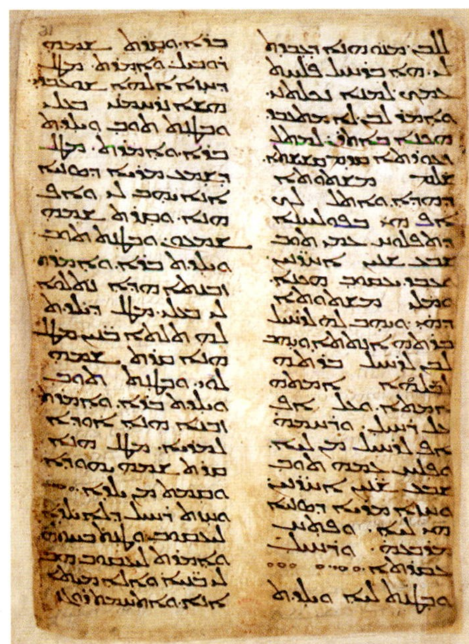

A Syriac Bible is signed by its scribe, a bishop named John, ca. AD 463–64.
The British Library, Public Domain

The Continuing Translation Tradition

At the heart of the church's response to the Great Commission is the work of the Bible translator. While Jesus did not specifically call for his disciples to engage in translation, the Great Commission (Matt. 28:16–20) makes the task necessary. Jesus emphasized the need for understanding the message of the kingdom of God (13:18–23). This mission of the church from its very beginning serves as the mother of translation.

Today agencies such as the United Bible Societies and SIL International/Wycliffe Bible Translators facilitate this task globally. At times, translators learn the language into which they hope to translate Scripture and translate from the Hebrew and Greek. In other cases, bilingual men and women translate the biblical text from a common language (e.g., Spanish) into a local tongue (e.g., Garifuna, spoken in some parts of Guatemala), under the supervision of a translation consultant.

There are about 6,900 languages in the world, and around 2,300 have at least one book of the Bible translated. This represents 90 percent of the world's population. Despite the great advances in Bible translation techniques, much work remains to be done by those women and men who, as the seventh-century bishop of Seville, Isidorus said, stand *inter partes* ("between the two sides"; 10.123). At the same time, many language groups have multiple translations available to them, with new versions being produced at a rapid rate to address the concerns and needs of various readers. In fact, the large number of translations available to English readers makes selection between them difficult. While grateful for this abundance, students and church members may well wonder whether supply has superseded the need.

The earliest translations of the Bible into English come from the Anglo-Saxon monk Caedmon (seventh century) and the great early church historian of England, the Venerable Bede (eighth century). John Wycliffe (fourteenth century) tried to make the Bible accessible to readers of his day as a hedge against abusive ecclesiastical authority. In the sixteenth century William Tyndale, an Oxford graduate, faced persecution because of his translation of Scripture based on the original Hebrew and Greek. These early translators displayed a passion for the gospel and the conviction that their labors and the personal cost were small in comparison to the great need.

In 1611 translators completed the most well-known English translation, the King James Version (KJV). The *Textus Receptus* (see above on textual criticism) served as the textual base for this translation. But this is not the Greek text used by most contemporary Bible translators. Most translators today recognize that the Majority Text sometimes includes words, phrases, and sometimes even paragraphs that were not part of what the biblical author wrote. What appears to be an omission in contemporary translations is really a refusal to add what a biblical author did not write (see sidebar on "What Happened to the Verse"). They use either the critical edition of the New Testament published by the United Bible Societies or the Nestle-Aland text, both of which take into account the vast manuscript discoveries since the seventeenth century. They are examples of an eclectic text that represents the best application of the principles of textual criticism.

What Happened to the Verse

In the KJV Romans 8:1 reads: "*There is* therefore now no condemnation to them which are in Christ Jesus, who walk not after the flesh, but after the Spirit." The NIV reads here: "Therefore, there is now no condemnation for those who are in Christ Jesus." This shorter version reflects a recognition by the translators that the best manuscript evidence we have for Romans 8:1 does not support the inclusion of "who walk not after the flesh, but after the Spirit." Two families of the Greek text support the shorter version.

The exclusion of those last words in the KJV does not mean that the translators wished to take something out of Paul's letter; rather, they did not want to add something in Romans that Paul did not write. This decision is the result of examining the Greek manuscripts that have survived the centuries and using the principles of textual criticism. Compare also 1 John 5:7–8 in the KJV and NIV and read a commentary on John 7:53–8:11. The task of textual criticism and translation go hand in hand.

Commonly used contemporary translations such as the New Revised Standard Version (NRSV), the English Standard Version (ESV), the New International Version (NIV), the Common English Bible (CEB), and the New Living Translation (NLT) all utilize the current editions of these Greek texts.

Translation Theory

How can we translate the New Testament in a way that is both faithful to the biblical authors' meaning and understandable to the contemporary reader? This central question is simple and elusive. Bible translators must decide on a philosophy of translation to guide their work. This task is daunting, since we can only approximate the meaning of the source language (in this case, Greek) in the receptor language (contemporary English). An Italian dictum voices a somewhat cynical view—"Traduttore, traditore" ("Translators, traitors")—since a translator can never get in all the meaning of the original.

When a person speaks or writes, the language or linguistic "code" supplies evidence of what she or he wishes to communicate. The process of understanding what someone says includes not only decoding the words and sentences but also making proper inferences. So, for example, if you say to a friend sitting next to you in class, "It's 8:30," you may mean, "It's time for class to begin," or, "The professor is late." You expect your classmate to understand what you mean by making the proper inferences. In both these cases contextual information comes into play (this particular class begins at 8:30 a.m. and the professor is not in the room).

We always communicate more than what our words say. So it is with the New Testament. When Paul said to the Philippians, for example, that one day every knee will bow and every tongue confess that "Jesus Christ is Lord" (Phil. 2:11), he expected the Philippians to understand his meaning of the term "Lord." "Lord" (*kyrios*) was how the LXX translated the name of God, Yahweh (see Isa. 45 for this very citation in Phil. 2:11). Also, "Lord" was a common title given to multiple deities around the empire, such as the Egyptian "Lord" Serapis and sometimes even the emperor. For Paul and the Philippians, the claim that Jesus is Lord attaches to the concept of transcendent deity. In fact, he is the one who is above every other so-called god and lord (see 1 Cor. 8:4–6). The question the translator of any verse must wrestle with is whether to translate the words alone or whether to attempt, in a limited way, to supply some of the conceptual information for the contemporary reader that would have been accessible to the original readers.

The problem of translation is even more acute since the concept suggested by a term in one language is not usually equivalent to the translated word used in another language. Think about our ideas attached to the term "lord." The Merriam-Webster dictionary indicates that the term can refer to "one having power and authority over others" or "a man of rank or high position." But these concepts are not equal to the ancient concepts of deity and divine rule as suggested by *kyrios* in the Greek-speaking world of the first century. Translations can only approximate the meaning of the author's original utterance. The concept suggested by a term in one language will overlap the concept of the equivalent word in another language, but the two concepts are rarely the same in all their dimensions.

Translators deal with these issues in various ways. Some argue that the best approach is to seek "formal equivalence," that is, to translate as much as possible word for word from the source language into the receptor language. Others attempt to produce a translation that has "functional" or "dynamic equivalence." As Eugene Nida, a scholar who has been highly influential in the field of translation, says, such translations try to reproduce "in a receptor language [i.e., English] . . . the closest natural equivalent of the source language [i.e., Hebrew or Greek] message, first in terms of meaning, and second in terms of style."[9] Such translators seek to render the original thought for thought. A version like the New American Standard falls clearly on the formal equivalence side while the New Living Translation has functional equivalence as its goal.

Much debate has taken place in recent years about whether translations should use "gender-inclusive", or "gender-accurate," language (as do the NLT and the NRSV). For example, Paul addresses the *adelphoi* in Philippi (Phil. 1:12). Should we render this term "brothers" or "brothers and sisters"? What did Paul mean here? Did he intend to address both male and female believers or only the men? While in the past "brothers" included both men and women, recent shifts in the English language indicate to many that "brothers" is more gender-marked today. Therefore, many argue that in order to be faithful to Paul's meaning, *adelphoi* should be translated as "brothers and sisters."

Despite these challenges of translation, these various versions have enriched the church through the centuries. As the LXX version of the Old Testament served the early church, so too in our day the global church is being served by the translations of the New Testament into the languages of the world. The message of Jesus is heard through these translations. By God's grace this message is indeed "the power of God that brings salvation to everyone who believes: first to the Jew, then to the Gentile" (Rom. 1:16).

Romans 8:4—Questions of Translation

What is the best way to translate Romans 8:4? Should translators render the Greek term *sarx* by the gloss "flesh," or should they explain the word in some brief way to the English reader? What did Paul mean by "walking"? Compare the following translations in light of the philosophy of translation they represent:

KJV: "That the righteousness of the law might be fulfilled in us, who walk not after the flesh, but after the Spirit."

CEB: "He did this so that the righteous requirement of the Law might be fulfilled in us. Now the way we live is based on the Spirit, not based on selfishness."

NLT: "He did this so that the just requirement of the law would be fully satisfied for us, who no longer follow our sinful nature but instead follow the Spirit."

J. B. Phillips: "So that we are able to meet the Law's requirements, so long as we are living no longer by the dictates of our sinful nature, but in obedience to the promptings of the Spirit."

Questions for Discussion

1. What were the unique challenges to the preservation and copying of the New Testament text from AD 100 to 300?
2. If scholars discovered a new ancient manuscript that challenged the authenticity of some vital portion of the New Testament, how would we decide whether to change our Bibles? Who decides?
3. Explain the term "canon" and how it was used in the ancient world.
4. How did Eusebius (a fourth-century church historian) describe books being considered for inclusion in the New Testament?
5. Discuss the issue of gender-inclusive (or gender-accurate) language translations. Which kind of translation should we use in the church today and why? Be sure to reflect on the philosophy of translation that guides these decisions as well as whether changes in the English language warrant the use of gender-inclusive (or gender-accurate) language.

BIBLIOGRAPHY

The Text of the New Testament

Aland, K., and B. Aland. *The Text of the New Testament*. Grand Rapids/Leiden: Eerdmans/Brill, 1989.

Black, D. A., ed. *Rethinking New Testament Textual Criticism*. Grand Rapids: Baker, 2002.

Comfort, P. *A Student's Guide to Textual Criticism*. Nashville: Broadman & Holman, 2006.

Greenlee, J. H. *An Introduction to Textual Criticism*. 2nd ed. Peabody, MA: Hendrickson, 1995.

Metzger, B., and B. Ehrman. *The Text of the New Testament: Its Transmission, Corruption, and Restoration*. 4th ed. Oxford: Oxford University Press, 2005.

Porter, S. E. and A. W. Pitts. *Fundamentals of New Testament Textual Criticism*. Grand Rapids: Eerdmans, 2015.

Wegner, P. D. *A Student's Guide to Textual Criticism*. Downers Grove, IL: InterVarsity Press, 2006.

Canon

Barton, J. *Holy Writings Sacred Text: The Canon in Early Christianity*. Louisville: Westminster John Knox, 1997.

Bruce, F. F. *The Canon of Scripture*. Downers Grove, IL: InterVarsity Press, 1996.

Kruger, M. J. *Canon Revisited*. Wheaton: Crossway, 2012.

Kruger, J. J. *The Question of Canon*. Downers Grove, IL: InterVarsity Press, 2013.

McDonald, L. M. *The Formation of the Christian Biblical Canon*. Peabody, MA: Hendrickson, 1995.

Metzger, B. M. *The Canon of the New Testament: Its Origin, Development, and Significance*. Oxford: Clarendon, 1987.

Patzia, A. G. *The Making of the New Testament*. Downers Grove, IL: InterVarsity Press, 1995.

Translation

Carson, D. A. *The Inclusive Language Debate*. Grand Rapids: Baker, 1998.

Comfort, P. W. *Essential Guide to Bible Versions*. Carol Stream, IL: Tyndale, 2000.

Fee, G. D. and M. L. Strauss. *How to Choose a Translation for All It's Worth*. Grand Rapids: Zondervan, 2007.

Metzger, B. *The Bible in Translation*. Grand Rapids: Baker Academic, 2001.

Scorgie, G. G., M. L. Strauss, and S. M. Voth. *The Challenge of Bible Translation*. Grand Rapids: Zondervan, 2003.

Wegner, P. D. *The Journey from Texts to Translations*. Grand Rapids: Baker, 1999.

NOTES

1. B. Metzger and B. Ehrman, *The Text of the New Testament: Its Transmission, Corruption, and Restoration*, 4th ed. (Oxford: Oxford University Press, 2005), 50.

2. B. Metzger, *Manuscripts of the Greek Bible: An Introduction to Greek Paleography* (New York: Oxford, 1981), 74 (see p. 75 for a photo of Codex Vaticanus at Heb. 11:3).

3. See C. H. Turner, *A New Commentary on the Holy Scripture* (1928), as cited by S. Neill, *The Interpretation of the New Testament, 1861–1961* (Oxford: Oxford University Press, 1964), 79.

4. B. F. Wescott and F. J. A. Hort, *The New Testament in the Original Greek* (London: MacMillan, 1881), 31, cited by S. Neill, *The Interpretation of the New Testament, 1861–1961* (Oxford: Oxford University Press, 1964), 73.

5. F. F. Bruce, *The Canon of Scripture* (Downers Grove, IL: InterVarsity Press, 1988), 18.

6. Lee McDonald's translation of the statement. The rest of the passage is from the LCL. L. M. McDonald, *The Formation of the Christian Biblical Canon* (Peabody, MA: Hendrickson, 1995), 146.

7. Cited in Bruce M. Metzger, *The Canon of the New Testament: Its Origin, Development, and Significance* (Oxford: Clarendon Press, 1987), 237.

8. Translation from McDonald, *The Formation of the Christian Biblical Canon*, 221.

9. E. A. Nida and C. R. Taber, *The Theory and Practice of Translation* (Leiden: Brill, 1969), 210.

SCRIPTURE INDEX

MARK

LUKE

ACTS

ROMANS

1 CORINTHIANS

2 CORINTHIANS

GALATIANS

EPHESIANS

PHILIPPIANS

COLOSSIANS

1 THESSALONIANS

2 THESSALONIANS

1 TIMOTHY

2 TIMOTHY

TITUS

PHILEMON

HEBREWS

JAMES

1 PETER

2 PETER

1 JOHN

2 JOHN

3 JOHN

JUDE

REVELATION

NONCANONICAL ANCIENT SOURCES INDEX

SUBJECT INDEX